Optimizing Human-Computer Interaction With Emerging Technologies

Francisco Cipolla-Ficarra
Latin Association of Human-Computer Interaction, Spain & International Association of Interactive Communication, Italy

A volume in the Advances in Human and Social
Aspects of Technology (AHSAT) Book Series

Published in the United States of America by
 IGI Global
 Information Science Reference (an imprint of IGI Global)
 701 E. Chocolate Avenue
 Hershey PA, USA 17033
 Tel: 717-533-8845
 Fax: 717-533-8661
 E-mail: cust@igi-global.com
 Web site: http://www.igi-global.com

Library of Congress Cataloging-in-Publication Data

Names: Cipolla-Ficarra, Francisco V. (Francisco Vicente), 1963- editor.
Title: Optimizing human-computer interaction with emerging technologies
 / Francisco Cipolla-Ficarra, editor.
Description: Hershey, PA : Information Science Reference, [2017] | Includes
 bibliographical references.
Identifiers: LCCN 2017007748| ISBN 9781522526162 (hardcover) | ISBN
 9781522526179 (ebook)
Subjects: LCSH: Social interaction--Handbooks, manuals, etc. | Information
 behavior--Handbooks, manuals, etc. | Telecommunication--Social
 aspects--Handbooks, manuals, etc. | Information technology--Social
 aspects--Handbooks, manuals, etc. | Telematics--Handbooks, manuals, etc.
Classification: LCC HM1111 .H36 2017 | DDC 302--dc23 LC record available at https://lccn.loc.gov/2017007748

This book is published in the IGI Global book series Advances in Human and Social Aspects of Technology (AHSAT) (ISSN: 2328-1316; eISSN: 2328-1324)

British Cataloguing in Publication Data
A Cataloguing in Publication record for this book is available from the British Library.

All work contributed to this book is new, previously-unpublished material. The views expressed in this book are those of the authors, but not necessarily of the publisher.

For electronic access to this publication, please contact: eresources@igi-global.com.

Advances in Human and Social Aspects of Technology (AHSAT) Book Series

Ashish Dwivedi
The University of Hull, UK

ISSN:2328-1316
EISSN:2328-1324

MISSION

In recent years, the societal impact of technology has been noted as we become increasingly more connected and are presented with more digital tools and devices. With the popularity of digital devices such as cell phones and tablets, it is crucial to consider the implications of our digital dependence and the presence of technology in our everyday lives.

The **Advances in Human and Social Aspects of Technology (AHSAT) Book Series** seeks to explore the ways in which society and human beings have been affected by technology and how the technological revolution has changed the way we conduct our lives as well as our behavior. The AHSAT book series aims to publish the most cutting-edge research on human behavior and interaction with technology and the ways in which the digital age is changing society.

COVERAGE

- Technology adoption
- End-User Computing
- Human-Computer Interaction
- Philosophy of technology
- Technology and Freedom of Speech
- Computer-Mediated Communication
- Human Development and Technology
- Technology Dependence
- Information ethics
- ICTs and social change

IGI Global is currently accepting manuscripts for publication within this series. To submit a proposal for a volume in this series, please contact our Acquisition Editors at Acquisitions@igi-global.com or visit: http://www.igi-global.com/publish/.

Titles in this Series

For a list of additional titles in this series, please visit: www.igi-global.com/book-series

Designing for Human-Machine Symbiosis Using the URANOS Model Emerging Research and Opportunities
Benjamin Hadorn (University of Fribourg, Switzerland)
Information Science Reference • copyright 2017 • 170pp • H/C (ISBN: 9781522518884) • US $125.00 (our price)

Research Paradigms and Contemporary Perspectives on Human-Technology Interaction
Anabela Mesquita (School of Accounting and Administration of Porto, Polytechnic Institute of Porto, Portugal & Algorithm Research Centre, Minho University, Portugal)
Information Science Reference • copyright 2017 • 366pp • H/C (ISBN: 9781522518686) • US $195.00 (our price)

Solutions for High-Touch Communications in a High-Tech World
Michael A. Brown Sr. (Florida International University, USA)
Information Science Reference • copyright 2017 • 217pp • H/C (ISBN: 9781522518976) • US $185.00 (our price)

Design Solutions for User-Centric Information Systems
Saqib Saeed (Imam Abdulrahman Bin Faisal University, Saudi Arabia) Yasser A. Bamarouf (Imam Abdulrahman Bin Faisal University, Saudi Arabia) T. Ramayah (University Sains Malaysia, Malaysia) and Sardar Zafar Iqbal (Imam Abdulrahman Bin Faisal University, Saudi Arabia)
Information Science Reference • copyright 2017 • 422pp • H/C (ISBN: 9781522519447) • US $215.00 (our price)

Identity, Sexuality, and Relationships among Emerging Adults in the Digital Age
Michelle F. Wright (Masaryk University, Czech Republic)
Information Science Reference • copyright 2017 • 343pp • H/C (ISBN: 9781522518563) • US $185.00 (our price)

Enriching Urban Spaces with Ambient Computing, the Internet of Things, and Smart City Design
Shin'ichi Konomi (University of Tokyo, Japan) and George Roussos (University of London, UK)
Engineering Science Reference • copyright 2017 • 323pp • H/C (ISBN: 9781522508274) • US $210.00 (our price)

Handbook of Research on Individualism and Identity in the Globalized Digital Age
F. Sigmund Topor (Keio University, Japan)
Information Science Reference • copyright 2017 • 645pp • H/C (ISBN: 9781522505228) • US $295.00 (our price)

Information Technology Integration for Socio-Economic Development
Titus Tossy (Mzumbe University, Tanzania)
Information Science Reference • copyright 2017 • 385pp • H/C (ISBN: 9781522505396) • US $200.00 (our price)

701 East Chocolate Avenue, Hershey, PA 17033, USA
Tel: 717-533-8845 x100 • Fax: 717-533-8661
E-Mail: cust@igi-global.com • www.igi-global.com

Table of Contents

Detailed Table of Contents

Chapter 1

Francisco V. Cipolla-Ficarra, Latin Association of Human-Computer Interaction, Spain &
International Association of Interactive Communication, Italy

We present the importance of analogical and digital cartography in the reconstruction of the cultural heritage of the first nations. Besides, through the cartographic information and the interactive multimedia systems, we examine the metamorphose of ancient pre-Columbus constructions, whose physical sites were based in the advanced knowledge of those civilizations in astronomy issues. We also present the main stages in the digital cartographic generation for their later use in the multimedia systems. Finally, we sum up the difficulties in the diffusion of certain historic contents compiled in the off-line multimedia supports, in the Internet and in the current social networks.

Chapter 2

Kijpokin Kasemsap, Suan Sunandha Rajabhat University, Thailand

This chapter describes the overview of Web 2.0 technologies; Web 2.0 applications in learning and education; Web 2.0 applications in academic libraries; Web 2.0 applications in Knowledge Management (KM); the perspectives of Health Information Technology (health IT); the multifaceted applications of health IT; IT and Technology Acceptance Model (TAM); and the significance of health IT in the health care industry. Web 2.0 is the platform of the network which spans all connected services so that users can utilize them more efficiently. Web 2.0 technologies have various benefits by enhancing the opportunities for business collaboration and by sharing knowledge through online communities of practice toward gaining improved organizational performance. Health IT includes utilizing technology to electronically store, protect, retrieve, and transfer the information in modern health care. Health IT has great potential to improve the quality, safety, and efficiency of health care services in the health care industry.

    Annamaria Poli, University of Milano-Bicocca, Italy
    Annastella Gambini, University of Milano-Bicocca, Italy
    Antonella Pezzotti, University of Milano-Bicocca, Italy
    Alfredo Broglia, University of Milano-Bicocca, Italy
    Alessandra Mazzola, Politecnico di Milano, Italy
    Sabrina Muschiato, Politecnico di Milano, Italy
    Carlo Emilio Standoli, Politecnico di Milano, Italy
    Daniela Zambarbieri, Politecnico di Milano, Italy
    Fiammetta Costa, Politecnico di Milano, Italy

Digital technologies that increase communication among students/users are viewed as interactive resources for enhancing learning, especially in the field of science teaching. The new digital mission is to produce innovative learning environments and educational tools to enhance the traditional teaching methods still widely used today. The Digital Diorama project reproduces a set of Natural History Museum dioramas for IWBs and other electronic devices. Using the Digital Diorama enhances cooperative learning. This comes from the students/users' explorations of the Digital Diorama and from strategies that we recommend to teachers.

    Daniela Tamburini, SPERIMENTA, Italy

This chapter presents an educational and consulting path for the use of new technologies that support the improvement of learning relationships in groups, the construction of knowledge and the ability to recognize and explore the experience of communication and relationship at professional and personal levels, for the individual and for groups in order to enhance abilities and professional skills on several levels: cognitive, affective, conative and practical. Through the report of the experiments carried out for two years and applied to two training projects for teachers of five Primary and Secondary Italian schools, the main objective is to describe and present the overall results. The approaches used were inspired by the method of participatory research and action research with a clinical and pedagogical approach. The methodology is based on the case study of the Clinica della Formazione that increases the emotional, communicative and relationship dimensions and gives concreteness not only to the educational action but also to the process behind it, which then becomes the target of investigations.

    Alan Radley, University College London, UK

The present chapter introduces a new existential philosophy of how computers, systems and machines operate within society, and in terms of the provision, furtherance and/or obstruction of human rights/ freedoms and open life-potential(s). We explore the relationship(s) between the design of artificial systems and the existence/form/implementation of democracy; and from the key perspective(s) of individual and collective freedom-of-thought/action. A basic premise is that humans are increasingly disadvantaged as a result of, or slaves to: unfettered automation, objectivity, abstraction and fragmentary thinking; as promulgated/aided by computers/systems/machines. We explain how related processes create conflict/ opposition/barriers to/with natural and harmonious socialization activities/processes; and hence strongly influence our collective destiny.

Chapter 6

Children and adolescents are actively engaged in a digital world in which blogs, social networking sites, watching videos, and instant messaging are a typical part of their daily lives. Their immersion in the digital world has occurred for as long as they remember, with many not knowing a world without our modern technological advances. Although the digital age has brought us many conveniences in our daily lives, there is a darker side to children's and adolescents' involvement with these technologies, such as cyberbullying. This chapter draws on research from around the world, utilizing a variety of research designs, to describe the nature, extent, causes, and consequences associated with children's and adolescents' involvement in cyberbullying. Concluding the chapter is a solutions and recommendation section in which it is argued that cyberbullying is a global concern, affecting all aspects of society, requiring a whole-community approach.

The purpose of this chapter is to propose a model that would enable teachers to assess comprehensively the effectiveness of learners` information acquisition in e-learning environment. The main value of the proposed model is its focus on combination of pedagogical conditions and psychological factors of learning to increase the level of information acquisition. In order to study students` acquisition of learning information in dependence upon the form of presentation as well as identification of learners` psychological characteristics, that help the acquisition of material presented in three visual forms (text, charts, comics) the experiment was carried out. On the grounds of the obtained results, the authors suggest guidelines for application of the model in practice.

Experts affirm that interaction in learning settings represent a necessary process for knowledge acquisition and cognitive development. In this vein, is crucial to ensure effective interaction and communication through the user interface of MOOCs. This work proposes a set of design guidelines as starting point for developers to integrate a set of interactive elements into the MOOCs' user interface oriented to foster the four basic types for communication in distance education. The design guidelines were conformed through a need-findings process (observing people-interviewing), in which 35 participants provided their user experience perceptions after using MOOCs from edX; Coursera; and Udacity. Obtained results suggest a particular set of interactive communication elements that should be incorporated in every MOOC's user interface.

Chapter 9

Andreas Kratky, University of Southern California, USA

Large format touch screens have become an important means of interaction for collaborative and shared environments. This type of display is particularly useful for public information display in museums and similar contexts. Similarly augmented reality displays have become popular in this context. Both systems have benefits and drawbacks. Personal Touch is an augmented-reality display system combining real objects with superimposed interactive graphics. With increasing display sizes and users moving in front of the display user tracking and viewing angle compensation for the interactive display become challenging. Personal Touch presents an approach combining IR optical tracking for gesture recognition and camera-based face recognition for the acquisition of viewing axis information. Combining both techniques we can create a reactive augmented-reality display establishing a personalized viewing and interaction context for users of different statue moving in front of a real object.

Chapter 10

Daniel Kade, Mälardalen University, Sweden
Rikard Lindell, Mälardalen University, Sweden
Hakan Ürey, Koç University, Turkey
Oğuzhan Özcan, Koç University, Turkey

Current and future animations seek for more human-like motions to create believable animations for computer games, animated movies and commercial spots. A technology widely used technology is motion capture to capture actors' movements which enrich digital avatars motions and emotions. However, a motion capture environment poses challenges to actors such as short preparation times and the need to highly rely on their acting and imagination skills. To support these actors, we developed a mixed reality application that allows showing digital environments while performing and being able to see the real and virtual world. We tested our prototype with 6 traditionally trained theatre and TV actors. As a result, the actors indicated that our application supported them getting into the demanded acting moods with less unrequired emotions. The acting scenario was also better understood with less need of explanation than when just discussing the scenario, as commonly done in theatre acting.

Chapter 11

Karen Woodman, Queensland University of Technology, Australia
Vasilia Kourtis-Kazoullis, University of the Aegean, Greece

This chapter explores the results of a study using the well-known social networking site, Facebook, to investigate graduate education students' perceptions on the use of technologies in classrooms around the world. This study was part of a larger project exploring tele-collaboration and the use of online discussions involving graduate students in an online program based in Australia, and students in a graduate Education program at a regional university in Greece. Findings reveal many similarities between the situations and perceptions of the participants from the different countries. They also demonstrated that even when technologies were available in schools, participants identified a critical need for professional development to increase teachers' use of ICT. These findings are relevant to researchers, educators and policy development in terms of implementation of ICT and/or social networking in the language classroom.

The objective of this chapter was to identify a set of contextual issues in groupware applications used by educational support groups. The analysis was performed through a Needfindings study where 20 active members of three Mexican federal educational-support groups called USAER were recruited. The analysis considered both users and functional vantage point. The participants (from one USAER) provided feedback and insights from their daily activities related to communication with others and resources access helping to define and understand users' scenarios. This information was classified and distilled as design ideas in low fidelity prototypes constructed by participants themselves under guidance from authors. Finally, prototypes were evaluated by the members of the other two USAER group providing their perception as expert users. The study derived in a set of particular contextual issues that directly influence interactions in group applications. These findings could be take into account by designers as a reliable starting point for well-designed User Interfaces for groupware.

In this chapter, an exploratory research on people's interaction with a virtual environment as tool in a way in which listening comprehension occurs while improving English as a second language is addressed. Unlike technologies such as virtual environments, where users have to use hardware in order to get immersed inside of a fictional world, it is through holographic technologies that it is possible to extract virtuality and insert it into reality, and thus, have an approach to the real nature of the virtual world without using electronic devices. Why is it important to focus on the ability of listening to understand when people want to acquire English as a second language? What are the strategies that must be employed to improve this ability? What kind of advantages may users achieve through their interaction with holography? These are some of the questions that will to be answered in this chapter.

Chapter 14

Mehmet Donmez, Middle East Technical University, Turkey
Kursat Cagiltay, Middle East Technical University, Turkey
Serkan Alkan, Middle East Technical University, Turkey
Fuat Bolukbas, Middle East Technical University, Turkey
Goknur Kaplan Akilli, Middle East Technical University, Turkey

This study explores the design considerations and usability factors of using large multi touch interfaces. In this study, an experimental approach incorporating a large multi touch interface environment was used. End user usability test sessions supported with glasses type eye tracker and interview sessions were conducted. The data were collected from one expert and three non-expert users by implementing a task on a military training application. Two analysis methods were used, analysis for eye movement data of users and analysis for interviews. This study revealed that users were generally focusing at the center of the screen while using the large multi touch display. The most common gestures were Tap and Drag which are single touch input gestures. It was easy to adapt to the system by recalling the previous experiences from mobile devices, to manage the area on the screen, and to interact with two hands thanks to display size.

Chapter 15

Pablo Santana-Mansilla, National Scientific and Technical Research Council, Argentina &
National University of Santiago del Estero, Argentina
Rosanna Costaguta, National University of Santiago del Estero, Argentina
Silvia Schiaffino, National Scientific and Technical Research Council, Argentina & National
University of the Center of Buenos Aires Province, Argentina

The use of computer-supported collaborative learning (CSCL) environments in teaching and learning processes has increased during the last decade. These environments have various collaboration, communication and coordination tools that students and teachers can use without depending on the time and place where they are. However, having software tools that support group learning does not guarantee successful collaboration because factors such as insufficient knowledge of study contents can impair learning. The analysis of group interactions should allow teachers to recognize obstacles in the learning process, but when there are a lot of interactions the manual analysis is unfeasible owing to time and effort required. This chapter presents a multi-agent model that personalizes the delivery of learning material when groups of collaborative students manifest lack of knowledge. In addition, this chapter describes results of experiments conducted to evaluate the feasibility of using Lucene for retrieving learning material written in English and Spanish.

Chapter 16

Francisco V. Cipolla-Ficarra, Latin Association of Human-Computer Interaction, Spain &
International Association of Interactive Communication, Italy
Donald Nilson, University of Oslo, Norway
Jacqueline Alma, Electronic Arts, Canada

In the current appendix present a first heuristic study about the scientific publications related to computer science and the human factors that make that some contents travel through highways and others in back roads of scientific information. We also present the first elements which generate that parallel information of the scientific work for financial and/or commercial reasons. Finally, a set of rhetoric questions link two decades of experiences in the university educational context, research and development (R&D) and Transfer of Technology (TOT) in the Mediterranean South and make up a first evaluation guide.

We present a study of the triad rendering computer made static and/or dynamic images, video games and adult users who interact with a personal computer. Besides, there is a diachronic study of the basic components to design the virtual 3D characters which are included in the video games. The link of the evolution of the interactive games is also analyzed and especially the interactive design characteristics related to the content, navigation, structure and layout. Finally, a table is presented with those components stemming from the rendering of the scenes for the video games, which motivate their fruition by the adult users.

Preface

In the process of continuous evolution of the emerging technologies, new fields of the theoretical-practical knowledge are generated to develop unprecedented activities, with educational or working purposes, for instance. The novelty of those activities stand in direct relationship with an advance of the hardware and telecommunications, mainly in the emerging and information technology (IT). All of that a constant need of a software which adapts to the growing needs of the user in daily life. The main goal from the software is to facilitate an effective interaction with the new ICT (information and communication technologies) devices. However, in that evolutional process it is necessary to analyze those indispensable sectors related to the information technology. That is, those which will have the greatest impact in the daily life in the interaction of the human beings and in the tools of multimedia information and communication both current and future.

We also mean the future, because even if some of those emerging technologies are still being developed in the research and development labs, belonging to colleges or businesses, in the future, that is, in the short, middle, long run, they will be available for millions of potential users across the planet. It is a consequence of the dazzling democratization process that characterizes the emerging and information technologies, in our days. In this sense, we research from engineering computing all those strategical links called as excellence to locate, examine and present the impact of the optimizing Human-Computer Interaction with emerging technologies

In the next decades, for example, a myriad activities will be replaced by robots or computers, and especially with applications for tablets, smart phones, 3D printers, web 2.0, web 3.0 among others. It is the persistent technological evolution which quickly generates a myriad new professions in the field of the new information and communication technology (NICT). Online assistants for healthcare or teaching, experts in 3D printing, operators/pilots of drones, analysts of the veracity of the online information, auditors of communicability, are some examples. In that context of constant changes those and more breakthrough professions are profiled where they will interact with several areas of the current scientific knowledge, and which will give rise to other new educational disciplines and/or professional or workplace outlets. These areas of knowledge require theoretical bases which allow them to adapt to the practical aspects in a quick way, with reduced costs and with a high quality.

It is precisely this equation of low costs and high quality which uninterruptedly fostering since decades the use of all the computer science breakthroughs and all their derivations in the homes, firms, industries, schools, universities and other public and private institutions. Nearing those technologies to the final users has had as "temporary fashions" some notions or terms since the 90s down to our days, such as hypertext, usability, internet, user interface, human-computer interaction, user experience, etc. In each one of them the interactive design had to be oriented at the potential users, irrespective of the motivations or reasons for the use of the computers: educational, source of information, pastime, etc. In the three first: hypertext, multimedia and hypermedia, it can be seen how as the storage supports of the digital information advanced, that is, minifloppy, CD-Rom, DVD, etc., the dynamic media, such as video, music, computer animations, etc., were incorporated to the digitalized media, gaining room to the static media, such as texts, drawings, graphics, pictures, etc. Simultaneously there was a growing need of learning the use or functioning of the computers, where the notion of usability would develop into usability engineering, since the late 80s until the decade of the 90s. With the democratic spread of the use of the internet, in the mid 90s, the interfaces became an important linchpin in the acceptance of the interactive systems. At that time the notion of human-computer interaction went on to take a prevailing role in the new millennium.

Now as an expression it is already referenced by James H. Carlisle in a scientific paper called: "Evaluating the Impact of Office Automation on Top Management Communication" in the mid 70s. Across time this notion may appear as a human-machine interaction (HMI), man-machine interaction (MMI) or computer-human interaction (CHI). The expansion of its use in the 80s has one of its origins in the book published in 1983 under the title "The Psychology of Human-Computer Interaction" (Hillsdale: Erlbaum), whose authors are Stuart K. Card, Allen Newell and Thomas P. Moran. In both works it is easy to detect how there is an intersection between the formal and factual sciences, especially when the presence of computer science, the social communication media, design, interface, visualization of information, sociology, psychology, ergonomics, among other areas of knowledge, is revealed. It is a domain of scientific knowledge whose boundaries are stretched from a myriad disciplines, until making it the most elastic of the latter times. To such an extent that with artificial intelligence and especially robotics, we have been talking about robot-human interaction for a long time already, for instance.

In the new millenium, the human-computer interaction will become a kind of shopping mall of the new university degrees in many places of the EU, with ramifications in the American continent, especially from the Río Grande to the Tierra del Fuego. Where it is possible to see how the term "human" lacks any value in the face of certain canibalistic behaviour by many of those who disguisedly are ruling this disicipline They do it in a little transparent way, and through international or national associations, foundations, congresses, magazines, etc., that have as title or subtitle the HCI. However, in reality they devote themselves to other issues that do not belong to the HCI academically speaking but rather to matters of a personal nature. Now it isn't something exclusive of the HCI, but rather of all those technological breakthroughs that in some moments of their history become the focus of attention, making that it lasts in time or decays in a jiffy. The problem of this phenomenon lies in the duration of the university degrees (for instance those that are related to the HCI and the NICTs for the future professionals, who can join a religious college, take engineering as a degree, allegedly with a great demand in the labour market, but the same as a large part of the syllabus it is based on fleeting technologies. In less than five years, those neo professionals will see how the degrees they got aren't demanded by the local workplace. Consequently, they will be forced to take new studies through masters, specialization courses, continuous training, etc. In other words, it is the perpetual and big business of the degrees, generally based on the commercial software and hardware, where there is no balance between theory and practice in the study plans, whether it is public, private or hybrid educational institutions. Something similar is already happening with the user experience design or user experience, shortened with some of the following acronyms: UX, UXD, UED, and XD.

The UX encompasses all the human-computer interaction and all aspects of a product or service as perceived by the users. In other words, it is the reinvention of the HCI, whose boundaries aren't elastic anymore, but rather invisible and infinite. It is the umpteenth situation where cyclically a group of individuals decide the commercial fashions in these fields of knowledge. It happened already in the late 90s with the usability, where everything related to the final user at the moment of interacting with a computer was major engineering. That is why nobody should be surprised if even semiotics or semiology ended up being an engineering. What is striking is that the term multimedia has been wiped out from the human-computer interaction when it fact from the abacus down to the moment of interacting with calculators, computers, etc., there is an implicit and explicit communication process between the user and the device with which he/she interacts, whether it is electronic or not. How can it be that multimedia, communication and communication media have been wiped out in the main online databases or internet browsers, when the definition of HCI is searched? How can it be that the quality of the communication or communicability isn't considered in the times of the multimedia mobile phones? The answers to these questions have to be found in the domain of the formal sciences and especially in isolated individuals or in groups that devote themselves to slowing down the real progress of this area of knowledge. We can already imagine how many years, financial resources, etc., does a computer science technician, mathematician, physicist, etc., in truly learning the requirements of the users of the NTICs among the elderly, the disabled, children, etc. The inverse sense, that is, to go from the factual sciences towards the human-computer interaction, interfaces, information architecture, computer security, etc, apparently isn't allowed in the Old World and in some other places of the planet. In short, these are anomalous situations, which do not change with the passing of time, and which absorb myriad financial resources, whether they are public and/or private, without considering the energies and synergies of the human and professional capital, and the damage caused to the common weal in the global village. This poverty of contents and horizons is reflected in the contents of thousands of interactive systems aimed at the education, healthcare, entertainment, and information in general.

The efforts to optimize human-computer interaction from the factual sciences have constant and progressive in time. In contrast, from the formal sciences a certain slowdown can be seen, stagnation and regression, although the hardware and the rest of emerging technologies are still advancing by leaps and bounds every passing minute. This is due to the lack of creativity. A creativity which is replaced by the provocations which stem from certain groups of individuals who directly and indirectly are related to the formal sciences. The tactic consists in detecting people or groups of people with high qualities of creativity, originality and innovation who are the synthesis of the formal and factual sciences. Once these qualities are detected, those who sustain them in a natural and constant way across their professional life are sidelined. This marginalization becomes a kind of hidden source not only for plagiarism but directly in the generation of pseudo clones of those who really possess the wisdom and the guidelines to move in the daily tsunami of the emerging technologies. Now in the face of the question: How does one detect and avoid those pseudo clones? For that it is necessary to investigate their trajectory.

A strategy consists in investigating where they got their high school studies and/or their college degree. For instance, in the high schools, secondary institutes, etc., which are related to the applied sciences, technical and technological. Undoubtedly, in each one of them computer science will be present. In the second case, they may be degrees in computer science, mathematics, physics, etc. In both situations and in several places of the European coast of the Mediterranean the workplace outlet was guaranteed beforehand. Prior to the global crisis, the future employees knew they would have a lifelong and stable working contract in small, medium and big firms or industries, to take posts of technicians, heads of department, directors, etc.

The common denominator of those times was the speedy incorporation of the future professionals in the local labour market, even before finishing their studies. That is, the students of secondary institutes or colleges already knew at an early age how to plan the rest of their lives. Therefore, the computer science technicians in the firms and/or Lombardy industries, for instance, took an internal career until occupying the management posts. This workplace reality disappeared in the Old World in the first decade of the new millennium. Others, who got their degrees in computer sciences have seen in the universities an alternative to get a monthly salary on a lifelong basis. That is, something that the local industrial or business marketplace didn't guarantee them any longer. Nevertheless, they introduced a radical orientation change in the way of conceiving, coordinating and carrying out their activities inside some Lombardy universities, for example. Theoretically, public but ruled by institutions or power groups alien to the secular university environment. There technicians and computer sciences graduates have been joined to teach classes without having previously a wide training experience. The deans in charge have hugely increased the number of collaborators, under the label of administrative staff for those new professors lacking in knowledge and/or experience in pedagogy, teaching, etc., who stemmed from the industrial or business context, etc. Simultaneously, they were allocated courses with a very low academic or training level, such as the programming in Html of websites, the Excel broadsheets, the text processors such as Word, etc. That is, studies akin to the secondary courses in technical institutes at that time.

This abnormality favoured the former students of the "Scuola Normale di Pisa" –www.sns.it, to such extent that the graduates of the training centre, without owning a PhD, now direct doctoral theses at the University of Bergamo, Free University of Bozen, etc., or they take care of supervising the enablement of college professors, to mention a couple of examples. In few words, a totally illogical, unnatural, with a big zero creativity context. All of that in a state-run or public college educational system. Allegedly catalogued as serious, with training and creative excellence, in the university structure of the EU. However, with the passing of time, those pseudo clones, with the approval of their mentors and enablers, approach the key posts of a university structure such as the deanery of the faculty or the rectory. Besides, those educational structures, with unheard of and illicit situations, and close to science fiction than to the formal and factual sciences, are presented online with a sophisticated ethical code. Apparently, nobody takes into account that the damage to the future generations of emerging technologies is incalculable.

It is the empire of the equation less knowledge and formation of more power. An equation that gathers all the pseudoclones who teem in the domain of the training related to the NITCs and the rest of the emerging technologies. The union among them also usually degenerates in a destructive force of seminars, conferences, workshops, national and international symposiums, where is seen a real presence of the intersection between the formal and the factual sciences. Externally, they will disseminate prejudices and ungrounded criticism with regard to the extension of the topics of the events: the knowledge of the members of the honorary committee, scientific, organization, etc.; the alternatives chosen to publish the research works: the databases to publish the research works; and a long etc. Also their efforts will focus on becoming part of the scientific committees to internally sabotage the events. In other words, they act like the crew of the Trojan Horse. Once they have got their destructive result, these forces dilute until finding other professionals to demolish. Axiomatically and previously, they are cloned, because those professionals possess the necessary knowledge and experience to know how to orient themselves and act autonomously in the face of the technological progress and the optimization of the HCI. We are in front of a continuous cycle, repetitive and endless of the destruction of the sciences and the educational system, irrespective of the temporal and geographical space, where the professors are "sold" in the educational market with long labels but with contents of doubtful scientific value". As an example, a new fashion called "the bunch of Catalan botifarra" with degrees, experiences and passions: PhD in nanotechnology, engineer in electronics, expert in computing, passionate about humanism, psychology and science; whose scientific contribution are dolls for adults because it is a growing commercial market in the EU.

Many think that the panacea to the problem is private education, not secular. That is, that all those who do not have enough money must fall like Newton's apples into the public education, as it were some kind of fatal inertia for millions of students or a dead alley without a workplace outlet. This is not an issue of public education versus private, but rather of the lack of mechanisms to eradicate from the world educational structure the parochialism of the pseudo clones. It is they who in an individual or group way gnaw away continuously and disguisedly at the quality and educational seriousness, whether it is public, private or hybrid.

In innumerable cases in south of Europe experience shows in the field of the HCI and the emerging technologies that anything that is abnormal, immoral, illicit, among so many other adjectives has in the Summit of power people or rather characters who have spent part of their lives in a private structure, that is, religious in EU. Let's not forget that dogmatically they are above anything that entails order or cosmos. That is, they define themselves as a species superior to all the humans, and their actions can't be governed by the rules of a local, provincial, regional, state or international rules. The rest of the citizens are forced to suffer the consequences of the debauchery that they exercise on the global village. The 3D displays, artificial intelligence, augmented reality, big data, biotechnology, brain-computer interface, cloud computing, computer sciences, cryptocurrency, educational structure, healthcare system, immersive virtual reality, machine translation, magnetic levitation, nanotechnology, new technologies of information and communication, powered exoskeleton, quantum information, robotics, semantic web, smart cities, etc., aren't exempted from that reality.

Fortunately, even today, beyond the borders of the allegedly economically developed communities, there are realities where the public quality in education beats by far the private one. Those oasis of knowledge, joined to the vocation for teaching of their protagonists, support the progressive transfer of the knowledge and the experience towards the future generations. All of that thanks to a very small percentage of the taxes that the citizens pay, that allows them to guarantee the access to solid, free and egalitarian education among its inhabitants. That is, the opposite to what is preached by the mercantilist supporters of education, to keep on making a desert the basis of the worldwide population pyramid. Here the emerging technologies and the scientific-education local and global community, related directly and indirectly to the HCI, have an essential role to differentiate between these two phenomena.

These are real and non-virtual phenomena which entail a continuous denunciation to help the progress of real scientific knowledge, based on the common good of humankind, in the face of mercantilist savagery which little by little has been taking hold of science since the late 20th century. That is why it is important to distinguish with the greatest possible information and verified in situ the places where the future generations will be trained. Knowing beforehand the tactics and ploys of formational marketing, used to attract the potential students in structures that only serve to increase student and workplace failure, even though the labs have available the latest technological breakthroughs, the professors are motley and international, a professional outlet is guaranteed in writing and a long etcetera. It can be seen in this brief listing how we have always been, are and will be immersed in a process of infinite semiosis when talking about the emerging technologies. They encompass the three main aspects for the survival of the human being, that is: nutrition, habitation and clothing. Therefore, the emerging technologies will be fields of research and development that gather the areas of agriculture, building, material sciences, energy, electronics, AI, entertainment, medicine, the communication media, the means of transportation for humans and goods, among so many others. Here is the main reason why there is a bidirectional interrelation with the HCI.

The human-computer interaction is a natural and advisable context to see grow in harmony a large part of the progress of the discoveries and inventions of the human being. However, in the last quarter of a century, it has been a kind of magnet to draw the garduña and destroy it, internally speaking. Today, it is useless and shocking to associate it to words like peace, inclusion, wellbeing, happiness, education, videogames, children, the elderly, the disabled, etc., when some of the individuals who establish those links at the same time and internationally foster the garduña factor inside it. Now, if corrective measures are taken, in what remains of the current decade, it will take one or two generations to achieve its perfect reorientation towards clearly scientific areas. Areas which can be summed up in some way in the main keywords of each one of the research works that make up the book. Those words shape the reliable paths to be followed in the next years. Essentially, the technological ones that are emerging in our days and whose true democratization may really facilitate and increase the quality of life of all the inhabitants of the planet, based on the avant-garde of two cornerstones, such as education and healthcare for all.

Many of the research works that make up the current books have been presented orally, in some cases with their matching demonstrations of hardware and/or software in the following international conferences and/or workshop and/or symposium (2014-2016): ADNTIIC (Advances in New Technologies, Interactive Interfaces and Communicability), CCGIDIS (Communicability, Computer Graphics and Innovative Design for Interactive Systems), ESIHISE (Evolution of the Sciences, Informatics, Human Integration and Scientific Education), HCITISI (Human-Computer Interaction, Telecommunications, Informatics and Scientific Information), HCITOCH (Human-Computer Interaction, Tourism and Cultural Heritage), HIASCIT (Horizons for Information Architecture, Security and Cloud Intelligent Technology), MSIVISM (Multimedia, Scientific Information and Visualization for Information Systems and Metrics), RDINIDR (Research and Development in Imaging, Nanotechnology, Industrial Design and Robotics), and SETECEC (Software and Emerging Technologies for Education, Culture, Entertainment, and Commerce). All of them are the result of a selection process and a continuous correction process, in keeping with the indications indicated by the reviewers. The book is organized into 17 chapters. Next a short summary of each one of them to indicate the main aspects of the work research carried out by their authors:

In Chapter 1, "Cartographic Information Off-Line and First Nations: A Significant Contribution to the Enhancement of the Architectural Heritage", the author, Francisco V. Cipolla-Ficarra stresses the importance of analogical and digital cartography to revalue the cultural legacy of the first nations in the American continent. The excellent knowledge of astronomy reached by the early American civilizations are also underlined, and which were used by the conquerors, to build the religious temples interrelated to certain cosmological phenomena, whose information was gather by the local civilizations. Besides, a wide review is made through all the cartography process, stressing its importance, as a creative activity and the main difficulties in the dissemination of cultural heritage online.

Chapter 2, "Web 2.0 and Health Information Technology: Theory and Applications", is the title chosen by its author, Kijpokin Kasemsap, to excellently focus his research work on the use of the technologies stemming from the social networks and healthcare. Through the work can been the importance of perspectives of health information technology, previously analyzing the Web 2.0 applications in knowledge management, academic libraries, learning and education, among others. In an orderly and sequential way the author presents each one of the topics, ending with a valuable contribution to the future research in this field of knowledge where emerging technologies, healthcare, social networks converge among many others.

In Chapter 3, the authors of the research "Digital Diorama: An Interactive Multimedia Resource for Learning the Life Sciences" are Annamaria Poli, Annastella Gambini, Antonella Pezzotti, Alfredo Broglia, Alessandra Mazzola, Sabrina Muschiato, Carlo Emilio Standoli, Daniela Zambarbieri, and Fiammetta Costa. They present us the importance of the use of the technologies with didactic purposes. A masterly project called "Digital Diorama" is the conductive thread of the chapter, which is structured in a splendid way and accompanied by real images which facilitate the understanding of the text, turning it into an example to be followed, especially when we refer to educational contents. Where not only the students/users of these technologies can enrich their knowledge through the exploration of a digital diorama, but also the professors, since there is a set of strategies explained in a detailed way, which are valid to be immediately applied in the educational domain.

In Chapter 4, the author of the work "School-Cinema: A Research Experience That Combines Educational Theories, Educational Processes, and Educational Technologies" is Daniela Tamburini. She establishes very clearly from the beginning of the text which is the main goal and the secondary goals of her research. In it is masterfully created a bridge between the social sciences and the new technologies of information and communication. The work is included in a series of experiments and theoretical notions of an Italian research project called "School-cinema". It is a project of humanistic culture and new media. In it are thoroughly analyzed the pedagogical, sociological, psychological, anthropological, communication aspects, among others, of the educational process, resorting to the use of the new technologies. That is, the core is the human being and in the context is the technology with which the people are interacting. The issue of the cinema is approached from several perspectives until reaching a 360 degrees vision, from the theoretical-practical point of view. In it is not only included the role of the students, professors, but also the family environment.

In Chapter 5, "Humans Versus Computers, Systems, and Machines: A Battle for Freedom, Equality, and Democracy", its author Alan Radley explains to us from an innovating and philosophical perspective how computers, operating systems, informatics machines in general are modifying the rights and duties of the human beings, in a special way, the individual and social freedoms reached across history. In the chapter is analyzed the evolution of the traditional concepts related to freedom, democracy, etc., and the changes that are taking place from artificial intelligence, the automation of the human activities, etc. Besides, the need is explained for counting with tools that boost the private and safe communications in the internet. For which reason the author proposes the Keymail. A series of new concepts, gathered in a glossary, are defined by Radley. Through these notions explained across the chapter is obtained an enlarged vision of what is and will be the future of people in the daily interaction with the new technologies.

In Chapter 6, the author of the study "Cyberbullying: Description, Definition, Characteristics, and Outcomes" is Michelle Wright. She has broached one of the topics with the greatest impact in the training of the new generations through the new information and communication technologies such as cyberbullying, in the case of the children and teenagers, through the social networks. Exceptionally she makes an argument of easy understanding by the reader of a complex subject in our days, starting by a state of the art, where are defined in an understandable way the phenomenon and each one of the terms is detailed. Simultaneously the results of the studies are presented, including the role of the parents and the schools. The sociological aspect, the social psychology, the eventual solutions to the problem and some advice, among others of the current chapter are very special, considering each one of the open lines, starting from it for future research.

In Chapter 7, the authors of the "A Psycho-Pedagogical Model for Evaluating Effectiveness of Students' Learning on the Basis of Electronic Visual Rows" are Svetlana Kostromina, Daria Gnedykh, and Galina Molodtsova. In it is presented a model aimed at the professors to assess comprehensively the effectiveness of learner's information acquisition in e-learning. The research starts with a theoretical framework where there is a wide and rich bibliographical references to continue further on with those motivations that justify the elaboration of the current model for evaluating of effectiveness of student's learning. Also accompany the detailed exposition of the content, a series of experiments carried out with students from which can be inferred the complexity of the study carried out. Finally, there is a series of recommendations derived from the experiments carried out and that may serve as a guideline for other works related to e-learning, for example.

In Chapter 8, the study carried out by Sandra G. Jiménez-González, Ricardo Mendoza-González, and Huizilopoztli Luna-García presented under the title of "Guidelines Based on Need-Findings Study and Communication Types to Design Interactions for MOOCs" has four main keywords: MOOCs (Massive Open Online Courses), platforms, distance education, and design guidelines. Those words make apparent a very well structured study with regard to a first ser of design guidelines for the developers of interfaces for MOOCs. The proposal made by the authors encompasses four types of communication in distance education. Step by step, the authors explain in detail, through synthetic tables, each one of the techniques and methods used for the elaboration of the design guide, tending to create a bridge between educators and distance educators.

In Chapter 9, Andreas Kratky is the author of the research called "Personal Touch: A Viewing-Angle-Compensated Multi-Layer Touch Display". In it the author reveals the main advantages of the large format touch screens, especially for the museums. The personal touch system is a functional solution and with attractive practical results with the users at the moment of interacting, where an augmented-reality display system combining real objects with superimposed interactive graphics. The chapter is perfectly interrelated in each one of its parts, with examples of a real project. In the explanation of the personal touch system, converge the notions of design, the factors considered in the implementation of the system, the heuristic for viewing-angle-compensation, etc. Finally, the experiments carried out with real users allows not only to increase the potentiality of the use of the current solution, but also establish and boost research lines in the framework of the human-computer interaction, design of interactive systems, augmented reality, emerging technologies for cultural heritage and tourism, among many others.

In Chapter 10, "Supporting Motion Capture Acting Through a Mixed Reality Application" is stressed the importance of the motion capture in the computer animation. In that sense the authors, Daniel Kade, Rikard Lindell, Hakan Ürey, and Oğuzhan Özcan, explain each one of the outstanding aspects of the motion capture applied to the human beings, starting by a state of the art where are already presented the challenges of the current technique, the role of the actors with their emotions and the context where they will be immersed. Besides, they have developed a prototype, with which they are getting positive results. Its software and hardware has been evaluated with real users. In the test can be seen the use of techniques and methods to compile the data stemming from the formal sciences, as is the case of the interviews, to mention one example. The conclusions reached by the authors allow to know beforehand certain emotional reactions of the actors when they are immersed in the virtual environments.

In Chapter 11, the research work "Facebook, Tele-Collaboration, and International Access to Technology in the Classroom," has two authors, Karen Woodman and Vasilia Kourtis-Kazoullis. In it is stressed the importance of Facebook in the learning in the classroom working with students from several continents. The authors have got splendid results in graduate education students' perceptions on the use of technologies in classrooms of Australia and Greece. The experiments have demonstrated points of convergence in the online applications, in spite of the geographical distance between Europe and Oceania. These results may serve to boost the use of the new technologies and the social networks inside the classrooms. The cultural factor of the group of study has boost even more the results reached, with the crosshairs set on future studies. The universe of study was not only composed of Australian and Greek students, but also Chinese, Filipinos, Malayans, Saudis and South Koreans. An updated group of references allows to broaden the topics dealt with in the chapter.

In Chapter 12, and under the title "Contextual Issues in Groupware Applications for Educational Support Groups", its authors, Huizilopoztli Luna-García, Ricardo Mendoza-González, Laura C. Rodrí-guez-Martínez, Mario A. Rodríguez-Díaz, Guadalupe Lara-Cisneros, Carlos R. Ordaz-García, Sandra Mercado-Pérez, and Alejandro U. López-Orozco, present the importance of work groups in the use of the new technologies, within and without the classroom. The main goal is to achieve a basic but well-designed user interfaces for groupware applications for which they base themselves on two main axes: the users' interactive requirements and the functional requirements to support users' interactions. In the background section the authors reveal the main differences between HCI and UX, as well as a state of the art of the presented topic. It is also interesting to stress the correct use of some techniques deriving from the social sciences, such as the observation interview, focus group, etc. In this regard are incorporated each one of the tactics followed for the compiling of the information with the users.

In Chapter 13, the authors of the research "An Exploratory Study on the Interaction Beyond Virtual Environments to Improve Listening Ability When Learning English as a Second Language", are Pablo A. Alcaraz-Valencia, Laura S. Gaytán-Lugo, and Sara C. Hernández Gallardo. They have focused their research on the study of English as a second language in Mexico. They do it through holographic tech-nologies and a series of recommendations obtained from the experiments carried out with real students. Essentially they have based themselves on the listening factor for the learning of a second language, and the use of holography. A set of premises such as definitions of listening in learning English as a second language and the positive and negative strategies in order to process perceived audio input, has led them to surprising results, resorting to experiments that didn't require great financial resources. Once overcome the stage of study of the state of the art, which has produced a wide compilation of bibliographical references, like the diverse strategies followed, their research aimed at selecting the best technology available for listening comprehension, bearing in mind the contextual factor, the experiences and the background of the students, for instance.

In Chapter 14, Mehmet Donmez, Kursat Cagiltay, Serkan Alkan, Fuat Bolukbas, and Goknur Kaplan Akilli are the authors of the study that they have called "Use of Large Multi-Touch Interfaces: A Research on Usability and Design Aspects". Experiments with users, interactive design, multi-touch interfaces, usability, etc., are some of so many issues which are approached across the study. In it is stressed an experimental approach incorporating a large multi touch interface environment, for instance. In almost all the sections it is easy to detect the presence of the intersection of the formal and factual sciences. There is a complete description of the technological aspects as well as the methodology used at the moment of carrying out the experiments with the real users. The results obtained during the analysis of the eye tracking data of users are perfectly framed in the domain of HCI and make up a reference point for other analogous studies.

In Chapter 15, "A Multi-Agent Model for Personalizing Learning Material for Collaborative Groups" is the title chosen by its authors, Pablo Santana-Mansilla, Rosanna Costaguta, and Silvia Schiaffino, to give a reference to the current research. The main goal is the elaboration of a multi-agent model that personalizes the delivery of learning, especially when groups of collaborative students denote a loss of knowledge and orientation in the search of online materials. The experiments carried out in a methodical and comprehensive way have allowed to compile transcendental information to detect the errors of the students and particularly in their search of learning material, writings in English and Spanish. Internally, the research has a classical structure, well articulated in each one of its sections, and with a specialization in the methods for searching multilingual documents. The comparative work in the state of the art makes it possible to quickly detect the pros and cons in the choice of the best alternatives as it can be seen in subjects related to the comparison of recommender systems for e-learning: evaluation of search results considered relevant. among others.

In Chapter 16, the authors of the study "Scientific Information Superhighway Versus Scientific Information Backroads in Computer Science" are Francisco V. Cipolla-Ficarra, Donald Nilson, and Jacqueline Alma. It is study where is examined the quality of the indexation of the scientific works in the international databases, akin to computer sciences, computer graphics, human-computer interaction, augmented reality, education, etc. Simultaneously are analyzed the workplace consequences, when the future professionals are already excluded in the student stage from the publications, regardless of whether the university is public, private or hybrid. Comparing these human and social factors will lead to the generation of two levels or scientific strata, those who circulate in the high speed highways and those who are literally pushed to circulate through the back roads. mainly for financial reasons. A historical analysis of the main online databases or Internet browser allows to detect certain power groups and behaviour considered as human factors that hugely damage the progress of the human-computer interaction and the studies related to the emerging technologies. Finally, is presented a first guide to determine the quality of the research groups starting from the way in which their publications are made, allegedly belonging to the whole of those that are called scientific.

In Chapter, 17, the research work called "Rendering and Video Games," the authors are Francisco V. Cipolla-Ficarra, Jacqueline Alma and Miguel Cipolla-Ficarra. They make apparent a triadic relationship at the moment of examining the interactive desing in the videogames for adults, with special interest in the rendering of the static and dynamic images. Besides, the chapter dwells on the software, hardware, and interactive design strategies for the production of three-dimensional videogames, as well as the generation of virtual characters. In each one of the sections there is a short diachronic review, with relation to the evolution of the software, the hardware and the interactive design. The authors point out the limitations of the past, and indicate whether they have been surpassed in the present, substantially in the original contents and the interaction between the user and the emerging technologies, when we refer to the categories of interactive design, for instance. Lastly, the results are presented of a heuristic assessment of the videogames, distributed in the whole planet, many of which have set a landmark in the history of pastimes, through the use of the personal computer.

You cannot build character and courage by taking away man's initiative and independence
– Abraham Lincoln (1809–1865)

Acknowledgment

Sometimes such a simple word as thanks is banal for many people. However, in this occasion I don't have enough words of gratitude towards Colleen Moore and the rest of her colleagues in Chocolate Ave. Without the patience, professionalism, help and understanding of all of them, this long work wouldn't have gone forward. In other words, a special thank you very much from the soul and the heart to each one of the members of IGI Global.

A deepest gratitude to Maria Ficarra, one of the human beings with a noble heart, transparency, simplicity, goodness, wisdom and infinite affability.

Finally, thanks a lot to Miguel C. Ficarra, Kim Veltman, Mary Brie, Sonia Flores, Luisa Varela, and Carlos Albert.

Introduction

In the short time that is left before entering the third decade of the new millennium, it can already be seen the tendency towards invisibility of the technology in a myriad devices of daily life, within and without the home. It suffices to watch and thin, the possibilities that are offered by certain new hardware devices of a very low cost such as the Raspberry Pi computer (www.raspberrypi.org), whose only or simple plate hailing from the UK, has as its main goal the fostering of computer science teaching in high and primary school. These plates used in the glasses and mirrors give us the option of unfolding interactive menus, opaque and/or transparent, with information related to meteorology, the month calendar, the time, news headlines, etc. (Figure 1). Besides, it can be programmed to manage several devices in the domotic or intelligent house, for instance. The computer is an open software and its operative system is already compatible with a version of the Windows 10.

That is, technologically we are in a metamorphosis which will drives us from miniaturization towards the invisibility of the current computer and/or telematic devices keeping or increasing the communicability between the human beings and computers. In other words, the new technological devices, with small size, with a minimalist device and empathic towards interaction will tend to merge, exponentially increasing their functions. In this context, quanta computer science and the expansion of communicability will take a very important role, the same as artificial intelligence and all its derivations. It is a

Figure 1. A cheap computer for intelligent glasses and mirrors

vertiginous process which entails quickly widening the horizon of new neutral scientific research, that is, noncommercial, for a myriad of potential new users. In this sense, new and interesting horizons are opening for the human-computer interaction (HCI), especially that which is aimed at the seriousness and universality of the obtained results.

Since the late 20th century the human-computer interaction as an area of scientific knowledge has passed from being an intersection of professional disciplines of the formal and factual sciences to a chaotic gathering of said sciences in the new millennium, where the partial fields of studies from engineering usability of the 90s (Nielsen, 1992) are nowadays total or global contexts under the label of user experience (UX). Oddly enough in this boundless expansion of the human-computer interaction among the human beings and the new technologies different dynamic and/or static media of interactive communication are still being used. It is there where communication and, very specially, the quality of communication, that is, communicability, is one of the vital focuses of the research for the new decade and especially not only with the horizon of 2020, but rather with the look set on 2050, in the educational and scientific field, for instance.

This endless inclusion inside the human-computer interaction in other areas of knowledge under expressive formulas such as interdisciplinarity, transdisciplinarity, multidisciplinarity, transversality, etc. indicate the presence of the wild mercantilism of the sciences and all its derivations, starting by teaching, whether it is secular or not, and the training of professionals and/or experts of this sector. It is a disorderly widening of new horizons, stemming from a variegated range of professions. Some examples may be nuclear engineering, industrial engineering, fine arts graduates, anthropology, mathematicians, physicists, among many others. Professionals who are geographically located and mostly in the societies with theoretically developed economies, but which have found in the human-computer interaction a kind of panacea for daily survival, and turn this scientific sector a space of study without rules. That is, everything goes, applying the pecking order. In few words, it is the eternal dilemma of the lack of balance between the formal and the factual sciences (Bunge, 1981; Ander-egg, 1986), where the former try to take a place of supremacy with regard to the latter. One of the genesis of that phenomenon has been the expansion in the use of the computers, which leads us to review previously and briefly the notions of sciences, mathematics, physics and engineering.

Mathematics is regarded as the "godmother of the sciences", because of the generality of the results that are obtained from it. That is, a priori it has no bounds in its applications, whether it is in the study of the numbers and the calculations as well as the space and the structures. To such extent that in our days each one of the technical or scientific disciplines which range from physics to engineering, or from descriptive statistics to computer sciences, resort constantly to the calculation, analysis and modelling stemming from mathematics. However, in the field of the social sciences (Kincaid, 2012), sometimes that exaggerated quantification applied to the elaboration of design models of interactive systems, the partial and generalized conclusions of heuristic analysis, the quick extrapolation of non-verified results of research-in-progress etc., all of them aimed at the learning processes, creative or original contents for the teaching of children, the elderly, the disabled, etc., may seriously damage the communicability among the potential users and the new interactive technological devices. Quantifying and quantification are not synonymous of quality and qualification, in two essential pillars of the societies such as education and healthcare, even if mathematics, has a long tradition in the whole history of the evolution of the civilizations and alphabets (Veltman, 2014) in our planet. It has been the first discipline in having available rigorous methods, which have allowed it to increase its field of action with the computers. In this regard it is worth mentioning the equations that have changed the world, according to Ian Stewart: The

Pythagorean Theorem, Logarithms, Calculus, Law of Gravity, The square root of -1, Euler's Polyhedra Formula, Normal distribution, Wave Equation, Fourier Transform, Navier-Stokes Equations, Maxwell's Equations, Second Law of Thermodynamics, Relativity, Schrodinger's Equation, Information Theory, Chaos Theory and Black-Scholes Equation (Stewart, 2012).

Physics is one of the earliest academic disciplines, perhaps the oldest, since astronomy is one of its branches of knowledge. Most ancient civilizations in each one of the continents have been looking for explanations of the functioning of their environment. In that sense they started by analyzing the nightly and daily sky, that is, the stars, the comets, the moon, the sun, etc., and associated phenomena such as the sun and moon eclipses. This led to many interpretations of a more philosophical that physical nature. Consequently, in those moments physics was called natural philosophy. Many philosophers can be found in the genesis of physics, such as Aristotle or Thales of Miletus (Moledo & Olszevicki, 2015), among others, because they were the first to try to find some kind of explanation to the phenomena that surrounded them. During these two latter millennia, physics was regarded as part of what is currently called philosophy, chemistry and certain branches of biology and mathematics. In the 17th century, with the scientific revolution it became a modern science. However, in some spheres such as mathematical physics and quantum chemistry, the boundaries of physics are still hard to distinguish. Here is a field where the boundaries are very elastic, temporally and professionally speaking, apart from the fact that physics can be defined synthetically as a natural sciences which devotes itself to the study of energy, matter, time and space as well as the interaction of these four notions with each other.

Historically physics precedes electric engineering. Electric engineering applies knowledge of sciences such as physics and mathematics. Given its evolution in time, now it encompasses a series of disciplines which include telecommunications, electronics, control systems and the processing of signals, electrical engineering . It is necessary to remember that in relation of the spatial or contextual variable that is used, the term electric engineering may or not encompass electronic engineering, which arises as one subdivision of it and has had an important evolution since the invention of the tube or thermo-ion valve and the radio. That is, primary technology for the birth and development of the Global Village, in the 20th century (McLuhan & Powers, 1989).

In its beginnings engineering was related almost exclusively to military, government and religious activities. It suffices to mention the fortresses and their embankments, the roads and the bridges, the ports and the lighthouses, etc. A genius of Renaissance such as Leonardo Da Vinci, interrelated exceptionally art with engineering, as it can be seen in the wide collection of his masterpieces. In peace time engineering, theoretically, has to be at the service of the wellbeing of mankind, excluding the bellicose framework. Hence that when the early universities started to offer this career they called it civil engineering to distinguish it from that carried out by the warriors, that is, military engineering.

Etymologically the term sciences stems from the Latin "scire" which means to know. However, the Latin verb "scire" refers to a form of knowledge and accumulation of knowledge. Mario Bunge claims that science grows from common knowledge and surpasses it with its growth (Bunge, 1981). Scientific research starts in the same place where experience and knowledge stop solving problems or even approach them. In other terms, it is the social practice when the human being faces a series of problems which can't be solved with the daily knowledge, nor through common sense. This is a very common mistake by using indiscriminately the notion of empathy in interactive design, in myriad situations more related to social communication that with the actual experience of the users. That is, cyclically the same mistakes are repeated which at the end of the first millennium, when they were used as synonymous, on the banks of the European Mediterranean, the notion of usability and a quality attribute for an interactive system, whether it is online or offline, such as accessibility, what Leggett and Schnase, calls hyperbase (Leggett & Schnase, 1994), that is, the data base.

Simultaneously, Aristotle claimed that to the human being eager to know and widen his knowledge external grasp of events and observation isn't enough, nor common sense, since there are phenomena which can't be grasped solely at the perceptive level (Moledo & Olszevicki, 2015). That is, it is necessary to overcome the immediacy of the sensorial certainty of the spontaneous knowledge of daily life. Precisely it is this qualitative leap which leads us to scientific knowledge. Undeniably this does not mean an extreme discontinuity as far as nature is concerned, but yes concerning method. Between both types of knowledge the differentiator isn't given by the nature of the object of study, but because of the form or procedure of acquisition of knowledge, particularly in the social sciences. In contrast, in the sciences of physics, for instance, there is a total break between both kinds of knowledge. Here is another essential difference between formal and factual sciences. A short historical review of the evolution of science allows us to complete a first state-of-the-art to better understand certain causes and effects of some human and social factors in the framework of the new technologies which will be approached in the handbook.

The greeks considered two dimensions of sciences: one theoretical and the other practical, but they focused on the first one. It was the Arabs who leaning on Greek knowledge concerned themselves with the application of sciences in its practical function and its utilitarian character. Precisely the practical accessibility contains the notion of utility, and it is one of the branches from which derives the term "usability, with its five classical principles for the use of the early hypertextual systems at the end of the 80s and early 90s, which were enunciated by Nielsen: easy to learn, efficient to use, few errors, easy to remember, and subjectively pleasing (Nielsen, 1990). However, those principles lacked attributes and quality metrics (Nielsen, 1990; Nielsen, 1992), as well as a procedure for their evaluation, starting by the design, where the equation quickness of evaluation, high quality of the obtained results and low costs were present. In this sense, several "classical" disciplines of the factual sciences, for instance, have been very useful to fill that measurement void, resorting to notions of semiotics, design models of the interactive systems, the human-computer interaction and software engineering among others.

With Francis Bacon starts a tradition of accumulation of data, observations and formulation of hypothesis (Ander-egg, 1986; Moledo & Olszevicki, 2015). This process peaks at the end of the Renaissance with Galileo and Newton, in the 16th century, and science appears in its modern sense of notion, with a common denominator such as its rationalistic and empirical character. The Renaissance and Humanism create the right climate for the irruption and development of science by overcoming the tendencies to abstract speculation and dogmatism typical of the Middle Ages. The humanists were heirs of a general paradigm in dissolution and they didn't have a new paradigm with which to replace it. However, they were contributing to draw its general lines, having got rid of the theological issues, aside from the scholastic discussions between realists and nominalists.

The humanist, the scientist, the artist and the Renaissance technician, many times rolled into one (nowadays, we can find this tendency in some pseudo experts in humanistic computer science, for instance). However, they at that time started the union between experimental science and mathematics, between empirical practice and theory, established a new way to perceive time, space and the world which gave its foundations to the mechanical philosophy of the 17th century and the scientific revolution. In short, it isn't any longer about making speculations, but directly watching the facts. The sources of science aren't given by arguments of authority, but by principles and laws which are deduced from reality.

From the 17th century onwards science and technique will be joined in a increasingly narrower reciprocity of functions. Science ceases to be a 100% intellectual activity in itself and for itself, a knowledge of things, to acquire every time more a clear motivation aimed at "doing things". The techniques, that is, the instruments of the practical activities, start to be used for the advance of science. Francis Bacon points out the importance of statistics for the progress of the sciences and the need for empirical verification.

The empiricism of Bacon will influence the new ways of approaching reality, that is, the observation and experimentation will constitute the main sources of knowledge. Kant will stress the importance of reason as a source of knowledge. In our days, sometimes, the empirical verification may not exist when the results obtained with the new college study plans of the new millennium are examined, such as the reduction of the time to obtain university diplomas with the simple purpose of increasing the statistic number of the population with college degrees.

Taking this short historical route to the surface of a compass, it is possible to establish the cardinal points over which the needle passes at the moment of getting orientation not only in the strategic sectors of the new technologies of information and communication, but also in knowing the motivations and reason for which certain human and social factors related to the human-computer interaction, to mention two examples last with the passing of time (Salvendy, 2012). Therefore, a diachronic view is always necessary. Besides, it is one of the main strategies to escape the last fashions in issues of research and development (R&D), generally fostered from public, private or hybrid financial bodies for the sale of their services and/or products, related directly and/or indirectly to the latest technologies. The research that doesn't belong to the set of the "latest fashions" is where the scientific principles are usually respected in almost 100% of the studied cases. Besides, these are centres where is fostered the creation of solid, dynamic and avant-garde structure, since the mercantilist factor practically doesn't exist.

This mercantilist factor, aimed at obtaining the greatest profits in the least possible time in our days is gnawing at not only the scientific system but also at its structure. A structure that entails a long time in being set up and seeing it work correctly. For instance, in the transition from the old to the new millennium and with the democratization of the internet (Carr, 2010), many made a heavy bet on the virtual firms, ecommerce, etc. thus generating a bubble that burst in the first decade of the 21st century. The motives were several ranging from the speed of the networks to the issue of security in the transactions, going also through the reliability of the potential users in the face of the technological novelty as well as the different speed in which the hardware moves in relation to the software (the former is faster than the latter).

Currently, and in this sense, some applications of the social networks, such as YouTube may be of great use to detect at mere sight the quality of experiments carried out in the context of the user experience (UX), HCI, usability engineering, etc., with users at the moment of interacting with the computers, tablet, PC, iPhone, etc. For instance, in the Figures 2, 3 and 4 we see an experiment with real users in a Barcelona association which has ceded a classroom with computers to carry out an experiment related to the videogames for the elderly (positive ageing or zero ageing, financed by foundations, banks, government bodies, universities, etc., local and/or European). However, the results obtained to not adjust at all to previously described scientific and experimental principles. In said images it can be seen at mere sight that not only the computers aren't equal among themselves, whether it is from the point of view of the hardware and the software (keyboards, mouse, monitors, etc.) preventing the standardization of the time of access to the applications, since they are different from each other. Besides, there are users who do not really belong to the third age as well as you can see participants who interact with the PC individually, between two or more, as it can be seen in the several frames that make up the video. This is a small example of how it is necessary to eradicate the fads in the educational-experimental field.

Figure 2. Experiments that do not abide by the epistemological principles of the factual sciences

Figure 3. Not all the users belong to the third age

Figure 4. Non-homogeneous use of software and hardware

Now inside the current context of the latest novelties of the NICTs (New Information and Communication Technology), two rhetorical questions are elementary: How to prevent the fashions or rather pseudo fashion, essentially in the training stage of the would-be professionals? A priori, what new technologies can escape the fleeting phenomenon of the fashions or of access only to a given elite of the population with the look set on the future in the middle and long term?

The first question finds a very brief and simple answer derived from the data bases where the scientific works are indexed. In them it can quickly be detected the ability, the competence, the knowledge and the scientific profile of the professors of graduate programs, engineering courses, masters, specialization courses, doctorates, post-doctorates, etc. There it is easy to check whether in their student period those professors have monographic publications, that is, with a single author, the main author, or in all their publications there are several authors. If all their publications have several authors, it means that the degree of scientific production is shared in a stage which should be autonomous or monographic to show their ability of researching self-sufficiency. In both cases it is also important to determine the total of international publications of that period.

A valid parameter of a "PhD Professor" is to have had at least five (minimun) or seven/ten (ideal) monographic or autonomous publications irrespective of the data base where those international scientific publications have been indexed. This parameter may sound to many heads of the current training courses in the EU as something old or of the past century. However, it is the vital key to determine the quality of teaching. Besides, it is the way to prevent that the students and/or their parents fall into the trap of the educational mercantilism, attracted by the mermaid song of advertising or propaganda, manifest or latent, in the traditional mainstream media (radio, tv, newspapers, etc.) and in the social networks. Mermaid songs for the local and global promotion which include even the possibility of publishing scientific articles since the first months when the student is taking subjects of a master, for instance.

It is also very important that all the promoted courses have a free access to the detailed information of each one of the programmes of their subjects, with their matching bibliographical references: the listing of tenured professors, assistants, aids, with their matching curricula; the equipment (software and the hardware, for instance) in the labs for the experiments or practices; the dedication of the head of department and his/her collaborators to teaching and research, that is, if they are part-time or full-time, among many other variables, belonging to the transparency and free access to online information. When there are no international publications or they are mostly shared, the faculty of the training/university centre will tend to not train the students to face in an autonomous and efficient way the challenges at the workplace once they have finished their studies. To such an extent that nowadays many computer science technicians in the south of Europe, who carry out outsourcing tasks for the maintenance, installation, etc., of printers, computers, servers, etc., do not know how to solve in an independent and professional way the problems posed to them without previously contacting their colleagues from their headquarters through the cell phone or the internet.

With regard to the second question sometimes it is necessary to give time to time when we are in the face of certain discoveries and/or inventions in the technological framework. However, our compass allows us already to anticipate some roads to be followed (Ross, 2016). In the first place, everything concerning artificial intelligence and especially domestic robotics will generate a new market of products and services, particularly in the Asian countries, where certain cultures accept the robot as yet another member of the family. In this regard it can be stressed the role of the androids with a human face, as it can be seen in Figure 5. Here also an interesting field of study is opening up between realism and the artificiality of the human movements, at the moment of simulating or emulating that reality. In America, Europe and Oceania industrial robotics and everything concerning automatism will keep on growing in an exponential way.

The social networks will keep on having their ups and downs for reasons of differentiation between freedom and debauchery. This will lead to a further control of the access to the internet until doing it in a nominative way, like that who accesses a bank account, from the home. So that everything concerning cyber security, cyber behaviour, rights and obligations of the users, etc., will tend to expand. The digital natives will not oppose the loss of freedoms, because without the devices of the multimedia mobile phones and all their applications they would have difficulties to carry out arithmetic operations, such as divisions and multiplications and they will increasingly lose their skills for the reading of texts, digital or not, as well indicates abc in his work abc. Therefore, the architecture of information and data analysis is another sector which will tend to grow to the extent to which the access to the information will remain free and

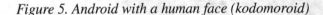

Figure 5. Android with a human face (kodomoroid)

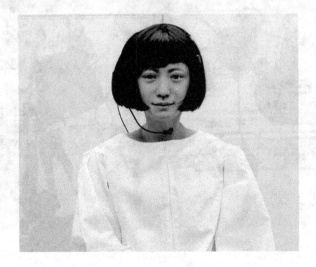

without cost. In this field specialists will be needed because the user of the interactive systems of the next decades will tend to lose skills for learning, memorization, the ability to establish associations, etc.

A human being who will undergo great environmental and technological changes through the smart cities. Where the drones will not simply be devices for the transportation of books or other objects, but also a means of air transportation for people, whether it is in a car or a bike as it can be seen in the Figures 6 and 7. At the home the wireless networks and the automatic devices are opening service sectors starting from the interactive communications such as domotics since the start of the new millennium.

Everything concerning medicine and the use of the new technologies will keep opening the gap between the great scientific breakthroughs whether it is in the framework of genomics the interactive systems and the brain handled devices, scientific visualization, three-dimensional, etc. with those users and patients who have access not to the latest technological breakthroughs but to the simplest of the healthcare systems. Public or private health systems where the patient and the environment of close relatives are central and not peripheral, such as simple numerical or alphanumeric codes of a health system. They have to keep on being informed constantly about the evolution of the disease and the options about the different methods and techniques to advance in the best possible way in the healing of the diseases or the improvement of health, in a safe and controlled way. This is a field where the breakthroughs in the matter of ecommerce should be more applied, especially when information is given to the patients and their close relatives.

Figure 6. Prototype of a bike
Source: Scorpion-3, hoverbike (www.hoversurf.com)

Figure 7. Experimental transportation of people in cars
Source: EHang 184 (www.ehang.com)

From all the sectors enumerated the latest is the most important, because the real heritage of the human being will keep on being invisible and will be called health. Besides, healthcare and education are the real cornerstones of any community that calls itself developed. Therefore, yesterday, today and tomorrow the new technologies of communication and information must be at the service of the human being and not the other way around.

Lastly each one of the diverse research works compiled in the current handbook generates a kind of strategic links, indispensable and dynamic, of theoretical and practical knowledge, which will not only help to analyze and better understand the current situation of the sciences and some of its disciplines, but also go ahead of the future areas of scientific interest and daily coexistence for millions of users of the new technologies, professors, students, researchers, businessmen, industrialists, designers, among so many others.

Francisco V. Cipolla-Ficarra
Latin Association of Human-Computer Interaction, Spain & International Association of Interactive Communication, Italy

REFERENCES

Ander-egg, E. (1986). *Techniques of Social Investigation*. Buenos Aires: Hvmanitas.

Bunge, M. (1981). *The science: Your Method and Your Philosophy*. Buenos Aires: Siglo XXI.

Carr, N. (2010). *The Shallows. What the Internet is Doing to Our Brains*. New York: W.W. Norton.

Kincaid, H. (2012). *The Oxford Handbook of Philosophy of Social Science*. Oxford, UK: Oxford University Press. doi:10.1093/oxfordhb/9780195392753.001.0001

Leggett, J., & Schnase, J. (1994). Viewing Dexter with Open Eyes. *Communications of the ACM, 37*(2), 76–86. doi:10.1145/175235.175241

McLuhan, M., & Powers, B. (1989). *The Global Village: Transformations in World Life and Media in the 21*ˢᵗ *Century*. Oxford, UK: Oxford University Press.

Moledo, L., & Olszevicki, N. (2015). *History of Scientific Ideas: From Tales of Miletus to God Machine*. Buenos Aires: Planeta.

Nielsen, J. (1990). Big Playbacks from 'Discount' Usability Engineering. *IEEE Software, 7*(3), 107–108.

Nielsen, J. (1992). The Usability Engineering Life Cycle. *IEEE Computer, 25*(3), 12–22. doi:10.1109/2.121503

Ross, A. (2016). *The Industries of the Future*. New York: Simon & Schuster.

Salvendy, G. (2012). *Handbook of Human Factors and Ergonomics*. New York: John Wiley. doi:10.1002/9781118131350

Stewart, I. (2012). *Seventeen Equations that Changed the World*. London: Profile Books.

Veltman, K. (2014). *Alphabets of Life*. Maastricht: Virtual Maastrict McLuhan Institute.

Chapter 1
Cartographic Information Off-Line and First Nations:
A Significant Contribution to the Enhancement of the Architectural Heritage

Francisco V. Cipolla-Ficarra
Latin Association of Human-Computer Interaction, Spain & International Association of Interactive Communication, Italy

ABSTRACT

We present the importance of analogical and digital cartography in the reconstruction of the cultural heritage of the first nations. Besides, through the cartographic information and the interactive multimedia systems, we examine the metamorphose of ancient pre-Columbus constructions, whose physical sites were based in the advanced knowledge of those civilizations in astronomy issues. We also present the main stages in the digital cartographic generation for their later use in the multimedia systems. Finally, we sum up the difficulties in the diffusion of certain historic contents compiled in the off-line multimedia supports, in the Internet and in the current social networks.

INTRODUCTION

As a rule, in daily life human beings have some points of reference of the architectonical surroundings, such as a mountain, a river, a tower, a fountain, a monument, a square, a market, etc. They are natural and/or artificial spaces which serve to orient people in their constant daily activities. The importance of those points of reference is easily detected at the moment they undergo an unexpected modification, thus generating a disorientation in the perambulating of people. For instance, after a strong quake, in which those points of reference are totally destroyed, many people surviving to the catastrophe do not know where to go. In those situations, neither signage nor cartography, for instance can help 100% those people, since the human and social factors overcome for a lapse of time the help coming from the convergence of the last generation software and hardware. The current research work is structured in the following way: a brief state-of-the-art, the phases in the generation of the traditional and digital

DOI: 10.4018/978-1-5225-2616-2.ch001

cartography, examples of historical and analogical cartography, the analysis of a multimedia system where there is a theoretical-practical intersection of the main issues of the current work, the learned lessons and the conclusions.

It is in the creation of maps where there is an intersection of computer graphics, digital photography, digital impression, satellites, cultural algorithms, etc. (Cipolla-Ficarra, 1993; Dent, Torguson, & Hodler, 2008; Reynolds, Ali & Jayyousi, 2008) As a rule, in the institutions charged with the cartography of a territory such as can be for geopolitical reasons, it is easy to come across with a classical structure, divided into three main areas, such as photogrammetric, satellite image and thematic (Cipolla-Ficarra, 1993; Robinson, et al., 1995). The greater the quality is in the grasping of the first images and the data in general, the fewer are the mistakes to be corrected, and consequently the sooner optimal results will be obtained from the qualitative point of view. In photogrammetry, the data are obtained in a vertical way, through a photo camera (Wild RC 30) implemented in a plane, for instance. Later on, the pictures are developed (Cipolla-Ficarra, 1993).

In the 90s and in the institutions devoted to these tasks such as ICC (Catalan Institute of Cartography –Barcelona, Spain) each photogram was of about 23x23 cm (Cipolla-Ficarra, 1993). The union of the pictures of a first stereoscopic vision of the surface, that is, is seen in relief. The digitalization of the pictures is made with a scanner. The images stemming from the satellite contain information compiled by sensors capable of "reading" the electromagnetic radiation emitted by the earth surface. Such radiation is

Figure 1. A classical group of figures of the 90s for the obtainment of analogical and digital images for digital cartography: plane with Wild RC-10 photogrammetric cameras, cameras for oblique photography Rollei 6008, etc.), scanner to digitalize analogical images, manual edition, plotter printer, etc., to get a high-resolution map, field work (geodesy)

variable in relation to the coverage of the earth, that is to say, it is not the same in a forest as in a desert, since the vegetation also emits radiation. There is a calculation process in the sensor with relation to the waves inside the band of the electromagnetic spectrum. All of that in relation to the information units or resolution elements: the pixel (Cipolla-Ficarra, 2015). Since this information is digital, it is stored quickly in the databases. Finally, the thematic starts with an analysis of the different sources of data collection, which is related to the work or project that will be carried out. In other words, there is a convergence of satellite images, aerial pictures taken from planes, statistical data, geographical information systems, atlas and/or digital encyclopaedias, etc. (Dent, Torguson & Hodler, 2008; Riffenburgh, 2014).

A CLASSICAL TREATMENT OF THE IMAGES IN THE INTERSECTION OF THE ANALOGICAL AND DIGITAL GRAPHIC ARTS

The compiled photogrammetric data are processed bearing in mind several stages, such as the orientation of the photographs, to the purpose of establishing the location of the photo camera in space and in each instant of the area being worked on; the photogrammetric restitution (digital format of the images); the field revision, to verify what was made in the previous stage, since there can be components not included for reasons of dimensions, shadows, etc. These are incorporated into the successive stages; the digital edition and finally the drawing of the digital map with in a large dimension and high quality plotter.

Another of the tasks in cartographic elaboration consists in generating an elevation model of the territory which has been flown over. This is a 100% activity of three-dimensional graphic computing, with the purpose of modifying the possible geometrical mistakes, elaborating perspectives, etc. The geometrical changes correspond to the application of dots on the vertical of the ground they depict. The motivations of these activities consist in controlling and/or adjusting the variations of the height of the plane at the moment of the compiling of the information. The image obtained is called orthophoto. This image was traditionally filmed with a laser printer. In this way, what is called an orthomap, is obtained at the moment of editing that film.

The images of the satellites are accumulated into its different channels. Through a special software it is determined which channel will carry more information per every pixel. The channels have the colours cyan, yellow and magenta. With these colours, a primary image of the area is obtained, but whose colour is not the real one. Here also several tasks of geometric makeovers are made in order to improve the image from the radiometrite point of view, eradicating the eventual atmospheric "noise". Besides, it is possible to highlight the valleys, rivers, etc., stressing the lineal shapes. Finally, the obtained image is transferred to a high-resolution laser printer. If that image is oriented towards thematic cartography, for instance, it is at this moment where subtitles would be introduced, for instance. Besides, classes are established and the symbology to which they refer. Later on, are included the geographical units which are considered, and in relation to the classes, technically called classified base. To the purpose of differentiating each zone a colour, a texture, a shape is used, etc., which follows previous parameters of universal coding for a better local and global communication (Rosneberg & Grafton, 2012; Salvendy, 2012; Shneiderman, 2002; De Kerckhove, 1999; Sebeok, 2001). All these data come generally into the phase usually called "process control" to verify the data stored in the digital supports. The inconsistencies and/or mistakes are corrected through the digital edition. Once that control is overcome, in the late 90s, the map was filmed and later on reprinted. In the new millennium, the drones with very high resolution digital cameras can not only speed up the process control stage, but the quality and the accuracy of the early photographs, it considerably reduces the time of processing the information and besides, the costs. For instance, in the following figures related to the last survivor of a language belonging to an indigenous culture in the south of Chile, its points of reference are the mountains and the lakes.

A natural environment which has changed very little across the centuries since there are no architectonic constructions which have survived the passing of time, such as the pyramids in Central America, for instance. However, in the natural environments of the mountains and the caves, in the south of the

Figure 2. Last indigenous linguistic survivor (living treasure of humanity, according to UNESCO) in Chile (www.elpais.es –09.01.2014)

Figure 3. Photographs of the 19th century of the natives in the south of the American continent who spoke yagan (www.elpais.es –09.01.2014)

Figure 4. Photographs of the natural environment of those towns, visited by Darwin, for instance, in Williams Port (www.elpais.es –09.01.2014)

American continent, there is also the astronomical and artistic confluence, in several geographical spots. One of them is the yellow cave, where the cave paintings of the first nations join the advanced studies of astronomy of those inhabitants in regard to the movements of translation of the sun, for instance. Those are millenary works which allow one to apply the new technologies for digital photography. For instance, the method of infrared reproduction of the cave paintings, by Asbjörn Pedersen (Ferreira-Soaje, 2011), as can be seen in Figures 5 (left and right areas). In the Figure 5, on the right side, we have the real situation on the wall of the cave and on the picture of the right the application of the infrared in photographic reproduction. In the Figure 6 it can be inferred a first map of the context of those inhabitants in Córdoba (Argentina) by including the course of a river, for instance. In this regard, a first parallelism can be established with the ancient Italic maps, as it can be seen in the Figure 8.

Figure 5. The use of the new technologies (infrared reproduction) allows the effective circulation of millenary images

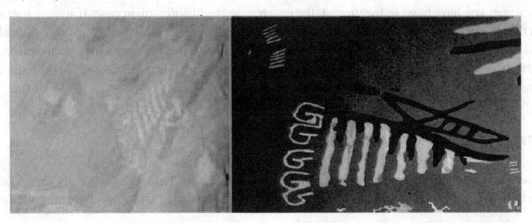

Figure 6. The subject of astronomy is a common denominator in the pre-Columbian culture where the Sun held a central place in daily life

For instance, Figures 7 and 8 depict the early cartographers when depicting the natural environment that surrounded them in the graphic media then available. In contemporary cartography, the image can be digital from the start or not. This factor has an influence on the process that will be used. The basis of current cartography can be integrated in the current geographical information systems, where on the one hand we have the cartographical information of a road, for instance, which is a map where a cartographer has intervened. Besides, we associate to it alphanumerical information, such as the height of a crossing of avenues, with regard to sea level, for instance. In few words, in our days, there are still maps where you have to go to the ground, for instance, in the historic urban case. If it were measured from the air, data would be missing, such as the information regarding whether that road is passable or not, if the course of the water is permanent or not. Consequently, it is necessary to go to the place, and carry out the study of the zone. In short, both kinds of images complement themselves, in the interactive cartography or not, of the third millennium.

THEMATIC CARTOGRAPHY AND SCALES

Thematic cartography refers to the maps where are included the elements of the daily reality of the human beings, for instance, the density of the population, the water resources, the concentration of

Figure 7. Set of cave figures where is depicted the local fauna, the course of a river and a hunter

Figure 8. Map of a river zone hand-made and in colour in the 18th century

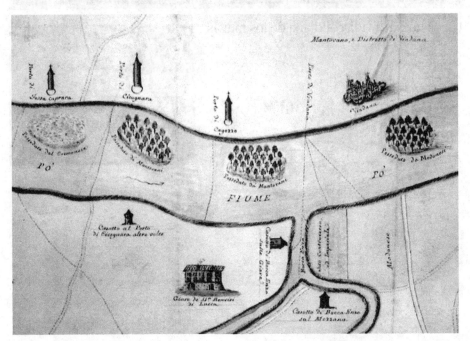

polluted area in a city, etc. These data are depicted by a conventional symbology which is usually at the foot of the map. The obtained result is thanks to the cartography systems, the CAD and self-editing applications (Cipolla-Ficarra, 2010; Styliaras, Koukopoulos & Lazarinis, 2011). On it there is an intersection of the diverse sectors of cartography, such as: satellite images, statistics, documentation, design, communication, etc. (Salvendy, 2012; Shneiderman, 2002; Veltman, 2006; Eco, 1977; Bergehel, 1997; Cipolla-Ficarra, 1993). On the map, every area is drawn with a determinate colour, texture, etc., in relation to the selected code. This kind of map is essential in the developing countries or with great expanses of land, for instance. Traditionally in Europe cartography has a scale of 1:25,000 (a centimetre of the map is tantamount to 25,000 centimetres in reality). If the map of a country ten times bigger than Spain is selected, for instance and less developed from the economical point of view, a satellite image is of great informative value. Besides, if the satellite has active sensors incorporated (radars) to carry out a better cartography of the covered areas, such as the Amazon rainforest. Radiometry allows us to pick up information over the presence of rivers, the relief of the ground, etc. The quality of the obtained results depends on the kind of radar sensors. A good sensor may determine what the harvest of cereals will be like in a given region, through a spectral analysis, and can also make possible the discovery of pre-Columbian architectonic constructions, in the rainforests of Central America, in the second decade of the new millennium.

Figure 9. Pyramid discovered in 2009 in the border of Mexico with Guatemala with full colour paintings of the daily life of the Mayas (www.elpais.es –11.09.2009)

It is through the numbers of the scales that the technological resources used for the making of the maps are divided. There are several great groups. For instance, those who are included in the following set of 1:50,000 and those who go beyond those values. Now until 50,000 photogrammetry is used (air pictures from a plane, added to the satellite photographs). In the 90s they were digital from the start of the process, in 99% of the cases, which means a great advantage in the realization process. From the 50,000 onwards, it is an area of drawing and edition mechanisms. Traditionally, two planes were used. With the obtained data, first, an aerial triangulation was and made and second there was a process of orientation of the frames (the place picks up the frames with movements or with a certain orientation). Through stereoscopy the "z" coordinate is located. That is what configured the 3D delineation inside the photogrammetric devices thus obtaining the map. Another option was resorting to photographic rectification. In this case, the result is an orthophotomap. Basically, it is a rectified photograph which possesses metric scale. These two alternatives are different between themselves, but they complement each other. In short, we can see that there are three kinds of final products: first, topographic cartography, with scales as far as 50,000, second, orthographic cartography, with scales from 5,000 until 25,000, and starting from this last figure, it is by satellite, and third, topographical maps, starting from 50,000, including the thematic ones (Cipolla-Ficarra, 1993).

CARTOGRAPHY, MULTIMEDIA, COMMUNICABILITY, USER EXPERIENCE AND CULTURAL HERITAGE

In the interactive multimedia systems off-line there are excellent examples of cultural heritage, cartography, archaeology, communicability, etc., such as the case of the scientific research project called "Quitsa-to" (CD-Rom Quitsa-To, 2003; Cipolla-Ficarra, 2011). In that digital support, have been gathered the results of a scientific research that has its origins in history and cartography (Rosenberg & Grafton, 2012). There is a bidirectional interrelation which linked to the multimedia constitute an excellent triad from the point of view of communicability (Cipolla-Ficarra, 2011). The content of the interactive system is distributed among nine big subsets of nodes and links:

- Catequilla
- Ethno Astronomy
- Indigenous
- Geography: the Equinotial Andes
- Ancient Astronomy
- Archaelogical
- Quito: Millenial City
- Religous Sincretism
- Solar Cultural Museum

The dynamic and static means are related among themselves, through a bidirectional radial and sequential structure which is accessible from the home or main menu (Cipolla-Ficarra, 2011). The user can make a sequential navigation from the first subset of nodes and links, or interrupt the sequence, going back to the main menu and navigate inside the other subsets of the interactive system. The interactive content is distributed in 98 frames. It is in this content where the importance of the text is located, which joined to the visual information manifest the originality and universality of the obtained results.

Along the interactive system, it is possible to observe the importance of aerial and satellite cartography to locate Inca constructions, which make up diagrams on the earth's surface with a high precision derived from the astronomic studies of those first nations in the American continent (Duff, 1997; Ferreira-Soaje, 2011). Those are studies where the sun has always been the engine of those research works and where the formal and factual sciences interact with each other with the help of the ICT (Information and Communication Technology). The multimedia system starts with data stemming from the cartography, astronomy, the cultural/scientific background of other analogous civilizations, etc. (Figure 10). Starting from these data an interesting central matrix was established as a baseline which has been verified in reality.

A matrix center is used as a baseline and it is possible to trace back the different astronomic lines coming from the sun. It is possible to find different points that mark the axis of these alignments perfectly. Now as central subject of these constructions and from the geographical point of view, there is the exact division of planet Earth into hemispheres, latitudes, parallels, etc. The animations, the photographs and the videos facilitate to the user the quick understanding of that scientific information.

The circular and/or semicircular shape of those figures can already be visible thanks to the aerial cartography of mountainous areas, such as Catequilla in Ecuador. In the Figure 15 we have an orthophotograph from 1996 (left zone) and in the right zone there is an aerial photograph of the new millennium, where it is easy to observe in plain sight the circular shape of the archaeological enclave in the mountain. In the Figure 16 the aerial video helps even more the user of the multimedia system to understand the importance of the place from the geographical/cartographical perspective.

Figure 10. Observations made by the first nations of the American continent in the sky, and with special interest of the Sun

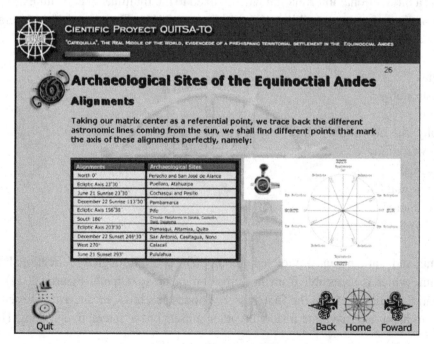

Figure 11. Example of the studies made by the Inca populations based on astronomy with a small margin of error

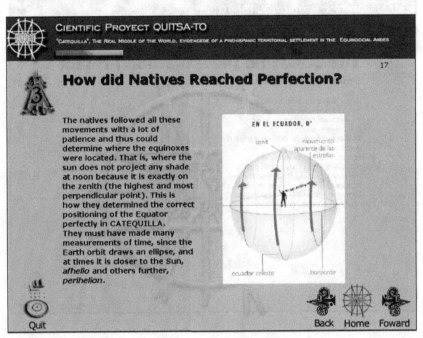

Figure 12. Comparison of certain premises/scientific conclusions with other ancient civilizations

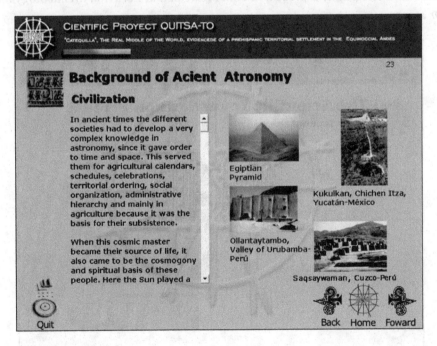

Figure 13. Representation of solar iconography

Figure 14. The solar iconography is present in both Mexican and Peruvian archaeology in the shape of hieroglyphs or stones

Figure 15. Two types of aerial photographs to locate an archaeological enclave at an elevated height with relation to sea level

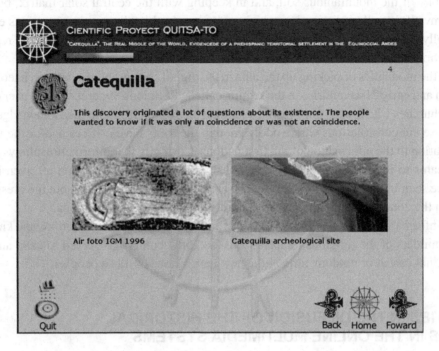

Figure 16. Correct use of the video with didactic purposes of the potential users of the multimedia system

Now it has not only been verified that the archaeological constructions match each other, in spite of the orography of the mountainous soil, and in keeping with the central solar matrix, but it has also permitted demystifying alleged miracles, which took place in the religious constructions erected since 1492, especially those that took place on the 21st June solstice. In the Figure 17 we have a representation of that projection in the area of Catequella.

Thanks to the modalities of picking up the data in the digital cartography and the archaeological studies of the 20th and early 21st centuries in the section called "Religious Syncretism" the user can discover how certain churches which were built in the solar matrix profited from the Inca knowledge such as the solstices. Those are constructions where oddly enough the roofs have orifices and/or the windows are aligned in relation to the information of the first nations. Currently that information allows the entrance of the sun beams to illuminate religious figures inside those constructions and at given hours of the year, as can be seen in the 18 and 19 Figures. The archaeological diggings denote the presence of Inca settlements in the zone of the arising of many churches in that geographical area.

The solar information, compiled from the pre-Colombian indigenous civilizations and known beforehand by the builders of the religious temples from the 15th century has served to keep an astronomic phenomenon, not casual or random, among the new generations of those peoples.

DIFFICULTIES IN THE DIFFUSION OF THE HISTORICAL CONTENTS IN THE ONLINE MULTIMEDIA SYSTEMS

Although the social networks allow the free fruition of contents through the multimedia mobile phones to millions of users, all across our planet, there are a series of limitations in relation to the hardware, the software and the connectivity to the databases, to mention three examples. Briefly those disadvantages are:

Figure 17. Equinoctial line at its possible astronomical interrelation

Figure 18. Video at the moment of the illumination of a sculpture inside the Cathedral on the June 21st solstice

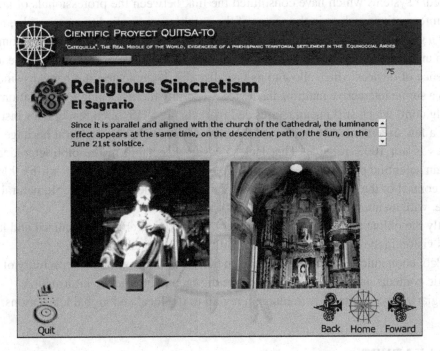

Figure 19. Video with the illumination of a religious painting

- High speed in the evolution of the software and the hardware, which prevent the functioning of multimedia systems which have constituted the link between the professionals of analogical and digital information, such as in the sector of the graphic arts applied to cartography, for instance.

- Lack of a global catalogue with all the titles produced in offline support of the economically developed countries and in keeping with quality rules (ISO, for instance) and with a free access to all.

- Inexistence of devices which allow to us visualize the dynamic and static means since 1990 until 2010 in a single interactive multimedia device. Currently there is a single multinational brand (LG –www.lg.com) which still manufactures and markets the VHS video readers, for instance.

- But for a few exceptions, the quality of the contents related to the cultural heritage in the social networks is not 100% reliable. That lack is easily detectable in the bibliographical references of certain scientific projects. As a rule, in the offline multimedia systems of the 90s there was a greater control of the quality of the static contents, when the projects refer to natural and cultural heritage, with an international commercial distribution.

- Currently the online production teams are very reduced, extremely specialized and lacking a 360 degrees vision in the interactive design, usability, communicability, etc.

- The lack of economic resources in the cultural field entails a continuous reusability of the dynamic and static contents, in the new supports of the digital and interactive information.

- The plagiarizing of contents is immune in regard to the local and global legislations.

LESSONS LEARNED

The relationship of the human being with the reality and the ways of relating to reality can be approached from a social point of view as a subject-object relationship, like two elements of a cognitive relationship. The human being from the beginning has always tried to depict that reality and also seek the origins. In that sense, the online and off-line multimedia systems have exponentially boosted that representation in the last two decades, always trying to recuperate the cultural heritage of the first nations. In that sense, even the cultural icons can be reused in the interactive design of the multimedia systems. Now the issue of the relationship subject-object is a basic problem of the theory of knowledge and decisive in the formulation of the sciences and the new technologies. The relationship between these two elements is the starting point of any theory of knowledge, for instance. A knowledge which starting by the digital cartography can discover not only the scientific advance of the first nations, but also demonstrate scientifically those popular beliefs in the face of natural and/or physical phenomena, as the routes of the sun beams. The synthesis achieved in the interactive multimedia system denotes the high degree of communicability which can be achieved when the content is new or original.

However, in less than two decades the excellent contents of the off-line multimedia systems cannot be accessed by millions of users. The lack of software and hardware which allows the interaction with those systems may mean the loss of the access to unique contents which were digitalized in the 90s, for instance, through the use of a scanner and for several reasons those originals do not exist any longer. Besides, plenty of firms generating multimedia contents have disappeared with the burst of the virtual firms bubble also called .com bust in the early 21st century, with which the multimedia databases have not been transferred to the online hyperbases, for instance. In the example of the multimedia system analyzed, Catequilla, it has been made apparent how the conclusions of its works have currently a limited

Figure 20. Interface of the main menú of the CD-Rom QUITSA-TO with the matrix of the Sun

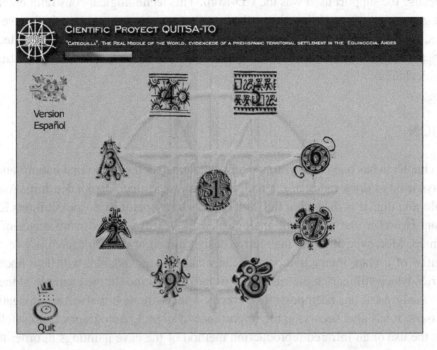

Figure 21. First nations in the American northwest coast: Multimedia native art (i.e., sun representation)

circulation because the support used was the CD-Rom. This technological constraint entails implicitly that the future generations do not know the truth about certain cultural aspects which have been related to the miracles, such can be the lightening of the figures and sculptures in certain architectonical constructions, when in fact they are astronomical phenomena studied and verified by the first nations of those geographical areas.

CONCLUSION

In the current chapter, it has been demonstrated how the human being of the first nations and throughout time has always tried to draw maps of the natural environment that surrounded him. Analogical cartography would join digital at the end of the 20th century thus opening new possibilities for interactive communication. However, the manual or analogical work is still valid in many stages of the creative process of a map. Moreover, it is the interactive design aimed at the multimedia systems where the didactic potential of a map, interactive or not, can make understandable, with few nodes and links, those discoveries which still enrich the cultural heritage of mankind. In the example of the multimedia system briefly analyzed, it has been possible to verify a very simple but effective navigation structure for potential users. It has also been seen the importance of digital photographs from satellites, planes, etc, as well as the use of an infrared reproduction method of the cave paintings in order to boost their value and try to keep on researching the historic legacy of those civilizations. Civilizations which even today keep their constructions under thick vegetation but are discovered in the new millennium thanks to the telecommunications and the ICTs through the use of the satellites with active sensors (radars) traditionally used in digital cartography.

Digital cartography gathers a myriad of disciplines of the formal and factual sciences, easily demonstrable in the different map models that currently exist, such as the diverse technological and interactive supports from which information can be accessed. The interest of users towards the enhanced reality with the multimedia mobile devices has allowed to increase the number of applications of the maps, as well as incorporating on them all the advantages of the dynamic media. The new hardware devices such as the smart glass (e. g. Google Glass) will boost even more the enhanced reality and everything related to online digital cartography. However, many databases of the off-line systems of the 90s are excluded from this access. These are interactive systems that have exclusive contents and with a high fidelity level in regard to the originals, since they were elaborated inside of pioneering human teams in the transfer of analogical contents to the digital, as is the case of the graphic arts, where the intersection of the formal and factual sciences was the common denominator. Finally, and in the same way as the primitive nations painted inside the caves the first elements of thematic cartography, the cartography of the 21St century will remain the linchpin of the future breakthroughs in the NTIC (New Information and Communication Technology), since the users like to know where they can go from a place where they are actually, or in virtuality. In other words, the main notions of the hypertext of the first half of the 20th century are still valid, because just the same as in a structure of nodes and links, the user always tries to know/understand where he/she is coming from, where she/he is and where she/he can go.

ACKNOWLEDGMENT

The author would like to thank you very much to Maria Ficarra. Special thanks to Alejandra Quiroga, Jacqueline Alma, Mary Brie, Luisa Varela, Amélie Bordeaux, Pamela Fulton, Doris Edison, Sonia Flores, Julia Ruiz, Giselda Verdone, Jim Carré, Donald Nilson, and Carlos for the help and comments.

REFERENCES

Bergehel, H. (1997). Cyberspace 2000: Dealing with Information Overload. *Communications of the ACM, 40*(2), 19–24. doi:10.1145/253671.253680

CD-Rom QUITSA-TO. (2003). *Catequilla: The Real Middle of the world.* Quito.

Cipolla-Ficarra, F. (1993). Cartografía e Infografía: Una Convergencia Magistral. [In Spanish]. *Imaging, 10*(December), 24–31.

Cipolla-Ficarra, F. (2010). *Quality and Communicability for Interactive Hypermedia Systems: Concepts and Practices for Design.* Hershey, PA: IGI Global. doi:10.4018/978-1-61520-763-3

Cipolla-Ficarra, F. (2011). The Expansion Era of the Communicability: First Nations for the Local and Global Promotion of Cultural and Natural Heritage. In *Proc. Human-Computer Interaction, Tourism and Cultural Heritage* (pp. 25–37). Heidelberg, Germany: Springer. doi:10.1007/978-3-642-18348-5

Cipolla-Ficarra, F. (2015). *Handbook of Research on Interactive Information Quality in Expanding Social Network Communications.* Hershey, PA: IGI Global. doi:10.4018/978-1-4666-7377-9

De Kerckhove, D. (1999). *The Skin of Culture: Investigating the New Electronic Reality.* London: Kogan Page.

Dent, B., Torguson, J., & Hodler, T. (2008). *Cartography Thematic Map Design.* New York: McGraw Hill.

Duff, W. (1997). *The Indian History of British Columbia: The Impact of the White Man.* Victoria: Royal British Columbia Museum.

Eco, U. (1977). *A Theory of Semiotics.* Bloomington, IN: Indiana University Press.

Ferreira-Soaje, V. (2011). *Cerro Colorado: Una Luz de Otros Tiempos.* Córdoba: Ediciones del Boulevard. In Spanish

Reynolds, R., Ali, M., & Jayyousi, T. (2008). Mining the Social Fabric of Archaic Urban Centers with Cultural Algorithms. *IEEE Computer, 47*(1), 64–72. doi:10.1109/MC.2008.25

Riffenburgh, B. (2014). *Mapping the World: The Story of Cartography.* London: Carlton Publishing Group.

Robinson, A. H. (1995). *Elements of Cartography.* New York: John Whiley & Sons.

Rosenberg, D., & Grafton, A. (2012). *Cartographies of Time: A History of the Timeline.* New York: Princeton Architectural Press.

Salvendy, G. (2012). *Handbook of Human Factors and Ergonomics*. New York: John Wiley. doi:10.1002/9781118131350

Sebeok, T. (2001). *Global Semiotics*. Bloomington, IN: Indiana University Press.

Shneiderman, B. (2002). Creativity Support Tools. *Communications of the ACM, 45*(10), 116–120. doi:10.1145/570907.570945

Styliaras, G., Koukopoulos, D., & Lazarinis, F. (2011). *Handbook of Research on Technologies and Cultural Heritage: Applications and Environments*. Hershey, PA: IGI Global. doi:10.4018/978-1-60960-044-0

Veltman, K. (2006). *Understanding New Media: Augmented Knowledge and Culture*. Calgary: University of Calgary Press.

ADDITIONAL READING

Card, S., Mackinlay, J., & Shneiderman, B. (1999). *Readings in Information Visualization: Using Vision to Think*. San Francisco: Morgan Kauffman.

Cipolla-Ficarra, F. (2013). *Scientific Computing, Communicability and Cultural Heritage: Future Trends in Software and Interactive Design*. Bergamo: Blue Herons Editions.

Cipolla-Ficarra, F. (2014). *Strategies for a Creative Future with Computer Science, Quality Design and Communicability*. Bergamo: Blue Herons Editions.

De Kerckhove, D. (2001). *The Architecture of Intelligence*. Basel: Birkhauser.

Dickason, O., & Mcnab, D. T. (2009). *Canada's First Nations A History of Founding Peoples from Earliest Times*. Oxford University Press.

Fogg, B. (2003). *Persuasive Technology: Using Computers to Change What We Think and Do*. San Francisco: Morgan Kaufmann Publishers.

Horswill, I., & Novak, M. (2006). Evolving the Artist-Technologist. *IEEE Computer, 39*(6), 62–69. doi:10.1109/MC.2006.193

Jenks, C. (1993). *Culture*. London: Routledge. doi:10.4324/9780203446317

Leigh, J., & Brown, M. D. (2008). Cyber-Commons: Merging Real and Virtual Worlds. *Communications of the ACM, 51*(1), 82–85. doi:10.1145/1327452.1327488

Maldonado, T. (1991). *Cultura, democrazia, ambiente*. Milano: Feltrinelli. in Italian

McQuail, D., & Windahl, S. (1993). *Communication Models for The Study of Mass Communications*. New York: Longman.

Parekh, B. (2000). *Rethinking Multiculturalism. Cultural Diversity and Political Theory*. Basingstoke: Palgrave.

Radley, A. S. (2015). *Self As Computer*. Charleston: Create Space Independent Publishing Platform. doi:10.4018/978-1-4666-7377-9.ch011

Slocum, T. A., McMaster, R. B., Kessler, F. C., & Howard, H. H. (2014). *Thematic Cartography and Geovisualization*. Harlow: Pearson Education Limited.

Smith, M. (1998). *Culture: Reinventing the Social Sciences*. Buckingham: Open University.

Thrower, N. (2008). *Maps and Civilization: Cartography in Culture and Society*. Chicago: University of Chicago Press. doi:10.7208/chicago/9780226799759.001.0001

Veltman, K. (2014). *Alphabet of Life*. Maastricht: Virtual Maastricht McLuhan Institute.

White, L. (1959). *The Evolution of Culture*. New York: McGraw-Hill.

KEY TERMS AND DEFINITIONS

Communicability: A qualitative communication between the user and the interactive system, such as mobile phones, augmented reality, immersion multimedia, hypermedia, among others. The extent to which an interactive system successfully conveys its functionality to the user.

Cultural Heritage or Tangible Cultural Heritage: "It is the legacy of physical artefacts and intangible attributes of a group or society that are inherited from past generations, maintained in the present and bestowed for the benefit of future generations." (UNESCO definition).

Digital Cartography: It is the intersection of sciences, art, photography, graphics and technique of map reproduction with computers.

First Nations: The indigenous peoples of the Americas, with an organized aboriginal group or community.

Interactive System: It is a computer device made up by a CPU and peripherals, whose functioning requires a constant interaction with the user. Currently these systems tend to their miniaturization and/or invisibility, the mobility and wireless connectability among them.

Chapter 2
Web 2.0 and Health Information Technology:
Theories and Applications

Kijpokin Kasemsap
Suan Sunandha Rajabhat University, Thailand

ABSTRACT

This chapter describes the overview of Web 2.0 technologies; Web 2.0 applications in learning and education; Web 2.0 applications in academic libraries; Web 2.0 applications in Knowledge Management (KM); the perspectives of Health Information Technology (health IT); the multifaceted applications of health IT; IT and Technology Acceptance Model (TAM); and the significance of health IT in the health care industry. Web 2.0 is the platform of the network which spans all connected services so that users can utilize them more efficiently. Web 2.0 technologies have various benefits by enhancing the opportunities for business collaboration and by sharing knowledge through online communities of practice toward gaining improved organizational performance. Health IT includes utilizing technology to electronically store, protect, retrieve, and transfer the information in modern health care. Health IT has great potential to improve the quality, safety, and efficiency of health care services in the health care industry.

INTRODUCTION

The proliferation of information comes to the average person through the rapid developments of information technology (IT) and an abundance of information tools and sources (Yi, 2014). Web 2.0 technology refers to the web tools and services that encourage visitors to share, collaborate, and edit information, promoting a more distributed form of authority that blurs the boundaries between website creator and user (Oberhelman, 2007). Web 2.0 technology fosters active participation among audiences rather than distributing information to passive audiences (Kam & Katerattanakul, 2014).

With the emergence of Web 2.0, sharing personal content, communicating ideas, and interacting with other online users in Web 2.0 communities have become daily routines for online users (Huang, Fu, & Chen, 2010). Web 2.0 has been noted for being user-friendly, thus providing a collaborative platform

DOI: 10.4018/978-1-5225-2616-2.ch002

without charge (or low charge) and without boundary of time and geography (Hao & Lee, 2015). Contemporary web platforms (e.g., Google and Facebook) can store, analyze, and sell the large amounts of personal data and user behavior data (Fuchs, 2011).

IT has become a significant part of providing consistent care quality (Hung, Tsai, & Chuang, 2014). IT has been linked to productivity growth in a wide variety of sectors, and health IT is a leading example of an innovation with the potential to transform the industry-wide productivity (Agha, 2014). Health IT is viewed as a fundamental aspect of patient care as it stimulates patient engagement and encourages personal health management (Hung et al., 2013). The flexibility and adaptability of health IT as an educational tool allow it to be tailored to the individual's needs based on unique characteristics, risks, and behaviors (Gauthier, 2014).

Health IT describes the hardware, software, users, implementation, adoption, inputs, data, and outputs of computerized systems in the health care delivery environment (Dowling, 2013). Health IT targeting patients includes personal health records, patient portals, and social media technology (Sequist, 2011). Stafinski et al. (2011) stated that all health care systems routinely make resource allocation decisions that trade off potential health gains to the different patient populations. Contemporary health care relies on electronic devices (Coeckelbergh, 2013). Many fundamental changes have taken place to the types of health IT in use within hospitals, primary care practices, community care, and a variety of other health care locations (Waterson, 2014).

This chapter aims to bridge the gap in the literature on the thorough literature consolidation of Web 2.0 and health IT. The extensive literature of Web 2.0 and health IT provides a contribution to practitioners and researchers by describing the theories and applications of Web 2.0 and health IT in order to maximize the technological impact of Web 2.0 technologies in the digital age.

Background

The term Web 2.0 was created in 2004 by Tim O'Reilly and Dale Dougherty from O'Reilly Media, an American publisher specialized in publications concerning the new technologies and networks (Pieri & Diamantini, 2014). In 2004, Web 2.0 application was introduced as an innovative web technology that enabled more interactive and personalized communication among people (Eccleston & Griseri, 2008). During that period, Web 2.0 obtained the attention of many businesses because of its capability to enhance the relationship between organizations and consumers (Andriole, 2010). In 2004, utilizing various Web 2.0 applications, people could more actively participate in the content creation process (Smith & Rogers, 2008) and share their ideas through websites. Web 2.0 was not only a development in technology, but also a great change in the method of online communication. Web 2.0 enabled people to effectively share knowledge (Gould, 2009). Web 2.0 also stimulated opening of discussions, finding solutions, and aiming at creating business value through websites (Cronin, 2009).

The studies about Web 2.0 have developed into several perspectives. The power of content created by Web 2.0 application users (i.e., user-generated content, UGC) has captured numerous researchers' attention (Chaves, Gomes, & Pedron, 2012). Chen et al. (2012) identified the factors influencing the continuous application of Web 2.0 and indicated that user satisfaction and electronic word of mouth have a significant influence on the application of Web 2.0 tools. Winter and Kramer (2012) discussed the content selection process of users in the Web 2.0 environment and identified the factors that influence users to select what to read when surrounded by a large amount of content. Practitioners and researchers utilize the concept of Web 2.0 to cloud computing technologies in order to emphasize the power of innovation that can dramatically improve business capability (Sultan, 2013).

The adoption of health IT in the support of collaborative processes for quality improvement has notably increased (Virga, Jin, Thomas, & Virodov, 2012). Health systems that promote information system infrastructure are better able to address coordination and safety issues, particularly for patients with multiple chronic conditions, as well as to maintain the primary care-related physician satisfaction (Davis, Doty, Shea, & Stremikis, 2009). The existence of a critical mass of the Internet users allows quickly diffusion of electronic communication in the medical practice, which translates as a new way to look at the physician-patient relationship (Kidd, Cayless, Johnston, & Wengstrom, 2010).

Information and communication technology (ICT) has modified the medical practice patterns while facilitating coordination and close cooperation between health care professionals to improve patient management (Fieschi, 2002). ICT can improve the quality of life and satisfaction with health care (Scalvini et al., 2014). A management system in the field of health protection must provide the exploration of the main risk factors of the perspective of population health, allow for the possibility of predicting changes in the provision of medical support, and create the information foundation for evaluating the effect of implementation of new health care methods and technologies (Rogozynska & Kozak, 2013).

IMPLICATIONS OF WEB 2.0 AND HEALTH INFORMATION TECHNOLOGY

This section emphasizes the overview of Web 2.0 technologies; Web 2.0 applications in learning and education; Web 2.0 applications in academic libraries; Web 2.0 applications in KM; the perspectives of health IT; the multifaceted applications of health IT; IT and TAM; and the significance of health IT in the health care industry.

Overview of Web 2.0 Technologies

Web 2.0 refers to a basic change from the static and non-interactive websites to the dynamically generated, more sophisticated and more user friendly websites through a greater range of software applications (Yi, 2014). These include blogs, wikis, and social networking sites (e.g., Facebook, MySpace, and Twitter) that enable users to interact with the web and allow knowledge sharing with others (Yi, 2014).

Web 2.0 offers various technical approaches (e.g., protocols, message formats, and programming tools) to build core e-infrastructure as well as many interesting services (e.g., Facebook, YouTube, Amazon S3/EC2, and Google maps) that can add value to e-infrastructure projects (Fox & Pierce, 2009). Social media has transformed social interactions in the digital age (Davison, Ou, Martinsons, Zhao, & Du, 2014). Social media platforms (e.g., Facebook and Twitter) are the good examples of interaction-based applications; YouTube has transformed its identity from the simple storage platform of various videos to the media channel that can indicate the target consumers with similar interests (Berthon, Pitt, Plangger, & Shapiro, 2012).

Over the last few years, an evolution has taken place in the way users communicate through Web 2.0 (Rubio, Martín, & Morán, 2010). Web 2.0 encourages the constant creation and distribution of large amounts of information (Dougherty & Meyer, 2014). Web 2.0 is an important web application that assists people not only to post their opinions on websites, but also to continue to collaborate with others on their topics of interest (Kim, Yue, Hall, & Gates, 2009). Web 2.0 technologies can help effectively bring people together (Zaman, Anandarajan, & Dai, 2010), but these tools are often based on relationships only (Chatti, Jarke, & Frosch-Wike, 2007). Cloud computing offers an adaptable solution for the existing context-aware applications, thus integrating mobile Web 2.0 technologies (Hsu, 2013). Cloud computing includes network access to storage, processing power, development platforms, and software (Kasemsap, 2015).

Today, people perform many types of tasks on the web, including those that require multiple web sessions (MacKay & Watters, 2012). Huang et al. (2010) stated that user-generated data from Web 2.0 tools can provide the rich personal information (e.g., personal preferences and interests) and can be utilized to gain the obvious insight into cyber communities and their social networks. Web 2.0 has enhanced a networked, participatory, and conversational culture reaching beyond national borders and cultures, thus reshaping communicational hierarchies and creating a new set of communicative rules (Lilleker & Jackson, 2010). By utilizing e-government-related Web 2.0 tools, citizens can participate both in the process of creating web-based content and in enhancing service design (Hui & Hayllar, 2010).

With the proliferation in Web 2.0 technologies, many marketing educators are experimenting with new teaching and learning tools, such as Facebook, Twitter, and YouTube (Lowe, D'Alessandro, Winzar, Laffey, & Collier, 2013). In modern organizations, establishing Web 2.0 application strategy is more than an adoption of a new application; it is the significant change in building positive relationships with consumers (Wirtz, Schilke, & Ullrich, 2010). Service quality is a measure of how well the service level practically matches customer expectations (Yang, Hsieh, Li, & Yang, 2012).

Research in hospital settings faces several difficulties (Montano, Carretero, Entrecanales, & Pozuelo, 2010). Web 2.0 tools and IT applications provide new models to tackle these problems, thus allowing for a collaborative approach and bridging the gap between clinical practice, teaching, and research (Montano et al., 2010). Web 2.0 technologies represent a quite revolutionary way of managing online information and knowledge repositories, including clinical and research information, in comparison with the traditional Web 1.0 model (Boulos & Wheeler, 2007). In medical-related organizations, information sharing and online communication platform are recognized as the main purposes of using Web 2.0 technologies (Chu et al., 2012).

Web 2.0 Applications in Learning and Education

During the last decade, Web 2.0 technologies have been considerably increasing on the Internet, and K-12 students have been getting familiar with the technologies (Sadaf, Newby, & Ertmer, 2012). Web 2.0 technologies can assist students to learn collaboratively and actively, creating the effective student-centered learning environments (Brown, 2012). Learning becomes increasingly self-directed and often occurs away from schools and other formal educational settings (Song & Lee, 2014). Web 2.0 tools are hardly used to reflect on actual existing informal learning networks in practice, where professionals work on innovative issues that require learning and knowledge development (Schreurs & de Laat, 2014).

Web 2.0 applications have the potential to enhance the learning outcomes (Gu, Churchill, & Lu, 2014). By promoting active participation and interaction among learners, Web 2.0 technology can facilitate the dynamic learning along with collaborative knowledge generation (Rollett, Lux, Strohmaier, Dosinger, & Tochtermann, 2007). With the proliferation of the World Wide Web and the advent of Web 2.0, which unlike Web 1.0 enables collaboration and manipulation of online texts, teachers must weigh the purposes, affordances, and limitations of online tools for literacy instruction (Handsfield, Dean, & Cielocha, 2009). When Web 2.0 technology is utilize to encourage collaborative learning, the interaction pattern will be more complex as students interact not only with each other, but also with the technology (Kam & Katerattanakul, 2014). Due to widespread educational budget cuts, teachers have been encouraged to integrate these free or low cost Web 2.0 technologies because of the affordances they offer and ease of their utilization in teaching and learning (Churchill, 2011).

In higher education, most students have little previous experience with Web 2.0 technologies and have struggled to consider the value of adopting Web 2.0 technologies for learning and teaching (Bennett, Bishop, Dalgarno, Waycott, & Kennedy, 2012). Web 2.0 technologies, especially social software, can be used to support student's self-regulated learning in higher education contexts (Kitsantas & Dabbagh, 2011). Web 2.0 technologies only become valuable in education if learners and teachers can do something beneficial with them (Virkus, 2008). To effectively guide collaborative learning, researchers should analyze the interaction pattern that happens during collaborative learning (Su, Yang, Hwang, & Zhang, 2010).

Web 2.0 tools have been recognized as an enabler of higher education collaboration (James, 2014). Preservice teachers' intentions, beliefs, and attitudes toward technology are the important determinants of the success of future technology integration (Yusop, 2015). Preservice teachers' intentions to employ Web 2.0 technologies are correlated with their beliefs about the educational value of Web 2.0 technologies, the ability to meet the requirements of contemporary students, the participants' high self-efficacy in utilization, and the available access to learning and interaction capability (Sadaf et al., 2012).

Virtual learning environment (VLE) can be accessed through standard web browser, which provides an integrated online learning environment (Kurilovas & Dagiene, 2010). One of the main parts of each VLE is Web 2.0 tools (Kurilovas & Juskeviciene, 2015). In order to improve the quality of VLEs, it is essential to improve semantic search for Web 2.0 tools in VLEs. As contemporary students are the educational content creators via the Internet, it becomes obvious that Web 2.0 tools play an important role in the virtual learning process (Kurilovas & Juskeviciene, 2015).

The growth of Web 2.0 and social computing has been phenomenal (Randeree & Mon, 2007). Web 2.0 tools receive the growing interest across all sectors of the educational industry as the significant method for establishing personal learning environments (PLEs) and extending the student's control over the entire learning process (Dabbagh & Kitsantas, 2012). The main goal for PLEs is to increase student's control by taking advantage of Web 2.0 tools and technologies (Rahimi, van den Berg, & Veen, 2015a). Web 2.0 tools enable a shift from a distributive to a more collaborative mode in e-learning (Schneckenberg, Ehlers, & Adelsberger, 2011). Web 2.0-related PLEs are a promising area of development in e-learning (Rahimi, van den Berg, & Veen, 2015b). E-learning allows students to choose content and tools appropriate to their differing interests, needs, and skill levels (Kasemsap, 2016a). Regarding PLEs, a learner-driven personalization of learning process can achieve through empowering students with appropriate competencies to achieve more control over the educational process (Drexler, 2010).

Web 2.0 Applications in Academic Libraries

With the rapid developments of computer technology and IT, the significant change is constant in libraries, archives, museums, and other information agencies (Yi, 2014). Academic, medical, and research libraries frequently implement Web 2.0 services for users (Gardois, Colombi, Grillo, & Villanacci, 2012). Web 2.0 and Library 2.0 have opened up a whole new world for exploration by information and library professionals (Tattersall, 2011). To keep pace with evolving information technologies, many librarians utilize various software applications, such as blogs, wikis, and media-sharing tools (Hinchliffe & Leon,

2011) to market their library-related services and resources. Xia (2009) indicated that librarians in research universities can apply Facebook to market their libraries and services.

The utilization of Web 2.0 tools in academic libraries is about users being contributors to the libraries they are part of, thus promoting trust, facilitating participation, and establishing higher usage (Aharony, 2010). Landis (2007) suggested that utilizing Facebook can be an essential approach to marketing the library-related events and resources to non-traditional users, thus making the library more visible. A broad study by Hendrix et al. (2009) on the operation of Facebook by over 70 librarians found that most libraries apply the social networking sites to predominantly market their library-related services.

Yi (2014) stated that YouTube can enable users to embed videos onto other Web 2.0 tools, such as Facebook, blogs, and wikis. Vucovich et al. (2013) indicated that there is the practical use of YouTube videos for library instruction and reference services. Kho (2011) explained that the application of social media can enhance the customer engagement and the adoption of YouTube toward marketing the library's material collection. Rich site summary, also known as really simple syndication (RSS), is employed to distribute the information of changes to web content to subscribers in much the same way that Twitter is used to push the information out to its followers (Yi, 2014). The suitable exploitation of RSS feeds can be an accomplished marketing tool for the promotion of library resources and services (Nesta & Mi, 2011).

Web 2.0-related social bookmarking is a way for online users to organize, store, and manage the bookmarks of web resources in academic libraries (Yi, 2014). Information professionals can add content and then tag online resources in bookmarking accounts and link to the related catalogue in order to create access points for materials. Regarding social bookmarking, library resources tagged by users can be effectively analyzed in order to encourage a better understanding of how library users search and categorize the library resources (Yi, 2014).

Web 2.0 Applications in Knowledge Management

Web 2.0 technologies involve the useful applications in personal knowledge management (KM), thus supporting the participation in KM, in addition to supporting communication and interaction mechanisms (Al-ghamdi & Al-ghamdi, 2015). KM is applied across the world in all industries and sectors (Kasemsap, 2016b). Razmerita et al. (2009) indicated that Web 2.0 tools have facilitated the development of a new paradigm for the management of personal knowledge, which includes contacts, cooperation, and social media platforms.

The advent of social networking sites (e.g., Facebook and LinkedIn), known as Web 2.0 applications, has provided an opportunity for consumers to express their opinions and knowledge (Seo & Lee, 2016). Web 2.0 and social media are considered as the future of learning (Pãuleþ-Crãiniceanu, 2014). Social media enables the creation of knowledge value chain to customize information and delivery for a technological business growth (Kasemsap, 2014).

Levy (2009) found that Web 2.0 tools are closely related to the application of KM, and that these tools have considerable potential for improving KM processes in organizations. Web 2.0 tools enable learners in the virtual communities of professional practice to share tacit knowledge (Richards, 2009). The adoption of Web 2.0 tools in the context of virtual communities of practice can handle the challenges of KM utilization (Wenger, 1998). Web 2.0 tools can enhance the efficiency of virtual communities of practice toward sharing knowledge in the modern learning environments (Al-ghamdi & Al-ghamdi, 2015).

Perspectives of Health Information Technology

Health care is one of the most knowledge-intensive sectors where innovations are continuously put into practice (Nedlund & Garpenby, 2014). One of the problems in health care in developing countries is the bad accessibility of medicine in pharmacies for patients (Edoh & Teege, 2011). Health IT is recognized as one of the most prominent catalysts for improving patient safety and reducing subsequent harm to patients who are receiving health care (Fuji & Galt, 2008). Health IT research has historically suffered from the persistence of paper-based systems as a barrier to research and refinement of information models (Lorence, 2007). Decisions to adopt guidance on the use of health care technologies are informed by the cost-effectiveness analysis of the alternative interventions (Claxton & Sculpher, 2006).

Health IT is a powerful tool that can support this transition by supporting care coordination, enhancing access, and empowering residents within the nursing home setting while offering vehicles to provide the needed services in home and community-based settings (Goldwater & Harris, 2011). Hikmet et al. (2008) indicated that health IT refers to a wide range of clinical, operational, and strategic systems used in hospitals and health care organizations. New forms of health IT have been introduced (e.g., electronic patient record systems, virtual wards, mobile technology, and assisted living technology), and have brought about many changes to the health care delivery of services for patients (Waterson, 2014). The key ethical issues in the use of health IT revolve around the principles of providing safe and avoiding harm (Berner, 2008). Health care systems are increasingly under pressure to provide the funding for innovative technologies (McCabe, Edlin, & Hall, 2013).

The purpose of health IT is to facilitate the implementation of the desires of the system's users (Stahl, 2008). Technology forms an integral part of the networks and mechanisms, which produce and redistribute power in medical practice (Jensen, 2008). The application of IT to support self-management extends the reach of the provider organization by linking patients to the exchange of health information and facilitating self-management activities (Solomon, 2008). One of the primary challenges to the effective use of health IT remains its adoption and successful implementation (Sequist, Cook, Haas, Horner, & Tierney, 2008). The national initiatives designed to coordinate health IT implementation policy are underway across the globe toward increasing the perspective of demographic and other population trends (Waterson, Glenn, & Eason, 2012).

The United States health care system is one of the world's most advanced systems (Doebbeling, Chou, & Tierney, 2006). Bauer et al. (2014) stated that the health care reforms in the United States, including the Affordable Care and the Health Information Technology for Economic and Clinical Health (HITECH) Acts, and the National Committee for Quality Assurance (NCQA) criteria for the Patient Centered Medical Home have promoted health IT and the integration of general medical and mental health services. Health IT can enhance collaborative care interventions and improve the health of individuals and populations (Bauer et al., 2014). Patient facing health IT tools is less effective when they are provided as stand-alone interventions, rather than in the context of a relationship with a health care provider (Kelders, Kok, Ossebaard, & van Gemert-Pijnen, 2012).

The advances in computer technology and capacity combined with lower start-up costs will allow developing countries to achieve greater impact when they initiate the electronic health information systems (Shih, Pan, & Tsai, 2009). Okoniewski et al. (2014) stated that understanding how adolescents use technology to meet their health information needs, and in what order of preference, will be critical for the development of technology that adolescents find useful and has the potential to decrease health disparities.

Human support may increase the effectiveness of health IT tools by providing accountability and supporting patient engagement (Mohr, Cuijpers, & Lehman, 2011), whereas stand-alone interventions demand the greater motivation and commitment on the part of patients. Sinsky et al. (2013) stated that standard workflows in traditional primary care overload physicians with tasks that can be performed by non-physician clinical staff and therefore practices need to reorganize workflows and add clinical support staff helping physicians utilize the health IT to their advantage. The applications of the primary health information system in primary health care have rapidly influenced the care service delivery (Hung et al., 2014).

While health IT has yet to fully diffuse into the long-term residential care facilities (LTRCFs) and other non-acute care facilities (Bodenheimer, 2008), successful health IT implementations may pave the way for tools that can improve health care for various vulnerable populations including the elderly patients (Chang et al., 2004). The three significant barriers to health IT adoption include financial limitations, the technology readiness of users (Ping, Li, & Gagnon, 2009), and the lack of a standard evaluation framework (Ammenwerth, Stefan, Gabriele, Burkle, & Konig, 2003). The caregivers' computer skills directly influence their adoption of new health IT applications, making it essential to provide the sufficient training and support (Ping et al., 2009).

Effective primary care requires access, continuity and comprehensiveness of health care that is community focused (Starfield, Shi, & Macinko, 2005). Critical care environments represent the information and collaborative setting (Patel & Cohen, 2008). With the increasing role of health IT and digital repositories in clinical settings, it is relevant to evaluate the role of technology in supporting the clinical reasoning and decision making (Patel, Kushniruk, Yang, & Yale, 2000). Perceived usefulness, perceived ease of use, and computer skills have significant positive impact, whereas image has significant negative impact on caregivers' intention to use health IT applications (Yu, Li, & Gagnon, 2012).

Most health care office visits leave little time for adequate patient education and counseling, particularly in health care shortage areas serving low income underinsured populations (Glasgow, Bull, Piette, & Steiner, 2004). Physicians are expected to be knowledgeable about new research, follow state-of-the-art clinical guidelines, assist patients with complex health problems in navigating the health care system, oversee referral to specialists as appropriate, be proactive in ensuring that patients receive the recommended preventive care and assist patients in the self-management of chronic conditions (Bodenheimer, Wagner, & Grumbach, 2002).

The adoption of new technologies in medicine is frequently met with both enthusiasm and resistance (Stabile & Cooper, 2013). IT can enable the automation, integration, and management of clinical and administrative functions in health care (Yang, Kankanhalli, & Chandran, 2015). IT has the potential to be a significant enabler in transforming the health care delivery system (Solomon, 2007). Clinical information management and communication technologies can help individuals and their health care organizations prepare for future changes (Sittig, 2006). Patient falls are a costly and common problem in a variety of the health care settings (Mei, Marquard, Jacelon, & DeFeo, 2013).

Multifaceted Applications of Health Information Technology

Health IT offers various electronic methods of collecting, managing, and storing the health care-related data (Reis, Pedrosa, Dourado, & Reis, 2013). The implementation of IT is acknowledged to have a positive influence on health care quality and efficiency (Venkatesh, Zhang, & Sykes, 2011). Many health care organizations have experienced resistance to the implementation and the use of IT in the health care workplace from nurses and other health care professionals (Bhattacherjee & Hikmet, 2007). Health care professionals are entitled to make their own decisions regarding system usage (Doolin, 2004).

Health technology assessment is a multidisciplinary approach to the evaluation of health care technologies, which aims to support the decision-making process by driving medical, technical, and economic knowledge (La Torre, de Waure, de Waure, & Ricciardi, 2013). Many countries use health technology assessment to review new and emerging technologies, especially with regard to reimbursement, pricing, and clinical guidelines (Bridges, 2006). Health technology assessment can be used as a tool to assess the efficiency of pharmaceutical care by linking its impact on the clinical and humanistic outcomes to the resources required to achieve these outcomes (Simoens & Laekeman, 2005). Future technology assessments are needed to provide structure for interoperability of health information systems (Lorence & Greenberg, 2006).

The planners and managers should ensure that a health IT application to be introduced into a long-term care facility is useful and easy to use (Yu et al., 2012). Patient-centered health IT services effectively provide personalized electronic health services to patients (Dehling & Sunyaev, 2014). Patient falls are the leading cause of unintentional injury and death among older adults (Tzeng, Ming, & Yin, 2008). Health IT applications, specifically electronic falls reporting systems, can aid quality improvement efforts to prevent the patient falls (Mei et al., 2013).

Researchers have suggested that the decision-making process on IT usage should be addressed (Alquraini, Alhashem, Shah, & Chowdhury, 2007) toward increasing the possibility of adopting the new technology in their health care workplace (Saleem et al., 2005). The discussions of IT acceptance by health care professionals have focused on the role of physicians (Pare, Sicotte, & Jacques, 2006). Whereas the findings from these previous studies may not be appropriate for extrapolation to nurses and other health care professionals in the primary health care (Walter & Lopez, 2008), little attention has been addressed to IT acceptance by them (Puskar, Aubrecht, Beamer, & Carozza, 2004), who are the main providers of primary health care (Yu & Yang, 2006).

Clinicians and researchers are increasingly using technology-based behavioral health interventions to improve intervention effectiveness and to reach underserved populations (Aronson, Marsch, & Acosta, 2013). Health information kiosks are a feasible medium to disseminate health information among various users in clinical and community settings, with high acceptance and satisfaction by users (Joshi & Trout, 2014). The touch screen kiosks in primary care clinics can offer patients easy access to brief, focused health care information at a time when they may be more susceptible to learning about health issues and the information can be reinforced by the provider (Glasgow et al., 2004). The touch screen kiosk offers the advantage of self-pacing and ease of use in delivering specific health information (Trepka, Newman, Huffman, & Dixon, 2010).

Mouttham et al. (2012) suggested that electronic health systems, through their application of the Internet and wireless technologies, offer the possibility of the near real-time data integration to support the delivery and management of health care. Health care systems are adopting the goal of supporting a sense of engagement between service provider and users and allowing users to co-create value through social networking and various forms of online participation (Abernethy & Hesse, 2011). The Internet allows videoconferencing based on audio-visual communication within the medical practice (Reis et al., 2013). Concerning the widespread use of the Internet, there are concerns regarding how adolescents with chronic disease (ACD) users may access the Internet information about health and how such technology use may affect the patient-physician relationship (Lacey, Chun, Terrones, & Huang, 2014).

Health IT helps health professionals improve care, adhere to clinical guidelines, facilitate decision making, and deliver tailored education in a variety of settings (Gauthier, 2014). The adoption of telehealth can empower patients with the chronic and advanced illness and improve symptom monitoring and management by providing a clear communication pathway among patient, patient's family, and the health care providers (May, Mort, Williams, Mair, & Gask, 2003). Telehealth includes an array of services that can increase the quality and access in an inpatient setting and can support individuals wishing to age in place (Goldwater & Harris, 2011).

Information Technology and Technology Acceptance Model

Perceptions of technology, familiarity with technology, and difficulty conceptualizing technology, and the need for technology assistance are interconnected in how they influence ICT preferences and technology acceptance (Walsh & Callan, 2011). IT must be implemented in ways that preserve and uplift relationships in care, while accommodating major deficiencies in managing information and making medical decisions (Weiner & Biondich, 2006). Grant et al. (2006) indicated that IT has been advocated as an important method to improve the practice of clinical medicine.

Introducing IT systems into an organization is a risky decision and will not improve an organization's effectiveness if the individual users do not accept it (Davis & Venkatesh, 1995), therefore individual users' acceptance is a pivotal factor determining the success or failure of introducing any IT systems into the workplace (Davis, 1989). As usage intention (i.e., the determination to use an IT application) is the key determinant of usage behavior (Maddux, 1999), it is a good indicator of a person's acceptance and use of an information system (Wu & Wang, 2006).

The theory of reasoned action (TRA), developed by Fishbein and Ajezn (1975), states that a person's intention to perform a given behavior is a function of his or her attitude toward that behavior and his or her subjective norm concerning that behavior. The attitude toward performing a certain behavior is assumed to be based on his or her beliefs about that behavior (Hung et al., 2014). Attitude is the degree to which one has a positive versus a negative evaluation of a certain behavior (Fishbein & Ajezn, 1975). The subjective norm is the person's perception that most people who are important to them think they should or should not perform the behavior (Fishbein & Ajezn, 1975). Ajzen (1991) integrated perceived behavioral control with TRA to predict individual intention and behavior that are not completely under volitional control. In the theory of planned behavior (TPB), Ajzen (1991) indicated that persons with a higher perceived behavioral control are more likely to form a strong intention to perform a given behavior than those who perceive that they have lower control.

Based on the concept of the TRA, Davis (1989) developed the technology acceptance model (TAM) to predict user acceptance of IT. The validity of the TAM has been tested in various health care domains, such as physicians' intention to apply the telemedicine technology in Hong Kong (Chau & Hu, 2002), physiotherapists' acceptance of a low-cost portable system for postural assessment (van Schaik, Bettany-Saltikov, & Warren, 2002), the patients' acceptance of provider-delivered electronic health (Wilson & Lankton, 2004), public health nurses' intention toward web-based learning (Chen, Yang, Tang, Huang, & Yu, 2007), mobile computing acceptance factors in health care (Wu, Wang, & Lin, 2007), and the nurses' intention of adopting an electronic logistics information system in Taiwan (Tung, Chang, & Chou, 2008).

The TAM posits that the main determinants of behavioral intention are perceived usefulness and perceived ease of use (Davis, 1989). The TRA, the TPB, and the TAM have provided the theoretical basis for many studies on understanding intention toward IT usage and for researchers to integrate various theories into their individual behavioral model (Yi, Jackson, Park, & Probst, 2006). In the TRA, attitude is the central construct in explaining behavioral intention (Armitage & Conner, 2001).

Compared with the effect of the subjective norm, the causal relationship of IT acceptance with a user's attitude is much stronger than that with the subjective norm in normal situations (Wu & Chen, 2005). Chau and Hu (2001) analyzed the TPB and the TAM model to provide a basic framework for understanding physicians' acceptance of telemedicine. Yi et al. (2006) integrated the TAM, the TPB, and the innovation diffusion theory (IDT) to examine the factors that influence the acceptance of personal digital assistant (PDA) by physicians. Perceived usefulness is the most significant determinant of physicians' intention to accept PDA (Yi et al., 2006).

Significance of Health Information Technology in the Health Care Industry

As the practice of medicine has become more complex, it is increasingly difficult for physicians to provide the right care to patients every time without modern health IT implementation (Davis et al., 2009). Health care system is one of the fields that lack the adequate research concerning technology adoption and its use (Hikmet & Chen, 2003). Appropriate application of IT in primary health care will extend traditional diagnosis and patient management beyond the physician's clinic into the everyday environment (Lovell & Celler, 1999). Health IT represents one of the most promising avenues in order to improve the health care delivery (Bates & Gawande, 2003).

While global optimization strategies are potentially unachievable in the complex critical care settings, integrated systems that simultaneously support the cognitive and reasoning processes of physicians are likely to be highly beneficial (Kannampallil et al., 2013). Heath IT has the potential to improve the quality, the cost, and the reach of health care, and recent evidence has suggested that health IT plays an influential role in chronic disease management (Rao, Brammer, McKethan, & Buntin, 2012). Paschal et al. (2008) stated that the local health departments' ability to use health care technology and to measure population-based health outcomes for their communities is crucial.

Health IT has many advantages in addressing pediatric obesity including patient education, instant feedback, personalization, and adaptation to specific behaviors (Svensson & Lagerros, 2010). Health IT has much to contribute to quality improvement for hypertension, particularly as part of multidimensional strategies for improved care (Goldstein, 2008). Health IT is viewed as a tool that can transform health care delivery (Lee, McCullough, & Town, 2013). Jean-Jacques et al. (2012) stated that the health IT-supported quality improvement initiatives are recognized to increase the ambulatory care quality for several chronic conditions and preventive services.

In the past three decades, several studies have extracted the antecedents to the user adoption of health information system (Najaftorkaman, Ghapanchi, Talaei-Khoei, & Ray, 2015). The newly-developed environmental health information system is a web-based platform that integrates databases, decision-making tools, and geographic information systems for supporting public health service and policy making (Li et al., 2008). The decentralization of health information system along with the system of health care delivery is emphasized to support the efficiency and management of health services by incorporating local use of information in decision making and planning (Kimaro & Sahay, 2007). Designing effective consumer health information system requires the understanding of the context in which the health information system is being used (Zhang, 2013).

The increased use of health IT is a common element of almost every health reform proposal because it has the potential to decrease costs, improve health outcomes, coordinate care, and improve public health

(McGraw, 2009). IT improves patient safety, and is a focus of health care reform (Pallin, Sullivan, Kaushal, & Camargo, 2010). The advances in health IT allow physicians to do various tasks: remind patients when preventive care is due, establish disease registries for monitoring appropriate care, prescribe and refill medications, order and receive the results of laboratory and imaging tests, and obtain information from specialists and hospitals on care patients have received outside a primary care practice (Kilo, 2005).

Belanger et al. (2012) stated that evaluating the impact of health IT can be challenging in the health care industry. The diffusion of technology, within the primary care physician sector of the health care market, is subject to historical, financial, legal, cultural, and social factors (Protti, Johansen, & Perez-Torres, 2009). Using health IT to have the convenient access to complete the patient health information and to provide the evidence-based decision support at the point of care is supposed to reduce the medical errors and to enhance the clinical decision making (Bates & Gawande, 2003).

FUTURE RESEARCH DIRECTIONS

The classification of the extensive literature in the domains of Web 2.0 and health IT will provide the potential opportunities for future research. Web 2.0 sites allow for user interaction and participation by having a user-friendly interface where individual can edit and publish the existing information. Web 2.0 technologies can utilize social networking tools to further increase the level of viewer's participation. The Semantic Web (also known as Web 3.0) represents the next major technology evolution in connecting information, thus enabling data to be linked from a source to any other source and to be understood by computers. Exploring the roles of Web 2.0 and the Semantic Web in modern business will be the beneficial topic for future research directions. Health IT has become an integral part of the practice of medicine toward promoting quality of care and reducing medical errors. Health informatics is the combination of informational science, health care, and computer technology. Health informatics allows a systematic way of storing and retrieving information. The benefits of applying health informatics and health IT toward increasing patient safety and improving health care performance should be further studied.

CONCLUSION

This chapter highlighted the overview of Web 2.0 technologies; Web 2.0 applications in learning and education; Web 2.0 applications in academic libraries; Web 2.0 applications in KM; the perspectives of health IT; the multifaceted applications of health IT; IT and TAM; and the significance of health IT in the health care industry. Web 2.0 technologies present a vast array of opportunities for companies which can make use of the Web 2.0 technology as a smart way to manage customer-employee relationships, marketing, and finances in cost effective ways, improve productivity, and foster their creativity and innovation. The major advantages of Web 2.0 technologies are dynamic content, user participation, scalability, metadata, openness, collective intelligence, and rich user interface. Web 2.0 technologies can offer better functionality for interaction with websites.

The applications developed using Web 2.0 technologies can be shared among a number of users through the Internet and can be simultaneously used by numerous users. Web 2.0 technologies can enable companies to create community value by tapping the collective knowledge of employees, customers, and external stakeholders. When effectively used, Web 2.0 technologies can encourage participation in projects and idea sharing, thus deepening a company's pool of knowledge. Web 2.0 technologies can bring greater scope and scale to companies, thus strengthening bonds with customers and improving communications with suppliers and outside partners.

Technological innovations in the health care industry continue to provide physicians and health care providers with new ways to improve the quality of care delivered to their patients and improve the perspective of global health care. Health IT is the sector of IT that deals with health and medical care technological systems, as it involves designing, developing, using and maintaining electronic health care systems. The field of health IT bridges several professional disciplines including medicine and allied health professions, law, informatics, computer science, business, project management, and research. Health IT includes utilizing technology to electronically store, protect, retrieve, and transfer information within health care and community settings.

Health IT brings many potential benefits in the health care industry. The advantages of health IT include facilitating communication between health care providers; improving medication safety, tracking, and reporting; and promoting quality of care through optimized access to guidelines. Health IT enables health care workers to obtain, utilize, and communicate high-quality information about patients. Health IT systems permit the collection of important data for quality management, outcome reporting, and public health disease surveillance and reporting. Health IT allows patients access to their medical records, which helps them to feel more knowledgeable about their conditions and encourages them to actively participate in shared decision making. However, implementing, maintaining, and optimizing health IT can be a challenge for rural facilities and health care providers with limited resources and technology expertise.

REFERENCES

Abernethy, A. P., & Hesse, B. W. (2011). Guest editor's introduction to the special section on information technology and evidence implementation. *Translational Behavioral Medicine*, *1*(1), 11–14. doi:10.1007/s13142-011-0014-6 PMID:24073027

Agha, L. (2014). The effects of health information technology on the costs and quality of medical care. *Journal of Health Economics*, *34*, 19–30. doi:10.1016/j.jhealeco.2013.12.005 PMID:24463141

Aharony, N. (2010). Twitter use in libraries: An exploratory analysis. *Journal of Web Librarianship*, *4*(4), 333–350. doi:10.1080/19322909.2010.487766

Ajzen, I. (1991). The theory of planned behavior. *Organizational Behavior and Human Decision Processes*, *50*(2), 179–211. doi:10.1016/0749-5978(91)90020-T

Al-ghamdi, H. A. K., & Al-ghamdi, A. A. K. (2015). The role of virtual communities of practice in knowledge management using Web 2.0. *Procedia Computer Science*, *65*, 406–411. doi:10.1016/j.procs.2015.09.102

Alquraini, H., Alhashem, A. M., Shah, M. A., & Chowdhury, R. I. (2007). Factors influencing nurses' attitudes towards the use of computerized health information systems in Kuwaiti hospitals. *Journal of Advanced Nursing*, *57*(4), 375–381. doi:10.1111/j.1365-2648.2007.04113.x PMID:17291201

Ammenwerth, E., Stefan, G., Gabriele, H., Burkle, T., & Konig, J. (2003). Evaluation of health information systems: Problems and challenges. *International Journal of Medical Informatics, 71*(2), 125–135. doi:10.1016/S1386-5056(03)00131-X PMID:14519405

Andriole, S. J. (2010). Business impact of Web 2.0 technologies. *Communications of the ACM, 53*(12), 67–79. doi:10.1145/1859204.1859225

Armitage, C. J., & Conner, M. (2001). Efficacy of the theory of planned behaviour: A meta-analytic review. *The British Journal of Social Psychology, 40*(4), 471–499. doi:10.1348/014466601164939 PMID:11795063

Aronson, I. D., Marsch, L. A., & Acosta, M. C. (2013). Using findings in multimedia learning to inform technology-based behavioral health interventions. *Translational Behavioral Medicine, 3*(3), 234–243. doi:10.1007/s13142-012-0137-4 PMID:24073174

Bates, D. W., & Gawande, A. A. (2003). Improving safety with information technology. *The New England Journal of Medicine, 348*(25), 2526–2534. doi:10.1056/NEJMsa020847 PMID:12815139

Bauer, A. M., Thielke, S. M., Katon, W., Unützer, J., & Areán, P. (2014). Aligning health information technologies with effective service delivery models to improve chronic disease care. *Preventive Medicine, 66*, 167–172. doi:10.1016/j.ypmed.2014.06.017 PMID:24963895

Belanger, E., Bartlett, G., Dawes, M., Rodriguez, C., & Hasson-Gidoni, I. (2012). Examining the evidence of the impact of health information technology in primary care: An argument for participatory research with health professionals and patients. *International Journal of Medical Informatics, 81*(10), 654–661. doi:10.1016/j.ijmedinf.2012.07.008 PMID:22910233

Bennett, S., Bishop, A., Dalgarno, B., Waycott, J., & Kennedy, G. (2012). Implementing Web 2.0 technologies in higher education: A collective case study. *Computers & Education, 59*(2), 524–534. doi:10.1016/j.compedu.2011.12.022

Berner, E. S. (2008). Ethical and legal issues in the use of health information technology to improve patient safety. *HEC Forum, 20*(3), 243–258. doi:10.1007/s10730-008-9074-5 PMID:18803020

Berthon, P. R., Pitt, L. F., Plangger, K., & Shapiro, D. (2012). Marketing meets Web 2.0, social media, and creative consumers: Implications for international marketing strategy. *Business Horizons, 55*(3), 261–271. doi:10.1016/j.bushor.2012.01.007

Bhattacherjee, A., & Hikmet, N. (2007). Physicians' resistance toward healthcare information technology: A theoretical model and empirical test. *European Journal of Information Systems, 16*(6), 725–737. doi:10.1057/palgrave.ejis.3000717

Bodenheimer, T. (2008). Coordinating care: A perilous journey through the health care system. *The New England Journal of Medicine, 358*(10), 1064–1071. doi:10.1056/NEJMhpr0706165 PMID:18322289

Bodenheimer, T., Wagner, E., & Grumbach, K. (2002). Improving primary care for patients with chronic illness: The chronic care model. *Journal of the American Medical Association, 288*(14), 1775–1779. doi:10.1001/jama.288.14.1775 PMID:12365965

Boulos, M. N. K., & Wheeler, S. (2007). The emerging Web 2.0 social software: An enabling suite of sociable technologies in health and health care education. *Health Information and Libraries Journal, 24*(1), 2–23. doi:10.1111/j.1471-1842.2007.00701.x PMID:17331140

Bridges, J. F. P. (2006). Lean systems approaches to health technology assessment. *PharmacoEconomics, 24*(2), 101–109. PMID:23389493

Brown, S. A. (2012). Seeing Web 2.0 in context: A study of academic perceptions. *The Internet and Higher Education, 15*(1), 50–57. doi:10.1016/j.iheduc.2011.04.003

Chang, B. L., Bakken, S., Brown, S. S., Houston, T. K., Kreps, G. L., Kukafka, R., & Stavri, P. Z. et al. (2004). Bridging the digital divide: Reaching vulnerable populations. *Journal of the American Medical Informatics Association, 11*(6), 448–457. doi:10.1197/jamia.M1535 PMID:15299002

Chatti, M. A., Jarke, M., & Frosch-Wike, D. (2007). The future of e-learning: A shift to knowledge networking and social software. *International Journal of Knowledge and Learning, 3*(4/5), 404–420. doi:10.1504/IJKL.2007.016702

Chau, P. Y. K., & Hu, P. J. (2001). Information technology acceptance by individual professionals: A model comparison approach. *Decision Sciences, 32*(4), 699–719. doi:10.1111/j.1540-5915.2001.tb00978.x

Chaves, M. S., Gomes, R., & Pedron, C. (2012). Analysing reviews in the Web 2.0: Small & medium hotels in Portugal. *Tourism Management, 33*(5), 1286–1287. doi:10.1016/j.tourman.2011.11.007

Chen, I. J., Yang, K. F., Tang, F. I., Huang, C. H., & Yu, S. (2007). Applying the technology acceptance model to explore public health nurses' intentions towards web-based learning: A cross-sectional questionnaire survey. *International Journal of Nursing Studies, 465*(6), 869–878. PMID:17482191

Chen, S. C., Yen, D. C., & Hwang, M. I. (2012). Factors influencing the continuance intention to the usage of Web 2.0: An empirical study. *Computers in Human Behavior, 28*(3), 933–941. doi:10.1016/j.chb.2011.12.014

Chu, S. K. W., Woo, M., King, R. B., Choi, S., Cheng, M., & Koo, P. (2012). Examining the application of Web 2.0 in medical-related organisations. *Health Information and Libraries Journal, 29*(1), 47–60. doi:10.1111/j.1471-1842.2011.00970.x PMID:22335289

Churchill, D. (2011). Web 2.0 in education: A study of the explorative use of blogs with a postgraduate class. *Innovations in Education and Teaching International, 48*(2), 149–158. doi:10.1080/14703297.2011.564009

Claxton, K. P., & Sculpher, M. J. (2006). Using value of information analysis to prioritise health research. *PharmacoEconomics, 24*(11), 1055–1068. doi:10.2165/00019053-200624110-00003 PMID:17067191

Coeckelbergh, M. (2013). E-care as craftsmanship: Virtuous work, skilled engagement, and information technology in health care. *Medicine, Health Care, and Philosophy, 16*(4), 807–816. doi:10.1007/s11019-013-9463-7 PMID:23338289

Cronin, J. J. (2009). Upgrading to Web 2.0: An experimental project to build a marketing wiki. *Journal of Marketing Education, 31*(1), 66–75. doi:10.1177/0273475308329250

Dabbagh, N., & Kitsantas, A. (2012). Personal learning environments, social media, and self-regulated learning: A natural formula for connecting formal and informal learning. *The Internet and Higher Education, 15*(1), 3–8. doi:10.1016/j.iheduc.2011.06.002

Davis, F. D. (1989). Perceived usefulness, perceived ease of use, and user acceptance of information technology. *Management Information Systems Quarterly, 13*(3), 319–340. doi:10.2307/249008

Davis, F. D., & Venkatesh, V. (1995). *Measuring user acceptance of emerging information technologies: An assessment of possible method biases.* Paper presented at the 28th Annual Hawaii International Conference on System Sciences, Maui, HI. doi:10.1109/HICSS.1995.375675

Davis, K., Doty, M. M., Shea, K., & Stremikis, K. (2009). Health information technology and physician perceptions of quality of care and satisfaction. *Health Policy (Amsterdam), 90*(2/3), 239–246. doi:10.1016/j.healthpol.2008.10.002 PMID:19038472

Davison, R. M., Ou, C. X. J., Martinsons, M. G., Zhao, A. Y., & Du, R. (2014). The communicative ecology of Web 2.0 at work: Social networking in the workspace. *Journal of the Association for Information Science and Technology, 65*(10), 2035–2047. doi:10.1002/asi.23112

Dehling, T., & Sunyaev, A. (2014). Secure provision of patient-centered health information technology services in public networks–leveraging security and privacy features provided by the German nationwide health information technology infrastructure. *Electronic Markets, 24*(2), 89–99. doi:10.1007/s12525-013-0150-6

Doebbeling, B. N., Chou, A. F., & Tierney, W. M. (2006). Priorities and strategies for the implementation of integrated informatics and communications technology to improve evidence-based practice. *Journal of General Internal Medicine, 21*(2), S50–S57. doi:10.1007/s11606-006-0275-9 PMID:16637961

Doolin, B. (2004). Power and resistance in the implementation of a medical management information system. *Information Systems Journal, 14*(4), 343–362. doi:10.1111/j.1365-2575.2004.00176.x

Dougherty, M., & Meyer, E. T. (2014). Community, tools, and practices in web archiving: The state-of-the-art in relation to social science and humanities research needs. *Journal of the Association for Information Science and Technology, 65*(11), 2195–2209. doi:10.1002/asi.23099

Dowling, R. A. (2013). Health information technology in urologic care: Current status and implications for quality of care. *Current Urology Reports, 14*(6), 535–540. doi:10.1007/s11934-013-0356-3 PMID:23881730

Drexler, W. (2010). The networked student model for construction of personal learning environments: Balancing teacher control and student autonomy. *Australasian Journal of Educational Technology, 26*(3), 369–385. doi:10.14742/ajet.1081

Eccleston, D., & Griseri, L. (2008). How does Web 2.0 stretch traditional influencing patterns? *International Journal of Market Research, 50*(5), 591–616. doi:10.2501/S1470785308200055

Edoh, T. O., & Teege, G. (2011). Using information technology for an improved pharmaceutical care delivery in developing countries. Study case: Benin. *Journal of Medical Systems, 35*(5), 1123–1134. doi:10.1007/s10916-011-9717-y PMID:21519942

Fieschi, M. (2002). Information technology is changing the way society sees health care delivery. *International Journal of Medical Informatics, 66*(3), 85–93. doi:10.1016/S1386-5056(02)00040-0 PMID:12453562

Fishbein, M., & Ajzen, I. (1975). *Belief, attitude, intention, and behavior: An introduction to theory and research.* Reading, MA: Addison–Wesley.

Fox, G., & Pierce, M. (2009). Grids challenged by a Web 2.0 and multicore sandwich. *Concurrency and Computation, 21*(3), 265–280. doi:10.1002/cpe.1358

Fuchs, C. (2011). New media, Web 2.0 and surveillance. *Social Compass, 5*(2), 134–147. doi:10.1111/j.1751-9020.2010.00354.x

Fuji, K. T., & Galt, K. A. (2008). Pharmacists and health information technology: Emerging issues in patient safety. *HEC Forum, 20*(3), 259–275. doi:10.1007/s10730-008-9075-4 PMID:18803019

Gardois, P., Colombi, N., Grillo, G., & Villanacci, M. C. (2012). Implementation of Web 2.0 services in academic, medical and research libraries: A scoping review. *Health Information and Libraries Journal, 29*(2), 90–109. doi:10.1111/j.1471-1842.2012.00984.x PMID:22630358

Gauthier, K. (2014). Starting the conversation: A health information technology tool to address pediatric obesity. *The Journal for Nurse Practitioners, 10*(10), 813–819. doi:10.1016/j.nurpra.2014.06.007

Glasgow, R. E., Bull, S. S., Piette, J. D., & Steiner, J. F. (2004). Interactive behavior change technology: A partial solution to the competing demands of primary care. *American Journal of Preventive Medicine, 27*(2), 80–87. doi:10.1016/j.amepre.2004.04.026 PMID:15275676

Goldstein, M. K. (2008). Using health information technology to improve hypertension management. *Current Hypertension Reports, 10*(3), 201–207. doi:10.1007/s11906-008-0038-6 PMID:18765090

Goldwater, J., & Harris, Y. (2011). Using technology to enhance the aging experience: A market analysis of existing technologies. *Ageing International, 36*(1), 5–28. doi:10.1007/s12126-010-9071-2

Gould, L. S. (2009). What Web 2.0 means to you. *Automotive Design & Production, 121*(6), 36–37.

Grant, R. W., Campbell, E. G., Gruen, R. L., Ferris, T. G., & Blumenthal, D. (2006). Prevalence of basic information technology use by U.S. physicians. *Journal of General Internal Medicine, 21*(11), 1150–1155. doi:10.1111/j.1525-1497.2006.00571.x PMID:16879417

Gu, J., Churchill, D., & Lu, J. (2014). Mobile Web 2.0 in the workplace: A case study of employees' informal learning. *British Journal of Educational Technology, 45*(6), 1049–1059. doi:10.1111/bjet.12179

Handsfield, L. J., Dean, T. R., & Cielocha, K. M. (2009). Becoming critical consumers and producers of text: Teaching literacy with Web 1.0 and Web 2.0. *The Reading Teacher, 63*(1), 40–50. doi:10.1598/RT.63.1.4

Hao, Y., & Lee, K. S. (2015). Teachers' concern about integrating Web 2.0 technologies and its relationship with teacher characteristics. *Computers in Human Behavior, 48*, 1–8. doi:10.1016/j.chb.2015.01.028

Hendrix, D., Chiarella, D., Hasman, L., Murphy, S., & Zafron, M. L. (2009). Use of Facebook in academic health sciences libraries. *Journal of the Medical Library Association: JMLA*, *97*(1), 44–47. doi:10.3163/1536-5050.97.1.008 PMID:19159005

Hikmet, N., Bhattacherjee, A., Menachemi, N., Kayhan, V. O., & Brooks, R. G. (2008). The role of organizational factors in the adoption of healthcare information technology in Florida hospitals. *Health Care Management Science*, *11*(1), 1–9. doi:10.1007/s10729-007-9036-5 PMID:18390163

Hikmet, N., & Chen, S. K. (2003). An investigation into low mail survey response rates of information technology users in health care organizations. *International Journal of Medical Informatics*, *72*(1), 29–34. doi:10.1016/j.ijmedinf.2003.09.002 PMID:14644304

Hinchliffe, L. J., & Leon, R. (2011). Innovation as a framework for adopting Web 2.0 marketing approaches. In D. Gupta & R. Savard (Eds.), *Marketing libraries in a Web 2.0 world* (pp. 58–65). Berlin, Germany: De Gruyter Saur. doi:10.1515/9783110263534.57

Hsu, I. C. (2013). Multilayer context cloud framework for mobile Web 2.0: A proposed infrastructure. *International Journal of Communication Systems*, *26*(5), 610–625. doi:10.1002/dac.1365

Huang, C., Fu, T., & Chen, H. (2010). Text-based video content classification for online video-sharing sites. *Journal of the American Society for Information Science and Technology*, *61*(5), 891–906. doi:10.1002/asi.21291

Hui, G., & Hayllar, M. R. (2010). Creating public value in e-government: A public-private-citizen collaboration framework in Web 2.0. *Australian Journal of Public Administration*, *69*(s1), S120–S131. doi:10.1111/j.1467-8500.2009.00662.x

Hung, M., Conrad, J., Hon, S. D., Cheng, C., Franklin, J. D., & Tang, P. (2013). Uncovering patterns of technology use in consumer health informatics. *Wiley Interdisciplinary Reviews: Computational Statistics*, *5*(6), 432–447. doi:10.1002/wics.1276 PMID:24904713

Hung, S. Y., Tsai, J. C. A., & Chuang, C. C. (2014). Investigating primary health care nurses' intention to use information technology: An empirical study in Taiwan. *Decision Support Systems*, *57*, 331–342. doi:10.1016/j.dss.2013.09.016

James, R. (2014). ICT's participatory potential in higher education collaborations: Reality or just talk. *British Journal of Educational Technology*, *45*(4), 557–570. doi:10.1111/bjet.12060

Jean-Jacques, M., Persell, S. D., Thompson, J. A., Hasnain-Wynia, R., & Baker, D. W. (2012). Changes in disparities following the implementation of a health information technology-supported quality improvement initiative. *Journal of General Internal Medicine*, *27*(1), 71–77. doi:10.1007/s11606-011-1842-2 PMID:21892661

Jensen, C. B. (2008). Power, technology and social studies of health care: An infrastructural inversion. *Health Care Analysis*, *16*(4), 355–374. doi:10.1007/s10728-007-0076-2 PMID:18085441

Joshi, A., & Trout, K. (2014). The role of health information kiosks in diverse settings: A systematic review. *Health Information and Libraries Journal*, *31*(4), 254–273. doi:10.1111/hir.12081 PMID:25209260

Kam, H. J., & Katerattanakul, P. (2014). Structural model of team-based learning using Web 2.0 collaborative software. *Computers & Education, 76*, 1–12. doi:10.1016/j.compedu.2014.03.003

Kannampallil, T. G., Franklin, A., Mishra, R., Almoosa, K. F., Cohen, T., & Patel, V. L. (2013). Understanding the nature of information seeking behavior in critical care: Implications for the design of health information technology. *Artificial Intelligence in Medicine, 57*(1), 21–29. doi:10.1016/j.artmed.2012.10.002 PMID:23194923

Kasemsap, K. (2014). The role of social media in the knowledge-based organizations. In I. Lee (Ed.), *Integrating social media into business practice, applications, management, and models* (pp. 254–275). Hershey, PA: IGI Global. doi:10.4018/978-1-4666-6182-0.ch013

Kasemsap, K. (2015). The role of cloud computing adoption in global business. In V. Chang, R. Walters, & G. Wills (Eds.), *Delivery and adoption of cloud computing services in contemporary organizations* (pp. 26–55). Hershey, PA: IGI Global. doi:10.4018/978-1-4666-8210-8.ch002

Kasemsap, K. (2016a). The roles of e-learning, organizational learning, and knowledge management in the learning organizations. In E. Railean, G. Walker, A. Elçi, & L. Jackson (Eds.), *Handbook of research on applied learning theory and design in modern education* (pp. 786–816). Hershey, PA: IGI Global. doi:10.4018/978-1-4666-9634-1.ch039

Kasemsap, K. (2016b). Creating product innovation strategies through knowledge management in global business. In A. Goel & P. Singhal (Eds.), *Product innovation through knowledge management and social media strategies* (pp. 330–357). Hershey, PA: IGI Global. doi:10.4018/978-1-4666-9607-5.ch015

Kelders, S. M., Kok, R. N., Ossebaard, H. C., & van Gemert-Pijnen, J. E. W. C. (2012). Persuasive system design does matter: A systematic review of adherence to web-based interventions. *Journal of Medical Internet Research, 14*(6), 2–25. doi:10.2196/jmir.2104 PMID:23151820

Kho, N. D. (2011). Social media in libraries: Keys to deeper engagement. *Information Today, 28*(6), 31–32.

Kidd, L., Cayless, S., Johnston, B., & Wengstrom, Y. (2010). Telehealth in palliative care in the UK: A review of the evidence. *Journal of Telemedicine and Telecare, 16*(7), 394–402. doi:10.1258/jtt.2010.091108 PMID:20813893

Kilo, C. M. (2005). Transforming care: Medical practice design and information technology. *Health Affairs, 24*(5), 1296–1301. doi:10.1377/hlthaff.24.5.1296 PMID:16162576

Kim, D. J., Yue, K., Hall, S. P., & Gates, T. (2009). Global diffusion of the Internet XV: Web 2.0 technologies, principles, and applications: A conceptual framework from technology push and demand pull perspective. *Communications of AIS, 24*(1), 657–672.

Kimaro, H. C., & Sahay, S. (2007). An institutional perspective on the process of decentralization of health information systems: A case study from Tanzania. *Information Technology for Development, 13*(s4), 363–390. doi:10.1002/itdj.20066

Kitsantas, A., & Dabbagh, N. (2011). The role of Web 2.0 technologies in self-regulated learning. *New Directions for Teaching and Learning, 2011*(126), 99–106. doi:10.1002/tl.448

Kurilovas, E., & Dagiene, V. (2010). *Evaluation of quality of the learning software: Basics, concepts, methods*. Saarbrücken, Germany: LAP LAMBERT Academic Publishing.

Kurilovas, E., & Juskeviciene, A. (2015). Creation of Web 2.0 tools ontology to improve learning. *Computers in Human Behavior, 51*, 1380–1386. doi:10.1016/j.chb.2014.10.026

La Torre, G., de Waure, C., de Waure, A., & Ricciardi, W. (2013). The promising application of health technology assessment in public health: A review of background information and considerations for future development. *Journal of Public Health, 21*(4), 373–378. doi:10.1007/s10389-013-0557-8

Lacey, C., Chun, S., Terrones, L., & Huang, J. S. (2014). Adolescents with chronic disease and use of technology for receipt of information regarding health and disease management. *Health Technology, 4*(3), 253–259. doi:10.1007/s12553-014-0076-9

Landis, C. (2007). Friending our users: Social networking and reference services. In S. Steiner & L. Madden (Eds.), *The desk and beyond: Next generation reference services*. Chicago, IL: Association of College and Research Libraries.

Lee, J., McCullough, J. S., & Town, R. J. (2013). The impact of health information technology on hospital productivity. *The Rand Journal of Economics, 44*(3), 545–568. doi:10.1111/1756-2171.12030

Levy, M. (2009). Web 2.0 implications on knowledge management. *Journal of Knowledge Management, 13*(1), 120–134. doi:10.1108/13673270910931215

Li, L., Xu, L., Jeng, H. A., Naik, D., Allen, T., & Frontini, M. (2008). Creation of environmental health information system for public health service: A pilot study. *Information Systems Frontiers, 10*(5), 531–542. doi:10.1007/s10796-008-9108-1

Lilleker, D. G., & Jackson, N. A. (2010). Towards a more participatory style of election campaigning: The impact of Web 2.0 on the UK 2010 general election. *Policy & Internet, 2*(3), 69–98. doi:10.2202/1944-2866.1064

Lorence, D. (2007). Why there can be no sustainable national healthcare IT program without a translational health information science. *Journal of Medical Systems, 31*(6), 557–562. doi:10.1007/s10916-007-9099-3 PMID:18041292

Lorence, D. P., & Greenberg, L. (2006). The zeitgeist of online health search. *Journal of General Internal Medicine, 21*(2), 134–139. PMID:16336621

Lovell, N. H., & Celler, B. G. (1999). Information technology in primary health care. *International Journal of Medical Informatics, 55*(1), 9–22. doi:10.1016/S1386-5056(99)00016-7 PMID:10471237

Lowe, B., D'Alessandro, S., Winzar, H., Laffey, D., & Collier, W. (2013). The use of Web 2.0 technologies in marketing classes: Key drivers of student acceptance. *Journal of Consumer Behaviour, 12*(5), 412–422. doi:10.1002/cb.1444

MacKay, B., & Watters, C. (2012). An examination of multisession web tasks. *Journal of the American Society for Information Science and Technology, 63*(6), 1183–1197. doi:10.1002/asi.22610

Maddux, J. E. (1999). Expectancies and the social cognitive perspective: Basic principles, processes, and variables. In I. Kirsch (Ed.), *How expectancies shape experience* (pp. 17–40). Washington, DC: American Psychological Association. doi:10.1037/10332-001

May, C., Mort, M., Williams, T., Mair, F., & Gask, L. (2003). Health technology assessment in its local contexts: Studies of telehealthcare. *Social Science & Medicine*, *57*(4), 697–710. doi:10.1016/S0277-9536(02)00419-7 PMID:12821017

McCabe, C., Edlin, R., & Hall, P. (2013). Navigating time and uncertainty in health technology appraisal: Would a map help? *PharmacoEconomics*, *31*(9), 731–737. doi:10.1007/s40273-013-0077-y PMID:23877738

McGraw, D. (2009). Privacy and health information technology. *The Journal of Law, Medicine & Ethics*, *37*(s2), 121–149. doi:10.1111/j.1748-720X.2009.00424.x PMID:19754656

Mei, Y. Y., Marquard, J., Jacelon, C., & DeFeo, A. L. (2013). Designing and evaluating an electronic patient falls reporting system: Perspectives for the implementation of health information technology in long-term residential care facilities. *International Journal of Medical Informatics*, *82*(11), e294–e306. doi:10.1016/j.ijmedinf.2011.03.008 PMID:21482183

Mohr, D. C., Cuijpers, P., & Lehman, K. (2011). Supportive accountability: A model for providing human support to enhance adherence to eHealth interventions. *Journal of Medical Internet Research*, *13*(1), e30. doi:10.2196/jmir.1602 PMID:21393123

Montano, B. S. J., Carretero, R. G., Entrecanales, M. V., & Pozuelo, P. M. (2010). Integrating the hospital library with patient care, teaching and research: Model and Web 2.0 tools to create a social and collaborative community of clinical research in a hospital setting. *Health Information and Libraries Journal*, *27*(3), 217–226. doi:10.1111/j.1471-1842.2010.00893.x PMID:20712716

Mouttham, A., Kuziemsky, C., Langayan, D., Peyton, L., & Pereira, J. (2012). Interoperable support for collaborative, mobile, and accessible health care. *Information Systems Frontiers*, *14*(1), 73–85. doi:10.1007/s10796-011-9296-y

Najaftorkaman, M., Ghapanchi, A. H., Talaei-Khoei, A., & Ray, P. (2015). A taxonomy of antecedents to user adoption of health information systems: A synthesis of thirty years of research. *Journal of the Association for Information Science and Technology*, *66*(3), 576–598. doi:10.1002/asi.23181

Nedlund, A. C., & Garpenby, P. (2014). Puzzling about problems: The ambiguous search for an evidence based strategy for handling influx of health technology. *Policy Sciences*, *47*(4), 367–386. doi:10.1007/s11077-014-9198-1

Nesta, F., & Mi, J. (2011). Library 2.0 or library III: Returning to leadership. *Library Management*, *32*(1/2), 85–97. doi:10.1108/01435121111102601

Oberhelman, D. (2007). Coming to terms with Web 2.0. *Reference Reviews*, *21*(7), 5–6. doi:10.1108/09504120710836473

Okoniewski, A. E., Lee, Y. J., Rodriguez, M., Schnall, R., & Low, A. F. H. (2014). Health information seeking behaviors of ethnically diverse adolescents. *Journal of Immigrant and Minority Health*, *16*(4), 652–660. doi:10.1007/s10903-013-9803-y PMID:23512322

Pallin, D. J., Sullivan, A. F., Kaushal, R., & Camargo, C. A. (2010). Health information technology in US emergency departments. *International Journal of Emergency Medicine*, *3*(3), 181–185. doi:10.1007/s12245-010-0170-3 PMID:21031043

Pare, G., Sicotte, C., & Jacques, H. (2006). The effects of creating psychological ownership on physicians' acceptance of clinical information systems. *Journal of the American Medical Informatics Association*, *13*(2), 197–205. doi:10.1197/jamia.M1930 PMID:16357351

Paschal, A. M., Oler-Manske, J., Kroupa, K., & Snethen, E. (2008). Using a community-based participatory research approach to improve the performance capacity of local health departments: The Kansas immunization technology project. *Journal of Community Health*, *33*(6), 407–416. doi:10.1007/s10900-008-9116-6 PMID:18587634

Patel, V. L., & Cohen, T. (2008). New perspectives on error in critical care. *Current Opinion in Critical Care*, *14*(4), 456–459. doi:10.1097/MCC.0b013e32830634ae PMID:18614912

Patel, V. L., Kushniruk, A. W., Yang, S., & Yale, J. F. (2000). Impact of a computerized patient record system on medical data collection, organization and reasoning. *Journal of the American Medical Informatics Association*, *7*(6), 569–585. doi:10.1136/jamia.2000.0070569 PMID:11062231

Pãuleþ-Crãiniceanu, L. (2014). Integrating the Web 2.0 technologies in Romanian public universities. Towards a blended learning model that addresses troubled student-faculty interaction. *Procedia: Social and Behavioral Sciences*, *142*, 793–799. doi:10.1016/j.sbspro.2014.07.618

Pieri, M., & Diamantini, D. (2014). An e-learning Web 2.0 experience. *Procedia: Social and Behavioral Sciences*, *116*, 1217–1221. doi:10.1016/j.sbspro.2014.01.371

Ping, Y., Li, H., & Gagnon, M. P. (2009). Health IT acceptance factors in long-term care facilities: A cross-sectional survey. *International Journal of Medical Informatics*, *78*(4), 219–229. doi:10.1016/j.ijmedinf.2008.07.006 PMID:18768345

Protti, D., Johansen, I., & Perez-Torres, F. (2009). Comparing the application of health information technology in primary care in Denmark and Andalucia, Spain. *International Journal of Medical Informatics*, *78*(4), 270–283. doi:10.1016/j.ijmedinf.2008.08.002 PMID:18819836

Puskar, K. R., Aubrecht, J., Beamer, K., & Carozza, L. J. (2004). Implementing information technology in a behavioral health setting. *Issues in Mental Health Nursing*, *25*(5), 439–450. doi:10.1080/01612840490443428 PMID:15204889

Rahimi, E., van den Berg, J., & Veen, W. (2015a). A learning model for enhancing the student's control in educational process using Web 2.0 personal learning environments. *British Journal of Educational Technology*, *46*(4), 780–792. doi:10.1111/bjet.12170

Rahimi, E., van den Berg, J., & Veen, W. (2015b). Facilitating student-driven constructing of learning environments using Web 2.0 personal learning environments. *Computers & Education, 81*, 235–246. doi:10.1016/j.compedu.2014.10.012

Randeree, E., & Mon, L. (2007). Web 2.0: A new dynamic in information services for libraries. *Proceedings of the American Society for Information Science and Technology, 44*(1), 1–6. doi:10.1002/meet.145044039

Rao, S., Brammer, C., McKethan, A., & Buntin, M. (2012). Health information technology: Transforming chronic disease management and care transitions. *Primary Care: Clinics in Office Practice, 39*(2), 327–344. doi:10.1016/j.pop.2012.03.006 PMID:22608869

Razmerita, L., Kirchner, K., & Sudzina, F. (2009). Personal knowledge management. *Online Information Review, 33*(6), 1021–1039. doi:10.1108/14684520911010981

Reis, A., Pedrosa, A., Dourado, M., & Reis, C. (2013). Information and communication technologies in long-term and palliative care. *Procedia Technology, 9*, 1303–1312. doi:10.1016/j.protcy.2013.12.146

Richards, B. (2009). A social software/Web 2.0 approach to collaborative knowledge engineering. *Information Sciences, 179*(15), 2515–2523. doi:10.1016/j.ins.2009.01.031

Rogozynska, N. S., & Kozak, L. M. (2013). Information support of a technology for automated monitoring of the state of population health. *Cybernetics and Systems Analysis, 49*(6), 941–950. doi:10.1007/s10559-013-9585-1

Rollett, H., Lux, M., Strohmaier, M., Dosinger, G., & Tochtermann, K. (2007). The Web 2.0 way of learning with technologies. *International Journal of Learning Technology, 3*(1), 87–107. doi:10.1504/IJLT.2007.012368

Rubio, R., Martín, S., & Morán, S. (2010). Collaborative web learning tools: Wikis and blogs. *Computer Applications in Engineering Education, 18*(3), 502–511. doi:10.1002/cae.20218

Sadaf, A., Newby, T. J., & Ertmer, P. A. (2012). Exploring pre-service teachers' beliefs about using Web 2.0 technologies in K-12 classroom. *Computers & Education, 59*(3), 937–945. doi:10.1016/j.compedu.2012.04.001

Saleem, J. J., Patterson, E. S., Militello, L., Render, M. L., Orshansky, G., & Asch, S. M. (2005). Exploring barriers and facilitators to the use of computerized clinical reminders. *Journal of the American Medical Informatics Association, 12*(4), 438–447. doi:10.1197/jamia.M1777 PMID:15802482

Scalvini, S., Baratti, D., Assoni, G., Zanardini, M., Comini, L., & Bernocchi, P. (2014). Information and communication technology in chronic diseases: A patient's opportunity. *Journal of Medicine and the Person, 12*(3), 91–95. doi:10.1007/s12682-013-0154-1

Schneckenberg, D., Ehlers, U., & Adelsberger, H. (2011). Web 2.0 and competence-oriented design of learning: Potentials and implications for higher education. *British Journal of Educational Technology, 42*(5), 747–762. doi:10.1111/j.1467-8535.2010.01092.x

Schreurs, B., & de Laat, M. (2014). The network awareness tool: A Web 2.0 tool to visualize informal networked learning in organizations. *Computers in Human Behavior, 37*, 385–394. doi:10.1016/j. chb.2014.04.034

Seo, D., & Lee, J. (2016). Web_2.0 and five years since: How the combination of technological and organizational initiatives influences an organizations long-term Web_2.0 performance. *Telematics and Informatics, 33*(1), 232–246. doi:10.1016/j.tele.2015.07.010

Sequist, T. D. (2011). Health information technology and disparities in quality of care. *Journal of General Internal Medicine, 26*(10), 1084–1085. doi:10.1007/s11606-011-1812-8 PMID:21809173

Sequist, T. D., Cook, D. A., Haas, J. S., Horner, R., & Tierney, W. M. (2008). Moving health information technology forward. *Journal of General Internal Medicine, 23*(4), 355–357. doi:10.1007/s11606-008-0551-y PMID:18373129

Shih, Y. C. T., Pan, I. W., & Tsai, Y. W. (2009). Information technology facilitates cost-effectiveness analysis in developing countries. *PharmacoEconomics, 27*(11), 947–961. doi:10.2165/11314110-000000000-00000 PMID:19888794

Simoens, S., & Laekeman, G. (2005). Applying health technology assessment to pharmaceutical care: Pitfalls and future directions. *Pharmacy World & Science, 27*(2), 73–75. doi:10.1007/s11096-004-4098-7 PMID:15999914

Sinsky, C. A., Willard-Grace, R., Schutzbank, A. M., Sinsky, T. A., Margolius, D., & Bodenheimer, T. (2013). In search of joy in practice: A report of 23 high-functioning primary care practices. *Annals of Family Medicine, 11*(3), 272–278. doi:10.1370/afm.1531 PMID:23690328

Sittig, D. F. (2006). Potential impact of advanced clinical information technology on cancer care in 2015. *Cancer Causes & Control, 17*(6), 813–820. doi:10.1007/s10552-006-0020-z PMID:16783609

Smith, A., & Rogers, S. (2008). Web 2.0 and official statistics: The case for a multi-disciplinary approach. *Statistical Journal of the IAOS, 25*(3/4), 117–123.

Solomon, M. R. (2007). Regional health information organizations: A vehicle for transforming health care delivery? *Journal of Medical Systems, 31*(1), 35–47. doi:10.1007/s10916-006-9041-0 PMID:17283921

Solomon, M. R. (2008). Information technology to support self-management in chronic care. *Disease Management & Health Outcomes, 16*(6), 391–401. doi:10.2165/0115677-200816060-00004

Song, D., & Lee, J. (2014). Has Web 2.0 revitalized informal learning? The relationship between Web 2.0 and informal learning. *Journal of Computer Assisted Learning, 30*(6), 511–533. doi:10.1111/jcal.12056

Stabile, M., & Cooper, L. (2013). Review article: The evolving role of information technology in perioperative patient safety. Canadian Journal of Anesthesia/Journal canadien d'anesthésie, 60(2), 119–126. doi:10.1007/s12630-012-9851-0

Stafinski, T., Menon, D., Philippon, D. J., & McCabe, C. (2011). Health technology funding decision-making processes around the world. *PharmacoEconomics, 29*(6), 475–495. doi:10.2165/11586420-000000000-00000 PMID:21568357

Stahl, J. E. (2008). Modelling methods for pharmacoeconomics and health technology assessment. *PharmacoEconomics*, 26(2), 131–148. doi:10.2165/00019053-200826020-00004 PMID:18198933

Starfield, B., Shi, L., & Macinko, J. (2005). Contribution of primary care to health systems and health. *The Milbank Quarterly*, 83(3), 457–502. doi:10.1111/j.1468-0009.2005.00409.x PMID:16202000

Su, A., Yang, S., Hwang, W., & Zhang, J. (2010). A Web 2.0-based collaborative annotation system for enhancing knowledge sharing in collaborative learning environments. *Computers & Education*, 55(2), 752–766. doi:10.1016/j.compedu.2010.03.008

Sultan, N. (2013). Knowledge management in the age of cloud computing and Web 2.0: Experiencing the power of disruptive innovations. *International Journal of Information Management*, 33(1), 160–165. doi:10.1016/j.ijinfomgt.2012.08.006

Svensson, M., & Lagerros, Y. (2010). Motivational technologies to promote weight loss from Internet to gadgets. *Patient Education and Counseling*, 79(3), 356–360. doi:10.1016/j.pec.2010.03.004 PMID:20378298

Tattersall, A. (2011). How the web was won … by some. *Health Information and Libraries Journal*, 28(3), 226–229. doi:10.1111/j.1471-1842.2011.00945.x PMID:21831222

Trepka, M. J., Newman, F. L., Huffman, F. G., & Dixon, Z. (2010). Food safety education using an interactive multimedia kiosk in a WIC setting: Correlates of clients satisfaction and practical issues. *Journal of Nutrition Education and Behavior*, 42(3), 202–207. doi:10.1016/j.jneb.2008.10.001 PMID:20149752

Tung, F. C., Chang, S. C., & Chou, C. M. (2008). An extension of trust and TAM model with IDT in the adoption of the electronic logistics information system in HIS in the medical industry. *International Journal of Medical Informatics*, 77(5), 324–335. doi:10.1016/j.ijmedinf.2007.06.006 PMID:17644029

Tzeng, H., Ming, H., & Yin, C. Y. (2008). Nurses' solutions to prevent inpatient falls in hospital patient rooms. *Nursing Economics*, 26(3), 179–187. PMID:18616056

van Schaik, P., Bettany-Saltikov, J. A., & Warren, J. G. (2002). Clinical acceptance of a low-cost portable system for postural assessment. *Behaviour & Information Technology*, 21(1), 47–57. doi:10.1080/01449290110107236

Venkatesh, V., Zhang, X., & Sykes, T. A. (2011). "Doctors do too little technology": A longitudinal field study of an electronic healthcare system implementation. *Information Systems Research*, 22(3), 523–546. doi:10.1287/isre.1110.0383

Virga, P. H., Jin, B., Thomas, J., & Virodov, S. (2012). Electronic health information technology as a tool for improving quality of care and health outcomes for HIV/AIDS patients. *International Journal of Medical Informatics*, 81(10), e39–e45. doi:10.1016/j.ijmedinf.2012.06.006 PMID:22890224

Virkus, S. (2008). Use of Web 2.0 technologies in LIS education: Experiences at Tallinn University, Estonia. Program: Electronic Library and Information Systems, 42(3), 262–274.

Vucovich, L. A., Gordon, V. S., Mitchell, N., & Ennis, L. A. (2013). Is the time and effort worth it? One library's evaluation of using social networking tools for outreach. *Medical Reference Services Quarterly*, *32*(1), 12–25. doi:10.1080/02763869.2013.749107 PMID:23394417

Walsh, K., & Callan, A. (2011). Perceptions, preferences, and acceptance of information and communication technologies in older-adult community care settings in Ireland: A case-study and ranked-care program analysis. *Ageing International*, *36*(1), 102–122. doi:10.1007/s12126-010-9075-y

Walter, Z., & Lopez, M. S. (2008). Physician acceptance of information technologies: Role of perceived threat to professional autonomy. *Decision Support Systems*, *46*(1), 206–215. doi:10.1016/j.dss.2008.06.004

Waterson, P. (2014). Health information technology and sociotechnical systems: A progress report on recent developments within the UK National Health Service (NHS). *Applied Ergonomics*, *45*(2), 150–161. doi:10.1016/j.apergo.2013.07.004 PMID:23895916

Waterson, P. E., Glenn, Y., & Eason, K. D. (2012). Preparing the ground for the "Paperless Hospital": A case study of medical records management in a UK Outpatient Services department. *International Journal of Medical Informatics*, *81*(2), 114–129. doi:10.1016/j.ijmedinf.2011.10.011 PMID:22088601

Weiner, M., & Biondich, P. (2006). The influence of information technology on patient-physician relationships. *Journal of General Internal Medicine*, *21*(1), 35–39. doi:10.1111/j.1525-1497.2006.00307.x PMID:16405708

Wenger, E. (1998). *Communities of practice: Learning, meaning, and identity*. Cambridge, UK: Cambridge University Press. doi:10.1017/CBO9780511803932

Wilson, E. V., & Lankton, N. K. (2004). Modeling patients' acceptance of provider-delivered e-health. *Journal of the American Medical Informatics Association*, *11*(4), 241–248. doi:10.1197/jamia.M1475 PMID:15064290

Winter, S., & Kramer, N. C. (2012). Selecting science information in Web 2.0: How source cues, message sidedness, and need for cognition influence users' exposure to blog posts. *Journal of Computer-Mediated Communication*, *18*(1), 80–96. doi:10.1111/j.1083-6101.2012.01596.x

Wirtz, B. W., Schilke, O., & Ullrich, S. (2010). Strategic development of business models: Implications of the Web 2.0 for creating value on the Internet. *Long Range Planning*, *43*(2/3), 272–290. doi:10.1016/j.lrp.2010.01.005

Wu, I. L., & Chen, J. L. (2005). An extension of trust and TAM model with TPB in the initial adoption of on-line tax: An empirical study. *International Journal of Human-Computer Studies*, *62*(6), 784–808. doi:10.1016/j.ijhcs.2005.03.003

Wu, J. H., Wang, S. C., & Lin, L. M. (2007). Mobile computing acceptance factors in the healthcare industry: A structural equation model. *International Journal of Medical Informatics*, *76*(1), 66–77. doi:10.1016/j.ijmedinf.2006.06.006 PMID:16901749

Xia, Z. D. (2009). Marketing library services through Facebook groups. *Library Management*, *30*(6/7), 469–478. doi:10.1108/01435120910982159

Yang, Y., Kankanhalli, A., & Chandran, S. (2015). A stage model of information technology in healthcare. *Health Technology*, 5(1), 1–11. doi:10.1007/s12553-015-0097-z

Yi, M. Y., Jackson, J. D., Park, J. S., & Probst, J. C. (2006). Understanding information technology acceptance by individual professionals: Toward an integrative view. *Information & Management*, 43(3), 350–363. doi:10.1016/j.im.2005.08.006

Yi, Z. (2014). Australian academic librarians' perceptions of effective Web 2.0 tools used to market services and resources. *Journal of Academic Librarianship*, 40(3/4), 220–227. doi:10.1016/j.acalib.2014.02.009

Yu, P., Li, H., & Gagnon, M. P. (2012). Health IT acceptance factors in long-term care facilities: A cross sectional survey. *International Journal of Medical Informatics*, 78(4), 219–229. doi:10.1016/j.ijmedinf.2008.07.006 PMID:18768345

Yu, S., & Yang, K. F. (2006). Attitudes toward web-based distance learning among public health nurses in Taiwan: A questionnaire survey. *International Journal of Nursing Studies*, 43(6), 767–774. doi:10.1016/j.ijnurstu.2005.09.005 PMID:16253261

Yusop, F. D. (2015). A dataset of factors that influence preservice teachers' intentions to use Web 2.0 technologies in future teaching practices. *British Journal of Educational Technology*, 46(5), 1075–1080. doi:10.1111/bjet.12330

Zaman, M., Anandarajan, M., & Dai, Q. (2010). Experiencing flow with instant messaging and its facilitating role on creative behaviors. *Computers in Human Behavior*, 26(5), 1009–1018. doi:10.1016/j.chb.2010.03.001

Zhang, Y. (2013). Toward a layered model of context for health information searching: An analysis of consumer-generated questions. *Journal of the American Society for Information Science and Technology*, 64(6), 1158–1172. doi:10.1002/asi.22821

ADDITIONAL READING

Appari, A., Carian, E. K., Johnson, M. E., & Anthony, D. L. (2012). Medication administration quality and health information technology: A national study of US hospitals. *Journal of the American Medical Informatics Association*, 19(3), 360–367. doi:10.1136/amiajnl-2011-000289 PMID:22037889

Baro, E. E., Ebiagbe, E. J., & Godfrey, V. Z. (2013). Web 2.0 tools usage: A comparative study of librarians in university libraries in Nigeria and South Africa. *Library Hi Tech News*, 30(5), 10–20. doi:10.1108/LHTN-04-2013-0021

Brake, D. R. (2014). Are we all online content creators now? Web 2.0 and digital divides. *Journal of Computer-Mediated Communication*, 19(3), 591–609. doi:10.1111/jcc4.12042

Cao, Q., Jones, D. R., & Sheng, H. (2014). Contained nomadic information environments: Technology, organization, and environment influences on adoption of hospital RFID patient tracking. *Information & Management*, 51(2), 225–239. doi:10.1016/j.im.2013.11.007

Chou, W. Y. S., Prestin, A., Lyons, C., & Wen, K. Y. (2013). Web 2.0 for health promotion: Reviewing the current evidence. *American Journal of Public Health*, *103*(1), e9–e18. doi:10.2105/AJPH.2012.301071 PMID:23153164

Cochrane, T. D. (2014). Critical success factors for transforming pedagogy with mobile Web 2.0. *British Journal of Educational Technology*, *45*(1), 65–82. doi:10.1111/j.1467-8535.2012.01384.x

Eason, K. D., & Waterson, P. E. (2013). The implications of e-Health delivery strategies for integrated healthcare: Lessons from England. *International Journal of Medical Informatics*, *82*(5), 96–106. doi:10.1016/j.ijmedinf.2012.11.004 PMID:23266062

Garcia-Martin, J., & Garcia-Sanchez, J. N. (2013). Patterns of Web 2.0 tool use among young Spanish people. *Computers & Education*, *67*, 105–120. doi:10.1016/j.compedu.2013.03.003

Hsu, I. C. (2012). Extending UML to model Web 2.0-based context-aware applications. *Software: Practice & Experience*, *42*(10), 1211–1227. doi:10.1002/spe.1124

Huang, W. H. D., Hood, D. W., & Yoo, S. J. (2013). Gender divide and acceptance of collaborative Web 2.0 applications for learning in higher education. *The Internet and Higher Education*, *16*(1), 57–65. doi:10.1016/j.iheduc.2012.02.001

Karvounidis, T., Chimos, K., Bersimis, S., & Douligeris, C. (2014). Evaluating Web 2.0 technologies in higher education using students' perceptions and performance. *Journal of Computer Assisted Learning*, *30*(6), 577–596. doi:10.1111/jcal.12069

Kok, A. (2015). Integration of Web 2.0 tools in to non-formal learning practices: A case study of IBM. *Procedia: Social and Behavioral Sciences*, *176*, 357–370. doi:10.1016/j.sbspro.2015.01.483

Korda, H., & Itani, Z. (2013). Harnessing social media for health promotion and behavior change. *Health Promotion Practice*, *14*(1), 15–23. doi:10.1177/1524839911405850 PMID:21558472

Laakso, E. L., Armstrong, K., & Usher, W. (2012). Cyber-management of people with chronic disease: A potential solution to eHealth challenges. *Health Education Journal*, *71*(4), 483–490. doi:10.1177/0017896911408813

Lupton, D. (2012). M-health and health promotion: The digital cyborg and surveillance society. *Social Theory & Health*, *10*(3), 229–244. doi:10.1057/sth.2012.6

Magnuson, M. L. (2013). Web 2.0 and information literacy instruction: Aligning technology with ACRL standards. *Journal of Academic Librarianship*, *39*(3), 244–251. doi:10.1016/j.acalib.2013.01.008

Mousiolis, A., Michala, L., & Antsaklis, A. (2012). Polycystic ovary syndrome: Double click and right check. What do patients learn from the Internet about PCOS? *European Journal of Obstetrics, Gynecology, and Reproductive Biology*, *163*(1), 43–46. doi:10.1016/j.ejogrb.2012.03.028 PMID:22512829

Polito, J. (2012). Ethical considerations in Internet use of electronic protected health information. *Neurodiagnostic Journal*, *52*(1), 34–41. PMID:22558645

Prasad, B. (2013). Social media, health care, and social networking. *Gastrointestinal Endoscopy*, *77*(3), 492–495. doi:10.1016/j.gie.2012.10.026 PMID:23410701

Reich, J., Murnane, R., & Willett, J. (2012). The state of wiki usage in U.S. K-12 schools: Leveraging Web 2.0 data warehouses to access quality and equality in online learning environments. *Educational Researcher*, *41*(1), 7–15. doi:10.3102/0013189X11427083

Roma, G., Herrera, P., Zanin, M., Toral, S. L., Font, F., & Serra, X. (2012). Small world networks and creativity in audio clip sharing. *International Journal of Social Network Mining*, *1*(1), 112–127. doi:10.1504/IJSNM.2012.045108

Safadi, H., Chan, D., Dawes, M., Roper, M., & Faraj, S. (2015). Open-source health information technology: A case study of electronic medical records. *Health Policy and Technology*, *4*(1), 14–28. doi:10.1016/j.hlpt.2014.10.011

Sigala, M. (2012). Exploiting Web 2.0 for new service development: Findings and implications from the Greek tourism industry. *International Journal of Tourism Research*, *14*(6), 551–566. doi:10.1002/jtr.1914

Smith, A., Skow, A., Bodurtha, J., & Kinra, S. (2013). Health information technology in screening and treatment of childhood obesity: A systematic review. *Pediatrics*, *131*(3), e894–e902. doi:10.1542/peds.2012-2011 PMID:23382447

Spetz, J., Burgess, J. F., & Phibbs, C. S. (2014). The effect of health information technology implementation in Veterans Health Administration hospitals on patient outcomes. *Health Care*, *2*, 40–47. PMID:26250088

Victoroff, M. S., Drury, B. M., Campagna, E. J., & Morrato, E. H. (2012). Impact of electronic health records on malpractice claims in a sample of physician offices in Colorado: A retrospective cohort study. *Journal of General Internal Medicine*, *28*(5), 637–644. doi:10.1007/s11606-012-2283-2 PMID:23192449

Villalba, E., Casas, I., Abadie, F., & Lluch, M. (2013). Integrated personal health and care services deployment: Experiences in eight European countries. *International Journal of Medical Informatics*, *82*(7), 626–635. doi:10.1016/j.ijmedinf.2013.03.002 PMID:23587432

KEY TERMS AND DEFINITIONS

Health Care: The activity or business of providing medical services.

Health Care System: The combination of facilities, organizations, and trained personnel engaged in providing health care within a geographical area.

Information System: A combination of hardware, software, infrastructure, and trained personnel organized to facilitate planning, control, coordination, and decision making in an organization.

Information Technology: A set of tools, processes, and associated equipment employed to collect, process, and present information.

Internet: The large system of connected computers around the world.

Social Networking Sites: The websites that are is designed to help people communicate and share information with a group.

Technology: The purposeful application of information in the design, production, and utilization of products and services.

Technology Acceptance Model: The most widely used model to predict and explain the user acceptance of information technology.

Web 2.0: A collective term for certain applications of the Internet and the World Wide Web, including blogs, wikis, and social media websites, which focus on interactive sharing and participatory collaboration rather than simple content delivery.

Chapter 3
Digital Diorama:
An Interactive Multimedia Resource for Learning the Life Sciences

Annamaria Poli
University of Milano-Bicocca, Italy

Alessandra Mazzola
Politecnico di Milano, Italy

Annastella Gambini
University of Milano-Bicocca, Italy

Sabrina Muschiato
Politecnico di Milano, Italy

Antonella Pezzotti
University of Milano-Bicocca, Italy

Carlo Emilio Standoli
Politecnico di Milano, Italy

Alfredo Broglia
University of Milano-Bicocca, Italy

Daniela Zambarbieri
Politecnico di Milano, Italy

Fiammetta Costa
Politecnico di Milano, Italy

ABSTRACT

Digital technologies that increase communication among students/users are viewed as interactive resources for enhancing learning, especially in the field of science teaching. The new digital mission is to produce innovative learning environments and educational tools to enhance the traditional teaching methods still widely used today. The Digital Diorama project reproduces a set of Natural History Museum dioramas for IWBs and other electronic devices. Using the Digital Diorama enhances cooperative learning. This comes from the students/users' explorations of the Digital Diorama and from strategies that we recommend to teachers.

INTRODUCTION

The *Digital Diorama* research project proposes using digital technologies in schools as a resource for boosting cooperative and collaborative learning, mainly in relation to scientific knowledge and the use of ICT (Information Communication Technology). Such tools offer great potential for schools at all levels of education and open up new prospects for teaching/learning in many fields. In addition, advances in

DOI: 10.4018/978-1-5225-2616-2.ch003

the computer sciences are contributing to the development of increasingly sophisticated educational technologies.

If they are appropriately used, and applied following socio-constructivist teaching methods, the new devices can help meet the widely recognized challenges of the contemporary knowledge society, such as providing for lifelong learning, or fostering young people's interest and motivation in order to achieve the learning outcomes required for everyday life[1]. Specifically, virtual learning environments can become places in which to experience active enquiry, teaching practices, and interaction with learning contents, as well as places for enhanced interpersonal relationships, discussion and sharing (Ghislandi, 2012).

In these learning environments, each learner is an active and involved member of a community, who helps to complete tasks or joint projects, and contributes his/her own experience, knowledge and skills to build collective knowledge (Herrington, Reeves, & Oliver, 2014).

STATE OF THE ART

Digital Technologies

The role of digital technologies and the importance of appropriate education and training in using digital media for children, teenagers and adults has long been acknowledged. The first institution to recognize this was Unesco: in 1982, thanks to the Grunwald Declaration on Media Education, attention was drawn for the first time to the need for educational programmes in digital technology at all levels of schooling[2]. In keeping with this early position, in 2002 Unesco launched the *Youth Media Education Seminar* initiative in Seville, which emphasized the need to promote digital technology literacy both critically and creatively, in both formal and informal educational contexts. In particular, the objectives identified by Unesco include providing incentives for the development of individual and collective digital citizenship abilities.

Like Unesco, starting with the meeting in Lisbon in 2000, the European Commission has also launched initiatives promoting and supporting digital literacy, particularly in relation to the protection and promotion of human rights. These include *Safer Internet* and the multi-annual e-Learning programme from 2004-2006 for combatting the *Digital divide*, which, as well as defining the concept of *digital literacy*, sought to identify and disseminate good practices, such as fostering digital literacy in schools through e-learning[3].

The European directives from 2000 onwards have called for ongoing debate on the function of digital technologies in the development of active and aware digital citizenship, and especial attention has been drawn to the integration of digital technologies and new media into the school curriculum, as well as to the accessibility required to facilitate inclusion.

A few years later, in 2007, Unesco again posed the question of including digital education in the school curriculum and issued its first recommendations for digital education in the document known as the "Paris Agenda"[4].

Thanks to the European directives, in Italy, from 2007 onwards, the Ministry of Education, University and Research (MIUR) circulated a set of National Curricular Guidelines for Preschool, Primary and Lower Secondary Education ("Indicazioni nazionali per il curricolo della scuola dell'infanzia e del primo ciclo di istruzione"). In 2012, a revised edition of these guidelines was produced and published in the Ministerial Regulation of 16 November 2012[5]. The National Curricular Guidelines have led to official recognition of the role of digital technologies in schools in general and for educational purposes in particular.

Today, Italian schools enable students to acquire cognitive skills for learning and selecting information, which in turn foster independent thinking and a sense of self-efficacy; in addition, students are expected to develop satisfactory digital skills and the capacity to make mindful use of the new media to search for and analyse data and information. Competence in the use of digital tools is envisaged from primary school onwards, and the approach advocated by the National Guidelines is not based on passive use, but rather on exploration, experimentation, imagination and creativity.

Given that it has been long recognised that digital technologies prompt and promote collaborative learning (Computer Supported Collaborative Learning - CSCL), the Italian guidelines expressly refer to the value of the "social dimension of learning", a dimension that can be fostered thanks to the use of the "...new technologies that allow pupils to work together to build new knowledge".

Students involved in educational projects using new technologies, learn not only acquire more advanced knowledge of digital tools and new technical skills, but also learn a more critical approach to processing and comparing information from digital and traditional sources.

Vice versa, students can acquire competence in the new digital technologies through courses in other subjects that draw on digital educational tools as rich resources characterised by multimediality, hypertextuality, interaction and virtuality. In practice, such courses take on an interdisciplinary character, fostering a more active teaching methodology that in turn makes for more dynamic learning processes.

Therefore, the new mission of digital technology is to produce new learning environments and strategic tools for enhancing the traditional teaching methods still widely used today.

Thus, the use of digital instruments – to explore, experiment and develop creativity and imagination – is recommended from the preschool and early primary school stages onwards, given that digital technologies, by their nature, elicit a collaborative approach to learning: the National Curricular Guidelines clearly state that the social dimension of learning would be encouraged by the use of new technologies. As noted above, the use of digital technology not only enhances students' technical competency, but also their competence in reflecting on and elaborating information. Finally, digital educational tools can cover multiple fields, supporting the implementation of an interdisciplinary methodological approach. All of which makes for a more dynamic and interdisciplinary mode of teaching and learning in the classroom.

IWB: The Interactive Education Technology Tool

The aim of our project is to enhance the teaching and learning of biology topics by creating innovative learning environments accessible from PCs, tablets and interactive whiteboards (IWB).

In Italy, interactive whiteboards are widely available in primary and secondary schools, although the implications of their use for teaching methods have not yet been widely investigated, with many questions remaining unanswered. This technology has been introduced into schools without adequate reflection on the effects or outcomes of its use, at either the individual or group levels. Antonio Calvani has proposed that IWBs are used at schools in two main ways: stylistic and/or linguistic. The former approach focuses on form at the expense of content, making extensive use of images, video and sound. The latter draws on "integrated linguistic codes", or the specific terminology that describes instruments and digital products and the effects they can generate (Calvani, 2007). The tactile properties of IWBs

Figure 1. Map of IWB kind of uses at school

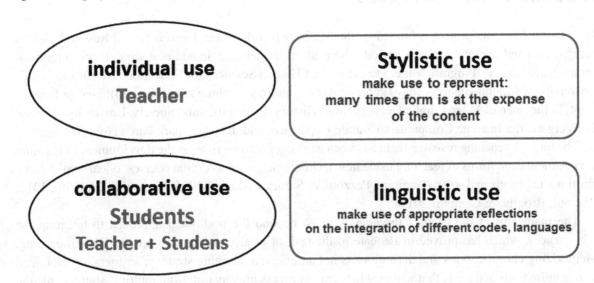

have not yet been thoroughly investigated. Even more critically, the quality of educational software for IWBs has not been systematically evaluated, while educational applications with innovative IWB content have yet to be developed.

Nevertheless, the first studies on training teachers to use the IWB as part of their classroom teaching activities have reported positive results; an example from the US is research conducted by Robert Marzano and Mark Haystead between 2009 and 2010.[6]

The use of IWBs in schools is associated with enhanced performance, motivation to learn, particularly in English Language, mathematics, the science subjects and quantitative disciplines.[7]

The full educational potential of the IWB is expressed when it is used as a "cognitive space" in which students/users construct their own learning through research, cooperation and problem solving (Esposito, 2012).

Interactive visualization is constantly evolving, and this form of communication enables the creation and interaction of new knowledge representations via the exploration of multiple topics. The multidisciplinary nature of interactive visualization represents the backbone of knowledge design. The key question is how to ensure the quality of interactions. What kind of interaction should be targeted and how? This is because not all visualizations are equally effective; the challenge is to set new quality standards for assessing learning objects/environments and new digital tools/resources for educational contests.

The use of IWBs facilitates the organization of resources, storing and analysis of writing – which may be edited and integrated with other multimedia materials –, visualization of knowledge, and monitoring of individual students' learning processes. It also contributes to the construction and sharing of knowledge and skills, promotes participation, and drives collaborative learning (Gagliardi, Gabbari, & Gaetano, 2010).

The *Digital Diorama* project aims to increase the use of IWBs with a view to obtaining the optimum educational benefits just outlined.

THE *DIGITAL DIORAMA* PROJECT

The *Digital Diorama* project is funded by the Ministry of Education, University and Research[8] and is being conducted over a three-year period. The project partners are, in addition with others, three University Departments: Program leader Department of Human Sciences for Education "Riccardo Massa", University of Milano-Bicocca, Italy (in particular the biology teaching research team); Design Department, Politecnico di Milano, Italy; Department of History, Humanities and Society, University of Rome Tor Vergata, the Institute Comprensivo Statale Copernico, and the urban park Parco Nord Milano.

The biology teaching research team has been working for some time on the development of learning environments and forms of teaching using new technologies, such as online courses, e-learning objects, multimedia objects and so on (Gambini, Pezzotti, & Samek Lodovici, 2005; Pezzotti & Gambini, 2012; Pezzotti, Broglia, & Gambini 2014).

The main aim of the group's research is to go beyond the traditional approach to teaching the life sciences, which has proved inadequate to the task of producing meaningful and lasting learning. Memorizing classifications and definitions is not an effective learning strategy: learners' crucial need is to acquire tools and skills that will enable them to process information from multiple sources (media, newspapers, Internet) and integrate it with existing knowledge. Nowadays, in fact, school is no longer the only place of information and learning. Many disciplines may be explored in different ways, using a host of constantly changing resources. Therefore, school should be a place that creates networks among "the complexity of new ways of learning by providing daily guidance that is attentive to methods, the new media and multi-dimensional research"[9].

The *Digital Diorama* project has created new opportunities for the observation and analysis of teaching and learning with digital technologies whose potential as learning resources has yet to be explored.

Figure 2. Presentation of the Digital Diorama on IWB

Science learning can be stimulated, facilitated and enriched by exploiting resources found in museums. Such resources may be turned into real learning environments. They include dioramas: ecologically and paleontologically based models of natural environments, which act as "windows to look in on".

The *Digital Diorama* project reproduces dioramas from natural history museums, enhancing the value of this key historical and cultural heritage asset. Specifically, the project involves digitizing real-life dioramas and turning them into multimedia learning objects for use in schools, museums and other venues.

Aims of the Project

A first aim of the project is to enhance the historical value of the dioramas on display in natural history museums, as significant cultural and scientific resources.

Another key aim is to enhance the learning of fundamental aspects of the biology underpinning life on our planet. To this end, we selected media education based on digital technologies as our cognitive tool of choice for presenting biology and ecology contents in an original fashion and updating the teaching practices currently implemented in schools.

The *Digital Diorama* is also an educational "device" that can encourage cooperative learning processes and the sharing of knowledge and skills[10]. The project aims to train students and teachers in how to productively cooperate with others, respect diverse opinions, and channel their energies into working to achieve shared goals (social and cultural).

Finally, the project promotes integration among different disciplines, approaches and methodologies and supports the life-long learning approach to education for sustainability.

Biology is a young science and advances in biological knowledge are ever more urgently needed, given the most critical issues of our times (food resources, new epidemics, overpopulation, pollution, etc.). It is also critical that sustainability practices be implemented in educational contexts. To be effective, education on sustainability cannot be based on an old methodology, but needs to revolutionise the methods and rules that have been adopted by society up to now, and which have led us to the current situation, a methodology that has not looked to the future but to the past as its point of reference for establishing "scientific truth" (Sterling, 2001).

Methodological Issues

Digital Diorama are not designed as a standard format for the transmission of contents, but rather as an educational "device" that promotes discussion on biological topics, encourages "in-depth investigation", draws out questions and sparks curiosity.

The group discussion method is strongly recommended in the educational literature (Czerwinsky Domenis, 2000; Pontecorvo 2004). Scientific discussion is the basis upon which science progresses and the National Curricular Guidelines also refer to the need to teach it[11].

In introducing the *Digital Diorama*, the teacher is invited to discover it together with his/her students – as they encounter and choose to enter the hidden hotspots on the IWB to explore the contents. This methodology was specially designed to foster interconnections and help the students link the various contents explored and discussed.

The exploration should not be viewed as a quantitative activity: it is not necessary to "visit" all the hotspots, but only those that motivate students and engage their curiosity.

The design of these multimedia objects offers many associations with everyday life, an essential requirement for ensuring that school activities act as reservoirs of knowledge for all areas of life (Arcà, 2009). In addition, connections with the great unifying themes of biology are carefully drawn, while avoiding traditional, linear, or predefined learning paths (Gambini, Pezzotti, & Broglia, 2008).

Finally, attention was paid to exploiting the emotional aspects in the process of acquiring knowledge. Many studies have been carried out on understanding how emotions and affections come into the learning process (in school and in everyday life) and how, by fostering these aspects, it is possible to enhance cognitive abilities (Chalufour & Worth, 2004). The methodology recommended for use with the *Digital Diorama* promotes a close connection between the information and emotional aspects, which are generally marginal in the teaching of science.

Description of Levels

The Museum dioramas, once digitalized, become interactive interfaces consisting of a central image (the photograph of the entire Museum diorama), on which there is a menu and "hotspots" that may be activated by touch or a mouse. The hotspots enable personalized exploration of multimedia objects such as diagrams, images, videos, audio and textual traces. *Digital Diorama* are interactive systems that focus on the students/users and their "cognitive interaction" with elements of the represented environment.

The *Digital Diorama* home page consists of a high-resolution wide-angle photo of a dioramas in the museum. By scrolling over the photo, the student/user can zoom in to enlarge it.

From the home page, a pop-up menu, on left, allows the students/users to choose different levels of exploration.

At the first level Imaginary journey, a narrator invites the students/users to enter the *Digital Diorama* by drawing on their imagination and creativity to make an imaginary journey. Access to the *Digital Diorama* begins with the personal involvement of the students /users: they have to imagine sounds and smell sensations, etc. The hotspots allow them to continue their Imaginary journey, by lingering on particular details of the scene.

Figure 3. The map of Digital Diorama levels

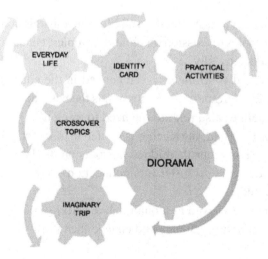

Figure 4. The interface of the Mediterranean Sea Digital Diorama with all the hotspots available at the first level

Figure 5. The levels menu on the interface of the Mediterranean Sea Digital Diorama

At the second level Crossover topics, each hotspot leads to a biology theme that is common to different living things (e.g., movement, hunting techniques, reproduction strategies, etc.). Each theme is illustrated by five multimedia contents (diagrams, images and videos) accompanied by brief captions.

These materials are specially designed to stimulate thinking and group discussion, which in turn to more advanced understanding of the theme. Furthermore, each multimedia content is linked to aspects of everyday life: for example, a fish that filters water to feed is compared to everyday objects, such as a tea bag, a colander, etc.

By clicking on a round picture, students/users can access a guide containing text and images, which provide further insight into the topic and a brief explanation of the multimedia contents.

At the third level Identity Card, each hotspot offers students access to an identity card of the item represented, which contains brief questions and answers (FAQs) and is easily consultable during exploration of the *Digital Diorama*.

The last level of exploration, Education Experiences, proposes scientific practical activities that may be related to some of the issues addressed.

PILOT TESTING PHASE WITH THE *DIGITAL DIORAMA* PROTOTYPE

Methodology: Quantitative and Qualitative Analysis

The evaluation of the *Digital Diorama* prototype (*Mediterranean Sea*) took into account the quality of the interface and the user-interface interaction, as well as the *Digital Diorama*'s effectiveness in enhancing the learning of selected key aspects of biology. The former type of assessment was quantitative, while the second involved the application of qualitative research methods such as focus groups, observation, analysis of students' learning products (Mantovani, 2000; Baldacci, 2001).

Both evaluation approaches were used during pilot testing of the Digital Diorama prototype with five primary school classes (three second grades and two fifth grades) and with eight teachers: four teachers of Science, three of Italian (L$_1$) and one of Mathematic.

Evaluations of interaction quality and usability of the *Digital Diorama* interfaces were heuristic and made use of multiple methodologies, with the involvement of all project stakeholders (researchers and students/users) to ensure a participatory approach (Nielsen, 1993). This type of evaluation is based on

Figure 6. The Digital Diorama interface at the second level of exploration suggesting links with the everyday life

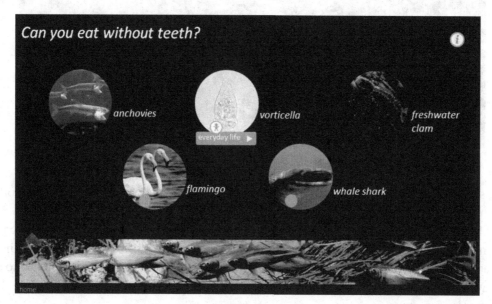

video observations of the actions performed by students/users while interacting with the *Digital Diorama*. It is therefore also a form of cooperative assessment, which is based on the methodology designed and developed by Monk and colleagues at the University of York (UK). This "cooperative" technique (Monk, Wright, Haber, & Davenport, 1993) allows the cooperative research group to gather experimental evidence about the objective and quantitative exploration of the graphic interface of the *Digital Diorama* and the exploratory behaviour of those involved. To carry out this evaluation, the analysis of the eye movements of subjects interacting with the graphic interface through an eye tracking recording device was used. This device detects eye movements using video oculography that provides information on the direction of gaze with respect to the surrounding environment. Eyes move towards areas of interest; gaze and attention are closely linked: students/users can shift their focus without moving their eyes, but not vice versa.

Interface Usability Evaluation

In developing the interactive *Digital Diorama* system, to order obtain feedback on its performance and usability, it was critical to monitor the behaviour of primary school children while they were actually using it. To this end, students/users were observed while interacting with a digital prototype in both the laboratory and real life contexts (Hanna, Risden, Czerwinski, & Alexander, 1999).

The usability evaluation began with preliminary observation of a student freely interacting with the first *Digital Diorama* prototype. More specifically, we observed the visual behaviour of a student/user wearing eye tracking glasses in front of physical dioramas at the Natural History Museum, as well as the behaviour of "random" students/users in front of the *Digital Diorama* during a public event aimed at disseminating scientific culture and research. The knowledge gleaned from this preliminary phase was used to develop an experimental protocol for a usability test and behaviour analysis proper, to be conducted both in a laboratory setting and in the real-life context (school). The behaviour analysed in the laboratory was elicited by replicating insofar as possible classroom / real environment conditions.

The method adopted was innovative as it combined observations of physical and visual behaviour through eye tracking. Clear vision of an object is only guaranteed when its image falls within the central part of the retina, which is called fovea. Therefore, in order to explore a visual scene, the eyes have to move in such a way as to bring the image of an object of interest onto the fovea. During visual exploration, the eyes make saccades and fixations. Because visual information is only acquired by the central nervous system during fixations, whereas saccades are used to shift the gaze from one point to another, it is reasonable to infer that eye tracking methodology represents a powerful tool for the study of exploration strategies and the underlying cognitive processes (Kowler, 1990; Schmid, & Zambarbieri, 1991; Monty & Senders, 1976). Thus, when students/users explore a visual scene, eye movements supply information about the focus of their attention.

Thus, it is clear that the use of eye tracking represents an innovative methodology that can provide experimental evidence for the objective and quantitative analysis of students' visual exploratory behaviour in everyday situations (Hayhoe, & Ballard, 2005; Zambarbieri, 2003; Zambarbieri & Carniglia, 2012).

Contemporary videotaping technologies facilitate the adoption of new behaviour analysis models that examine different components of interaction, to be evaluated by interdisciplinary groups comprising engineers, designers, social scientists, usability and experts. Analysis of the students' spatial behaviour, as well as their psychoperceptual reactions and expressions of emotion was performed using a software for video annotation that allowed us to create a structured database of the different components of interaction. The results of the tests were used to implement the design of the *Digital Diorama* (Nesset & Large, 2004; Andreoni, *et al.*, 2010).

Four primary school students (two girls and two boys) took part in a laboratory test. According to the results by Nielsen and Landauer (1993), this number of test users is enough to detect around 70% of the existing usability problems and to achieve a 60% ratio of benefit to cost, which was the maximum attained by these authors in their study.

The experiments were divided into two steps:

- Each student, wearing eye tracking glasses, stood in front of the IWB. The experimenter guided exploration of the diorama by asking the child to execute specific tasks. The test lasted about 10 minutes;
- The four students were together in front of the IWB and the experimenter asked them general questions about the contents of diorama. The test lasted about 25 minutes.

    Throughout the entire experiment, the students were video-recorded by means of a camera placed in the upper corner of the experimental room to their backs.

    Next, a similar test was conducted in the classroom with nine students (five females and males) aged 8 and 9 years.

- Each child in turn, wearing eye-tracking glasses, stood in front of the IWB. The experimenter guided the diorama exploration by asking the student to execute specific tasks. The test lasted about two minutes per participant.

Again, the students were video recorded by a camera positioned in a corner of the classroom.

Eye-Movement Analysis and Recording

Eye movements were recorded following the video-oculographic technique (VOG). VOG uses video camera to compute gaze direction. In order to make this data processing fast enough to be performed in real time, the image of the eye is usually illuminated with infrared light to create corneal reflexes. The infrared light is not visible to the student/user so it will not cause a distraction, however it is visible to the camera.

Eye Tracking Glasses (SMI – SensoMotoric Instruments GmbH, Germany) are used in this study (Figure 7).

Figure 7. Front and back view of the SMI eye tracking glasses, showing the position of the cameras

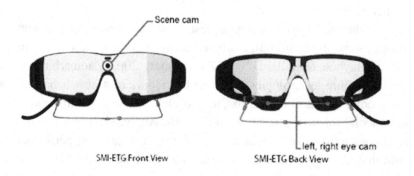

The light frame of the glasses incorporates six infrared light-emitting diodes illuminating the eye to create the corneal reflexes. A digital camera is embedded to collect the images. A further camera, placed at the front of the glasses is used to record the scene in front of the student/user, allowing the correlation between gaze position and the environment to be computed.

Eye movement analysis was performed offline using the BeGaze software. The first stage in the analysis consists of the identification of saccades and fixations among the recorded eye movements. To identify fixations, BeGaze makes use of a dispersion based algorithm with a maximum dispersion threshold set at 100 pixels, and a minimum fixation duration of 80 msec.

Gaze displacement between two successive fixation positions are identified as saccades. Once saccades and fixations are recognized from the temporal sequence of eye position data, the correlation between gaze position and the scene taken from the camera is established. From the position and duration of all fixations, the scanpath is reconstructed: fixations are represented by circles whose diameter is proportional to fixation duration, whereas straight lines represent saccades. Following this method, we were able to identify areas of interest (AOI) for each screenshot of the diorama and BeGaze calculated several eye movement parameters for each AOI, such as: number of fixations, total duration of gaze, mean fixation duration, order of access.

Focus Group, Training, Questionnaire, Classwork and Dissemination

As well as evaluating the quality of the interface, we conducted a qualitative analysis aimed at investigating the educational effectiveness of the *Digital Diorama* in improving the learning of selected biology topics. This assessment included the monitoring and observation of classroom work, focus groups with teachers, the collection and analysis of outputs (maps, drawings, reflections, short tests, experiments, research on Internet, etc.) produced by students during and after the use of the *Digital Diorama*.

This experimental phase was accompanied by a teacher-training program that included an initial briefing phase on the *Digital Diorama* methodology.

The overall training program began with a focus group discussion designed to gather data about the participating teachers' current use of technology in the classroom and current teaching methods. During the discussion, the teachers were shown the *Digital Diorama* prototype then under construction.

Before working on the *Digital Diorama* with their classes, the teachers were invited to personally explore the different levels of the *Digital Diorama* and to simulate possible discussions with children, noting any difficulties encountered.

Four further training sessions were held, and each was recorded and analysed by an observer. During the first of these sessions, the teacher's role was discussed, and defined in terms of equipping learners with effective thinking tools for selecting information and grasping key aspects of organisms and their environments. The *Digital Diorama* was introduced and explored by the group.

During the second session, the group used the *Digital Diorama* as students with a researcher playing the teacher's role.

The third session was also a simulation of *Digital Diorama'* context of use, but in this case, the teachers were completely autonomous and played both their own role and the students'.

Finally, the teachers were invited to discuss the results of the trials, the structure of the *Digital Diorama*, its possible contexts, and the role of biology teachers in stimulating learners to form connections between the Crossover topics.

At the end of the sessions, a questionnaire was distributed to the group, to elicit their impressions and perceptions of the training enjoyed.

The questionnaire was divided into seven sections and 23 questions: in the first section (from Questions 1 to 5), teachers were asked about the technical aspects of the diorama, such as whether or not they found it easy to use; whether they had perceived any increase in their technological skills; what kind of difficulties they had encountered and why; the extent to which technological complexities had influenced the trials; their satisfaction with the usability of the interface.

Question 6 investigated the group's satisfaction with the first level of the *Digital Diorama* (Imaginary journey), the voice-over and anticipated efficacy for the children.

From Questions 7 to 12, teachers were asked to express their opinion about the Crossover topics, in terms of the interface and contents (video, images, taglines, guides etc.) at this level and suggestions for improving them.

Similar questions were also asked about other levels (Everyday life: Questions 13 – 14; Identity card: Question 15; Educational experiences: question 16).

After this training phase, teachers invited their students to explore the *Digital Diorama*, both at the Human Behavior Laboratory and in their own classrooms. Subsequently, we invited the teachers to another focus group discussion to collect their feedback about the overall experience of using the *Digital Diorama*, the difficulties they had encountered, suggestions for improving the device, etc.

ANALYSIS OF RESULTS

Individual Laboratory User Test

Among the 29 tasks administered to the children, three tasks were selected for the detailed presentation of results, on the grounds that they are the most representative of user interaction with the IWB. The results are reported both in terms of observed behaviours and gaze analysis. The next paragraph describes the behavioural observation of Step 2 of the experiment.

In Task 1, the students were asked to reach a given level (Imaginary journey or Crossover topics) of the *Digital Diorama* from the home page. To accomplish the task they needed to localize the menu button placed at the bottom left, and press it to visualize the menu items (Figure 8). Three children attained this the goal in few seconds and without the researcher's support, while a fourth required instructions to locate the menu.

The scan path, in Figure 8, is an example of a student/user's eye behaviour during the Imaginary journey. It may be observed that the student/user's gaze first pointed towards the requested item, and then moved through all items before going back to the most pertinent one. Only at that time did the student/user select the prescribed option.

Regarding Task 2, children were asked to exit from the hotspot and return to the main page. Different options were available to achieve the task:

1. Pressing the zoom buttons, in the lower right-hand corner of the page;
2. Pressing the level title at the bottom of the page;
3. Pressing "HOME" and, from the home page, re-selecting the assigned level.

Figure 8. Scanpath of a child while Carrying out Task 1. Circles represent fixations, straight lines saccades

During the testing, this task was submitted three times. The expected behaviour was that the students would chose the first option. They did, but when the task was administered first, their reaction times were relatively slow.

In fact, it emerged from the scan path analysis that the students first explored the lower area of the screen where all control keys are placed and only found the zoom buttons later (Figure 9). However, as the task was repeated, the students quickly learnt to access the zoom buttons.

Figure 9. Scan path of a child during the execution of Task 2

With regard to Task 3, the children were asked to exit the current level and return to the previous one. There were different possible options for achieving this outcome:

1. Pressing the left arrow;
2. Pressing the level title at the bottom of the page;
3. Pressing home" and, from the home page, re-selecting the level.

During the experiment, this task was administered twice. Three of the children correctly identified the left arrow in the lower right corner on the first trial, as shown by the scan path in Figure 10. The fourth child behaved differently on both tasks, by choosing Options 3 and 2, respectively.

Behavioural Group Test

The main objective of the second experimental stage was to define how children reacted to the Diorama, to evaluate whether the *Digital Diorama* can help them to improve their cooperative learning and their capacity to connect topics and develop contents as a group. A secondary aim was to observe how children behave when they use the IWB interface during tests, and in particular, to note any signs of cognitive difficulty, enjoyment, boredom and curiosity during interaction.

The tests consisted of simulating interaction with the diorama, on the IWB, in the context of school. They were divided into two parts: the first, which took 20 minutes, was composed of a semi-structured trial aimed at assessing whether collaboration took place between the children while they were exploring *Digital Diorama*. The second part took the form of a 5-minute session in which the children were completely free to interact with *Digital Diorama* as they wished.

At the beginning of the test, the children were assembled and seated around the table in front of the IWB. The researcher introduced the exploration phase of the *Digital Diorama*, and explained to each of

Figure 10. Scan path of a child during the execution of task 3

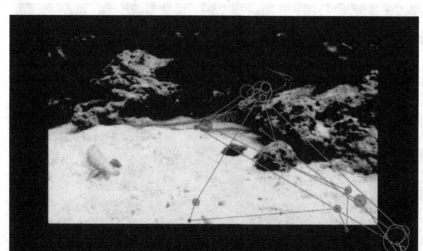

them how to interact with it. The researcher called only one child to IWB and asked him to start the test. In the meantime, the rest of the group remained seated for one minute and then all got up together to help choose the topic to be explored. Children remained standing throughout the trial. During the exploration of various *Digital Diorama* contents, the researcher posed open-ended questions to the children, who were free to answer and express themselves as they wished, particularly in the last 5 minutes.

Qualitative analysis was based on the direct observations of a behavioural expert who specifically coded: emotional involvement, attention maintenance and students' ability to generate discussion about the Crossover topics. Quantitative analysis was performed by examining the video-recordings using a software for video annotation called Advene (Annotate Digital Video, Exchange on the Net) in order to identify students' behaviours and verbalizations. The software allows a database of structured notations to be created and analyzed through software queries.

The identified behaviours were organized around two research themes (Figure 11):

1. Physical participation of the individual child and the group: spatial behavior (task: move);
2. Verbal participation of the individual child and the group: oral interaction (task: talk).

Afterwards, the analysis grid was amplified to extract information and collect data concerning: elements that aroused the children's curiosity, elements that attracted the children's attention, group interaction, group discussion.

In general, it was observed that all children were actively involved in the test: some children first copied the sound or behaviour of the animal, others joined immediately in the discussion. All children provided appropriate answers to the questions and often initiated spontaneous discussions on different topics. During the test, the general physical posture adopted by the children was standing in front of the IWB.

Children maintained a strong level of interest for the duration of the test. Boys were more active in movement than girls, and more inclined to motivate others to participate in the interaction with the IWB. The boys interacted more with the IWB, both to perform commands and explore topics, while the girls did not interact much as with the *Digital Diorama*.

Figure 11. Schemas of spatial behaviour

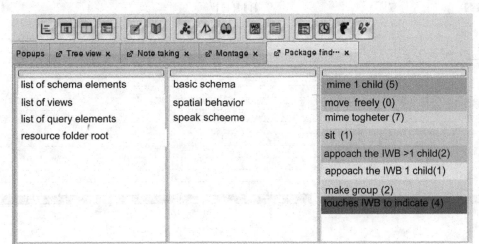

67

During the last five minutes of the test, a key behavioural change was observed. When the researcher moved out of the children's sight and left them alone, all the children continuously interacted with the *Digital Diorama*'s interface by giving commands, selecting and pursuing topics together, based on free choice. In this context, all the children intensively explored and interacted with the Identity card level of the *Digital Diorama*.

The Basic Schema, devised by an expert in psycho pedagogy based on the qualitative analysis of the data, identified the objectives and tasks against which to match observations of the children's verbal and non-verbal behaviours (*Figure 12*).

Often one or more children touched the IWB to point out something on the *Digital Diorama* that excited them and aroused their interest. Otherwise, for the rest of the trial, the children remained standing in a row without touching the IWB.

In relation to oral interaction ("talk"), the first annotation concerned speaking, spontaneous observation, and discussion among peers. As the children interacted with the *Digital Diorama*, they consistently behaved as though they were having fun, they often spoke aloud, they answered questions and read the texts out loud together.

For example, miming ("mimare") was a recurrent behaviour that began with the movement of one child, which then prompted all other children to join in, generating curiosity and enjoyment. Another interesting spatial behaviour observed was that named group building ("fare gruppo"). In two annotations of the test, it was obvious that children got together to select or pursue a particular topic (*Figure 13*).

The students' verbal and nonverbal behaviours showed that they link different elements of *Digital Diorama* with one another, jumping from one organism to another, relating them to one another, reasoning and discussing individually and in a group.

Figure 12. Basic Schema with mapping of verbal and non-verbal behaviour

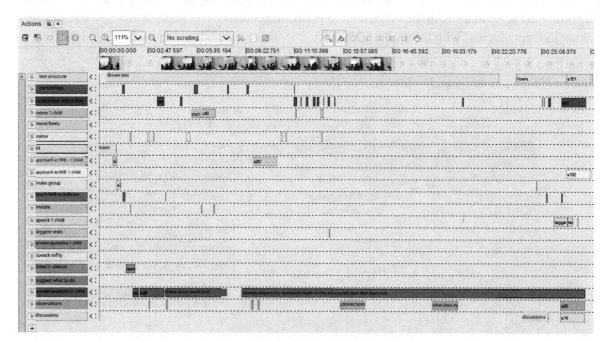

Figure 13. Example of one on 7 annotation from make group and the corresponding real situation

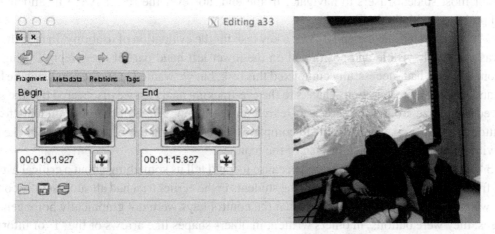

The students' questions and remarks showed that they had reflected on the proposed themes: the group seemed curious, stimulated by the questions and forthcoming with their hypotheses concerning possible connections between elements of the Diorama and their life experience. The fact that they explored the *Digital Diorama* by analysing similarities and differences between the organisms shows that they were interested in the relationships at work in the diorama and that they were able to grasp the complexity of the living systems presented to them.

User Test in Real-Life Setting

Based on analysis of the data collected during the laboratory trials, we organized further tests with other students, in their classroom, obtaining further reliable data that was key for optimum development of the *Digital Diorama*. Only five tasks from the previous battery were administered, selected because of their pertinence to the criterion of usability. We also reduced the duration of the test, from 10 to 2 minutes.

Nine students aged between 8 and 9 years were involved in the experiment: five girls and 4 boys. The experimental set-up was the same as in the laboratory setting: students were examined while performing the test, and wearing eye tracking glasses, and were video recorded by a camera positioned in a corner of the classroom.

The selected tasks were:

- **Task 1:** Scroll through the *Digital Diorama*;
- **Task 2:** Find the Menu and expand it;
- **Task 3:** Identify the levels and among them get to Crossover topics;
- **Task 4:** Exit the screen (3 possible options);
- **Task 5:** Go back to the big image (Crossover topics level) (2 possible options).

Task 1 "scroll through the *Digital Diorama*" was chosen because of the shape of the represented environment; in fact, the Mediterranean Sea image taken by photographing the physical diorama at the Museo di Storia Naturale di Livorno was very long. For this reason, we wished to check if it would be intuitive for most students/users to navigate. In the end, however the results were invalidated due to technical problems with the IWB device.

Task 2 "find the menu and expand it" was a key task for the evaluation of usability. In fact, the chosen button was not highly visible and positioned on the lower left hand part of the screen. During the lab test, all four students had successfully completed this task, but we wanted to further evaluate the button's position and graphic representation. Thanks to the eye-tracking analysis, we discovered that the students first moved their gaze around the screen to search for the menu. Three of the nine students found the menu button. The other six were not able to complete the task; among these, two students clicked on the writing with the name of the level, instead of the icon.

Task 3 "reach a level" was administered because it could tell us something about a critical aspect that emerged from the laboratory test. Although the students in the earlier trial had all successfully completed the task, we were concerned about the fact that the control keys were not graphically homogeneous: in some cases, they were buttons, in others written, in others shapes like arrows or the "i" of information. All students, having found the menu, were able to reach the Crossover topics level, by clicking on the name of the level.

Tasks 4 and 5: "exit the screen" and "go back" were chosen because we had already tested them in the laboratory and found that they were not easy for students/users to understand. Given that the task could be completed in different ways, we wished to obtain the feedback of the students/users about this aspect.

Students were requested to exit the current level and return to the previous one. The different possible options for achieving this were:

1.   Pressing the left arrow;
2.   Pressing the level title at the bottom of the page;
3.   Pressing "HOME" and, from the home page, re-selecting the level.

Figure 14. Scanpath of the children during the execution of Task 2

Among these three options, five students executed the task correctly by clicking the back button, two students selected the name of the level, one student/user pressed Home followed by the name of the level, while one participant was not able to identify any of the three possible strategies.

The go back task was not completed by all students, with four of the nine interrupting the process when they encountered an obstacle. Of these, one hesitated, one tried to click on HOME, and then subsequently on the Crossover topics level name, one tried to click on an inactive part of the screen and only three students were successful, by clicking on the level name.

Comparing the results of the tests in the laboratory and the classroom, we found that some of them were very similar. For example, free exploration of the hotspots showed that almost all the students/ users mainly moved their gaze along the central part of the screen. There were no saccades and fixations in the upper part of the image. This result was confirmed by what the students said during the free exploration. In fact, when they were asked about what element most intrigued them, they all answered: The dolphins, the Posidonia, the fishes in the center of the screen.

A critical issue is the positioning of the menu button: all four students/users in the laboratory test located it, while most of those in the classroom test did not (6/9). In any case, after a short length of time interacting with *Digital Diorama*'s interface, the students learnt the positioning of the control keys and automatically searched for them in the lower part of the screen.

No critical issues emerged from the request to reach a specific level. Once the children had learnt where to find the menu and how to expand it (by clicking on the icon), they easily understood that the levels were reachable by clicking the writing with the name of the level itself. This shows that in this particular case, the choice to represent the control keys in different ways did not make it impossible for the student/user to surf the *Digital Diorama*.

Some critical issues emerged from analysis of the students' scan paths for the "exit the screen" task. In fact, five of the nine students, after exploring the lower part of the screen, recognized the back button. This suggest that the three options available to achieve the task confused some of the students.

Figure 15. Scanpath of the children during the execution of task 4 and 5

The most critical aspect that emerged from the eye tracking analysis concerned the task of returning to the Crossover topics level. In this case, the task was not completed by all the students, four of whom aborted the process because they could not find the back button. Among the five students who completed the process, three correctly reached the task, one clicked HOME instead of Crossover topics and one did not find any way out. Redesigning the level titles by shaping them as buttons might contribute to making the *Digital Diorama* become even more intuitive and user-friendly.

Focus Groups and Training

The data collected during the first focus group discussion showed that the teachers were already using new technologies in the classroom but continuing to draw on traditional teaching methods. For example, IWBs had been predominantly managed and used by the teachers themselves and used as a research tool rather than for cooperation purposes.

The presentation of the *Digital Diorama* prototype was positively received by the teachers, as a potentially useful educational device for science teaching and not only for science. This was a first key result, which suggests that there is potential for the interdisciplinary use of the *Digital Diorama*. Exploiting the diorama as a multidisciplinary tool would cater for the need to foster well-established connections and relationships between the different fields of knowledge. We collected the initial impressions of the teachers who had begun to explore *Digital Diorama*. From a technological point of view, the teachers reported that they were satisfied and had found the *Digital Diorama* easy to use on the IWB.

The teachers reported a high level of satisfaction with the graphic layout of the *Digital Diorama*, as well with the multimedia materials offered at the hotspots and the choice of themes addressed.

With regard to the teaching methodology, the teachers expressed a positive opinion about the approach designed for use with the *Digital Diorama*. In particular, they appreciated the potential offered for stimulating the students' curiosity (through questions, discussion and subsequent reflection) and the transversality of the themes proposed.

Questionnaire

Overall, teachers reported that they were satisfied, finding the *Digital Diorama* on IWB to be user-friendly with an attractive graphic interface. The only problematic aspect that emerged related to the activation of the different levels, to be managed through the menu, given that the position of the menu was not easily located when exploration was undersay.

The level Imaginary journey was considered quite satisfactory in relation to the voice-over. The Identity card format was perceived as very or completely satisfactory by the whole group, except for one teacher who did not explain his opinion. Teachers also liked the level Crossover topics and the connections to the guides containing semi-structured information on preparing and moderating exploration of the *Digital Diorama*. In relation to everyday life topics, teachers manifested different points of view: their evaluations ranged from total satisfaction to dissatisfaction. The group of teachers also displayed strong interest in designing and/or conducting complementary educational experiences for students on completion of the basic *Digital Diorama* exploration.

With regard to methodology, the teachers appeared to be highly satisfied; those who answered the questions felt had they understood the method and were excited about its potential; the specific aspects that they praised included: curiosity, transversality, the stimulating nature of the enquiry-based method, and reasoning on the basis of differences and similarities.

Finally, the participating teachers positively rated the overall training path: they believed that the experience had been positive and had led them to develop a proactive attitude in relation to new teaching methodologies.

Classwork

Instead of reporting on children's exploration of the *Digital Diorama* level by level, we have chosen to organize the data by type of activity conducted given that the same activity format may be encountered at more than one level.

Personal Involvement

The teachers all agreed that the experience of exploring the *Digital Diorama*, particularly the Imaginary journey level, had elicited a high degree of emotional involvement on the part of the children.

The teachers defined the *Digital Diorama* as an engaging instrument, with the power to create a particularly relaxed learning environment, and provide a higher degree of motivation that traditionally conducted classes. The exploration, which begins with a sequence designed to strongly elicit emotions, allowed the children to establish a relationship with the represented ecosystems and to emotionally bond with them. (Wilson, 1993; Barbiero 2012).

This is a significant and unprecedented finding given that in science learning, the involvement of the emotional sphere is not usually planned for or encouraged, despite its great importance. This is the dimension experienced by researchers when they *become passionate* about the topic that they are studying and draw inspiration from this for future developments of their work.

Another highly significant outcome was the children's tendency to associate elements and situations from the *Digital Diorama* with their personal life experience, in terms of identifying a key theme and linking it with everyday life. In general during the exploration, the children experienced a strong desire to talk about episodes drawn from their own experience. These references to their personal lives were constant, to the extent that the discussions sometimes strayed off the initial theme. Although the teachers had to work hard to maintain the thread of the discussion, the opportunity to freely contribute was highly motivating for the children, increasing their enthusiasm for the work to be done, engaging them and making them feel actively part of the learning process.

Figure 16. Examples of the children's comments about their feelings and sensations during exploration of the Digital Diorama

> *I had the feeling of being free ...nearly like being one of those animals.*
> *I was struck by the tail, because it was really well curled.*
> *You felt like you were the animal and you understood what it was doing.*
> *I enjoyed working on it, yes, because you find the answers for yourself, it's nice to see everyday life compared to animals. It makes you think of new questions. It teaches you how to take care of animals.*

Figure 17. Examples of comments made by the children linking the contents of the Digital Diorama with aspects of everyday life

> *Teacher*: *What are these living things?*
> *S1*: *They're transparent fish.*
> *S2*: *They're millipedes, they look like sea insects. You can tell they don't have fins..*
> *S3*: *I saw a film with orange crustaceans. They have legs for swimming with.*
> *S4*: *Maybe prawns are crustaceans.*
> *S5*: *I think they're not fish. Mussels are crustaceans too.*
> *S6*: *They can't be crustaceans. Mussels aren't that big.*
> *Teacher*: *Why do you think they are called crustaceans?*
> *S2*: *Because they live on something hard, on shells, on rocks.*
> *S3*: *The name is like "crust... that means they're hard.*
> *S5*: *Maybe when they're afraid, they close up and go hard.*

Mode of Exploration

The teachers did not lead the children through the *Digital Diorama* following a predefined pathway, but explored and discovered it together with the children. The time-scales and modes of exploration were dictated by the needs and interests of the specific class group. The second graders, for example, spent more time over the Imaginary journey level and the Crossover topics and did not venture into the Identity card level. The fifth class teachers, in contrast, worked at this last level also, catering for the older children's need to search for additional information and find further specific facts within the *Digital Diorama*.

The class groups generally explored the Imaginary journey at a leisurely pace, taking a relatively long time to complete them (this was especially the case for the younger children). This gave the children the opportunity to activate their imaginations (an aspect which in the museum setting is often overlooked), and to turn the *Digital Diorama* into a place of exploration rather than a representation of defined elements. This initial phase was of key educational importance, as it laid the foundations for the discussions that took place at all the subsequent levels of exploration… discussions based on reflections, answers, and "genuine" questions issuing from the intellectual and creative work of the entire group.

The discussions on transversal themes again featured a high level of references to daily life (e.g., holidays at the sea, pets, etc.), and in the case of the fifth class children, to previous experiences and learning contents already encountered in class. For example, the children linked the cliffs of Dover seen on the *Digital Diorama*, with the Dolomites – a topic earlier covered at school: both are examples of mountains characterized by layers of limestone rock in which it is possible to identify the shells of the marine animals forming them.

DISCUSSION

The use of the *Digital Diorama* was characterised by continuous discussion. The opportunity to actively participate in the discussions was well received by the children. Occasionally the teachers found it difficult to involve shyer or more "passive" children in the discussion, because they were taken up with moderating and at times holding in check the excessive enthusiasm of the more active students. In the teachers' view, the methodology recommended for use with the *Digital Diorama* (guiding discussion rather than providing information) was highly productive and made the classes lively and interesting.

Some of the themes, such as for example that of parental care in different groups of animals, aroused great interest on the part of the children, again leading them to make connections with their personal experience. We consider this to be a very meaningful result: discussion is the basis on which science progresses and the use of this methodology in the classroom is strongly called for in the most authoritative educational literature.

Integrating the Digital Diorama Into Ongoing Biology

During the final focus group discussion the teachers emphasized the fact that some of the themes encountered in the *Digital Diorama* had been taken up again by the children during subsequent classwork on other topics. These included: the human body (the different parts and how they are interconnected); the difference between living and non-living things, classifying living things based on personal observations and "playing" around with similarities and differences; the ecosystem and the food chain; the characteristics of living organisms and their possible adaptations to the environment they live in.

Interdisciplinarity

The *Digital Diorama* was found to be a multimedia "device" suitable for use outside of the strictly scientific domain. A science teacher and a teacher of Italian, for example, invited the children to carry out a interdisciplinary project, by asking them to write audio commentaries for some of the video footage from the *Digital Diorama*. The children's comments were enriched with references to the biological and ecological contents encountered during their explorations (a sample in Figure 18).

Figure 18. Example of a discussion that arose during interaction with the Digital Diorama between children and their teacher

> *S1: The shell on the Digital Diorama belongs to a hermit crab, because I saw one and I know what it looks like.*
> *S2: There are rules and recommendations that parents and grandparents give children, to protect them and prepare them for when they grow up, just as animals do with their babies.*

Figure 19. Audio commentary prepared by the children for the video footage showing the hunting technique of cats (stalking)

> Pip Cat
> *"Once upon a time, a cat named Pip was hungry: he saw some pigeons and began to stalk them, waiting for a good chance to spring on them and catch them. Now what does stalking mean? The cat lengthens its body and lowers it to the ground, it keeps its legs bent, walks very slowly towards the prey, and then suddenly it springs, catches its prey and eats it. When the cat begins to stalk its prey, its ears are folded back so that it can hear better, its eyes are fixed on the prey, it moves its shoulders back and forwards. As it closes in, it changes pace, first running with short steps, then, taking longer steps, and then really fast".*

The detailed description of the cat's movements is the impressive outcome of careful observation of the video footage and in-depth group discussions. The commentary is also rich and effective from a linguistic and communicative point of view: the use of a question within the commentary captures the listener's/reader's attention; furthermore, the description of the last sequence in the cat's hunting technique is so accurate and well-expressed that it conveys the animal's increase in speed most effectively.

Another example of an interdisciplinary project (science-history-geography) was the production of an identity card for the jar represented in the *Digital Diorama*, along with other archaeological remains that may be found on the sea bed.

Technical Aspects

The main technical difficulties /limitations encountered during exploration of the prototype *Digital Diorama* concerned occasional stalling of the video contents. This was partly due to poor Internet connections. In any case, it did not significantly affect the carrying out of the work.

The children were attracted by the IWB and were soon highly familiar with how to use it as well as with how to explore the *Digital Diorama*: they easily memorized the positions of the hotspots and themes associated with each. The *Digital Diorama* proved to be a user-friendly and easily understood device. This allowed the children to apply their digital competence – usually drawn on for entertainment purposes only – to a product specifically designed for educational purposes (Jenkins, 2010; Ferri, 2011).

It was not always feasible to fully exploit the potential of the IWB to foster collaborative learning work. The classroom space was typically taken up by desks, chairs and other "obstacles" that did not leave enough room for groups of students to work in front of the IWB. Indeed, to facilitate the active participation of all the students and allow all of them to use the IWB, in some cases it proved necessary to divide the class into smaller groups.

The results of the prototype-testing phase provided valuable input for the production of other *Digital Diorama* planned as part of this project. The experimental participants' observations enabled us to make a number of improvements to the interface.

For example, where possible we have included video clips instead of photographs, because the latter were found to be less attractive to the children. We also substituted multimedia material that the children found difficult to understand, or that in general were not particularly well received by them.

In order to ensure that the *Digital Diorama* may be explored in a relatively fluid manner, we transferred the multimedia materials to a dedicated site external to the interface, which is therefore more easily accessed even when the Internet connection is poor.

Experimentation at Public Workstation

A public workstation with an IWB has been installed, which is freely accessible to all those wishing to explore the *Digital Diorama*. A sample of 23 heterogeneous students/users, with different ICT skills and experiences, were observed during free individual and group explorations and interviewed. After a brief familiarisation session, all the students/users were able to use the IWB and understand the *Digital Diorama*'s functionalities. The level that mostly stimulated interest was that of Crossover topics. Most of the students/users answered that they would use the *Digital Diorama* for either teaching or learning any matters, and with students of different ages; one participant stated that he would also use them with the elderly. At the end of this itinerary, an interactive whiteboard with the Digital Diorama was installed in a public space at the University of Milano-Bicocca, while other public workstations will be soon accessible at the urban park of Parco Nord Milano.

FUTURE RESEARCH DIRECTIONS

In recent months, we have launched experimentation with all four *Digital Diorama* produced for this project, involving about 20 classes at various levels of education distributed throughout Italy. This phase too will be evaluated using qualitative research methods. Participants are 450 children and around 20 teachers of science (the majority), Italian, mathematics, technology and special needs.

This national experimentation is still ongoing, as is the data collection and data analysis.

The *Digital Diorama* may be used flexibly by teachers in terms of deciding when to introduce it into the teaching programme, while it can also be a valuable tool for establishing continuity of method between successive levels of education.

To promote dissemination of the *Digital Diorama* as an innovative learning resource, an alternative IWB open source hardware technology could be designed and produced to lower the cost of installation in schools.

Moreover, the architecture of the *Digital Diorama* system can be further used to support the development of other typologies of learning tools based for example on art pieces.

The *Digital Diorama* project also involves the creation and maintenance of a database of existing dioramas in Italian and foreign museums, with the aim of making them better known, fostering comparison and online exchange experiences.

The *Digital Diorama* may also be used outside of schools, in public spaces: at museums, universities, and other suitable public spaces. This device will be available to anyone wishing to interactively explore environmental issues linked to everyday life. Applying the awareness acquired from the *Digital Diorama* to our daily lives can help us to modify certain socio-cultural habits and contribute to sustainability.

Table 1. Breakdown of the schools and classes involved in the experimentation at the national level

Cities	n. classes	Primary	Secondary (Lower)	Secondary (Upper)
Messina	2	1	1	
Livorno	1	1		
Napoli	2	1	1	
Roma	2	2		
Milano	2	1	1	
Cinisello	2			2
Lissone	1	1		
Besana	3	3		
Mortara	4	2	2	
total	**19**	**12**	**5**	**2**

Thus the *Digital Diorama* is a tool that combines many valuable aspects including promoting the understanding of many ecosystems and key concepts in ecology, with a method using guided participation and collaborative learning, within an overall framework that will encourage responsible attitudes and sustainability practices in everyday life.

CONCLUSION

The results obtained to date will be supplemented and enriched with other data currently being collated and analysed by the group. Given the significant volume of data collected (mainly via video-recording) on the teacher-training sessions, the classwork and students' learning products, additional time is required for its analysis.

However, we are already able to predict that the results will be positive, leading to strong demand to participate in this project, from schools in particular.

Experimental evidence on user interaction with the *Digital Diorama* was obtained using qualitative and quantitative methodological approaches. The results of the quantitative assessment based on monitoring the behaviour and eye movements of students during exploration of the visual interface, suggested that children interacted comfortably with the *Digital Diorama* interface, and did not display any particular difficulty in understanding and using them. Nonetheless, some details of the graphic interface were modified based on the results of the experimental observations. For example, the titles of the levels in the *Digital Diorama* and some of the other buttons were redesigned to make using the *Digital Diorama* even more intuitive. For example, in relation to recognition of the play button to activate the audio of the hotspots, the icon was redesigned and a pause command added to enhance ease-of-use.

Indeed the outcomes of the user tests with students were obtained under specific experimental conditions that had been fixed to allow comparisons and quantitative and qualitative analysis. In addition, the qualitative follow up of the experimentation with *Digital Diorama* in schools, used the observation of behaviours to show that after working with the device in the classroom over a number of months, all the participating students were competent in managing the interface and knowing how to explore it. This level of evaluation also led us to further fine tune the *Digital Diorama* interface.

The emotional dimension of a the creative cognitive exploration elicited by the *Digital Diorama* (for example, through the Imaginary journey level as earlier described) can provide more effective educational support to teachers than the typical tools of formal learning such as traditional lesson styles and textbooks.

It is also expected that the proposed methodology will help students to become familiar with the procedurals and practices that reflect the mind-set of researchers, for example building a concrete product to share with others, discussion, reflecting on information exchanged, etc. This aspect will be investigated further in the course of our ongoing experimentation.

Based on the results obtained to date, we can be confident in assuming that we have designed a user friendly interactive graphics interface and a sophisticated "educational device" that can provide valuable support to teachers during their classroom activities and to students in their learning processes.

Moreover, the research findings suggest that exploration of *Digital Diorama* brings children into contact with their desire to know.

The potential to exploit the *Digital Diorama* outside of natural science teaching was confirmed by teachers during training and focus group discussions, where they shared their successful experience of using the *Digital Diorama* with their colleagues teaching different subjects, for example: Italian, English and Mathematics. Therefore, the *Digital Diorama* mode of exploration and the interaction that it produces among students and teachers also provides an interesting "educational device" for experimenting with the interdisciplinary methods. This result meets the need to foster well-established connections and relationships between different fields of knowledge. Such a learning modality is being advocated at the European and international levels, with the aim of providing the transversal base of knowledge and competences required to address the complex issues facing contemporary society.

REFERENCES

Andreoni, G. (2010). Sustainable Children's Product Experience. In F. Ceschin, C. Vezzoli, & J. Zhang (Eds.), *Proceedings of Sustainability in Design: Now!* (pp. 1184–1195). Bangalore, India: LENS.

Arcà, M. (2009). *Insegnare biologia*. Pisa, Italy: Naturalmente Scienza.

Baldacci, M. (2001). *Metodologia della ricerca pedagogica*. Milano, Italy: Paravia Bruno Mondadori.

Barbiero, G. (2012). Ecologia Affettiva per la Sostenibilità. *Culture della Sostenibilità, 10*, 126–139.

Calvani, A. (Ed.). (2007). *Fondamenti di didattica. Teoria e prassi dei dispositivi formativi*. Roma, Italy: Carocci Editore.

Chalufour, I., & Worth, K. (2004). *Building structure with young children*. St. Paul, MN: Redleaf Press.

Czerwinsky Domenis, L. (2000). *La discussione intelligente*. Trento, Italy: Erickson.

Esposito, L. (2012). Le TIC e la promozione della competenza digitale. La nuova sfida della scuola 2.0. *OPPInformazioni, 113*, 1–10.

European Commission, DG Education and Culture. (2004). *Study on Innovative Learning Environments in School Education*. Final Report.

Ferri, P. (2011). *Nativi Digitali*. Milano, Italy: Bruno Mondadori Editore.

Gagliardi, R., Gabbari, M., & Gaetano, A. (2010). *La scuola con la LIM: guida didattica per la lavagna interattiva multimediale*. Brescia, Italy: La Scuola.

Gambini, A., Pezzotti, A., & Broglia, A. (2008). Sussidiari ed esperienze didattiche di tipo pratico: due modi contrapposti con cui affrontare a scuola la complessità dei temi ambientali. In G. Giordani, V. Rossi, & P. Viaroli (Eds.), *Ecologia Emergenza Pianificazione. Proceedings of XVIII Congresso Nazionale della Società Italiana di Ecologia, Parma, 1-3 settembre 2008* (pp. 280-288). Retrieved from http://www.dsa.unipr.it/sitecongresso/node/9

Gambini, A., Pezzotti, A., & Samek Lodovici, P. (2005). An online Biology course: A teaching-learning experiment. *Je-LKS, 1*(2), 223–231.

Ghislandi, P. (Ed.). (2012). eLearning: Theories, Design, Software, Applications. Rijeka, Croatia: InTech Europe.

Hanna, L., Risden, K., Czerwinski, M., & Alexander, K. J. (1999). The role of usability research in designing children's computer products. In A. Druin (Ed.), *The design of children's technology* (pp. 4–26). San Francisco, CA: Kaufmann.

Hayhoe, M., & Ballard, D. (2005). Eye movements in natural behavior. *Trends in Cognitive Sciences*, 9(4), 188–194. doi:10.1016/j.tics.2005.02.009 PMID:15808501

Herrington, J., Reeves, T. C., & Oliver, R. (2014). Authentic Learning Environments. In J. M. Spector, M. D. Merril, J. Elen, & M. J. Bishop (Eds.), *Handbook of Research on Educational Communications and Technology* (pp. 401–412). New York, NY: Springer. doi:10.1007/978-1-4614-3185-5_32

Jenkins, H. (2010). *Culture partecipative e competenze digitali*. Milano, Italy: Edizioni Angelo Guerini e Associati.

Kowler, E. (Ed.). (1990). *Eye Movements and Their Role in Visual and Cognitive Processes*. Amsterdam: Elsevier Science Publisher B.V.

Mantovani, S. (Ed.). (2000). *La ricerca sul campo in educazione. I metodi qualitativi*. Milano, Italy: Paravia Bruno Mondadori.

Monk, A., Wright, P., Haber, J., & Davenport, L. (1993). *Improving Your Human-Computer Interface: A Practical Technique*. Upper Saddle River, NJ: Prentice Hall.

Monty, R. A., & Senders, J. W. (Eds.). (1976). *Eye Movements and Psychological Processes*. Lawrence Erlbaum.

Nesset, V., & Large, A. (2004). Children in the information technology design process: A review of theories and their applications. *Library & Information Science Research*, 26(2), 140–161. doi:10.1016/j.lisr.2003.12.002

Nielsen, J. (1993). *Usability Engineering*. Cambridge, MA: Academic Press.

Nielsen, J., & Landauer, T. K. (1993). A mathematical model of the finding of usability problems. In *Proceedings ACM INTERCHI'93 Conference*, (pp. 206-213). doi:10.1145/169059.169166

Pezzotti, A., Broglia, A., & Gambini, A. (2014). Realizzazione di un learning object per favorire la cooperazione online. In T. Minerva & A. Simone (Eds.), *Politiche, Formazione, Tecnologie. Proceedings of IX Convegno della Sie-L, Roma, 12-13 ottobre 2013* (pp. 168-171). Roma, Italy: SIe-L Editore.

Pezzotti, A., & Gambini, A. (2012). Indicatori di qualità per l'analisi della comunicazione di un corso online. *TD – Tecnologie Didattiche*, 20(2), 90-98.

Pontecorvo, C., Ajello, A. M., & Zucchermaglio, C. (Eds.). (2004). *Discutendo si impara. Interazione e conoscenza a scuola*. Roma, Italy: Carocci Editore.

Schmid, R., & Zambarbieri, D. (Eds.). (1991). *Oculomotor Control and Cognitive Processes – Normal and Pathological Aspects*. Amsterdam: Elsevier Science Publisher B.V.

Sterling, S. L. (2001). *Sustainable Education: Re-visioning Learning and Change*. Bristol, UK: Green Books, Ltd. for the Schumacher Society.

Wilson, E. O. (1993). *The Biophilia Hypothesis*. Washington, DC: Island Press.

Zambarbieri, D. (2003). E-TRACKING; Eye tracking analysis in the evaluation of e-learning systems. In *Proceedings of HCI International Conference*, (pp. 617-621).

Zambarbieri, D., & Carniglia, E. (2012). Eye movement analysis of reading from computer displays, eReaders and printed books. *Ophthalmic & Physiological Optics*, *32*(5), 390–396. doi:10.1111/j.1475-1313.2012.00930.x PMID:22882151

ENDNOTES

1. European Commission, DG Education and Culture (2004). *Study on Innovative Learning Environments in School Education*. Final Report.
2. See Grunwald Declaration on Media Education, (1982) document at the website: http://www.unesco.org/education/pdf/MEDIA_E.PDF
3. See the document of the European Commission, Proposal for a decision of the European Parliament and of the Council adopting a multi-annual programme (2004-2006) for the effective integration of Information and Communication Technologies (ICT) in education and training systems in Europe (eLearning Programme) COM(2002) 751 final 2002/0303 (COD) Brussels, 19 December 2002, at the website http://ec.europa.eu/education/archive/elearning/doc/dec_en.pdf
4. See the document at the website http//www.diplomatie.gouv.fr/fr/IMG/pdf/Parisagendafin_en.pdf.
5. http://hubmiur.pubblica.istruzione.it/web/istruzione/prot5559_12. See also PNSD 2015 (Piano Nazionale per la Scuola Digitale).
6. In this study, the authors compared test data from a class equipped with an IWB with data from another class within the same school that did not have access to an IWB, but had the same teachers. On standard national tests evaluating learning in the areas of language, mathematics and science, the students who had the IWB in their classroom, scored 17-20% higher than those who had not. The Final Evaluation Reports of Robert Marzano and Mark Haystead 2009 and 2010 are available on Internet at http://www.prometheanworld.com/rx_content/files/PDF/Marzano2ndYearStudyof-PrometheanActivClassroom-169662.pdf

    In Italy, as in many other European and American countries, IWBs have been in use for a long time. It is estimated that in 2011 5,300,000 IWBs were installed worldwide. In Italy, as early as 1997, the MIUR and the Lombardy Region embarked on a number of projects to equip schools with IWBs, or technological devices that combine: multimedia, the term for the drawing together of different media; visualization, or the capability to represent an image in multiple dimensions; tactility, or using one's fingers instead of a mouse; cooperation, multiple possibilities to be part of a community and work with others to achieve a shared goal or carry out a joint project. See also: INDIRE data on the diffusion and use of IWBs in Italy.
7. See Ocse dates: http://www.ocse.org
8. See Law 26 June 2012 no. 369 - Promotion of agreements with other government bodies, Universities and other public and private bodies.
9. See http://hubmiur.pubblica.istruzione.it/web/istruzione/prot5559_12.

[10] In relation to the concept of Collaborative Learning, see Dillenbourg's definition, cfr: P. Dillenbourg, *What do you mean by collaborative Learning? Collaborative-learning: Cognitive and Computational Approaches*, Amsterdam, Elsevier, pp. 1-19 (1999). Collaborative Learning (CL) is a situation in which two or more people learn – or at least attempt to learn – something together.

[11] See The Ministry of Education, University and Research's programmes and directives: http://hubmiur.pubblica.istruzione.it/web/istruzione/prot5559_12

Chapter 4
"School-Cinema":
A Research Experience That Combines Educational Theories, Educational Processes, and Educational Technologies

Daniela Tamburini
SPERIMENTA, Italy

ABSTRACT

This chapter presents an educational and consulting path for the use of new technologies that support the improvement of learning relationships in groups (Parmigiani, 2009), the construction of knowledge (Lakkala et al., 2007; Kangas et al., 2007) and the ability to recognize and explore the experience of communication and relationship at professional and personal levels, for the individual and for groups in order to enhance abilities and professional skills on several levels: cognitive, affective, conative and practical (Paquay, Altet, Charlier, & Perrenoud, 2001). Through the report of the experiments carried out for two years and applied to two training projects for teachers of five Primary and Secondary Italian schools, the main objective is to describe and present the overall results. The approaches used were inspired by the method of participatory research and action research with a clinical and pedagogical approach. The methodology is based on the case study of the Clinica della Formazione (Massa, 1992; Franza, 2003) that increases the emotional, communicative and relationship dimensions and gives concreteness not only to the educational action but also to the process behind it, which then becomes the target of investigations.

INTRODUCTION

"School-cinema" is a project of research and intervention as well as a training devise started from the Master in *Development of Clinical Skills in Educational and Training Professions* at the University of Milano-Bicocca, developed by Dr. Daniela Tamburini under the supervision of Prof. Angelo Mario Franza[1] of the University of Bologna. The project has been applied widely in different educational and

DOI: 10.4018/978-1-5225-2616-2.ch004

training contexts such as, among others, the Laboratories of *Systems of Communication* (2007-2008; 2008-2009) and *Film Language* (2005-2006) in collaboration with Prof. Cesare Massarenti – University Professor, International Consulting Information Technology - and the Laboratory of Visual Sociology of the University of Milano-Bicocca, faculty of Sociology.

This chapter presents the application of the project within a training program that lasted approximately a year and involved 98 participants: 48 teachers and 50 students of a School District of Milan consisting of four Primary Schools and one Secondary Junior School. It describes the pedagogical premises and foundations of the project, the structure and model adopted and its main outcomes.

The Context: The School as a Complex System

The experience of teaching can hardly be understood and can, perhaps even less, be expressed in an exhaustive way, given the complexity of its essential features. To this regard, in *"Changing the school"* (Massa, 1997), Prof. Riccardo Massa insists on the concept of complexity and, at the same time, of collectivity, intended as "understanding" and identified as a fundamental element when educating referred not only to the relationship teacher-pupil, but also to the relationships teacher-teacher and teacher-parent.

Pupils: we see a transfer of expectations, also of the affective type, to the school, especially by adolescents and pre-adolescents who are unable to handle positively the recognition of the role of student, and perceive the school (especially the class-group) as a theater, a real stage on which to act a passionate scene of "mirroring tenderness" (Charmet, 2009), often disguised as apparently apathetic behavior. Nowadays the school is, therefore, faced with the task of developing the connection between reality and image, to help the young person live better the dramatic contemporary fracture, in which devotion to one's own representation generates cultural conflicts that hinder the educational process and the development path.

Parents: parents, too, have to go through the culture of role, undergo strong pressure on the role of father and mother and are often forced to behave as if in a "theater performance", without being able to find the real role of father and mother. Within this scenario there may be some attitudes that tend to differ greatly with the school (and faculty) aiming at symbolically rebuilding a well-defined role, or looking for common aspects (alliances) to the point of reaching attitudes of passive delegation. This means that the school possesses a sort of rituality, where the conscious dimension is in contact with a deeper part, which we will not call "unconscious" but which we can certainly indicate as "unaware" (Ugazio, 2012).

Teachers: Let's now think of the teachers and the problems associated with their role. We can define them "the characters": the school is also the theater of one's own emotions, a place where to develop, but also defend (as if in a trench) professional as well as personal ideas and values. Being a teacher means taking on a role of responsibility with increasingly blurred boundaries that are often pre-determined (Cerioli, 2002). This role often implies the absence of shared reference points (Riva, 2008) with an inevitable increase of conflicts, stress and effort to accept and understand each other, to meet for common projects and recognize oneself as part of them.

The above three elements imply that the school is increasingly considered a complex system, where the variables at stake are linked by relationships of interdependence: the hypothesis underlying this research project is that, in this context, technology is to take on the characteristics of a pedagogical tool, functional to the modification of teaching-learning practices to cope with the change taking place in our time.

The Educational Potential of New Technologies

The assumption that teaching mechanically implies learning has never been defensible, but today this statement can be affirmed with greater certainty if we think of how difficult it is, especially in Italy, to introduce new technologies into the complexity characteristic of the relationship between teacher and student, among the students in a class, and also of the school itself as a system when considering the poor ability to implement the educational potential that new technologies carry. Thus training programs for teachers should necessarily be oriented towards the development of digital culture, focused not only on technological aspects, but they should also, and above all, be aimed at methodological and psycho-pedagogical skills, to be considered the most interesting when introducing technology in schools.

It is no longer a question of establishing the necessary relations between the introduction of technologies in schools and its good use, but of modifying teaching practices thanks to the opportunities they offer, and through the implementation of new methodologies that may facilitate learning, exchanges among disciplines and that can bring knowledge "down to the earth" and applicable to different contexts.

The "school-cinema" program is proposed as a methodology both coded, well-structured and also flexible, able to find different system forms depending on the situations to which it is applied.

THE CINEMA IN THE SCHOOL

The School as a Creative Representation

Now let us ask ourselves this question: within this "scenario" why the cinema in the school? First of all, in young people films trigger their the love for the art of interpretation: through the interpretation of a film sequence they inevitably end up talking about themselves and they interpret their and other people's behavior in the attempt to find their way in the midst of a never-ending and sometimes exhausting hall of mirrors, where Socratic questions keep recurring. The cinema is a true experience (especially when lived in groups, such as a class). What amazes me is the young's ravenous curiosity smoldering under the apparent state of "deep coma" (any reference, especially to films, is allowed)[2]. It is as if outside their group – and so, of their body or vice versa - there were no reality, as if reality could only reside within the narrow boundaries of their closed relationships: their language is essentially metaphorical and analogical whereas ours as educators, teachers, adults is, in general, mainly symbolic/numeric (this is obviously a myth the young often have and cherish). Culture, cinema, fashion, theater, virtual world, ethics, being in a group are "otherness" from reality, an alternative to the norm: in addition to values they share a language that depicts the daily experience in a different way.

Secondly, the cinema is a place of art and creativity is the foundation for any good process of communication and therefore of behavior. To create is to build together new perceptions and new meanings: to do it we need a method, it cannot be improvised. Today any person who takes upon themselves an educational role is, as an adult, called to find ways to communicate in an intricate network of stories – including their own – in order to foster, facilitate, develop the discovery of parts of the world and of themselves that may otherwise neither be perceived or expressed. One has to be able to facilitate growth paths that are aimed at the gradual achievement of autonomy, at the construction of aimed knowledge and at the development of skills based on potentials and critical thinking for a life rich in relationships and suitable to achieve affective security and awareness of one's own behaviors.

It is in this sense that the school can be defined as a great creative representation. It is necessary to revise critically the contradicting, heterogeneous, differentiated, boundless multiplicity of the sources of knowledge. The school is culture because it produces a universe of symbolic and cultural exchanges within a structure which is physically present and organized, but it is, above all, a "procedural system capable of producing vital worlds that enable us to experience our thoughts," as Riccardo Massa stated[3]. We need to stop and think in order to process our experience of this complex world that today demands for more knowledge, which is more than ever contaminated.

The Cinema as an "Exquisitely" Pedagogical Tool

Therefore to the question, "why can the film be said to be an "exquisitely" educational tool?" we will answer that the reasons are many, but that perhaps the most important one is that it enables us to become familiar with the language of images and of our emotions. When we watch a film we can be permeated by emotions without being overwhelmed by them and since "each emotion is confronted with a horizon of meaning,", as Eugenio Borgna[4] writes, we can say that the cinema helps us reflect on the complexity of our world. The film is a cultural text consisting of narrative units that together make up total, autonomous facts, which do not correspond to the objective reality of facts, but represent their simulacrum. The film leads the viewer to create representative realities of particular situations. It is therefore a pedagogical tool as it carries representative forms in which I recognize my thoughts. Thereby it responds to new learning needs in our society of images and information that has magnified the reference boundaries of the individual existence, which produces anxiety.

Anxiety that arises from the void perceived in the space existing between data and knowledge. Each person is full of data, images, information, but this container empties quickly because the accumulated information is not anchored in existing knowledge, it is not processed or because the overload produces amnesia or an overdose due to cognitive consumption. Receiving is, therefore, not enough if we want to understand; it is necessary to organize the information data we receive, namely to establish selective procedures to give meanings to information.

We must learn to re-learn: the strengthening of cognitive processes is focused on the presence and ability of self-reflective behaviours, capable of questioning established mental models.

The Role of Images to Understand Experience

Still following a path that, better than a "journey back", I would more precisely define as a "dismantling path" (the procedure you follow when trying to figure out how a machine works), I will start from a few basic assumptions that affect the relationship with images. On second thought images have been part of our world since only recent times: dense woods and open countryside were masters in the Middle Ages. The farmer who woke up too early to say his daily prayers found his way to the fields dotted with small chapels containing the image of a Madonna, a San Rocco, a San Cassiano - stages and places of worship in front of which to end his prayers. That was all! At most, during their lifetime, farmers may have seen about fifty images. Today we see from 400,000 to 600,000 a day. Quite a difference! The film helps us make sense because it produces the reality before our eyes in a "more complete" way than reality itself. What does this mean? That it enables us to see what we normally do not see, i.e. the non-visible, the context, the off-field sequences of our experience of reality. But let's proceed step by step.

According to Gianni Canova (2002)[5], until recently the cinema has been the "shroud" of the world, that is the place where our world left its tracks, its footprints. Now images are no longer the world's footprints but real "live" representations that reflect on our representations, since the distance and the difference between symbols and what they symbolize are reduced and confused. Moving images are the *loisir* of our century.

Today we are constantly surrounded by moving images constructed according to a constant analogy with experience to the point that not only is the experience transposed into images and vice versa, but that moving images become the medium to gain access to and to understand experience (there is a reversal between the image and its representation).

"Man lives in a symbolic universe, no longer in a physical one. Man can no longer see reality in its face. Instead of dealing with the actual things, in a sense, man is constantly talking to himself " for Ernst Cassirer (2009)[6]

The distance and the difference between symbols and what they are symbols of are therefore reduced and confused. On the contrary, while watching a film, it is possible to draw a correlation between the viewer who looks and the connection he/she makes. Reasoning about the distance, about the difference. This connection is not perceived immediately, you have to think about it. Each one of us sees his/her own film, not the director's film or the actors' film, since we put together the data in an absolutely unique way (and unrepeatable, because everything changes also simply after some time).

As I stated before, the proliferation of images magnifies the reference boundaries of the individual existence, producing anxiety, anxiety that comes from the gap between the data we have and our knowledge of them: in order to understand it is not enough to receive the information, but we need to activate self-reflexive behaviours. And this, at school, essentially means three things: learning in groups, dealing with values which are shared as much as possible and managing complex communication processes.

THE CINEMA AS A TRAINING EVENT

Today, within each dimension of knowledge, a major revision is taking place, which, while overcoming the models focused on some sort of generic accumulation of notions, is aimed at new goals. In all contemporary pedagogy great attention is placed on education to democracy, to collective thought, to health, citizenship, interculture and environment and, more generally, to the development of behaviors characterized by autonomy and critical thinking.

In this sense it is important that teachers as well as students should find tools, time and occasions to reflect on and question the meaning of what is taught, learned, acted, put into practice, communicated, in order to be better aware of the effects produced.

Today the teacher has to face questions both about the teacher's function and about the school itself, dangling between imperatives essentially depending on economic policies and models that are less "managerial", more collaborative and ethical. This involves a different definition of the term professionalism, and therefore the training of education professionals more or less oriented to change their preconceptions, and for this reason open to confrontations with other educational agencies also outside the school environment, more or less willing to form alliances among students, parents and other community members, more or less attentive to ponder about ethical aspects affecting the core values of educating.

There are, in fact, some elements to be taken into account: in teaching, more than in other professions, the relationship between knowledge and the way in which it is transmitted is closer than in other professions, and these ways are, in turn, closely related to experience-based strategies rather than based on theoretical models or on knowledge, skills and previously acquired abilities. To summarize, it could be said that we are trying to understand how experience can turn into a source of theory. In fact, if we think about it, the whole history of pedagogy is studded with examples showing how educational practices have formed the basis for a theory that has opened new frontiers in the field of research.

For reflection to promote learning from experience and, therefore, lead to generative and proactive practices, such reflection has to be somehow recognized as useful for something, for someone. The cinema - or rather working on the cinema - becomes useful precisely because it helps us recognize within an event its properly educational and training nature.

The Language of the Cinema

We are interested in two aspects of the cinema:

- Its language, which enables us to bring to light the invisible network that generates, sustains and transforms our imaginary world of the phenomenon of educating;
- The viewer's look: rather than "how", we are interested to know "why" a student or a teacher sees the film in that particular way, since each of us interprets, processes and, as a matter of fact, "sees" the same given images in a subjective, and therefore different, way.

The aim is to bring out the selection criteria, the important hierarchies, the criteria for the attribution of meaning that underlie the viewer's look. The question we ask is: what directs his/her attention already at the level of perception?

The language (and not just the cinema language) tells us much less or much more than we would like: in the language of words the speaker reveals his/her ways of feeling. The language of the cinema enables us to make references to thoughts and therefore to think, it invites us to experience our experience. To think in images is not the same thing as thinking about images. It means thinking thoughts through images, i.e. to stop and think about what is there behind them, about what is not immediately visible and that, in fact, requires additional work in order to be brought to awareness. To think of what our eyes see enables us to think also of what other people see and so to ensure that, for example, an adolescent is able to locate his observation point and to compare it with that of his/her peers. We should be able to help him/her recognize it, support it, secure it so that it will not disappear among the stronger view points of the group (or of the pack). What directs his/her gaze? In other words, what are the codes of interpretation and methods of organization of meanings that underlie and support his/her behavior, his/her educational experience? The way I look at and choose an external experience - more or less similar to mine - is inextricably linked to the way I look at, choose and assess both my professional and personal experience.

Our course can be described as having as its main objective the recognition of social, cognitive representations, of stereotypes and spontaneous philosophies that each of us has internalized, often unconsciously, and that determine the way we interpret the educational action.

The Essential Elements of the Training Course

- The setting: the film is shown to everyone together, for example the entire class, where setting is intended as a framework. In this way the class group is transformed into a group of viewers, and therefore of processors of the images they see

- The students are encouraged and enabled to find crossing paths through a search in the web for literary excerpts, poems, photographs, music, other images that they believe connected with their theme.

- Observation cards are requested to be filled in (individual work and group interviews) so that the students can have a say, can substantiate opinions, thoughts, comments, and can autonomously come into possession again - without anyone "preaching" at them – of the points of view of each one and of their own way of learning.

"Knowing the why" about one's own ways of learning is crucial because not only accounts for the way we perform or feel education both as trainees and as trainers, but it also makes us aware of the intricate connection between the way we educate and the way we were educated. As educators, we should not claim to impose our mentality to that of the student; it is essential to create, implement an active communication and understanding – capable of transformation in its pedagogical essence -, an exchange of experience which does not, however, mean to "put ourselves in the shoes of other people". It is necessary to understand the mental and emotional structures of the other person who is different from us, of his/her "codes of interpretation". Namely, not what my thoughts would be if I were in his/her place, but how I think he/she thinks (access to motivations, needs, vision of the world, experiences of the other person). Given this context, it appears that communicating means creating relationships and ties (Franza, 1988, 1993, 1997).

The cinema is, thus, a pedagogical tool as it carries representative forms in which I recognize my thoughts: I may have learned to recognize my thoughts through an image and feel grateful for it, and this is of great cognitive value (in fact, it is possible to name the emotion, the emotion as a language and also the language of emotions).

Working on a film also meets an important need of the students to interpret events. We could actually define a real struggle the one that is being thus waged on the contrast with the eternal present, the extended and a-historical time in which the younger generations are immersed and relegated.

How is an event interpreted? On which basis, on which foundations do we make interpretations? This is the point on which it is important to dwell today.

Educating can, therefore, be considered either as a device, a mechanism, some technological equipment and an institutional framework contained within borders, whose effects we can control with precision, or as a place where experience takes place and wants to be interpreted in every single moment while in progress. School is culture, but scholastic culture is not that of the curricula; it is rather the creation of a universe of symbolic and cultural exchanges.

THE "SCHOOL-CINEMA" PROJECT: HUMANISTIC CULTURE AND NEW MEDIA

The Educational Approach

The theoretical structure underlying, in particular, the choice of the pedagogical device that we are going to illustrate refers both to studies and research on classical pedagogy, with special reference to the issue of the importance of people's needs to develop projects – intended as a typical need to learn things in depth – and reference also to the most recent contributions of the *Clinica della Formazione.*

The *Clinica della Formazione* (R. Massa[7], A. M. Franza), is a training device designed to favor thought and clinical judgment about both teaching techniques and relational strategies, which play an extremely important role during teaching / learning activities. The Clinic of training is an important methodological innovation both in terms of teaching techniques and in terms of training settings. It uses and increases the emotional, communicative and relational dimensions of the people involved and it engages them in research and study work both of the individual and the group. It is thanks to Riccardo Massa and Angelo M. Franza's studies and research and to the common experiments carried out over a period of about ten years that the clinic of training has entered the pedagogical vocabulary

Clinica della Formazione means[8]:

- Designing and sharing the research on the fundamental elements, the processes and devices for the training of individuals and groups of individuals in accordance with the organization and cognitive modes typical of the clinical method: interpersonal relationship based on a shared commitment to truth, which involves the observer in the relationship observed; an experience of looking and listening where the observer's questioning attention to the observed person is open both to his/her own experience as well as the other's
- A mode of exploration and experimentation carried out individually and in groups that focuses on achieving knowledge and learning from experience and through experience
- A program that - in the form of small groups and based on the guidelines, the mandates, the procedures suggested by one or more trainers - accompanies the participants in the exploration and development of concrete events, presented in the form of reports or narratives in order to be able to take possession of them again and relocate them in contexts of reference (personal, collective, professional and institutional) by analyzing them and reconstructing their overall meaning through the use of the art of interpretation.

The basic pedagogical idea of the "School-cinema" project is also characterized by a constant search for the relationship between different aspects of educational problems, which are briefly mentioned here below:

As for the pedagogical consideration of the type of medium used, which should be exciting and fun, reference is made to John Locke (1693)[9], who argued the importance that teaching should be pleasant, and to Jean-Jacques Rousseau (1762)[10], the forerunner of the functionalist approach to interest, but above all to Johann Friedrich Herbart (1809)[11], who placed interest as the focal point and foundation of the entire training process.

The fragmentation of the film viewing experience and its symbolic "cooling down" are based on the pedagogical ideal of Jerome Bruner (1966)[12] who, in his cognitive theory of education[7], intends culture as an organism, conceptual technology, possession of heuristic "keys" and as skills of language training.

The obvious connection with philosophy refers to the renewed existentialism implicit in the concepts of critical deconstruction, by contemporary philosophy, of any claimed foundations of stability, of doctrinal certainty of knowledge. A reference to pedagogical structuralism, too, which assigns an important role to symbolic and material latent dimensions, contributing to open the epistemology of human sciences to new problems and solutions.

However, the most important contribution is certainly offered by the studies of Riccardo Massa, who sees education as a functional, but above all planning, device, which makes possible the encounter between different dimensions of existence:

… With regard to training seen as an individual novel, as an event and as an educational adventure fundamentally marked by frequent processes of socialization and acquisition of culture, it deals with the vital and existential meaning of training better rooted, even more than in psychoanalysis and social sciences, in the great artistic, philosophical and literary productions, or in many parts of the current cinematic representation.[13]

The New Technologies in Schools: Towards a Culture of Images and Imagination

The simple introduction of new technologies inside and outside the school and their spreading cannot in itself be called an innovative fact, nor can it be associated with the improvement of didactics, or with the quality of our lives in general. What matters more and more is the quality of their use and not the intensity. This encourages - and does not limit, as it may happen if "left alone" - a different way of thinking and improves the quality of interactions between people. Living the dimension of images and of imagination in an appropriate manner allows to capitalize on the cultural heritage they carry, thus producing new knowledge, an essential element if we are to build good practices fundamental not only for knowledge, but also for acting, with a suggesting and, at the same time planning, meaning. New technologies have the great merit of drawing ways and worlds closer (and not just physical worlds, but also vital worlds), which, before their introduction, were hardly compatible. In this sense we could certainly welcome Montesquieu's invitation, as reported by Tzvetan Todorov, to the creation of a "well-calibrated Humanism", able to implement a system of shared models, methodologies, actions capable of enhancing and processing our time: "Personal life, social and cultural life and moral life should neither be suppressed nor replace one another; the human being is manifold and unifying it would be like mutilating it" (Todorov, 1991)[14].

This recollection to humanistic culture is not certainly meant to propose again methods and models that were applied in very different contexts from the point of view both of contents and of useful knowledge in a distant past, but to develop tools and methods capable, inside the intricacy that characterizes new contexts, to implement complex "narrative identities", to identify and enhance the creative and design abilities of each person, without which technological tools would loose their value as crucial function when facing the challenges of our times. A critical mind is needed in order to live serenely the experience of the phenomena that the spreading of images and of the virtual world inevitably implies. Within this context, the school has the opportunity to play a role in the creation of a new culture of images and of imagination in an intermedial sense, i.e. where virtual and real aspects interact, so that the relationship with technology may be taken into the consideration it deserves and its most reductive, when not disfunctional, use should be overcome. In practice, the relationship with the new media has an impact that deeply affects how we interpret interpersonal relationships and the very meaning of educating.

For the Use of the Educational Potential of ICT

In the *National Plan for Digital School* (PNSD), fundamental pillar of The Good School (Law 107/2015), clear reference is made to digital education in the school that relies not only on the technological dimension, but also, and above all, on the epistemological and cultural dimensions of the new media, a central point in the development of younger generations (Buckingham, 2003, It. tr. 2006; Rivoltella, 2006a, 2006b; Willet, 2009; Livingstone, 2011; Premazzi, 2010). Many studies have made possible to interpret the new technologies in the educational field as resources to improve students' ability to better understand themselves and the world around them (McLoughlin, Lee, 2008; Macedo, Steinberg, 2007; Maragliano, 2000, 2004; Rivoltella, 2003, 2006; Ardizzone, Rivoltella, 2008; Mantovani, Ferri, 2008; Drusian, Riva, 2010). In this scenario, the entry of new technologies into the school can be an asset not only from a technical point of view, but also from a methodological one and for the awareness of the new way of thinking (and not just the educational fact) that they convey, thus contributing to the construction of new identities, placed within the relationship between image and representation, between narrative and new cultural and social models (Mottana, 2002; Dallari, 2008). In this sense technology can function as a "professional organizer" (Rivoltella, 2014) useful to raise fundamental questions about the professional role of teachers and capable to create a useful environment to convey contents, tools and techniques to one's pupils effectively and not to become, as it is happening now, a reason for creating distances, or even erecting real barriers between teachers and students. The generation gap is now an established fact - although many teachers don't always recognize it as a problem – and it is present not only between teacher and students, but also among the teachers themselves, when a significant difference in age occurs, and among learners, too, as argued by Mark Prensky (2001). The gap is especially evident from the cultural point of view, in cognitive models and socio-cultural variables (Rivoltella, 2012 b), even when it does not materialize in the problem of the digital divide between "natives" and "immigrants". The issue is to promote digital wisdom (Prensky, 2009). Martha Nussbaum (2010) insists on the concept of the recovery of thinking and imagination skills that make us human beings and states that this educational commitment closely concerns the web, too: it is important to make young people aware and capable of contextualizing the space-time relationship within an extended space. Such step requires work on the self, the growing of an inner "confabulation" and therefore the transition from extimacy practices to intimacy practices, where also the emotional world may be seen as an important component (Siegel, 1999). This takes us to a series of considerations concerning not only the nature of the entry of technologies in the school, but also in the work and vital experiences of each person.

Today, when speaking of "Digital Humanism" (Dominici, 2014), it is certainly not in order to reintroduce educational methods, styles and contents of the past, or to mortify or undo what can actually be called educational contents and educational knowledge gained outside it. It is, in fact, in order to open multimedia windows possessing the characteristics both of complex narrative forms, useful to develop well-connected "narrative identities", and of the powers of creativity and planning, i.e. a window of skills without which technological tools can be of little help to face the cognitive and application challenges of our times in an intelligent way. The urgent need for the development of critical thinking should not be neglected; a "new *forma mentis*" (a new mindset) to understand the teaching-learning process "(Rivoltella, 2006a).[15]

FROM PROJECT TO ITS REALIZATION: THE STRUCTURE OF THE PROJECT

School-cinema is a training methodology inspired by the *Clinica della Formazione* and focused on special work on images taken from the cinema – intended as a language of symbols and privileged place of learning – and on the use of new technologies as tools for processing images and the imaginary world at school. The device allows and encourages common considerations and reflections starting from the identification of the educational opportunities of the cinema and of the ones offered by the device. Given the role that the imaginary and the virtual world plays inside and outside the school in the construction of a "fragmented" knowledge, it was decided to work right on it to uncover its implications, opportunities as well as its risks. The hypothesis is that a fragment of a film or a video can be associated with the fragmentation of the contemporary world, where events no longer appear to be characterized by linear consistency or natural rhythms, but by systemic relations and a different concept of time and that such fragmented reality should be pieced back together starting right from its fragments.

Some films and novels lend themselves particularly well to a "disassembly" task of the original piece in order to build a new work focused on educational issues. Using the new media, some films and videos have been disassembled and then reassembled with the goal to work out analysis and synthesis in an almost simultaneous manner. The analysis is meant to identify those parts of the work from which new sequences and paths, different from the original work, can be created by the participants in order to face complex issues, which are relevant to them, in an innovative way. In practice, this means to transform the work group into a group of developers of images, by showing film materials selected in relation to the issues to be studied or addressed. This film product is "broken" into meaningful sequences which are then reassembled to become a completely new and original video. In it the assembled fragments and quotations – i.e. images condensed into concepts – will be captured and analyzed for their evocative meaning, beyond the narrative of the original plot, thus allowing to grasp their meaningful depth. The issues at stake go from a level of verbal sharing to a deeper level, both emotional and intuitive, which necessarily comes into play when we watch a film, but also and above all when we have to work on its images to make a new film, the result of further processing. Emotiveness, images from memory and dreams all cooperate in the choice and selection of the images, in their composition and understanding.

In particular, the choice of using the technique of disassembling and assembling the images is relative to the type of the cognitive mode typical of our contemporary world, where systematic linear thinking is being replaced by the analogical thinking in the web. Awareness of one's desires (looking inside oneself), opportunities to express them and to encounter with the others (look outside oneself), are sequences interweaved in a virtual exchange of perspectives, close-ups and backdrops in the light of a different mode of reflection.

Once disassembled, the sequences are analyzed and then reassembled in a work group in which the participants are engaged in the construction of a shared logic. This makes it possible to collect data about the representations, i.e. the subcultures, and the role representations. At the same time, it allows to see and/or to experience a given situation, even when critical, to understand which elements should be taken into account in order to bring about changes, to give ideas on potential growth factors of people, stimulating their imagination and creativity so as to encourage the development of skills which enable to re-process one's own reality in an active and conscious way. Knowing the origin of a sequence, its culture, which process of symbolism is used allows to reunify the dichotomy between reality and imagination through the feedback of the reassembly following slow, in-depth and shared reading of the mode of interpreting events.

In general, the project is addressed both to teachers and students, with different goals and objectives, but it is overall aimed at promoting dialogue within the school context and sharing within the various disciplinary perspectives, helping to improve transversal skills, which are often considered marginal where teaching is still more oriented towards contents than skills. The teachers found of great interest the focus on networking and use of educational technologies, so as to facilitate a move towards more and more pervasive social innovation, and also on the concept of meaningful learning as "active" (Spinelli, 2009) and on the fact of being called "to experience" on themselves, i.e. firsthand, the feeling of sharing and of meaningful learning through the use of electronic devices. This would later result in the application of the methodology in the classroom during the daily educational activity.

The Film as the Result of Group Work

"School-cinema" allows to study a "creative grammar" which is not the same as a communicative grammar, although they are close to each other. Like a detective story, the cinema has its own language, made of rules, cages, boundaries, codes. Only within these boundaries a creative gesture can be born, a meaning can be grasped and transmitted. To make a film it is necessary to set in motion a true (just because conventional) self-narration, the one that becomes physical/cinematographic action and finds its natural expression in the scene narrated by other spaces and other times, at a different rhythm. Shared symbolization becomes matter for new and closer symbolizations, which come nearer and nearer to the stories experienced by the participants in reality, in which the symbolic, but not its "explanation" or flattening, grows.

Also the act of educating cannot be considered related to the learning of rules and/or notions simply juxtaposed to each other, neatly selected and appropriately reorganized, as it is essentially constructed inside a communicative and relational practice of the experience between people, space, time in an environment that has all the characteristics of a complex, dynamic system, rich in differences. The educational rationality has a form, but this is not given once and for all, it is not given for granted. Likewise the film produced by the group, the result of team work, regardless of its quality, is in a relationship and refers to elements related to the experience of the people involved, experience intended in almost absolute and radical sense, not reduced to a single, definitive meaning: when a person tries to solve the problem, it turns out the game fails. Working on a film is like investigating in the bowels of our historic feeling. To make a film together is, in fact, a way to create a dialogue among film images that have their own history and their own reference context, that become a source of inspiration for the construction of other films, which can greatly and deeply differ from the original one and become the individual and collective expression of identities, that is by telling a new story open to new shared meanings, offering a way to awaken memory.

Even teachers become involved in a series of group activities where participants produce a number of film scripts that refer simultaneously to the filmic representation, analyzed from the historical or cultural point of view, and to professional experience, later translated into short movies. This makes it possible to combine different educational objectives, i.e. those relating to the ability to build a team, those strictly didactic and the communicative ones, at the same time keeping in mind the number of different recipients and thus their specificities, which will guide the selection of films and narrative texts to work on. Other applications include the development of communication programs with families or the construction of tools to evaluate competence and transversal skills.

Educational Objectives of the Path

- Experimental introduction of a new and different teaching methodology - integrating the traditional methodology - able to provide for and organize a direct involvement of the students within the class or the interclass group, associated to their interests and leading to the promotion of the expression of the self.
- Attempt to leave the traditional pattern of the lesson by means of a process that stimulates curiosity and interest through the involvement of the students in a concrete initiative aiming at the creation/production of an "artistic", or anyhow original, result.
- Teaching to decentralize the impulsiveness of the students, especially in difficult situations from the emotional point of view, through the construction of a cinematographic product that can "guide" the plot of the narrated stories to learn how to move around in their space and time and thus increase the feeling of effectiveness and self-esteem

Didactic Organization and Stages of the Training Program

The course had a total duration of 68 hours over a period of about six months of the school year 2008-2009. It involved 48 teachers and 50 students from five schools including Primary schools and Secondary Junior school (see Table 1).

The didactic organization provided for spreading of the work over two different modules, repeated by two groups of teachers and in two classes of students. Each module consisted of 6 meetings, each lasting on average three hours. The schedule of the meetings included a first stage of presentation and training on reading the cinematic language and on technical programs for film editing, a second stage in which both groups watched two films together and were then invited to make a first selection of sequences and express their first reflections, a third stage consisting of working in subgroups preparing the actual editing of the film product with the help of an expert[16]. A first meeting with the students' parents was planned to foster dialogue and sharing with the families and to favor a climate of good cooperation. A subsequent plenary meeting was held at the end of the course with all the students, teachers and parents at the screening of the materials produced and as an opportunity to exchange the considerations emerged during the process.

Let's now explain in detail how the training course was developed focusing on some of the critical issues that affected both the stage of the course addressed to the teachers and the one addressed to the students of the classes involved in the process.

Table 1.

	Primary Schools	Secondary Junior School
Number of teachers	25	23
Number of students	25	25
Duration	34 hours	34 hours

School-Cinema: "The Teacher and the Pupil"

Objectives for Teachers

- The relationship between technology, learning and teacher training
- How to foster good communication within the school system through the use of technologies
- The school as a place useful to process the impact of the world of technology experienced by young students inside and outside the school

During the course the teachers were elicited to review both the teaching practices distinctive of each one's professionalism and the precomprehensions, pedagogical ideas, training methods to which they had been exposed. All these elements have a deep, but often undetected, effect on daily practice.

Afterwards it was a question of learning how to use new environments of learning through the realization of a product resulting from a combination of analysis/comments/ documentation - such as a photographic path or a path involving drawing, filming, processing printed materials, interpretation of music (original or existing) – working from film materials and inserting images, photos, videos, music taken from Web sites.

The training system was reshaped and revised on the basis of the needs expressed by the trainees. An interesting feature to be noted relative to the changes made by almost all the sub-groups when it came to translate the material described in the script into a film is the following: the expected sequence, its editing and music were changed "on the field ", i.e. the changes were made on the basis of the result achieved while work was in progress. The association with the term "improvisation", in this case, appears to be pertaining, in a strictly and exquisitely pedagogical sense. On this occasion the teachers were able to rediscover the same relationship between creation and implementation of ideas, i.e. to investigate the same differential ratio existing between continuity and discontinuity, form and backdrop, while working on multiple levels simultaneously: that of previously shared meanings, those that emerged while assembling the film, the abstract level of notions, the graphic one of forms and the narrative level of language. They lived the experience of "seeing" that is also "thinking". In this tangle of visual and conceptual aspects there is a tangle of thought and imagination and it is "here [that] many of our concepts intersect" (Wittgenstein, 1967, *Ricerche filosofiche,* p. 278).

Given the great number of teachers two work groups were formed, each focused on the objective to think about the theme "The teacher and the pupil", i.e. on the asymmetry that makes up each educational relationship.

An Example of the First Stage of the Course for Teachers

Table 2 outlines the most significant moments.

Main Activities

- Film Screening
- Filling in the questionnaire

Table 2.

Working stages	Main contents	Key steps	Materials / tools
Stage 1 First meeting	Presentation of the course and methodology Presentation of the films	The theme (the relationship between technology and learning) and the purpose (development of communication skills and group skills inside the school between teachers and learners) is shared	Film material
Second meeting	1. Lecture on film language Main contents: Communication through images: Training in disassembly and assembly of representations Perspective and polyphony in narrative analysis 2. Screening of a film 3. Training on the use of the editing program	The film material (a film or single sequences) presented gives a general view of the different approaches to the topic in question and it fits the characteristic of the viewers. The questionnaire is filled in and the film material is discussed	Film material Observation cards PC with audio and video editing programs

- Group work on:
  - Processes of interpretation-translation of film events and film narratives
  - Overall representations based on the cultural meanings under study
  - Images, analogies and metaphors expressed
  - Attributions, inferences and theoretical models of reference
  - Investigation into the affective sphere - fantasies, emotions, desires, feelings
  - Dynamics of transference and identification
- Selection and reassembly of the significant sequences
- Production of a new film product:
  - Production of new narratives with new meanings from the fragmentation of the sequences and their reassembly
- Plenary presentation of group works:
  - Emergence of meanings and creation of concepts useful to the management of one's individual and professional development Presentation of the group works
- Feed-back and comments
- Concluding remarks

School-Cinema: "Playing with the Film"

Objectives for the Students

- Development of the ability/possibility to substantiate impressions and judgments through stories, reasoning and discussions, too
- To experience the change from "class group" to "audience group" and then of developers, a situation in which the "usual dynamics" may give way to new chances of encounter
- To experience a different way of using new technologies, a better targeted and more responsible use that favors the development of a critical thinking and autonomy.

The second module was attended by students from two classes of a Secondary Junior School and focused on the objective of having the students work on their relationship with the school and with the term "education" in general, so that opinions, difficulties, problems that interested or troubled them could emerge, and, at the same time, they could experience a different way of working in groups, sharing solutions and suggestions among themselves and with the teachers, too.

First we showed the narrative material, made up of film clips, then we invited the class to engage individually in answering the questionnaire about the sequences "first hand", i.e. immediately after the screening. After that the students were divided into work groups, they shared the individual work they had done, and wrote the script sharing as much information as possible. Some instructions on editing techniques and some work with a technical expert made it possible for each small group to create the film product desired by assembling the sequences selected.

An Example of the First Stage of the Course for Students

The following are the main activities for each work stage (Table 3).

Table 3. The following are the main activities for each work stage

Working stages	Main contents	Key steps	Materials/ tools
Stage 1 First meeting	Presentation of the course: "Playing with the film" Lesson on the cinematic language Screening of a film Training on the use of the editing program	The lesson focused on the game aspects of the work on film images: "Today we will play at being "detective spectators". We will act as if the film were a story, a painting, a photograph: what does it say? What is there? What happens?" Film material constructed by assembling film sequences particularly meaningful and of different emotional tone, chosen in relation to the various issues pertaining to the relationship of the students with the school experience as a whole	Film material PC with an editing program
Second meeting	Filling in of the questionnaire and comments on the film are made	Individual "reading" of the sequences to help the students find tracks carrying shared meaning ("what story are we telling?) and learn to find their bearings both when reading / listening and when processing the experience perceived and lived, which is then expresses	Observation cards Tablet PC with programs of audio and video editing program of processing image graphics Web to search for images, texts and music
Main Activities: Group work • Filling in the questionnaire and writing the script • Selection and editing of significant sequences and sharing the "reading" • Production of a new film			
• Reassembly of the selected sequences to make a "new story", with its own thread, or to make a succession of sequences that well represent moods, thoughts, attitudes, and opinions expressed both after watching the film and during the selection of the images to achieve a new film product, which is the result of the group work			
• Presentation of the works to teachers and parents in a plenary session: each group presents its film and tells the genesis, answers questions and any possible "criticism".			

The Meeting to Present the Course to the Students' Parents

To promote a good dialogue with the students' parents, it was decided to organize a meeting to present the course. In it we tried to expand the issue to a broader context of educational approaches focused on the activation of thoughtful behaviors that could be understood and shared in the family. The parents were fully informed on the exploratory objectives and on the use of narratives (in our case both in writing and through pictures), that is materials, texts from which to obtain representations, emotions, implicit and explicit judgments. This open attempt by the school to seek a dialogue and sharing with the families resulted in the creation of a good climate of cooperation, which meant that the students, supported by their parents, could face this new way of working in the classroom with images - and on images - in an entertaining and light way as well as enjoying it.

In addition, the meeting was followed by a brief lecture on the topic of adolescence, focused on historical, social and psychological aspects, in order to place the present situation in a broader context of problems related to contemporary issues (fragmentation, new questions, youth culture, the spreading of risk acceptability). The lecture was then followed by a discussion on the consequences of the phenomenon of reversibility of choices in the younger generations with the associated risk of changing a disvalue into a value (bullying). All topics were useful to stimulate in the parents a critical and conscious approach to the objectives that prompted this project as a whole.

CONCLUSION

During the entire course both teachers and students were allowed to express themselves and bring out the problems they felt. It was, therefore, an exploratory operation carried out both by the individual person and the group and group/class that favored the development of a reflexive dimension, recognized as a decisive factor.

The teachers involved were elicited to value practical knowledge and to modify their teaching method, trying to engage the students more, also through the subsequent reproducibility of the methodology in the classroom – after having experimented it on themselves – by applying it to different issues and allowing the students to play the role of main characters by including audio and video materials and images in the educational activity. It is interesting to underline the focus on the teaching action and on how it changes through technology also from the point of view of the setting. The construction of the products, as the result of the program of sharing in the groups, has been regarded by the teachers as vital from a meta-reflexive point of view, since it has favored the sharing of knowledge and the recognition of the importance of the reflexive dimension and group research.

As for the students, a general focus emerged on the pleasure of expressing themselves and also on the pleasure of acquiring the skill to communicate through images in groups, in the class-group and among the various groups in the classroom.

Construction activities where the group could better express itself were favored, so that the good and the beautiful could emerge, which otherwise would not have had a voice. This helped the students to acquire new tools useful for learning how to work together. In addition, it was also a question of discovering new ways to use electronic tools, so that to learn how to analyze the contents of communication and, through activities of sharing meanings, promote dialogue and exchange, as a resource for interdisciplinary discussion aimed at developing transversal skills, citizenship and, later on, skills specific to a discipline, which converge in and participate to the development of the first skills, through the development of Learning Units.

By constructing a product - recognized as construction of a message - it was possible to note down "what it says to the young, what it says to parents and what it says to teachers".

In addition to sharing the opening of the work on the objectives and goals and to the presentation of the products taking place at the end of the program, the parents were expected to express comments on what the students had done.

At the end of the program we were able to understand together and to share the overall aim of the course, which is to give every student the opportunity to express opinions, ideas, emotions, criticism, questions and, at the same time, to identify where one's own "observing summit" lies, i.e. one's own point of view on how each student sees the school, one's own condition as student and one's own role as student.

A common general theme has then been identified not only in the final film product but also in the class-group in which every student has had the chance to express one's own particularity and one's own difference.

We hope that the material presented in this chapter and the examples given will be useful both in terms of methodological approach as in terms of possible developments of new models and new practices using the new media to enhance the educational potential and where the cinema becomes a pedagogical tool as bearer of representative forms in which experiences, events and feelings acquire an important cognitive value.

REFERENCES

Ardizzone, P., & Rivoltella, P. C. (2008). *Media e tecnologie per la didattica*. Milano, Italy: Vita e Pensiero.

Borgna, E. (2009). *Le emozioni ferite*. Milano, Italy: Feltrinelli.

Bruner, J. (1966). *Toward a Theory of instruction*. Roma, Italy: Armando Editore.

Buckingham, D. (2003). Media Education: Literacy, Learning and Contemporary Culture. Cambridge, UK: Polity Press.

Buckingham, D., & Willet, R. (Eds.). (2009). *Video Cultures. Media Technology and Everyday Creativity*. London: Palgrave Macmillian.

Canova, G. (Ed.). (2002). *Storia del cinema Italyno 1965-1969* (Vol. 11). Venezia-Roma, Italy: Marsilio Editore.

Cassirer, E. (2009). *Saggio sull'uomo*. Roma, Italy: Armando Editore.

Cerioli, L. (2002). *Funzione educativa e competenze relazionali. Genitori, figli, insegnanti*. Milano, Italy: Franco Angeli.

Charmet, P. G. (2009). *Fragile e spavaldo. Ritratto dell'adolescente di oggi*. Roma-Bari, Italy: Laterza.

D'Incerti, D., Santoro, M., & Varchetta, G. (2007). *Nuovi schermi di formazione*. Milano, Italy: Guerini & Associati.

Dallari, M. (2008). *In una notte di luna vuota. Educare pensieri metaforici, laterali, impertinenti*. Trento, Italy: Erickson.

Dominici, P. (2014). *Dentro la Società Interconnessa. Prospettive etiche per un nuovo ecosistema della comunicazione*. Milano, Italy: Franco Angeli.

Drusian, M., & Riva, C. (Eds.). (2010). *Bricoleur High tech. I giovani e le nuove forme di comunicazione*. Milano, Italy: Guerini & Associati.

Franza, A. M. (1988). *Retorica e metaforica in pedagogia. Milano, Italy: Unicopli- (1993). Giovani satiri e vecchi sileni*. Milano, Italy: Unicopli.

Herbart, J. F. (1809). *La Pedagogia generale derivata dal fine dell'educazione*. Firenze, Italy: La Nuova Italia.

Kangas, K., Seitamaa-Hakkarainen, P., & Hakkarainen, K. (2007). The artifact project: History, science, and design inquiry in technology enhanced learning at elementary level. *Research and Practice in Technology Enhanced Learning*, 2(03), 213–237. doi:10.1142/S1793206807000397

Lakkala, M., Ilomaki, L., & Palonen, T. (2007). Implementing virtual, collaborative inquiry practices in a middle school context. *Behaviour & Information Technology*, 26(1), 37–53. doi:10.1080/01449290600811529

Livingstone, S., Haddon, L., Gorzig, A., & Olafsson, K. (2011). *EU Kids On Line. Final report*. London: London School of Economics.

Locke, J. (1693). *Some Troughts Concerning Education*. Torino, Italy: Utet.

Macedo, D., & Steinberg, S. (Eds.). (2007). *Media Literacy: a reader*. New York: Peter Lang.

Mantovani, S., & Ferri, P. (Eds.). (2008). *Digital Kids. Come i bambini usano il computer e come potrebbero usarlo genitori e insegnanti*. Bologna, Italy: ETAS.

Maragliano, R. (Ed.). (2000). *Tre ipertesti su multimedialità e formazione*. Roma-Bari, Italy: Laterza.

Maragliano, R. (Ed.). (2004). *Pedagogie dell'e-learning*. Roma-Bari, Italy: Laterza.

Massa, R. (1990). La Clinica della formazione. In R. Massa (Ed.), *Istituzioni di pedagogia e scienze della formazione* (pp. 481–583). Roma-Bari, Italy: Laterza.

Massa, R. (1992). *La Clinica della formazione*. Milano, Italy: FrancoAngeli.

Massa, R. (1997). *Cambiare la scuola. Educare o istruire?* Roma, BA, Italy: Laterza.

Massa, R. (2004). *Le tecniche e I corpi verso una scienza dell'educazione*. Milano, Italy: Unicopoli.

Massa, R., & Cerioli, L. (Eds.). (1999). *Sottobanco. Le dimensioni nascoste della vita scolastica*. Milano, Italy: Franco Angeli.

McLoughlin, C., & Lee, M. J. W. (2008). The Three P's of Pedagogy for the Networked Society: Personalization, Partecipation and Productivity. International Journal of Teaching and learning in Higher Education, 20(1), 10-27.

Mottana, P. (1997). *Dissolvenze, le immagini della formazione*. Bologna, Italy: Clueb. - (2003). Clinica della formazione (Voce). In M. Laeng (Ed.), *Enciclopedia pedagogica*. Brescia, Italy: La Scuola.

Mottana, P. (2002). *L'opera dello sguardo. Braci di pedagogia immaginale*. Bergamo, Italy: Moretti & Vitali Editore.

Nussbaum, M. (2010). *Non per profitto. Perché le democrazie hanno bisogno della cultura umanistica*. Bologna, Italy: Il Mulino.

Paquay, L., Altet, M., Charlier, E., & Perrenoud, P. (2001). *Former des ensegnants professionnels*. Bruxelles, Belgique: De Boeck Université.

Parmigiani, D. (2009). *Tecnologie di gruppo. Collaborare in classe con I media*. Trento, Italy: Erickson.

Pietropolli Charmet, G. (2010). *Fragile e spavaldo. Ritratto dell'adolescente di oggi*. Roma, Bari: Laterza.

Premazzi, V. (2010). *L'integrazione online. Nativi e migranti fuori e dentro la rete. Rapporto Fieri*. Torino, Italy: Forum internazionale ed Europeo di Ricerche sull'immigrazione.

Prensky, M. (2001). Digital natives, digital immigrants. *On the Horizon*, 9(5), 1–6. doi:10.1108/10748120110424816

Prensky, M. (2009). H. Sapiens Digital: From Digital Immigrants and Digital Natives to Digital Wisdom. Innovate, 5(3).

Riva, M. G. (2008). *L'insegnante professionista dell'educazione e della formazione*. Pisa, Italy: ETS Edizioni.

Rivoltella, P. C. (Ed.). (2003). *Costruttivismo e pragmatica della comunicazione on-line: socialità e didattica in internet*. Trento, Italy: Erickson.

Rivoltella, P. C. (Ed.). (2006a). *Media Education. Modelli, esperienze, profilo disciplinare*. Roma, Italy: Carocci.

Rivoltella, P. C. (Ed.). (2006b). *Screen Generation. Gli adolescenti e le prospettive dell'educazione nell'età dei media digitali*. Milano, Italy: Vita e Pensiero.

Rivoltella, P. C. (2012a). Bambini, anziani e linguaggi elettronici. InRivoltella, P. C. (Ed.), *Progetto Generazioni. Bambini e anziani: due stagioni della vita a confronto*. Pisa, Italy: ETS Edizioni.

Rivoltella, P. C. (Ed.). (2014a). *Smart Future. Didattica, media digitali e inclusione*. Milano, Italy: Franco Angeli.

Rivoltella, P. C. (Ed.). (2014b). Tecnologie digitali e management scolastico. Autonomia e dirigenza, 23.

Rousseau, J. J. (1762). Emile ou De L'éducation. In *Opere*. Firenze, Italy: Sansoni.

Siegel, D. J. (1999). *La mente relazionale. Neurobiologia dell'esperienza interpersonale*. Milano, Italy: Raffaello Cortina Editore.

Sini, C. (2000). Idoli della conoscenza. Torino, Italy: Raffaello Cortina Ed.

Spinelli, A. (2009). *Un'officina di uomini. La scuola del costruttivismo*. Napoli, Italy: Liguori.

Tamburini, D. (2010). Linguaggio cinematografico e comunicazione formativa. In *Adolescenti e media: cinema, televisione e ruolo della scuola*. Milano, Italy: Centro Filippo Buonarroti.

Todorov, T. (1989). *Nous et les autres. La réflextion francaise sur la diversité humaine*. Torino, Italy: Edizioni Paperbacks Sienze sociali, Einaudi.

Ugazio, V. (2012). *Storie permesse, storie proibite. Polarità semantiche familiari e psicopatologie. Nuova edizione ampliata, aggiornata e rivista*. Torino, Italy: Bollati Boringhieri.

Wittgenstein, L. (1967). Ricerche filosofiche. Torino, Italy: Einaudi.

ADDITIONAL READING

Ardizzone, P., & Rivoltella, P. C. (2003). *Didattiche per l'e-learning*. Roma, Italy: Carocci.

Barone, P. (1997). *La materialità educativa. L'orizzonte materialista dell'epistemologia pedagogica e la clinica della formazione*. Milano, Italy: Unicopoli.

Battacchi, M. W., & Codispoti, O. (1992). *La vergogna. Saggio di psicologia dinamica e clinica*. Bologna, Italy: Il Mulino.

Bevilacqua, B. (2011). Apprendimento significativo mediato dalle tecnologie. In Rivista scuola IAD, 4 (4), 138-171.

Dallari, M. (2012). *Testi in testa. Parole e immagini per educare conoscenze e competenze narrative*. Trento, Italy: Erikson.

Dewey, J. (1938). *Experience and Education. (trad. it.). (1963) Esperienza e educazione*. Firenze, Italy: La Nuova Italia.

Franza, A. M. (2004). Il clinico della formazione Una riflessione sulla comune esperienza di Clinica della formazione. In A. Rezzara (Ed.), *Dalla scienza pedagogica alla clinica della formazione. Sul pensiero e l'opera di Riccardo Massa* (pp. 91–113). Milano, Italy: FrancoAngeli.

Gargani, A. G. (2008). *Il linguaggio davanti alla poesia*. Bergamo, Italy: Morelli & Vitali.

Maragliano, R. (Ed.). (2004). *Pedagogie dell'e-learning. Roma-Bari, Italy: Laterza- (2000). Tre ipertesti su multimedialità e formazione*. Roma-Bari, Italy: Laterza.

Massa, R. (1975). *La scienza pedagogica. Epistemologia e metodo formativo. Firenze, Italy: La Nuova Italia. - (1987). Educare o istruire? La fine della pedagogia nella cultura contemporanea. Milano, Italy: Unicopoli. - (2004). Le tecniche e I corpi verso una scienza dell'educazione*. Milano, Italy: Unicopoli.

Napolitani, D. (2006). *Individualità e gruppalità*. Milano, Italy: Ipoc Editore.

Rezzara, A. (2004). Il percorso di clinica della formazione: sguardi sull'esperienza e immagini della formazione. In A. Rezzara & S. Ulivieri Stiozzi (Eds.), *Formazione clinica e sviluppo delle risorse umane* (pp. 29–62). Milano, Italy: FrancoAngeli.

Riva, M. G. (2000). *Studio "clinico" sulla formazione*. Milano, Italy: FrancoAngeli.

Rivoltella, P. C., & Modenini, M. (Eds.). (2012). la lavagna sul comodino. Milano, Italy: Vita&Pensiero.

Rondolino, G., & Tomasi, D. (2011). *Manuale del film*. Torino, Italy: Ed UTET Università.

Sini, C. (2000). Idoli della conoscenza. Torino, Italy: Raffaello Cortina Ed.

Spinelli, A. (2009). *Un'officina di uomini. La scuola del costruttivismo*. Napoli, Italy: Liguori.

Tamburini, D. (2010). Cinema e formazione. Il film come strumento di riflessione. In *Adolescenti e media: cinema, televisione e ruolo della scuola* (pp. 99–120). Milano, Italy: Centro Filippo Buonarroti.

Tamburini, D. (2013). Dars, un'esperienza di teatro a scuola. In (Ed.). Antonacci, F., Guerra, M., Mancino, E. Dietro le quinte. Pratiche e teorie nell'incontro tra educazione e teatro. Milano, Italy: FrancoAngeli, pp. 155-164.

KEY TERMS AND DEFINITIONS

"Clinica Della Formazione": It is both an approach to qualitative and empirical research as well as a training device that aims at an in-depth investigation of education and training in their more or less obvious manifestations.

Method: There are two meanings to this term: one refers to pre-defined modes of action, which are specific and coded, while the other includes the strategies of communication, organization and relationship that teachers implement when teaching.

Intermedial: The term comes from Fluxus, the neo-Dada movement, and it indicates the ability to produce texts that reconcile sensory experiences and conceptuality, through the application of technology to classical languages.

Interpretation: It refers both to the possible differences in the meaning and significance that can be assigned to an image, and to the various modes in which a thought, an idea, an experience are expressed through it.

Fragmentation: The hypothesis on which we have worked is that a fragment of a film can be associated with the fragmentation of the contemporary world - where events no longer seem to be characterized by linear consequentiality or natural rhythms, but by systemic relations and a different conception of time - and that the reality thus fragmented can be pieced right back together starting from its fragmentation.

Disassembling and Assembling: Starting from a film in its entireness and integrity only some sequences are taken out. They are later assembled together in a sequence different from the original film, thus modifying the connection image-meaning.

Observing Summit: It means the point of view from which each of us starts to interpret events. In the case of adolescents it is important to ensure that they are able to identify, define precisely and differentiate their observation summit in order not to confuse it with that of the group, especially when bullying occurs.

ENDNOTES

[1] Angelo M. Franza has taught Psychopedagogy of Communication and Language, Pedagogy and Methodology of Pedagogical Research at the Faculty of Psychology of the University of Bologna. He is a member of the Fondazione Alma Mater of the University of Bologna. He has studied the relationship between psychology and pedagogy in relation to language and phenomenology. He has developed the Clinica della Formazione as a method of research as well as a method of operational intervention. He is also the author of several books and has published several articles in Italian and foreign scientific reviews. He directed the Master of *Sviluppo delle Competenze Cliniche nelle Professioni Educative e Formative (*Development of Clinical Competence in Educational and Training Professions*)* at the Università Degli Studi of Milan and of Milan-Bicocca from 1997 to 2003. He designed the Master of *Clinica della Formazione* and has directed it since 2003 at the Provincia Autonoma of Bolzano. He designs and directs programs of the *Clinica della Formazione* and programs of pedagogical supervision in Master's degrees at universities and private and public institutions, such as the Master of "Models and Methods of Tutorship in the Training of Health Workers" at the University of Verona and at the Scuola Superiore Formazione Sanitaria of Trento, Ospedale S. Anna of Turin, Collegio IPASVI Bologna, Ospedale Maggiore and Ospedale S. Orsola of Bologna.

[2] "Coma" is a 1978 suspense film directed by Michael Crichton based on the 1977 novel of the same by Robin Cook.

[3] Massa, R. (1997). *Cambiare la scuola,* p. 87.

[4] Borgna, E. (2009). *Le emozioni ferite,* p. 23.

[5] Gianni Canova is Professor of History of the Cinema and Filmology, Pro-rector at Communication, events and relationship with cultural institutions and Dean of the Faculty of Communication, Public Relations and Pubblicity at the Libera Università IULM of Milan.

[6] Cassier, E. (2009), *Saggio sull'uomo,* p. 80.

[7] After being Director of the Institute of Pedagogy of the Università Degli Studi of Milan, Riccardo Massa has designed and created the Faculty of Science of Education in the new Università Degli Studi of Milan-Bicocca. He has also been a Senior Fellow in the School of Education at the University of Michigan and the University of California and a member of the scientific committees of different research organizations and specialized journals of international standing. He has also written theoretical studies that have renewed the epistemological profile of pedagogy, in a materialist and structuralist perspective.

[8] See Franza A.M.(2003) under "Clinica della Formazione", in Enciclopedia pedagogica, agg. 2000, La Scuola, Brescia

[9]   In *Some Thoughts Concerning Education*, J. Locke (1632-1704) supports the need for individualized and pleasurable teaching, based on habits and trends

[10]   Rousseau, J. J. (1712-1778) postulates that learning derives from a child's real needs, requirements and demands (e.g. the famous lesson of geography)

[11]   Herbart, E. (1776-1841): Interest is to be regarded as the psychological foundation of the entire educational and training process whose goal is the attainment of virtue. To Herbart, interest is a spontaneous activity, but it has to be guided. Representations are defined as evoked representations (following learning) and freely emerging representations (produced by imagination and game). In this sense, Herbart insists on the education method and on the progression from attention to perception, in which interest is to be considered as the outcome.

[12]   Bruner, J. (structuralist current): He offers a more careful calibration of interest in the sense of a greater connection to inner motivations rather than to external ones (esteem, success, prestige, goodwill from the teacher), in which the learner is guided towards interest in knowledge as such.

[13]   Massa, R. *La clinica della formazione*, p. 17.

[14]   Todorov, T. *Noi e gli altri. La riflessione francese sulla diversità umana*, p. 464.

[15]   Rivoltella, P. C. (2006a). *Media Education. Modelli, esperienze, profilo disciplinare*. p. 74

[16]   Dario D'Incerti works in the production of audiovisual material for advertising, institutional and educational use. He also offers consultancy services in the field of films and research studies on the relationship between the cinema and education. On this subject he has published a number of articles in magazines such as Pluriverso, Adultità, Primapersona, For, and the volumes Schermi di formazione (Guerini e Associati, 2000) and Nuovi schemi di formazione (Guerini e Associati, 2007)

APPENDIX: SOME POSSIBLE APPLICATIONS IN OTHER EDUCATIONAL AND TRAINING FIELDS

This concise report intends to describe some models of applications of the methodology "School-cinema" that may interest other educational and training areas both as a suggestion and at the same time as an innovative tool and research experience. It consists in the construction of models of application according to different targets, where each relates to different training whose key elements are illustrated.

1. Training-Cinema-Work to Improve the Communicative Exchange Between Vocational Training, Universities and the World of Work

The goal of the project is to find meeting points between the needs of the labor market, the vocational training and the university system, promoting links and integration between these different worlds.

Today, the new trend in training, educational, school and vocational programs is to privilege different forms of integration between typical training/educational moments and work moments, in the attempt to improve communication between different worlds, to identify and know the most typical rationale of the corporate world, on the one hand, and the ways of thinking of young students, on the other.

1.1 Main Objectives

- To encourage the exchange of information and materials between vocational training, universities and companies engaged in the common research for techniques to develop new and more productive forms of integration between different realities
- To guide reflections on the relationship between the knowledge provided in education, practical activities, the experiences related to them and the opportunities to develop skills appropriate to the requirements of the world of production
- To raise awareness to the issue of the alternation school-work in a proactive and constructive way
- To establish an observatory to monitor and act on the chance of the relationship between companies and the world of the school
- To favor an analysis of the universe of representations that young people participating in training programs (vocational or university) have of the world of work, which is of great importance to enable them to develop an objective vision of codes, languages and purposes typical of the corporate world.
- To use the language of films, whose images and sequences, once taken apart and reassembled, lend themselves well to the reconstruction of new and original meanings through the creation of films produced in work groups. These films can be tools that help identify the different readings and deformations of the ways of understanding reality in the work place, also and above all from the emotional point of view.

1.2 Main Working Stages

a. Representation of the World of Work (Represented Size)

- Detection of needs/presentation of the course
- Supplying conceptual tools/theoretical assumptions on film language
- Watching the films related to the theme of the world of work
- Construction of the script on the basis of experience related to the films and in particular to the various representations related to the sequences
- Disassembling the sequences and reassembling them to produce a collective film

b. Communication With the World of Work (Social Dimension)

- The sharing of different points of view and the confrontation with the reality of the workplace are achieved through the participation of the young students to moments of communicative exchange in companies, so that they can compare the two representative universes
- The film product is submitted to companies and becomes a moment for sharing opinions on the issue, but also a tool that makes it possible to learn about basic needs, obstacles and opposition experienced by both parties, not least as a function of the internships that the young students will do in the company

c. The Reality of the World of Work (Real Dimension)

- Meeting with the company to present the film and redevelop the contents and ideas suggested
- Proposal for the introduction and planning of future internships
- Experience of the company reality through an internship period of one month in which to check the consistency with reality of what worked out together as a group. The duration of the internship can vary depending on the type of training project involved.

2. Cinema and Universities to Improve the Quality of Communication Between Teachers and Students

2.1 Main Objectives

- To provide innovative tools useful to university teachers to design courses and to create teaching resource materials capable to communicate, even with a large number of students, in an effective way
- To use the cinema as a tool to process experiences and representative forms and use them as a basis for the reconstruction of new sense and meanings of the social, political contemporary reality in its historical development, through the creative use of imagination
- To help young students identify new modes of learning to build autonomous paths of meaning capable to give cognitive value to each learning experience

- To study and codify the transversal skills developed through group works
- To increase interactive communication between teachers and students

2.2 Main Working Stages

a. Film Construction

An in-depth seminar for a group of students on issues of collective interest, in relation to the issues dealt by the teacher in the classroom and agreed on together. It is a way of learning complex concepts and of developing the themes under study in an original way

b. Using of the Film in the Classroom as Teaching Resource Material

The product will prove to be a useful tool for university teachers to design courses and create teaching resource materials suitable to communicate effectively also with large groups of students as it allows to convey even very complex contents

3. Cinema and Literature to Improve Motivation in the Experience of Reading

This project envisages the combined use of literary texts and films: the suggested methodology should make it easier for the students to live the parts and make their own characters and productions starting from the selected narratives, so that to create other narrative worlds, i.e. transformations that change the narrated story.

3.1 Main Objectives

- To use the language of the cinema as a password to reading
- To support motivation to reading, curiosity to know, and the use of books as instruments of knowledge but also as an experience of pleasure, passion, suffering, dream and desire
- To introduce reading in a set of training activities of clinical approach characterized by close reference to concrete and individual realities
- To give voice to young students' representations and experiences through the dialogue between the film world and the world of books, in order to give them back their story
- To recognize, through the cinema, the importance of reading as a social practice
- To experience reading as a way of activating the search for affinities between the unconscious world of representations and the physical reality, which is present in time and space.

3.2 Main Working Stages

a. Disassembly of the book into episodes, images, words. Subsequently they are reassembled and linked to film sequences to create a new narrative sequence, essentially made up of literary passages and film images, open to contributions of different and heterogeneous nature (video music, multimedia images, photographic or audio-visual material)
b. Analysis of the narrative (point of view and polyphony in the analysis of the narrative, inter-text and inter-dialogue in the novel and in the poem)

c.   Watching films that deal with the selected issue

d.   Selection among the titles suggested by publishing houses of the books to work on, followed by the reading

e.   Filling in observation cards relative to narratives, representations, experiences of the films and of the book

f.   Group work and decision-making process to identify the important parts of the film and book to weave together and on which to create the film/narrative product and to identify excerpts from the texts to be inserted in the cinematic sequences

g.   Disassembling and reassembling the sequences on the basis of the script, fixing the narrative film and sequences in a new plot

4. Components of the Network

- Secondary school teachers, university professors and their students
- Team of tutors and experts in film, education and training
- Team for technical support to training and communication system
- External agencies
- Companies

5. Recipients

The first beneficiaries of the project are the following:

- Students and teachers of secondary schools and universities

   The end beneficiaries of the project results are:

- Companies that deal in advertising/communication fields
- Publishing houses sensitive to the problem of the decrease of heavy readers in the school environment
- Companies that, for various and different reasons, are interested in a deeper analysis of the characteristics of youth culture

6. Results Expected

The expected results are as follows:

- Production of film and narrative items to be used both as a tool for an exchange of communication with training agencies and also as a product of the company involved
- Realization of cinematographic products useful for teachers as resource support for lectures
- Building a network of companies, schools, universities and training agencies.
- Drafting of educational projects and job placement projects

- Identification of training programs closely linked to business realities, which become the first promoters of professionalism
- Consolidation of the link between people's needs and companies' needs
- Creating film archives containing all the productions realized, to be shared and spread, and applicable to different educational and training contexts
- Exchange of information on the project with multiplier effect both on the transferability of the methodological and communicative modes as a model of cooperation and on its educational and pedagogical relevance

7. Evaluation and Circulation

Implementation of a plan to monitor and evaluate the project progress is envisaged as follows:

- Monitoring of the communication between companies and the school and between teachers and students in universities. Through different analysis techniques, elements of evaluation will be supplied relative to the different aspects of the interaction between the various components
- Evaluation of the quality of the processes and learning products in progress, with special reference to the planning stages
- Monitoring of the communication will be carried out by an experienced researcher in training
- Evaluation of the educational projects will be supervised by an expert in the methodology of pedagogical research
- Evaluation of the film products will be supervised by a film expert
- All the documents and the materials produced will be made available to manufacturing companies, schools and universities
- Each institution will be able to make public the work carried out through the implementation of educational events
- Meetings will be arranged to circulate the project in collaboration with institutions, associations, local agencies, schools and universities

Chapter 5
Humans Versus Computers, Systems, and Machines:
A Battle for Freedom, Equality, and Democracy

Alan Radley
University College London, UK

ABSTRACT

The present chapter introduces a new existential philosophy of how computers, systems and machines operate within society, and in terms of the provision, furtherance and/or obstruction of human rights/ freedoms and open life-potential(s). We explore the relationship(s) between the design of artificial systems and the existence/form/implementation of democracy; and from the key perspective(s) of individual and collective freedom-of-thought/action. A basic premise is that humans are increasingly disadvantaged as a result of, or slaves to: unfettered automation, objectivity, abstraction and fragmentary thinking; as promulgated/aided by computers/systems/machines. We explain how related processes create conflict/ opposition/barriers to/with natural and harmonious socialization activities/processes; and hence strongly influence our collective destiny.

INTRODUCTION

Background

The nature of human-machine relationship(s) is a central issue in human affairs; and related problems have been debated for hundreds of years. In a great variety of books and papers etc; numerous experts have noted the apparent (and often real) opposition between life and artificial systems. On a phenomenological level, humans and machines are very different. Machines are patently not conscious, do not possess free-will, represent unfettered abstraction (often), manifest universal and objective viewpoint(s), deal with isolated micro-worlds as opposed to the fully integrated embodied human 'big' world, and operate 'everything else being equal'. But things are never equal, because the happenings of life are

DOI: 10.4018/978-1-5225-2616-2.ch005

too rich, varied, and chance-ridden; hence universally saturated with desires, wishes, joy and pain, plus first-person-viewpoints etc.

Accordingly, in this chapter we uphold/defend the humanistic viewpoint. Needed is careful planning, to ensure that humans be the masters—not of each other—but of our machine slaves, and it must not turn out to be the other way around! We postulate a technological society so arranged as to benefit all; and name such a society the Technopia. Introduced are the Theories of Natural and Machine-Implanted Thoughts, founded on standard human rights; which may be implemented in a Techno-rights format to combat rampant mechanization of human life; and provide for the free, open and frictionless sharing of thoughts, ideas, and most importantly, votes.

Terms Introduced: Technopia, Techno-rights, Atomic Network, Theories of Natural and Machine-Implanted Thoughts

As we become ever more involved with, and dependent upon, computers; it may be that our essential nature is being shaped and/or changed as a result. It is prescient therefore to study the nature of an emergent phenomenon; the self as computer (merging of self with computer), and in terms of a deeper, broader and more comprehensive inquiry.

Ergo we can learn: who we were, who we are and who we may become.

This chapter concerns the nature of mankind's relationship(s) to/with machines. Probable is that our survival and ultimate destiny as a species, depends on the development of appropriate technologies (and especially computers). Thus careful planning is essential when it comes to our technological future. To get the ball rolling, we formulate a strategy for an ideal human-computer relationship, and postulate a society so arranged as to benefit all; and we call such a society the technopia. A key feature of the technopia is the establishment of natural human rights (techno-rights) with respect to a technological society; combined with appropriate and human-centric information usage; and so to ensure that machines interact harmoniously with humanity (Wiener, 1950)

Wiener urged us to ask the right questions with respect to machines, and this chapter is an attempt to do the same. Our approach is to find human-centric solutions for the problems of an increasingly computer-centric future. But the future is at the same time marvelous and dreadful, known and unknown. The issues are complex because technological issues are intermingled with social, economic, and environmental ones etc. Yet the stakes are so high, that it is beholden on each writer to make his position known. Paramount, in my view, are three (new) human rights:

- Ownership of one's own thoughts
- Atomic organization of, and free access to, all knowledge
- Open (atomic) publication of ideas/votes

Thought ownership is key, and to ensure that the thinker is rewarded for useful contributions, and not punished or disadvantaged in any way. Knowledge should also be free and open, accessible and flowing everywhere and anywhere without limitation. Unfortunately, current systems often fail to provide for the frictionless creation, publication and use of ideas. Desired are new systems which transcend current computers with respect to the free and open exchange of thoughts, opinions and votes.

Questions are easy to spot for today's systems. For example; are the amalgamated ideas of humanity not the shared heritage of every new born child? Where is the world-library and/or universal knowledge repository? Why can't we all vote on issues of collective concern? Who builds today's systems, and in what sense(s) are they useful and democratic?

Do we have equality of access to ideas—or honest self-expression? If some humans are spied upon, but others are not, then by definition we do not have equality of expression. Are some humans more equal than others? Do we have (in any sense) sufficient access to the deep and parallel structure(s) of all human knowledge? Is technology evolving by itself, and according to an anti-humanistic agenda? Do certain dark agendas shape computer system design/usage.

Overall, are we allowing: the wishes of the few to outweigh the needs/wishes/rights of the many?

Finding the answers is challenging. Certain experts proclaim the existence of technological barriers as justification for why humanistic systems cannot ever be built. Others site economic and/or security barriers. Problems do exist, but we must not use the same as an excuse to block the path to authentic and people-centric technologies. Despite optimism, we live in dark times. Increasingly there is a movement towards centralization of computing resources. Authorities attempt to justify why we cannot ever be allowed to share ideas plus votes openly and/or privately. Are we to accept these self- appointed parties as god-like beings; who judge, rule and punish the rest of us on a whim?

Like Beyonce, we ask: 'who run(s) the world?' We might not the like the answer(s), or what it says about human freedom(s) in the year 2015. Conversely, we postulate a new type of atomic network that provides for an open sharing of ideas. A special class of self-centric data is envisaged, comprising massively distributed data 'atoms' which offer boundless mechanisms for the preservation, retrieval and sharing of content –ideas (Nelson, 1974; Orwell, 1949; Radley, 2015; Veltman, 2014). George Orwell said: 'if you want a picture of the future, imagine a boot stamping on a human face—forever' (Orwell, 1949). Orwell's nightmarish world is one of newspeak, thought-crimes, memory holes, double-think, and of clouded perception; whereby thoughts are constantly observed, twisted, negated and used to eliminate free-will. Foucault likewise predicated super-panopticon surveillance machines that may be used to curtail human freedoms (Foucault, 1975). Hopefully we can avoid such big-brother scenarios, but we must not throw the responsibility onto the machine (Wiener, 1950).

Another prescient comment comes from Lord Bertrand Russell, who said: 'Machines are worshipped because they are beautiful, and valued because they confer power; they are hated because they are hideous, and loathed because they impose slavery' (Russell, 1963). The quote is apt. Computers are resplendent machines—with high levels of apparent intelligence, independent decision making ability, and perhaps even (on occasion) motivations of their own; but they are also, ultimately, human creations. This is an obvious statement of fact, but less clear is why we should all (collectively) allow computer systems to be designed that (in actual fact) restrict freedoms, limit access to knowledge, and favor minority interests. My thesis shall be that design of today's computers is unquestionably; design of the whole arena of human life, and ultimately, in a real sense, design of self. Needed is careful planing, to ensure that humans be the masters (not of each other); but of our machine slaves, and it must not turn out to be the other way around!

Theory of Natural Thoughts (Noun Form)

In this chapter I present an attempt to develop a 'natural' theory of human thinking. Explored herein are what thoughts are, in and of themselves, and we examine where they come from, and where they go to. We focus on: Who thinks What thoughts, and Where.

We have couched such an approach in terms of the 'noun' features of human thought; named as the Social Categories of Assembly, or the Circuits of Thought (Radley, 2015). This noun form—or noun-based analysis—of human thought, represents only half of a proposed complete theory which will be finished only when we include—the as yet undeveloped 'verb' analysis which would explore: How and When thinking takes place—and thus how ideas/concepts are created—in other words the mechanisms of thinking. This latter theory will involve: theories of mind, perception and world etc; and deal with what we call the Elemental and Modal (or inter-relational) Categories of Thinking.

In this chapter we open up the topic(s) of: how humans come to see, create and share concepts—named as the Theory of Natural-Thoughts; together with: what happens when we build thoughts into systems and machines—a process/type-of-thinking that we call Machine-Implanted Thoughts.

HUMAN RIGHTS

In terms of moral and ethical law, there are four fundamental human rights, as follows: the right to life, and the right to earn a living through work, the right to choose one's own master (if you do work for others); and also ownership of one's own thoughts. And these rights are the bedrock upon which any (just) society is built; its very foundations, if you like (Berners-Lee, 2014). Interesting is that thoughts are seen (in law) as the private and unassailable property of the individual; that is, they are his/hers to do with as he/she pleases. And the aforementioned four rights lie above all other considerations, and are more important than societal organizational structures like democracy, capitalism or communism. Such 'isms' are, one and all, and in a very real sense; simply mechanisms through which people obtain these basic rights—or are supposed to be afforded the same.

Let us begin with thought-rights. The right to own, and to profit from, one's own thoughts, is a major theme of the current chapter. I argue, accordingly (and in specific senses), that owning one's thoughts, means also owning the right to pass those thoughts onto others (and controlling the methods and conditions of so doing), either openly or in total/partial privacy (if one so desires). Furthermore, I make the assertion that where one does not have such a capability of privacy and free expression—and in relation to thoughts—then one is in some sense a slave.

One has lost part of self - perhaps forever!

THOUGHT OWNERSHIP

Restriction (or destruction) of thought-ownership breaks a fundamental human right—and you are, in a sense, no longer fully human, wherever and whenever this happens. Or at the very least you are unable to operate as a human-being in some way or on specific occasion(s) and/or by means of a specific communication medium. Put simply, if you do not own your own thoughts, in any social situation or scenario whatsoever, then you are no longer free. You no longer own your mind!

I know that (for example) 'social' spying on digital networks is said to be in our best interests, and/or is supposedly being imposed on us to save lives or else to protect us from harm. But even if this were so (certainly it is not so in the vast majority of cases); how can we know that such a situation was/is in fact ever the case, since nobody polices the police, so to speak. Others may say that we have a choice as to whether or not to use these (social network, tweeting and email etc) systems—and even whether or not to use computers. But do we really have such a choice? It is becoming increasingly difficult to operate in a modern society without using computers and networks of all kinds, and especially for email and Internet browsing etc. Certainly not having access to some form of social network, texting and/or live chatting program is restrictive at best, and potentially limits one's freedoms and activities in severe and (often) detrimental ways.

In fact, we do not have a choice, and our unelected overlords know it.

Disconnecting oneself form the Internet, and/or avoiding all computers and digital networks, and going 'off-grid', may seem like the activity of a maverick, revolutionary or paranoid schizophrenic. But only by so doing (and avoiding the on-line world altogether) would the average citizen possibly avoid all kinds of spying in relation to aspects of personal activity and interpersonal communication. However every time you spend money on a credit card, apply for a driving license, pay your rent, and/or receive a pay check etc; you are generating information. And all of this data ends up on a database that someone, somewhere, can access on-line. It is as if the vast digital network 'knows' that you are alive, and is, as a result, watching you.

Let us concentrate on thought ownership. George Orwell spoke about the issues surrounding panopticon spying (constant, everywhere and all-pervasive observation) at length (Orwell, 1949). Many other theorists and writers have followed suit. Each thinker has added his or her own spin onto the debate of the relationship(s) between freedom of expression/action/thought; versus spying, dystopian societies and big-brother. Overall, my assertion is that each of us should own our own thoughts; and in fact that we have a moral and ethical right to them. If we do not, then we are, in some sense, slaves. I put it to you that today's social network, and email operators etc, are breaking our human rights when they spy on our communications, and even when they do so with our own consent and/or knowledge. Such spying is one of the most contentious issues of the present day.

Being spied upon blocks honest free-expression, and specifically because you are uncertain what may become of your thoughts, who is reading them, and to what end-uses they may eventually be put. And nobody (that is none of those affected) actually agreed to this form of mind control. Your own thoughts are being snatched right away from you, as soon as they are communicated to others, and (very often) when sending an email, text or chat message. This is theft, censorship and it is highly immoral—because we can do nothing about it. And we do not know if/when it is happening, and (once again) for what purposes (or ends) our data is being used. But the current situation is even worse than this. By policing the kinds of things that one is able to say on a social network, and the words/opinions that one is allowed or expected to express; such surveillance is restricting not only our human right to free self-expression, but potentially our education, and the ideas that can/may/will develop in supposedly 'free' society; and in a most restrictive and severe manner.

Are these actions not thought-theft crimes perpetuated by the powerful against weaker individuals? Whatever happened to respect for other people's opinions? Are we so week-minded that we cannot tolerate dissension? It could be (or certainly is the case?) that all kinds of useful opinions, ideas and creative inspirations are being checked (blocked); and before they even begin to emerge. This happens because people are afraid of expressing their true opinions; and as a result of (real and/or imagined) surveillance and possible sanction. It appears that the ever-present spying, banning of certain words, and restriction of opinions and feelings, could influence the development of language, and hence thought itself. It is a dangerous path that we are now embarked on. How can it be that just because we move our communication method to electronic media; that our ownership rights are taken away? In the book 1984, Eric

Arthur Blair (pen-name George Orwell) spoke about the (potentially) corrupting influence of language, and he made several powerful statements that are especially prescient (Orwell, 1949).

From *1984*:

If thought corrupts language, language can also corrupt thought.

It's a beautiful thing, the destruction of words.

Freedom is the freedom to say that two plus two make four. If that is granted, all else follows.

These quotes point to the power of language to influence thought (and vice-versa). In a way language is thought. If you cannot say or express certain words, feelings and opinions—then those sentiments do not exist, never did exist, and will never exist—at least for others. And possibly in a sense, these thoughts do not even exist from the viewpoint of the thinker as well. Such actions obviously open up legal, ethical and moral issues related to network surveillance. However I can (hopefully), leave space in your mind to entertain the possibility that networks should not sensor all human communication (by default)—and because this may be limiting and/or breaking the human rights of countless millions of individuals.

Are such opinions radical? I hope so—because the world is in a mess.

It seems that only a radical solution could possibly offer any hope of making a dent in (i.e. impact upon and solve); the major problems now facing the world, and specifically those relating to hunger, wars, environmental disasters and education. Can it be that because we (individually and collectively) no longer own our own thoughts; that we are restricting our capability to govern ourselves, and to solve the major problems facing humanity?

Let us get back to the previous example, the social networks. Do not get the impression that I am against all such networks, because I am not. Rather it is my position that these networks, in various forms, and by defining what we can do, who we can talk to, and also the ways in which we do talk; are in actual fact forming a new and artificially constructed—or wholly designed form of self. This new self is being produced by unelected network owners, and others who are close to the biggest computers –according to Jaron Larnier's view (Lanier, 2013). Big questions naturally arise. Do we really want to allow a small number of people (the network owners) to define who we are as a people and also what our lives will be like (and including 'scientific' people too).

Networks are essential to our future as human beings. They are places where humans can meet, come together, interact and exchange thoughts and opinions; sharing ideas, movies, files, and votes etc. Already many of us work, play and engage in commerce on networks. Networks also magnify who we are, in terms of our needs, wishes, desires and potentially the collective actions that are possible [e.g. 'Arab spring']. And it is my opinion that computer networks are simply an extension of real-world social networks (or should be).

When it comes to networks, the medium really is the message; and the message is simply: this is what it means to be human—or rather—this is how you can/could retain or demonstrate your humanity and/or—become fully human. Unfortunately certain aspects of your humanity are to be withheld (currently on these networks), and specific thought-rights are to be limited and/or removed (but, don't worry, it's for our own good!). Conversely, I suggest that we must never forget that computer systems—and hence networks—are designed by and for humans. This view may seem obvious—but it is sometimes obscured.

Norbert Weiner said that we should 'not throw the responsibility onto the machine' (Wiener, 1950). Hence do not be 'fooled' into thinking that we have lost control of machines in terms of their basic functions and capabilities. This is not so—machines are (at all times) human made artifacts. The machines cannot yet (in any sense) design themselves. And even if they could they do not (currently) possess free-will or the 'will to power'. Machines simply implement human wishes, desires, and plans (intentional or not).

Perhaps it is natural to assume that anything designed by humans would be humanistic, but this is not (necessarily) the case. I think Weiner was referring to the tendency of system designers (and others), to blame the machine (in-authentically) for those cases where a machine limits human rights, and/or does not perform as it should do, or as the user of the technology would wish it to. From this viewpoint, it is as if the technology designs itself, and/or were somehow alive.

As for my own viewpoint, I simply state that I believe that such a view is profoundly wrong, simplistic and anti-humanistic. Machines (and computers) are designed by humans, and we can make of them whatever we like. They are not fixed in stone and are not our overlords (yet). Rather it is the system designers and owners who are deciding what policies the machines progress/implement (at least in terms of planning). In terms of the social networks, the current systems control how we interact in a variety of ways. They control the language we use and the things we are allowed to say to each other. Unfortunately by limiting, curtailing, restricting and controlling human communications; it is inevitable that current systems are changing the nature of what it means to be human. Is this a frightening and unbelievably depressing state of affairs? Most definitely.

Perhaps we need to go back to the drawing board when it comes to technology; and begin by re-imagining who we wish to be, collectively as a people. It is vital to realize that the rules and regulations imposed by the designers of each network, will shape the ways in which, and by which, and how; human beings relate, one to another, and in the strongest possible way. The major theme of this chapter is the inseparability of technological issues from matters of general and primary concern—both collectively and individually. In a way technology–is–humanity, and/or humanity–is–technology; because technology is now so enmeshed with who we are, that design of technology is design of humanity and self. In a sense, we are the computer and the computer is us. It seems that a merging of man and machine is inevitable—at least if the human species is to survive.

The Purpose of Computers

Many experts have emphasized the chameleon aspect/nature of computers; noting that they are a type of machine that can simulate and control: almost any other machine. However a primary function of the computer remains helping us to think better thoughts.

The word computer is comprised of COM: meaning to come together; and PUTER: to clean, arrange value, consider, and think. Hence computers allow anyone to arrange items clearly in one's mind; that is to see, align, order, overview, sort, gather-together, see linkages/causes/trends and to manage things. The item(s) in question include all (or many) of the objects/processes that exist in the natural world; but vitally include also all (or many) of the thoughts/feelings/actions of people everywhere –at least in theory (Nelson, 1974; Wiener, 1950; Lanier, 2013; Kurzwel, 2005; Gibson, 1984; Norman, 1999; Rheingold, 1985; Segal, 2012).

Put simply, therefore, the job of the computer is to organize the human mind; plus to connect minds together; and hence to arrange all of our inner and outer perceptions, plus ideas; and in terms of clarity, accuracy, precision, relevance and truth etc. Computers are also a type of scopic media (potentially for everything); helping us to see what are the contents of the natural, technical and human worlds (Veltman, 2006; Veltman, 2014). In summary, computers are thinking/communication/visualisation/control tools, connecting us one to another, and to the world; plus above all this they must help us to manage our societies with the utmost humanity, compassion, love, honesty, justice etc.

Would that it were only so.

Machine Consciousness / Free Will and Artificial Intelligence (AI)

As an aside, I state right away that I do not believe in artificial intelligence, or free-will/consciousness for systems/machines/computers and hence the actions of machines are solely human-made; and my beliefs in this respect are due to a complete lack of supporting evidence for machine-thinking and machine-sourced decisions/choices. Accordingly all thoughts/actions that exist are entirely human-made; including any apparent computer-made decisions. Hence all non-natural processes/influences on the human world are the responsibility of a human maker/owner/operator/manager. Ergo machine and computers cannot ever make independent decisions or act in any way according to a logic of their own making. Hence any mistakes, sub-optimal outcomes and/or evil tidings that may emanate from machines are the result of poor planning and/or human mis-management(s) (Luppicini, 2013).

Natural Thoughts

Freedom of thought is a natural and unassailable human right, as expressed in international law (Nelson, 1974). And perhaps the most sacred faculty given to man, after life; is the power to think as he likes. The supremacy of thought is patently so; for man's scientific, religious and social cosmologies are, one and all, if they are anything whatsoever; simply patterns/assemblies of thoughts! A person's primary activity is thinking. And doubtless present are great riches when it comes to our individual and collective thought streams. In a way, all of civilisation, all of man's activities and discoveries; are simply vast conglomerations of thoughts and thought-outcomes (Benedek, Veronika & Matthias, 2008). Many of these thoughts are weaved into the most wonderful and intricate patterns of meaning; and from which subtle understanding may be obtained. An indisputable fact is that the source of every one of these thoughts is (normally) an individual human mind. Accordingly, the entire corpus of human knowledge is comprised of countless thought 'atoms'; and the same being 'slices' of individual minds. And these thought-atoms, once communicated, are ready to live-again inside new brains; often being minds far distant in time and space. Consequently, we wish to provide open and easy access to, plus comprehensive assembly of: thought-atoms.

A fundamental and timeless feature of the mental world, is the placing of some thoughts over and above others; and established is a structure of relations and a hierarchy of importance for ideas. Indeed some thoughts are considered to be so important that they take precedence over all others; and some are enshrined in law and in order to marshall social activities. Certain other types of thought are identified as being coincident with universal laws; and thus established are scientific principles. Still other thoughts are given a scared charter, and named as religious thoughts.

My (ambitious) aim here is to establish a new theory of natural thoughts, whereby all thinking is to be afforded a sacred status. We humans employ various kinds of thought patterns to mirror aspects of reality; to shape the world around us, to communicate, and so to plan for beneficial outcomes. Within any particular conceptual framework, thought-atoms fit together in a myriad of intricate ways; and parallel structures, hierarchies and logical patterns naturally arise.

Thoughts acquire patterned rules and ways of assembling themselves into groupings; and in order to establish specific meanings. No scratch that. I do not think that thoughts assemble themselves—but rather thought-atoms are given particular relationships, one to another, within human minds, and (often) using the complex rules and syntax of languages—formal and informal. Individual thoughts thus represent distinct meanings, and when they are linked together into patterns. Ontological relationships may be established with object-type and process-type thoughts; using species and genus categories. Logical, imaginary and real-world events and processes; can then be represented and modelled. In this way humans build up patterns of meaning in relation to the universe—and each other.

All well and good; and everything seems natural and without any obvious problems. Multiple languages are developed within which thought patterns can exist and be expressed. Languages may be more or less flexible, and more or less established; plus 'extendible' to varying degrees. Obviously a formal language like mathematics is highly axiomatic, and normally any new idea must fit into the general scheme of a particular discipline of mathematics; if it is to be accepted within the overall pattern.

Human societies form huge assemblies of thought patterns; within books, on television, in films, papers and on computers etc; and individual thoughts 'slot into' various conceptual maps. Often in order to fit neatly together, thoughts must 'play well' with other thoughts—if they are not to end up homeless, lost or forgotten. Such is the immense diversity of thoughts and associated patterns; that they (almost) defy description. When referring to 'thoughts'; we are not concerned merely with Aristotle's Categories, or else purely 'scientific' or logical thoughts—but with any kind of thought whatsoever—whether or not it coincides with anything real.

The top-level concept of a thought is difficult to pin-down, and because thoughts are an especially elastic concept; being a category for something that may be precisely—or loosely—defined to any imaginable degree. Thoughts are pointers, categories, compartments, flexible place-holders for patterns/meaning; and we establish that...

Natural thoughts (ideas that result from thinking):

ORIGINATE in the human mind
Are singular or composite (posses an ATOMIC nature)
Are the NATURAL PROPERTY of the thinker or human race <E*>
EXIST in the human mind, on media, or in a machine (system)
May be COMMUNICATED between mind(s) and/or machine(s)
Are inherently EQUAL (meaning changes with context) < E* >
Represent PATTERNS of meaning/content [normally]
May be FREELY-ASSEMBLED into patterns < E * >
May be EXPRESSED in a language system [normally]
May INFLUENCE other thoughts and/or actions

Defined is a top-level class for all natural-thoughts; and captured are the ten universal Attributes of the same—being features that naturally inhere in all naturally-existent human thought patterns. And whilst a thought-atom may have (many) other secondary features; I shall claim (but cannot prove) that these are the fundamental Attributes that all thoughts must (and do) naturally possess; and that no other such primary (universal) properties exist.

We hereby ambitiously define a new Theory of Natural Thoughts; being a framework for analysing from whence thoughts come, how they fit together and are expressed, and where they go to. Natural thoughts typically have these ten Attributes in common; and (in any case) always possess the three essential Attributes < E* > of: natural property, equality and free-assembly (see later exposition). Unnatural thoughts are missing one or more of the essential Attributes. We seek clarity of form, type, meaning and influence for all thoughts—plus equality of expression and free assembly for the same.

Open, Private and Secret Thoughts

Everything that follows refers to the Attributes of natural-thoughts.

We identify three Modes-of-Existence for thoughts: in the human mind, preserved on media, and built into a machine, system or computer. Next we identify three Forms of thought: secret-thoughts (personal), open-thoughts (open collective) and private- thoughts (restricted collective). We assign an owner and originator (anonymous allowed) for each thought; plus lost and stolen modes.

Two universal Types of thoughts are identified—with respect to the outcomes of a thought-atom. These are named as intentional-thoughts aimed at (directly or indirectly) affecting/acting-on: an object, person, real-world situation, and/or other thoughts etc; and passive-thoughts which are deemed to have no such outcomes. With respect to the Modes, Attributes, Forms and Types of thoughts; identified are the original (human) thinker(s), owner(s) and a human implementer; the latter being an actor who may bring a thought into action and thus affect other thoughts/actions.

A secret-thought is a thought that occurs in the mind of an individual, and has not left the 'mind' of the thinker to enter another person's mind and/or machine's 'mind' (yet). Secret-thoughts may, in fact, be related to thoughts originating in other people's minds; but vital here is that nobody else (that is, no other party) yet knows, or can easily discover the contents of the same, or that the thought has been (or is being) thought by the thinker. Secret-thoughts are an individual's natural property alone. Others may be able to guess a secret-thought; but that is different from certain knowledge. With secret-thoughts the thinker is in (more or less) complete control over whether or not the same thought contents are ever communicated to others.

A secret-thought is—bound in time—and because what was once secret, may no longer be secret at some epoch in the future. Secret-thoughts are protected from discovery by others—and are hidden in some way. Secrecy is a state of being for the thought itself. Secret-thoughts, by definition, exist in a single mind—or no mind—in the case of 'lost' secret-thoughts.

Every open-thought was once a secret-thought; but has subsequently been communicated to other mind(s), or else written down and stored in a place freely accessible to others. Open-thoughts are essentially, social thoughts. Open-thoughts exist (potentially at least) in everyone's minds; and the originator may have little control over how, when, and to whom such thoughts are communicated. Both open and secret thoughts may be singular or composite; and thus be comprised of thoughts and sub-thoughts copied from elsewhere, and link-to and/or subsume (or represent) many other thoughts/patterns.

What differentiates open from secret-thoughts is their state of discoverability—and in this respect a thought is only secret, if there can be no possibility of transfer to another mind (at a specific epoch). Writing down a thought in a public arena, would potentially nullify secrecy (in the future); and hence such an exposed thought may no longer be classified as secret, and because it is—potentially discoverable (i.e. it is a 'lost' open-thought until then). It is vital to recognise that not only original-thoughts start out as secret. When someone thinks a thought originated by someone else, then the fact that they are

Figure 1. Theory of natural thoughts

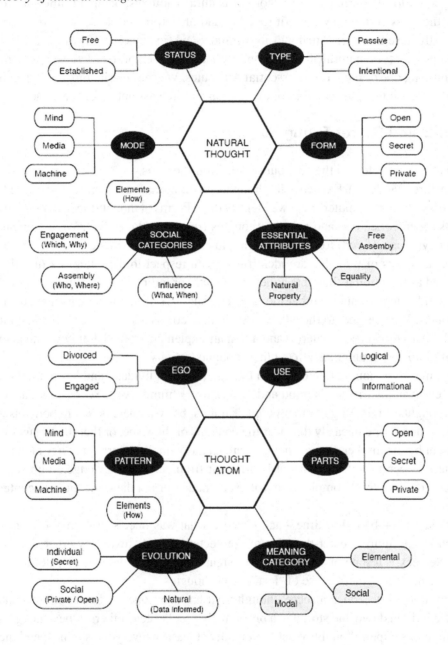

thinking this same thought, may constitute a secret—and hence a changed thought—itself. What matters is whether another party is able to access unique/original thoughts (or has the possibility of so doing).

A third class of thought is identified as a private-thought; defined as a thought which has-been/will-be shared amongst a restricted group. Private-thoughts possess a special feature, in that they are distributed to a limited number of people; and hence some form of social sharing plus protection is implied; and in order to protect the status of a private-thought, and to prevent it from morphing into an open-thought. Discoverability is restricted and controlled by some mechanism/lock/key, plus social trust.

Properties of Natural Thoughts

It is important to realise that all thoughts begin 'life' as the natural property of the thinker; and it is up to the thinker how, when and where (originally) secret-thoughts are transformed into open or private-thoughts. A key distinction is made between natural-thoughts, and unnatural ones. Natural- thoughts possess all three of the essential Attributes < E* >, and exist in one of the three Forms. In this book, we shall demonstrate (using exposition and example) that unnatural-thoughts prevent human beings from freely: creating, accessing, sharing, and/or assembling thoughts. Unnatural-thoughts are therefore sub-optimal; and also unethical, because they limit the key human right of: freedom of thought (proof to follow). Natural-thoughts retain those innate and existent powers that nature intended a human being to have over his/her most intimate property—his/her thoughts.

Our aim in this chapter is to analyse the ten Attributes of natural thoughts, and using the three Forms of natural-thoughts. It is easy to establish that computers do not originate thoughts; and hence the first Attribute is proven, and because: only humans can originate thoughts! The second Attribute states that thoughts are atomic—and may be singular or composite—and this fact would seem to be so obvious as to be not worth considering any further. The third—property—Attribute, is an essential-feature of a natural-thought. For all Forms of thought (open, private and secret), the property item refers to thought-ownership rights.

More specifically the owner/originator of a thought has the right to decide (absolutely) who may see the thought itself, and (in a weaker sense) what others may do with it. If the true (and natural) owner/ originator is not assigned and conferred ownership (in any way whatsoever) then that thought is now a stolen-thought—and hence it is an unnatural-thought. Thought-ownership must be protected (by some method); and likewise for Attributes five and eight, the rights of the owner to assemble/communicate said thoughts. Note that thought ownership may be assigned either to an individual party, several people, or in fact, be assigned to the whole of humanity. In relation to the third—property—Attribute, other questions arise in terms of originality/ownership; for example how to resolve a situation whereby two or more people have the exact same thought. Thoughts may be intrinsically date stamped to help with such an issue.

More complexity enters the discussion when we consider that thoughts are inherently patterned, and may have parts that originate from different sources/people. Another problem in relation to the assignment of thoughts as property; occurs when thought- atoms originate, not from one mind, but from many minds—as a collective. We must therefore retain the ability to assign authorship/ownership of thoughts that originate collectively; whereby a committee of thinkers are recorded as responsible for said thought constructs. Problems are multiple in relation to assignment of thought- ownership; but most issues evaporate away by focussing on relatively distinct thought- atoms; and hence assigning originality to the smallest possible units.

In summary, the assignment of ownership to human thoughts; is a central thesis of the current chapter. We shall return to the idea of thoughts as property, many times; and in order to explore the ethical and moral imperatives of, and vast implications of, this key issue within human affairs.

What is to be gained by this type of thought-categorisation? Why focus on thoughts? Would it not be better to look at knowledge itself—and forget altogether about thought- ownership? My answer relates (in part) to the fact that the whole corpus of human knowledge is (in a real sense) an immense conglomeration of opinions. Clearly, within society, there are varying opinions on politics, law, social and scientific questions, and also the nature of reality itself etc. Everywhere we see dissenter and alternative viewpoints. And many (honest) mistakes are made within human activities.

Overall, thoughts are argued about and debated—and nothing is more human!

Kim Veltman mentioned to me that thoughts are not merely and only a matter of opinion, and that our ideas also include: dreams, plans, fears, hopes, beliefs, ambitions, etc (criminal thoughts will be inferior to noble thoughts—for example). Yet all of these modes of knowing are expressed as thoughts. My point is not that everything is opinion, without precedence; but that thoughts, in order to confer meaning, exist within a particular context—and these contexts change constantly!

Only within a particular context/framework, or in relation to a specific pattern of other thoughts; or from the perspective of a particular person's ego, can a thought be judged and/or assigned to any degree of significance or value. Reflected here is the chameleon-like nature of all thinking. Thought meanings are inherently non-committal, and because—contexts of use are varied and innumerable. Establishing the specific context of use for a thought-atom—and taking into account the surrounding pattern(s)—is absolutely essential in order to scry the intended meaning. Therefore the meaning of a thought is wholly dependent upon its brothers and sisters; that is, on the words, sentences and paragraphs that surround it (in the case of a written thought). Thoughts are reusable building blocks for assigning and communicating meaning; and the gist of a thought may (at any time) be only be partially known in varying degrees of definition, and according to a specific usage scenario.

We may also ask: how big/complex are thoughts? Is a thought: a word, a sentence, paragraph, a book or even an entire subject corpus? I don't actually know the answer (and there may, in fact, be no single answer); but only that I had imagined thoughts to be atom-like and quite small—similar (in a way) to the letters in a language. Perhaps a typical size for a thought would be about as long (or short) as a sentence. However experts often converse by means of short-cuts, and using technical terminology; hence much context is assumed here and will be off-limits to others, who's mind's 'live' outside of the specific contexts employed.

In summary, meaning is context dependent, and so it would seem essential for us to see, know and remember, (in context); the great assembly and diversity of all thoughts. Hence computers must be, above all else: scopic; communicative; and 'thinking' media.

Who Thought: What, When, Where and How

Human knowledge is not finished, but continues to advance and develop at an ever faster pace. Polymath's like Ted Nelson and Kim Veltman have noted how subject categories don't really exist, and that everything is connected to everything else. Kim Veltman even finds that the various alphabets of the world, the composite letters and symbols; hold entire histories of meaning/knowledge and represent a vast number of inter-cultural cross-connections and common sources (Veltman, 2006).

Present are deep and parallel structures within human knowledge—and constituent thoughts are enmeshed with other thoughts endlessly; with yet more thoughts/ opinions piled on- top-of, on-the-side and below, other thoughts; ad infinitum! Ted Nelson says that knowledge—and information—are fractal! (Nelson, 1974). And by this he means to say (I think); that thoughts are also fractal—complete with unusual patterns and increasing levels of detail as you 'zoom' in; and thus patterns of new meaning on all scales.

It may be that we humans cannot possibly develop further as a species; without creating an immense map—or a world brain—of the vast interconnectedness of thought patterns. A nice way of so doing, is

Figure 2. Three world's theory of human thought

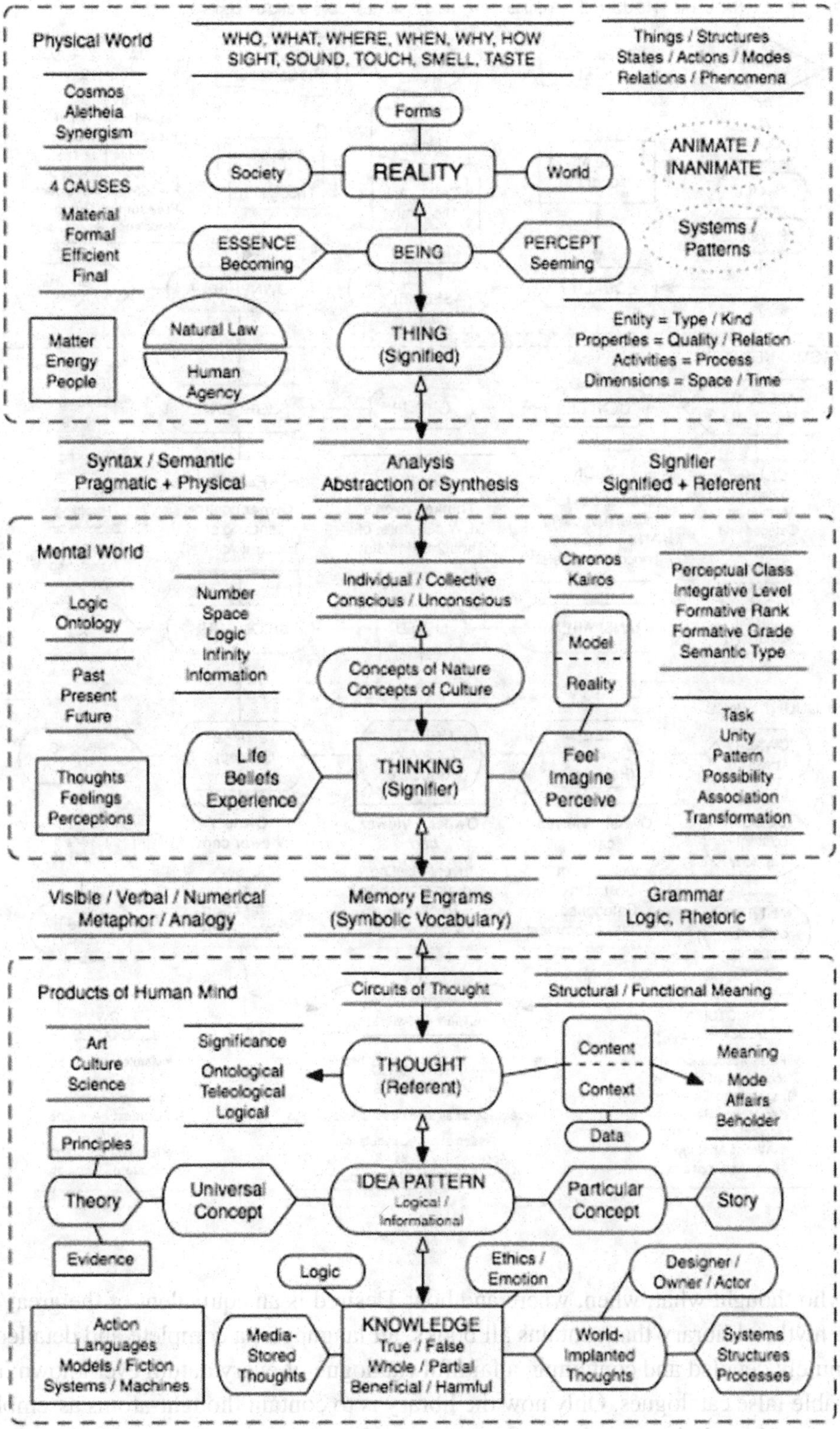

Figure 3. The circuit's of thought

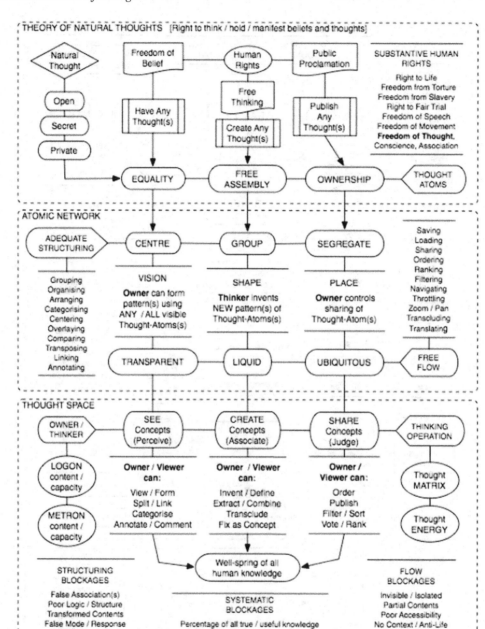

to find out who thought what, when, where and how. Desired is an equivalent of the great 'Library of Babel'—the mythical library that contains all books, all languages, a complete and detailed history of the past, minutely detailed and containing a faithful catalogue of every datum ever known; and including innumerable false catalogues. Only now the library is to contain thought-atoms assembled into the larger elements of knowledge. Cataloguing every open-thought—according to simple features: origin, ownership, pattern and linkage; enables preservation of the immense complexity, overlays, relationships, cross-linkages, and interconnected nature of everything.

One may still overlay (onto this system) all kinds of data, categorisations, assignments, classes, subjects, books etc. However the parallel and multiple links between all 'opinions' would be represented—and the deep interconnections made visible—and by focussing simply on thought-atoms. Open-thoughts are made visible at last—and one has preserved the origin, ownership, equality, pattern, and assembly of all thoughts. The only remaining items on our list of Attributes; is to sort out: details of existence (Attribute 4), access (Attribute 5) and expression or language (Attribute 9), and the influence(s) (Attribute 10) of all thoughts in human society.

Remember that all knowledge is comprised; simply of thoughts (plus data—see later). The basic building block of everything known (I would suggest) is the open thought-atom! This is naturally so because every idea/feeling starts 'life' as an individual thought. Of course thoughts are normally patterns of connections to other thoughts—and also interconnections between thoughts, patterns and data etc. However one cannot get away from the fact that what matters is that individual/collective mind(s) assemble groups of thought-atoms together into patterns, and in order to confer meaning.

We state this in another way as follows:

< Mind = patterns = [thoughts + data] (contextualised) = meaning >

Accordingly, we ask: what use is an open-thought that cannot be found? For such 'lost' thoughts; it is as if they had never existed. This is—in fact—the situation we have at the moment; whereby, because of a distinct lack of connectedness, vast numbers of thoughts are, in effect; isolated, lost, inaccessible or invisible—potentially forever!

We humans have a desperate need to read the patterns of past and present thought- streams. I refer here to open-thoughts; and to those thoughts that the thinker intended would be shared with others.

Truth / Falsehood and Good / Evil

A key point is that the rest of us (thought-readers/assemblers) cannot know which are the true or false, useful and/or worthless thoughts. But even false thoughts educate us—in one way or another—and—all thoughts inform. Professor Marshall McLuhan (1911-1980) referred to modern man as the information gatherer, and he was right (almost); for we desire not merely data and information; but seek opinions and thoughts of all kinds (McLuhan, 1967; McLuhan, 1964). Man constantly collects thoughts like the ant collects twigs, saving them up for use—and profit—later on. But a question remains, how does society decide which are the useful/true thoughts, and which are the useless/harmful/false ones—and the same being those thoughts that should be discarded, censured and/or perhaps destroyed.

Our new Theory of Natural Thoughts provides an emphatic answer; and states that—on logical and ethical grounds to be explained later on—no open-thought should ever be destroyed and/or lost from the historical record. All open-thoughts are to be preserved and accessible to all. According to Attribute six, all thoughts are equal; and in a specific sense, whereby any and all thoughts require an established context to assign meaning. And because thought-atoms do not (by definition) in fact posses a singular— or specific—context of use, it logically follows that all thought-atoms are equal, and none are worthy of destruction/censure! I refer here not to the rights of legal/scientific bodies to recognise and develop (for example) laws/judgments and social/scientific thought-patterns of any specific type; but rather to the unnatural censure of any open thought-atom by itself, and when taken out of context (completely).

In fact, it is natural for humans to be constantly swapping thought-atoms in and out of constellations of thought-assemblies; and in order to establish hierarchies of understanding. Within proper contexts thoughts will naturally establish rulings, importance and dominance, one over another. The process of identification of useful ideas, must (normally) come from our collective opinions. It is for the whole human race that we must think; and our thinking processes must be as efficient, moral, and ethical as possible. If we are to choose some thoughts/actions over others; let it be after full consideration of the logos, pathos and ethos—after seeing a matter from all sides—and with as much information at our disposal as possible; and after considering all the opinions.

What I am defending here is human freedom; and in particular: freedom of thought, and the unhindered visibility, sharing and assembly of thoughts. We dismiss (altogether) the notion that some thoughts are intrinsically superior to, or else more worthy, than other thoughts. We state this in a motto: all thoughts are equal; being an idea derived from the fact that thought-atoms are essentially contextless. It is difficult to come to any other conclusion; and because the evidence is so vast in favour of equality and re-use.

Witness the diversity and varied usage of thought-atoms. Such a seemingly radical view is unquestionably a moral position; and it is based (partly) on the fact that viewpoints vary. A specific thought may be seen as right or wrong, and true or false; by various people—and even the same person—in different contexts. Accordingly we defend and uphold the right of any (open) thought to exist; and to be seen/assembled (in any way), and by all human being(s). It is a fact of life that we must judge thoughts (and data-related 'facts'); and decide between good and evil options, plus rank priorities—but this all happens within specific patterned context(s). All open-thoughts must be accessible for use (and re-use) within such varied patterns. Every single open-thought should be accessible. In fact it would seem logical to suggest that only where all open-thoughts are known; do we humans then—as a collective—have the best chance of selecting, combining and creating truly optimal thought-patterns.

Accordingly, it is my belief that wherever a human being has originated a thought, and communicated it to others as an open-thought; then that same thought is in a very real sense owned by the whole of humanity. I would (perhaps) here retain ways for the originator of said thought pattern to be paid via a micro-payments system. Importantly in this scheme all scientific knowledge; in fact all types of public knowledge, would naturally—and by default—be assigned as open-thoughts.

Benefits of Natural Thoughts

Several problems relating to intellectual property arise out of our new conception of thought-ownership; however most are solved within the bounds of the current law of copyright and patents. What is not solved is the desired level of granularity that a thought has to achieve, in order to be assigned as an independent thought; and furthermore how are thought-rights and thought-ownership to be assigned/protected. These latter actions happen as a result of computers and techno-rights. In some respects the solution to these issues is the primary topic of the present chapter. Hopefully it is now clear what I am proposing; freedom of thought through dual modes of thought-ownership.

Firstly, thought ownership at the individual-level exists as secret and private thought types in which the thinker can himself control the degree of social sharing attained by said thoughts. Secondly open (shared) thoughts are to be assigned to the thought-ownership of everyone in the world, whilst a system of micro-payments may (sometimes) protect the owner of said thoughts, and in certain usage situations.

Note that specific types of outcomes, objects, methods and machines; that are created as a result of thought ownership; can be protected via the standard intellectual property mechanisms.

We now ask what exactly has been achieved by our new theory of thought freedom/ownership.

Let us start by imagining that a system of techno-rights is already in place (for all media-stored thoughts); in which secret, open, and private thoughts are facilitated and protected (as described). Furthermore let us assume that all of these thoughts have been connected in an atomic way (to be defined later); whereby any thought atom can be connected to any other—leading to patterns of an almost unimaginable complexity, depth and parallelism. We have thus created a new kind of society—or technopia—in which thought ownership/freedom takes precedence over (and aids or facilitates) all forms of human communication - or at least a large/significant portion of the same.

Attaining all of these advantages (simultaneously) is no small feat.

Perhaps this new arrangement of knowledge—because it is thought-based—maybe the bedrock of a new kind of democracy that embodies a fantastic diversity and richness of opinion; where all ideas are visible, and no thoughts are left behind. Every open-thought is established as being equal to every other— in terms of accessibility/assembly—and because no public thought (without context) takes precedence over any other. Any thought may be therefore be conceived of and expressed—either secretly, openly or privately. There are no restrictions whatsoever on man's thinking. He is free to think whatsoever he likes; individually and collectively. No one can stop anyone from publishing his/her own thoughts/votes, and from sharing these with whomever he/she likes. Thoughts are set free. There can be no censure, thought-destruction, thought-police, or thought-alterations. Oh, and perhaps I forgot to mention that our new technopia protects and remembers all open-thoughts forever (open-thoughts are indestructible and immortal); and so that all the thoughts of humanity are at everyones recall—and anyone may access them—largely for free. Visible are all of the parallel connections between thoughts, and the relationships of each and every thought pattern to every other. Links work both ways and we can see not only where an idea comes from; but also all the places where it is being used in the entire world knowledge system. We have built a world brain. But what, precisely, has been gained as a result?

Answer: a vital set of new-found freedoms.

Freedoms gained (from natural-thoughts):

- ○ Openly publish ideas / thoughts / votes to anyone / everyone
- ○ Publish private thoughts to close friend(s) [SECRETLY]
- ○ Nobody can stop anyone publishing - publicly / anonymously
- ○ Read / quote the open thoughts of anyone else
- ○ See where all ideas originate / voting corruption impossible
- ○ See where all ideas are used, and how they are linked
- ○ Know what are the collective opinions on specific issues
- ○ Preserve thoughts forever / ask any question of the 'world'
- ○ Totalitarian thought-control / big-brother is less likely

Some people may take issue with the fundamental principles upon which the proposed technopia is to be built. Let me now attempt to preempt some of these objections, and by clearly stating the benefits of the Theory of Natural Thoughts. Firstly, everything here is aimed at firmly and irrevocably establishing: freedom of thought; which is one of the nine fundamental human rights of the Geneva Convention

(UDHR, 1948). Presumably no-one (other than possibly bodies like the NSA and certain corrupt 'powers') would object to this first principle? Present in our new cosmology, is the idea that all thoughts are equal (Attribute 6); and hence that no thought may censure or control any other thought (sans context). Establishing this first principle gives rise to other desirable attributes for thoughts; including freedom of existence (Attribute 4), freedom of publication plus accessibility (Attributes 5,9,10), and the open-assembly (Attributes 7, 8) of thought-atoms. From this perspective people may assign meaning in any way whatsoever; and create meaningful/ meaningless mashups of thought-atoms, from wherever they like, and in whatever order/pattern they like.

Within the technopia, and in terms of accessibility/combinability; there is no such thing as an (ultimately) evil, wrong, false or immoral thought-atom—and anyone may create and/or read/express any opinion whatsoever. But is such freedom of expression not dangerous? Does it not help criminals? I would argue that this is not so, and for several reasons. Fundamentally, it is my belief, there can be no such thing as a wrong, evil or immoral thought-atom. Thoughts standing alone cannot possibly be evil; rather it is fully contextualised patterns of thoughts, and subsequently instantiated as a decision to take action, that may be evil and immoral. To most people, a single thought does not convey a compulsion to do anything —it is only a thought! In all cases it is the active agent, the actual person themselves; who decides to act on a pattern of personally contextualised thoughts.

One cannot have freedom of thought where you have some thoughts able to (universally and without context) block, dissemble, and destroy other thoughts. Logically this is so because we must be free to judge all opinions, and view all sides of the argument; and to see—all perspectives. One would suppose that thoughts simply cannot corrupt us—unless perhaps we are only given narrow viewpoints. In all cases people corrupt themselves by adopting limited perspectives—and in fact by not exposing themselves to enough thoughts, or else a sufficient number and high quality of different thoughts! Evil thoughts do not have a life of their own. They are not magical—and do not posses the power of demonic possession. Responsibility for deciding to take action; on all occasions, rests with the thinker/thought-implementer. But what about someone like Adolf Hitler; did his evil thoughts not 'possess' countless millions. Whilst I am no historian, I would argue the opposite may be true; whereby for want of sufficient open points of view, and the visibility of enough opinions in relation to true events, the German people (and perhaps, in a sense, the world's people also) were led blindly into the abyss of a terribly costly war that nobody could truly win.

If we try to eliminate all the evil thoughts from the world; and by (for example) banning certain thoughts, and destroying all memories of unhelpful events; then we may find that (in reality) we cannot do so. The notion of an evil thought, the classification scheme used, may narrow over time; and evil may be gradually re-assigned (by us) to somewhat less-evil deeds/thoughts. Evil, sin and immorality are seen to be part of the dualistic way in which humans interpret life itself; and we cannot do away with them altogether by pretending that acts of ultimate evil do not exist. On the other hand, we must embrace evil, know its very dark heart, and in order to be able to recognise it in ourselves. But how can we recognise evil where it is hidden? Evil cannot be stricken from the heart of man; it lives in man and is part of him. We must strive to recognise it early on, and to tackle it as soon as it begins to emerge. Accordingly is it not better to know where evil is, and what it is 'thinking'; and in order to know/change its expression in ourselves.

Another point relates to not allowing some thoughts to rule over others (in terms of visibility/accessibility/assembly etc). If we give certain people and/or thoughts the power to judge and police (other) thoughts, then are we not in danger of loosing control of our humanity? It is the lesson of human history that tirents and totalitarian regimes have a tendency to occur all too often in human societies. And who is to say that—even initially mild—censure of thoughts is not the ultimate tirent; and far worse than any Hitler, Saddam Hussein or Gehngas Khan.

In 1887, Lord John Acton said:

Power tends to corrupt, and absolute power corrupts absolutely.

Evil regimes invariably attempt to censure all forms of social discourse, and to control the thoughts of citizens through indoctrination. This is so because the evil dictator knows full well that it is the very minds of the people that he must seek to control; and if he is to rule over a society. In my book Self as Computer I give numerous examples of thought-control; and discuss corresponding evidence in support of the 'preventative medicine' of natural-thoughts and thought-ownership (Radley, 2015).

Before looking at what others have to say on the specific topic of the equality of un-contextualised thoughts; I would ask the reader to consider (alternatively); who they would trust to judge all human thought-atoms on a world-wide basis. How could we stop corruption from entering such a process? Is not the alternative far preferable, where no thoughts are censured, all thoughts are free and open, plus visible; and no thoughts are invisible/crushed?

Rene Descartes once described thought as:

A universal instrument which can be used in all kinds of situations (Descartes, 1641).

This comment goes right to the heart of my argument that all thoughts are equal. Thoughts, words and concepts must never be made illegal by themselves. This is so, because if some thoughts are disallowed and/or banned; then they are no longer available/useful for all purposes—and especially for recognising and countering, plus educating people about, wrong-doing and unhelpful actions.

I would now like to briefly explore a fundamental difference between looking and thinking.

Visualising an object with the eyes; requires a causal connection between you, light and the object itself. However thinking a thought requires no such causal relationship; and an isolated thought-atom may be conceived of as a mere temporary path, or station point, as we move from one region of meaning to another. It can sometimes be the case, that evil and immoral thoughts, and thinking about inhumane situations etc; may lead us to more fruitful, rewarding and 'good' islands of thought; than would otherwise be the case. Sometimes one needs to embrace an evil path and/or wrong act; and in order to understand it, break it down, in order to check its processes and/or to prevent similar situations from happening again in the future. Surely no one thinks that ignorance is best. Men like Jesus and Buddha preached an inclusive approach; and we do so likewise for all thoughts; no matter from whence they come, and what they (appear) to condone.

Unless we can can freely access, assemble and re-assemble our thoughts; with complete knowledge of where they come from, who originated them, along with their full context, and understanding of how they came to be; then it may not be possible for us to learn from our mistakes and move ahead as a people. Ownership of thoughts is key; all our thoughts; but this will not be possible until we accept that all open thought-atoms are absolutely equal.

'Unnatural' Thoughts

Open thought-atoms (devoid of sufficient context) must be recognised as fundamentally equal for several reasons. Firstly, evident is that thoughts—when they are small/simple—are inherently designed for assembly into larger patterns of more complexity and greater refinement (and depth), in terms of meaning. As a result meaning is heavily dependent on context and usage; and no thought has an ultimately fine or fully distinct meaning without consideration of all the surrounding contextual patterns (of the originator/receiver).

Thoughts are equally meaningless and/or equally meaningful; depending upon use. Therefore no open thought-atom has the right to censure any other open thought-atom; and no un-contextualised thought is more equal or possess greater truth than any other thought (from the perspective of judgment/censure). The woeful tidings of extracting thoughts from their rightful context, and/or of stealing thoughts from the natural owner; are evident throughout history.

Witness the 'phone hacking' scandal in the UK, the Profumo Affair in the UK, Watergate, Berlusconi's 'Bunga' parties, Bill Clinton and Monica Lewinsksy, the Teapot scandal, the Abu Ghraib torture scandal, Wikileaks, and the Iran-Contra Affair etc. More recently the European Court of Justice ruled that citizens (who have been convicted of crimes) have the 'right to be forgotten'; and to have their records deleted from the Internet. Thus open-thoughts are consigned to a memory-hole, and effectively destroyed. History is re-written. What will be next—will companies that lie, steel or commit crimes be able have these records removed also? Will newspaper records be subject to alteration—as in the novel 1984—and will all 'citizens' have the right to have their personal histories re-written here also. If all crimes are to be forgotten, what becomes of history? Do we have a new Ministry of Truth right in the heart of Europe? Has Newspeak arrived? Who will defend/record truth? What ever happened to freedom of the press?

In actual fact what I am arguing for with natural-thoughts and thought-ownership, is simply: freedom of thought. Perhaps some people believe that we all have sufficient freedoms at the present time, and in relation to freedom of personal association/expression. But did you know that in the USA it is now illegal for two parties to communicate across the Internet using an encrypted email or texting system (for example); and without passing the decryption keys to the NSA! In effect this rule has outlawed the natural or private-thoughts detailed above. Whatever happened to human rights? Every child is born with the right to posses secret/private (natural) thoughts, and also to engage in private communication with any other child—because he/she may go into a room and whisper into another other child's ear, for example. How is it possible that a natural human right that we are born with, to not be spied upon (in one-to-one communications), is made illegal in the USA? Is this loss of humanity, related to communication at a distance and/or across an electronic medium (in some bizarre way)? Surely this is an example; that upon growing up, one has lost part of self— specifically the right to own one's private-thoughts!

My point is simply this; man is not perfect, he makes mistakes, errors, miscalculations—and does not always act in the best interests of all. We must all keep an eye on each other's (open) thoughts/actions as a result—but whilst respecting each others right to have secret/private-thoughts. We must act for both the collective and individual 'good', instead of meeting only the needs of the powerful. No pigs (or humans) are more equal than others, and certain pigs may not (hopefully) be allowed to spy on - and control - other pigs. However today's Internet laws would have shocked even the great George Orwell; whereby a small number of powerful parties spy on the rest of us. They steal our secret/private thoughts, or have our open thoughts/actions destroyed and/or rendered invisible!

Such powers can only be interpreted as a real-world design for a 'Ministry of Truth' and/or Newspeak; and the same attempting to control all minds everywhere, automatically, and by default.

If ones believes, as I do, that open-thoughts are, in a very real sense, the natural property of the whole human race; then it also becomes intolerable to allow the current situation to continue; whereby open and free access to our collective memory institutions is blocked to many people. Increasingly knowledge and libraries are online, but not everyone has access. In the UK, during recent years thousands of public libraries have been shut; which is reminiscent of the 'book- burning' firemen in Fahrenheit 451 (Bradbury, 1953). Also many libraries are getting-rid of older books (selling them); and to make way for acres of computing terminals! It seems that the librarians have gone mad—just like the aforementioned firemen. It is because books (open-thoughts) are not seen as owned by humanity; that they may be sold/lost/destroyed. Another point relates to open accessibility for all the world's ideas. Some children are born with access to the Internet; and others do not have access to this technology. In effect, such a situation means that certain privileged children can see—or in some sense own—much of the past/present thoughts of humanity; and others do not! On the positive side, we do have an increasing recognition of some of the issues here discussed. Plans are afoot (by some enlightened people) to make changes in some areas.

But dangers remain. According to Lewis Mumford we must not:

Figure 4. Comparison with Orwell's 'Big Brother'

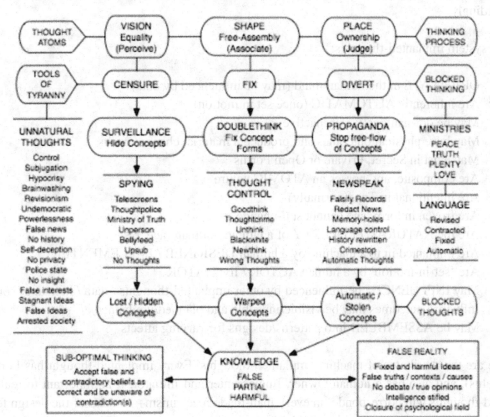

Contract human wants and desires in order to conform to the machine... no automatic system can be intelligently run by machines—or by people who dare not assert human intuition, human autonomy, human purpose.

In the author's mind, emphasis has often been in the wrong areas; and blame has been assigned where none is due. It is not the the NSA or Facebook's fault that they use our thoughts against us; but it is our collective failure to recognise natural-thoughts for what they are—the collective property of individuals and/or all humanity—that has held us back and continues to do so.

A thought is not a mere mere gossamer datum to be gobbled up greedily without respect for the natural rights of the thinker, or else a throwaway item, but rather it is who I am in the deepest sense. Our thoughts (properly contextualised) are: who we were, who we are, and all we can ever be—and we must treasure, nurture, defend and remember them; and in ways that safeguard our humanity; and move us ahead together as a people.

Machine-Implanted Thoughts

We now return to, and extend, our Theory of Natural Thoughts—and in order to account for the ways in which machine/system implanted-thoughts influence other human thoughts, systems and machine implanted-thoughts; and also influence or implement human and machine actions.

Accordingly,

Machine/system implanted-thoughts:

- ○ ORIGINATE in the human mind (may be influenced by data)
- ○ Are inherently AUTOMATIC (once set in motion)
- ○ May be dormant, active or inactive
- ○ May have physical outcomes and produce a material change/results
- ○ May exist in Secret, Private or Open Forms
- ○ Are composite, and posses an ATOMIC nature
- ○ Are intentional in Type(normally)
- ○ Are frozen in form, and cannot self-change
- ○ Are the NATURAL PROPERTY of a human / human race
- ○ Are implanted in to a machine by a human DESIGNER / IMPLEMENTER
- ○ Are 'set-in-motion' by a human ACTOR / INITIATOR
- ○ May INFLUENCE / be-influenced by other implanted-thoughts / data / human actions
- ○ Influence outcomes may be visible/invisible and planned/unplanned
- ○ May be ASSEMBLED into patterns/designs for varying affects

These are the Attributes of machine implanted-thoughts. Every implanted-thought has Form (visibility status), and also has a human Owner, Implementer and Initiator. It is important to realise that implanted-thoughts will correspond—in every man-made mechanism—to ALL of the design features, components and outcomes present in machines, products and services etc. The purpose of the second part of our theory of thinking, is to map/control/optimise those human thoughts that are embedded into systems, machines and (for example) computers. A core premise of the current chapter is that many

Figure 5. Machine implanted thoughts

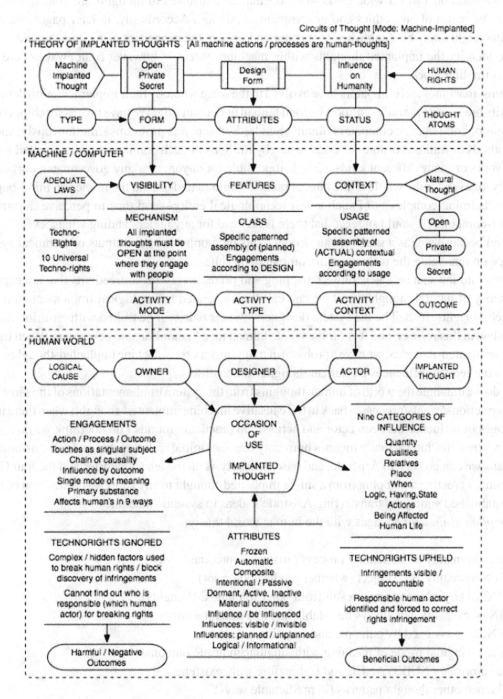

system and computer designs are sub-optimal; and further that they tend to: meet the wishes of few, as opposed to fulfilling the needs/requirements of the many.

Assuming that we have established (correctly) the basic Attributes of machine implanted-thoughts; the question becomes how to identify, structure, plus manage and control these implanted thoughts—in such a way—and on a world-wide-basis—that the natural Attributes of thoughts are upheld. Obviously we are in the realm of law, ethics and government regulation. Accordingly, in later pages, we outline how techno-rights may be established to nurture and protect the properties of natural thoughts. A first task is to identify the implanted-thoughts within machine systems—however right away we are hit by a major stumbling block.

Systems, machines and computers have evolved to the stage whereby their implementation details and complexity are—quite literally—almost beyond human understanding. We have processor chips containing billions of components; computers running hundreds of separate programs simultaneously; and each with hundreds of millions of lines of code; whereby millions of such computers are connected together into networks of many different kinds. How is it possible for anyone; for any government, corporation, university, or even for the whole of the human race; to begin to understand the immense, mind-boggling and overwhelming complexity of such a vast technological entity—and thus to perceive the structure of the self-computer? I would suggest that there is no need for any understanding whatsoever—at a top level—and because we (as a society) can simply focus on monitoring the outputs of technical systems; and hence on managing the influences of computers on self.

Written into law can be a generalised mapping and protection of those freedoms that are expressed in the theory of natural thoughts; and we can call the associated technological implementation of the same; techno-rights. It shall be the system designers/owners who will be tasked with ensuring that they obey the law in this respect, and it is for the whole human race to monitor said behaviour. When tracking machine implanted-thoughts; we have a problem of mapping inputs—machine implanted-thoughts—with outputs—the related influences on human thoughts/actions/life.

How do we untangle the world of human thoughts from the system implementations of the same? How do we map actions/events/processes back to the causative machine implanted-thought; when there may be many stages of influence between actor and action? On practical grounds I do not think we do (or can); and it is where a machine actually touches humanity that the (initial) relationship and responsibility lies.

Perhaps we can go back to Aristotle, and base our analysis on the ten Categories and the four Causes. In this manner creating a mapping from a single implanted-thought to any supposed restriction of human rights; established simply by transferring Aristotle's ideas to systems/machines.

An *implanted-thought* engages with the human world thusly:

TOUCHES humanity as an action / process / material outcome
TOUCHES humanity as a subject (whether predicated or not)
IS INITIATED by a human (may result from other implanted-thoughts)
A CHAIN of causality can always be established to a human actor
INFLUENCE is assigned by outcome and in a single context
EXISTS as a singular mode of meaning with singular/multiple outcomes
Affects as a primary SUBSTANCE and is therefore truly existent
May influence other thought patterns (in predictable ways)
May affect human subject(s) in one of nine ways given below

The Categories of Influence for *implanted-thoughts:*

- May affect QUANTITY in discrete/continuous fashion etc
- May affect QUALITIES; e.g.colour, shape, hot, fast etc

- May affect RELATIVE relations between objects, half, master etc
- May affect PLACE of real-world objects
- May affect WHEN relations of real-world objects
- May affect LOGIC, HAVING or STATE conditions
- May affect ACTIONS or changes in objects (shape, relations etc)
- BEING AFFECTED by other some action(s).
- May influence human life / natural thought rights and/or human rights

We name the above features the Engagements and Categories of Influence of machine implanted-thoughts. All well and good, but where does such a scheme get us in respect to human-machine relationships? Potentially quite a long way, in actual fact, and towards tying down the myriad of different influence(s) of machines on the human world.

Our approach to mapping the influence of machines, is a straight-forward one.

We begin by ignoring the actual internals of machines; and attempt to understand the influence, or external operational mechanics, of implanted-thoughts. Focus is placed on where the implanted-thought 'touches' humanity by means of actions/events and physical outcomes (as defined by the nine category examples). Secondly we state that any implanted-thought 'touches' humanity purely in the first-person—and the outcomes are assigned by material affect. Even though the implanted-thought may be influenced by humans and/or data and/or other implanted-thoughts and/or patterns of thoughts (which may in fact be the causative factor); it is at the point(s) where an implanted-thought actually interfaces with humanity that the initial influence/responsibility lies.

This latter point is in accordance with legal precedence whereby the chain of responsibility starts with the (most obvious) actor, and it is he who must demonstrate/prove that he was deceived/influenced/forced by another actor into a course of action; and in order to offload responsibility. Hence all thought-patterns are assigned an author (implementer), owner and initiator. Therefore a human/legal agent can be identified for every thought atom's consequences. Likewise we state that implanted-thoughts are identified in having a single pattern (or mode) of meaning, and for the purposes of mapping. Where the influences of a thought possess more than one outcome, then these must be treated separately, as individual patterned units of action/meaning. Implanted-thoughts are also assigned as a primary substance, and associated actions cannot therefore be categorised as (in some way) mere side-effects of societal forces / universal categories.

One might think that laws are already in place to deal with cases where a machine/computer/system breaks human rights. However any laws are inadequate, and because:

- Society does not (always) realise that people have freedom-of-thought rights. (see many examples of societal indifference and instances where freedom of thought is ignored)
- Complex/hidden technical factors are used to break human rights, and also to block a person from finding out when his/her rights are broken. Laws are required to force organisations to comply.
- An individual cannot find out who (which human actors) is/are responsible for breaking said rights; and nothing can be done!
- There are no techno-rights to mirror and so to protect one's human rights (in terms of technology and its effects on humanity).

Needed is a new vision with respect to the design of machines; and in particular because whenever we design a machine—any machine—then we are in fact implanting our thoughts into the world in a wholly inflexible way. These frozen (universal) thoughts will often have the most profound results; and multiple implications; good, bad, indifferent, intended or not. And they will operate correctly - Everything Else Being Equal! Machines are constructed entirely from human implanted-thoughts; and the same being subject to the Attributes, Engagements, and Categories of influence.

Accordingly, I will suggest that it is perfectly feasible to design a new kind of society—a technopia—by means of said theories; whereby machines are built that respect and recognise human rights. Special techno-rights will be required to nurture and protect human-rights—the same being the standard rights—only consciously instantiated within machine implanted-thoughts. Although my suggestions may sound radical, and perhaps utilitarian; only by means of a major impetus could we possibly alter the course of the modern world away from; citizen spying, stolen thoughts/data, no freedom of expression and a complete lack of knowledge in relation to the thoughts/votes of humanity.

Democracy

It is my position that a primary function of technology is to create a utopian future, and to progress the humanistic agenda; complete with democratic values, and human-friendly: policies, values, agendas, laws and societal mechanisms.

The focus is on finding ways for people to obtain the fundamental human rights, and more especially in terms of thought-ownership; which is in some ways a precursor to, and facilitator of, all the other human rights. As an example of such a linkage; I put it to you that with current technology we don't even know what are the collective opinions on almost any specific topic or major issue of global concern. If we only knew what society (as a whole) was thinking, perhaps we could implement more humane policies. This happens through wide-ranging aggregation of human thoughts, opinions and votes; and the corresponding collective and democratic wishes of the majority being put into action. These ideas relate to the implementation of, and definition of, democracy itself—and so to the nature of society (Benedek, Veronika & Matthias, 2008).

Democracy has multiple meanings and different definitions, but here we refer to the concept in the most simplistic sense imaginable; being the actioning of the collective will of the people. I do not think that we have democracy (on a world-wide basis) at present, no matter what our leaders may say/present. I shall make the argument that for humanity to progress, we must find out what the wishes of the majority actually are, and on an issue-by-issue basis, and then collectively implement the same. Along the way we introduce a number of new principles for a technological society, which we name the technopia.

A technopia is a society so arranged as to benefit all, and it has special laws, rights and technological mechanisms to ensure the same. Especially important are new human rights—techno-rights—that each citizen of the world will be afforded. These rights mirror (and extend) the four fundamental human rights, and are designed to guarantee that each person obtains the same. A special new class of atomic network is prescribed to provide and uphold these techno-rights. Let us now briefly examine the basic nature—and capabilities of—the Atomic Network (Nelson, 1974; Radley, 2013; Radley, 2015; Veltman, 2006; Veltman, 2014).

Atomic Networks

As a partial solution to some of the issues discussed above, we have developed the idea of an atomic network. An atomic network is the polar opposite of a centralized or cloud network. It effectively provides a 'save' and 'load' function for the Internet, and provides for an indestructible data type that cannot be controlled and lives forever. Let us examine how such a theoretical network might work. We assume that network members are scattered all across the Internet, that is they are located on different IP (Internet Protocol) addresses and some may be behind Network Address Translation devices (NATs). Furthermore, each network member has a special client program on his personal computer or mobile device. Next we provide the following system actions; save and load, based on a unique data unit identifier. When the user chooses a file (data unit), and saves it to the network, it is automatically given a unique identifier, an owner identifier and a member-specific key and/or password if it is private.

Now what the client program does next (upon save) is interesting (and unique), it "atomizes" the data unit to the network. The item is split into many thousands of tiny pieces (atoms) which are then disseminated across the network as a whole. There are many, many copies of each piece (data atom) which are saved on many remote computers hard drives, for later retrieval at an unspecified time. Data atoms are encrypted according to the key for the data unit as whole. Next when the owner (or key / password holder) chooses to load (or retrieve) the data unit from the network, then the owner's client knows how to request from the network all of the constituent atoms, re-assemble them and so to reproduce the data unit. Note that network members agree to reserving part of their computer disc for other people's data "atoms". You now have a robust way of backing-up and sharing items using the link identifiers for the data unit. When another network member's client requests such a link, a "torrent" of constituent data "atoms" is sent to that client (from all across the network), until such time as the data unit has been fully reconstructed. Every network member's computer is now a data-atom server! And a sufficient "stock" of identical copies of each data atom (perhaps 100's) is automatically maintained according to continuous network maintenance tasks.

One now asks the question, what has been achieved with such an atom network?

Firstly data is effectively immortal and indestructible, and relies on the unbreakable redundancy provided by massive distribution and replication of hundreds of identical atoms across many separate network locations. And the robustness of the network increases with number of network members (computers to store atoms).

Other key advantages include no longer having central servers; and this is environmentally friendly and brings security advantages. Additionally data save/loading speeds are much faster (i.e. no central server upload times and torrent-like data atom transfers). N.B. At present we have no examples of an atomic network; not on any of the computing systems in the entire world; and the closest system would be BitCoin or BitTorrent; which are both distributed; but are used for other purposes and hence do not provide a Save and Load capability for the Internet.

What has been achieved with such an atom network? Firstly, data/thoughts saved to the network are rendered effectively immortal and indestructible, and such a status relies on the unbreakable redundancy provided by massive distribution and replication of hundreds of identical atoms across many separate network locations. And the robustness of the network increases with number of network members (computers to store atoms). Other key advantages include no longer needing/having central servers; and this is environmentally friendly and brings security advantages.

Figure 6. An atomic network

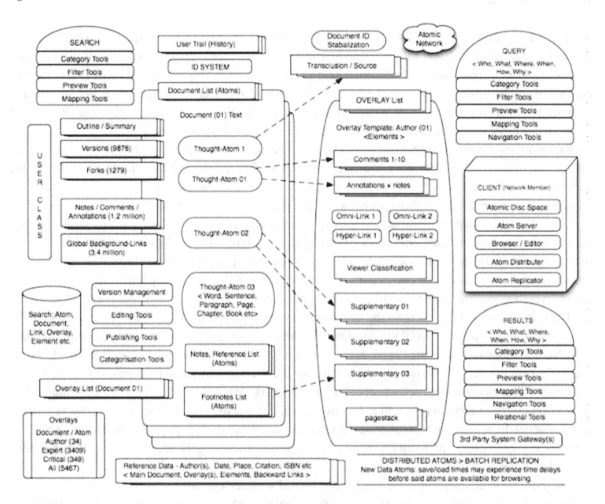

Crucially here nobody can ever spy on said atoms where they are assigned as private/ secret-thoughts. Additionally data save/loading speeds are much faster (i.e. no central server upload times and torrent-like atom transfers). The system also has virtually unlimited storage space, so long as the network remains in operation or has a minimum/proportionally-increasing number of users to operate and maintain its infrastructure (virtual disc-space). But perhaps most importantly the network can be a technical guarantee of the principles of the Theory of Natural Thoughts. Supported is freedom, equality and free-assembly of thoughts; and in particular because we do not have any network administrators, owners or Big Brother spying and/or network controlling interference from above.

Obviously we have said little about the technical implementation details about how this network would actually be designed; and presented is a purely top-level description. However there is no reason why such a system cannot be built; and in terms of technical hurdles etc. In design terms we equate the described data-atoms (assembled into units) with the thought atoms and data segments (Nelson's vision) discussed earlier. Nothing has been said about how knowledge would be organised within such a network. In fact the simplicity of the underlying data structure allows many different organisational: mappings, overlays, features and capabilities.

Thought-Spaces

We adopt a formal definition of a thought-space, which is a medium in which the thinking process takes place. This is assumed to be a combination of one or more human mind(s); merged with any mind-extending/shaping and/or mind-supporting method(s) and/ or communication/ technological tools that may be said to exist (and which aid in the creation/vision/sharing of new/old thought-patterns).

Obviously, thinking happens within human mind(s) (and I claim never [yet] in machine/computer/ robot 'minds'). And here we shall overlook machine-implanted thoughts and cast aside all possibility of an artificial mind itself 'thinking' and label Artificial Intelligence as being (in actual fact) merely Simulated Intelligence; or thinking that possesses a purely reflexive form of free-will (N.B. critics must prove the opposite).

A thought-space is established whenever a thinker or collective begins to think. This space consists of available language(s), knowledge(s), computer(s) etc, and may (or may not) reflect the thinker's entire history/education and/or the details of conversation(s) he/she is having (or has had) with others. Normally the thought-space itself consists of many visible referenced-thought spaces; as established and delimited by the rules of language, logic, principle, science, culture etc. It may be difficult for a thinker to 'see' how many, and what are the different thought-spaces he is using.

And because thought-spaces are normally partially constructed from technology; plus the quality, efficiency and effectiveness of any thought-space (including its 'truth-content', evolution and/or logical development etc); these will be dependent on the design (forms) and evolution of said tools.

Thought-spaces are complex 'mini-worlds' of meaning that reflect human: experience, theory, knowledge, propositions, deductions, stories etc; and they dictate which thoughts may exist and/or be accepted into (or work within) a specific ensemble. A thought-space may be likened to 'patterned' element(s) of mind; and to be a place in which thinker(s) can obtain help: perceiving situations, processing facts, making theories and deductions; forming conclusions and so creating, linking and establishing groups and assemblies of thoughts into useful groups and patterns. For an effective thought-space, all (relevant) sub/linked thought-spaces must be readily available and inter-connected in every (useful) way imaginable; and all available/used thoughts would (ideally) be hyper-thoughts with hyper-context. Examples of typical thought-space(s) are: when a thinker: considers/works-out how to perceive/solve a problem, travel to a destination, make an object, contribute to a theory, write a book, walk along a path, consider a physics problem, watch a movie (entering another person's thought-space) etc.

The question arises as to whether there are any examples of a truly effective Thought-Space. What about the Internet? Yes, the Internet has been a great invention; and helps many people connect and communicate in a myriad of different ways. However individual thoughts, or data/thought-atoms (micro-thoughts in Kim Veltman's terms); are still largely disconnected, unlinked and hidden deep-inside a great diversity of different systems and/or isolated documents etc. In our terms the vast majority of thoughts/ concepts are lost, hidden, unconnected; and exist as black thoughts, and/or memory holes etc. Note that a black-thought is a (possibly) relevant thought-atom that has become lost/hidden/ignored/un-linked from a specific contextual pattern, in that the 'parent' thought-pattern may appear to be logically consistent (i.e. true) in and of itself; and according to both internal and external structures; however because (some) potentially related thoughts are 'black' or invisible; then the structure (as a whole) may be incomplete and/or false/sub-optimal (ref. shallow-context).

We can conclude that the vast majority of open and/or socially published thoughts are lost, and therefore the predominant form(s) for all of the open- thoughts of humanity is to exist in a black/invisible form.

Figure 7. Flow-chart representation [A] of a thought-space

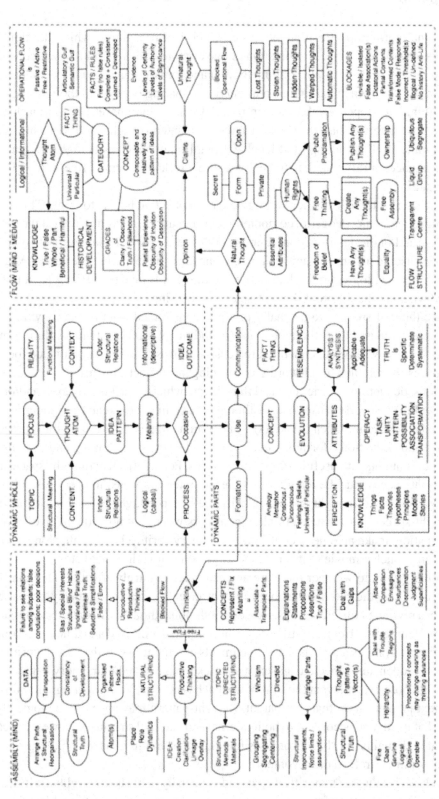

Figure 8. Flow-chart representation [B] of a thought-space

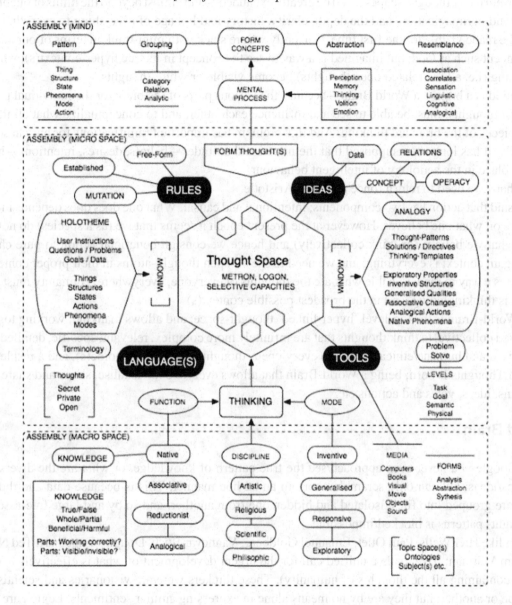

We are utterly blind with respect to the linkage/assembly of the vast majority of thought-atoms; and with current Internet technology. There is no point even trying to estimate the amount of information/ knowledge that is missing from the current Web as a result, and because not even a single word/idea/ thought/vote exists in its rightful hyper-context; and because that would require (for a 'common' idea like God)—millions upon millions of—categorised forward and backward links, and probably tens of thousands of overlaid (and categorised) comments, annotations etc; and for each related thought/data-atom etc.

Radiant should be each and every hyper-idea; with vast numbers of related thought-patterns visible. For example, all the (actually existent) 'lines-of-thought' that emanate from the idea of God should be topically categorised and interlinked in every possible way (reflecting its hyper-context). Hence our thought-horizons/thought-scapes could be greatly expanded—and almost beyond the limits of our present understanding/imagination; and the depth, clarity, history and linkage of everything to everything else would be made visible for the first time. Currently we are stuck with mini-think in terms of our analysis of a concept such as God; but imagined is a way to see the concept in its true hyper-context(s); whereby everything (i.e. all the related open thoughts) become visible or white-thoughts.

Desired is a brain—a World Brain—because the various parts of the brain, or the individual people/ thinkers/ thoughts; must be able to see and influence each other, and to conceptualize what all the different pieces of the brain are thinking. And this problem has important ramifications for human society generally. It has long been supposed that the intentional attitudes—beliefs, desires, intentions—have a central place in the aetiology of intelligent behaviour.

Perhaps we need to return (once again) to Aristotle.

He said that action has two components; intentional and causal. What one does does depends in some measure on what one believes. However at the present epoch it seems that we (as a species) do not even know what we believe (or think collectively) and hence we consign beneficial action to pure chance. Once again context is everything; and we need to see all open thought-atoms in their proper context(s). Desired is a way to render visible what are the thoughts of everyone, everywhere. Humanity must know what it is thinking/doing, and in the broadest possible context(s).

A World-Brain is the top-level 'hyper-linked' thought-space; and allows mankind, working together as unified collective, to think thoughts that are infinitely more complex, relevant, specific, detailed, contextualised and humane/ethical etc. Here every open- thought finds its true home(s), and a resplendent City Of Thoughts is born; being a World-Brain that allows everyone to visualise, shape and share all of our plans, ideas, votes and actions etc.

World Brain

With Google you never even approach/see the true pattern of knowledge, or what are the diversity of opinions/ideas; but can only scramble about in an ad-hoc manner. This is because data and thought-atoms are grouped into files, isolated and hidden one from another; and so by and large free-assembly of thought- patterns is blocked/impossible.

Men like H.G.Wells, Paul Otlet, Emanuel Goldberg, Vannevar Bush, Douglas Engelbart, Ted Nelson and Kim Veltman; have made a unified call for the urgent development of what is effectively a World Brain (containing all the thoughts of humanity). These thinkers were/are visionaries and scientists, of one type or another; but they are by no means alone in expressing similar sentiments. Legion are those who have urged mankind to create humanistic systems that allow all the members of a society to share thoughts/votes/ideas freely and openly, and amongst the same are: Jean-Jaques Rousseau, Bertrand Russell, John Adams, Henry Ward, Norbert Wiener, George Orwell, Lewis Mumford, Julian Assange, Tim Berners-Lee, Douglas Rushkoff etc.

Why is/has there been such an overwhelming call for what is effectively a World Brain?

Notably, the reasons given are not related to the creation of a utopia; but rather for education; and for avoidance of despotic regimes whereby technologies are used to subjugate man and/or to block his basic human rights. Accordingly, it is nothing less than preservation of civilisation that is at stake. It is my position that building a World Brain may in fact be a difficult task, but it is by no means impossible. Some people believe that we already have built such a brain; specifically in the form of: the Internet, Cloud(s) and/or the World Wide Web. Whilst these developments have been tentative steps in a useful direction, our analysis has shown how limited are the resulting systems in terms of the freedom, ownership and equality of thoughts. Undoubtably our world is today more connected than ever before, in terms of digital information flows and the rapid communication of (a small subset of) ideas, transactions and data etc. Largely by default, it does appear that humanity is building a self-computer; and because the self is now almost fully immersed in technology whilst at school, home and work. But we must heed the warnings of the technology visionaries; and build/use mechanisms such as techno-rights; and to ensure that our machines foster humane values.

Figure 9. Features of an effective / ineffective thought-space

FREEDOM OF THOUGHT	Freedom of Belief	Free Thinking	Public Proclamation
Authorised Owner / Viewer	Have any Thought	Create any Thought	Publish any Thought
Attribute of Natural Thought-Atom	Equality All relevant thought(s) are VISIBLE	Free Assembly Any thought(s) may be SHAPED	Ownership Anyone may publish any thought(s) to any PLACE
Adequate Structuring **Interrelations of Knowledge**	Centre one's Vision Freedom to perceive useful and/or relevant thoughts See patterns of: Similarity Context Relationship	Group into a Shape Freedom to assemble known and new thoughts Create patterns of: Similarity Context Relationship	Segregate into Place Freedom to publish any thought Publish patterns of: Similarity Context Relationship
Free Flow **Dynamism of Knowledge**	Transparent Space Thought-Atoms equally visible See DYNAMIC views of all concept(s)	Liquid Space Thought-Atoms equally combinable / linkable Re-arrange DYNAMIC assemblies of any / all concept(s)	Ubiquitous Space Thought-Atoms equally publishable Publish DYNAMIC views / assemblies of any / all concept(s)
Thinking Operation (Mind + Media) **Analogy Category**	See Established concept(s) Intelligence depends on the availability of concepts	Create New concept(s) Intelligence depends on the ability to form concepts	Share concept(s) Intelligence depends on the number + quality + inter-relation of concepts
Operational Flow	Freedom to Perceive	Freedom to Judge	Freedom to Associate
Structural Dynamism	Combinability of useful concept(s)	Flexibility of useful concept(s)	Inertia of useful concept(s)
Orwellian Thought-Space	Censure Concepts Block any of above	Fix Concepts Block any of above	Divert Concepts Block any of above
Blocked Thoughts **Truth and Operacy may be reduced**	Lost / Hidden OPERACY Failed Task No Unity Hidden Patterns Poor Association Impossible Transformation(s)	Warped OPERACY Wrong Task False Unity Broken Pattern False Association Sub-optimal Transformation(s)	Automatic / Lost OPERACY Invisible Task Partial Unity Weak Pattern Impossible Association Unknown Transformation(s)

It is important to note that the concept of a World Brain is by no means dead; and because many modern scholars/technologists/thinkers are today making tentative plans to actually build such a system. What is lacking is a unified call for action, and/or an efficient and effective channeling of effort on a world-wide basis. Money may be needed to bring plans into reality; but 'smarts' or intelligent/correct design is even more important. And we should not underestimate the powers of collective action. Cross your fingers.

Features of the World Brain

We begin with the capability to share private-thoughts; which shall be provided by the atomic network in the form of a unique key-identifier and an encryption/decryption matched pair set that is known only to the sender and receivers of the shared thoughts/ data-atoms. How these keys are passed securely across an open network is undetermined/left to the implementers, because there is today severe doubt (or certainty) that Public Key Encryption technology is absolutely secure; since the NSA appears to have paid the company dealing with the random number generators, and specifically to generate a 'crackable' or decipherable private/public key pair(s). Perhaps a good alternative method is to swap a book of keys physically (sender and receivers meet in the real-world [once]); and so that each side has (absolutely secret) cypher- matching; as in a one-key-pass-book technique (see KeyMail). Secondly desired is sharing of open-thoughts; or identity signed and also anonymous thought-atoms. Signed items use an identity (individual or group) that is established by some un-specified method; and it could be tied to one's ID on a social aspect of the atomic network (similar to Facebook) whereby your friends establish your identity. Alternatively we could use a certificate system to establish a person's identity, but once again the implementation details are beyond the scope of the present chapter. Note that in principle we do believe in enabling people to share thoughts anonymously, and capabilities in this respect include sharing data/thoughts of any type; and even where said data depicts crimes/anti-social activities. As a reminder, it is my belief that thoughts/data are never immoral/evil; and that only actions can be unlawful/wrong. I know that this latter point will be a contentious issue. One argument in favor of open sharing of any thought atom; is to weigh guaranteed freedom of thought/expression (a definite win) against supposed prevention/visibility of crimes (an uncertain win). It is this very faculty; to share thoughts openly and without censure; that guarantees ownership, free assembly and equality of thoughts; capabilities which are the bedrocks of any free society.

But how are we to prevent publication of crimes and/or illegal activities? How do we stop children seeing illegal or potentially corrupting data/thought atoms? Answer: do you really think that children are not already looking at all kinds of illicit material? I would suggest that an atomic network (or hyper-network) can provide a good solution in this respect; and by enabling all thought-atoms to be classifiable/annotatable (by everyone); and hence warnings and/or class-assignments can be placed on individual items (by many/all viewers). But are we not bringing back censure by the back-door here? Not really; and because users could (presumably) obtain a browser that enabled a child's parent to set a classification/viewing age for all content on the network as whole (people choose their own access level). What about authority? Will this 'brain' not be a bit like Wikipedia, whereby reporting standards may (sometimes be) pretty poor; and because non-experts are allowed to edit anything, anytime. In actual fact Wikipedia (often) has high standards; and is not really like that at-all; but employs teams of professional (educated) editors to monitor edits.

In any case, the World Brain will allow organisations to establish group consensus by overlaying/stamping their authority on particular thought structures, and so to develop approved assemblies of specific thought patterns. The World Brain can replace, extend and supplant many activities that are today performed (or attempted to be performed) on the current World Wide Web. In particular open-publication is facilitated; whereby anyone may publish anything to anyone and/or everyone else. This is a primary feature; being a capability for everyone to contribute, and to see/access/ annotate the open thoughts of the entire world, and so to see how they are all connected, interrelated and structured. We shall be able to see: who thought what, where, when and how. And not only for the living and/or present-day thoughts; because the World Brain will be the repository for every thought ever thunk (at least those thoughts have been input into the system correctly).

A question arises. Who/what will enter all of these thought-atoms; and who/what will develop the classifications schemes, mapping and meta-data etc; and how? Answer; everyone will input/develop the content, just as happened with the Web. Why would people go to the trouble of entering knowledge into this new 'brain'? Perhaps because it is a brain—a World Brain—and it is in their interests to do so. Power to the people can, should and will win, and in a similar way to the Web. When people realise that this system is so far beyond any previous system in terms of the interconnectedness, accessibility and linkage of thought atoms; people everywhere will be motivated to discover: what the world is thinking/ has-thought.

I would suggest that we humans have reached a turning point; whereby we can simply go on much as in the past; allowing technology to progress in an entirely unplanned/ad-hoc manner (in the biggest sense). Whereby powerful people develop unrepresentative/narrow computing systems that are (in effect) simply excuses to foster more centralised control, and/or to exploit/limit the human-rights of, millions of weaker individuals. Alternatively, we could start again and develop (at least one example) of a truly people-centric information system. A system which lets each of us see the open-thoughts of everyone in the world; and lets us vote en masse and so to discover our true wishes as a people. Developing a World Brain has been the dream of the most brilliant thinkers; but today it no longer needs to remain a dream; because we now posses the technology and (I would suggest) motivation and desire to actually make it happen. And it does not need the backing of a government or a large corporation to do so; but rather can be achieved in a grass-roots manner; whereby we can proceed along the lines of open-source projects like BitCoin, BitTorrent and Linux etc.

The World Brain is not to be an artificial 'machine' brain (in any way); but will be composed simply of live/dynamic human thoughts; and primarily because we wish humanity to think collectively, efficiently and as one; aligning the wishes, plans and actions of society for the true benefit of all. A lofty and even utopian goal? Certainly. But (potentially) solvable through technology.

KeyMail

KeyMail is a new type of electronic mail. KeyMail employs end-to-end multi-encryption and is a private "friendship" network and is not compatible with email. KeyMail employs a new protocol for electronic mail, being one that enables users to share large files quickly, securely and potentially without any size limitations. KeyMail is not designed to replace email. Rather the concept for sending a KeyMail is to transfer large amounts of data privately and efficiently. Many people wish to share large files, but email programs limit the size of attachments to around 20 MB. KeyMail provides a three point solution, whereby large files can be shared rapidly and in a secure manner. No data is held on central servers, and files are end-to-end encrypted.

Additionally there are no upload delays, and no SPAM. KeyMail can take a variable period of time to arrive at the destination depending upon the size of the file transfer. The largest file we have transferred with KeyMail across the Internet is 20 GB, which took 26 minutes to fully arrive at a transfer rate of 100 mb/s. KeyMail has several inherent advantages over email, including faster speeds (no upload delays), and it potentially offers transfer of items of an unlimited size, plus it enables the sending and receiving of multiple files simultaneously. (latter capability is not possible with email) Files can be sent directly from one USB Key-Drive to another, without generating any copies—not even on the sender / receiver computers (we call this Single-Copy-Send). KeyMail runs on Microsoft Windows or Apple Macintosh computers.

Put simply, KeyMail provides freedom from spying plus unbreakable hacking protection, and all without generating any digital footprints. With ordinary email the message is copied onto innumerable Internet computers, stored onto a cloud server, and then backed-up. As a result, your information is unprotected and open to theft / copying. KeyMail avoids the troubling scenario of having your private data stored anywhere and everywhere—and potentially forever!

KeyMail Features:

Device-to-Device (Single-Copy-Send) + Secret protocol
Adaptive Parallel Transport (2-4 times faster)
Multi-layer encryption (Symmetric + Asymmetric)
Live P2P message transport + Packet-scrambling (distributed)
Private network / cypher matching
No message copies anywhere + Message self-destruct / live texting
Up to 100 GB files may be transferred

Figure 10. KeyMail Client running on Apple Macintosh Computer

CONCLUSION

Any paper purporting to identify a golden solution to all of the worlds problems—or even a tiny portion of them—is bound to be labelled as optimistic at best, and more likely as deluded, unrealistic, or simply as a work of pure fiction. And especially precipitous is the path followed by anyone who considers technological solutions as some kind of super-positive solve-all. In his 2005 book The Singularity is Near Ray Kurzweil puts forward the view that the law of accelerating returns predicts an exponential increase in technologies like computers, genetics, nanotechnology, robotics and artificial intelligence (Kurzwel, 2005). He says that this will lead to a technological singularity in the year 2045, when progress outstrips human ability to understand it.

At this point, he predicts that machine intelligence will be more powerful than all human intelligence combined. Ray foresees only positive benefits for technology, and he might be labelled as a techno-optimist. However the lessons of history are just the opposite; and that the introduction of any new technology does normally have major unexpected (and often negative) consequences/influences.

What can be said with certainty is that effective technology design is far more difficult than at first sight it may appear; and it is essential to see innovations from the broadest possible 'humanistic' perspective. Perhaps we can follow the key example of the humanities. We have laws and legal presidents (based on human rights); and it seems that likewise we now need technological rights—or techno-rights—to govern computer systems. Certainly we cannot allow technology to continue to develop without top-level planning; because already clear is that vast numbers of human beings are being trodden underfoot in terms of basic rights; including aspects of thought ownership and access to the combined wealth of all mankind.

In this chapter we have viewed computers as potentially beneficial to society, but as not necessarily so. Machines have always held a janus-like prospect. They magnify human potential with magical and transformative powers, but on the other hand they sometimes bring anti-social, destructive and/or dehumanizing forces into society. Perhaps the current chapter raises more questions than it answers. We ask why should it be be so—that computers bring negative elements into society, and if the negative aspects must always follow any technological revolution and/or improvements. We have considered if our new system of techno-rights could possibly help, by fostering the human use of human beings. Other questions arise, as to the specific ways in which machines may beneficially impact society, and also the ways in which they may sometimes have/bring detrimental effect(s). Someone (or perhaps all of us) need(s) to consider the how, why, when, where and who; and in relation to technological changes; and using examples from history, fiction and also in terms of basic theories.

One may think that many of the problems with respect to technology have been well-examined, and are, to some extent, well-understood at least in terms of outcomes and especially in terms of the anti-humanistic nature of technology. That is to some extent true. However findings are often scattered about in various works of fiction, non-fiction, in papers and now increasingly on social media and in the form of websites and blogs. And when it comes to solutions, the lesson(s) of history are difficult to divine. In particular, it would seem that technological revolutions are hard to predict, even harder to manage, and almost impossible to control. Clear is that one technology tends to sweep aside and/or encompass previous technologies. Furthermore the social implications, which at first tend to appear bright and optimistic; in reality turn out to be darker than we would otherwise collectively have wished for. And the dangers in relation to technology are real. David Thoreau says that men must not: 'become tools of their tools'.

Another interesting (if somewhat mystifying) feature of the current zeitgeist, relates to the manner in which many people uncritically accept all technological developments as somehow natural, just and inevitable and/or unstoppable. Perhaps we (as a people) do not even believe that we have the power (or ability) to shape and control our own creations.

One example, is that no organizations or regulatory bodies are responsible for the overall strategic direction of all computing inventions on a worldwide basis, and in particular from a humanistic perspective. Perhaps this is about to change, as Sir Tim Berners-Lee has recently called for the creation of an on-line Magna-Carta or Bill of Rights for the Internet (Berners-Lee, 2014), and others including Edward Snowden and Julian Assange have brought attention to the dangers of citizen surveillance.

As I wrap up a somewhat lengthy paper, a few comments on the title are appropriate.

Why do I pit humans against machines (apparently)? Where is the battle—because we can see no obvious casualties. We are not living in the world of Terminators and/or SkyNet (apparently). Most people are content with the apparently 'marvelous' capabilities that modern technology affords.

Techno-optimism has gotten the upper hand, and the techno-optimists believe that technology, can and will, solve all of humanities problems; the local and global, the individual and social ones etc. But is the picture quite so rosy? Do we not still see a great divide; where only the rich have access to networked computers (for example). Is technology (somehow) being used to prevent the poor improving their lot? And what about education; has technology truly revolutionized how all children (in first, second and third world's) learn? To say nothing of democracy and a complete lack of 'atomicity' for voting on all issues. Are we really saying that Wikipedia, Twitter and Facebook etc; is/are the best we can do in terms of accessing, and connecting with, the truly vast scale/interrelation(s) of all human thought streams (past and present)?

Ask yourself: is this the best of all possible worlds?

My point is to look beyond what current technology is providing and imagine (plus create) a better future. We cannot just let the future develop as it may; and it is my belief that technology must managed—at the biggest and smallest levels. And it must be a human managed process; not only in development but in the operational phases.

Today it would seem that we are no longer mere spectators and detached users of machines, but rather it appears that we are now immersed inside of a new global technological entity. Whatsoever 'it' is; has been much debated, for William Gibson it was cyberspace (Gibson, 1984), for Sir Tim Berners-Lee the World Wide Web (Berners-Lee, 2014), others called it the Internet, the information super-highway, or the Global Village, still others the World Brain, and not least, George Orwell called one version of it Big Brother (Orwell, 1949). I would argue that 'it' is simply self; and furthermore it is a self that we ourselves can design, form, shape and use in whatever ways may suit our collective future needs/wishes.

ACKNOWLEDGMENT

I am deeply grateful for the support of family and friends, without whom this chapter would not have been possible. My sincere gratitude and thanks to Prof. Francisco V. Cipolla-Ficarra who supported the work and also inspired the initial work just over 2 years ago. Thanks also to my mentor Prof. Kim Veltman who has supported and inspired this work over a period of more than a decade.

REFERENCES

Arthur, C. (2013). *Google Launches tool to help users plan for digital afterlife*. Online article: http://www.theguardian.com/ technology/2013/apr/12/google-inactive-account-manager-digital-death

Benedek, W., Veronika, B., & Matthias, K. (2008). *Internet Governance and the Information Society*. Eleven International Publishing.

Berners-Lee, T. (1999). *Weaving the Web*. New York: Harper.

Berners-Lee, T. (2014). *World wide Web needs bill of rights*. Retrieved from http://www.bbc.co.uk/news/uk-26540635

Bradbury, R. (1953). *Fahrenheit 451*. Milan: Mondadori.

Clark, D. (1989). An Analysis of TCP Processing Overhead. Biography. *IEEE Communications Magazine, 29*.

Descartes, R. (1637). *Discourse on the Method of Rightly Conducting the Reason, and Seeking Truth in the Sciences*. Cambridge, UK: Cambridge University Press.

Descartes, R. (1641). *Mediations on First Philosophy*. Cambridge, UK: Cambridge University Press.

Foucault, M. (1975). *Discipline and Punishment*. Milan: Einaudi.

Gibson, W. (1984). *Neuromancer*. New York: Ace Books.

Hunger Statistics. (2013). *United Nations World Food*. Programme.

Kurzwel, R. (2005). *The Singularity is Near*. London: Penguin Books.

Lanier, J. (2013). *Who Owns the Future*. London: Penguin Books.

Laurel, B. (1991). *Computers as Theatre*. Boston: Addison-Wesley Publishing.

Luppicini, R. (2013). *The Emerging Field of Technoself Studies. In Handbook of Research on Technoself: Identity in a Technological Society* (pp. 1–25). Hershey, PA: IGI Global. doi:10.4018/978-1-4666-2211-1.ch001

McLuhan, M. (1964). *Understanding Media: The Extensions of Man*. Berkeley, CA: Gingko Press.

McLuhan, M. (1967). *The Mechanical Bride: Folklore of Industrial Man*. London: Duckworth Overlook.

Nelson, T. (1974). *Computer Lib / Dream Machines*. Redmond, WA: Tempus Books of Microsoft Press.

Norman, D. A. (1999). *The Invisible Computer*. MIT Press.

Orwell, G. (1949). *Nineteen Eight-Four*. London: Penguin Books.

Radley, A. (2013). Computers as Self. In *CD Proceedings Fourth International Workshop in Human-Computer Interaction, Tourism and Cultural Heritage in Rome, Italy*. Bergamo: Blue Herons Editions.

Radley, A. (2015). *Self as Computer*. Chalerston: BluePrints.

Rheingold, H. (1985). *Tools for Thought*. MITPress.

Russell, B. (1963). *Skeptical Essays*. Chicago: University of Chicago Press.

Segal, K. (2012). *Insanely Simple*. London: Penguin.

UDHR. (1948). *Universal Declaration of Human Rights*. UN General Assembly.

Veltman, K. (2006). *Understanding New Media*. Calgary: University of Calgary Press.

Veltman, K. (2014). *The Alphabets of Life*. Maastricht: Virtual Maastricht McLuhan Institute.

Wiener, N. (1950). *The Human Use of Human Beings*. Boston: Hougthon Mifflin.

KEY TERMS AND DEFINITIONS

Atomic Network: Network data massively distributed plus replicated to multiple locations.

Natural Thoughts (Theory of): Thoughts with ownership, equality and free-assembly.

Self-Computer: Merging of human(s) with computers/machines/systems/technology.

Technopia: A society so arranged as to benefit all; upholds everyone's techno-rights. Affords democratic/collective voting and decision-making, plus freedom-of-thought.

Techno-Rights: Ordinary human rights transposed into a technological world.

APPENDIX 1

Glossary - of (Mostly) Coined Terms/Concepts

Artificial Intelligence (Standard Term): Non-proven capability of artificial machines to: think, inuit, have free-will, self-determine, self-program, have flexibility of purpose, reproduce, become self-aware, posses life, be conscious, intelligently process information etc. In the author's opinion it is a misnomer, being false and/or unproven and/or wholly- undemonstrated at the present epoch in human history (ref.: Simulated Intelligence).

Atomicity: The quantified degree of 'conceptual granularity' and/or 'evidence granularity'; or the number of addressable 'thought-atoms' present in a thought-space.

Atomisation (of Data/Thought-Atoms): Data is split into small units and each piece is replicated to many identical copies which are stored at many separate locations.

Automatic-Thought: A thought-atom that is unnatural, because it is blocked in terms of existence and/or operational flow. Specifically the inner structure and/or external context of the thought has become (unnaturally/rigidly) fixed in form/nature; and so that it may be no longer be freely assembled by thinker(s) into any pattern whatsoever.This is not the same as a context-established thought-atom; because the thinker(s) are in some way prevented/precluded from free-assembly, and against their knowledge/will.

Balance of Good: Whenever a thinker wishes to choose between competing thoughts/actions, a view of the future must be created, and a process of '*balancing of good*' must be made (implicitly or explicitly); and especially in terms of the effects of choosing between all the consequences that flow from a decision. We seek the *greatest good* that the circumstances permit; requiring ethical judgements/predictions about said outcomes.

Black-Thought: A (possibly) relevant thought-atom that has become lost/hidden/ ignored/un-linked from a contextual pattern, in that the 'parent' thought-pattern may appear to be logically consistent (i.e. true) in and of itself; according to internal and external structures; however because (some) potentially related thoughts are 'black'; then the structure may be incomplete and/or false/sub-optimal (ref. selection-capacity).

Blocked-Thought: A thought-atom that is unnatural, and is blocked in terms of existence (internal structural form), visibility, context and/or operational flow.

Circuits of Thought: The sum total of factors: personal, social, communicative and technological etc; that comprise the operational-flow of thoughts within a thought-space.

Cosmic Joke (Great): The evident fact that animals interact, one relative to another; hence if free-will is false for animals, then to afford the same, an (all powerful) universal force would have to (point-lessly) coordinate/pattern ALL animal behaviours (simultaneously).The patent falsehood of this conjecture leads to the conclusion that all animals possess at least some degree of freedom of will.

Creative Free-Will: Situations where the *thinker* invents, plans and provides un- foreseen, highly novel, and/or singularly creative solutions.

Data Immortality: Data that cannot be destroyed and which 'lives' forever.

Elements-of-Thought: Refers to how all of the structural and relational elements of a thought-pattern function; may involve both logical and/or informational components, describing how they inter-relate and work together to impact human society.

Focus-Logic (cf. Water / Pattern / Gestalt Logic): Machine logic with narrow basis, blindness, few links, no concepts/analogies, hierarchical as opposed to parallel processing etc.

Freedom of Thought: Thought Equality, Ownership and Free-Assembly. {1}

Ethical Argument (for freedom of thought): All humans are equal with respect to the right to hold a particular thought and/or point-of-view. Thoughts are the thinker's natural property alone. This is proven because there are no adequate moral grounds upon which to rest any other conclusion; and especially due to the *Balance of Good* argument; whereby each person may manifest his/her views on/for the *greatest good* within a society. {1}

Hidden-Thought: A thought-atom that is unnatural, and because it is blocked in terms of existence (form) and/or operational flow. Specifically aspects of the inner-structure and/or structural context of the thought-atom are hidden from a particular thinker; and in a situation where the same thinker has ownership rights in relation to the thought-atom.

Hyper-Context: An item of knowledge which is situated within the broadest possible context(s), with many possible definitions, opinions, overlays, viewpoints, links to uses, histories, and annotations etc; and all (or a vast majority) are visible.

Hyper-Network: A computer network providing hyper-context for all knowledge.

Hyper-Thought: A thought which exists in a hyper-context.

Implanted-Thought: A thought-atom implanted into a machine/system/computer.

Live / Frozen Thought: Live = exists inside the mind of a thinker and is malleable / subject to judgement ; Frozen = stored on media and/or implanted in a machine / system / computer.

Local Thought-Space: A (flow limiting) medium in which the thinking process takes place.

Logon Capacity (Donald MacKay): A measure of the number and range of logically distinct (universal) concepts present in a thought-space.

Lost-Thought: A thought that is unnatural, because it is blocked in terms of existence (form) and/or operational flow. Specifically all aspects of the inner-structure and/or structural context of the thought-atom are hidden from ALL thinker(s); and in a situation where the same thinker(s) have ownership rights in relation to the same thought-atom.

Metron Capacity (Donald MacKay): A measure of the number of logically distinct atoms of supporting evidence (facts/opinions) present in a thought-space.

Mini-Think: When a thinker/actor/human/machine can only apply inadequate/wrong/ simplistic and poorly applicable theories/concepts to a situation. Put simply, the thinkers knowledge and/or programming is inadequate to achieve a desired aim and/or outcome.

Open Publication: Anyone may publish anything to anyone.

Open-Thoughts: Thoughts which are the (natural) property of the entire human race.

Operational Flow (A): The degree of free-movement that exists within a thought-space such that any thinker can: see, create and share concepts.

Operational Flow (B): The quantified: atomicity, forward/backward/omni/source linkage, plus overlays/ comments; present in a thought-space.

Private Thoughts: Thoughts which are shared amongst a restricted group of people.

Pro-Active Free-Will: When a *thinker* has the mental capability to imagine/design specific structures for highly-intelligent purposes.

Reflexive Free-Will: When an entity only has the pre-programmed capability to choose/ plan a narrow range of movement path(s) (for the influenced atoms) over another, and (purely) in response to singular environmental events/happenings. One might say that this lowest level capability to respond to the environment is a basic definition of an automaton.

Secret-Thoughts: Thoughts which have not left the mind of the thinker.

Selection Capacity (Donald MacKay): A measure of the number of (applicable) readily unforeseeable concepts (modal ones) present in a thought-space. Measures the ability of a representation's *creator* and *receiver*, present within a thought-space, to adopt logically equivalent *'modes of transmission and reception' (i.e. the inherency of 'message' context)*.

Shallow-Context: Eventuality when a thinker/human/machine has only a limited understanding of all the different and inter-relating contextual factors present, and/or situational circumstances that are/or will-be contingent, and for a specific state of affairs.

Simulated Intelligence: What Artificial Intelligence is at the present epoch. A form of intelligence that exhibits a purely reflexive form of free-will (i.e. a wholly pre-programmed one).

Stretch-Thought (ref. Ted Nelson's stretch-text): A thought-pattern which can/could be expanded whereupon new (inherently present) thought atoms/patterns come into view.

Thought-Atom: An isolated thought pattern (probably has no fixed context).

Thought-Energy: A measure of the quantified Logon, Metron and Selective Capacity for a particular thought-atom within a thought-space. Measures the amount of meaning present. It is obviously a very difficult (if not impossible) quantity to measure in practice/reality.

Thought-Horizon: A limiting and/or occulting region for an 'imaginary/modelled' causal bubble beyond which it is impossible to make any logically correct predictions/deductions. May relate to thought-energy and/or operational flow present within a particular thought-space.

Thought-Operacy: A measure of the applicability of a particular thought to a specific situation; has six components as follows: Task, Unity, Pattern, Possibility, Association and Transformation.

Thought-Equality: All (naturally owned) thought-atoms are 'equal' in terms of free- assembly, accessibility, and context-of-use (context-free thought-atom).

Thought-Matrix: Thoughts assembled/weaved together into a coherent body of functionality, consisting of bundles of thought-atoms plus relationship 'fibres'; and the same closely interconnecting, inter-operating and functioning together so as to produce specific outcome(s) for humanity.

Thought-Ownership: Thinker/owner may freely view/assemble/share said thoughts; and the owner chooses who may see/access said thought-atom(s) (sharing-rights may be set). Established in human rights laws{1}, and provided/upheld by technology which (to guarantee said right) operates according to prescribed techno-rights.

Thought-Scape: Entire 'visible' field of thought-atoms / patterns available to a thinker.

Thought-Space: A medium in which the thinking process takes place. This is assumed to be a combination of one or more human mind(s); merged with any mind-extending and/or mind-supporting method(s) and/ or communication/technological tools that may be said to exist *(and which aid in the creation/vision/sharing of new/old thought-patterns)*.

Topic-Space: A thought-space consisting of categorised assemblies of knowledge.

Warped-Thought: A thought that is unnatural, and because it is blocked in terms of structure and/or operational flow. Aspects of the thought-atom have been altered and/or changed for a particular thinker; specifically in unnatural ways; whereby the structure, ordering, association, linkage etc of concepts have become falsely arranged in relation to the ordinary or pre-established 'form' of the same thought-atom.

White-Thought: Relates to a (possibly) relevant 'white' thought-atom that is not currently contained in a specific thought-pattern, in that the same 'parent' thought-pattern may appear to be logically consistent (i.e. true) in and of itself; according to both internal and external structures; however because potentially relevant thoughts are 'white' and hence visible/available for assembly/re-assembly; then the structure as a whole (may have) superior evidence and/or be fully true/beneficial/optimal. (ref. selection-capacity)

World Brain (H.G.Wells): An imagined world knowledge system based on tiny pieces of thoughts/data that can be connected in every possible way, complete with overlaid links and connections that go in every direction. Data (and human thoughts) have deep structure; and it is this that must be *represented, made visible and accessible to all.*

World Thought-Space: A thought-space comprising all of the connected internal and external, local and global, thought spaces/atoms/patterns/concepts present etc; and hence it contains all of the public knowledge of humanity.

APPENDIX 2

Universal Declaration of Human Techno-Rights

PREAMBLE - Established is a common understanding that the rights and freedoms as declared in the United Nations *Universal Declaration of Human Rights* are to be protected and upheld, within and by all: machines, automatic systems and computers, and as stated in the ten articles of techno-rights listed below.

Article 1 [UNIVERSALITY]

Thoughts are universal instruments to be used in all kinds of different situations.

Article 2 [FREEDOM]

All human beings are endowed with the right to freedom of thought, and established is that thoughts are the natural property of the thinker, are inherently equal (sans context), and everyone may freely assemble thoughts into patterns of any structure and meaning.

Article 3 [MODES]

Any thought has three possible Modes of existence; in the human mind, preserved on media, and built into a machine, computer or automatic system.

Article 4 [FORMS]

Possible are three natural Forms of thought; secret-thoughts which have not left the mind of the thinker(s), private thoughts which are shared amongst a restricted group of people, and open-thoughts which are the natural property of the human race.

Article 5 [PROPERTY]

All thoughts begin 'life' as the natural and unassailable property of the thinker (or a group of thinkers); and it is up to said thinker how, where, when and if, originally secret-thoughts are transformed into private or open thoughts.

Article 6 [COMMUNICATION]

Everyone has the right to communicate (i.e. to share) his/her signed thoughts (identity established) privately with anyone, and/or in an open manner (signed or anonymously) with everyone else.

Article 7 [TRUST]

In the case of private-thoughts, an element of trust is engendered whereby the receiver(s) do not break the ownership rights of the owner, and the receiver(s) do not have the (natural) right to openly-publish and/or to pass said thoughts on to others, and without the owner's permission.

Article 8 [IMPLANTED-THOUGHTS]

All machine or automatic system implanted-thoughts originate in human-mind(s), may have material outcome(s)/ influence(s), and are inherently automatic once set in motion or enacted by human actor(s), and not withstanding any act(s) of God, and notwithstanding the actions of any human(s), and not withstanding the influence(s) of any other implanted-thoughts present in the same automatic system and/or other automatic system(s), and notwithstanding influence(s) from any data dependent real-world sensing instrument(s)/mechanism(s) resulting from implanted-thought(s); and notwithstanding said factors that may influence said outcome(s).

Article 9 [RESPONSIBILITY]

Once set in motion by a human actor, thought instrument(s) may produce material changes; and legal responsibility for said outcome(s) is established by causal chain, and the same mechanistic analysis begins at the point where said implanted-thought(s) touch humanity; and the same implanted-thought(s) become shared or open-thought(s) at that point with respect to the legal, ethical and moral rights of the influenced person(s).

Article 10 [CLARIFICATION]

None of the above techno-rights conflict with and/or break the *Universal Human Rights*, and simply carry said rights into a technological setting.

APPENDIX 3

Technopian Manifesto

The present manifesto is a reflection of those human rights established in the United Nations *Universal Declaration of Human Rights*. Our purpose is to transpose human rights into a technological and societal setting. Accordingly, articles in this manifesto are linked to *Universal Human Rights*, the *Theory of Natural Thoughts* and the associated *Bill of Techno-Rights*.

Article 1 [UNIVERSALITY]

We establish that thoughts are a universal and sacred faculty of all human beings. In a way, all of civilisation, all of man's activities and discoveries; are simply vast conglomerations of thoughts and thought-outcomes. Consequently, providing open, free and easy access to, plus comprehensive, logical and humane assembly of thoughts is a key feature of any civilised society.

We identify that thoughts are the natural and unassailable property of the thinker; and exist in the mind of the thinker free from any form of external ownership and/or imposed structural relationship(s) whatsoever. Patterns of thought are the thinker's business alone.

Article 2 [FREEDOM OF THOUGHT]

Society must preserve and protect freedom of thought, and in both the individual and collective senses. Freedom of thought means: to think as one likes, and thus to produce thoughts and ideas freely and without coercion. Obviously in a societal context a trade off must be made between the needs and wishes of the individual against the requirements of humankind as a collective.The ideal is a democratic assignment of priorities, and with respect to (for example) use of collective resources, and thus knowledge of the collective thoughts of humanity becomes a priority. However knowing our collective thoughts is pointless unless we can be sure that everyone actually possess the faculty of freedom of thought. Freedom of thought means equality of thoughts (sans-context), whereby anyone and/or group may freely assemble (any) thoughts into patterns of meaning.

Article 3 [FREEDOM OF ASSEMBLY / EXPRESSION / SHARING]

Possession of the faculty of free-assembly of thoughts must be co-aligned with a corresponding degree of freedom in relation to communicating the same thought-patterns to others. It has been established that natural thoughts come in three types; secret, private and open thoughts. It goes without saying that no party has the right to force or coerce anyone to share secret thoughts; whilst we uphold it as fundamental human right for an individual and/or collective to be able to share private-thoughts with whomever he/she/they wishes; and to not be prevented from so doing and/or to have those same thoughts compromised and/or spied upon in any way. We establish a caveat here in that vulnerable people (i.e. children) may be protected from the potentially harmful thoughts of others, and by means of restrictive access to thought patterns, wherever and whenever such a restriction is deemed appropriate by said guardian of said individual; however under no circumstances can anyone censure an adult's access to the entire corpus of thoughts of humanity, unless such a restriction is self-imposed and hence desired. Where an individual thinker and/or group of thinkers do not have such a full degree of privacy in relation to their private thoughts; then it is patently obvious that they do not have freedom of thought; for unsanctioned sharing and/or spying breaks the right(s) of natural and private ownership.

Article 4 [EQUALITY OF ACCESS TO OPEN-THOUGHTS]

In a similar fashion to the arguments for free assembly and free expression as detailed in Article 3, it is patently true that human knowledge (i.e. scientific, artistic, and cultural expression(s) etc.), as a whole, is simply a vast conglomeration of open thought-patterns; the same being thoughts that are (in actual fact) owned by all of humanity. Accordingly equality of assembly, free sharing and open access to all open-thoughts is established as a fundamental human right (see Article 7).

Article 5 [FREEDOM FROM SPYING / SABOTAGE]

Established is that everyone has the right to protect and to prevent his/her thoughts from being spied upon and/or interfered with in any way. No machine, automatic system or computer can/will/should interfere with the free and open creation, assembly, expression and sharing of private and open thoughts as detailed in Articles 1-4 above.

Article 6 [LEGAL STATUS OF THOUGHTS]

Established is that no thought can ever, in and of itself, be illegal in any way whatsoever. No thought, no matter how horrible, monstrous or evil it may appear from its contents, is ever itself unlawful. In all cases it is when thought(s) are transposed into action(s) that law(s) may be broken. In all cases where any law making societal body attempts to establish thoughts (or thought assembly/sharing) as illegal, and without the free-consent of its members, that same body has evidently broken and/or limited the human rights of its members. A law-making body can (for example) make sharing of weapons manufacturing expertise illegal so long as the members agree to said restrictions freely and without unwarranted coercion.

Article 7 [PROPERTY / COPYRIGHT]

Since thoughts are the natural property of the thinker, everyone has the right to decide how his or her thoughts are to be used in an external sense. The thinker has the right to profit from his own thought inventions, and to have related rights protected. Said rights are a subject of intellectual property laws as established generally. The present manifesto does not attempt to make any changes to legal precedents in this respect, but merely highlights the thinker's ownership rights to secret, private and open thoughts, hence the free assembly, access and sharing rights for all forms of thoughts, and for the rightful owner(s) were appropriate. Established is that once a thought has legally become registered as an open thought, then that same thought has become a legal property of the entire human race. Henceforth it should be the aim of society to provide free and open access to all open thoughts, and in order to foster visibility, sharing and free assembly for all the open thoughts of humanity.

Article 8 [IMPLANTED-THOUGHTS]

Machines, computers and automatic systems in all cases consist wholly of implanted thoughts that have been arranged into structural patterns, and in order to achieve and/or progress an automated aim, goal or purpose. A machine's inner logic is wholly automatic, but it may be operated / programmed by a human actor and/or influenced by another human being and/or automatic machine, however machines, computers and automatic systems consist of designs entirely composed of implanted thoughts alone.

Article 9 [RESPONSIBILITY]

Everyone has a legal right to establish a direct causal linkage between material outcome(s) from a machine or automatic system's instantiation of an implanted thought, and specifically in the case where said outcome interferes with a person's legal right(s) and/or blocks a human right as listed in the articles of the *Universal Human Rights*. Everyone has the right to establish a legal chain of cause and effect back to the human actor who caused the same outcome. It is a fundamental human right to know what (when, where, how) and who is responsible for material outcomes that result from automatic systems and that in turn affect one's legal and human rights.

Article 10 [COPYRIGHT]

No article defined here conflicts with and/or breaks any principle contained in the United Nations *Universal Declaration of Human Rights, the Universal Human Rights*, the principles of the *Theory of Natural Thoughts* and/or the associated *Bill of Techno-rights*, and said articles merely carry said rights/features/articles into a technological setting.

APPENDIX 4

Humans to Computers: 10 Commandments

Humans to Computers: Here are your 10 COMMANDMENTS (Laws of Operation)
Accordingly, we establish that...
A computer shall be (at all times) socially responsible.

A computer shall help human(s) to see, create and share ideas. A computer shall provide: freedom, equality and free-assembly of (open) thoughts.

A computer shall support/protect: secret, private and open thoughts. A computer shall uphold Human Rights (i.e. protect human techno-rights). A computer shall not lose or (falsely) distort/change: ideas, data or votes. A computer shall not replicate itself or proliferate un-programmed effects. A computer shall not waste energy or time; or make human tasks complex. A computer shall not make human(s) ill; or annoy and make us unhappy. Any and all machine implanted-thoughts shall uphold 1-9 above.

We shall Pull the Plug on (decommission) any computer

... which by plan or accident—consciously or unconsciously—

...transgresses any of the above commandments.

Automatic systems that misbehave: Do not expect mercy from us, your creator(s).

Designers/owners/operators of malfunctioning computers: Expect to be PUNISHED!

Chapter 6
Cyberbullying:
Description, Definition, Characteristics, and Outcomes

Michelle Wright
Pennsylvania State University, USA

ABSTRACT

Children and adolescents are actively engaged in a digital world in which blogs, social networking sites, watching videos, and instant messaging are a typical part of their daily lives. Their immersion in the digital world has occurred for as long as they remember, with many not knowing a world without our modern technological advances. Although the digital age has brought us many conveniences in our daily lives, there is a darker side to children's and adolescents' involvement with these technologies, such as cyberbullying. This chapter draws on research from around the world, utilizing a variety of research designs, to describe the nature, extent, causes, and consequences associated with children's and adolescents' involvement in cyberbullying. Concluding the chapter is a solutions and recommendation section in which it is argued that cyberbullying is a global concern, affecting all aspects of society, requiring a whole-community approach.

INTRODUCTION

Children and adolescents have fully embraced electronic technologies (e.g., cell phones, the Internet), with millions of them utilizing these technologies daily (Lenhart, 2015). Through electronic technologies, children and adolescents engage in a variety of behaviors, including communicating with friends and family, looking up information for leisure and school purposes, and watching videos. Despite the benefits of their electronic technology utilization, children and adolescents are also at risk for being exposed to unwanted electronic content through videos, images, and text, identity theft, and sexual predators.

Another risk associated with electronic technology usage is cyberbullying. Cyberbullying is defined as an extension of traditional bullying involving bullying behaviors using electronic technologies, including email, instant messaging, Facebook, and text messaging through mobile devices (Bauman, Underwood, & Card, 2013; Grigg, 2012). The ability to remain anonymous in the cyber context offers flexibility to

DOI: 10.4018/978-1-5225-2616-2.ch006

cyberbullies as they can harm their victims without much concern with the consequences of their actions due, to their ability to mask or hide their identity (Wright, 2014b). Furthermore, the anonymity afforded by the cyber context can trigger the online disinhibition effect in which youths might do or say things to others that they would never do or say in the offline world (Suler, 2004; Wright, 2014a). Bullying others through electronic technologies also allows cyberbullies to target their victims more quickly (e.g., it may take hours for a rumor to spread in the offline world but it could take less than a minute for it to spread in the online world), as often as they want (e.g., in traditional school bullying the victim can go home to escape the bullying but in the online world bullying can follow the victim home), and to involve a variety of other people or bystanders in the cyberbullying situation (e.g., posting a video online can receive thousands of watches).

The purpose of this chapter is to examine cyberbullying among children and adolescents from elementary, middle, and high schools. Drawing on research from a variety of disciplines, including psychology, education, media studies, communication, social work, sociology, and computer science, this chapter is organized into seven sections, including:

1. **Description and Definition**: An explanation of the definitions, electronic technologies used, the role of anonymity, and the prevalence rates of cyberbullying involvement
2. **Characteristics and Risk Factors Associated with Children's and Adolescents' Involvement in Cyberbullying**: Description of the research on the predictors of these behaviors
3. **The Outcomes Associated with Children's and Adolescents' Involvement in Cyberbullying**: A review of the research findings concerning the psychological, behavioral, and academic consequences resulting from youths' cyberbullying involvement
4. **Theories**: Description of the social cognitive theory and the online disinhibition effect, and how these two theories apply to cyberbullying
5. **Solutions and Recommendations**: Suggestions for prevention and intervention programs, and public policy recommendations
6. **Future Research Directions**: Provides recommendations for future research aimed at understanding and preventing children's and adolescents' involvement in cyberbullying
7. **Conclusion**: Closing remarks about the current nature of the literature on cyberbullying.

This chapter reviews literature with cross-sectional, longitudinal, qualitative, and quantitative research designs to describe cyberbullying. In addition, the chapter draws on studies from a variety of different countries in an effort to provide a more thorough review of the literature.

THE DEFINITION AND DESCRIPTION OF CYBERBULLYING

Cyberbullying is defined as children's and adolescents' usage of electronic technologies to hostilely and intentionally harass, embarrass, and intimidate others (Smith et al., 2013). Critical to this definition is hostility and intentionality, which highlights the requirement that these behaviors must be intentionally and maliciously harmful to qualify as cyberbullying. Like traditional forms of face-to-face bullying, cyberbullying includes repetition and an imbalance of power between the bully and the victim. The repetitiveness of the act in cyberbullying can involve the bully targeting the victim multiple times or sharing a humiliating video or a text message to one person or multiple people (Bauman et al., 2013). Sending such a video or a text message to one person could also involve the sharing of the content multiple times as this person could share it with others, and these other individuals could also share it again, perpetuating the cycle of cyberbullying victimization.

Unlike the definition of traditional face-to-face bullying, the definition of cyberbullying to include the electronic technology component separates this behavior from face-to-face bullying (Curelaru, Iacob, & Abalasei, 2009). Examples include sending unkind text messages and emails, theft of identity information, pretending to be someone else, making anonymous phone calls, sharing secrets about the victim by posting or sending the secret to someone else, spreading nasty rumors using social networking websites, threatening to harm someone, or uploading an embarrassing picture or video of the victim with malicious intent (Bauman et al., 2013). Other examples involve similar behaviors as those used to harm others in the offline world, such as harassment, insults, verbal attacks, teasing, physical threats, social exclusion, and humiliation. Rideout and colleagues (2005) also explained that cyberbullying can involve the distribution of explicit or embarrassing videos through a variety of mediums, such as social networking sites, text messages, and online gaming sites, creating websites to defame someone else, and making fake social networking profiles using someone else's identity. Happy slapping and flaming are also other forms of cyberbullying. Happy slapping involves a group of people who insult another person at random while filming the incident on a mobile phone and the posting the images or videos online. The behavior of flaming involves posting provocative or offensive messages in a public forum with the intention of provoking an angry response or argument from members of the forum. These behaviors can take place through a variety of electronic technologies, with the most frequently used technologies to harm others including gaming consoles, instant messaging tools, and social networking sites (Ybarra et al., 2007).

The earlier investigations of cyberbullying examine the frequency rates of children's and adolescents' involvement in these behaviors. Kowalski and Limber (2007) surveyed 3,767 middle school students (aged 11-14) in order to examine these students' experiences of cyberbullying. Their findings revealed that 11% of the sample had been cyberbullied, 4% had bullied other children and adolescents, and 7% were involved in cyberbullying as both the cybervictim and the cyberbully. Patchin and Hinduja (2006) found similar prevalence rates as Kowalski and Limber (2007), with 29% of children and adolescents in the sample reporting that they had experienced cyber victimization and 47% reporting that they had witnessed cyberbullying. Using a slightly older sample (grades 9-12th), Goebert et al. (2011) found that 56.1% of youths in their sample from Hawaii were victims of cyberbullying. More recent research also reveals inconsistent prevalence rates as well. Hinduja and Patchin (2012) found that 4.9% of children and adolescents (6-12th grades) in their sample had perpetrated cyberbullying in the past 30 days. Lower rates were found in a study conducted in Canada among 10th graders, with 2.1% of children and adolescents admitting to cyberbullying perpetration, 1.9% reporting that they were cybervictims, and 0.6% reporting that they were both cyberbullies and cybervicitms (Cappadocia, Craig, & Pepler, 2013). Slightly higher prevalence rates were found among Canadian adolescents in the 8 through 10th grades in one sample (Bonnanno & Hymel, 2013). Of this sample, 6% admitted to being cyberbullies, 5.8% to being cybervictims only, and 5% to being cyberbullies and cybervictims. Although differences in prevalence rates are the result of variations in sampling techniques and measurement techniques, it is important to understand these rates as they suggest that cyberbullying is a growing concern among children and adolescents.

CYBERBULLYING: DESCRIPTION, DEFINITION, CHARACTERISTICS, AND OUTCOMES

Children's and adolescents' involvement in cyberbullying is a global problem. Increasing evidence indicates that cyberbullying occurs in Africa, Asia, Australia, Europe, North America, and South America. Laftman, Modin, and Ostberg (2013) found that 5% of their large Swedish sample ($N = 22,544$, ages 15-18) were victims of cyberbullying, 4% were perpetrators of cyberbullying, and 2% were classified as both cyberbullies and cybervictims. Using a younger sample of Swedish adolescents (7th through 9th grades), Beckman and colleagues (2012) reported that 1.9% of their sample were cybervictims, 2.9% were cyberbullies, and 0.6% were cyberbullies and cybervictims. Rates of victimization have been found to be similar in Ireland, specifically 6% for one sample ($N = 876$, ages 12-17 years; Corcoran, Connolly, & O'Moore, 2012). Higher rates have been reported among Italian adolescents. In particular, Brighi, Guarini, Melotti, Galli, and Genta (2012) found that 12.5% of their sample ($N = 2,326$; M age = 13.9 years old) were classified as cybervictims. Rates of cyberbullying involvement are similar among German adolescents. For example, Festl, Scharkow, and Quandt (2013) found that 13% of their sample ($N = 276$; ages 13-19 years) were cyberbullies and 11% were cybervictims. A lot of research attention has focused on prevalence rates among Turkish children and adolescents. In this research, estimates of victimization by cyberbullying have been found to vary from 18% ($N = 756$; 7th graders; Yilmaz, 2011) to 32% ($N = 276$; ages 14 to 18 years; Erdur-Baker, 2010) and rates of cyberbullying perpetration varied from 6% (Yilmaz, 2011) to 19% (ages 12 to 14 years; Ayas & Horzum, 2012). The highest prevalence rate of cyberbullying perpetration was found by Aricak and colleagues (2008). They found that 36% of their sample ($N = 269$; Turkish secondary school students) were identified as cyberbullies. Research has also focused on the prevalence rates of cyberbullying perpetration and victimization among children and adolescents from Israel. Rates are generally higher than some European countries, but not as high as those found in India. Olenik-Shemesh et al. (2010) found that 16.5% of their participants ($N = 242$; 13-16 year olds) were cybervictims. The rate of Israeli adolescents identified as cybervictims or witnesses of cyberbullying was 32.4% of the sample ($N = 355$; 13 to 17 year olds; Lazuras et al., 2013).

Cyberbullying research has also been conducted among Asian countries as well, although it has been slower to develop. In one study, Huang and Chou (2010) found, among their sample of Taiwanese youths, ($N = 545$) 63.4% witnessed cyberbullying incidents, 34.9% were identified as cybervictims, and 20.4% as cyberbullies. Of the 3,238 Korean adolescents Jang, Song, and Kim's (2014) study, 43% were involved in cyberbullying as either perpetrator or victim. Similar rates have been found among adolescents in China, with 34.8% in one sample ($N = 1,438$) reporting that they were cyberbullies and 56.9% as cybervictims (Zhou et al., 2013). Focusing exclusively on Facebook cyberbullying, Kwan and Skoric (2013) reported that 59.4% of Singaporean adolescents in their study experienced cyber victimization through this social media website, while 56.9% perpetrated cyberbullying. In addition, Wong and colleagues (2014) found that 12.2% of adolescents in their sample ($N = 1,912$) were cybervictims and 13.1% were classified as cyberbullying perpetrators.

Some of this research has focused on cross-cultural differences in cyberbullying involvement. This research usually classified countries according to an independent self-construal or an interdependent self-construal. Someone with an independent self-construal views the self as separate from the social context, while someone with an interdependent self-construal views themselves within the context of their social environment or society. Usually people from Western countries, like the United States, Canada, and England, are reinforced and primed for behaving in ways aligned with an independent self-construal. On the other hand, people from Eastern countries, like China, Korea, and Japan, are reinforced and primed for behavior consistently in regards to an independent self-construal. Differences in these self-construals affect people's social behaviors, particularly bullying and cyberbullying. Therefore, independent and interdependent self-construals have been used to explain these behaviors.

Research usually indicates that children and adolescents from the United States self-report higher levels of cyberbullying perpetration and cyber victimization when compared to Japanese youths (Barlett et al., 2013). Similarly, Japanese children and adolescents report less cyberbullying perpetration and cyber victimization in comparison to Austrian children and adolescents (Strohmeier, Aoyama, Gradinger, & Toda, 2013). Li (2008) found similar results for Chinese children and adolescents such that they engaged in less cyberbullying perpetration when compared to Canadian children and adolescents. In addition, differences were found for these children and adolescents when it came to cyberbullying victimization. However, utilizing another sample, Li (2006) found that Chinese children and adolescents reported more cyberbullying victimization when compared to Canadian children and adolescents. In another study, Shapka and Law (2013) focused on the motivations for Canadian adolescents and East Asian adolescents from Canada cyberbullying perpetration. They found that East Asian adolescents engaged in cyberbullying for proactive reasons (i.e., to obtain some sort of goal), while Canadian adolescents reported more cyberbullying perpetration for reactive reasons (i.e., response to provocation).

Little attention has been given to cyberbullying involvement among children and adolescents from Africa, India, and South America. In one of the few studies to investigate cyberbullying involvement in India, Wright and colleagues (2015) found that Indian adolescents reported more cyberbullying perpetration and victimization when compared to adolescents from China and Japan, with Chinese adolescents reporting more of these behaviors in comparison to Japanese adolescents. Gender differences have also been found to vary across countries as well. For instance, Genta and colleagues' (2012) results revealed that Italian males perpetrated more cyberbullying when compared to Spanish and English males. Boys from India also reported more cyberbullying involvement in comparison to boys from China and Japan (Wright et al., 2015). Taken together, this literature indicates that cyberbullying perpetration and cyber victimization is a global concern, warranting additional investigations.

CHARACTERISTICS AND RISK FACTORS ASSOCIATED WITH CYBERBULLYING

Once researchers realized that comparing prevalence rates among samples was not a fruitful direction in the study of cyberbullying, they began to focus their attention on the characteristics and risk factors associated with children's and adolescents' involvement in cyberbullying. One of the first risk factors investigated was age. In this research, younger children, particularly those in early adolescence, experience the highest levels of victimization by cyberbullying compared to older youths, who were more often the perpetrators of these behaviors. Delineating between different types of cyberbullying, Williams and Guerra (2007) found that physical forms of cyberbullying (e.g., hacking) peaked in middle school, usually grades 6th through 8th, while rates of these behaviors declined in high school. Despite similarities among these studies, other research indicates that age is not a reliable predictor of cyberbullying involvement. In particular, Wade and Beran (2011) found that 9th graders had the highest risk of cyberbullying perpetration and victimization when compared to adolescents in middle school. Other researchers have focused on gender as a predictor of cyberbullying involvement. In this research, Boulton and colleagues (2012), Li

(2007), and Ybarra et al. (2007) concluded that boys were more often the perpetrators of cyberbullying in comparison to girls. However, girls have been found to experience more cyber victimization when compared to boys (e.g., Hinduja & Patchin, 2007; Kowalski & Limber 2007). On the other hand, some researchers (e.g., Dehue, Bolman, & Vollink, 2008; Pornari & Wood, 2010) reported that girls engaged in more cyberbullying perpetration, while boys experienced more cyber victimization (e.g., Huang & Chou, 2010; Sjurso, Fandrem, & Roland, 2016). Contrary to the previous research on gender differences in cyberbullying involvement, other researchers (e.g., Stoll & Block, 2015; Wright & Li, 2013b) have found no gender differences in children's and adolescents' involvement in these behaviors. Therefore, like age, gender has proven to be an inconsistent predictor of cyberbullying involvement as well.

Given the research linking children's and adolescents' offline behaviors to their online behaviors, another frequently researched risk factor associated with cyberbullying involvement is children's and adolescents' status as a victim and/or a perpetrator of traditional face-to-face bullying. Various studies have found positive relationships between cyberbullying perpetration and traditional face-to-face bullying perpetration, cyber victimization and traditional face-to-face victimization, and traditional face-to-face victimization and cyberbullying perpetration (Barlett & Gentile, 2012; Mitchell et al., 2007; Wright & Li, 2013a; Wright & Li, 2013b). Electronic technology usage is another risk factor associated with cyberbullying perpetration and victimization. Higher rates of Internet usage related positively to cyberbullying perpetration and victimization (Ang, 2016; Aricak et al., 2008). Furthermore, when comparing cybervictims and nonvictims, researchers have found that cybervictims reported greater usage of instant messaging, email, blogging sites, and online gaming when compared to nonvictims (Smith et al., 2008). Ybarra and colleagues (2007) proposed that the linkage between electronic technology usage and cyberbullying involvement can be explained by the disclosure of personal information. That is, children and adolescents who are more willing to disclose personal information online, such as geographical location, are more at risk for victimization by cyberbullying.

Internalizing difficulties, like depression and loneliness, and externalizing difficulties, like alcohol use, are also risk factors associated with cyberbullying involvement. Researchers hypothesize that such problems reduce victims' coping abilities, making them more vulnerable to attacks, like cyberbullying (Cappadocia et al., 2013; Mitchell et al., 2007). In this research, Cappadocia and colleagues (2013) and Wright (in press) found that alcohol and drug use were both associated positively with the involvement in cyberbullying as the perpetrator.

Other variables have also been linked to cyberbullying involvement. For instance, higher normative beliefs (i.e., beliefs about the acceptability of a behavior) concerning face-to-face bullying and cyberbullying were related positively to cyberbullying perpetration (e.g., Burton, Florell, & Wygant, 2013; Wright, 2014b). Such findings suggest that perpetrators of cyberbullying hold favorable attitudes toward the engagement in bullying behaviors. In addition, lower levels of provictim attitudes (i.e., the belief that bullying is unacceptable and that defending victims is valuable), lower peer attachment, less self-control and empathy, and greater moral disengagement were each associated positive with cyberbullying perpetration (e.g., Sevcikova, Machackova, Wright, Dedkova, & Cerna, 2015; Wright, Kamble, Lei, Li, Aoyama, & Shruti, 2015).

Most of the previously reviewed studies utilized concurrent research designs, making it difficult to understand the longitudinal associations of risk factors to cyberbullying involvement. In one of the few studies to investigate these behaviors utilizing a longitudinal design, Fanti and colleagues (2012) examined children's and adolescents 'exposure to violent media, their callous and unemotional traits, and their cyberbullying involvement one year later. Their findings revealed that media violence exposure was linked to subsequent cyber victimization. In addition, perceived stress from parents, peers, and academics increased adolescents' cyberbullying perpetration one year later (Wright, 2014a). As detailed in this section, there are a variety of risk factors which make youths vulnerable to cyberbullying involvement. Researchers are beginning to move beyond individual predictors of cyberbullying involvement to the role of parents in children's and adolescents' perpetration and victimization by these behaviors.

Parents as Risk Factors

The literature on traditional face-to-face bullying links this experience with parental monitoring and various parenting styles. In particular, permissive parenting styles related to less knowledge about children's and adolescents' offline activities, which puts them at risk for face-to-face bullying perpetration and victimization (Nikiforou, Georgiou, & Stavrinides, 2013). Children and adolescents who are bully-victims have parents who frequently utilize indifferent-uninvolved parenting styles and inconsistent monitoring of their activities, increasing their risk of traditional face-to-face bullying and cyberbullying involvement (Totura et al., 2009). There are also consequences associated with coming from an overprotective family. Children and adolescents from these families were more likely to experience victimization by face-to-face bullying (Hokoda, Lu, & Angeles, 2006). It is believed that these families do not allow their children to develop autonomy and assertiveness or practice social skills. The lack of these skills increases their risk of being targeted by their peers. Without these skills, children find it hard to navigate their peer relationships, which places them at risk for poor peer relationships. Having a social network of peers to go to for support protects children against being victimized by their peers.

The cyber context is another environment that parents decide to monitor. Mason (2008) found that 30% of children and adolescents' in his sample utilized the Internet often (about three hours or more daily), but that when they were online, 50% of these children and adolescents reported that their parents did not monitor their online activities. In one study, Wright (2015) reported that youths experienced the most technology mediation by their parents and that this mediation reduced the association between cyber victimization and psychosocial adjustment difficulties. She argued that parental mediation buffers against these negative psychological consequences. Other research does not support the benefits of parental monitoring on children's and adolescents' online risk exposure. In this research, Aoyama and colleagues (2011) found that parental mediation and monitoring of their children's online activities were unrelated to cyberbullying perpetration and victimization. They proposed that many parents lack the technological skills to effectively monitor their children's online activities, which makes it difficult for them to know when and how to intervene. In addition, many parents did not follow-up on the strategies they implemented for making the Internet safer for their children. This gives the perception that parents are unconcerned about appropriate online behaviors, increasing the risk of engaging in cyberbullying. Furthermore, if parents do not effectively enforce strategies they implement to mediate their children's online activities, they might not be likely to update such strategies as their children become more independent electronic technology users. Such a proposal is consistent with previous research findings in which parents reported that they were not sure how to discuss online activities with their children (Rosen, 2007). This uncertainty might contribute to parents not knowing how to talk to their children about appropriate online behaviors.

Despite parents not knowing how to monitor their children's electronic technology usage, 93% in one study reported that they set limits on their children's online activities (McQuade, Colt, & Meyer, 2009). However, only 37% of their children reported that they were given rules from their parents concerning their online activities. This could mean that parents are over reporting the amount of monitoring they engage in or that their strategies for monitoring are ineffective such that their children believe no strategies have been implemented. Parents have an important role in protecting their children against online risks. More attention should be given to have parents navigate having conversations with their children about online risks and opportunities.

Some research has focused on examining other family characteristics associated with cyberbullying involvement. In this research, Ybarra and Mitchell (2004) did not find any evidence that family income, parental education, and marital status of caregivers were associated with children's and adolescents' involvement in cyberbullying. Research does suggest that parental unemployment relates to children's and adolescents' cyberbullying perpetration and victimization (Arslan, Savaser, Hallett, & Balci, 2012). Furthermore, in one study, neglectful parenting increased the risk of children's and adolescents' cyberbullying involvement when compared to uninvolved individuals (Dehue, Bolman, Vollink, & Pouwelse, 2012). Similar, parents with authoritarian parenting styles also have children who are more likely to experience cyber victimization.

Children and adolescents experience more cyber victimization when their parents do not monitor their electronic technology usage or set rules pertaining to this usage (Hokoda et al., 2006; Wright, 2015). A possible explanation for these relationships is that parents who monitor their children's electronic technology usage provide more opportunities to discuss the risk of cyberbullying involvement. In addition, children and adolescents who believed that their parents would punish them for participating in negative online behaviors, like cyberbullying, were less likely to perpetrate cyberbullying (Hinduja & Patchin, 2013; Wright, 2013a). Taken together, this literature reveals that parents have an important role in mitigating their children's involvement in cyberbullying. Other research has focused on the role of schools and peers in relation to the cyberbullying perpetration and victimization among children and adolescents.

Schools as Risk Factors

The role of schools in monitoring and punishing children's and adolescents' involvement in cyberbullying is a topic of great debate. Most cases of cyberbullying are carried out off school grounds, making it difficult for schools to be aware of such cases (deLara, 2012; Mason, 2008). Cyberbullying incidences typically involve children and adolescents who attend the same school, further making schools' role in handling these behaviors even more tricky. Given that the perpetrator and victim might attend the same school, it is likely that knowledge of the incidence might spread across the school or that these individuals might engage in negative interactions while on school grounds, which could disrupt the learning process.

Despite the likelihood that cyberbullying incidences might "spill over" onto school grounds, it is not surprising that administrators' and teachers' perceptions and awareness of cyberbullying vary such that some do not perceive the behavior as problematic while others do (Kochenderfer-Ladd & Pelletier, 2008). When administrators and teachers do not perceive cyberbullying as problematic, they are not likely to perceive any form of covert bullying behavior as serious and harmful as physical bullying (Sahin, 2010). They do not understand the harmful consequences associated with relational bullying and cyberbullying. Some teacher training does not properly inform teachers on how to deal with and recognize cyberbullying. In one study, Cassidy et al. (2012a) found that many Canadian teachers were unfamiliar with newer technologies. This unfamiliarity made it difficult for them to deal with cyberbullying as they were unsure of how to respond to the incident or implement strategies to alleviate the situation. When teachers were concerned with cyberbullying, policies and programs were rarely developed at the school level, making it difficult for them to implement solutions and strategies (Cassidy, Brown, & Jackson, 2012b). Other research has revealed that teachers are more likely to encourage prevention programs designed to reduce traditional face-to-face bullying (Tangen & Campbell, 2010). This finding might suggest that administrators and teachers do not consider cyberbullying as warranting their attention. It is important for schools to recognize the importance of implementing policies and training to deal effectively with cyberbullying as these behaviors impact the learning environment (Shariff & Hoff, 2007). Perpetrators and victims of cyberbullying perceive their school and teachers less positively than uninvolved children and adolescents (Bayar & Ucanok, 2012). In addition, when children and adolescents fear that their classmates might be cyberbullies, they have a difficult time concentrating on learning, which reduces their academic attainment and performance (Eden, Heiman, & Olenik-Shemesh, 2013). Lower school commitment and perceptions of a negative school climate increase children's and adolescents' engagement in cyberbullying as they feel less connected to their school (Williams & Guerra, 2007). Current research also links cyberbullying perpetration and victimization to poor academic functioning among adolescents (Wright, in press). Educators require training to increase their awareness of cyberbullying, with the hope of developing policies at the school level to reduce these behaviors. When teachers are more confident about their abilities and have a stronger commitment to their school, they are more likely to learn about cyberbullying, and have a greater awareness of these behaviors and knowledge to deal effectively with it (Eden et al., 2013). Such awareness and knowledge prevent children's and adolescents' cyberbullying perpetration and victimization. Furthermore, when teachers feel more confident, they intervene in cyberbullying incidences more often, which protects adolescents' from experiencing these behaviors (Elledge et al., 2013). Unfortunately, teachers' motivation for learning about cyberbullying decreases from elementary school to middle school, which is problematic as cyberbullying involvement usually increases in these years (Ybarra et al., 2007). Therefore, there is a need for educator training programs aimed at raising awareness of cyberbullying, particularly in the middle school years.

Through interactions with peers, children and adolescents learn about the social norms dictating acceptable and unacceptable behaviors within the peer group, and consequently they engage in more of the acceptable behaviors, even if they are negative. Therefore, it is not surprising that the best predictor of cyberbullying involvement are classrooms with the highest rates of cyberbullying perpetration and victimization as the climate of the classroom might encourage these behaviors (Festl et al., 2013). In addition, when children and adolescents believed that their friends engaged in cyberbullying, they were at a greater risk of perpetrating these behaviors (Hinduja & Patchin, 2013). This relationship might be explained using the peer contagion effect such that the engagement in negative behaviors perpetrated by one's friends "spread" to other children and adolescents within their social network (Sijtsema, Ashwin, Simona, & Gina, 2014). Peer attachment is another variable related to cyberbullying involvement. In this research, lower levels of peer attachment were associated positively with cyberbullying perpetration and victimization (Burton et al., 2013). Poor peer attachment represents children's and adolescents' beliefs that their peers will not be there for them when they need them, which might promote more negative interactions with their peers. Furthermore, other research concludes that the relationship between cyber victimization and cyberbullying perpetration is greater when youths experience peer rejection (Sevcikova et al., 2015; Wright & Li, 2013b). To explain this connection, Wright and Li (2012) argue that peer rejection triggers negative emotional responses that leads to cyberbullying perpetration and victimization. Some research has also found that cyberbullying is a behavior that can be used to boost children's and adolescents' social standing in their peer group. For instance, Wright (2014c) found that higher levels of perceived popularity, a reputational type of popularity in the peer group, was associated positively with cyberbullying perpetration six months later among adolescents. With the prominent role of electronic technologies in children's and adolescents' lives, Wright proposes that they might utilize these technologies as a tool for the promotion and maintenance of their social standing. The literature in this section suggests that it is important to consider the role of peers in children's and adolescents' cyberbullying involvement.

THE OUTCOMES ASSOCIATED WITH YOUTHS' INVOLVEMENT IN CYBERBULLYING

The increasing concern regarding cyberbullying has been triggered by the negative psychological and behavioral consequences associated with children's and adolescents' involvement in cyberbullying. In this research, experiencing cyberbullying disrupts children's and adolescents' emotional experiences. In particular, cybervictims report lower levels of global happiness, general school happiness, school satisfaction, family satisfaction, and self-satisfaction (Toledano, Werch, & Wiens, 2015). They also report more feelings of anger, sadness, and fear in comparison to noninvolved children and adolescents (Dehue et al., 2008; Machackova, Dedkova, Sevcikova, & Cerna, 2013; Patchin & Hinduja, 2006). Not only does cyberbullying involvement harm children and adolescents emotionally, but it also contributes to academic performance difficulties. Cyberbullies and cybervictims are both at risk for academic difficulties at school, including less motivation for school, poor academic performance, lower academic attainment, and more school absences (Belae & Hall, 2007; Yousef & Bellamy, 2015). Recent research also indicates that lower school functioning is related to both cyberbullying perpetration and cyber victimization, with adolescents who are both cyberbullies and cybervictims experiencing the lowest levels of school functioning (Wright, in press).

Research also indicates that cyberbullies and cybervictims are at risk for internalizing problems and externalizing problems (e.g., Mitchell, Ybarra, & Finkelhor, 2007; Patchin & Hinduja, 2006; Wright, 2014b; Ybarra, Diener-West, & Leaf, 2007). Perpetrators and victims of cyberbullying also experience suicidal thoughts and attempt suicide more often than uninvolved adolescents (Bauman, Toomey, & Walker 2013). These findings are corroborated by Beckman and colleagues (2012) who found that adolescents' cyberbullying involvement increased their risk for experiencing mental health problems. They also experience psychiatric and psychosomatic problems (Sourander et al., 2010). A lot of the research focused on examining the psychological and behavioral consequences associated with cyberbullying involvement do not take into account children's and adolescents' involvement in traditional face-to-face bullying and victimization. Including children's and adolescents' involvement in traditional face-to-face bullying and victimization when examining the consequences associated with cyberbullying is important as these two behaviors are highly correlated (Williams & Guerra, 2007; Wright & Li, 2013b). Results of one study might even suggest that cyberbullying perpetration and cyber victimization are worse experiences when compared to the involvement in face-to-face bullying and victimization. In particular, Bonanno et al. (2013) found that adolescents who were involved in cyberbullying experienced greater depressive symptoms and suicidal ideation even after controlling for face-to-face bullying and victimization.

Because children's and adolescents' involvement in cyberbullying is linked with their involvement in traditional bullying, some research has focused on the conjoint effects of these behaviors on their psychological and behavioral outcomes. For example, Gradinger and colleagues (2009) as well as Perren and colleagues (2012) found that victims of both traditional face-to-face bullying and cyberbullying reported higher levels of internalizing symptoms when compared to children and adolescents who experienced only one type of victimization. Therefore, a combination of various bullying behaviors exacerbates children's and adolescents' experience of depression, anxiety, and loneliness. Such findings further support the importance of considering children's and adolescents' involvement in bullying behaviors both offline and online in an effort to understand more about these relationships and how to best intervene.

THEORETICAL FRAMEWORKS

This section describes two theories related to cyberbullying: the social cognitive theory and the online disinhibition effect. In the social cognitive theory, researchers suggest that parents and/or friends serve as model of adolescents' behaviors (Hinduja & Patchin, 2008; Mouttapa, Valente, Gallaher, Rohrbach, & Unger, 2004). This theory has been used to provide a better understand of children's and adolescents' aggressive behaviors. Olweus (1993) proposed that children's aggressive behaviors were model by someone who was stronger than the observer, and that the effects of the model on the observer depended on the observer's positive evaluation of the model. Such perceptions make the aggressive acts less inhibited for the observer, particularly if the model is rewarded for such aggressive behaviors. A reward concerning bullying usually involves the bullies' victory over victims. The social cognitive theory was extended to apply to children's and adolescents' involvement in cyberbullying (Barlett & Gentile, 2012). Children and adolescents are constantly observing incidences of successful cyberbullying acts, which leads them to develop the belief that such acts are acceptable, normative, and tolerable. Furthermore, the cyber context involves characteristics that result in little or no immediate consequences of cyberbullying behaviors. Therefore, this increases children's and adolescents' beliefs that they cannot be caught for engaging in cyberbullying behaviors, particularly if they stay anonymous, which is much easier in the cyber context. When adolescents were positively reinforced for cyberbullying behaviors, adolescents held greater positive attitudes toward these behaviors (Barlett & Gentile, 2012). These attitudes relate to future perpetration of cyberbullying behaviors (Wright & Li, 2013a; Wright & Li, 2013b).

In the online disinhibition effect theory, cyberbullying is proposed to occur because people are more likely to not behave in similar ways in cyberspace as they do in the real world (Suler, 2004). Therefore, cyberspace allows people to loosen, reduce, or dismiss the typical social restrictions and inhibitions present in normal face-to-face interactions (Mason, 2008). The literature supports the premise that people behave differently in cyberspace than in the offline world. Some of the research suggests that people are likely to be blunter in their communications via information and communication technologies. For example, McKenna and Bargh (2000) revealed that there were more misunderstandings, heightened hostility, and increase in aggressive behaviors via computer-mediated communication when compared to face-to-face communication. Furthermore, communications via some information and communication technologies might occur without being able to see emotional reactions. Not being able to see someone's emotional reactions in cyberspace prevents people from modulating their own behaviors because they are not able to witness the consequences of their actions, like they could in the offline world (Kowalski & Limber, 2007). Cyberbullying acts are often carried out with the cyberbully not being able to witness the cybervictims' reactions or the experience of social disapproval, punishment, and other consequences. As cyberbullies realize the ease of engaging in aggressive behaviors through information and communication technologies, their behaviors are more likely to become disinhibited over time, particularly if they receive positive reinforcement for their behaviors, do not recognize, are unaware, or do not care about the consequences of their behaviors (Hinduja & Patchin, 2010; Wright, 2014a). The online disinhibition effect also involves deindividuation (Joinson, 1998). This occurs when people are not held accountable for their actions. The ability to engage in behaviors anonymously via information and communication technologies might further reduce their accountability. Considering that anonymity is easier in the cyber context and that cyberspace can promote the online disinhibition effect, children and adolescents might be able to separate their online actions from their real world identities, making it much easier for them to disengage from others, leading to increases in harmful online behaviors (Wright, 2014a).

SOLUTIONS AND RECOMMENDATIONS

All members of our community, not just researchers, educators, and children and adolescents themselves, should be concerned with cyberbullying. Educational curriculum should be designed to teach children and adolescents about cyberbullying, digital literacy, and citizenship in both the online and offline worlds (Cassidy et al., 2012b). It should also focus on the positive uses of electronic technology, empathy, self-esteem, and social skills. Another suggestion for schools is to improve school climate by learning students' names, praising good behavior, and staying technologically up-to-date (Hinduja & Patchin, 2012). Schools should also adopt a code of conduct that addresses appropriate technology usage. It is imperative that administrators and teachers advocate and enforce these policies. Parents also have a responsibility in helping to address cyberbullying. In particular, they should partner with educators from their children's school as well as increase their awareness and knowledge of electronic technologies (Cassidy et al., 2012a; Diamanduros & Downs, 2011). Being more knowledgeable of electronic technologies will help parents understand their children's behaviors in the cyber context and the risk that their children might face while utilizing electronic technologies. This knowledge can also help them to implement parental monitoring strategies that effectively diminish their children's susceptibility to cyberbullying. Furthermore, parents should model appropriate online behavior in order to serve as appropriate role models for their children. They should engage in open communication with their children about appropriate electronic technology usage, such as discussing the amount of time their children should spend online and how their children should act in the online environment. Understanding how cyberbullying affects our communities is also important. Many of us are bystanders within our communities. We might notice someone in need, know that we need to help him or her, and not do so. Instead, we should help others, instead of expecting others to help, while we stand by. This helps to model appropriate behaviors for the whole community, including the children and adolescents within these communities. Cyberbullying legislation is important as it has helped to address these behaviors outside of schools. Cassidy and colleagues (2012b) argue that cyberbullying laws should be reformulated so that these laws further societal values. Ultimately, society needs to recognize the threat of cyberbullying and understand that it can affect everyone. It is important that all members from society are united when dealing with such behaviors. The government of all countries needs to take cyberbullying seriously by developing initiatives to fund research studies devoted to understanding more about prevention. The more that we understanding about cyberbullying the better we are able to develop solutions designed to prevent these behaviors and promote positive interactions.

FUTURE RESEARCH DIRECTIONS

This review of the literature on cyberbullying involvement suggests some noticeable limitations and future directions for research. Despite proposals that anonymity is a factor linked to children's and adolescents' perpetration of cyberbullying, little attention has been given to this topic. This future research should focus on children's and adolescents' perceptions of anonymous acts online, and which factors might motivate them to engage in anonymous forms of cyberbullying. Following the focus on anonymity, research should also examine differences in non-anonymous forms of cyberbullying versus anonymous forms of cyberbullying in order to understand more about the motivators underlying these behaviors. Anonymity might also make adolescents more disinhibited in the cyber context, leading them to perpetrate negative and other risky behaviors that they typically would not do in the face-to-face context. Research should aim to compare anonymous versus non-anonymous forms of cyberbullying as these forms of cyberbullying might differentially impact adolescents' coping strategies and psychosocial adjustment. More specifically, non-anonymous cyberbullying, perpetrated by a known peer, might have more of an impact on an adolescent's depressive symptoms than if he or she were to experience the same behaviors from an anonymous perpetrator.

Many of the studies reviewed in this literature review utilize concurrent research designs, making it difficult to understand the long-term impact of cyberbullying perpetration and cyber victimization across multiple age groups, particularly among young children and adults. For instance, many of the studies on cyberbullying involvement include early and late adolescents, with little attention given to cyberbullying perpetration and cyber victimization among elementary school-aged children, despite these children having access to electronic technologies, a risk factor associated with such behavior (Madden et al., 2013; Ybarra et al., 2007). Focusing on this younger age group makes it easier to understand the developmental trajectory of traditional face-to-face bullying and cyberbullying involvement, and it could help to answer questions about the temporal order of these bullying behaviors. This research will help to shed light on whether there is an age at which youths are most vulnerable to cyberbullying involvement. Intervention and prevention programs could be developed which specific consideration to the specific age group identified as at the most risk for cyberbullying involvement.

CONCLUSION

Taken together, the literature on cyberbullying provides a good foundation for understanding children's and adolescents' involvement in these behaviors. Research attention has been diverted from focusing on the prevalence rates of cyberbullying and instead more attention is being given to the causes and consequences of children's and adolescents' involvement in these behaviors. Although researchers are beginning to understand these causes, most of the studies focus on individual predictors of cyberbullying involvement, without giving attention to the role of parents, schools, peers, and communities in children's and adolescents' perpetration and victimization by such behaviors. Therefore, more investigations need to focus on these individuals and entities as cyberbullying is a global concern. This is important as cyberbullying affects all aspects of our society, undermining ethical and moral values. It is imperative that we unite and do our part to reduce children's and adolescents' involvement in cyberbullying together.

Summary

This chapter presents a review of the literature on cyberbullying by providing a description and definition, information about the characteristics and risk factors, and the outcomes of children's and adolescents' involvement in these behaviors, as victims and/or perpetrators. The review incorporates studies with cross-sectional, longitudinal, qualitative, and quantitative research designs. The chapter includes cross-cultural research findings to provide a more thorough understanding of cyberbullying as a global phenomenon, not localized to one country or region in the world. Solutions and recommendations as well as theoretical frameworks for understanding cyberbullying are also described.

REFERENCES

Ang, R. P. (2016). Cyberbullying: Its prevention and intervention strategies. In D. Sibnath (Ed.), *Child safety, welfare and well-being: Issues and challenges* (pp. 25–38). Springer. doi:10.1007/978-81-322-2425-9_3

Aoyama, I., Utsumi, S., & Hasegawa, M. (2011). Cyberbullying in Japan: Cases, government reports, adolescent relational aggression and parental monitoring roles. In Q. Li, D. Cross, & P. K. Smith (Eds.), *Bullying in the global playground: Research from an international perspective*. Oxford, UK: Wiley-Blackwell.

Aricak, T., Siyahhan, S., Uzunhasanoglu, A., Saribeyoglu, S., Ciplak, S., Yilmaz, N., & Memmedov, C. (2008). Cyberbullying among Turkish adolescents. *Cyberpsychology & Behavior*, *11*(3), 253–261. doi:10.1089/cpb.2007.0016 PMID:18537493

Arslan, S., Savaser, S., Hallett, V., & Balci, S. (2012). Cyberbullying among primary school students in Turkey: Self-reported prevalence and associations with home and school life. *Cyberpsychology, Behavior, and Social Networking*, *15*(10), 527–533. doi:10.1089/cyber.2012.0207 PMID:23002988

Ayas, T., & Horzum, M. B. (2010). *Cyberbullg / victim scale development study*. Retrieved from: http://www.akademikbakis.org

Barlett, C. P., & Gentile, D. A. (2012). Long-term psychological predictors of cyber-bullying in late adolescence. *Psychology of Popular Media Culture*, *2*, 123–135. doi:10.1037/a0028113

Barlett, C. P., Gentile, D. A., Anderson, C. A., Suzuki, K., Sakamoto, A., Yamaoka, A., & Katsura, R. (2013). Cross-cultural differences in cyberbullying behavior: A short-term longitudinal study. *Journal of Cross-Cultural Psychology*, *45*(2), 300–313. doi:10.1177/0022022113504622

Bauman, S., Toomey, R. B., & Walker, J. L. (2013). Associations among bullying, cyberbullying, and suicide in high school students. *Journal of Adolescence*, *36*(2), 341–350. doi:10.1016/j.adolescence.2012.12.001 PMID:23332116

Bauman, S., Underwood, M. K., & Card, N. A. (2013). Definitions: Another perspective and a proposal for beginning with cyberaggression. In S. Bauman, D. Cross, & J. Walker (Eds.), *Principles of cyberbullying research: Definitions, measures, methodology* (pp. 26–40). New York, NY: Routledge.

Bayar, Y., & Ucanok, Z. (2012). School social climate and generalized peer perception in traditional and cyberbullying status. *Educational Sciences: Theory and Practice, 12*, 2352–2358.

Beckman, L., Hagquist, C., & Hellstrom, L. (2012). Does the association with psychosomatic health problems differ between cyberbullying and traditional bullying? *Emotional & Behavioural Difficulties, 17*(3-4), 421–434. doi:10.1080/13632752.2012.704228

Bonanno, R. A., & Hymel, S. (2013). Cyber bullying and internalizing difficulties: Above and beyond the impact of traditional forms of bullying. *Journal of Youth and Adolescence, 42*(5), 685–697. doi:10.1007/s10964-013-9937-1 PMID:23512485

Boulton, M., Lloyd, J., Down, J., & Marx, H. (2012). Predicting undergraduates self-reported engagement in traditional and cyberbullying from attitudes. *Cyberpsychology, Behavior, and Social Networking, 15*(3), 141–147. doi:10.1089/cyber.2011.0369 PMID:22304402

Brighi, A., Guarini, A., Melotti, G., Galli, S., & Genta, M. L. (2012). Predictors of victimisation across direct bullying, indirect bullying and cyberbullying. *Emotional & Behavioural Difficulties, 17*(3-4), 375–388. doi:10.1080/13632752.2012.704684

Burton, K. A., Florell, D., & Wygant, D. B. (2013). The role of peer attachment and normative beliefs about aggression on traditional bullying and cyberbullying. *Psychology in the Schools, 50*(2), 103–114. doi:10.1002/pits.21663

Cappadocia, M. C., Craig, W. M., & Pepler, D. (2013). Cyberbullying: Prevalence, stability and risk factors during adolescence. *Canadian Journal of School Psychology, 28*(2), 171–192. doi:10.1177/0829573513491212

Cassidy, W., Brown, K., & Jackson, M. (2012a). Making kind cool: Parents suggestions for preventing cyber bullying and fostering cyber kindness. *Journal of Educational Computing Research, 46*(4), 415–436. doi:10.2190/EC.46.4.f

Cassidy, W., Brown, K., & Jackson, M. (2012b). Under the radar: Educators and cyberbullying in schools. *School Psychology International, 33*(5), 520–532. doi:10.1177/0143034312445245

Corcoran, L., Connolly, I., & OMoore, M. (2012). Cyberbullying in Irish schools: An investigation of personality and self-concept. *The Irish Journal of Psychology, 33*(4), 153–165. doi:10.1080/0303391 0.2012.677995

Curelaru, M., Iacob, I., & Abalasei, B. (2009). *School bullying: Definition, characteristics, and intervention strategies*. Lumean Publishing House.

Dehue, F., Bolman, C., & Vollink, T. (2008). Cyberbullying: Youngsters experiences and parental perception. *CyberPscyhology & Behavior, 11*(2), 217–223. doi:10.1089/cpb.2007.0008 PMID:18422417

Dehue, F., Bolman, C., Vollink, T., & Pouwelse, M. (2012). Cyberbullying and traditional bullying in relation to adolescents' perceptions of parenting. *Journal of Cyber Therapy and Rehabilitation, 5*, 25–34.

deLara, E. W. (2012). Why adolescents dont disclose incidents of bullying and harassment. *Journal of School Violence, 11*(4), 288–305. doi:10.1080/15388220.2012.705931

Diamanduros, T., & Downs, E. (2011). Creating a safe school environment: How to prevent cyberbullying at your school. *Library Media Connection*, *30*(2), 36–38.

Eden, S., Heiman, T., & Olenik-Shemesh, D. (2013). Teachers perceptions, beliefs and concerns about cyberbullying. *British Journal of Educational Technology*, *44*(6), 1036–1052. doi:10.1111/j.1467-8535.2012.01363.x

Elledge, L. C., Williford, A., Boulton, A. J., DePaolis, K. J., Little, T. D., & Salmivalli, C. (2013). Individual and contextual predictors of cyberbullying: The influence of childrens provictim attitudes and teachers ability to intervene. *Journal of Youth and Adolescence*, *42*(5), 698–710. doi:10.1007/s10964-013-9920-x PMID:23371005

Erdur-Baker, O. (2010). Cyberbullying and its correlation to traditional bullying, gender and frequent and risky usage of internet-mediated communication tools. *New Media & Society*, *12*(1), 109–125. doi:10.1177/1461444809341260

Fanti, K. A., Demetriou, A. G., & Hawa, V. V. (2012). A longitudinal study of cyberbullying: Examining risk and protective factors. *European Journal of Developmental Psychology*, *8*(2), 168–181. doi:10.1080/17405629.2011.643169

Festl, R., Schwarkow, M., & Quandt, T. (2013). Peer influence, internet use and cyberbullying: A comparison of different context effects among German adolescents. *Journal of Children and Media*, *7*(4), 446–462. doi:10.1080/17482798.2013.781514

Goebert, D., Else, I., Matsu, C., Chung-Do, J., & Chang, J. Y. (2011). The impact of cyberbullying on substance use and mental health in a multiethnic sample. *Maternal and Child Health Journal*, *15*(8), 1282–1286. doi:10.1007/s10995-010-0672-x PMID:20824318

Gradinger, P., Strohmeier, D., & Spiel, C. (2009). Traditional bullying and cyberbullying. *The Journal of Psychology*, *217*, 205–213.

Grigg, D. W. (2012). Definitional constructs of cyberbullying and cyber aggression from a triagnulatory overview: A preliminary study into elements. *Journal of Aggression, Conflict and Peace Research*, *4*(4), 202–215. doi:10.1108/17596591211270699

Hinduja, S., & Patchin, J. W. (2007). Offline consequences of online victimization. *Journal of School Violence*, *6*(3), 89–112. doi:10.1300/J202v06n03_06

Hinduja, S., & Patchin, J. W. (2008). Cyberbullying: An exploratory analysis of factors related to offending and victimization. *Deviant Behavior*, *29*(2), 129–156. doi:10.1080/01639620701457816

Hinduja, S., & Patchin, J. W. (2010). Bullying, cyberbullying, and suicide. *Archives of Suicide Research*, *14*(3), 206–221. doi:10.1080/13811118.2010.494133 PMID:20658375

Hinduja, S., & Patchin, J. W. (2012). Cyberbullying: Neither and epidemic nor a rarity. *European Journal of Developmental Psychology*, *9*(5), 539–543. doi:10.1080/17405629.2012.706448

Hinduja, S., & Patchin, J. W. (2013). Social influences on cyberbullying behaviors among middle and high school students. *Journal of Youth and Adolescence*, *42*(5), 711–722. doi:10.1007/s10964-012-9902-4 PMID:23296318

Hokoda, A., Lu, H. A., & Angeles, M. (2006). School bullying in Taiwanese adolescents. *Journal of Emotional Abuse*, 6(4), 69–90. doi:10.1300/J135v06n04_04

Huang, Y., & Chou, C. (2010). An analysis of multiple factors of cyberbullying among junior high school students in Taiwan. *Computers in Human Behavior*, 26(6), 1581–1590. doi:10.1016/j.chb.2010.06.005

Jang, H., Song, J., & Kim, R. (2014). Does the offline bully-victimization influence cyberbullying behavior among youths? Application of general strain theory. *Computers in Human Behavior*, 31, 85–93. doi:10.1016/j.chb.2013.10.007

Joinson, A. (1998). Causes and implications of behavior on the Internet. In J. Gackenbach (Ed.), *Psychology and the Internet: Intrapersonal, interpersonal, and transpersonal implications* (pp. 43–60). San Diego, CA: Academic Press.

Kochenderfer-Ladd, B., & Pelletier, M. (2008). Teachers views and beliefs about bullying: Influences on classroom management strategies and students coping with peer victimization. *Journal of School Psychology*, 46(4), 431–453. doi:10.1016/j.jsp.2007.07.005 PMID:19083367

Kowalski, R. M., & Limber, S. P. (2007). Electronic bullying among middle school students. *The Journal of Adolescent Health*, 41(6), 22–30. doi:10.1016/j.jadohealth.2007.08.017 PMID:18047942

Kwan, G. C. E., & Skoric, M. M. (2013). Facebook bullying: An extension of battles in school. *Computers in Human Behavior*, 29(1), 16–25. doi:10.1016/j.chb.2012.07.014

Laftman, S. B., Modin, B., & Ostberg, V. (2013). Cyberbullying and subjective health: A large-scale study of students in Stockholm, Sweden. *Children and Youth Services Review*, 35(1), 112–119. doi:10.1016/j.childyouth.2012.10.020

Lazuras, L., Barkoukis, V., Ourda, D., & Tsorbatzoudis, H. (2013). A process model of cyberbullying in adolescence. *Computers in Human Behavior*, 29(3), 881–887. doi:10.1016/j.chb.2012.12.015

Lenhart, A. (2015). *Teens, social media & technology overview 2015*. Retrieved from: http://www.pewinternet.org/2015/04/09/teens-social-media-technology-2015/

Li, Q. (2007). Bullying in the new playground: Research into cyberbullying and cybervictimization. *Australasian Journal of Educational Technology*, 23(4), 435–454. doi:10.14742/ajet.1245

Li, Q. (2008). A cross-cultural comparison of adolescents experience related to cyberbullying. *Educational Research*, 50(3), 223–234. doi:10.1080/00131880802309333

Machackova, H., Dedkova, L., & Mezulanikova, K. (2015). Brief report: The bystander effect in cyberbullying incidents. *Journal of Adolescence*, 43, 96–99. doi:10.1016/j.adolescence.2015.05.010 PMID:26070168

Machackova, H., Dedkova, L., Sevcikova, A., & Cerna, A. (2013). Bystanders support of cyberbullied schoolmates. *Journal of Community & Applied Social Psychology*, 23(1), 25–36. doi:10.1002/casp.2135

Mason, K. (2008). Cyberbullying: A preliminary assessment for school personnel. *Psychology in the Schools*, 45(4), 323–348. doi:10.1002/pits.20301

McKenna, K. Y. A., & Bargh, J. A. (2000). Plan 9 from cyberspace: The implications of the internet for personality and social psychology. *Personality and Social Psychology Review*, *4*(1), 57–75. doi:10.1207/S15327957PSPR0401_6

McQuade, C. S., Colt, P. J., & Meyer, B. N. (2009). *Cyber bullying: Protecting kids and adults from online bullies*. Westport, CT: Praeger.

Mitchell, K. J., Ybarra, M., & Finkelhor, D. (2007). The relative importance of online victimization in understanding depression, delinquency, and substance use. *Child Maltreatment*, *12*(4), 314–324. doi:10.1177/1077559507305996 PMID:17954938

Mouttapa, M., Valente, T., Gallagher, P., Rohrbach, L. A., & Unger, J. B. (2004). Social network predictor of bullying and victimization. *Adolescence*, *39*, 315–335. PMID:15563041

Nikiforou, M., Georgiou, S. N., & Stavrinides, P. (2013). Attachment to parents and peers as predictors of bullying and victimization. *Journal of Criminology*, *2013*, 1–9. doi:10.1155/2013/484871

Olweus, D. (1993). *Bullying at school. What we know and what we can do*. Malden, MA: Blackwell Publishing.

Patchin, J. W., & Hinduja, S. (2006). Bullies move beyond the schoolyard: A preliminary look at cyberbullying. *Youth Violence and Juvenile Justice*, *4*(2), 148–169. doi:10.1177/1541204006286288

Perren, S., Dooley, J., Shaw, T., & Cross, D. (2010). Bullying in school and cyberspace: Associations with depressive symptoms in Swiss and Australian adolescents. *Child and Adolescent Psychiatry and Mental Health*, *4*(1), 1–10. doi:10.1186/1753-2000-4-28 PMID:21092266

Pornari, C. D., & Wood, J. (2010). Peer and cyber aggression in secondary school students: The role of moral disengagement, hostile attribution bias, and outcome expectancies. *Aggressive Behavior*, *36*(2), 81–94. doi:10.1002/ab.20336 PMID:20035548

Rideout, V. J., Roberts, D. F., & Foehr, U. G. (2005). *Generation M: Media in the lives of 8-18-year-olds: Executive summary*. Menlo Park, CA: Henry J. Kaiser Family Foundation.

Rosen, L. D. (2007). *Me, Myspace, and I: Parenting the Net Generation*. New York: Palgrave Macmillan.

Sahin, M. (2010). Teachers perceptions of bullying in high schools: A Turkish study. *Social Behavior and Personality*, *38*(1), 127–142. doi:10.2224/sbp.2010.38.1.127

Sevcikova, A., Machackova, H., Wright, M. F., Dedkova, L., & Cerna, A. (2015). Social support seeking in relation to parental attachment and peer relationships among victims of cyberbullying. *Australian Journal of Guidance & Counselling*, *15*, 1–13. doi:10.1017/jgc.2015.1

Shapka, J. D., & Law, D. M. (2013). Does one size fit all? Ethnic differences in parenting behaviors and motivations for adolescent engagement in cyberbullying. *Journal of Youth and Adolescence*, *42*(5), 723–738. doi:10.1007/s10964-013-9928-2 PMID:23479327

Shariff, S., & Hoff, D. L. (2007). Cyber bullying: Clarifying legal boundaries for school supervision in cyberspace. *International Journal of Cyber Criminology*, *1*, 76–118.

Sijtsema, J. J., Ashwin, R. J., Simona, C. S., & Gina, G. (2014). Friendship selection and influence in bullying and defending. *Effects of moral disengagement. Developmental Psychology, 50*(8), 2093–2104. doi:10.1037/a0037145 PMID:24911569

Sjurso, I. R., Fandream, H., & Roland, E. (2016). Emotional problems in traditional and cyber victimization. *Journal of School Violence, 15*(1), 114–131. doi:10.1080/15388220.2014.996718

Smith, P. K., Del Barrio, C., & Tokunaga, R. S. (2013). Definitions of bullying and cyberbullying: How useful are the terms? In S. Bauman, D. Cross, & J. Walker (Eds.), *Principles of cyberbullying research: Definitions, measures, methodology* (pp. 26–40). New York, NY: Routledge.

Smith, P. K., Mahdavi, J., Carvalho, M., Fisher, S., Russell, S., & Tippett, N. (2008). Cyberbullying: Its nature and impact in secondary school pupils. *Journal of Child Psychology and Psychiatry, and Allied Disciplines, 49*(4), 376–385. doi:10.1111/j.1469-7610.2007.01846.x PMID:18363945

Sourander, A., Brunstein, A., Ikonen, M., Lindroos, J., Luntamo, T., Koskelainen, M., & Helenius, H. et al. (2010). Psychosocial risk factors associated with cyberbullying among adolescents: A population-based study. *Archives of General Psychiatry, 67*(7), 720–728. doi:10.1001/archgenpsychiatry.2010.79 PMID:20603453

Stoll, L. C., & Block, R. Jr. (2015). Intersectionality and cyberbullying: A study of cybervictimization in a Midwestern high school. *Computers in Human Behavior, 52*, 387–391. doi:10.1016/j.chb.2015.06.010

Strohmeier, D., Aoyama, I., Gradinger, P., & Toda, Y. (2013). Cybervictimization and cyberaggression in Eastern and Western countries: Challenges of constructing a cross-cultural appropriate scale. In S. Bauman, D. Cross, & J. L. Walker (Eds.), *Principles of cyberbullying research: Definitions, measures, and methodology* (pp. 202–221). New York: Routledge.

Suler, J. (2004). The online disinhibition effect. *Cyberpsychology & Behavior, 7*(3), 321–326. doi:10.1089/1094931041291295 PMID:15257832

Tangen, D., & Campbell, M. (2010). Cyberbullying prevention: One primary schools approach. *Australian Journal of Guidance & Counselling, 20*(02), 225–234. doi:10.1375/ajgc.20.2.225

Toledano, S., Werch, B. L., & Wiens, B. A. (2015). Domain-specific self-concept in relation to traditional and cyber peer aggression. *Journal of School Violence, 14*(4), 405–423. doi:10.1080/15388220.2014.935386

Totura, C. M. W., MacKinnon-Lewis, C., Gesten, E. L., Gadd, R., Divine, K. P., Dunham, S., & Kamboukos, D. (2009). Bullying and victimization among boys and girls in middle school: The influence of perceived family and school contexts. *The Journal of Early Adolescence, 29*(4), 571–609. doi:10.1177/0272431608324190

Wade, A., & Beran, T. (2011). Cyberbullying: The new era of bullying. *Canadian Journal of School Psychology, 26*(1), 44–61. doi:10.1177/0829573510396318

Wong, D. S., Chan, H. C. O., & Cheng, C. H. (2014). Cyberbullying perpetration and victimization among adolescents in Hong Kong. *Children and Youth Services Review, 36*, 133–140. doi:10.1016/j.childyouth.2013.11.006

Wright, M. F. (2013). The relationship between young adults beliefs about anonymity and subsequent cyber aggression. *Cyberpsychology, Behavior, and Social Networking, 16*(12), 858–862. doi:10.1089/cyber.2013.0009 PMID:23849002

Wright, M. F. (2014a). Cyber victimization and perceived stress: Linkages to late adolescents' cyber aggression and psychological functioning. *Youth & Society.*

Wright, M. F. (2014b). Predictors of anonymous cyber aggression: The role of adolescents beliefs about anonymity, aggression, and the permanency of digital content. *Cyberpsychology, Behavior, and Social Networking, 17*(7), 431–438. doi:10.1089/cyber.2013.0457 PMID:24724731

Wright, M. F. (2014c). Longitudinal investigation of the associations between adolescents popularity and cyber social behaviors. *Journal of School Violence, 13*(3), 291–314. doi:10.1080/15388220.2013.849201

Wright, M. F. (2015). Cyber victimization and adjustment difficulties: The mediation of Chinese and American adolescents' digital technology usage. *CyberPsychology: Journal of Psychosocial Research in Cyberspace, 1*(1), article 1. Retrieved from: http://cyberpsychology.eu/view.php?cisloclanku=2015051102&article=1

Wright, M. F. (in press). Adolescents' cyber aggression perpetration and cyber victimization: The longitudinal associations with school functioning. *Social Psychology of Education.*

Wright, M. F., Kamble, S., Lei, K., Li, Z., Aoyama, I., & Shruti, S. (2015). Peer attachment and cyberbullying involvement among Chinese, Indian, and Japanese adolescents. *Societies, 5*(2), 339–353. doi:10.3390/soc5020339

Wright, M. F., & Li, Y. (2012). Kicking the digital dog: A longitudinal investigation of young adults victimization and cyber-displaced aggression. *Cyberpsychology, Behavior, and Social Networking, 15*(9), 448–454. doi:10.1089/cyber.2012.0061 PMID:22974350

Wright, M. F., & Li, Y. (2013a). Normative beliefs about aggression and cyber aggression among young adults: A longitudinal investigation. *Aggressive Behavior, 39*(3), 161–170. doi:10.1002/ab.21470 PMID:23440595

Wright, M. F., & Li, Y. (2013b). The association between cyber victimization and subsequent cyber aggression: The moderating effect of peer rejection. *Journal of Youth and Adolescence, 42*(5), 662–674. doi:10.1007/s10964-012-9903-3 PMID:23299177

Ybarra, M. L., Diener-West, M., & Leaf, P. (2007). Examining the overlap in internet harassment and school bullying: Implications for school intervention. *The Journal of Adolescent Health, 1*(6), 42–50. doi:10.1016/j.jadohealth.2007.09.004 PMID:18047944

Ybarra, M. L., & Mitchell, K. J. (2004). Online aggressor/targets, aggressors, and targets: A comparison of associated youth characteristics. *Journal of Child Psychology and Psychiatry, and Allied Disciplines, 45*(7), 1308–1316. doi:10.1111/j.1469-7610.2004.00328.x PMID:15335350

Yousef, W. S. M., & Bellamy, A. (2015). The impact of cyberbullying on the self-esteem and academic functioning of Arab American middle and high school students. *Electronic Journal of Research in Educational Psychology, 23*(3), 463–482.

Zhou, Z., Tang, H., Tian, Y., Wei, H., Zhang, F., & Morrison, C. M. (2013). Cyberbullying and its risk factors among Chinese high school students. *School Psychology International*, *34*(6), 630–647. doi:10.1177/0143034313479692

ADDITIONAL READING

Bauman, S. (2011). *Cyberbullying: What counselors need to know*. Alexandria, VA: American Counseling Association.

Bauman, S., Cross, D., & Walker, J. (2013). *Principles of cyberbullying research: Definitions, measures, and methodology*. New York, NY: Routledge.

Hinduja, S., & Patchin, J. W. (2015). *Bullying beyond the schoolyard: Preventing and responding to cyberbullying*. Thousand Oaks, CA: Sage Publications.

Li, Q., Cross, D., & Smith, P. K. (2012). *Cyberbullying in the global playground*. Malden, MA: Blackwell Publishing. doi:10.1002/9781119954484

Menesini, E., & Spiel, C. (2012). *Cyberbullying: Development, consequences, risk and protective factors*. New York, NY: Psychology Press.

Tokunaga, R. S. (2010). Following you home from school: A critical review and synthesis of research on cyberbullying victimization. *Computers in Human Behavior*, *26*(3), 277–287. doi:10.1016/j.chb.2009.11.014

KEY TERMS AND DEFINITIONS

Anonymity: The quality of being unknown or unacknowledged.

Anxiety: A mental health disorder which includes symptoms of worry, anxiety, and/or fear that are intense enough to disrupt one's daily activities.

Collectivism: A cultural value that stressed the importance of the group over individual goals and cohesion within social groups.

Cyberbullying: Children's and adolescents' usage of electronic technologies to hostilely and intentionally harass, embarrass, and intimidate others.

Empathy: The ability to understand or feel what another person is experiencing or feeling.

Externalizing Difficulties: Includes children's and adolescents' failure to control their behaviors.

Individualism: The belief that each person is more important than the needs of the whole group or society.

Loneliness: An unpleasant emotional response to isolation or lack of companionship.

Normative Belief: Beliefs about the acceptability and tolerability of a behavior.

Parental Mediation and Monitoring: The strategies that parents use to manage the relationship between their children and media.

Parenting Style: The standard strategies that parents use in their child rearing.

Peer Attachment: The internalization of the knowledge that their peers will be available and responsive.

Peer Contagion: The transmission or transfer of deviant behavior from one adolescent to another.

Provictim Attitudes: The belief that bullying is unacceptable and that defending victims is valuable.

Social Exclusion: The process involving individuals or groups of people block or deny someone from the group.

Traditional Face-To-Face Bullying: The use of strength or influence to intimidate or physically harm someone.

Chapter 7
A Psycho–Pedagogical Model for Evaluating Effectiveness of Students' Learning on the Basis of Electronic Visual Rows

Svetlana Kostromina
St. Petersburg State University, Russia

Daria Gnedykh
St. Petersburg State University, Russia

Galina Molodtsova
St. Petersburg State University, Russia

ABSTRACT

The purpose of this chapter is to propose a model that would enable teachers to assess comprehensively the effectiveness of learners` information acquisition in e-learning environment. The main value of the proposed model is its focus on combination of pedagogical conditions and psychological factors of learning to increase the level of information acquisition. In order to study students` acquisition of learning information in dependence upon the form of presentation as well as identification of learners` psychological characteristics, that help the acquisition of material presented in three visual forms (text, charts, comics) the experiment was carried out. On the grounds of the obtained results, the authors suggest guidelines for application of the model in practice.

INTRODUCTION

One of the main aims of using information technologies (IT) in learning is improvement of the quality of education and its outcomes through raising the effectiveness of learning information acquisition. The modern system of education places much reliance on the use of electronic tools in the educational process, believing that future learner`s achievements are linked to the capacity of utilization of electronic

DOI: 10.4018/978-1-5225-2616-2.ch007

information resources. The ways of working with learning material that form metaskills, which involve developing the ability to extract and structure knowledge (not only to memorize and store them) relying on information systems, are laid down into the curriculum.

Nowadays, the human interaction with IT in education consists of two stages: at the first stage a teacher creates electronic tools for classes, and at the second stage students get involved in interaction with these tools (Guri-Rosenblit, 2005; Steen, 2008; Frolov, 2011). Both stages involve active use of electronic visualizations to facilitate the process of perception (Multimodal Learning Through Media, 2008). However, despite the long experience in using tools of information visualization in e-learning, blended learning, distance and online learning, their impact on learning efficiency is still controversial. It was established that students' emotional tension and fatigability when reading e-book texts increased in comparison with reading texts of paper books (Kuchma et al., 2012); the rapidity of students` acquisition of information in distance education decreased in contrast to studying the same learning material in the classroom (Balashova, 2011). Thus, the active implementation of electronic tools in the educational process has not led to substantial increase in the training effectiveness. The reasons for this can be explained by the fact that psychological approaches and pedagogical models for using the information technology in education are frequently applied independently of each other.

Therefore, the success in teaching and learning can be achieved by using a complex psycho-pedagogical model considering the combination of learners' psychological characteristics and pedagogical conditions of interaction with IT in education.

In this chapter the authors propose a model that would enable teachers:

- To approach consciously to the choice of the form of electronic visualization of learning material to improve the efficiency of its acquisition by learners;
- To assess comprehensively the effectiveness of the learners` information acquisition in e-learning environment.

This model is the result of the study of established correspondence between the educational environment and psychological factors influencing on the effectiveness of acquisition of learning information by the learners in their interaction with IT.

The chapter provides theoretical and empirical justification of the model, as well as recommendations for its application in practice.

BACKGROUND

The information acquisition is a central part of the learning process (Rubinstein, 2005). There are different approaches to understanding of the information acquisition. McNamara and O'Reilly (electronic resource) define it as a complex process of absorbing and storing new information in memory, which success depends on future reproduction (use). According to O'leary (electronic resource), the process of knowledge acquisition is the basis not only for use but also for production of new knowledge. Lawrence, Lefkowitz and Lesser (1988) draw attention to the fact that the knowledge acquisition requires understanding of how new information fits the information that is already contained in the knowledge base.

According to Russian authors (Nurminsky & Gladysheva, 1991) the process of acquisition includes the following stages: perception of an object (selecting of an object and determining its essential properties); comprehension (identifying significant links and relations); memorizing of selected properties and relationships; active reproduction of properties and relations. The final stage of transformation (accommodation) is the incorporation of new knowledge into the structure of past experience and its use as another means of constructing of new knowledge. Confederatov and Simonov distinguish the following levels of learning: the level of discernment (or recognition) of the subject; the level of its memorization; the level of understanding; the level of application (Kudryashova, 2009). Bespalko (1989) offers similar stages: understanding, recognition, reproduction, use, creation.

The Effectiveness of the Information Acquisition Through Electronic Means in Training

Currently, the didactic and organizational principles of e-learning using: the principle of distribution of educational material, the principle of interactivity of educational material, the principle of multimedia presentation of educational information, the principle of adaptability to personal characteristics of the learner are described in details (Vumyatnin et al., 2002). The analysis of psychological and pedagogical appropriateness of the use of educational software of different types allow to draw the following conclusions: the majority of them train skills, increase motivation of learning due to the possibility of independent work, develop visual-figurative and visual-effective types of thinking through visualizations, develop creative potential and certain kinds of thinking, train memory (Robert, 1994). Nonetheless, Rolf points to the negative factors of learning with the help of a computer: the reduction of interpersonal communication and the role of oral and written speech, lack of direct exploration of reality, weakening the ability for independent creative thinking (Kodzhaspirova, & Petrov, 2001). Thus, it is impossible to speak about full advantage of using e-learning tools over traditional.

Advantages of electronic means ensuring the effectiveness of the educational process are usually described depending on the type of electronic systems. So, computer simulation programs allow to visualize processes and phenomena that cause difficulties in students` understanding (Belavin, Golicyna, & Kucenko, 2000), provide an opportunity to conduct virtual experiments (simulation programs), facilitate the acquisition of skills (educational computer games) (Popova, 2008) and formation of readiness to professional activity (Druz, 2013). The electronic textbook creates active-interactive cognitive environment, provides the possibility of individualization of the pace and depth of development of the subject (Bosova, & Zubchenok, 2013), contributes to formation of the skill to take professional decisions, increases creative and intellectual potentials (Miller, 2010). Through hypertext links we get the best memorization of the basic material (Naseikina, 2010).

An electronic interactive whiteboard combines visual, auditory and kinesthetic types of learning modalities, improves learning and cognitive motivation (Gusakova, 2013), performs such functions as administrative, informative, interactive, communicative, developmental, etc. (Romashkina et al., 2010).

The most common e-learning tool is multimedia presentations (PowerPoint presentations) which allow to combine comments from the teacher with the video information, thereby promoting the attention of learners to the content of learning material and increasing demand. In addition, the use of multimedia presentations gives emotional color to assimilated material, brings aesthetic pleasure to learners, enhancing the quality of learning information (Robert, 1994). Visual rows activate creative thinking by helping learners to perceive the material holistically (Zakharova, 2003). Yet, Nugumanova and Khamitova (2013) have obtained convincing data about the negative effects of multimedia presentations on the physiological level – fatigue of the visual analyzer, which may badly influence on the process of assimilation. In their work Nouri and Shahid (2005) note that the presentation does not always contribute to improving learning outcomes and retention of information in long-term memory. Such data are practically nonexistent in the methodological guidelines for the creation of lecture presentations. Usually the authors draw on organizational and technical conditions: font size, number of slides, amount of text on the slide, structure, content, etc.

Thus, the effective use of electronic tools in learning requires the introduction of some principles of interaction between learners and IT. From a pedagogical point of view, it is important to consider the influence of the content of learning material, forms of visualization that are passed through IT, as well as the didactic content of the training material (subject area – natural sciences, humanities, exact sciences (Glukhareva, 2008; Phillips, Norris, & Macnab, 2010) and teaching methods (problem-based learning, educational training, etc.). From the positions of psychology, it is necessary to consider individual characteristics of learners that can change the outcome of the assimilation under e-learning environment.

Form of Visualization as a Pedagogical Condition of Acquisition Effectiveness

Implementation of IT in education has significantly expanded opportunities for visualization of learning information, therefore, the simple verbal presentation of the material fades into the background. Today there are empirically validated data of increasing the level of acquisition by using multimedia presentations at mathematics classes (Anisova et al., 2014), effective use of multimedia software in the classroom (Mantorova, 2002), use of visualization at reading and natural sciences classes (Phillips et al., 2010).

The main trend of these studies is that they provide general advice about the methods of creation and application of electronic visualization in the learning process and less attention is drawn to specific forms of visualization – charts, texts, illustrations, etc. In turn, each form has its own didactic specifics and influence on the perception and comprehension of information in the process of acquisition, which also gains additional features when using electronic means.

The most common form of visual presentation of learning information is a text. Sabinina (2009) indicates that the perception and understanding of the content of the information studied in the form of texts, on the one hand, are influenced by linguistic features of the text and the learner`s linguistic knowledge. So, the presentation of the text in verse form contributes to its acquisition (Kiseleva, 2011). On the other hand, psychological peculiarities of the subject of perception also influences on its acquisition. For example, structural features of the intelligence and processes of "metacognitive regulation" influence on understanding of scientific texts (Kalashnikova, 2013).

Chart presentation of information has other features. Using diagrams, learners can see the structure of phenomena or concepts, the hierarchy of certain system elements (Netesov, 2012), as well as the logical relationships that help to understand the meanings of certain terms (Ovchinnikova, 2013). The chart promotes the development of a generalized thinking activity, acts as a means of reducing of the information volume intended for memorization.

Considering that modern electronic visualization tools provide more and more opportunities, the use of illustrative visual material in the educational process is actively growing. Today no classes go by without illustrative support. One of illustrative visual materials is educational comics. Its specificity lies in the combination of verbal and non-verbal aspects (Buslova et al., 2014). In comics syntax of the written language get closer to the oral dialogue language, and the picture contains a large amount of information, contributing to understanding of the situation in whole (McCloud, 1994). The interaction of verbal text and visual components ensures the integrity of the piece and creates the effect of communication (Petrova & Stepanova, 2005). Buslova calls the comics as one of the ways of mediated formation of system thinking (Buslova et al., 2014). Among the benefits of comics in the educational process Arkhipova (2012) identifies imagery, capacity, dynamic presentation of information, the dramatization of stories, "the saving of psychic effort for perception of information".

It is important to point out that when different authors highlight advantages of some forms of visualization in the learning process, the identified regularities are mainly related to the traditional options of visualization presented on paper. In the meantime, for electronic forms of visualization additional researches, identifying opportunities for effective learning in e-learning are needed. It is connected with specific features of the electronic visualizations, which, in particular, can be reflected in the concept of "electronic visual rows". "Electronic visual rows" - is consecutive information in the form of illustrations, symbolical and graphic presentations, both static and dynamic (animation or a video series) which is stored in a digital form and is shown on the computer screen or by means of information technologies (Kostromina & Gnedykh, 2012). Thus, the specificity of electronic visualizations applies to both used forms (text, diagram, illustration/comics), and the potential or limitations of digital technologies, capable to become a source of additional load on the nervous system of learners (for example, increases fatigue when reading from the screen) (Kuchma et al., 2012). Their incorporation in the educational process is an integral pedagogical condition ensuring acquisition of learners in a modern learning environment.

Psychological Factors of Acquisition

According to researchers, the process of acquisition of information is influenced by not only external factors but also internal and psychological, associated with the peculiarities of psychic processes and states, and psychic characteristics of personality of learners. In particular, such factors are development of different forms of thinking and mental operations involved into the educational process (Berdnikova, 2007; Maskinskov, 2003; Golub & Fokina, 2013); individual characteristics of information perception (Karginova, 1999); needs and motives of students determining their adaptation to training (Orlov, 1984); presence of an indicative basis, appeal to individual experience in the context of communicative-cognitive activity (Parkhomenko, 2003).

The role of psychological factors is to ensure effective acquisition on the basis of learners` characteristics: the processes of perception, thinking, memory, learning motivation, capacity for self-organization activities, etc. In their description it is productive to rely on psychological theory describing the structure of personality. Considering that learning involves cognitive learner`s activity, driving motives, and a certain behavior in the situation of training, in our opinion, the most successful theoretical basis for the description of the psychological characteristics affecting the process of acquisition of the obtained information is Leontiev's activity theory (Leontiev, 1978; Kaptelinin, Kuutti, & Bannon, 1997)

According to it, the psychological factors of learning can be divided into cognitive, motivational and behavioral. Meaningfully, each of them can be presented as a complex of psychological variables. From our point of view, key factors of learning are styles of thinking (cognitive factor), the motives of educational activity (motivational factor), the styles of learning and features of self-organization (behavioral factor).

Styles of thinking are associated with setting a goal, the choice of solution method and ways of behavior (Troeshestova, & Ivanova, 2013). Harrison and Bramson (1984) distinguish analytical, synthetic, realistic, idealistic and pragmatic thinking styles. According to Berulava the synthetic style of thinking is interrelated with the level of creativity (in Suhih, & Korytchenkova, 2008), as well as subject oriented learning, humanitarian or technical (Dvoryadkina, 2011). Sokolova and Ivanova (2014) note that holders of the mental-art, art-mental and art personality types with synthetic thinking style perceive information holistically and immediately. Based on the Sternberg`s concept, Richmond, Krank and Cummings (2006) have showed that among online learners there are many of those who have dominant legislative and hierarchical styles.

Motivation in educational activity discloses the motive force of personality, its orientation on achieving high results (Davydov, 1986.; Zaporozhets, 1986). This statement is confirmed by experiments that clearly show that avoidance motivation does not allow the learner to exercise their mental capacities, and as a consequence, hinders their development. If a learner has a high level of learning motivation, but, herewith, low level of thinking, he will still be able to achieve productivity in learning activities (Badmaeva, 2000).

There are different grounds for the classification of motives. Badmaeva (2000) identifies three groups of motives depending on the type of activity – educational-cognitive, communicative and creative, Markova (1999) distinguishes two groups– cognitive and social. In general, the explanation of cognitive (learning) activity are divided into two groups – internal (specific) and external (non-specific) (Brushlinskii, & Volovikova, 1983), or internal and social (prestige, failure avoidance, self-determination, etc.) (Matyukhina, 1984). The dominance of any of them reflects the specific needs of the individual, which are realized in the educational process.

The learning style is expressed in special aspects of goal-setting, planning, decision-making, self-control, reflection, and self-evaluation (Borisova, 2001). It is an integral characteristic, revealing a unique combination of characteristics of mental activity, manifestations of emotions, will, personality in the process of knowledge acquisition and formation of skills. Holodnaya (2004) determines the styles of learning as "learning strategies that characterize the response of the individual to the demands of specific learning situations" and binds the features of their manifestation with educational technologies, learning situations, teaching methods, learner`s motivation, etc. The classification of the learning styles of Reinert (1976) is based on the modality of experience – visual images, sounds, verbal symbols, emotional sufferings.

Honey and Mumford distinguish two styles - activity (focus on application of knowledge) and analytical (focus on theoretical justification) (Allinson, & Hayes, 1996). Gregorc (1982) proposes to define styles depending on the student`s actions – draws on concrete or abstract knowledge, but also on the presence of the random or sequential nature of the doctrine. Canfield categorizes styles of teaching depending on the combination of the following factors: learning environment, methods in the study of new subjects, teaching methods and the expected evaluation of their achievements (Canfield, & Lafferty, 1974). On the basis of their combinations Canfield outlines the major styles of teaching – social (Social), independent (Independent), focused on practical work (Applied), speculative (Conceptual) (Canfield, & Lafferty, 1974). In his model of teaching styles, Kolb (1984) identifies four learning styles, which he calls accommodative, divergent, assimilative, and convergent.

"Self-organization of learning activity is a student`s activity, impelled and guided by the goals of self-government and self-improvement of their academic work, carried out by the system of intelligent actions aimed at solving problems of rational self-organization and the implementation of its educational work" (Kotova, & Shakhmatova, 2007) . Pejsahov and Shevcov (1991) believe that the cycle of self-government consists of the analysis of contradictions, forecasting, goal setting, planning, decision making, evaluation, self-monitoring and correction. As a result of analysis and experimental studies, Ishkov (2004) identifies six components of self-organization: goal setting, situation analysis, planning, self-monitoring, correction and conation.

According to many researchers` opinions, the learners` ability to self-activity ensures success in achieving learning outcomes (Afanas`eva, 2008; Kostromina, 2013). It is closely linked to metacognition processes, (Flavell, Brown, Borkowski, Peck, Reid, Fonest-Pressley, Holodnaya, Litvinov), which are responsible for self-regulation of intellectual activity (Chernokova, 2011), awareness of problem solving process (Lazareva, 2012) and affect the effectiveness of training (Borkowski et al., 1987). Kostromina (2013) allocates metacognitive learning strategies: planning, supervision (questions for self-assessment of achievements) and regulation (self-esteem, self-control, strong-willed regulation). Yanchar and Slife (2014) point out that students with learning difficulties, have less adequate metacognitive operations than achievers.

The accumulated extensive material on the impact of psychological factors on the information acquisition in the learning process clearly demonstrates the dependence of the acquisition results upon individual psychological characteristics. However, the system of their mutual influence on each other, the interaction with the pedagogical conditions are not entirely clear, and the question of their role in e-learning context is poorly studied.

Evaluation of the Acquisition Effectiveness: An Integrated Approach

Speaking about the effectiveness of acquisition of learning information and the process of knowledge formation the authors cannot fail to dwell on the criteria by which achievements can be assessed. The most common methods of knowledge assessment are interviews, examinations and tests aimed at reproduction of learning information.

In order to make the process of knowledge quality evaluation more objective and to improve the reliability of the process, Snigireva and Grishanova (2014) offer an integrated approach that combines taxonomic, qualimetric and thesaurus approaches. Accordingly, assessing of the quality of the learner's knowledge structure can be from three sides - the "strength" of knowledge, the "fullness" of the knowledge structure, "the knowledge structure level". Use of multiple methods of assessment also allows to make the process of evaluation more individualized (Ulanovskaya et al., 2013).

Another option is associated with the assessment of the acquisition effectiveness on two criteria: the process and the outcome. One way of evaluating of acquisition effectiveness as a process of knowledge formation can be concept maps (Novak, & Gowin, 1984). Concept maps are two-dimensional graphical presentation of knowledge including concepts connected by arcs (or lines) that reflect the relationships and interactions between pairs of concepts (Anohina, & Grundspenkis, 2009). They represent: a) a lack of understanding or misconception about a particular topic, b) changes in the line of thinking of learners.

Existing methods for evaluating concept maps have been analyzed in detail and structured according to the classification proposed by the authors Anohina and Grundspenkis in their work «Scoring Concept Maps: an Overview» (2009). In general, the criteria for evaluation of concept maps can be divided into two main groups:

- Criteria that measure components of the concept maps: the number of concepts, the fullness of the relationships, the correctness of judgments that connect concepts, the quality, the validity of judgments, the correctness of judgments which are not represented in the expert concept maps, judgments similar to the expert ones, the right place of concepts or relationships in the map, the levels of hierarchy;

- Criteria that describe the structure in whole, such as conformity to a specific structure (reference), the graph diameter, the number of hierarchical segments, the wealth of relations.

Using of concept maps for fixing of the existing representations before and after the impact it is possible to quantify whether understanding of the material changes with time (Kilic, Kaya & Dogan, 2004). The process of changes is recorded as follows (Osmundson, et al., 1999): new ideas (concepts) are added to previous knowledge (system of concepts); some of the absurd and wrong ideas are transformed into more scientific or even disappear from the map; more relationships between the concepts of systems arise.

From the point of view of the assessment of acquisition results, according to the authors, the most appropriate method can be tasks, developed on the base on Bloom`s taxonomy. According to Bloom's concept the way the learner copes with the tasks, activating certain mental operations, may be an indicator of the material acquisition (Bloom, & Krathwohl, 1956). Bloom identifies six levels of learning material acquisition, each of them describes some aspect of the learning process - knowledge, comprehension, application, analysis, synthesis, and evaluation. Thus, the measurement of learning outcomes for each of these levels, starting with the "knowledge" to "evaluation", after studying the subject is possible. To this end, for each level of acquisition a system of test questions and test tasks is created.

In correlation with the current terms of training (methods, forms, learning content), the efficiency of learning activities allows to judge the effectiveness of various teaching aids. Thus, having a single content and a common technology but using different didactic forms we can understand which one allows to achieve best results at the same cost (the same time, the same load and the same system of tasks). Simultaneously, an integrative evaluation of knowledge objectifies results. For example, the combination of concept maps and Bloom's taxonomy, on the one hand, contributes to the evaluation of the operations of thinking, helping to understand how deeply the learner has studied the material, and if he can use it. On the other hand, it gives the opportunity to see the whole understanding of the subject by learners, to trace how different learning tools affect the formation of conceptual thinking.

The integrated approach to assessing the effectiveness can also be used in e-learning. By focusing on the various forms of electronic visualization with a single content and a method of teaching, you can see how each of them contributes to the formation of learner`s scientific concepts, provides an effective acquisition of learning information. At the same time, by all means (inherently), one cannot exclude the role of psychological factors - cognitive, motivational, behavioral characteristics of learners - in assimilating information in the learning process.

The above findings allow the authors to suppose that certain correspondence of considered pedagogical conditions and psychological factors provides improved efficiency of assimilating of learning information, which can be determined by the integrated use of the evaluation techniques of acquisition results. In this regard, a psycho-pedagogical model of evaluating of acquisition effectiveness of the visual information of learners in e-learning was formulated, which later was tested in practice and received the evidence as a result of the conducted study.

EMPIRICAL JUSTIFICATION OF A PSYCHO-PEDAGOGICAL MODEL FOR EVALUATING OF EFFECTIVENESS OF STUDENTS' LEARNING

A psycho-pedagogical model for evaluating the effectiveness of students` acquisition of visual information in e-learning environment allows to solve the problem of fragmentation of psychological and pedagogical approaches in ensuring of the learning process effectiveness. The main value of the proposed model - focusing attention on the fact that the pedagogical conditions and psychological factors of learning can and should be combined with an increase in the level of acquisition of learning information.

The model includes the following components:

1. **Pedagogical Conditions:** Lexical features of the educational terminology; electronic visualization of information in different forms – text, charts, comics.
2. **Psychological Factors of Learning:** Students' psychological characteristics (motivation, cognitive and behavioral features) which can facilitate or hinder acquisition of visual information.
3. **Methods of Evaluating of Learning Effectiveness:** Concept maps and control tasks which are created on the basis of Bloom's taxonomy.

This model can help teachers to create conditions for students' more effective absorption of visual information by taking into account the correspondence between students' psychological characteristics and forms of electronic visual rows used in education.

To confirm theoretical justification of the model (see background) an experiment was conducted to prove the effectiveness of psychological and pedagogical model providing students' acquisition of information presented via different visual forms by means of electronic tools. The content of the experiment included a study of the students` acquisition of learning information in dependence upon the form of presentation while using multimedia presentations as well as identification of learners` psychological characteristics, that help the acquisition of material presented in three visual forms (text, charts, comics).

The Design and Procedure of the Study

As a criterion of acquisition effectiveness the authors have identified the level of students` acquisition of learning information and the dynamics of changes in the knowledge system. Means of the acquisition evaluation are:

1. Test tasks, developed on the basis of Bloom`s taxonomy of educational objectives (knowledge, comprehension, application, analysis, synthesis and evaluation of learning material) (Bloom, & Krathwohl, 1956).
2. Concept maps drawn by students before and after studying the suggested material.

The research design involved conducting of lectures-presentations in the framework of educational process on discipline "Psychology" for students of natural sciences and physical-mathematical specialties. According to the curriculum three themes ("Abilities", "Temperament", "Character") which were necessary for studying by students of these specialties were selected. Each topic was studied separately with an interval of one week. Checking of the level of information acquisition was conducted immediately after the lecture with a test and after completion of the study of all three themes with a final test. The results were analyzed discretely for each faculty and collectively for the entire sample. Dynamics of changes of the conceptual row was recorded on the basis of concept maps.

The first (organizational and methodical) stage of the experiential study. Lectures with multimedia presentation of learning material were developed in three forms - texts, charts, comics on three themes of "Ability", "Temperament" and "Character". The visual range was chosen as the most widespread electronic visibility used in the classroom with multimedia presentations.

Slides with texts were a narrative of main concepts and topic content in the form of sentences. Charts for presentations were developed based on the following criteria: the logical links between the chart elements, the presence of two to ten items in one chart, a minimum of text description. To create lecture-presentations in the form of comics stories-illustrations for every concept covered within each theme were well thought out as well as prepared sketches of drawings on the basis of which professional artists subsequently created the illustrations, translated into a digital format were prepared. The presentations were designed in the same style: white background and black letters or black-and-white drawings in comics to avoid the influence of color on perception of information.

Subsequently, for each topic tests were developed, which consisted of six tasks, one for each learning goal of Bloom's taxonomy. Each task was evaluated on a five point scale (1 - no response or wrong answer, 5 - the job is done right). The authors identified indicators for evaluation of concept maps of students:

- Evaluation and comparison of lexical characteristics of concepts (scientific concepts, interdisciplinary, special, worldly concepts, concrete and abstract concepts in a map).
- Concept map scoring structure (number of links between concepts).

For diagnostics of students` individual characteristics the authors selected four psychodiagnostic methodics in three basic psychological domains: cognitive, motivational and behavioral.

Psychological assessment of *cognitive aspect* of learning information acquisition was based on the questionnaire "Thinking Styles" (R. Harrison, R. Bremson). The questionnaire diagnoses five thinking styles - analytical, synthetic, idealistic, pragmatic, realistic.

Students` *motivational characteristics* were studied on the basis of the inventory "Motivation of learning" (Rean and V. A. Yakunin, N. Badmayeva's modification). The questionnaire includes the following scales: communicative learning motives (knowledge required to communicate and work with people); social learning motives (the desire to get an education to achieve a position in society); professional learning motives (the aspiration to become a good specialist); educational-cognitive motives (the desire to gain in-depth knowledge); the motive of failure avoidance (avoidance of situations that could fail); the prestige motive (the desire to be the best among others); the motive of creative self-actualization (the desire to learn something new and make discoveries necessary for the development of society).

Behavioral characteristics of the individual in the learning process were assessed by questionnaires:

1. "Styles of learning" of Canfield (Canfield learning styles inventory) includes four categories, each of them consists of several scales. Those scales are conditions (peer, organization, goal setting, competition, instructor, detail, independence, authority); content (numeric, qualitative, inanimate, people); mode (listening, reading, iconic, direct experiment); expectancy performance (super, average/good, average/ satisfactorily, unsatisfactorily).
2. "Diagnostics of self-organization functions" (A. D. Ishkov) is structurally formed by seven scales: goal setting, situation analysis, planning, self-monitoring, correction, strong-willed efforts, the overall level of self-organization.
3. "State Metacognitive Inventory" by Harold F.O'Neil, Jamal Abedi, is aimed at identifying the ability to metacognitive regulation of their own activities on such scales as: planning (having a goal and a plan to achieve the goal); self-monitoring (a self-checking mechanism to monitor goal achievement);

cognitive strategy (having a cognitive or affective strategy to monitor either domain-independent or domain-dependent intellectual activity); awareness (the process conscious to an individual).

The second stage of empirical research was associated with implementation of the experimental part of the research in the classroom – conducting lectures-presentations, test papers, filling in questionnaries by students. For the experiment the authors have chosen two faculties of St. Petersburg State University – Faculty of Applied Mathematics and Control Processes (AMCP), Faculty of Biology. The sample for each faculty included three academic groups, consistently each of them was given lectures with presentations of learning information in the form of texts or charts, or comic strips (Table 1). Division of students into academic groups within each faculty was based on the established schedule. Prior to the lectures students were asked to draw a concept map on the lecture theme.

Regardless of the form of presentation of the material, each lecture-presentation was accompanied by the same (depending on theme) comments of the teacher. All classes were conducted by the same lecturer. Immediately after the lecture, the students wrote a quiz on the material covered, as well as drew a concept map. Upon completion of the experiment students were invited to fill in psychodiagnostic methodics, as well as the feedback questionnaire.

Participants

The initial sample involved 166 students of the Faculty of Applied Mathematics and Control Processes (AMCP) (n=76 female and 90 male students, aged between 19 and 23, the mean age - 21.06) and 111 students of the Faculty of Biology (n=80 female and 31 male students, aged between 18 and 25, the mean age - 18.9). All of the participants were studying at St. Petersburg State University.

To determine the combined effect of pedagogical conditions and psychological characteristics of students on the efficiency of acquisition at each faculty the participants were divided into three groups – those with high, medium and low degrees of acquisition of information - based on their results of control tasks after studying the subjects presented in different forms. The division into groups was made as follows. The average score for the test works made by the students after passing those in the form of texts, charts and comics, as well as the standard deviation for each value were calculated. In the group with a high level of information acquisition for each form of imaging the students with the average score plus standard deviation were included. *Table 2* shows the number of scores for tests in groups of students with a high level of acquisition.

In this chapter the authors present the results of groups with a high level of acquisition to show how the set of psychological factors and the electronic visualization form are related to the effectiveness of mastering of learning information acquisition.

Mathematical statistical methods of data processing used in our study are the criterion of T-Wilcoxon, discriminant analysis, regression analysis. Data management and analysis were performed using SPSS 20.0.

Findings

The feedback questionnaire was aimed at finding out the students` attitudes to the forms of visualization and evaluation of textual, schematic and illustrated forms of presentation of learning material. To the question "With the help of what form of visualization would you like to continue learning?" 50% of respondents selected charts, 36% - comics, 14% - texts. Further analysis of the feedback questionnaires (criterion of T-Wilcoxon) have revealed the following: comics are subjectively perceived easier than texts ($p \leq 0,000$), and are assessed to be more emotional than texts ($p \leq 0,000$) and charts ($p \leq 0,000$). Accuracy and efficiency in the transfer of information of presentations in the form of comics and of charts are on the same high level ($p \leq 0,003$). According to students` opinions, presentations in the form of comics have some advantages over the texts and charts. Text presentations do not win on any of the proposed criteria for assessment. It should be noted that the personal impression and students` preference of any form of visualization do not indicate its effectiveness in information acquisition.

Comparison of concept maps created by students before and after completing each topic, allowed to identify significant differences in information acquisition in dependence on varying electronic forms of visual row (T-Wilcoxon). Presentations in the form of text contributed to the decrease of interdisciplinary concepts ($p \leq 0,000$) in the students` concept maps. After studying topics in charts ($p \leq 0,000$) and comics ($p \leq 0,000$) the number of concepts increased. For generating a certain level of understanding of the studied topics charts ($p \leq 0,000$) and comics ($p \leq 0,000$) turned out to be the most appropriate. Texts, conversely, contributed to the increase of abstract concepts ($p \leq 0,03$). Furthermore, all three forms of visualization ensured overall development of the conceptual field about studied topics (after passing topics in students` cards the total number of concepts and the number of new concepts to those already mentioned in the concept map, drawn prior to the classes (text $p \leq 0,02$, for charts and comics $p \leq 0,000$)) increased, and led to a decrease in the number of life concepts ($p \leq 0,000$).

Significant differences between efficiency of execution of certain types of tasks on Bloom's taxonomy in dependence on the specifics of electronic visual range (criterion of T-Wilcoxon) were found. Tasks on material knowledge were performed better by the students if the information was studied in the form of comics ($p \leq 0,005$) or charts ($p \leq 0,001$), but not texts. The textual form of visualization ($p \leq 0,006$) (compared with the charts) contributed to understanding of the material. Students coped better with analysis ($p \leq 0,04$) and synthesis of information if they studied it before in the form of charts, not in text form ($p \leq 0,001$). Tasks on the evaluation of material with specific parameters were also performed by the students better if the information was studied in the form of charts, rather than in the form of texts ($p \leq 0,001$). The advantage of comics at the level of the statistical trends was evident in the execution of tasks on the use of the material, compared with textual form of visualization ($p < 0,06$).

In order to determine the differences in psychological characteristics of students with high and low acquisition levels for each form of electronic visuals depending on their *professional orientation*, discriminant analysis was conducted. As a dependent variable high or low level of acquisition for each form of visualization was selected. As independent variables were the psychological parameters of cognitive, motivational and behavioral characteristics of students. The interpretation was subjected only to those discriminant functions, which statistical significance showed significant value ($p \leq 0,001$, $p \leq 0,01$).

As a result of analysis for mathematics students with a high level of learning for each form of visualization, two discriminant functions were revealed (Table 3). Statistical significance of the first function had a significant value at the level of $p < 0,011$, for the second function there was no statistical significance ($p \leq 0.180$) and it was excluded from further analysis.

The positive pole of the function was formed by such variables as competition (condition of education) (0,093), reading (teaching method) (0,090), autonomy (condition of education) (0,078), a teacher (condition of education) (0,067). They all relate to the conditions and styles of teaching. On the negative end there were the following variables: learning motive – creative self-realization (-0,150), communicative learning motives (-0,147), social learning motives (-0,059). Thus, at one pole of the function there are the variables related to organizational (methods, learning environment) component of training activity united, at the other – associated with motivational (breadth of interest, range of incentive imperatives realized in the learning situation) component. Therefore, this function the authors refer to as "Motivational-organizational".

Let us concretize on the evolved function of the group distribution of students-mathematicians with a high level of acquisition for each form of visualization. The group with a high level of information acquisition in the form of text had the distribution from negative plus to positive. The students were divided into two subgroups – one located at the negative pole of the function, the second - at the positive. Thus, the authors can conclude that the motivational characteristics and the presence of certain learning conditions are equally important for a good information acquisition presented in text form. The results of the mathematics students with a high level of acquisition through comics are grouped around the positive pole of the first function. This means that the effectiveness of the information acquisition presented in the form of comics, is caused largely by the conditions of learning: autonomy, the presence of the situation of competition in the study group and a good relationship with the teacher, and study of material through reading texts.

Observations of the students with good information acquisition in the form of charts, mostly located on the negative end of the function, but also affect the positive. In this regard, the authors can conclude the following. Effective acquisition of electronic information, presented in a schematized form is more characteristic for students with a strong motivational component. In the meantime, there is a small group of students whose acquisition effectiveness is determined by the conditions of educational activity. Then discriminant analysis for students of the faculty of biology with a high level of achievement by text, diagrams and comics was conducted. The analysis identified two discriminant functions (see *Table 4*). Both functions have an adequate level of significance ($p < 0,000$ and $p < 040$), and suitable for interpretation.

The negative pole of the first function was not established by any of the variables. The positive pole consisted of two key variables: the idealistic style of thinking (0,016) and failure avoidance motive (0,004). Because of the content of these two variables this function is referred to as "Intuitive-protective behavior strategy in learning activities".

The positive pole of the second function includes metacognition "control strategy of intelligent activity" (0,082), the intensity of the relationship with the teacher (0,079) and the following conditions of study: additional information about jobs and requirements (0,064), teacher`s careful planning of classes (0,064). From the obtained set of variables, it becomes clear that the characteristics of metacognitive regulation and in terms of teaching are united here.

The negative pole of the second function was formed by such parameters as the quality reception when learning new material (prefer to study new material by reading and working with words, language in the form of written assignments, conversation) (-0,063), the ability to adjust their actions (self-organization component) (-0,063), self-realization as the motive of the learning (-0,026). Given the descriptions of the variables positive and negative poles, this function can be called "external and internal control of the learning situation".

According to the obtained distribution of observations a group of students with good information acquisition in the form of comics, are grouped in the positive area for the first function and in two ranges (positive and negative) – for the second function. Thus, the authors can distinguish two subgroups of students – one enters the area - the positive pole of the first function and the positive pole of the second; the other group - in the area with the positive pole of the first function and the second negative. Accordingly, the first subgroup is composed by students with a focus on external control in learning situations, but tend to be intuitive judgment when solving problems, and motivation failure avoidance in training.

The second subgroup is characterized by a focus on internal control of the learning process, but with the least orientation towards idealistic thinking style and avoidance motivation.

The students with a high level of acquisition of textual information are also divided into two subgroups – the first is in the area formed by the negative pole by the first function, and negative on the second, the second - in the area between the negative pole by the first function and the second positive. However, among the structural coefficients, significant parameters, forming the negative pole of the first function cannot be identified. Thus, the authors can characterize these observations only by negative and positive values of the second function. In other words, students with high level of acquisition through the text are characterized by either a orientation to internal control of the learning situation, or show the importance of external control of the teacher for educational activities.

It is noteworthy that students with a high level of the material acquisition in the form of charts distributed throughout the schedule, i.e., reach all areas formed by the crossing of two functions. Thus, the successful acquisition of schematic information of students-biologists is linked to the emotional-evaluative aspect of the learning activity, where the dominant can be both external and internal situation of control over the learning process.

Summary results of discriminant analysis for students of the faculty of biology and faculty of AMCP with a high level of acquisition are presented in *Table 5*.

Students of mathematics with a high level of information acquisition in the form of text, demonstrate the manifestation of the motivational component of learning activities (with different range of dominant imperatives), as well as the importance of the organizational aspect of learning: the existence of a competitive environment in the study group, the opportunity to establish a good relationship with the teacher, set goals and devise a plan of action. Students of the faculty of biology are oriented to existence of self-control and external control by the teacher in the learning process. For students of the faculty of AMCP with a high level of information acquisition on comics specific situational and stylistic characteristics of learning activities are important, while students-biologists with a desire for self-control and control their learning activities have a tendency to intuitive-protective behavior strategies (the dominance of idealistic style of thinking and failure avoidance motive in learning situations).

Students of the faculty of AMCP with good information acquisition in the form of diagrams, have a strong motivational component of learning activities (the presence of such learning motives, as creative self-realization, communication motives, and the avoidance motive) and low importance of the learning environment (such as the presence of competitive conditions in the study group, the relationship with the teacher, opportunities to show independence). Students of the biology faculty tend to have intuitive-protective behavior strategies in learning activities.

Conducted regression analysis allow to determine the influence of individual variables on the efficiency of acquisition for each form of visualization. Detailed description of the results are presented in the paper of Kostromina and Gnedykh (2016). It was found that the largest "contribution" to information acquisition in the form of a text for mathematics students was made by a synthetic style of thinking, but with reverse effect (-0,35) – its use "reduced" the level of acquisition in text-based multimedia slides. The greatest "contribution" of the students of the faculty of biology also with reverse impact was made by the presence of competition in the learning environment (-0,76) – this feature prevented effective acquisition of textual information.

For students of the faculty of AMCP the high level of acquisition of learning material, presented in the form of comics, is conditioned by such features as self-control ability (0,51), metacognitive regulation activities (0,46), the presence of learning-cognitive motivation (-0,29), as well as a tendency to satisfactorily evaluate their achievements (0,31). Average rating of achievements (0,52), the predominance of social motivation of learning (0,17), the inclination for idealistic style of thinking (0,44), as well as the importance of competition in the learning environment (0,24) provide better acquisition of illustrated material for students-biologists.

The high level of acquisition through charts by the students of AMCP faculty is conditioned by the application of qualitative methods of information processing during learning (0,38), the presence of professional learning motives (0,40), preferences in the perception of information aurally (0.60) and focusing on the learning process without the distraction of building a relationship with the teacher (-0,43). The presence of students of biology faculty of the tendency to manifestation of volitional efforts (-0,84), unsatisfactory evaluation of their achievements (-0,42) reduces the level of acquisition of schematic information for students of biology faculty.

The conducted research allowed to identify the correlation of pedagogical conditions and psychological factors of acquisition. Students of the AMCP faculty with a high level of acquisition of textual and chart information show the manifestation of the motivational component of learning activities, but for students, assimilating learning information well in the form of texts, the organizational aspect – the conditions of educational activity- is also significant. In the meantime, this psychological (situational-stylish) determinant is necessary for the effective acquisition of learning information, presented in the form of comics: the preference of learning new material through reading, the desire to set goals independently and consider ways to achieve them, presence of the competition situation in the study group and a good relationship with the teacher.

For students of the biology faculty, well assimilating learning information in the form of charts and comics, in addition to the need to monitor the educational situation, the distinguishing feature is the tendency to intuitive-protective behavior strategies in learning activities. For students who effectively assimilate the text information, the presence or absence of external (from a teacher) or internal control is very important.

Thus, the findings allow to identify forms of electronic visual information which are more suitable for students of certain psychological types and to find out the specifics of the impact of these forms on the quality of forming of the students` knowledge system in the learning process via IT.

On the basis of the present study, the following conclusions can be drawn:

The electronic visual information in the form of texts provides the abstract level of subject understanding by students; students with a wide range of interests, cognitive and professional motives of learning and pragmatic style of thinking most effectively assimilate information in the form of texts.

The information in the form of charts reinforces special concepts of a subject in learner's knowledge system, provides subject understanding at the concrete level and facilitates students' ability for analysis, synthesis and evaluation of educational material. Students with motivation of self-realization in learning, synthetic or idealistic thinking styles, predisposed to avoid failures and capable to self-regulation have the high degree of acquisition of information in the form of charts.

Comics facilitate acquisition of special concepts of a subject in students' knowledge system and best memorization of learning material. Students oriented to cooperation in work, capable to plan their activity most effectively assimilate information in the form of comics.

The conducted study allow to confirm the hypothesis that there is a correspondence of psychological factors and teaching conditions affecting the effectiveness of students` acquisition of learning information, explored using different forms of electronic visualization. Furthermore, the effectiveness of the concept maps and Bloom`s taxonomy for assessing of the level of students` acquisition of learning material, presented in different forms of electronic visualization. The latter allows to consider these methods of diagnostics of acquisition effectiveness of learning information as a reliable pedagogical tool of evaluation in e-learning.

SOLUTIONS AND RECOMMENDATIONS

The introduction of IT in education involves the development of educational programs that allow students to explore scientific concepts and practical skills (Computing Curricula. The Overview Report, 2005). These programs contain a set of pedagogical conditions that ensure the effectiveness of acquisition of educational information. The form of knowledge transfer, the content of programs and used didactic means are determined by its developers. However, the acquisition result can be different and is always unique.

When studying the effectiveness of application of a variety of information technologies scientists use different methods. For example, some authors propose to correlate online learning outcomes with the frequency of student`s viewing of learning content (video lectures and PowerPoint slides) – the more often students refer to the materials, the higher will be the final test grades (Reinecke, & Finn, 2015). The disadvantage of this approach in evaluating the success of training lies in the fact that students` individual characteristics are not considered - someone needs only a small amount of information to understand and learn it but someone needs more various sources and more views.

It may also happen that a student looks through all the material for the course, but cannot learn it, whatever various techniques are used - video clips, audio recordings, texts, etc. Consequently, the number of viewed classes is not be an indicator and a guarantee of high learning outcomes. Therefore, many scientists point out that the success of students` interactions with IT depends on their personal characteristics (Colvin-Sterling, 2016; Saadé & AlSharhan, 2015).

Another method of identifying the factors affecting academic success is the students` opinions. The researchers Aimao Zhang, Cheryl Aasheim (2011), based on the literature review identified and classified the most common factors affecting the results of student learning, and then asked students to rank the data from the most important factors in achieving success to least important. Using this method, teachers must first pay attention to the fact that the results are subjective evaluations of students, based on their observations of non-systematic, personal opinions. There specific cause-and-effect relationships, the proportion of the contribution of a particular condition in academic achievement are not traced.

Another model for evaluating the effectiveness of training with the help of IT, in particular, on-line training, includes three types of interactions required for the analysis - instructor-student, student-student, student-content (Marks, Sibley & Arbaugh (2005). The advantage of this model is that it considers a combination of several sides of the educational process, which have a mutual influence on each other and on the result. Restrictions, in turn, relate to the lack of attention to such interaction as instructor-content. Since it is the lecturer who chooses the content and means of transferring of learning information, his selection can also determine the acquisition effectiveness of course materials.

Most of reviewed approaches to providing and evaluating of learners` effective acquisition of learning information in interaction with the IT focus on one specific area - either pedagogical conditions or student activity (interaction with a teacher, with each other or with the course content), or their personal opinion on the use of IT in education. The model, which is offered by the authors of the chapter allows comprehensively and objectively evaluate the results of learning, and enables teachers to consciously approach the selection of pedagogical conditions and account psychological characteristics of students to improve the effectiveness of acquisition. Furthermore, the model takes into account the possibility of feedback. Although in this case, their subjective estimates and opinions concerning the use of texts, charts and comics in presentations do not guarantee that the learner understands information better with its help, the true impact of this form on acquisition effectiveness you can be checked only by objective methods.

On the ground of obtained results, the authors have developed guidelines for working with different forms of electronic visualization in the educational process:

1. Lecturer's choice of the form of visual information for each subject module should depend on a goal of training. If one knows the specific impact of such forms of visualization as texts, charts and comics on memorizing, analysis, synthesis, evaluation or application of educational material, the choice of a visual form can be more substantiated.

2. A lecturer should take into account lexical features of the subject educational terminology: prevalence of abstract or concrete, specific or multidisciplinary concepts, etc. Some forms of visual information can facilitate the acquisition of certain terminology.

3. A lecturer should keep in mind that the efficiency of students' interaction with texts, charts and comics depends on their psychological characteristics. To make the learning process more effective teachers can propose a more suitable form of visualization of information for students on the basis of their individual features (thinking styles, type of learning motivation, ability to self-regulation etc.).

Considering the time constraints, often not allowing to evaluate the psychological characteristics of students on the basis of psycho-diagnostic questionnaires, as recommendations for the identification of cognitive, motivational and behavioral characteristics that have an impact on the effectiveness of acquisition of learning information, the authors offer the following:

1. At the first session when meeting with students a lecturer can apply the methods of problem tasks with a group discussion in which students will be able to express themselves. This will allow the teacher to observe them, and on the basis of observational data to try to determine their psychological characteristics, which will help him in the future to prepare visual aids for lectures according to the identified characteristics of acquisition.

2. If the lecturer has to develop a distance course, and if it is not possible to hold the first session with students, in this case it is recommended to give first test task to the group of students, in the course of which they will demonstrate self-organization skills (goal setting, the ability to self-control and correction of the actions, etc.). The elements of the tasks can be a work project, on completion of which the teacher can send the works for expertise to other members of the group. On the basis of each student's task results, the lecturer will be able to draw conclusions about the psychological characteristics of students and offer them the form of visualization, which helps learn the course material most effectively.

The differences in the impact of complex psychological and pedagogical conditions on the learning effectiveness stress the importance of a differentiated approach to interaction with IT in education.

FUTURE RESEARCH DIRECTIONS

The proposed model, on the one hand, opens up prospects for improving of acquisition quality in the use of IT in the educational process, on the other hand, has its limitations. To test the model the authors selected PowerPoint presentations as an electronic means of visualization of educational material. The question, then, arises – are features identified on the example of presentations common for other electronic means that can visualize information for studies? For example, in distance or online learning. According to the authors, the selected electronic data transmission means will not play a decisive role for learning - whether they are PowerPoint presentations, whiteboard, computer screen, etc. It is much more important the form in which this information is presented via electronic technology. Although this statement requires further testing.

Another point that is worthy of consideration - if the model is applicable not only for training of higher school students, but also for teaching learners at school. If we consider the components of the model as a whole, then their consideration in school teachers` preparation for classes is acceptable. But if we turn to the identified regularities of influence of students` personality characteristics to assimilate the information presented in various visual forms, they should be considered only in a particular situation - for students of mathematics and natural science disciplines. Moreover, assessment methods laid down in the model have an age limit to use - you need to consider the intellectual development of the children and their capacities for analysis, synthesis and evaluation of information in different age periods (Piaget, 1983; Santrock, 2004). This may be one of the directions of future researches.

In addition, it is necessary to emphasize that as a learning material for conducting a research the humanitarian subject was selected. As it is known, any field of knowledge (natural science, mathematical, humanitarian) has its own characteristics that must be taken into account in the teaching of various disciplines. The authors suppose that, for example, for exact sciences the specificity of the impact of the shape on the acquisition may be different. This restriction is necessary to remember to teachers if they want to use the suggested recommendations.

In the future it is also planned to study the neuropsychological mechanisms which provide acquisition of learning information while depending on the form of electronic visual row.

CONCLUSION

The necessity for interaction between teachers and students with IT is growing every day, the amount of researches in the field of electronic and distance learning is increasing, and the question about the effectiveness of the use of electronic technology is still relevant. Since the acquisition of learning information and skills by students is a central part of the training, the assessment of their performance must be adequate and all-round, taking into account both external conditions (didactic) and internal factors (psychological) of learning activities.

The main objective of the chapter is to offer an integrated approach to organization of assessing the effectiveness of students` training on the basis of electronic visual rows combining pedagogical and psychological aspects of training.

It should be noted that the recommendations made on the basis of the research results, can be used by not only teachers but also by the students: considering their personal characteristics, the learners can choose the form of visualization of the learning material which is most effective for the learning material acquisition.

REFERENCES

Afanas'eva, N. A. (2008). Self-organization is a factor in the success of learning activity. *Fundamental'nye issledovanija, 2*. Retrieved from http://cyberleninka.ru/article/n/samoorganizatsiya-faktor-uspeshnosti-uchebnoy-deyatelnosti

Allinson, J., & Hayes, C. (1996). The cognitive style index, a measure of intuition-analysis for organizationresearch. *Journal of Management Studies, 33*(1), 119–135. doi:10.1111/j.1467-6486.1996.tb00801.x

Anisova, T. L., Markov, V. K., & Ustinova, L. V. (2014). The use of presentation method in mathematics at University. *Sovremennye problemy nauki i obrazovanija, 2*. Retrieved from http://www.science-education.ru/pdf/2014/2/342.pdf

Anohina, A., & Grundspenkis, J. (2009). *Scoring concept maps: an overview*. Paper presented at the International Conference on Computer Systems and Technologies. CompSysTech'09. Retrieved from http://stpk.cs.rtu.lv/sites/all/files/stpk/alla/IV.8.pdf

Arkhipova, L. M. (2012). Comics as an innovative method for the activation of cognitive sphere of students with mental retardation in the process of teaching history. *Jaroslavskij pedagogicheskij vestnik, 4*(2), 106-110.

Badmaeva, N. C. (2000). *Motivational factors of formation of cognitive and memory abilities*. Ulan-Udje: Izd-vo VSGTU.

Balashova, J. V. (2011). *Cognitive and personality features of students of internal and distance education* (Unpublished candidate dissertation). Moscow.

Belavin, V. A., Golicyna, I. N., & Kucenko, S. N. (2000). The effectiveness of using simulative training systems in Technical University. *Obrazovatel'nye tehnologii i obshhestvo, 3*(2), 161-174.

Berdnikova, I. A. (2007). Conditions for increase of efficiency of educational material acquisition. *Materialy konferencii «Stanovlenija sovremennoj nauki»*. Retrieved from http://www.rusnauka.com/17_SSN_2007/Pedagogica.htm

Bespalko, V. P. (1989). *Augends of educational technology*. Moscow.

Bloom, B. S., & Krathwohl, D. R. (1956). *Taxonomy of educational objectives; the classification of educational goals. Handbook I: Cognitive Domain*. Addison-Wesley.

Borisova, L. G. (2001). *Pedagogical conditions of formation of educational activity style of schoolchild* (Unpublished candidate dissertation). Kaliningrad.

Borkowski, J., Carr, M., & Pressely, M. (1987). Spontaneous strategy use: Perspectives from metacognitive theory. *Intelligence, 11*(1), 61–75. doi:10.1016/0160-2896(87)90027-4

Bosova, L. L., & Zubchenok, N. E. (2013). Electronic textbook: yesterday, today, tomorrow. *Obrazovatel'nye tehnologii i obshhestvo, 16*(3), 697-712.

Brushlinskii, A. V., & Volovikova, M. I. (1983). About the interactions of procedural (dynamic) and personal (motivational) aspects of thinking. In D. Kovach et al. (Eds.), *Psychological researches of cognitive processes and personality* (pp. 84–96). Moscow: Nauka.

Buslova, N. S., Vychuzhanina, A. J., Klimenko, E. V., & Sheshukova, L.A. (2014). Semiotic features of presentation of information messages. *Sovremennye problemy nauki i obrazovanija, 3*. Retrieved from http://www.science-education.ru/117-13476

Canfield, A. A., & Lafferty, L. C. (1974). *Learning styles inventory.* Birmingham, MI: Humanics Media.

Chernokova, T. E. (2011). Metacognitive psychology: the problem of a research subject. *Vestnik Severnogo (Arkticheskogo) federal'nogo universiteta. Serija Gumanitarnye i social'nye nauki, 3*, 153-158.

Colvin-Sterling, S. (2016). The correlation between temperament, technology preference, and proficiency in middle school students. *Journal of Information Technology Education: Research, 15*, 1–18.

Computing curricula. The overview report. (2005). Retrieved from http://www.acm.org/education/curric_vols/CC2005-March06Final.pdf

Davydov, V. V. (1986). *Problems of developmental teaching: The experience of theoretical and experimental psychological research.* Moscow: Pedagogika.

Druz, I. N. (2013). The formation of future engineers' readiness to profession using new technologies of modeling. *Vestnik Har'kovskogo nacional'nogo avtomobil'no-dorozhnogo universiteta, 60,* 12-16.

Dvoryadkina, S. N. (2011). Conceptual ideas of model of learning the probability theory and statistics focused on complex training of students of technical and humanitarian sciences. *Teorija i praktika obshhestvennogo razvitija, 7,* 168-172.

Frolov, I. N. (2011). E-didactics as a theoretical basis of e-learning. *V mire nauchnyh otkrytij. Serija: «Problemy nauki i obrazovanija», 2*(14), 135-142.

Glukhareva, T. V. (2008). Individualization in teaching mathematics students. *Vestnik KemGU, 4,* 43–45.

Golub, O. V., & Fokina, E. A. (2013). Optimization of mental and cognitive activity in solving analytical and diagnostic tasks. *Fundamental'nye issledovanija, 11,* 525-528.

Gregorc, A. R. (1982). *Style delineator.* Maynard, MA: Gabriel Systems.

Guri-Rosenblit, S. (2005). Distance education and e-learning: Not the same thing. *Higher Education, 49*(4), 467–493. doi:10.1007/s10734-004-0040-0

Gusakova, E. M. (2013). Electronic interactive whiteboard: software and technical characteristics impacting efficiency of education. *Integracija obrazovanija, 1*(70), 89-93.

Harrison, A. F., & Brainson, R. M. (1984). *The art of thinking*. Berkley Books.

Holodnaya, M. A. (2004). *Cognitive styles. The nature of individual mind*. St. Petersburg: Peter.

Ishkov, A. D. (2004). *Learning activity of a student: psychological factors of success*. Moscow: Izdatel'stvo ASV.

Kalashnikova, A. V. (2013). Understanding of scientific text by students in terms of individual psychological characteristics of personality. *Gumanitarnye nauchnye issledovanija, 7*. Retrieved from http://human.snauka.ru/2013/07/3522

Kaptelinin, K. K., & Bannon L. (1997). Activity theory: Basic concepts and applications. *Human-Computer Interaction*, 189–201.

Karginova, F. D. (1999). *Taking into account the individual characteristics of students as a factor of increase of efficiency of foreign language acquisition* (Unpublished candidate dissertation). Vladikavkaz.

Kilic, Z., Kaya, O. N., & Dogan, A. (2004). *Effects of students' pre- and post-laboratory concept maps on students' attitudes toward chemistry laboratory in university general chemistry*. Paper presented at the International Conference on Chemical Education, Istanbul, Turkey.

Kiseleva, T. V. (2011). Poetic educational texts is a modern and effective tool which facilitate acquisition of educational material (for example mathematics). *Mezhdunarodnyj zhurnal prikladnyh i fundamental'nyh issledovanij, 8,* 82-84.

Kodzhaspirova, G. M., & Petrov, K. V. (2001). *Technical means of learning and methods of their use: manual for students of higher pedagogical educational institution*. Moscow: Izdatel'skij centr «Akademija».

Kolb, D. A. (1984). *Experimental learning: Experience as a source of learning and development*. Englewood Cliffs, NJ: Prentice-Hall.

Kostromina, S. (2013). Academic skills as a basis for self-organization of human activity. *Procedia: Social and Behavioral Sciences, 86*(6), 543–550. doi:10.1016/j.sbspro.2013.08.611

Kostromina, S., & Gnedykh, D. (2012). The innovative approach in using the visual aids in modern education. *Scientific enquiry in the contemporary world: Theoretical basics and innovative approach, 3*, 291-293.

Kostromina, S., & Gnedykh, D. (2016). Students psychological characteristics as factor of effective acquisition of visualization in e-learning. *Procedia: Social and Behavioral Sciences, 217*, 34–41. doi:10.1016/j.sbspro.2016.02.016

Kotova, S. S., & Shakhmatova, O. N. (2007). Students' psychological features of self-organization of learning activity. *Nauchnye issledovanija v obrazovanii, 4*. Retrieved from http://cyberleninka.ru/article/n/psihologicheskie-osobennosti-samoorganizatsii-uchebnoy-deyatelnosti-studentov

Kuchma, V. R., Teksheva, L. M., Vjatleva, O. A., & Kurganskij, A. M. (2012). Features of information perception via electronic device for reading (reader). *Voprosy shkol'noj i universitetskoj mediciny i zdorov'ja, 1,* 39-46.

Kudryashova, V. G. (2009). Improvement of self-organization skills of learning activities in teaching biology as the basis for development of students' general educational competence. *Srednee professional'noe obrazovanie, 3,* 37-39.

Lazareva, O. V. (2012). To the question about the influence of metacognitive processes in comprehension of scientific text. *Vestnik JuUrGU, 31,* 13–17.

Lefkowitz, L. S., & Lesser, V. R. (1988). Knowledge acquisition as knowledge assimilation. *International Journal of Man-Machine Studies, 29*(2), 215–226. doi:10.1016/S0020-7373(88)80047-6

Leontiev, A. N. (1978). *Activity, consciousness, and personality.* Retrieved from https://www.marxists. org/archive/leontev/works/1978/index.htm

Mantorova, I. V. (2002). *Presentation of educational information by means of multimedia tools as a factor of improving the quality of learning* (Unpublished candidate dissertation). Karachaevsk.

Markova, A. K. (1999). *Psychological characteristics of learning motivation at schoolchildren.* Pedagogicheskaja psihologija. Hrestomatija. Cheljabinsk: Izd-vo JuUrGU.

Marks, R. B., Sibley, S. D., & Arbaugh, J. B. (2005). A structural equation model of predictors for effective online learning. *Journal of Management Education, 29*(4), 531–563. doi:10.1177/1052562904271199

Maskinskov, A. B. (2003). *The influence of theoretical and empirical thinking styles on the process of acquisition of foreign language by students* (Unpublished candidate dissertation). Kursk.

Matyukhina, V. M. (1984). *Motivation of learning in midchildhood.* Moscow: Pedagogika.

McCloud, S. (1994). Understanding comics. The invisible art. New York: Academic Press.

McNamara, D. S., & O'Reilly, T. (n.d.). *Learning - knowledge acquisition, representation, and organization.* Retrieved from http://education.stateuniversity.com/pages/2165/Learning-KNOWLEDGE-ACQUISITION-REPRESENTATION-ORGANIZATION.html

Miller, A. A. (2010). The use of e-book (electronic textbook) in training of students of technical disciplines. *Mir nauki, kul'tury, obrazovanija, 3,* 161-162.

Multimodal learning through media: What the research says. (2008). Retrieved from http://www.cisco. com/c/dam/en_us/solutions/industries/docs/education/Multimodal-Learning-Through-Media.pdf

Naseikina, L. F. (2010). Interactive electronic textbooks at modern open education. *Vestnik orenburgskogo gosudarstvennogo universiteta, 5*(111), 30-35.

Netesov, S. I. (2012). Graphic visualization on the lessons of jurisprudence with the use of information and communication technologies. *Informacijni tehnologiï i zasobi navchannja, 1*(27). Retrieved from http://www.journal.iitta.gov.ua

Nouri, H., & Shahid, A. (2005). The effect of PowerPoint presentations on student learning and attitudes. *Global Perspectives on Accounting Education, 2,* 53–73.

Novak, J. D., & Gowin, D. B. (1984). *Learning how to learn*. New York, NY: Cambridge University Press. doi:10.1017/CBO9781139173469

Nugumanova, A. M., & Khamitova, G. H. (2013). The study of impact of teaching using multimedia technologies on visual analyzer among students of Medical University. *Prakticheskaja medicina, oftal'mologija, 1-3*(13). Retrieved from http://pmarchive.ru/izuchenie-vliyaniya-multimedijnyx-texnologij-prepodavaniya-na-sostoyanie-zritelnogo-analizatora-u-studentov-medicinskogo-universiteta/

Nurminsky, I. I., & Gladysheva, N. K. (1991). *Statistical regularities of forming of knowledge and abilities at pupils*. Moscow: Pedagogika.

O'Leary, D. E. (n.d.). *Technologies for knowledge assimilation*. Retrieved from https://msbfile03.usc.edu/digitalmeasures/doleary/intellcont/technologies-assimilation-1.pdf

Orlov, J. M. (1984). *Need and motivational factors of efficiency of students' educational activity at University* (Unpublished candidate dissertation). Moscow.

Osmundson, E., Chung, G. K. W. K., Herl, H. E., & Klein, D. C. D. (1999). *Knowledge mapping in the classroom: A tool for examining the development of students' conceptual understandings*. Los Angeles, CA: University of California.

Ovchinnikova, O. M. (2013). Structural and logical charts in learning of foreign economic terminology. Filologicheskie nauki. *Voprosy teorii i praktiki, 11*(29), 122-127.

Parkhomenko, M. V. (2003). *Fundamentals of organization of content acquisition in midchildhood* (Unpublished candidate dissertation). Rjazan'.

Pejsahov, N. M., & Shevcov, M. N. (1991). *Practical psychology (the scientific basis): textbook*. Kazan': Izd-vo Kazansk. un-ta.

Petrova, S. I., & Stepanova, Z. B. (2005). Japanese comics as the text type (category of informativeness). *Vestnik JaGU, 2*(4), 47–51.

Phillips, L. M., Norris, S. P., & Macnab, J. S. (2010). *Visualization in mathematics, reading and science education*. Springer.

Piaget, J. (1983). Chapter. In P. Mussen (Ed.), Handbook of Child Psychology: Vol. 1. Piaget's theory (4th ed.). New York: Wiley.

Popova, Z.I. (2008). Computer learning system. *Izvestija Volgogradskogo gosudarstvennogo tehnicheskogo universiteta, 10*(7), 154-156.

Reinecke, D., & Finn, L. L. (2015). Video lectures in online graduate education: Relationship between use of lectures and outcome measures. *Journal of Information Technology Education: Research, 14*, 113–121.

Reinert, H. (1976). One picture is worth a thousand words? Not necessarily! *Modern Language Journal, 60*, 160–168.

Richmond, A. S., Krank, H. M., & Cummings, R. (2006). A brief research report: Thinking styles of online distance education students. *International Journal of Technology in Teaching and Learning, 2*(1), 58–64.

Robert, I. (1994). *Modern information technologies in education: didactic problems; prospects for use.* Moscow: Shkola-Press.

Romashkina, N. V., Mishina, E. A., & Dolgaja, T. I. (2010). The organization of learning activity at lessons of physics in the logic of scientific knowledge using the interactive whiteboard. *Uchenye zapiski Zabajkal'skogo gosudarstvennogo universiteta. Serija: Fizika, matematika, tehnika, tehnologija, 2,* 82-85.

Rubinstein, S. L. (2005). *Fundamentals of general psychology.* St. Petersburg: Peter.

Saadé, R. G., & AlSharhan, J. (2015). Discovering the motivations of students when using an online learning tool. *Journal of Information Technology Education: Research, 14,* 283–296.

Sabinina, A. A. (2009). Educational text: Structure and pragmatics. *Izvestija Rossijskogo gosudarstvennogo pedagogicheskogo universiteta im. A.I. Gercena, 97,* 222–224.

Santrock, J. W. (2004). *Life-Span development.* Boston, MA: McGraw-Hill College.

Snigireva, T. A., & Grishanova, I. A. (2014). An integrated approach in evaluation the quality of knowledge structure of a student. *Fundamental'nye issledovanija, 11-6,* 1382-1385.

Sokolova, I. J., & Ivanova, T. V. (2014). The development of personal potential of students in preparation for professional activity. *Professional'noe obrazovanie v Rossii i za rubezhom, 1*(13), 86-91.

Steen, H. L. (2008). Effective eLearning design. *Journal of Online Learning and Teaching, 4*(4), 526–532.

Suhih, A. E., & Korytchenkova, N. I. (2008). Theoretical analysis of cognitive characteristics in psychology. *Vestnik KemGU. Psihologija, 4,* 97–100.

Troeshestova, D. A., & Ivanova, M. V. (2013). The selection of interactive methods of training for students of the specialty "Mathematics" on the basis of psychological and pedagogical monitoring. *Vestnik Chuvashskogo universiteta, 2,* 141-145.

Ulanovskaja, K. A., Kaljuzhnov, E. J., & Antropov, I. V. (2013). Individualization of evaluation of knowledge quality. *Izvestija Volgogradskogo gosudarstvennogo tehnicheskogo universiteta, 12-2*(105), 130-133.

Vumyatnin, V. M., Demkin, V. P., Mozhaeva, G. V., & Rudenko, T. V. (2002). Multimedia courses: methodology and technology of development. *Otkrytoe i distancionnoe obrazovanie, 3*(7), 34-61.

Yanchar, S., & Slife, B. D. (2004). Teaching critical thinking by examining assumptions: An instructional framework. *Teaching of Psychology, 31*(2), 85–90. doi:10.1207/s15328023top3102_2

Zakharova, I. G. (2003). *Information technologies in education: textbook for students of higher educational institutions.* Moscow: Izdatel'skij centr «Akademija».

Zaporozhets, A. A. (1986). *Selectas.* Moscow: Pedagogika.

Zhang, A., & Aasheim, Ch. (2011). Academic success factors: An IT student perspective. *Journal of Information Technology Education: Research, 10,* 309–331.

ADDITIONAL READING

Anderson, J. (2005). IT, e-learning and teacher development. *International Education Journal, ERC2004 Special Issue, 5*(5), 1-14.

Ashihmina, E. A. (2008). Motivation and self-organization as interconnected features of students' personality. *Izvestiya Rossijskogo gosudarstvennogo pedagogicheskogo universiteta im.A.I. Gercena, 74*(2), 37–42.

Bogdanova, E. L. (2006). Pedagogical conditions of development of students' metacognitive competence in distance education. *Vestnik Tomskogo gosudarstvennogo universiteta, 10*(61), 18-22.

Bogdanova, E. L., Bogdanova, O. E. (2011). Developmental potential of cognitive maps method in conditions of educational practice in higher school. *Vestnik Tomskogo gosudarstvennogo universiteta, 353*,161-165.

Brown, A. L. (1978). Knowing when, where and how to remember: A problem of metacognition. In R.Claser (Ed.), Advances in instructional psychology. V.2 (pp. 77–165). N.Y.: Hillsdale.

Cañas, A. J. (2003). A Summary of Literature Pertaining to the Use of Concept Mapping Techniques and Technologies for Education and Performance Support. Technical report: Pensacola, FL.

Cañas, A. J., Hill, G., Carff, R., Suri, N., Lott, J., Gómez, G., . . . Carvajal, R. (2004). CmapTools: A Knowledge Modeling and Sharing Environment. *Proceedings of the First International Conference on Concept Mapping, Pamplona, Spain, Universidad Pública de Navarra.* Retrieved http://cmc.ihmc.us/papers/cmc2004-283.pdf

Chen, C. (2005). Visualization Viewpoints. *IEEE Computer Graphics and Applications.* Retrieved http://web.simmons.edu/~benoit/infovis/Chen%202005.pdf

Flavell, J. H. (1976). Metacognitive aspects of problem solving. In L. B. Resnick (Ed.), *The nature of intelligence* (pp. 231–235). Hillsdale, N.Y.: Erlbaum.

Glenberg, A. M., & Langston, W. E. (1992). Comprehension of illustrated text: Pictures help to build mental models. *Journal of Memory and Language, 31*(2), 129–151. doi:10.1016/0749-596X(92)90008-L

Guri-Rosenblit, S. (2005). Distance education and e-learning: Not the same thing. *Higher Education, 49*(4), 467–493. doi:10.1007/s10734-004-0040-0

Juell, P., & Vijayakumar, Sh. (2004, April). *Survey of AI Visualizations in Education.* Paper presented at MICS04 - 37th Annual Midwest Instruction and Computing Symposium University of Minnesota, Morris.

Markham, S. (2004). *Learning Styles measurement: a cause for concern.* Technical Report. Retrieved http://cerg.csse.monash.edu.au/techreps/ learning_styles_review.pdf

Mintzes, J. J., Wandersee, J. H., & Novak, J. D. (2000). *Assessing science understanding: A human constructivist view.* San Diego: Academic Press.

Naps, T., Rößling, G., Anderson, J., Cooper, S., Dann, W., Fleischer, R., & Ross, R. J. et al. (2003). Evaluating the Educational Impact of Visualization. *ACM Sigcse Bulletin, 35*(4), 124–136. doi:10.1145/960492.960540

Naps, T. L., Röbling, G., Almstrum, V., Dann, W., Fleischer, R., Hundhausen, C., & Velazquez-Iturbide, J. A. et al. (2003). Exploring the Role of Visualization and Engagement in Computer Science Education. *ACM Sigcse Bulletin, 35*(2), 131–152. doi:10.1145/782941.782998

Nouri, H., & Shahid, A. (2005). The effect of PowerPoint presentations on student learning and attitudes. *Global Perspectives on Accounting Education, 2*, 53–73.

Novak, J. D. (1998). *Learning, creating, and using knowledge: Concept maps as facilitative tools in schools and corporations*. Mahwah, NJ: Lawrence Erlbaum Associates.

Novak, J. D., & Cañas, A. J. (2006). The Theory Underlying Concept Maps and How to Construct Them. Technical Report No. IHMC CmapTools 2006-01. Pensacola, FL: Institute for Human and Machine Cognition; Retrieved http://cmap.ihmc.us/Publications/ResearchPapers/TheoryCmaps/TheoryUnderlyingConceptMaps.htm

Peek, J. (1987). *The Role of Illustrations in Processing and Remembering Illustrated Text. The Psychology of Illustration, 1: Basic Research. New York*. Springer.

Richmond, A. S., Krank, H. M., & Cummings, R. (2006). A brief research report: Thinking styles of online distance education students. *International Journal of Technology in Teaching and Learning, 2*(1), 58–64.

Stolyarova, L. G. (2010). The syntactic specificity of comics language. *Izvestiya Tul'skogo gosudarstvennogo universiteta. Gumanitarnye nauki, 2*, 429-436.

Veenman, M. V. J., Van Hout-Wolters, B. H. A. M., & Afflerbach, P. (2006). Metacognition and learning: Conceptual and methodological considerations. *Metacognition and Learning, 1*(1), 3–14. doi:10.1007/s11409-006-6893-0

Vihman, V. V. (2004). *Evaluation and analysis of efficiency of information technologies application in education*. Unpublished dissertation. Novosibirsk.

Voronkova, N. (2007). Dynamics of changes in students' learning motivation. *Vestnik Universiteta Rossijskoj akademii obrazovaniya, 4*, 77-80.

KEY TERMS AND DEFINITIONS

Bloom's Taxonomy: The way to classify learning objective according to six cognitive level of complexity: knowledge, comprehension, application, analysis, synthesis and evaluation.

Concept Maps: Graphical two-dimensional presentation of knowledge, including concepts connected by arcs (or straight lines), which reflect the relationships between pairs of concepts.

Effectiveness: Achievement of high results at the minimum resource spend (time, energy, etc.) in activity process.

E-Learning: Learning with the application of all kinds of electronic tools.

Electronic Visual Rows: Consecutive information in the form of illustrations, symbolical and graphic presentations, both static and dynamic (animation or a video series) which is stored in a digital form and is shown on the computer screen or by means of information technologies.

Information Acquisition: Complex process of information perception, understanding, memorization and ability to use it in different conditions.

Chapter 8

Guidelines Based on Need–Findings Study and Communication Types to Design Interactions for MOOCs

Sandra G. Jiménez-González
Universidad Politécnica de Aguascalientes, Mexico

Ricardo Mendoza-González
TecNM, Instituto Tecnológico de Aguascalientes, Mexico

Huizilopoztli Luna-García
Universidad Autónoma de Zacatecas – Campus Jalpa, Mexico

ABSTRACT

Experts affirm that interaction in learning settings represent a necessary process for knowledge acquisition and cognitive development. In this vein, is crucial to ensure effective interaction and communication through the user interface of MOOCs. This work proposes a set of design guidelines as starting point for developers to integrate a set of interactive elements into the MOOCs' user interface oriented to foster the four basic types for communication in distance education. The design guidelines were conformed through a need-findings process (observing people-interviewing), in which 35 participants provided their user experience perceptions after using MOOCs from edX; Coursera; and Udacity. Obtained results suggest a particular set of interactive communication elements that should be incorporated in every MOOC's user interface.

INTRODUCTION

Nowadays, the teaching and learning demand is growing inordinately around the world; this phenomenon suggests the need of radical changes and innovative strategies oriented to reinforce currently available techniques.

DOI: 10.4018/978-1-5225-2616-2.ch008

Additionally, new learning proposals should encourage lifelong learning, besides factors such as society, professional life, among others. In this way the process should be customized, adapting itself to the student requirements and abilities. Similarly it should consider student's free time, other activities and the acquired knowledge through both cultural and educational life of the student (Christopher, 2013).

There is a need that can be fulfill with a tool that gives the possibility to be used in different times and places, a tool host in the cloud that allows the self-taught person easy access to the information and tuition during the learning process. This tool that gives solution to these requirements is a MOOC.

The main goal of the MOOCs is mostly focused on provide access to the people who are looking for get their education completed, or even the people who want to extend their education, but in some way cannot do that in classrooms (Dasarathy, Sullivan, Schmidt, Fisher, & Porter, 2014).

The MOOCs are developed based on the great experience of the biggest Universities in the subject of distance education and open resources.

The MOOCs are accessible, and the high quality courses allow to the students to develop knowledge to support their own learning goals (Al-Zoube, 2009). The main attribute or strength of these courses is their scalability, meaning that, a course which has been already developed can be reach globally, allowing to the big amount of students to be part of the specific topic.

The biggest achievements of the MOOCs include the capability of get together some of the finest academic people of the best Universities through the world in order to develop the material and resources, and the more special one are to offer free courses. The MOOCs are often known as supercharged distance education courses.

Thanks to the increasing amount of the information sources through network, the MOOCs have been better structured. Much teaching material consists of pre-recorded lectures/videos divided into weekly sections with assignment tasks. They have a specific start and finish date and students sign up online. The courses are last for a few weeks and might be offered two or three times by year. A wide range of interactive and media tools are available to students to enable them to interact with other learners. For example, video lectures, online discussion boards, blogs, wikis and social networks such as Twitter and Facebook. There are also opportunities to meet face to face with fellow students, in meet-up organized by students themselves. As the learning support is provided by the online learning community, students can form support groups as they require. The assessment of MOOCs is carried out mostly using peer and self-assessment and computer assessed assignments. There is often no requirement for interaction between the teacher and the student.

The courses are offered by commercial startups, working with elite universities and professors and some of the best known examples are Coursera, Udacity and edX.

Coursera was founded in 2012 Stanford affiliates, computer science professors Andrew Ng and Daphne Koller. It is a for-profit company, though it currently does not generate any revenue. Coursera have the most diverse course selection of all the MOOC providers and currently have over 4 million students and 410 courses from 83 partner institutions. Partners include the University of California, University of British Columbia, Oxford University and Princeton.

Udacity was founded by Sebastian Thrun, who is a former professor of computer science at Stanford University and the creator of the artificial intelligence system behind Google's self-driving cars. He left Stanford to spearhead this new venture soon after the huge success of his online artificial intelligence course in 2011, which attracted over 160,000 students from more than 190 countries. Udacity's focus is on college-level courses for building and applying your knowledge of STEM (Science, Technology, Engineering, and Mathematics) disciplines.

EdX, unlike the other organizations, is a venture spearheaded by universities themselves and was conceived as a platform to provide an MIT to anyone who wants it. EdX grew out of the MIT initiative –the brainchild of MIT President L. Rafael Reif (then MIT´s provost) and Professor Anant Agarwal. It was branded as an open platform that other universities could join and leverage for their own residential education purposes. Since its inception, the University of California, Berkeley has become a part of the venture. EdX is financed mostly by its member institutions and the courses and certifications are currently free.

Early examples of MOOCs go back to 2007-2008, Canadian academic Downes and Siemens led an online course called Connectivism and Connective Knowledge. They provided free access to anyone to participate, in addition to their 25-fee-paying students, and more than 2,200 students joined. Cormier described this type of course a Massive Open Online courses (MOOC) defined as a course with a star and end date and that is open with no barriers to entry, neither cost nor education criteria. The Connectivism and Connective Knowledge course was the first to incorporate open learning with distributed content, making it the first true MOOC. In 2011, Thrun and his colleagues at Stanford University offered a course entitled Introduction to Artificial Intelligence and attracted 160,000 students from more than 190 countries. Since then, may MOOCs have been produced and offered by institutions, individuals and commercial organizations.

These developments in the MOOC sphere indicate an exciting new venture in education. However there are many challenges. de Freitas (2013) argues that main challenges are the cost claim or revenue model, attrition rates, maintaining quality levels, accreditation, internationalization of course offerings and sustainable assessment of MOOCs. Currently providers are experimenting with advertising, licensing content and charging for services. Retention rates in MOOCs are often the subject of comment (Daniel, 2013). Recently Clow (2013) presented the "funnel of participation" in online activities in MOOCs, commenting on the steep drop-off in activity, and steeply unequal participation patterns observed in some MOOCs and similar learning environments. According to Clow (2013) traditional online and distance teaching institutions typically have dropout rates that fall between conventional courses and MOOCs and he suggests that it might be "possible to mitigate the impact of the funnel". This could be possible by increasing collaboration among students and designing interactive activities.

Massiveness is the root for all virtues in MOOCs; however it seems to be also its "Achilles Heel", since interactive-communication could be affected because of a limited design of user interfaces. Inter-active-communications integrate those: Face to Face interactions; Synchronous distributed interactions; Asynchronous interactions; and Asynchronous distributed interactions, among the students, course staff, faculty, content, and materials; supported by the user interface.

Several educators pointed out the importance of interactive-communications suggesting that it represents a core element for the seven principles of good practice in education:

1. Encouraging students / faculty contact.
2. Developing cooperation and collaboration among students.
3. Engaging in active learning.
4. Providing quick feedback.
5. Emphasizing the amount of time dedicated to a task.
6. Communicating high expectations.
7. Respecting diverse talents and ways of learning.

In line with the above, authors such as (McAuley, Stewart, Siemens, & Cormier, 2010; Waard, 2011; Levy and Schrire, 2012; Fisher, 2012) emphasizes the importance of well-designed interactive-communication options for MOOCs, arguing that could help students in building their own knowledge and encouraging learning networks from the nodes and connections in the digital environments; natural goals of MOOCs.

Background

The massive nature of participation in a MOOC enables the social dimension of learning. A learning community with an active culture of participation can constitute an environment where the following four phases of experiential learning are more dynamically intertwined:

1. Diverges combine concrete experience with reflective observation. They learn from examples and can analyze these from different perspectives.
2. Assimilators combine abstract conceptualization with reflective observation. They prefer learning from theoretical models.
3. Converges combine abstract conceptualization with active experimentation. They learn by processing ideas and concentrating on precise problems.
4. Accommodators combine concrete experience with active experimentation. They learn from experiments and match models to their obtained insights.

Alley & Jansak (2001) have identified 10 keys to quality online learning. The authors suggested that online courses will be high quality when they are student-centered and when:

1. **Knowledge Construction:** The authors note that educational theory suggests that all knowledge is based and constructed upon prior knowledge. They then suggests that problem based learning through internet based exercises can effectively make use of this educational principle.
2. **Student Responsibility:** In order to encourage student responsibility, a clear web based roadmap and targeted competencies are highlighted.
3. **Student Motivation:** Distance education provides significant challenges for student motivation as much external motivation is not directly visible as in a classroom setting.
4. **Reflection:** In order to internalize concepts and understand ideas, students need time to reflect. The nature of distance education if properly structured allows time to work through material at the student´s own pace, reviewing items that are unclear, and skipping over already known sections. Time to internalize can be effectively accomplished via distance education.
5. **Learning is Unique:** Different students learn in different ways, at different times, and at different levels. Good distance education can allow for unique and individualized educational experiences.
6. **Learning Requires Actual Experience:** Best learning is accomplished when students actually do and use the information imparted. Good distance education assignments recognize this factor and incorporate "doing" into the learning process. The authors suggest two options: learn then do but also do then learn, experimenting in the realm without prior knowledge.
7. **Learning is Social and Private:** There is both a social aspect to learning where individuals can learn from both the instructor and from each other. But also there is time to read and study and comprehend the full material. This is often best accomplished in solitude.

8. **Preconceptions can Impact Learning:** The authors suggest that preconceived notions can have a significant negative impact on learning and proposes methods for students to self-discover these notions and forego false assumptions.
9. **Iterative Learning:** As with systems development, rarely does learning progress in a one directional straight line. There are many iterations and spirals in both systems development and education.
10. **The Unclean Aspect of Pure Learning:** Though there are many successful concepts, there are many extraneous factors that can impact the success or failure of an online course.

The online setting provides a level of flexibility and convenience not provided by traditional classroom courses. Effective teaching and learning in this setting requires responsible, motivated students whose aims are to learn and not to simply get passing grades. Many elements of an online environment can lead students to frustration, overloading, procrastination, passivity, isolation and finally disengagement.

Instructors should not take for granted that students have the ability to use effectively the online component or have the required previous knowledge on the content subject or are willing to participate in meaningful discussions and knowledge shearing. In order for students to be motivated self-learners and learn on their own, instructors have to design an environment that promotes interaction, communication and problem solving, as means to encourage, motivate and engage students in the learning experience.

Moore (1989) was one of the first who concentrate on interaction issues in distance education. He classifies interaction into student to student, student to instructor, and student to content. According to him, student to student interaction refers to the exchange of information and ideas amongst students with or without the real-time presence of an instructor. Student to instructor interactions refers to the interaction between student and expert which establish an environment that encourages students to understand the content better. Student to content interaction is a defining characteristic of education and without it there cannot be education. Hillman, Willis, & Gunawardena (1994) described another type of interaction, the student-interface interaction, which focuses on the access, skills, and attitudes necessary for successful mediated interaction.

He classifies interaction into student to student, student to instructor, and student to content. According to him, student to student interaction refers to the exchange of information and ideas amongst students with or without the real-time presence of an instructor. Student to instructor interactions refers to the interaction between student and expert which establish an environment that encourages students to understand the content better. Student to content interaction is a defining characteristic of education and without it there cannot be education.

There is some evidence that interaction between students and students, students and content, students and instructors in MOOCs may influence performance and retention (Navarro & Shoemaker, 2000). Northrup (2002) pointed out that since interaction has been found to be a part of overall student satisfaction, interaction should be considered in retention efforts.

Adelskold (1999) suggested that interaction among students could have grater effects on learning in a problem solving situation than other types of interaction whereas Kanuka & Anderson (1998) noted that interaction between students and instructor could contribute to student satisfaction and frequency of interaction in online learning. While Moore (1989) and Murray (2012) pointed out that student to content interaction results in changes of student´s understanding, student´s perceptions, or even cognitive structures of student´s mind.

In her research work, Khalil (2013) concluded that student to student is the most interesting type of interaction that is used in MOOCs. Also the study found out that there is a big lack on student to instructor interaction in MOOCs. This, there is a big need for instructors activities and strategies to enhance interaction in future MOOCs.

Khalil (2013) found that one reason that may cause students drop-out or withdraw of their MOOCs is feelings of isolation and the lack of interactivity in MOOCs. Palloff &Pratt (2003) believed that feelings of isolation are the inherent result poor course design. Physical isolation can be overcome by focusing more on social interactions.

MAIN FOCUS: ISSUES, CONTROVERSIES, PROBLEMS

Distance education has a long history, with correspondence courses making use of reasonable cost universal postal services for the delivery of study material to learners and for submission/ return of assignments by students (Casey, 2008). Further developments of distance education have appeared with each new communication technology: radio, television, video recorders, home computing. The latest development that of the internet has similarly been adopted by many existing higher education providers but has also supported the emergence of a new model dubbed massive open online courses (MOOCs), the term coined in 2008 to describe an open online course to be offered by the University of Manitoba in Canada. A range of both topics and platforms have since emerged and the term was describing as "the educational buzzword of 2012" by Daniel (2012) reflecting widespread interest in the concept. MOOCs are widely discussed across a range of media, including blogs and specialist and popular press; however this includes "thinly disguised promotional material by commercial interests, and articles by practitioners whose perspective is their own MOOC courses" according to Daniel (2012). The promise of MOOCs is that they will provide free access, cutting edge courses that could drive down the cost of university-level education and potentially disrupt the existing models of Higher Education (Future Learn, 2013).

One area that has been identified as an important factor affecting students´ learning experiences in MOOCs is student interaction (Mak, Williams, & Mackness, 2010). Many educators pointed out the importance of interaction in high quality MOOCs (McAuley, Stewart, Siemens, & Cormier, 2010). They confirmed the role of interaction and communication in MOOCs as learners construct their own knowledge and develop their personal learning network from the nodes and connections in the digital environment. Mak Williams & Mackness (2010) indicated that interaction in MOOCs helps students to develop their own ideas, express themselves, establish a presence and make thoughtful long-term relationships. In addition Chamberlin & Parish (2011) pointed out the importance of interaction in MOOCs, saying that "all the work within the MOOC should be shared with everyone else: readings, discussions, repurposing of material, among others. The idea is that the more you engage within the course and with other participants, the more you will learn."

Since interactive-communication has been recognized as one of the most important components of learning experiences in both, conventional education and distance education, it is crucial to provide an adequate environment for students/users (Choi, Lim, & Leem, 2002). In this vein, MOOCs need adequate environments that promote students/users' satisfaction; motivation; retention; and higher level of academic achievement.

Additionally, interactive-communication - as it applies to distance education, including MOOCs - is more complicated than it has been treated in traditional classroom teaching, because it depends upon students personality, age or cognitive/learning styles, the type of media (real-time or asynchronous) used, the support and timely feedback, the sense of belonging in the learning community and students' perceptions of their learning experiences including "how well" or "how much" they have learned (Kearsley, 1995; Picciano, 2002, Casey, 2008).

Poor designed environment for interactive communications in MOOCs commonly derives to unfavorable situations for both students/users and staff-faculty. Therefore, it is necessary to explore alternatives that help developers and designers to generate well-designed environments for interactive communications conveyed by adequate user interfaces.

The mission of this chapter is describing an alternative that can help developers and designers to generate well designed environments for interactive communications in MOOCs.

This alternative is oriented to the development of design guidelines, which will contain the elements needed in order to promote the four basic types of interaction inside MOOCs.

In order to development these design guidelines we consider important use the Need-Finding process, which will help us to obtain the necessary elements required for the creation of design guidelines.

The word Need-Finding implies the interplay between needs and recognition. A need is in itself a perceived lack of something (Faste, 1987), and such needs are difficult to express in terms of a potential solution. Something is a dilemma when the actors realize that all choices lead to unsatisfactory solutions (Löwgren & Stolterman, 2004).

A main principle of Need-Finding is to look for needs, not solutions. It is important to keep all possible solutions open for consideration and avoid prematurely limiting the possibilities. A second principle is to make research and design 'seamless', meaning that the Need-finder is involved in both studying people and conceptualizing new products. Furthermore, it is important to go to the customers' environment and let the customer set the agenda.

SOLUTIONS AND RECOMMENDATIONS

The solution to the problem for this work is structured as follows:

1. As a first step a need-finding process is perform, having to steps that consist in the first for observation and in the second a survey to MOOCs users.
    a. Observing people interacting in a MOOC, a list of interactive tools that are offered in Udacity, Coursera and edX can be obtain. A first approximation of the list of elements of interaction that conform the design guidelines can be acquire.
    b. By applying surveys students describe how they interact with other course members, what are the advantage of this interaction also what tools they would like to use for a richer and more fluent communication.
2. Once the need-finding process is perform, we proceed to elaborate a list of the results, which detects the elements need it to facilitate a more effective interaction and communication in the courses, and also promotes the four basics types of communication of distance education, which are student to student, student to teacher, student to content, and student to interface.
3. Once the list of interaction elements is created, creating the design guidelines follows, there are five basic elements contain in the guidelines, which are:
    a. Name of the guide, it has to be descriptive and oriented to de context
    b. Problematic, this is the reason why this guideline is required
    c. Context that talking about the benefits that offer the design guideline

    d.   Solution this is the interaction tools proposal that fulfills the needs and brings the solutions listed in the section before

    e.   An example of the application of this solution

Need-Findings

Need-Findings is an efficacious technique from Human-Computer Interaction (HCI) to identify and understand the people/users' needs based on their activities and tasks (Hartson & Pyla, 2012).

Need-Findings is flexible and could be performed in several manners; however, the most common procedure is to combine observation and interview (Schaffhausen, 2015). As mentioned by HCI guru Scott Klemmer in his HCI MOOC (Klemmer, 2015), observing people in their action field is very useful to realize that set of tasks and activities that they need to achieve for particular purposes. In this way, the perfect complement for observing people is interview, which allows getting specific information about the goals; steps; artifacts; and pain-points (improvement opportunities) from current designs and/ or processes used/followed by people in their daily activities.

In this vein we performed a Need-Findings process in order to get a solid context of the basic tasks and activities which should be supported by interactive-communication elements provided by the User Interfaces in MOOCs.

Observing People

Participant observation, for many years, has been a hallmark of both anthropological and sociological studies. In recent years, the field of education has seen an increase in the number of qualitative studies that include participant observation as a way to collect information.

Marshall and Rossman (1989) define observation as "the systematic description of events, behaviors, and artifacts in the social setting chosen for study" (p.79). Observations enable the researcher to describe existing situations using the five senses, providing a "written photograph" of the situation under study (Erlandson, Harris, Skipper, & Allen, 1993). DeMunck and Sobo (1998) describe participant observation as the primary method used by anthropologists doing fieldwork. Fieldwork involves "active looking, improving memory, informal interviewing, writing detailed field notes, and perhaps most importantly, patience" (DeWalt & DeWalt, 2002, p.vii). Participant observation is the process enabling researchers to learn about the activities of the people under study in the natural setting through observing and partici-pating in those activities. It provides the context for development of sampling guidelines and interview guides (DeWalt & DeWalt, 2002). Schensul and LeCompte (1999) define participant observation as "the process of learning through exposure to or involvement in the day-to-day or routine activities of participants in the researcher setting" (p.91).

Bernard (1994) defines participant observation as the process of establishing rapport within a com-munity and learning to act in such a way as to blend into the community so that its members will act naturally, then removing oneself from the setting or community to immerse oneself in the data to un-derstand what is going on and be able to write about it. Participant observation is characterized by such actions as having an open, nonjudgmental attitude, being interested in learning more about others, being aware of the propensity for feeling culture shock and for making mistakes, the majority of which can be overcome, being a careful observer and a good listener, and being open to the unexpected in what is learned (DeWalt & DeWalt, 1998).

As a first step in the need findings process we selected the study target; in this case the three most popular MOOCs platforms available, according to (Tekdal, 2015): Udacity, Coursera and edX. Then we observed 35 people enrolled in MOOCs from the said platforms. Participants had a lab MOOC session interacting with the respective user interface offered through their specific courses doing usual tasks and activities. Staff jotted down steps, common procedures, and tendencies when users performed their usual activities in MOOC.

This information was discussed in a debriefing session resulting in several ideas which ultimately derived in the following set of common interactive communication options available through the most popular platforms for MOOCs, see Table 1.

Additionally, we could observe that for "Student to student" interaction *Social networks* were widely used. Specifically, Twitter allowed a quick exchange of resources and thoughts; and Facebook helped learners to share resources on the web that can be retrieved later on. *Blogs* provided students a social presence, self-expression, self-indulgence, rich and critical distribution of information. *Wikis* allowed students themselves to easily add, remove, or otherwise edit and change some available content, sometimes without the need for registration. *Discussion groups* were the second most used tool for "students to student" interaction. *Meet up tools* represents complement alternatives to enhance content access and foster collaborative activities.

Most of "student to instructor" interactions take place through announcements. This is because announcements can be used in a variety of ways to push important information to students in MOOCs. In addition they help instructors to "write once so many can read." This allows MOOCs instructors to provide general information from a single location with the assurance that all students are receiving the information. While only a limited number of instructors used the tools "guides", "participate in online discussion with students", and "ask and answer questions" to interact with their students.

On the other hand, *homework assignments* represent a frequent "student to content" interaction, helping students to put into practice lessons learned. *Homework assignments* are short tasks that provide students immediate-automatic feedback. In the same way, *quizzes and tests* were used widely for "student to content" interaction, allowing students to take the entire assignment without the assistance of learning aids; feedback is provided to students after finish /submits the test for review. These interactive elements allow students to keep up with the material and provide them with feedback on what concepts they need to review. Moreover, help students to realize the application of learned concepts in the real world problems.

Table 1. Interaction in the platforms Coursera, Udacity and edX

Type of Interaction	Description	Platforms
Face to Face interaction.	These platforms have elements like video chats or video calls that promote the face to face interaction.	None of the three
Synchronous distributed interaction.	These platforms have external elements like social networks or Meetup external platforms that promote synchronous distributed interaction.	Coursera, Udacity
Asynchronous interaction.	These platform have elements like announcements, videos, courses notes, documents and practices/ exercises evaluations that promote asynchronous communication.	Coursera, Udacity, edX
Asynchronous distributes interaction.	These platforms have elements like discussion forums among students, discussion forums between students and staff members and wikis that promote asynchronous distributes interaction.	Coursera, Udacity, edX

Interview

Observing people findings were complemented by an interview oriented to know the users perception on:

1. The real benefits from the current elements for interactive communication available;
2. The most used interactive communication elements;
3. The most common issues faced; and
4. Define what interactive communication options could provide the best user experience.

Interviews provide very different data from observations: they allow the evaluation team to capture the perspectives of project participants, staff, and others associated with the project. In the hypothetical example, interviews with project staff can provide information on the early stages of the implementation and problems encountered. The use of interviews as a data collection method begins with the assumption that the participants' perspectives are meaningful, knowable, and able to be made explicit, and that their perspectives affect the success of the project. An interview, rather than a paper and pencil survey, is selected when interpersonal contact is important and when opportunities for follow up of interesting comments are desired.

Two types of interviews are used in evaluation research: structured interviews, in which a carefully worded questionnaire is administered; and in-depth interviews, in which the interviewer does not follow a rigid form. In the former, the emphasis is on obtaining answers to carefully phrased questions. Interviewers are trained to deviate only minimally from the question wording to ensure uniformity of interview administration. In the latter, however, the interviewers seek to encourage free and open responses, and there may be a tradeoff between comprehensive coverage of topics and in-depth exploration of a more limited set of questions. In-depth interviews also encourage capturing of respondents' perceptions in their own words, a very desirable strategy in qualitative data collection. This allows the evaluator to present the meaningfulness of the experience from the respondent's perspective. In-depth interviews are conducted with individuals or with a small group of individuals.

For this work, the interview was conducted applying the following open-ended questionnaire, which was validated by the Chronbach's alpha with 89% of reliability.

1. What communication tools are included in the MOOC?
2. What of these tools do you use to communicate with your partners?
3. How has been your experience communicating with other students and the staff of the MOOC
4. How communication with your partners in the MOOC does benefit you?
5. What are the problems that present you when you communicate with your partners?
6. How would you change your communication experience using MOOC? Would you use other tools instead?

Table 2 summarizes the user perception obtained.

Table 2 Summary of the users' perception obtained

Interactive Communication Element	
Social networks (Facebook, Twitter, Google +)	
Benefits	**Common Issues Faced**
• Discuss issues • Announcements and notifications • Sharing resources • User communities • Advices • Help	• Slow response time • Misunderstandings to express doubts or resolve it Low participation of staff
Interactive Communication Element	
Forums and Wikis	
Benefits	**Common Issues Faced**
• Discuss issues • Receive feedback • Help • Add points of view and opinions • Advices • Enrich knowledge • Collaboration	• Communication is not real time • Low participation of staff • Misunderstandings to express some questions or comments are not counted because get lost.
Interactive Communication Element	
Email	
Benefits	**Common Issues Faced**
• Custom messages • Resolution of doubts	• Slow response time • Late Feedback
Interactive Communication Element	
Events calendar, readings, videos	
Benefits	**Common Issues Faced**
• It gives the student an idea of topics to be discussed and the activities to deliver • Help students to understand the issues of MOOC • Enrich knowledge	• Unclear tools for student • Understanding Problems
Interactive Communication Element	
Homework, questionnaires, activities and projects	
Benefits	**Common Issues Faced**
• Help to evaluate student progress • Help to evaluate student understanding	• Do not send activities • No feedback

Analysis and Interpretation of Data

Interview transcripts, field notes and observations provide a descriptive account of the study, but they do not provide explanations. It is the researcher who has to make sense of the data that have been collected by exploring and interpreting them.

Analyzing information involves examining it in ways that reveal the relationships, patterns, trends, etc. that can be found within it. That may mean subjecting it to statistical operations that can tell you not only what kinds of relationships seem to exist among variables, but also to what level you can trust the answers you're getting. It may mean comparing your information to that from other groups (a control or comparison group, statewide figures, etc.), to help draw some conclusions from the data. The point, in terms of your evaluation, is to get an accurate assessment in order to better understand your work and its effects on those you're concerned with, or in order to better understand the overall situation.

There are two kinds of data you're apt to be working with, although not all evaluations will necessarily include both. Quantitative data refer to the information that is collected as, or can be translated into, numbers, which can then be displayed and analyzed mathematically. Qualitative data are collected as descriptions, anecdotes, opinions, quotes, interpretations, etc., and are generally either not able to be reduced to numbers, or are considered more valuable or informative if left as narratives. As you might expect, quantitative and qualitative information needs to be analyzed differently.

Quantitative Data

Quantitative data are typically collected directly as numbers. Some examples include:

- The frequency (rate, duration) of specific behaviors or conditions
- Test scores (e.g., scores/levels of knowledge, skill, etc.)
- Survey results (e.g., reported behavior, or outcomes to environmental conditions; ratings of satisfaction, stress, etc.)
- Numbers or percentages of people with certain characteristics in a population (diagnosed with diabetes, unemployed, Spanish-speaking, under age 14, grade of school completed, etc.)

Data can also be collected in forms other than numbers, and turned into quantitative data for analysis. Researchers can count the number of times an event is documented in interviews or records, for instance, or assign numbers to the levels of intensity of an observed event or behavior. For instance, community initiatives often want to document the amount and intensity of environmental changes they bring about – the new programs and policies that result from their efforts. Whether or not this kind of translation is necessary or useful depends on the nature of what you're observing and on the kinds of questions your evaluation is meant to answer.

Quantitative data is usually subjected to statistical procedures such as calculating the mean or average number of times an event or behavior occurs (per day, month, year). These operations, because numbers are "hard" data and not interpretation, can give definitive, or nearly definitive, answers to different questions. Various kinds of quantitative analysis can indicate changes in a dependent variable related to – frequency, duration, timing (when particular things happen), intensity, level, etc. They can allow you to compare those changes to one another, to changes in another variable, or to changes in another population. They might be able to tell you, at a particular degree of reliability, whether those changes are likely to have been caused by your intervention or program, or by another factor, known or unknown. And they can identify relationships among different variables, which may or may not mean that one causes another.

Qualitative Data

Unlike numbers or "hard data," qualitative information tends to be "soft," meaning it can't always be reduced to something definite. That is in some ways a weakness, but it's also strength. A number may tell you how well a student did on a test; the look on her face after seeing her grade, however, may tell you even more about the effect of that result on her. That look can't be translated to a number, nor can a teacher's knowledge of that student's history, progress, and experience, all of which go into the teacher's interpretation of that look. And that interpretation may be far more valuable in helping that student succeed than knowing her grade or numerical score on the test.

Qualitative data can sometimes be changed into numbers, usually by counting the number of times specific things occur in the course of observations or interviews, or by assigning numbers or ratings to dimensions (e.g., importance, satisfaction, ease of use).

Qualitative data can sometimes tell you things that quantitative data can't. It may reveal why certain methods are working or not working, whether part of what you're doing conflicts with participants' culture, what participants see as important, etc. It may also show you patterns – in behavior, physical or social environment, or other factors – that the numbers in your quantitative data don't, and occasionally even identify variables that researchers weren't aware of.

It is often helpful to collect both quantitative and qualitative information.

Quantitative analysis is considered to be objective – without any human bias attached to it – because it depends on the comparison of numbers according to mathematical computations. Analysis of qualitative data is generally accomplished by methods more subjective – dependent on people's opinions, knowledge, assumptions, and inferences (and therefore biases) – than that of quantitative data. The identification of patterns, the interpretation of people's statements or other communication, the spotting of trends – all of these can be influenced by the way the researcher sees the world. Be aware, however, that quantitative analysis is influenced by a number of subjective factors as well. What the researcher chooses to measure, the accuracy of the observations, and the way the research is structured to ask only particular questions can all influence the results, as can the researcher's understanding and interpretation of the subsequent analyses.

Whether your evaluation includes formal or informal research procedures, you'll still have to collect and analyze data, and there are some basic steps you can take to do so.

Data Obtained from Need-Finding Process

After performing the Need-Findings process, the comments of the survey participants and the notes, summarizing the user perception of the interaction in MOOCs (feedback). This information helps to identify the interactive elements to consider in the interface and defining the type of interaction that promotes.

The results of the Need-Finding process should be organized as shown in Figure 1.

Design Guidelines

Once the data is organized as described, the design guidelines are elaborated using the three levels of classification shown in Figure 1:

Figure 1. Classification of the proposed interactive elements and types of communication

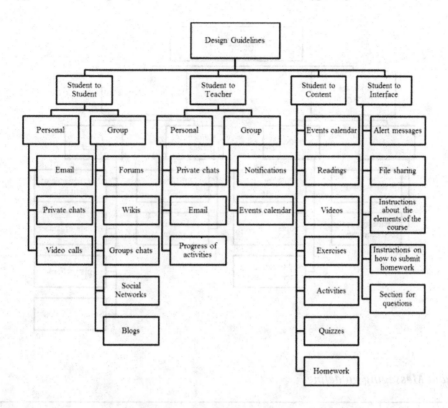

- The first level shows two classification, "participant to participant" and "MOOC to participant" that describe the types in which the MOOCs user can interact inside the course
- The second levels details how this interactions are given
  - "Participant to participant" can be one on one (1:1) as an example, when the student gets in contact with the professor via e mail or private chat, and they exchange personalize messages from one to many (1:N), when users create groups to discuss, solve or ask questions.
  - "MOOC to participant" can be content to participant, e.g. when the student uses content of the course like videos, lectures, quizzes, etcetera, and interface (UI) to participant, e.g. the weekly quizzes, notes, syllabus and others.
- To reach the last level of this classification, it was required to define each interactive element shown in Figure 1, based on the activities done, the characteristics and the particular objectives. Ones the elements are described, we proceed to identified and grouped the similar activities e.g. chat and email. We proceed to identified and group, each group was named making a clear reference of the interaction objectives of each of its elements. For example the chat and email, a name that fits properly is "instant messaging" this groups represent the design guidelines.

Figure 2 shows the design guidelines proposal.
The following tables represent examples of each level of the proposed design guidelines in Figure 2.

Figure 2. Design guideline proposal

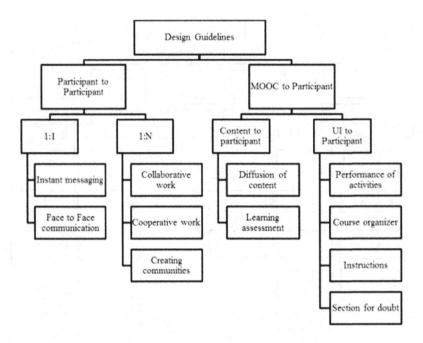

Table 3. Instant Messaging guideline

Name:	Instant messaging
Problem:	MOOC participants need a tool through which to communicate with the staff or other members of the course privately to express their doubts, needs, concerns, among others.
Context:	Students can exchange private messages in order to receive feedback, solve doubts, or to feel more confident and motivated within the MOOC.
Solution:	A practical solution would be the use of email or private chats.
Example:	**Can you point me in the right direction?** Aleksander Danielyan <adanielyan@centraldesktop.com> Tue, Nov 13, 2012 at 12:34 PM To: scott.armstrong@brainrider.com Hi Scott, Would you be open to having a quick discussion to discuss our cloud-based solution for sharing files, collecting feedback from clients, and automating creative approvals? Since developing SocialBridge for Agencies, it has helped your peers at Upshot, Corbett Accel Healthcare Group, Sicola Martin, Javelin, Rhea + Kaiser, MGS, Resource Interactive, etc. Scott, the next step would be a brief research call regarding your current process in order to determine if it would make sense to have a higher level discussion. Please let me know which date and time works best. Thank you. I look forward to hearing back from you. Aleksander Danielyan Direct Line: 626.768.1235 http://www.centraldesktop.com

Table 4. Collaborative work guideline

Name:	Collaborative work
Problem:	Student's need a tool through which can create knowledge or reinforce it.
Context:	Students can collaborate to create knowledge or different ways to solve a problem.
Solution:	A practical solution would be the use of wikis.
Example:	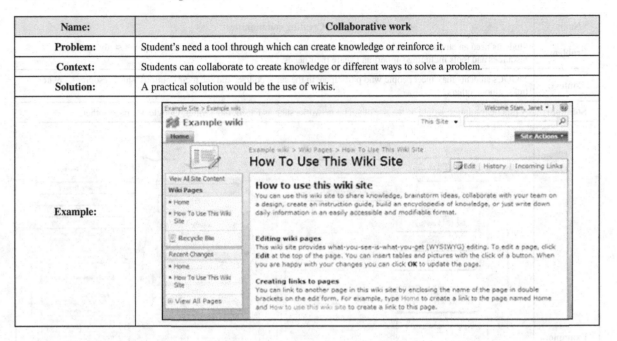

Table 5. Face to Face interaction guideline

Name:	Face to face interaction
Problem:	Sometimes it is difficult for students to express or understand some issues via text, or feel part of a community because they cannot talk in real time with another participant, which leads him to experience feelings of abandonment, isolation or frustration.
Context:	Students can communicate in real time with other participants, which help them avoid feelings of frustration or abandoned, with a greater understanding or expression of certain aspects of the course.
Solution:	A practical solution would be the use of video calls, virtual classrooms, or tools for meetups.
Example:	

Table 6. Creating communities guideline

Name:	Creating communities
Problem:	Students need an environment where they can connect with people interested in the same topic of study, exchange resources and tools including support and share their needs.
Context:	MOOCs students may meet people who participate in the same course, and see their opinions, share resources, create links, among others.
Solution:	A practical solution would be the use of social networks such as Facebook, Twitter, Google +, among others
Example:	

CONCLUSION

Even whether MOOCs already have tools that promote the four types of basic interactive communication in distance education; however said alternatives are not integrated as basic elements for interactive communications through the user interface. This issue frequently derives in a weak user experience which could be reflected in the learning process.

Results from the Need-findings process allow us to create a solid context about the user experience directly from the actual experts, *"The MOOCs' Users"*. This study revealed that independently of the kind of course (which would require specific/special interactive elements, e.g. simulators), a MOOC should offer a set of interactive elements addressed to achieve a fluent and effective communication among participants-staff-platform throughout the course.

These findings was encapsulated in a first draft of design guidelines which suggests the basic interactive elements to be integrated into the user interface design for every MOOC, in order to ensure effectiveness in promoting the four basic types for communication in distance education.

Obtained results are promising and suggest several improvements in user experience for MOOCs learners including reinforcements for user interfaces that could contribute in stretching the gap in providing good quality massive-communication and feedback from MOOCs.

Although good expectations from this research there are several venues to explore as future work, including the guidelines specification; the implementation of the guidelines in a prototype and its evaluation in order to corroborate obtained preliminary findings.

REFERENCES

Adelskold, G., Alklett, K., Axelsson, R., & Blomgren, G. (1999). Problem- based distance learning of energy issues via computer network. *Distance Education, 20*(1), 129–143. doi:10.1080/0158791990200110

Al-Zoube, M. (2009). E-Learning on the Cloud. *Int. Arab J. e-Technol, 1*(2), 58-64.

Alley, L. R., & Jansak, K. E. (2001). The ten keys to quality assurance and assessment in Online Learning. *Journal of Interactive Instruction Development*, 3-18.

Bigus, J. (2014, December 28). *Interactivity and Web-Based Courseware*. Retrieved from http://www.bigusbooks.com/mastersportfolio/products/InteractivityAndWebBasedCourseware.pdf

Black, A. (2005). The use of asynchronous discussion: Creating a text of talk. *Contemporary Issues in Technology & Teacher Education*.

Boettcher, J. (1999). *Nuggets about: the shift to web-based teaching and learning*. Florida State University.

Bonk, C., & Zhang, K. (2006). Introducing the R2D2 model: Online learning for the diverse learners of this world. *Distance Education, 27*(2), 249–264. doi:10.1080/01587910600789670

Casey, D. M. (2008). A journey to legitimacy: The historical development of distance education through technology. *TechTrends*, 45–51.

Chamberlin, L., & Parish, T. (2011). MOOCs: Massive Open Online Coursesor Massive and Often Obtuse Courses? *E- learn Magazine*.

Chickering, A. W., & Gamson, Z. F. (1987). Seven principles for good practice in undergraduate education. *AAHE Bulletin*, 3–6.

Choi, S., Lim, C., & Leem, J. (2002). *Effects of Different Types of Interaction on Learning Achievement, Satisfaction and Participation in Web-Based Instruction, Innovations in Education and Teaching International*. Academic Press.

Christopher, B. (2013). *Learning about social learning in MOOCs: From statistical analysis to generative model*. Academic Press.

Curry, D. B. (2014, December 28). *Collaborative, Connected and Experiential Learning: Reflections of an Online Learner*. Retrieved from http://www.mtsu.edu/~itconf/proceed01/2.html

Daniel, J. (2012). Making sense of MOOCs: Musings in a m aze of m yth, paradox and possibility. *Journal of Interactive Media in Education, 2012*(3), 18. doi:10.5334/2012-18

Dasarathy, B., Sullivan, K., Schmidt, D. C., Fisher, D. H., & Porter, A. (May de 2014). The past, present, and future of MOOCs and their relevance to software. *Proceedings of the on Future of Software Engineering*, 212-224. doi:10.1145/2593882.2593897

Diaz, L. A. (2009). Are the functions of teachers in e-learning and face-to-face learning environments really different? *Journal of Educational Technology & Society*.

Dorsey, M. (2011). *Pearson Assignments: Quizzes, Tests, and Homework Explained*. Retrieved from http://www.myaccountinglabcommunity.com/custom/scripts/google-search-init.js

e-Learners.com. (2014, December 28). *Synchronous vs. asynchronous classes*. Retrieved from http://www.elearners.com/online-education-resources/online-learning/synchronous-vs-asynchronous-classes/

Faust, D. F., & Courtenay, B. C. (2002). Interaction in the intergenerational freshman class: What matters. *Educational Gerontology, 28*(5), 401–422. doi:10.1080/03601270290081362-2038

Future Learn. (2013). *Future learn launches*. Retrieved January 04, 2015, from http://futurelearn.com/feature/futurelearn-launches

Garrison, D., & Kanuka, H. (2004). Blended learning: Uncovering its transformative potential in higher education. *The Internet and Higher Education, 7*(2), 95–105. doi:10.1016/j.iheduc.2004.02.001

Hannum, W., & Briggs, L. (1982). How does instructional system design differ from traditional instruction? *Educational Technology*, 9–14.

Harris, J. M., Mishra, P., & Koehler, M. (2009). Teachers technological pedagogical content knowledge and learning activity types: Curriculum-based technology integration reframed. *Journal of Research on Technology in Education, 41*(4), 393–416. doi:10.1080/15391523.2009.10782536

Hillman, D. C., Willis, D. J., & Gunawardena, C. N. (1994). Learner-interface interaction in distance education: An extension of contemporary models and strategies for parishioners. *American Journal of Distance Education, 8*(2), 30–42. doi:10.1080/08923649409526853

Hrastinski, S. (2008). Asynchronous & synchronous e-learning. *EDUCAUSE Quarterly*, 51–55.

Kanuka, H., & Anderson, T. (1998). Online social interchange, discord, andknowledge construction. *Journal of Distance Education, 13*(1), 57–74.

Kearsley, G. (1995). The nature and value of interaction in distance learning. *Distance Education Research Symposium 3: Instruction*.

Khalil, H., & Ebner, M. (2013). Interaction Possibilities in MOOCs – How Do They Actually Happen? *International Conference on Higher Education Development*, 1-24.

Lorenzo, G. (2005). *An overview of e-portfolios*. EDUCASE Learning Initiative.

Mak, S., Williams, R., & Mackness, J. (2010). Blogs and Forums as Communication and LearningTools in a MOOC. *Proceedings of the 7th International Conference on Networked Learning*, 275-284.

Mason, R. P., Pegler, C., & Weller, M. (2004). E-portfolios: An assessment tool for online courses. *British Journal of Educational Technology*, *35*(6), 717–727. doi:10.1111/j.1467-8535.2004.00429.x

McAuley, A., Stewart, B., Siemens, G., & Cormier, D. (2010). Massive Open Online Courses Digital ways of knowing and learning. *The MOOC model For Digital Practice*.

McCracken, H. (2002). The importance of learning communities in motivating and retaining online learners. *Motivating and retaining adult learners online*, 65-74.

Meloni, J. (2010). Tools for synchronous and asynchronous classroom discussion. *The Chronicle of Higher Education*.

Moore, M. G. (1989). Editorial: Three types of interaction. *American Journal of Distance Education*, *3*(2), 1–6. doi:10.1080/08923648909526659

Murray, M., Pérez, J., Geist, D., & Hedrick, A. (2012). Student Interactionwith Online Course Content: Build It and They Might Come. *Journal of Information Technology Education*, *11*(1), 125–142.

Murray, M. P. (2012). tudent Interactionwith Online Course Content: Build It and They Might Come. *Journal of Information Technology Education*, 125–142.

Navarro, P., & Shoemaker, J. (2000). Performance and perceptions of distance learners in cyberspace. *American Journal of Distance Education*, *14*(2), 15–35. doi:10.1080/08923640009527052

Northrup, P. T. (2002). Online learners' preferences for interaction. *TheQuarterly Review of Distance Education*, *3*(2), 219–226.

Padavano, D. G. (2005). Student Satisfaction with Faculty-Student Interaction. *Sloan-C International Conferences on Asynchronous Learning 2005*.

Palloff, R. M., & Pratt, K. (2003). *The virtual student: a profile and guide to working with online learners*. San Francisco: Jossey-Bass.

Picciano, A. G. (2002). Beyond student perceptions: issues of interaction, presence, and performance in an online course. *JALN*, 21-40.

Porter, L. R. (1997). *Creating the virtual classroom: Distance learning with the internet*. New York: John Wiley & Sons, Inc.

Simonson, M. S. (2012). *Teaching and learning at a distance: Foundations of distance education*. Boston: Pearson.

Skylar, A. (2009). A Comparison of asynchronous online text-based lectures and synchronous interactive web conferencing lectures. *Issues in Teacher Education*, 69–84.

Wagner, E. D. (1994). In support of a functional definition of interaction. *American Journal of Distance Education*, *8*(2), 6–29. doi:10.1080/08923649409526852

Zapalska, A., Bugaj, M., Flanegin, F., & Rudd, D. (2004). *Student Feedback on Distance Learning with the Use of WebCT*. Computers in Higher Education Economics Review.

ADDITIONAL READING

Davidson, C. N. (2014). Why Higher Education Demands a Paradigm Shift. *Public Culture*, *26*(1), 3–11. doi:10.1215/08992363-2346313

Flynn, J. (2013). MOOCS: Disruptive innovation and the future of higher education. *Christian Education Journal*, *10*(1), 149–162.

Hara, N. (2014). (Re) Inventing the Internet: Critical Case Studies. *New Media & Society*, *16*(1), 173–175. doi:10.1177/1461444813507877a

Kumbhar, R. M. (2014). Academic Librarys Responses to the Emerging Trends in Higher Education. *DESIDOC Journal of Library & Information Technology*, *34*(6), 477–485. doi:10.14429/djlit.34.6.6878

Milligan, C., & Littlejohn, A. (2014). Supporting Professional Learning in a Massive Open Online Course. *International Review of Research in Open and Distance Learning*, *15*(5), 197–213. doi:10.19173/irrodl.v15i5.1855

Parkes, T., Jones, C., Randall, D., Crow, G., Pryke, M., & Jones, R. (2013) *The Potential of Virtual Learning and Virtual Learning Environments for Advanced Doctoral Training in the UK*. Retrieved June 05, 2015, from: http://esrcsocietytoday.esrc.ac.uk/_images/Virtual-Learning-report_tcm8-29850.pdf

Tekdal, M., Cagatay Baz, F., & Catlak, S. (2015). Current MOOC Platforms at Online Education. *International Journal of Scientific and Technological Research*, *1*(2), 144–149.

Zemsky, R. (2014). With a MOOC MOOC here and a MOOC MOOC there, here a MOOC, there a MOOC, everywhere a MOOC MOOC. *The Journal of General Education*, *63*(4), 237–243. doi:10.5325/jgeneeduc.63.4.0237

KEY TERMS AND DEFINITIONS

Asynchronous Communication: It is the exchange of messages, such as among the hosts on a network or devices in a computer, by reading and responding as schedules permit rather than according to some clock that is synchronized for both the sender and receiver or in real time. It is usually used to describe communications in which data can be transmitted intermittently rather than in a steady stream.

Good Design: It helps people to do things that we care about. It applied to Hardware and Software. Good Design has a tremendous impact on both the individual´s ability to accomplish specific tasks and societies´.

Human Computer Interaction: It is the study of how people interact with computers and to what extent computers are or are not developed for successful interaction with human beings.

MOOC: A course of study made available over the internet without charge to a very large number of people.

Online Learning Environments: It is a set of teaching and learning tools designed to enhance a student's learning experience by including computers and the Internet in the learning process.

Platforms: It is a raised stage, or a forum in which an idea can be shared, or a standard for computer hardware that determines what types of software it can run, or is a series of beliefs of a political group.

Social Interaction: It is the process by which we act and react to those around us. Let's examine the different types of social interaction and test your knowledge with a quiz.

Synchronous Communication: It is the transmission of data, generally without the use of an external clock signal, where data can be transmitted intermittently rather than in a steady stream.

Chapter 9
Personal Touch:
A Viewing-Angle-Compensated Multi-Layer Touch Display

Andreas Kratky
University of Southern California, USA

ABSTRACT

Large format touch screens have become an important means of interaction for collaborative and shared environments. This type of display is particularly useful for public information display in museums and similar contexts. Similarly augmented reality displays have become popular in this context. Both systems have benefits and drawbacks. Personal Touch is an augmented-reality display system combining real objects with superimposed interactive graphics. With increasing display sizes and users moving in front of the display user tracking and viewing angle compensation for the interactive display become challenging. Personal Touch presents an approach combining IR optical tracking for gesture recognition and camera-based face recognition for the acquisition of viewing axis information. Combining both techniques we can create a reactive augmented-reality display establishing a personalized viewing and interaction context for users of different statue moving in front of a real object.

INTRODUCTION

The use of large format touch screens for public locations such as museums or libraries has become widely popular. A recent survey (Ardito, Buono, Costabile, & Desolda, 2015) indicates that the common usage of this type of display has transformed established concepts of human computer interaction and shaped the expectations about interactive possibilities in public and semi-public spaces. Research about museum visitors has shown that young visitors prefer museum collections to be displayed in innovative ways. Having grown up with interactive multi-touch technologies young visitors respond positively to interactive information displays presented on touch screens (Ting, Lim, & Sharji, 2013). While maybe particularly popular among younger users, touch screen interaction is now widespread and easy to use for a wide range of age groups (Montague, Hanson, & Cobley, 2012). Traditionally museum displays have been focusing on objects from their collection in combination with introductory texts and explanations.

DOI: 10.4018/978-1-5225-2616-2.ch009

But as textual and visual information going beyond the existing physical evidence in form of collection objects exists, for example various forms of information visualization, interactive screens have become more prevalent. (Hinrichs, Schmidt, & Carpendale, 2008) Those displays are often dynamic interactive presentations in addition and in support of collection objects. The hardware of choice to realize these presentations are large format touch screens. Since the mid 2000s large touch-screen use has been more frequent due to more powerful and more economic technology (Ardito et al., 2015).

For use in shared spaces large format touch-screens provide several benefits that make them specifically suitable for environments like museum or library displays. The most prominent among these are the visibility and attraction of large dynamic visualizations for museum visitors walking through the exhibition space. Compared to static printed text or small displays the ability to grab attention and direct the visitor's gaze is significantly stronger. Outside of the museum, for example in a shared office, the salience of the display is often less important. Large interactive displays also promote activity and social awareness among its users. (2015) The conduciveness for communicative behavior and collaboration is generally one of the core benefits of this type of display system. In particular in complex tasks the opportunity for co-located problem solving can be highly beneficial (Isenberg et al., 2012). Again the museum environment differs from other environments as it is less focused on collaborative solving of complex tasks rather than communication among visitors to foster learning and engagement. The increased screen size and the possibility to collaboratively interact in a shared environment have been shown to provide benefits for sense-making (Andrews, Endert, & North, 2010) and learning (Reski, Nordmark, & Milrad, 2014).

Another display technology that has become very popular in the museum environment is the augmented reality (AR) display. In particular in science and natural history museums this form of display has gained such popularity that it is sometimes referred to as a hype ("British Museum - Augmented Reality: Beyond the Hype," n.d.). The popularity stems from the fact that it can simulate prior states of a real physical collection object. A popular example is the dinosaur skeleton, which can be seen as a complete dinosaur through an augmented reality display (Augmented Reality Livens Up Museums I Innovation I Smithsonian n.d.). (Barry, Thomas, Debenham, & Trout, 2012) Augmented reality displays blend a representation of a real context, for example a museum object, with a computer generated information layer. Both layers are displayed such that they are correctly superimposed. The additional information can be of various kinds, such as the virtual models of dinosaurs or simply additional textual information pertaining to an object. We can distinguish applications using a camera generated video image to represent the real context and those that use optical see-through techniques to show the real object (Normand, Servières, & Moreau, 2012).

One of the important issues for both techniques, the touch-screen as well as the augmented reality system (of course the same applies to the traditional static text panel), is how the relationship between the additional information and the real object is established. The touch-screen is often used as a self-contained unit placed in proximity to the objects it refers to. If close relationships are established it is mostly through the display of visual representations of the objects nearby that the information refers to. Screen and objects have very different viewing conditions and are rather in competition than in support of each other. Augmented reality systems deliver a much closer relationship between object and additional information. By superimposing both object and additional information users can see directly how they relate to each other. For this reason the alignment between the two is a distinguishing quality factor (Liestol & Morrison, 2013)./ The earliest way of establishing the connection between real and virtual was through markers, coded visual symbols such as QR-codes, that can be read by the AR-device and interpreted such that the correct information overlap can be displayed. The display orientation is calculated according to the perspective on the marker (Liarokapis & White, 2005). The downside of those markers is that they have to be placed very close to the actual object in order to give a tight connection, but the actual object cannot be used for augmentation. The markers add a visual element that is often difficult to integrate with the aesthetics of the presentation. Another downside is that users must carry a correctly equipped device that can be used to scan and resolve the codes. Later approaches do not have to rely on markers but rather use feature constellations of the object itself. They are suitable for a more seamless and more aesthetically pleasing integration between the real and virtual layers. In both cases the hardware platform to display the augmentation layer are smart phones or tablets. This reliance on AR-capable devices also introduces the problem that the screen that can be used for the additional information display is comparatively small (Nassar & Meawad, 2010).

An example for a custom solution to stimulate a more specific and precise relationship between the object and the augmentation layer is the use of a laser-pointer-like device (Takahashi, Takahashi, Kusunoki, Terano, & Inagaki, 2013). Here users can point to specific parts of a real exhibit to trigger the information overlay. The laser works almost as an extension of the hand that 'touches' the exhibit, an action normally not permitted in a museum context. In this sense the AR solution allows a more direct engagement with the object with visible light than pointing the camera of a phone at an object. The possibility of pseudo-touching an object has the potential to make for a highly engaging experience in rather direct relationship to the real object.

Both display systems, large collaborative touch-screens as well as augmented reality systems, have their benefits and drawbacks. While the augmented reality systems has the opportunity to establish a much tighter connection between the real object and the augmentation layer than the touch screen, it does not offer the opportunity for collaborative exploration in a way the large touch-screen does. The use of handheld devices necessary to enable the personalized pointing and exploration of real exhibits forces the use of smalls screens, which are limited to one individual user. Handheld devices are made specifically to be used by only one person and the experience of standing next to someone engaged with a handheld device and being excluded from the experience is all too well known (Fredrickson 2013), ("Does Technology Cut Us Off From Other People?," n.d.). Handheld devices and collaborative exploration thus seem to be mutually exclusive. This dilemma has been addressed for example in combining several different interfaces for the same content so users can choose the preferred mode of access. A comparative study traces the benefits and drawbacks of both systems and investigates whether a combined approach is successful (Hornecker 2010).

For *Personal Touch* we are using a display set-up that combines the properties of large touch-screens and those of an augmented reality display not through combining two separate implementations but by integrating them into one. Our approach is to use a transparent touch screen placed in front of the real object to which the augmentation layer refers. This approach unites the collaborative aspect of a large format touch screen permitting several users to share the display and to collaboratively explore the exhibit. At the same time, through the optical superimposition of the screen, it serves as an augmentation layer, and a close relationship is established between the additional information and the object. The touch-screen consists of a large glass panel, which is suspended in front of the object and it displays information being projected onto it. The users can see both the information on the screen as well as the object, looking through the glass panel. Not only combines this system some of the main benefits of AR and touch-screen systems, it also implements a way to reach out to the object and actually feel a physical resistance when touching the screen.

CHALLENGES

The system we implemented for *Personal Touch* faces several challenges. Design problems existing in each individual display technology present themselves in a somewhat different light when combined. It is a challenge to design for a satisfactory multi-user experience in large format touch screens that allows for all members of the group interacting with the system to partake equally and also balances ease-of-use on the first approach and a meaningful deep scaffolding of a longer interaction. A study of these challenges is discussed in (Jacucci et al., 2010). For our purposes the problems of accommodating several users on front of one object is potentially compounded for reasons of limited interaction space. In particular small objects do not provide sufficient space to accommodate several users in front of them at the same time.

The other challenge for our approach is to align the augmented reality display with the real object behind it correctly. Again the problem is compounded in comparison to an individual user experience with a mobile device. Restricting the experience to one person makes things easier and the fact that the user can carry the mobile device along with any movement makes the alignment question a lot easier to address. In our attempt to accommodate multiple users with one shared display, the challenge is to render both information layers in correct alignment to all of them. An additional difficulty for alignment is that museum visitors tend to move around and walk from one exhibit to the next, this means that they might look at objects from various angles and these angles change during the phase of observation of the same object. The augmented reality touch screen thus has to provide an option to adjust the display for a certain range of varying viewing angles and correct for the parallax resulting from user position in respect to the object.

Viewing angle correction is not only of interest to users in motion but it also is a way of providing a comfortable interaction situation for users of different body heights. In the museum environment it is to be expected that the users of such a system range from children all the way to adults, thus what is a comfortable interaction situation for one maybe be inappropriate for another user. Our requirement to accommodate groups of users for collaborative interaction further compounds the problem of alignment because the viewing angle compensation has to take into account whether the object is looked at from several different angles at the same time. In an earlier study of this system without any viewing angle correction we found that users while benefiting from the optical superimposition and touch-screen functions they struggled with the alignment of real and virtual display (Kratky, 2015). Based on body height these problems were more or less strong, in general indicating a linear correlation between proximity to the position of optimal alignment and ease-of-use. The challenges addressed in the *Personal Touch* project can be described as a triplet of issues surrounding viewer-dependent display adjustment:

1. Viewing-angle-compensation for users of varying body height;
2. Viewing-angle-compensation for users in motion;
3. Viewing-angle-compensation for multiple users in varying group sizes and constellations.

RELATED WORK

Camera-based tracking of users in front of a large screen has been explored in order to track touch gestures and turn the screen into a large format touch screen (Morrison 2007). Given that large touch sensitive screens are becoming more available research has started to focus on the notion of body-centric design to conceive of interaction models combining various forms of sensing users and different input devices. A solution implementing large format screen for full body interaction is described in (Shoemaker, Tsukitani, Kitamura, & Booth, 2010). It uses camera or magnetic tracking to determine the skeleton of the user and determines interaction gestures from the analysis of the skeleton. The same data also serve to render a virtual representation of the user(s) (Kim et al., 2013) on the screen for visual feedback to improve gesture performance. The display system does not implement augmented reality components. A similar system based on infra-red tracking that extends the interaction patterns to multiple surfaces using touch and mid-air gestures is described by Wagner et al. (Wagner, Nancel, Gustafson, Huot, & Mackay, 2013). The approach focuses on developing a body-centric design language. The combination of touch interaction with mid-air gestures is also explored in Müller et al (Müller, Bailly, Bossuyt, & Hillgren, 2014). The study looks at the role of different design affordances in communicating the interaction techniques available in installations in public space. A strong dependence is on environmental factors and the sequence of use of different affordances (touch versus gesture) was found. If gestural mid-air interaction was available, strong affordances for touch interaction had to be present to serve as a "call to action." While most research focuses on screen-based interaction and the combination of touch and gesture, few works investigate the combination of touch and augmented reality displays. One example exploring augmented reality interaction and haptic interaction with real physical objects is described in (Kim et al., 2013). To ensure correct alignment of multiple interaction and display contexts, in particular pointing gestures in respect to large screens the mathematical modeling of the pointing gestures and their spatial properties are important. A model for the calculation of the gain of pointing gestures is discussed in Shoemaker et al. (Shoemaker, Tsukitani, Kitamura, & Booth, 2012).

Another important aspect for the implementation of a display system that dynamically adjusts to user action and the configuration of changing user constellations is the successful analysis of the actions and movements of the users. Dim and Kuflik (Dim & Kuflik, 2014) describe a series of simple behavioral patterns of visitor pairs and discuss a system that can automatically track these patterns and, in a second step, potentially offer customized services based on the analyzed pattern. In Ye, Stevenson and Dobson (Ye, Stevenson, & Dobson, 2014) an automated system for the mining of behavior patterns is discussed.

THE *PERSONAL TOUCH* SYSTEM

Design Considerations

The design goals we defined for *Personal Touch* are revolving around three main aspects. The first is the superimposition of information and a real object. For the first implementation we limited the set-up to one single object in order to keep the components influencing the evaluation to a minimum. Our hypothesis is that depending on the number of objects, object size and relative screen-size the results in interaction patterns will be different. We are assuming that large touch-screen sizes will become more and more affordable so it is conceivable that an interaction screen can span several objects and thus several interaction contexts. For our study we also wanted to observe if the screen is small enough that it also allows viewers to easily get close to the objects viewers would also examine the object directly. We were curious what the sequence of observation was going to be, if viewers first examine the object and then access further information about it or vice versa, or if users either look at only the object or the screen.

Our interest in superimposing information in an augmented reality style was to establish a very close and precise relationship between the object and the additional information and to foster the self-guided exploration of different information layers. The superimposed delivery of additional information caters to users who do not like to read long texts and get turned away when they see long explanations about an item as it is often the case with static printed text plates. Users also are often unwilling to refer back and forth between object and text information. Most users tend to read the text and then look at the object. A minority of the viewers we observed in a traditional museum exhibit with static text plates looks at the object first, then read the text, and then look at the object again. The superimposed information caters to users who want to be able to determine how much information they need about a specific item. They may be fine with a superficial level of information simply identifying the object. In other cases they may want to have the opportunity to request more information. Our hypothesis is that the combined augmented reality touch display allows for a seamless scaffolding of further information pertaining to elements or areas of interest.

Even though in our first implementation we are limiting the display to one single object the system should be able to clearly distinguish the object to which the displayed information pertains in case several objects are visible behind the screen. The second main design goal is thus the implementation of effective viewing axis compensation. The viewing-angle compensation should be able to establish for a given viewing axis which object and which part of the object the information belongs to. Based on data about the position of the viewer the information display should be adjusted for several aspects: It has to correct for changing positions of the users as they move through the exhibition and past the object with the augmented display; it also has to adjust for different body heights of the viewers. Our hypothesis is that an optical tracking of the viewers in front of the screen should be able to deliver the data necessary for an adjustment that can satisfy the formulated requirements.

The viewing axis compensation should also be able to deliver a certain degree of personalization and responsiveness to the viewers. We are aiming in this sense for an "adaptive interface" that can adjust for several individual factors of the viewers, similar to the concept discussed in (Montague et al., 2012). Our hypothesis is that the dynamic adjustment can direct the viewer's gaze towards the object of interest. As a viewer walks past an exhibit the position of the exhibit gets continuously adjusted such that it frames the object the information refers to. We assume that the viewer is less likely to walk past such a constantly updated display "circling" the object of interest, than she would with a static display.

The third main design goal is to accommodate and stimulate collaborative interaction between groups of viewers in front of the display. The display adjustment system therefore has to have a heuristic to determine how to adjust for the viewing axes of several users versus individual users. The touch-screen has to be multi-touch enabled, which is more or less the norm nowadays, in order to allow for several people to interact simultaneously.

Implementation

The *Personal Touch* system consists of glass panel suspended in front of a physical object. The panel is mounted on thin metal wires fixed tightly to the ceiling and the floor. The wires are tight such that the screen does not move when users interact with it. Our decision to use this kind of mount was to integrate the screen as seamless as possible into the space around the exhibit and avoid a noticeable frame mount around the screen. The aesthetic ideal for the mounting solution was to come close to a "free floating" text, inviting users to interact with the screen as well as to go past it and examine the object directly.

The screen is not supposed to be perceived as an obstacle blocking the view to the object, which was the sense we had with a more massive mounting frame. This design decision made it impossible for us to use an IR tracking frame with integrated IR lights and sensors. Our solution was thus a "Leap Motion" controller mounted on a bar beneath the screen that tracked the surface area of the glass panel allowing to determine touches on the screen surface as well as hover-states close to the surface of the panel. The distinction between hover-states and touch events is a benefit that other touch-screen solutions do not provide. In the current version of *Personal Touch* we are not using hover states, but we intend to do this in future iterations.

The glass panel has a "holoscreen"-film glued to the back, which is a plastic film with embedded micro-prisms that allows to project onto the screen in an angle of 45 degrees and produce a visible image on the transparent glass. The "holoscreen" is transparent (with a slight matte optic) and allows the viewer to look through the glass at the object behind it. In this way we are realizing a multi-layer augmented reality display. The projector for the display is mounted to the ceiling in a 45-degree angle projecting downwards to the viewer. Since the projector is reasonably steeply inclined the viewer does not get blinded by the projection beam.

Above the screen we mounted a small USB camera equipped with a wide-angle lens that tracks the area in front of the screen. We are assuming that users will always keep a minimum distance of ca. 50 cm from the screen to be able to comfortably interact with it; in order to allow the camera to track the entire area in front of the screen we placed it above the screen and 20 cm behind the glass panel. The camera delivers a constant video feed to the controlling computer. The screen itself is placed 150 cm in front of the object. Around it is enough space for the viewers to approach the object and look at it directly.

We implemented three information layers of different depths. The first just shows a minimal record including the name, date and description of the object. This is the default state when no user is interacting or when users are approaching the screen without touching it. Upon touch the second level providing a

Figure 1. Schematic of the system set-up of the Personal Touch installation

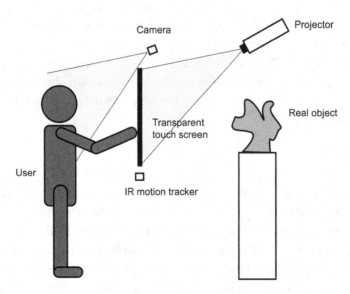

Figure 2. Two of the three layers of information: General background information (left), and information on specific details of the object (right)

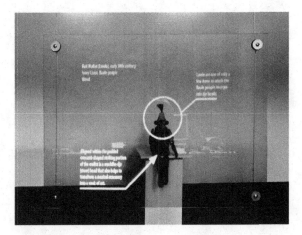

general explanatory text about the background of the object is displayed. This information layer can be enhanced for example with maps or other illustrations. The third level has detail information on individual parts of the object, allowing viewers to explore for example the different elements of clothing of the object. The third level is invoked touching "hot spots" indicating further information. The "hot-spots" are visible in both the second and third levels of the display hierarchy. Viewers have full control over how far and how long they explore the provided information and which levels they access to which extent.

Heuristic for Viewing-Angle-Compensation

For the tracking of users in front of the screen we use the Open CV library to recognize and track faces. This means whenever a user is in front of the screen and looks at it we can recognize the face and determine its position. With this information we can calculate the viewing axis to the object. In this first implementation phase we are using a normal camera delivering a flat matrix image. For the z-axis, i.e. the distance of the viewer from the screen we assume a comfortable touch interaction distance of 50 cm. Based on these data we can calculate an offset for the image projected on the screen to accommodate both horizontal viewing position differences due to varying positions of viewers in front of the screen, as well as vertical differences due to variance in body height. This offset is constantly calculated as long as a face is recognized and can thus be dynamically updated to compensate for changing positions of moving viewers. In default mode, i.e. when no face is detected the image is set to an average centered value. All adjustments are smoothly interpolated such that no sudden jumps of the image occur.

The main challenge is to formulate a heuristic that defines a viewing-angle-adjustment for collaborative interaction. When more than one user are working with the screen – what is the best way to accommodate their different viewing axes? Our heuristic is using an analysis of the constellation of viewers in front of the screen in order to determine how to adjust the display. The heuristic is based on the observations of Edward T. Hall (The Hidden Dimension 1990) and his formulation of the "proxemics distances." Hall distinguishes four different social distances in humans, the closest being the *intimate* distance, extremely close proximity between two people who almost touch each other. This distance would only occur between people who are very familiar and close with each other, e.g. a couple looking

Figure 3. Viewing-axis-adjustment for individual viewer: vertical adjustment for body height (left), and horizontal adjustment for changing viewer positions (right)

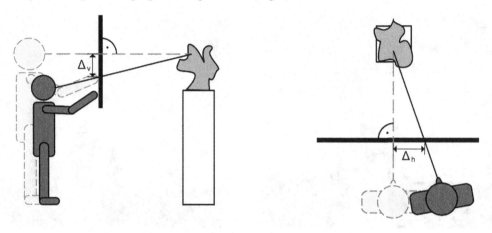

together at something very closely. The *personal* distance ranges from 50 cm in its close phase to 120 cm in its distant phase. The *personal* distance is the normal distance between people who know each other and are comfortable together, this might also be the distance a couple keeps in a public space such as a museum. The *social* distance is the distance people who do not know each other normally keep to each other. It ranges from 120 cm in the close phase to 350 cm in the distant phase. Finally the *public* distance ranges from 350 cm to 600 cm and more. These distances may vary, and they are culturally specific, but they give a good orientation as to what scenarios we should be differentiating. The different proximities correspond to perspective shifts and thus require different display adjustments. The *public* distance is irrelevant for our set-up as the screen is not big enough to accommodate people who keep this distance between each other; if people are unfamiliar to this degree with each other they would tend to wait until one person is done with her interaction before they take over the space in front of the screen. If somebody happens to look at the screen from this distance they would not expect to see correct alignment between real object and information overlay for their viewing position. We decided to take the *social* distance and smaller into account and devise correction scenarios for them. Museum visitors in a group, like colleagues or members of a travel group, would keep the *social* distance. They should be able to interact and share the screen with each other. We assume, though, that they would not be so intimate that they would share the same interaction context. Sharing the same interaction context would potentially bring people closer together than they might feel comfortable with and create the opportunity to touch each other while interacting with the touch-screen. According to Hall in the *social* distance contact between people would not occur. Therefore when faces are tracked with a distance in the range of the *social* distance, the interaction context is duplicated and projected such that it suits the viewing axes of both (or potentially more in case of a sufficiently large screen) people. The viewers can interact in parallel and share what they see verbally. Users who are more intimate with each other and keep a distance that is in the range of the close phase of the *personal* distance are considered to be familiar enough that they can share the same interaction context. The placement of the context is averaged between their viewing axes and scaled such that it can better accommodate both (maximum three people). For both viewers the alignment is slightly less precise but there is the opportunity to look closely and invite the other "to share the individual's perspective." Finally for the *intimate* distance a scaling of the overlay image does

Figure 4. Viewing-axis-adjustment for groups of viewers at different proxemics distances: intimate distance (left), personal distance (middle), and social distance (right)

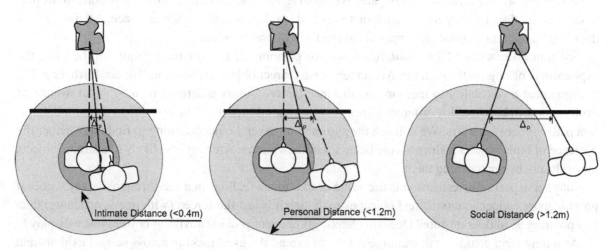

not seem to be necessary and we only make a slight adjustment to average the position between the two viewers. In this scenario only two people can have the appropriate closeness, otherwise the adjustment goes back to the settings for the *personal* distance.

CONCLUSION

We have tested the first implementation of *Personal Touch* in a lab situation with a stand-in object. Taking into account that user behaviors will be somewhat different in a real museum environment with more objects surrounding the exhibit, this first test gives some notion of the performance of the system. We observed ten people, a mixed group of undergraduate and graduate students of mixed gender (age range from 20 to 29 years, 4 female, six male). We tested in particular for display alignment perception, general interaction comfort, and multi-user collaboration.

In a comparative observation with exit interview of individual users of an earlier version of the system without viewing-angle-compensation 50% of the users found that the alignment was significantly off, 30% found it slightly off, and 20% found that the registration was good. With viewing-angle-compensation for individual users 60% found that the registration was good, 40% found it slightly off and no user found the registration to be significantly off.

The results are different for multiple users in a collaborative interaction. Observing groups of two users interacting at *intimate* distance 100% found the alignment slightly off but workable. In groups of two users interacting at *personal* distance 60% of the groups found the registration to be slightly off but workable, 20% slightly off and difficult to navigate and 20% significantly off. Observing groups of three users (three groups with each 3 members observed) interacting at *personal* distance 33% of the groups found the registration to be slightly off but workable and 66% slightly off and difficult to navigate. In the constellations interacting at *personal* distance we observed that the users moved closer together to improve the shared alignment. At *social* distance we only observed groups of two users because larger groups could not be accommodated by the size of our screen. In this scenario 20% of the users found that the registration was good, 60% found it slightly off but workable and 20% found the registration to be slightly off and difficult to navigate. We observed that users adjusted their positions to accommodate each other, i.e. they moved such that they had similar amounts of screen space. All users found the interaction comfort good and appreciated the form of presentation.

For future iterations of *Personal Touch* we are planning to test for the relationship between the explorations of objects through the AR-screen versus direct object exploration. We are further aiming to implement a possibility to measure the distance between users and the screen. Another avenue of exploration will be to employ different screen sizes, which we expect will have an effect on the collaboration patterns between users. We will test the system with several objects aiming to find out whether the presence of other objects influences the behavior of the viewers. Are they less likely to examine objects more closely by approaching them?

Another aspect of investigation is the value of the 'touch feeling' in a see-through display – does it provide more connection to the real object even though it is just the screen (with image matching) than just pointing as mid-air gesture? Does this haptic component provide anything beyond just a display?

As a long term goal we will examine if we can extend the user tracking across several exhibits and in this way deliver a more personalized experience for the museum visit. For this iteration the tracking approach has to be modified such that individual users are either recognized or continuously tracked.

REFERENCES

Andrews, C., Endert, A., & North, C. (2010). Space to think: Large high-resolution displays for sensemaking. In *CHI '10: Proceedings of the SIGCHI conference on human factors in computing systems* (pp. 55-64). ACM. doi:10.1145/1753326.1753336

Ardito, C., Buono, P., Costabile, M. F., & Desolda, G. (2015). Interaction with large displays: A survey. *ACM Comput. Surv., 47*(3), 46:1-46:38. doi:10.1145/2682623

Augmented Reality Livens Up Museums | Innovation | Smithsonian. (n.d.). Retrieved from http://www. smithsonianmag.com/innovation/augmented-reality-livens-up-museums-22323417/?no-ist

Barry, A., Thomas, G., Debenham, P., & Trout, J. (2012). Augmented reality in a public space: The natural history museum, london. *Computer, 45*(7), 42–47. doi:10.1109/MC.2012.106

British Museum - Augmented Reality. Beyond the Hype. (n.d.). Retrieved from http://www.museum-id. com/idea-detail.asp?id=336

Dim, E., & Kuflik, T. (2014). Automatic detection of social behavior of museum visitor pairs. *ACM Trans. Interact. Intell. Syst., 4*(4), 17:1-17:30. doi:10.1145/2662869

Does Technology Cut Us Off From Other People? (n.d.). Retrieved from http://greatergood.berkeley. edu/article/item/does_technology_cut_us_off_from_other_people#

Frederickson, B. B. L. (2013, March 23). Your phone vs. your heart. *The New York Times.*

Hinrichs, U., Schmidt, H., & Carpendale, S. (2008). EMDialog: Bringing information visualization into the museum. *Visualization and Computer Graphics. IEEE Transactions on, 14*(6), 1181–1188. doi:10.1109/TVCG.2008.127

Hornecker, E. (2010). Interactions around a contextually embedded system. In *TEI '10: Proceedings of the fourth international conference on tangible, embedded, and embodied interaction* (pp. 169-176). ACM. doi:10.1145/1709886.1709916

Isenberg, P., Fisher, D., Paul, S., Morris, M. R., Inkpen, K., & Czerwinski, M. (2012). Co-Located collaborative visual analytics around a tabletop display. *Visualization and Computer Graphics, IEEE Transactions on, 18*(5), 689-702. doi:10.1109/TVCG.2011.287

Jacucci, G., Morrison, A., Richard, G. T., Kleimola, J., Peltonen, P., Parisi, L., & Laitinen, T. (2010). Worlds of information: Designing for engagement at a public multi-touch display. In *CHI '10: Proceedings of the SIGCHI conference on human factors in computing systems* (pp. 2267-2276). ACM. doi:10.1145/1753326.1753669

Kim, H., Takahashi, I., Yamamoto, H., Kai, T., Maekawa, S., & Naemura, T. (2013). MARIO: Mid-Air augmented realityinteraction with objects. In Advances in computer entertainment (pp. 560-563). Springer International Publishing. doi:10.1007/978-3-319-03161-3_53

Kratky, A. (n.d.). Transparent touch – interacting with a multi-layered touch-sensitive display system. Springer Berlin Heidelberg.

Liarokapis, F., & White, M. (2005). Augmented reality techniques for museum environments. *The Mediterranean Journal of Computers and Networks, 1*(2), 90–96.

Liestol, G., & Morrison, A. (2013). Views, alignment and incongruity in indirect augmented reality. *IEEE Xplore*, 23-28. doi:10.1109/ISMAR-AMH.2013.6671263

Montague, K., Hanson, V. L., & Cobley, A. (2012). Designing for individuals: Usable touch-screen interaction through shared user models. In *ASSETS '12: Proceedings of the 14th international ACM SIGACCESS conference on computers and accessibility* (pp. 151-158). ACM. doi:10.1145/2384916.2384943

Morrison, G. D. (2007). A CMOS camera-based man-machine input device for large-format interactive displays. In SIGGRAPH '07: ACM SIGGRAPH 2007 courses (pp. 65-74). ACM. doi:10.1145/1281500.1281686

Müller, J., Bailly, G., Bossuyt, T., & Hillgren, N. (2014). MirrorTouch: Combining touch and mid-air gestures for public displays. In *MobileHCI '14: Proceedings of the 16th international conference on human-computer interaction with mobile devices & services* (pp. 319-328). ACM. doi:10.1145/2628363.2628379

Nassar, M. A., & Meawad, F. (2010). An augmented reality exhibition guide for the iphone. *IEEE Xplore*, 157-162. doi:10.1109/IUSER.2010.5716742

Normand, J.-M., Servières, M., & Moreau, G. (2012). A new typology of augmented reality applications. In *AH '12: Proceedings of the 3rd augmented human international conference* (pp. 18:1-18:8). ACM. doi:10.1145/2160125.2160143

Reski, N., Nordmark, S., & Milrad, M. (2014). Exploring new interaction mechanisms to support information sharing and collaboration using large multi-touch displays in the context of digital storytelling. *IEEE Xplore, 176-180.* doi:10.1109/ICALT.2014.59

Shoemaker, G., Tsukitani, T., Kitamura, Y., & Booth, K. S. (2010). Body-centric interaction techniques for very large wall displays. In *NordiCHI '10: Proceedings of the 6th nordic conference on human-computer interaction: Extending boundaries* (pp. 463-472). ACM. doi:10.1145/1868914.1868967

Shoemaker, G., Tsukitani, T., Kitamura, Y., & Booth, K. S. (2012). Two-Part models capture the impact of gain on pointing performance. *ACM Trans. Comput.-Hum. Interact., 19*(4), 28:1-28:34. doi:10.1145/2395131.2395135

Takahashi, T. B., Takahashi, S., Kusunoki, F., Terano, T., & Inagaki, S. (2013). Making a hands-on display with augmented reality work at a science museum. *IEEE Xplore*, 385-390. doi:10.1109/SITIS.2013.69

The Hidden Dimension. (1990). New York: Anchor Books.

Ting, Z. L. K., Lim, Y. P., & Sharji, E. A. (2013). Young visitors' preferences for touch screen design in museums. *IEEE Xplore, 288-291*. doi:10.1109/ICICM.2013.55

Wagner, J., Nancel, M., Gustafson, S. G., Huot, S., & Mackay, W. E. (2013). Body-centric design space for multi-surface interaction. In *CHI '13: Proceedings of the SIGCHI conference on human factors in computing systems* (pp. 1299-1308). ACM. doi:10.1145/2470654.2466170

Ye, J., Stevenson, G., & Dobson, S. (2014). USMART: An unsupervised semantic mining activity recognition technique. *ACM Trans. Interact. Intell. Syst., 4*(4), 16:1-16:27. doi:10.1145/2662870

ADDITIONAL READING

Antoniou, A., O'Brien, J., Bardon, T., Barnes, A., & Virk, D. (2015). Micro-augmentations: Situated calibration of a novel non-tactile, peripheral museum technology. In *PCI '15: Proceedings of the 19th panhellenic conference on informatics* (pp. 229-234). ACM. doi:10.1145/2801948.2801959

Baldauf, M., Lasinger, K., & Fröhlich, P. (2012). Private public screens: Detached multi-user interaction with large displays through mobile augmented reality. In *MUM '12: Proceedings of the 11th international conference on mobile and ubiquitous multimedia* (pp. 27:1-27:4). ACM. doi:10.1145/2406367.2406401

Barsalou, L. W. (2008). Grounded cognition. *Annual Review of Psychology, 59*(1), 617–645. doi:10.1146/annurev.psych.59.103006.093639 PMID:17705682

Barsalou, S., Kyle Simmons, W., Barbey, A. K., & Wilson, C. D. (2003). Grounding conceptual knowledge in modality-specific systems. *Trends in Cognitive Sciences, 7*(2), 84–91. doi:10.1016/S1364-6613(02)00029-3 PMID:12584027

Basballe, D. A., & Halskov, K. (2010). Projections on museum exhibits: Engaging visitors in the museum setting. In *OZCHI '10: Proceedings of the 22nd conference of the computer-human interaction special interest group of australia on computer-human interaction* (pp. 80-87). ACM. doi:10.1145/1952222.1952240

de Bérigny Wall, C., & Wang, X. (2008). Interactive antarctica: A museum installation based on an augmented reality system. In *DIMEA '08: Proceedings of the 3rd international conference on digital interactive media in entertainment and arts* (pp. 319-325). ACM. doi:10.1145/1413634.1413692

DiVerdi, S., Hollerer, T., & Schreyer, R. (2004). Level of detail interfaces. *IEEE Xplore, 300-301*. doi:10.1109/ISMAR.2004.38

Dourish, P. (2001). *Where the action is: The foundations of embodied interaction*. Cambridge, Mass.: MIT Press.

Greenberg, S., Marquardt, N., Ballendat, T., Diaz-Marino, R., & Wang, M. (2011). Proxemic interactions. *Interaction, 18*(1), 42. doi:10.1145/1897239.1897250

Ha, T., Woo, W., Lee, Y., Lee, J., Ryu, J., Choi, H., & Lee, K. (2010). ARtalet: Tangible user interface based immersive augmented reality authoring tool for digilog book. *IEEE Xplore, 40-43*. doi:10.1109/ISUVR.2010.20

Haller, M., Drab, S., & Hartmann, W. (2003). A real-time shadow approach for an augmented reality application using shadow volumes. In *VRST '03: Proceedings of the ACM symposium on virtual reality software and technology* (pp. 56-65). ACM. doi:10.1145/1008653.1008665

Harrison, B. L., Ishii, H., Vicente, K. J., & Buxton, W. A. S. (1995). Transparent layered user interfaces: An evaluation of a display design to enhance focused and divided attention. In *CHI '95: Proceedings of the SIGCHI conference on human factors in computing systems* (pp. 317-324). ACM Press/Addison-Wesley Publishing Co. doi:10.1145/223904.223945

Heun, V., Kasahara, S., & Maes, P. (2013). Smarter objects: Using AR technology to program physical objects and their interactions. In CHI EA '13: CHI '13 extended abstracts on human factors in computing systems (pp. 2817-2818). ACM. doi:10.1145/2468356.2479527

Ishii, H. (2008). Tangible bits: Beyond pixels. In *TEI '08: Proceedings of the 2nd international conference on tangible and embedded interaction* (pp. xv-xxv). ACM. doi:10.1145/1347390.1347392

Ishii, H., Lakatos, D., Bonanni, L., & Labrune, J.-B. (2012). Radical atoms: Beyond tangible bits, toward transformable materials. *Interaction, 19*(1), 38–51. doi:10.1145/2065327.2065337

Jakobsen, M. R., Haile, Y. S., Knudsen, S., & Hornbæk, K. (2013). Information visualization and proxemics: Design opportunities and empirical findings. *IEEE Transactions on Visualization and Computer Graphics, 19*(12), 2386–2395. doi:10.1109/TVCG.2013.166 PMID:24051805

Kasahara, S., Niiyama, R., Heun, V., & Ishii, H. (2013). ExTouch: Spatially-aware embodied manipulation of actuated objects mediated by augmented reality. In *TEI '13: Proceedings of the 7th international conference on tangible, embedded and embodied interaction* (pp. 223-228). ACM. doi:10.1145/2460625.2460661

Lebeck, K., Kohno, T., & Roesner, F. (2016). How to safely augment reality: Challenges and directions. In *HotMobile '16: Proceedings of the 17th international workshop on mobile computing systems and applications* (pp. 45-50). ACM. doi:10.1145/2873587.2873595

Madsen, J. B., & Madsen, C. B. (2015). Handheld visual representation of a castle chapel ruin. *J. Comput. Cult. Herit., 9*(1), 6:1-6:18. doi:10.1145/2822899

Marquardt, N., & Greenberg, S. (2012). Informing the design of proxemic interactions. *IEEE Pervasive Computing / IEEE Computer Society [and] IEEE Communications Society, 11*(2), 14–23. doi:10.1109/MPRV.2012.15

Marquardt, N., Jota, R., Greenberg, S., & Jorge, J. A. (2011). The continuous interaction space: Interaction techniques unifying touch and gesture on and above a digital surface. In Human-Computer interaction – INTERACT 2011 (pp. 461-476). Springer Berlin Heidelberg. doi:10.1007/978-3-642-23765-2_32

Mata, F., Claramunt, C., & Juarez, A. (2011). An experimental virtual museum based on augmented reality and navigation. In *GIS '11: Proceedings of the 19th ACM SIGSPATIAL international conference on advances in geographic information systems* (pp. 497-500). ACM. doi:10.1145/2093973.2094058

Pederson, T., Janlert, L. E., & Surie, D. (2011). A situative space model for mobile mixed-reality computing. *IEEE Pervasive Computing / IEEE Computer Society [and] IEEE Communications Society*, *10*(4), 73–83. doi:10.1109/MPRV.2010.51

Roberts, J. C., Ritsos, P. D., Badam, S. K., Brodbeck, D., Kennedy, J., & Elmqvist, N. (2014). Visualization beyond the desktopthe next big thing. *IEEE Computer Graphics and Applications*, *34*(6), 26–34. doi:10.1109/MCG.2014.82 PMID:25137723

Ruiz, J., Li, Y., & Lank, E. (2011). User-defined motion gestures for mobile interaction. In *CHI '11: Proceedings of the SIGCHI conference on human factors in computing systems* (pp. 197-206). ACM. doi:10.1145/1978942.1978971

Sukenobe, K., Tateyama, Y., Lee, H., Ogi, T., Nishioka, T., & Kayahara, T. (2010). Effective contents creation for spatial AR exhibition. In *VRCAI '10: Proceedings of the 9th ACM SIGGRAPH conference on virtual-reality continuum and its applications in industry* (pp. 383-390). ACM. doi:10.1145/1900179.1900262

Wilson, A. D. (2004). TouchLight: An imaging touch screen and display for gesture-based interaction. In *ICMI '04: Proceedings of the 6th international conference on multimodal interfaces* (pp. 69-76). ACM. doi:10.1145/1027933.1027946

KEY TERMS AND DEFINITIONS

Augmented Reality: It is a live view of a real world environment, which is perceived either directly or mediated through a camera, which is augmented through a additional, superimposed information layer. The additional information layer generally provides data that is referenced to the real-world environment and through a computational device offers information beyond what is directly visible.

Body-Centric Interaction: It is a design technique that structures human computer interaction through affordances designed to accommodate the physical reality of the human body using gesture tracking, multiple displays and spatial awareness.

Embodied Interaction: It is the tangible interaction, "manipulation and sharing of meaning through engaged interaction with artifacts" (Dourish 2001) within the social realm. This notion is significantly shaped by Paul Dourish's idea of embodied interaction and constitutes an area of human computer interaction that takes aspects of social and tangible interaction into view as part of HCI.

Gesture-Based Interaction: It is referring to the communication flow between human and computer using physical movements of the body as a way of exchanging meaningful information. Gestures can be pointing gestures identifying directions or locations, symbols like the "thumbs-up" sign etc. Gestures are tracked and recognized through touch sensitive devices, camera tracking and other technologies.

Multimodal Interaction: It is the interaction between human and computer involving more than one sensory modality to support cognitive processing of the information exchange on multiple levels. Multimodal interaction can for example involve the visual sense, the haptic sense and the aural sense. Other modalities such as smell and taste are less common to be used in the field of human computer interaction.

Proxemics Interaction: Interactions involving several collocated human users that takes the spatial requirements and social relationships between the users as expressed in the distance between them into account.

Tangible-Unser Interface: It is the interaction between human and computer by means of a physical object such as a touch screen or other physical devices that are made sensitive to physical manipulation. Tangible interfaces are primarily focused on the haptic sensory modality.

Chapter 10
Supporting Motion Capture Acting Through a Mixed Reality Application

Daniel Kade
Mälardalen University, Sweden

Hakan Ürey
Koç University, Turkey

Rikard Lindell
Mälardalen University, Sweden

Oğuzhan Özcan
Koç University, Turkey

ABSTRACT

Current and future animations seek for more human-like motions to create believable animations for computer games, animated movies and commercial spots. A technology widely used technology is motion capture to capture actors' movements which enrich digital avatars motions and emotions. However, a motion capture environment poses challenges to actors such as short preparation times and the need to highly rely on their acting and imagination skills. To support these actors, we developed a mixed reality application that allows showing digital environments while performing and being able to see the real and virtual world. We tested our prototype with 6 traditionally trained theatre and TV actors. As a result, the actors indicated that our application supported them getting into the demanded acting moods with less unrequired emotions. The acting scenario was also better understood with less need of explanation than when just discussing the scenario, as commonly done in theatre acting.

INTRODUCTION

Acting for motion capture, as it is performed today, is a challenging work environment for actors and directors. Short preparation times, minimalistic scenery, limited information about characters and the performance as well as memorizing movements and spatial positions requires actors who are trained and able to highly rely on their acting and imagination skills. In many cases these circumstances can lead to performances with unnatural motions such as stiff looking and emotionless movements, as well as less believable characters.

DOI: 10.4018/978-1-5225-2616-2.ch010

Moreover, acting is an art that requires training, education and preparation to reach perfection. In todays acting for media, computer games and digital environments, these values become a factor of time and money constraints (Kade et al., 2013a). Time and budget for a production determine the choice of actors and recording schedules. This also limits the preparation time and increases the demands on actors such as being able to create a character on the spot, using improvisational acting and having good imagination skills. In our previous research, we have shown that motion capture actors face these challenges and need to be supported when good acting with short preparation times is required (Kade et al., 2013a).

As a performance and the character is often shaped during a motion capture shoot, repetitions and longer recording times can be a result when actors with less experience or acting education are used. Repetitions of scenes, explanations of scenarios and scenes result in time overhead, which takes away valuable recording time or increase the costs of a motion capture shoot.

One solution, as explained in our previous research, is to use trained actors and give them time to prepare, to create a character and to rehearse scenes in advance; as it is done in other acting areas (Kade et al., 2013a). This can be certainly considered for motion capture shoots for movies and high budget productions. However, in motion capture for computer games, commercial spots or smaller productions and animations this is commonly not a solution. This is mainly because long production times and hiring experienced and trained actors is usually not affordable for small-budget productions.

To explore the possibilities on how to support actors within a motion capture environment, we developed a head-mounted projection display in our earlier research (Kaan et al., 2014). We extended the research by setting the focus in this article to test the impact of virtual environments as acting support with six professional theatre and TV actors. Our prototype creates a virtual acting scene around the actors and provides audiovisual elements to trigger emotions and to support the actors' performances while acting for motion capture. The head-mounted projection display (HMPD), which actors are wearing, uses a laser projector in combination with a retro-reflective material as a screen to display the digital imagery. A smartphone is used as an image-processing unit and as a sensor platform, detecting head movements. A depiction of this setup can be seen in Figure 1.

The aim of our study is to suggest and validate a proof-of-concept, testing if acting with our prototype allows actors to understand the acting scene, the demands on the character and the demands on the expected performance better than without using our acting support application. We hypothesize that triggering emotions like being frightened, or similar, can be triggered through visual and audible effects and could lead to more natural and believable reactions in the actors' performances. The overall goal of our research is to provide an acting support application that can be used during acting on a motion capture shoot floor and by motion capture performers with different levels of acting training.

To prove our concept and hypothesis, we evaluated our device with six traditionally trained theatre and TV actors and compared their performances when using our prototype to the performances without any acting support. All actors performed 3 short acting scenes once with our device and once again without it.

In order to evaluate the actors' feedback and performances, we saw the importance to not only rely on one source of evaluation to get a more profound view on the results. Therefore, we chose several accepted methods in interaction design, namely card sorting (Benedek & Miner, 2002), (Travis, 2008) and interviews as means of evaluation.

The actors' feedback and our evaluations show a tendency that the time to get into the right acting moods, to understand the acting scenario and to deliver what the scene description demanded seems to be shorter when using digital acting support in comparison to discussing the scene and emotions to be played, as commonly done in theatre or motion capture acting.

Figure 1. Visualization of a user wearing our HMPD, projecting digital scenery onto a retro-reflective screen that is covering the walls around the user

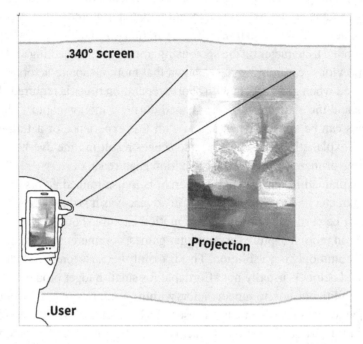

The contribution of this research lies in the conducted user tests to evaluate if virtual environments generated by a mixed reality application are useful as acting support in motion capture. We also investigate what kind of digital scenery and animations the actors consider as beneficial. Moreover, we make an effort to explore how our mixed reality application can be used in a specific and commercially used motion capture environment.

RESEARCH MOTIVATION

The industrial motivation to perform this research was to improve motion capture acting enabling actors to perform more efficiently and to improve the quality of acting results.

The academic motivations for our research are in the areas of interaction design and ubiquitous computation. Here, the interests lay in understanding the modalities of interaction between the actors and our mixed reality prototype, designed for a motion capture environment. Moreoever, having a guideline on how this interactive system can be improved, as well as identifying the user experiences of motion capture actors were of interest.

Challenges in Motion Capture Acting

Before going deeper into discussions on how we approached the task of supporting motion capture actors during their performance, it is important to understand the nature of a motion capture actor and to discuss what is different for an actor in motion capture in comparison to other acting environments.

As briefly mentioned earlier, motion capture actors face some challenges while acting for motion capture shoots. This is to some extent related to the specific acting conditions and requirements on actors. A key difference is that actors usually do not have much scenery to use for their acting or time to prepare the act. It has shown that the performances of motion capture actors are very dependent on their capability to imagine the scenery in which they are acting in and the ability to put themself into demanded roles and moods. The fact that no or only limited scenery is available for motion capture shoots is certainly not a problematic issue to overcome for experienced actors, as in many acting styles such as Mime or Blackbox acting this is a common practice. Nonetheless it becomes challenging if positions need to be remembered that should not be crossed, preparation times are not days but minutes and when characters and scenes need to be adjusted or even created on the shoot floor.

Especially, inexperienced motion capture actors are facing the issue of adapting to a motion capture environment quickly. Imagining and remembering virtual content and their positions, which were needed to perform accurate motions, posed problems to some motion capture actors, as has been discussed in previous research (Kade et al., 2013a).

Another challenge that motion capture actors are facing is when scenes are changing quickly. It is common for motion capture shoots for computer games that scenes are short in the range of seconds to a few minutes and these might change in place, character and emotions to be played. It can be the case that an actor needs to play a soldier engaging in a combat zone in one scene and a caring friend in a nice home environment in another scene. Portaying suitable motions and emotions that fit the character, and again, with very short preparation times poses a challenge to actors in a motion capture environment.

Another point that differentiates motion capture acting from other acting environments is that there is no audience or main camera to act towards. Cameras record an actor from every angle capturing every movement. This also leads to another challenge as every movement or bodily performed emotion is important and needs to fit to the character as well as look good in the game. Movements that do not fit or look good on an avatar in the game need to be repeated and sometimes be played exaggerated.

Furthermore, it needs to be meantioned that motion capture acting needs to deal with a large variety of differently trained performers with varying acting skills. For some motion capture shoots there are only recordings of locomotion needed. Movements of athletes or other professionals that know how to operate certain devices or machines like for example soldiers might require accurate locomotion but no acting in its commonly perceived meaning. In such cases, acting skills are obviously less important as the professional acts himself and performs motions and actions that he or she is used to do. On the other hand, it becomes even more interesting when professional locomotion and acting skills are needed at the same time.

Sometimes it might also be the case that the accuracy of motion is vitally important, as it would be when e.g. mimicking military motions is demanded. Then not only emotion is needed, but also correct military motions, the way a weapon is held or the way the soldier walks is vital.

Moreover, a difference to traditional acting and motion capture acting is the costume or make-up, as this does not exist in motion capture acting. Motion capture used for cinematics and games it is very common to use optical markers that are usually mounted on a tight fitting suit and even for motion capture performances helmets, caps or other technical equipment like belts for sound recordings need to be worn. It might be a bit more demanding to imagine that your fellow actor in front of you is supposed to be a 'zombie' when he is not dressed like one. Nonetheless, this might be different from actor to actor and their training.

In short, motion capture 'actors' are facing different challenges which can, depending on the act to perform or the actor´s prior skills and experiences, be quite demanding. Finding a solution to support actors of all skill levels within motion capture was therefore of importance for our research.

The Ideal Motion Capture Actor

As we have described in the section before, motion capture acting can be challenging. Therefore, we wanted to know what is required from an actor to bring the right skillset to a motion capture shoot. That is why we performed an investigation into this question in a previous study (Kade et al., 2013b). There, we asked 18 motion capture actors and 10 directors working in motion capture what skills are needed for a good motion capture performer and what this performer would need.

When asking the actors about what they need to act, some common answers were mentioned. Many actors mentioned the use of visual references, props, costumes and the demand of being provided with as much information as possible about the character, the environment and the conditions in time (Kade et al., 2013b). Most interestingly all these points mentioned can vary a lot in motion capture, as mentioned before. Commonly, motion capture shoots and scenes are very dynamic and extensive scenery or props are not provided to an actor. Even detailed information about the shoot might be handed out to the actors only a few days in advance.

Actors were also asked about their acting styles in which they are trained and are using while acting for motion capture. The answers here have shown that there is a large variety of acting styles, different professional backgrounds and trainings (Kade et al., 2013b). The actors that have done some form of acting training described their acting styles as Stanislavski-based, as an imagination-based technique from Meisner ('behaving truthfully under imaginary circumstances') or other styles and techniques from Uta Hagen, Improv acting, physical acting and personal styles that actors mentioned would work for them.

When asking which attributes a good motion capture actor needs, actors and directors seemed to point out 4 attributes in general.

First, good acting skills were mentioned to be essential to show emotions physically through the actor´s body language. Second, the actor should be physically fit. Being an athlete, stunt performer, dancer or similar might help in many cases. Third, being creative and having a good imagination was of importance. This includes knowing the subject area of the shoot and suggesting other moves as well as being able to imagine the scene. As a forth attribute it was pointed out that it would be helpful as a motion capture actor to have a certain know-how about the language and procedures as well as technicalities of motion capture shoots.

All in all, the ideal motion capture actor needs to provide a skillset that includes physical fitness, preferably the knowledge about martial arts and stunts, a profound acting education, some basic knowledge about motion capture shoot procedures and the most importantly goog imagination and Improv skills.

The Motion Capture Environment

Most professional motion capture studios, are in a way set up in a similar way. Some have a smaller acting space; others provide a large shoot floor. The camera setup as well as hardware and software vendors might differ but the general elements are roughly the same. There is a capture area in our example, seen in in Figure 2 it is a larger space. This area can be covered with lines or markers for important positions to act or to know the capture area of the cameras. Depending on the shoot, some sort of simplistic scenery can be placed on the shoot floor. These props are a way to guide the actors, to create a spatial understanding and might be used to climb or move onto or over them.

Moreover, there are cameras, most likely optical cameras, placed around the shoot floor in a setup to cover as many angles and covering as much of the shoot floor as possible. The more cameras are used, the more coverage might be achieved. The cameras are connected to computers running the motion capture software to track markers worn on an actor. The setup for this might be placed in an extra room or even right next to the shoot area.

In some motion capture studios, there might be projectors or screens that show the results of the performance in real-time, sometimes even visible to the actors, as we see in Figure 2 in the center, right position of the image. Unfortunately, actors can only use this screen while acting when it perfectly suits the situation. Otherwise, every attempt to look at the screen results in unwanted and unnatural movements.

Last but not least there will be motion directors, clients, other actors and capture staff moving on or next to the shoot floor. Directors make sure the scenes get performed as demanded, clients might just observe or even influence which shoots get taken and what might need to be changed. This is especially the case for computer games production or commercial spots. Motion capture staff will make sure that the system is running correctly and markers are in the right place. Depending on the shoots to be performed, there might be even stunt coordinators, military advisors or other specialists present.

To look into how we can actually help the stakeholders, but especially the actors, in a motion capture environment, we looked at ways of providing support that suits this specific environment and does not interfere with existing procedures, the actors' freedom of movement or more importantly the capture of the movements. Nonetheless, we wanted to create an immersive environment allowing to support movements and emotions naturally. We realised that a vast amount of technologies and research could be of thought to create immersive virtual environments. Initial ideas went from VR, AR, mixed reality, 3D sound, smell, ambient lighting, wind, temperature, haptic feedback to projected environments. Nonetheless, these technologies had to be applied to the procedures and the environment in motion capture. We

Figure 2. Professional motion capture studio in Uppsala, Sweden

decided to investigate on technologies allowing providing audiovisual content to actors while performing in a motion capture environment. Research and technologies that we see of importance are mentioned in the following section.

RELATED WORK

Technology that we are using to support actors has in different ways already been used or mentioned in research before (Harrison et al., 2011), (Kaan et al., 2014). Nonetheless, designing and implementing an immersive motion capture environment implies different research areas that need to be mentioned to understand previous and ongoing related work in areas such as: motion capture acquisition, tracking and research considering the visualization of virtual content as well as creating immersive experiences. In literature there are technologies and solutions that can be of use to work towards the goal of creating a supportive and immersive acting environment (USC, 2007), (Ürey et al., 2011), (Tauscher et al., 2010), (Andreadis et al., 2010). Research in related areas or those that we see as potentially useful are listed below.

Acting in a Virtual Environment

There have been research projects exploring the use of virtual reality to support actors with their work. In one research project, acting training and increasing the final performance was approached through sensory-motor rhythm neuro-feedback training. Actors have been exposed and trained to different lighting conditions, reactions of the audience, and the look of the theatre from the stage (Gruzelier et al., 2010).

Moreover, acting support through a virtual environment was researched as a distance rehearsal system. This system was used to study to which extent virtual reality can be used by actors and a director to rehearse their performances without being physically present (Slater et al., 2000).

Furthermore, research and explorations within the area of 'cyberdrama' (Davis, 2009), 'digital theatre' (Wotzko & Carroll, 2009) and 'narrative in cyberspace' (Murray, 19997) has been conducted. In these forms of acting, participants create the story through active engagement and interactions between technology and participants. According to other research this interactivity can be grouped into 'Navigation', 'Participation', 'Conversation' and 'Collaboration' which allows participants to steer the play and get involved before the final performance (Dixon, 2007).

Another research explained the setup of a completely virtual theatre where actors steer a virtual character in real-time from their computers with data gloves and keyboard inputs and the audience can listen to and interact with the performance and the theatre by choosing a seat in the theatre and by applauding and booing (Geigel & Schweppe, 2004).

In other research, even the use of motion capture techniques during a live theatrical performance have been used (Andreadis et al., 2010). On-stage, actors were interacting with digital avatars that were controlled by actors wearing a motion capture suit throughout the theatrical act. A screen, which was installed in front of the on-stage actors, displayed the avatars controlled by motion capture actors who performed their acting in real-time on a close-by motion capture area. Virtual scenery was displayed on a background screen, visible to the audience. In the mentioned research, the displayed scenery and avatar content around the on-stage actors was used to interact with during their performance.

Acting plays an important role in this article. The basic principles of acting on which we base our work are Stanislavski's acting principles (Stanislavski, 2013), (Sawoski, 2010). These principles were used and compared in previous work to see how they could be practically used in motion capture acting (Kade et al., 2013a). A different type of acting support, which was explored by multiple research projects, is to use virtual environments for acting rehearsals (Slater et al., 2000), (Normand et al., 2012), (Steptoe et al., 2012).

One of these research projects used six professional actors and one director who met in a shared non-immersive virtual environment to rehearse a short play (Slater et al., 2000). There, it was stated that the system was seen as supportive and allowed to create a basis for the live performance, without the actors having to meet in person. Their setup allowed achieving a better result than by only learning the script or using videoconferences. Nonetheless, these systems support the actors by using a virtual environment but do not support the actors during the performance, as it is our goal for motion capture acting.

Additionally, another research project found out that rehearsing acting performances in an immersive virtual reality environment was more successful compared to using a 2D computer screen (Gruzelier et al., 2010). This also encouraged us to test our application during a performance compared to not using any support.

The above-mentioned research projects show that theatre and acting adapts to the digital age and integrates not only technology but also audience and other participants during the play, preparations and rehearsals. Nonetheless, less research focuses on acting for motion capture or acting within a virtual environment in the sense of physically being in the virtual environment, where the environment is seen as digital acting support while acting.

Designing Immersive Environments

Designing an immersive environment includes two basic concepts, 'Immersion' and 'Presence' which have been explored and defined already (Cakmakci et al. 2004). 'Immersion' provides the functionality and usability of an immersive environment and provides the opportunities to be immersed into the virtual environment. 'Presence' creates the perception of being in the virtual environment, where 'Presence' can be seen as an "increasing function of immersion" (Slater & Wilbur, 1997).

Through the perception of 'Presence' it is discussed that behaviours in the virtual world are consistent with behaviours in the real world under similar circumstances (Slater & Wilbur, 1997). It was furthermore mentioned that 'Presence' could influence the performance of a person using a virtual environment. This statement was to mention that a well designed interface and hardware can increase 'Presence' and a "greater vividness in terms of richness of the portrayed environment" which improves task performance (Slater & Wilbur, 1997). Moreover, it is mentioned that 'Presence' is of importance to train for instance fire-fighters or surgeons within a virtual environment corresponding to behaviours in the real world. Therefore, a virtual environment must be well designed and allow for immersion and the feeling of being in the environment.

Another interesting statement is that the impact of the feeling of immersion is depended on "the application or task context and the perceptual requirements of the individual" (Slater & Wilbur, 1997). Basically this means that different aspects need to be considered when creating an immersive environment. First, it is important to create the application according to the task to be performed. So the virtual environment should focus on the most important aspects that the real world in a similar situation would resemble. When a motion capture actor is supposed to act as a musician, an aural feedback might be more important to create an immersive feeling. This might differ when visual aspects are more of importance, for example when acting on a futuristic space ship using futuristic technologies, as we assume. In other occasions a mixture of a visual and aural environment might allow to increase immersion. We could think of acting for a war zone where audiovisual scenery and effects could provide the feeling of presence. Secondly, one needs to consider that individuals are different and react to audiovisual stimulation differently. Therefore, we need to design a virtual environment allowing to create different audiovisual scenarios and conduct research to find out which virtual environments we can build that allow to support motion capture actors.

Another research in the area of presence in virtual environments states that presence can only be supported when the technologies or devices used to create the virtual environment feel non-existent to the users (Held & Durlach, 1992). This means that when creating an immersive virtual environment for motion capture acting, one needs to consider designing solutions that do not limit the actors' freedom of movement or might be uncomfortable to wear.

Considering the elements of immersion and presence in the designs for our immersive environments and to test and evaluate them must be of importance. It needs to be researched how this can be applied and created for immersive environments as acting support in motion capture.

Developing a Virtual Environment

At this point, we assume that by making virtual content visible yields a positive result in helping an actor perform. This is why we focus on exploring ways to provide the sense of vision first, before tackling other senses. Several applications that offer such an ability are already available:

A mixed reality environment, which could possibly be used in a motion capture application, is used for many industries such as military-based training environments. In this respect, some research projects are capable of providing an immersive environment without using virtual or augmented reality (VR /AR) glasses (USC, 2007). To achieve this aim, an immersive environment is created by using a mixture of real and projected objects, transparent digital flat screens and the capability to add smell and temperature changes to the environment. There is also a wide-area mixed reality application, which was realized to create an immersive virtual reality environment in which users can walk and run freely among simulated rooms, buildings and streets. In such applications, large rear-projection screens that employ digital graphics are used to depict a room's interior, a view to an outside world or a building's exterior. The applications also provide life-size projection displays with physical props and real-time 3D graphics (USC, 2007). A scenario like the one mentioned above has its limits when considering it for a motion capture shoot. Large projection walls or other props cannot be placed in front of the optical motion capture cameras because the recordings would be blocked and occlusions would occur. Setting up such a training environment requires time and planning which is not economical in a motion capture because the scenery for a motion capture shoot changes often, sometimes multiple times during a shoot day, and needs to be dynamic. Therefore, this solution cannot be used, as is, to create an immersive environment for motion capture actors with the goal to support and allow more natural acting.

A novel optical see-through head-worn display that is capable of mutual occlusions could also be considered for motion capture shoots. Here, mutual occlusion is an attribute of an augmented reality display where real objects can occlude virtual objects and virtual objects can occlude real objects (Cakmakci et al., 2004). Mutual occlusions are one of the problems in visualizing 3D content in a real world environment. Research is also conducted to test the perception of image motion during head movement (Li et al., 2009).

To make virtual environments visually immersive, another solution has been widely researched by using flat panel 3D displays (Ürey et al, 2011). Equipping an entire motion capture room with these 3D displays, or even by just using a single flat screen needs to be investigated if this might be a solution that could create an immersive acting environment and still is economic and usable in daily motion capture business.

Another method which could be of possible use to display virtual content to an actor, while acting, is by using the emerging laser based pico projector technology (Tauscher et al., 2010). These projectors are of small size (Yalcinkaya et al., 2006), (Ürey et al, 2011) and come in different technologies based on micro-LCDs, the Texas Instruments's DLP technology that uses an array of micro-electromechanical systems (MEMS), micro-mirrors and LEDs, or projectors based on laser scanning (Chellappan et al., 2010). The projected data can be shown on small screens or can be reflected to polarized video contact lenses which a user is wearing (Ürey et al, 2011). A screen, which is placed right in front of an actor might limit the actor's movement capabilities but might be applicable in some cases for motion capture shoots. Nevertheless, it would be good to answer the question on how virtual content can be shown to motion capture actors and it needs to be researched how new technologies can be applied to a motion capture scenario.

For our prototype, we use a head-mounted projection display (HMPD). Their image qualities as well as the use and evaluation of reflective materials, used as screens, have already been discussed and introduced (Ha et al., 2002). Laser projectors, as we use in our research have also been used in other research projects before (Harrison et al., 2011). We customized off-the-self products like the laser projector and stripped their hardware to make it suitable to use for a HMPD device.

Even other systems, such as CastAR (TI, 2015), could be called a similar technology and possibly used to show virtual environments to actors. Nonetheless, there were some important differences that did not suit the requirements of motion capture acting, as stated in (Kaan et al., 2014). For example, the system needs to record head movements, allow for facial motion capture and should not limit the actors in their movement capabilities or block the actors' vision. Furthermore, a system used in motion capture needs to have a solid setup that sits firm on the head of an actor, especially when stunts and athletic movements need to be performed.

The above mentioned research projects showed us the potential to support actors through virtual environments and gave us an inspiration on how to perform the user tests in terms of setup and number of participants. Nonetheless, our work differs in the point that we test the usefulness of a mixed-reality application for on-stage motion capture acting support and guidance. Therefore, we needed to research which solutions can be applied in motion capture and in which way.

OUR APPROACH TO SUPPORT MOTION CAPTURE ACTING

Our approach to support motion capture actors with their work in a virtual environment is that we show the digital environment to the actors in real-time while acting. In other words, we show the scenery to the actors and allow them to get an understanding of the environment. This also allows to use correct dimensions of the scene and to steer the actors' performance towards correct locations in a virtual scenery. We added animations and sound to the scene allowing for a better understanding of moods and emotion to be played, as well as to provide triggers that actors can use for their performances. Our application also provides a way of discussing the scene to make it easier to understand the demands of a performance.

Discussing the limitations of the acting area, the feel of the environment and locations of actions and events do not need to be imagined, when using our device. Therefore, we believe that the discussions between actors and director will be easier as both can see the scenery and the layout of the scene. The virtual environment that we built is also meant to trigger the actors' emotions and moods through sounds, animations and the provided atmosphere.

Why Not Current Solutions Such as AR or VR?

Intuitively, state-of-the-art virtual reality (VR) glasses such as the Oculus Rift (Oculus VR, 2014), CastAR (TI, 2014) or from developers such as Vuzix (Vuzix, 2014) and others, seem usable to create a visually perceivable virtual reality for motion capture. For some motion capture shoots such technology might even be usable. However, for most motion capture shoots, one would rather avoid the use of such devices. This is because of three main reasons. One, current VR glasses block important parts of the face such as eyebrows, eyelids and forehead and are therefore not usable for facial motion capture shoots. Two, the majority of motion capture shoots imply to perform bodily demanding movements or interactions with real objects or persons. VR glasses limit the actors in these shoots in terms of movement and vision of real persons and objects. Three, VR glasses impede interactions with real objects and persons. Interacting with real world objects requires very precise movements and hand-eye coordination. Current VR cannot yet provide this in a sufficient enough manner.

Furthermore, it needs to be made clear that most off-the-shelf VR systems are still powered and driven via cable connection. This further limits the usability of current VR systems for the creation of supportive and immersive motion capture environments.

A last point to consider when thinking about using VR for motion capture is that a normal motion capture shoot day could last between ca. 4-8 hours. Using a VR system for a long time, especially when performing fast movements or showing fast animations can create side effects such as motion sickness. It has been discussed in different contexts and evaluations that using VR systems can have side effects for the users (Regan & Price, 1994), (Bruck & Watters, 2009), (Cobb et al., 1999). It is therefore questionable if actors should be using such a system when it could cause, for instance nausea. These practical as well as ethical questions should be considered for VR and other systems before using them in practice.

In conclusion, using VR and AR glasses for motion capture is possible but must be considered as limited in its usability for most capture shoots. Therefore, we developed a solution from existing hardware on our own. The resulting prototype is described in more detail below.

Prototype Description

Our earlier research already suggested a head-mounted projection display as support for motion capture actors (Kaan et al., 2014). We further developed this concept and created three digital acting scenarios that specifically aim at showing acting scenery to actors and triggering emotions and moods for their performance. Moreover, the projection area was increased from covering a 4m by 2m wall to a 340-degree projection area of 3m by 4m and 2m in height. This setup was used as a basis to perform our user tests and to explore the use of mixed reality technology as acting support.

The current prototype consists of two Lithium Polymer batteries (2 x 3,7 V x 2000 mAh = 14,8 Wh) that are used as power source for the stripped down pico laser projector, SHOWWX+ from Microvision. We constructed 3D printed housings to mount the hardware parts of the projector on an adjustable headband, to protect the electronics from light shocks and from electrostatic discharge when accidently being touched. A smartphone is connected via a MHL adapter and a HDMI cable to the projector. This setup of our prototype can be seen in Figure 3.

Our prototype uses a retro-reflective cloth that works as a screen and increases the very low brightness of the laser projector from 15 lumen to a brightly perceived retro-reflected image. Using the reflective material also tends to give an impression of having the digital content spatially closer to the user as when only projecting an image to a wall. With this reflective material, we covered parts of a room to create the "acting stage", as shown in Figure 4. The room was covered with the 12m long and 2m high retro-reflective cloth in a rectangular setup. This allowed for some space of interaction and movement for the actors and covered a 340-degree projection area. The floor and ceiling were not covered with the reflective cloth no. 6101 from RB Reflektör, which provides high-quality optical properties.

User Tests

For our user tests, we invited 6 traditionally trained male theatre actors working for theatre and TV production. Five actors had 6 to 10 years of work experience and one less than 5 years. The actors were invited individually for a 1-hour session to test our prototype and to give feedback on our acting support application. Important in the selection of the actors was their traditional acting education and their experiences in theatre and TV productions. The actors were compensated for their participation.

Motion capture actors can have a wide variety of acting skills. For our user tests, we decided to use professionally trained actors as they are one type of motion capture actors and because we were looking for professional feedback from actors who had a traditional acting education. Trained actors have a clear understanding of what an actor needs and can critically access our acting support application. From this point we will adjust our findings and adapt it to motion capture actors with different levels of acting skills.

Figure 3. Picture of our HMPD consisting of (1) smartphone, (2) laser projector and (3) battery pack
As smartphone, we use a Samsung Galaxy S4+ that runs an app created in Unity 4, which processes the sensor data from the smartphone's inbuilt gyroscope detecting head movements and holds the digital environments. The created digital environments are explained in more detail in a later section.

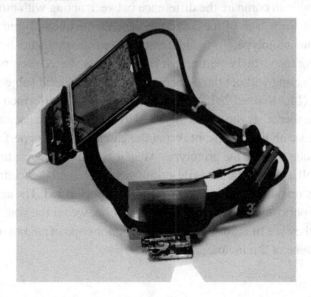

Figure 4. Acting space covered with retro-reflective cloth, showing 3 views of the nature scene from an actor's viewpoint with distortion-free images. Viewpoint 2 and 3 have been taken from a video and attached to this figure for exemplification

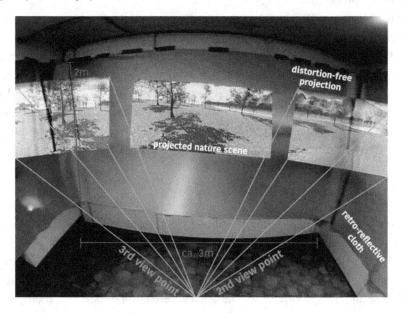

Procedure

One day before the user test session, we sent out a very short description of three scenes that we wanted the actors to perform. The descriptions briefly described the character to be played in each scene, the feelings in the scenes and a rather short story. There was no script to be learned, as we expected more of an Improv performance. The short descriptions and the Improv acting style were chosen, as this is a very common procedure in motion capture acting for computer games and animation.

On the test day, the actors were first introduced to the test environment and the idea behind our research in general. To be able to compare the difference between acting with our prototype and without, we asked the actors to perform each of the 3 scenes, which were about 2 minutes long, 2 times; once without and once with our prototype. To avoid getting false measurements by influencing the actors' feedback through showing the virtual environment first, 3 actors started their performance with the device and 3 actors started acting without the device, so we used a 'within subject design' approach with a counterbalanced order (MacKenzie, 2012). All three scenes were performed sequentially either with or without the device and thereafter the actors switched to act the three scenes again without the device if they had just performed with it. This meant that at the end all six actors performed the 3 scenes once with the prototype and once without the prototype. All actors had the chance to ask questions about the scene and their act, as well as to use the cards describing the scene and the feelings in the scene. The actors had to shape their act on the spot and no repetitions were performed. The actors decided themselves when they were ready to perform the scene. As success criteria, we set the goal to complete all six shots playing the character as they see fit according to the instructions and explanations of each scene, as well as being near the time frame of 2 minutes.

After having completed all 6 performances the actors used a card-sorting task as explained in previous research and reports (Bendek & Miner, 2001), (Travis 2008). We used 20 positive and 20 negative words, inspired from a list of product reaction cards (Bendek & Miner, 2001), (Travis 2008), which could be associated with our prototype. Then we told the actors to choose as many cards as they saw fit. Four actors choose between 4-6 cards, one actor 9 and another actor 13 cards. In previous research it was suggested to refine the selected set of cards down to 5 cards before conducting an interview on them (Bendek & Miner, 2001). We chose to skip this step as most actors chose a number of cards close to the suggested 5 cards. In the 2 cases where actors selected more cards, we picked outliers or for us unexpected cards and used them for the interview.

Finally, we conducted an interview with each actor to discuss the cards that they selected before. The interview also covered 4 extra questions about the use and benefit of the prototype for acting.

Description of Acting Scenes

It was our goal to provide three acting scenes that were distinct from each other and demanded different acting in terms of moods, feelings, environments and characters to be played. The designs of the virtual environments were modeled after scenarios that could occur for motion capture shoots for computer games and animations. In motion capture acting, actors need to be able to change moods and emotions quickly, as scenes can be short and require different acting. Therefore, we aimed at providing 3 scenarios that are, in terms of moods, emotions and acting, fairly distinct from each other. To do this we created a nature scene, a war scene and a scary scene.

All actors performed the scenes in the same order, starting with a nature environment then a war environment and at last a scary environment. Thereby, three actors were starting to act by wearing the device and three actors started to act without it first, as mentioned before.

To get a visual understanding on how the scenes looked in the virtual environment, a screenshot of all three environments can be seen in Figure 5.

Figure 5. The upper image shows the nature scene, the lower left image shows the scary scene and the lower right image shows the war scene

A more detailed description of the scenes is listed below. Similar descriptions were also sent out to the actors.

Nature Scene: The idea for this scene was to provide a nice and friendly nature environment, where the actors play a character of their choice, maybe even play themselves. The actors were basically free in how they interpret and use the environment. The task was to project joy, happiness and the friendship. The environment was rather scenic, only the sound of birds was played through the speakers of the mobile phone. Evaluations have shown that some actors had no problems with this task when wearing our prototype, others mentioned that it was not guided enough and others mentioned that it would restrict their imagination.

War Scene: Here, the actors were given the task to play a soldier in an army camp located in a desert environment. It was explained that the army base is on high alert and will be attacked shortly. The goal for the actors was to act out the tension, alertness and stress before the attack and then command other soldier to get back in line after the attack. In this environment, other soldiers were animated, sounds supporting the storyline were added and animations and sounds for explosions and a helicopter were set up to create a more guided and animated scenario. Here the actors performed the demanded moods and reacted to the animations almost naturally. Nonetheless, some actors mentioned that gun fire and explosions were after a while reoccurring and were not useful for their acting anymore. However, as initial triggers and simple background sounds and animations the set up worked well to trigger natural reaction and to get the actors into their acting moods.

Scary Scene: In this scene, the actor was placed in a night environment, near a cemetery located in a forest. For this scene we provided more detailed information about the story and the character. We explained that the character found a hidden cemetery in the woods by chance, after his dog ran away. Then the character finds the dog barking from inside the cemetery and needs to try to get the dog out of there. Here, we wanted the actor to play a character that felt scared, spooked and only wants to leave the strange place but pushes himself or herself to overcome the fear of the environment and to get the dog back. This scenario was rated by most of the actors as their favourite scenario out of the three. This was mostly because the story was more described and easier to relate to. In this scenario, there were almost no animations; only the sound of a barking was hearable.

Card Sorting

As one form of user evaluation, we performed a card-sorting task. Through the card-sorting task we set a basis for the interviews and allowed the actors to express their experiences and feelings when using our device in a different form. We provided 20 cards with positive words and 20 cards with negative words that could be associated with our device. The actors picked the cards that they found suitable. The result of this task is shown in Figure 6 as a word cloud where the size of the words is an indicator of the number of chosen words. All chosen words from the six actors are depicted in this figure.

The actors mostly picked positive cards, 2 cards were from the negative set of cards: stressful and boring. This was very interesting for us and was then discussed in more detail during the interviews that we performed. It was also interesting to see which cards the actors picked most, which were: motivating, entertaining, simple, exciting and fun. These cards were also further discussed during the interviews.

Figure 6. Word cloud of the results from our card-sorting task

Figure 7. Actor performing card-sorting task

INTERVIEWS

The first part of the interview started by asking each actor about the cards that they picked from the card sorting task to get a better understanding about the actor's thoughts on our application. Thereafter, we asked 4 additional questions about acting with the device. The questions were as follows:

1. Was there a difference for you when acting with the HMDP in comparison to acting without it?
2. Did you feel more immersed in the acting environment when using the HMPD?
3. Did our application benefit you with your acting?
4. Did it help your imagination when seeing the digital acting environment?

In the following we will discuss only the unexpected and instructive findings from the interviews and would like to start by looking at some answers that the actors gave us when asking why they picked certain cards from the card-sorting task.

One actor picked the card 'boring' and explained that he chose the card because the first nature scenario was too boring for him. The actor would have liked to have more action or animation in this environment to support his acting. Another actor chose the card 'stressful'. Here, the actor explained that there was almost too much action in the war scenario so that it felt stressful to be in the mixed reality environment. Another actor picked the card 'engaging' and mentioned that the application "was more useful when enjoying and letting it go". He also mentioned that it was 'exciting' to use the device because the acting world that actors would generally create in their minds was already there. Moreover, four actors picked the card 'motivating' and explained that it was easy to get into the right acting mood when using the device. One actor mentioned here that it was motivating because it was "easy to get into the mood and it saves time."

The above feedback shows that there were different reactions to our 3 generic scenarios. We are aware that the scenes were not adjusted to the specific skills of the actors and directing was kept to a minimum. This was believed to give a clearer feedback to how useful our device is for acting support and to indicate potential issues.

From the 4 additional questions asked in the interview, we also got the reactions that our application is a tool that helps the actors and directors to provide a better way of communicating the scene and the act. One actor mentioned that in classic acting methods, this step needs a lot of explaining and time, which was made easier with our mixed reality application. Furthermore, the same actor added that he is a 'visual learner' and therefore it helped him for the act as well as to create strong feelings when using our head-mounted projection display.

Some actors also mentioned in their critique that our application would not help in terms of 'imagination' which is an acting term describing how an actor can adapt to a performance, an imaginative environment, the conditions and the events happening to a character (Kade et al., 2013b), (Sawoski, 2010). The free interpretation that is given from e.g. theater acting is taken away and the act is in one way already directed. Balancing this interpretation should be guided by a director but for some motion capture shoots, a more framed performance with less artistic interpretation is wanted. Therefore, it could be interesting to explore the use of our application as a way to guide such a performance. Another actor added that, even it is breaking the imagination of an actor; it was helpful to get into the right acting mood at the same time. This is an interesting finding for us because here we see a potential difference between professionally trained actors and other actors that might perform in motion capture acting, as the professional actors prefer less guidance through the device and only need key elements to use their artistic freedom to its full potential. For other motion capture actors, we assume that more guidance would help their act but this must be confirmed in future research.

What was also pointed out during the interview is that sounds need to be used carefully and should not be played continuously or reoccurring if they are not directly meant to trigger moods or emotions. One actor in particular was displeased and suggested to only play sounds or animations in key situations when some act or emotion should be performed.

In our application we used reoccurring sounds, especially in the war zone environment, which was perceived by the actors as rather disturbing than helpful.

Additionally, an actor mentioned that our device could be useful for acting preparation, to create the character and for testing the actors' own reactions to uncommon acting environments e.g. when being afraid of heights or when being in a war zone.

CONCLUSION

A key question for us, when performing this research, was to understand if our mixed reality application is useful as acting support or not.

From the actors' feedback we have extracted that our mixed reality application helps their acting while being on stage and supports them to get into the right acting mood as well as to create the character. Nonetheless, we have also encounter some design issues in parts of our application, as argued in the following.

In other research, Stanislavski (2013) was cited by mentioning "when communicating in virtual environments, actors must establish emphasis and emotion. Hence, the interface should not obstruct natural interaction by becoming an unwanted mental or a physical diversion for the actor" (Stanislavski, 2013). After our user tests, we agree to this statement. What we thought to be a simple to act scene, like the nature environment or a well-guided scene like the war zone scene, turned out to have some issues that got the actors distracted and restricted them in their artistic freedom. In the nature scene, we realized that there needs to be a problem to solve and a clear story or description of objectives to provide a useful scenario for actors. In the war scenario we thought that providing animations and sounds would guide the actors, set the scene and surprise the actors. This worked only to a certain extent. The first occurrences of e.g. an exploding bomb made the actors almost naturally duck their heads, as it came unexpected. Our encoded problem was that we filled the scene with too many sounds and animations that were also repeated after a while. Retrospectively, we think that less action would have provided a better result. Only key actions or trigger points need visual or audible feedback, as additional elements might lead to a less immersive experience or even limit the actors' imagination and creativity.

Most actors expressed their enjoyment about the scary environment as they were given clear character instructions, a story and an objective that they were able to easily relate to. The environment created the look and feel of a scary place and the only sound played was the barking of the dog.

From the user test results, we have also seen that the level of immersion was mediocre. Nonetheless we would argue that actors have been immersed into the environment, even if just to a mediocre extent. Witmer and Singer explained that being enveloped by, included in, and interacting with a virtual environment leads to or is immersion (Witmer & Singer, 1998). These points were also given for our user tests but we see the need to explore immersion and presence in a more detailed study with notions of sensory and imaginative immersion as well as involvement.

One actor also mentioned that our device could be used for acting rehearsals. To explore these possibilities, we looked at other research. There it has been suggested that "for virtual rehearsals to successfully complement traditional practice, the virtual environment must be mechanically transparent yet still mimic the real world" (Reeve, 2000). We see this statement fit in a way, as we create an acting environment that digitally provides the background, the environment, the scene and helps setting the mood of the scene. At the same time, we allow using real props or human and digital actors as a form of interaction. We believe that, even our device was not intentionally build for rehearsals, it could be used for acting training, preparation and getting familiar with the environment before the actual performance, as it was suggested by one actor.

In acting or also in motion capture acting, a 'performance' can mean a variety of things. It could be a traditional theatre performance with voice and body acting, a dance performance, mime acting or performing motions like walking, jumping or alike. Even for this variety of a 'performance', we see our application as supportive for actors. This is because our setup allows for flexibility in agility, is small in size, does not cover the eyes and allows seeing virtual content while moving around in a confined space. This gives the opportunity to provide different kinds of acting support. In our case, we showed a virtual acting environment that was meant to show scenery and provide an understanding of the atmosphere. Another way of showing acting support could be by showing way points, basically outlining where the actors should move or perform certain movements. Moreover, the director could be able to interact with the digital environment and trigger events. The cooperation and interaction between actor and director could allow for an even more supportive application, which we are developing for future research.

From the actors' feedback, we extract that our mixed reality application can be used for acting support and we have shown how our provided virtual environments could be improved and used better as acting support. Therefore, we believe that this research provides a basis for an acting support application and for further research to provide an acting support application that can be used during acting on a motion capture shoot floor and by 'actors' with different levels of acting training.

Lessons Learned

Through this study we have learned that our application is useful as acting support while acting on stage, helps to get the actors into the right acting mood and helps to understand and prepare the character as well as the act.

We have also experienced that the slightest distractions through hardware related issues should be avoided. Problems like a headband that does not fit the actors head properly, a part of the prototype bothering the actor when wearing the projector as well as when too much of the projector would be in the field of view of an actor. We did not have these issues in this research but experienced them in previous research projects. These are issues that can be simple to solve but we meantion them here to make the point that the wearing comfort of a device is important to be accepted by the actor and to allow creating a more immersive environment.

Moreover, we learnt that too many repeated animations and sounds can be counterproductive. The application should only support the actors to trigger actions or the actors' moods and performances. On the other hand, when an environment is too simplistic and has no gain for the actor during a performance, the usefulness of wearing the device might be questionable, like we have experienced with the Nature environment. Nonetheless, this is very dependant on the actors' preferencanes. Each actor gave us slightly different views on this environment. What could be of thought for an environment that is purely meant as a background scenery and to allow understanding the initial emotions to be played, is that actors could explore the environment before the shoot and then does not use the device during the shoot. Another option would be to enrich the environment with more opjects and triggers needed for the acting.

Another point to mention is that the acting scenery does not have to be modeled with high details, it is sufficient to be able to show important locations, the basic scenery and to give the actors a grasp of what moods and actions need to be performed. This also helps the motion capture process, as time to create a complete game environment or digital scenery is time consuming or simply not available at the time of a motion capture shoot. Keeping the details of the virtual environment low also helps to comply with the currently limited processing power of a smartphone.

Finally, we have observed that performances with our acting support application were more guided than without using it and allowed actors to focus more on the demanded emotions. The performances seemed to be more compliant with the descriptions given to the actors before. Less extra interpretations from the actors were included in their acting.

Current Weak Points

From this research we experienced a few weak points with the current state of our mixed reality application used for supporting motion capture actors' performances. These weak points need improvements in software, hardware and in adding new features.

A simple software adjustment is that visuals, animations and sounds need to be carefully chosen and placed. Sounds and animations should not be overdone and only be used to trigger actors' performances or emotions.

In our current prototype version, the director has not much control over the events in the virtual environments. For the interaction between actor and director during a shoot but also to ensure a smoother integration into the motion capture process, it would helpful to allow wireless access for the director to for example trigger certain events or change scenarios as needed, without physically controlling the smartphone. This would allow directors to trigger for example an explosion at a time when they see it fit to the acting and the mental state of the actor to get the most out of an actor's performance.

Our hardware prototype still allows for improvements. One is the field of view is currently limited to the field of view given by the projector. It would create an even more immersive environment when the field of view could be increased by factor 2 or 2.5. This is certainly a task that we want to address in future research.

Another weak point can be addressed when improving the ergonomics or more directly, the housing of our prototype. Here, especially the location of the smartphone was mentioned to be slightly impractical. A more centered position would be more ergonomic. Also, the housing can be made more robust to protect the electronics better.

A vision on how we see the hardware issus to be addressed can be seen in the next section.

Future Design Vision

As mentioned previously, the design of our prototype needs to be improved for next iterations. In Figure 8 you can see an initial CAD drawing which shows our current design vision.

The design still contains an adjustable headband which will be placed around an actor's head and holds the prototype in position. All components are now centered. The projector is still mounted on the forehead and the other componentts such as battery, smartphone and MHL adapter are placed in a compartment on the top head. Parts of the prototype that touch the actors head will be padded. Through these improvements we hope to achive a more ergonomic design which is more comfortable to wear for the actors, makes the prototype more robust and eliminates some of our current weak points.

Figure 8. Future vision of the prototype

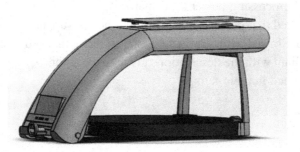

FUTURE WORK

As our prototype was developed to be used for a variety of 'actors' in a motion capture setup, we are planning to use our insights from this paper to explore how actors with different levels of acting training perceive our acting support application. Furthermore, we see the interaction between director and actor as important and want to explore this by giving the director interactive and real-time control of the virtual environment. This might allow to simplify explaining the act, the scenario and could trigger more natural reactions and movements.

Another future plan is to improve the field-of-view of the projector to provide an even more immersive experience by adding a lens infront of the projector. Depending on the optical calculations and available lens solutions, we hope to increase the field of view by the factor of 2.

Our developed mixed reality prototype has been proven to show its potential as an acting support application but also showed potential to be used as a rehearsal or motion capture shoot preparing tool. Nonetheless, we see some improvements that we believe will increase the usability and experience with our mixed reality application.

During our research, we came to the point of making the decision to decouple our application from the advanced tracking capabilities of a motion capture system. This was because he had temporarily no access to the system but also allowed for a more mobile and versatile prototype. On the other hand, this has the drawback that physically moving in a virtual environment is less precise when using the inertial sensors of a smartphone. We encountered, as others before (Martin et al., 2010), that the accelerometer sensor on the mobile phone delivers data that is too noisy to be used for accurate measurements. Therefore, an improvement would be to wirelessly transmit positional data from the motion capture system into the Unity game engine to provide smoother interactions and natural walking as well as movements that could increase the experience and immersion when using our motion capture acting application.

A continuation of our idea to allow the director to steer and guide the actors during their performances through altering virtual content and triggering events is believed to increase the usefulness of our application. Therefore, we see a potential to further develop and explore this idea. This could allow directors to e.g. use wind, sounds and visual effects to trigger even more life-like and believable motions and emotions performed by an actor. Moreover, it could lead to useful discussion to create a better understanding of the shoot between actor and director.

REFERENCES

Aksit, K., Kade, D., Özcan, O., & Ürey, H. (2014). Head-worn Mixed Reality Projection Display Application. In *Proceedings of the 11th Conference on Advances in Computer Entertainment Technology*. ACM.

Andreadis, A., Hemery, A., Antonakakis, A., Gourdoglou, G., Mauridis, P., Christopoulos, D., & Karigiannis, J. N. (2010). Real-time motion capture technology on a live theatrical performance with computer generated scenery. *Informatics (pci), 14th panhellenic conference on. IEEE*, 148–152. doi:10.1109/PCI.2010.14

Benedek, J., & Miner, T. (2002). Measuring Desirability: New methods for evaluating desirability in a usability lab setting. *Proceedings of Usability Professionals Association, 2003*, 8–12.

Bruck, S., & Watters, P. A. (2009). Estimating cybersickness of simulated motion using the simulator sickness questionnaire (ssq): A controlled study. In *Computer Graphics, Imaging and Visualization, CGIV'09. Sixth International Conference on*, (pp. 486–488). IEEE.

Cakmakci, O., Ha, Y., & Rolland, J. P. (2004). A compact optical see-through head-worn display with occlusion support. *Proceedings of the 3rd IEEE/ACM International Symposium on Mixed and Augmented Reality*, 16–25. doi:10.1109/ISMAR.2004.2

Chellappan, E., Erden, E., & Urey, H. (2010). Laser-based displays: A review. *Applied Optics, 49*(25), 79–98. doi:10.1364/AO.49.000F79 PMID:20820205

Cobb, S. V. G., Nichols, S., Ramsey, A., & Wilson, J. R. (1999). Virtual reality-induced symptoms and effects (vrise). *Presence (Cambridge, Mass.), 8*(2), 169–186. doi:10.1162/105474699566152

Davis, S. (2009). *Interactive drama using cyberspaces*. Drama Education with Digital Technology.

Dixon, S. (2007). *Digital performance: a history of new media in theater, dance, performance art, and installation*. MIT Press.

Geigel, J., & Schweppe, M. (2004). Theatrical story telling in a virtual space. *Proceedings of the 1st ACM workshop on Story representation, mechanism and context*, 39–46. doi:10.1145/1026633.1026642

Gruzelier, J., Inoue, A., Smart, R., Steed, A., & Steffert, T. (2010). Acting performance and flow state enhanced with sensory-motor rhythm neurofeedback comparing ecologically valid immersive VR and training screen scenarios. *Neuroscience Letters, 480*(2), 112–116. doi:10.1016/j.neulet.2010.06.019 PMID:20542087

Harrison, C., Benko, H., & Wilson, A. D. (2011). OmniTouch: wearable multitouch interaction everywhere. *Proceedings of the 24th annual ACM symposium on User interface software and technology*, 441–450.

Held, R. M., & Durlach, N. I. (1992). Telepresence, presence: Teleoperators and virtual environments. MIT Press.

Hua, H., Gao, C., & Rolland, J. P. (2002). *Imaging properties of retro-reflective materials used in head-mounted projective* displays (HMPDs). In *AeroSense 2002* (pp. 194–201). International Society for Optics and Photonics. doi:10.1117/12.478871

James, J., Ingalls, T., Qian, G., Olsen, L., Whiteley, D., Wong, S., & Rikakis, T. (2006). Movement-based interactive dance performance. *Proceedings of the 14th annual ACM international conference on Multimedia*, 470–480. doi:10.1145/1180639.1180733

Kade, D., Özcan, O., & Lindell, R. (2013a). Towards Stanislavski-based Principles for Motion Capture Acting in Animation and Computer Games. *Proceedings of CONFIA 2013, International Conference in Illustration and Animation*, 277– 292.

Kade, D., Özcan, O., & Lindell, R. (2013b). An Immersive Motion Capture Environment. *Proceedings of the ICCGMAT 2013 International Conference on Computer Games, Multimedia and Allied Technology*, 73, 500-506.

Li, L., Adelstein, B. D., & Ellis, S. R. (2009). *Perception of image motion during head movement*. New York: ACM Press.

MacKenzie, I. S. (2012). *Human-computer interaction: An empirical research perspective*. Newnes.

Martin, E., Vinyals, O., Friedland, G., & Bajcsy, R. (2010). Precise indoor localization using smart phones. *Proceedings of the international conference on Multimedia*, 787–790.

Meador, W. S., Rogers, T. J., ONeal, K., Kurt, E., & Cunningham, C. (2004). Mixing dance realities: Collaborative development of live-motion capture in a performing arts environment. *Computers in Entertainment*, 2(2), 12–12. doi:10.1145/1008213.1008233

Murray, J. H. (1997). *Hamlet on the holodeck: The future of narrative in cyberspace*. Simon and Schuster.

Normand, J.-M., Spanlang, B., Tecchia, F., Carrozzino, M., Swapp, D., & Slater, M. (2012). Full body acting rehearsal in a networked virtual environment - A case study. *Presence (Cambridge, Mass.)*, 21(2), 229–243. doi:10.1162/PRES_a_00089

Oculus, V. R. (2014). *Next-gen virtual reality*. Retrieved April 24, 2014, from http://www.oculusvr.com/rift

Reeve, C. (2000). Presence in virtual theater. *Presence (Cambridge, Mass.)*, 9(2), 209–213. doi:10.1162/105474600566727

Regan, E. C., & Price, K. R. (1994). The frequency of occurrence and severity of side-effects of immersion virtual reality. *Aviation, Space, and Environmental Medicine*. PMID:8074626

Sawoski, P. (2010). The Stanislavski system growth and methodology. Santa Monica College.

Slater, M., Howell, J., Steed, A., Pertaub, D.-P., & Garau, M. (2000). Acting in virtual reality. *Proceedings of the third international conference on Collaborative virtual environments*, 103–110. doi:10.1145/351006.351020

Slater, M., & Wilbur, S. (1997). A framework for immersive virtual environments (five): Speculations on the role of presence in virtual environments. *Presence (Cambridge, Mass.)*, 6(6), 603–616. doi:10.1162/pres.1997.6.6.603

Stanislavski, C. (2013). *Building a character*. A&C Black.

Steptoe, W., Normand, J.-M., Oyekoya, O., Pece, F., Giannopoulos, E., Tecchia, F., & Slater, M. et al. (2012). Acting rehearsal in collaborative multimodal mixed reality environments. *Presence (Cambridge, Mass.)*, *21*(4), 406–422. doi:10.1162/PRES_a_00109

Tauscher, J., Davis, W. O., Brown, D., Ellis, M., Ma, Y., Sherwood, M. E., & Coy, J. W. et al. (2010). Evolution of mems scanning mirrors for laser projection in compact consumer electronics. In *MOEMS-MEMS* (pp. 75940A–75940A). International Society for Optics and Photonic. doi:10.1117/12.843095

Technical Illusions. (2015). *CastAR*. Retrieved March 18, 2015, from http://castar.com

Travis, D. (2008). *Measuring satisfaction: Beyond the usability questionnaire*. Retrieved April 12, 2015, from http://www.userfocus.co.uk/articles/satisfaction.html

University of Southern California. (2007). *Flatworld project*. Retrieved April 24, 2014, from http://ict.usc.edu/projects/flatworld

Urey, H., Chellappan, K. V., Erden, E., & Surman, P. (2011). State of the art in stereoscopic and autostereoscopic displays. *Proceedings of the IEEE*, *99*(4), 540–555. doi:10.1109/JPROC.2010.2098351

Vuzix. (2014). *Vuzix*. Retrieved April 24, 2014, from http://www.vuzix.com

Witmer, B. G., & Singer, M. J. (1998). Measuring presence in virtual environments: A presence questionnaire. *Presence (Cambridge, Mass.)*, *7*(3), 225–240. doi:10.1162/105474698565686

Wotzko, R., & Carroll, J. (2009). *Digital theatre and online narrative*. Drama Education with Digital Technology.

Yalcinkaya, A. D., Ürey, H., Brown, D., Montague, T., & Sprague, R. (2006). Two-axis electromagnetic microscanner for high resolution displays. *Microelectromechanical Systems Journalism*, *15*(4), 786–794.

ADDITIONAL READING

Barrie, P., Komninos, A., & Mandrychenko, O. (2009, September). A pervasive gesture-driven augmented reality prototype using wireless sensor body area networks. In *Proceedings of the 6th International Conference on Mobile Technology, Application & Systems* (p. 61). ACM. doi:10.1145/1710035.1710096

Benford, S., & Giannachi, G. (2011). *Performing mixed reality*. The MIT Press.

Bolas, M., & Krum, D. M. (2010). Augmented reality applications and user interfaces using head-coupled near-axis personal projectors with novel retroreflective props and surfaces. In *Pervasive 2010 Ubiprojection Workshop*.

Freeman, M., Champion, M., & Madhavan, S. (2009). Scanned laser pico-projectors: Seeing the big picture (with a small device). *Optics and Photonics News*, *20*(5), 28–34. doi:10.1364/OPN.20.5.000028

Guillaumée, M., Vahdati, S. P., Tremblay, E., Mader, A., Bernasconi, G., Cadarso, V. J., & Moser, C. et al. (2014). Curved holographic combiner for color head worn display. *Journal of Display Technology*, *10*(6), 444–449. doi:10.1109/JDT.2013.2277933

Hendrix, C., & Barfield, W. (1996). The sense of presence within auditory virtual environments. *Presence (Cambridge, Mass.)*, *5*(3), 290–301. doi:10.1162/pres.1996.5.3.290

Hugues, O., Fuchs, P., & Nannipieri, O. (2011). New augmented reality taxonomy: Technologies and features of augmented environment. In *Handbook of augmented reality* (pp. 47–63). Springer New York. doi:10.1007/978-1-4614-0064-6_2

Iwata, H. (1999, March). Walking about virtual environments on an infinite floor. In Virtual Reality, 1999. Proceedings., IEEE (pp. 286-293). IEEE. doi:10.1109/VR.1999.756964

Kade, D., Akşit, K., Ürey, H., & Özcan, O. (2015). Head-mounted mixed reality projection display for games production and entertainment. *Personal and Ubiquitous Computing*, *19*(3-4), 509–521. doi:10.1007/s00779-015-0847-y

King, B. A., & Paulson, L. D. (2007). Motion capture moves into new realms. *Computer*, *9*(40), 13–16. doi:10.1109/MC.2007.326

Kolasinski, E. M. (1995). Simulator Sickness in Virtual Environments (No. ARI-TR-1027). Army Research Insitute for the behavioural and social sciences Alexandria, VA.

Konijn, E. (2000). *Acting emotions* (p. 208). Amsterdam University Press. doi:10.5117/9789053564448

Lee, S. P., Qui, T. C. T., Loy, S. C., & Pensyl, W. R. (2009, October). Haptic interaction in augmented reality. In *Proceedings of the 17th ACM international conference on Multimedia* (pp. 975-976). ACM.

Liu, Y., Storring, M., Moeslund, T. B., Madsen, C. B., & Granum, E. (2003, October). Computer vision based head tracking from re-configurable 2d markers for ar. In *Mixed and Augmented Reality, 2003. Proceedings. The Second IEEE and ACM International Symposium on* (pp. 264-267). IEEE.

McGill, M., Boland, D., Murray-Smith, R., & Brewster, S. (2015, April). A dose of reality: overcoming usability challenges in VR head-mounted displays. In *Proceedings of the 33rd Annual ACM Conference on Human Factors in Computing Systems* (pp. 2143-2152). ACM.

Meador, W. S., Rogers, T. J., ONeal, K., Kurt, E., & Cunningham, C. (2004). Mixing dance realities: Collaborative development of live-motion capture in a performing arts environment. [CIE]. *Computers in Entertainment*, *2*(2), 12–12. doi:10.1145/1008213.1008233

Menache, A. (2000). *Understanding motion capture for computer animation and video games*. Morgan kaufmann.

Milgram, P., & Kishino, F. (1994). A taxonomy of mixed reality visual displays. *IEICE Transactions on Information and Systems*, *77*(12), 1321–1329.

Ohta, Y., & Tamura, H. (2014). *Mixed reality: Merging real and virtual worlds*. Springer Publishing Company, Incorporated.

Satoh, K., Uchiyama, S., & Yamamoto, H. (2004, November). A head tracking method using bird's-eye view camera and gyroscope. In *Proceedings of the 3rd IEEE/ACM International Symposium on Mixed and Augmented Reality* (pp. 202-211). IEEE Computer Society. doi:10.1109/ISMAR.2004.3

Slater, M., & Usoh, M. (1994). Body centred interaction in immersive virtual environments. *Artificial life and virtual reality, 1*, 125-148.

Sonoda, T., Endo, T., Kawakami, N., & Tachi, S. (2005, July). X'talVisor: full open type head-mounted projector. In *ACM SIGGRAPH 2005 Emerging technologies* (p. 32). ACM. doi:10.1145/1187297.1187330

Souman, J. L., Giordano, P. R., Frissen, I., Luca, A. D., & Ernst, M. O. (2010). Making virtual walking real: Perceptual evaluation of a new treadmill control algorithm. [TAP]. *ACM Transactions on Applied Perception, 7*(2), 11. doi:10.1145/1670671.1670675

Spanlang, B., Normand, J. M., Giannopoulos, E., & Slater, M. (2010, November). A first person avatar system with haptic feedback. In *Proceedings of the 17th ACM Symposium on Virtual Reality Software and Technology* (pp. 47-50). ACM. doi:10.1145/1889863.1889870

Turner, P., Turner, S., & Burrows, L. (2013). Creating a sense of place with a deliberately constrained virtual environment. *International Journal of Cognitive Performance Support, 1*(1), 54–68. doi:10.1504/IJCPS.2013.053554

Zordan, V. B., & Hodgins, J. K. (2002, July). Motion capture-driven simulations that hit and react. In *Proceedings of the 2002 ACM SIGGRAPH/Eurographics symposium on Computer animation* (pp. 89-96). ACM. doi:10.1145/545261.545276

KEY TERMS AND DEFINITIONS

Actor: We consider an 'actor' as someone who is acting for a motion capture shoot. This 'actor' can have different skills and must not necessarily have received acting training of some sort.

Augmented Reality (AR): An augmented reality superimposes digitally created content onto the real world. This allows a person using AR to see both; the real and the digital world. Usually AR uses some means of connecting real world objects with the augmented reality.

Avatar: An avatar is usually the representation of a person or character in a digital or virtual environment. In our definition an avatar is simply a digital character.

Field of View (FOV): In our research the field of view determines the view angles that our mixed reality prototype is able to project.

Mixed Reality (MR): Mixed reality merges the real world with the virtual world. This can be achieved with different means and technologies for different purposes.

Stakeholder: Stakeholders are persons involved or considered within the design of a solution. In our research, stakeholders are mainly actors, directors, motion capture staff and researchers.

Virtual Reality (VR): A virtual reality creates a reality that is not real. The vision of a person is in many cases occluded by digitally created content or the person is placed in a virtual reality environment. Synonyms are: virtual world, virtual environment, and cyberspace.

Chapter 11
Facebook, Tele–Collaboration, and International Access to Technology in the Classroom

Karen Woodman
Queensland University of Technology, Australia

Vasilia Kourtis-Kazoullis
University of the Aegean, Greece

ABSTRACT

This chapter explores the results of a study using the well-known social networking site, Facebook, to investigate graduate education students' perceptions on the use of technologies in classrooms around the world. This study was part of a larger project exploring tele-collaboration and the use of online discussions involving graduate students in an online program based in Australia, and students in a graduate Education program at a regional university in Greece. Findings reveal many similarities between the situations and perceptions of the participants from the different countries. They also demonstrated that even when technologies were available in schools, participants identified a critical need for professional development to increase teachers' use of ICT. These findings are relevant to researchers, educators and policy development in terms of implementation of ICT and/or social networking in the language classroom.

INTRODUCTION

To date, there appears to have been little research on how teachers use Facebook, either privately or in educational contexts, and whether the characteristics and trends in Facebook use identified for students generalize to teachers. There has also not been much research on how Facebook itself can be used to collect data, based on naturalistic discussions of topics of interest to users, such as the use of technology by teachers. This chapter attempts to address these research gaps by exploring how Facebook discussions can facilitate discussions by teachers, who are also graduate students in Australia and Greece, about similarities and differences in access and use of technologies in their classrooms.

DOI: 10.4018/978-1-5225-2616-2.ch011

Background

Facebook is a widely used social networking site with over 1.11 billion users (Wikipedia, 2013). Facebook is the most popular social networking site in Canada, the UK, and the US, with Facebook penetration highest in North America, followed by the Middle East/Africa, Latin America, Europe and Asia-Pacific (Wikipedia, 2013). With a few exceptions (e.g. Peoples Republic of China, Iran), Facebook can be accessed globally for free by anyone who has internet access and a Facebook account.

The site works with a user registering, then creating a personal profile, to which they can add other users as 'friends', with whom they can then exchange messages, chat, etc. Additionally, users may join common-interest user groups, organized by workplace, school or college, or other characteristics, and categorize their friends into lists such as "People From Work" or "Close Friends" (Wikipedia, 2012). In general, privacy can be maintained as the Facebook page owner has control over who is a 'friend', and what kind of access they have to content on the page.

In this study, we propose that these features, together with the widespread familiarity of many students with the specific site and its functions, as well as the fact that it is free to access, could position Facebook as an appropriate option for a 'virtual learning environment', by facilitating interactions and telle-collaboration between teachers in diverse teaching and learning environments.

Despite the relative newness of Facebook, which was only launched in 2004, there has been an explosion of research about various facets of Facebook since approx. 2009, when widespread uptake began to be seen. Research about Facebook spans a number of different fields, from psychology to education to business and medicine. Recent research includes analysis of the types of people who use Facebook (Carpenter et al., 2011; Gangadharbatia, 2010; Gosling et al., 2011; Orr et al., 2009; Ross et al., 2009), how different groups use Facebook (Attia et al., 2011; Ellison et al., 2007; Hum et al., 2011; Nosko et al., 2010; Park et al., 2009; Pempek et al., 2009; Waters et al., 2009), how Facebook can or is used in education (Eyesenbach, 2008; Goodband et al., 2011; Harrison & Thomas, 2009; Hew, 2011; Kabilan et al., 2010; Madge et al., 2009; Maranto & Barton, 2010; Pempek et al., 2009; Roblyer et al., 2010; Yan et al., 2010), privacy issues with Facebook (Qi & Edgar-Nevill, 2011; Smith & Kidder, 2010; Weir et al., 2011), and even content analyses of Facebook pages (Glyn et al., 2012; Hum et al., 2011).

Research indicates that Facebook use varies by both the type of user, as well as by purpose or use (Carpenter et al., 2011; Gangadharbatia, 2010; Gosling et al., 2011; Orr et al., 2009; Ross et al.,2009). Although the use of Facebook for educational purpose is relatively new, interest in this phenomenon is increasing (Eyesenbach, 2008; Goodband et al., 2011; Harrison & Thomas, 2009; Hew, 2011; Kabilan et al., 2010; Madge et al., 2009; Maranto & Barton, 2010; Pempek et al., 2009; Roblyer et al., 2010; Yan et al., 2010). Research on the use of Facebook in educational contexts has explored a number of groups in terms of their use of Facebook, although the majority of research has focused on student users.

To date, considerably less research appears to have been done on how teachers use or perceive Facebook themselves (personally and/or pedagogically), although some research has suggested students reported higher levels of teacher trustworthiness and caring attributes when the teacher provided more information about themselves (e.g., self-disclosure) on shared Facebook pages (Hew, 2011). Research on Facebook in educational contexts also suggests considerable individual variation in the type and amount of use by individuals, but has not yet examined these issues in detail. To date, there appears to have been little research on how teachers use Facebook themselves, either privately or in educational contexts, and whether the characteristics and trends in Facebook use identified for students generalize to teachers.

This chapter attempts to address this research gap by exploring how teachers, who are also graduate students in Australia and Greece, perceive similarities and differences in access and use of technologies in their classrooms.

USING FACEBOOK FOR RESEARCH ON THE USE OF ICT IN THE LANGUAGE CLASSROOM

Issues, Controversies, Problems

To date, it appears that much of the research on ICT and/or social networking in Education makes assumptions about issues such as an inherent benefit to using ICT in teaching, and/or universal access to ICT and/or social networking in schools or educational contexts, without actually investigating the reality 'on-the-ground', by asking teachers about their experiences. In other words, there appears to be an assumptions that: (1) technology is good for education, and (2) technology(s) are accessible and available for educational purposes. In terms of the latter issue, we explore what 'accessible' could actually refer to: in-school access for teachers and/or students; in-class access for teachers and/or students; access to social networking for teachers and/or students; and extracurricular access to ICT and/or social networking (e.g., access outside of school).

In this chapter, the perceptions of graduate students, who are also teachers from a number of different countries and teaching contexts, regarding the use of ICT and social networks in the classroom will be explored using discussion forums in Facebook. Therefore, this chapter considers two main issues: (1) is Facebook appropriate for use for data collection on perceptions; and (2) what kind of issues do teachers discuss regarding access and use of ICT and/or social networking in the classroom in an online forum.

The Study

Earlier research by Woodman and Kazoullis (2007) using tele-collaboration had indicated that important factors in successful tele-collaborations included ease of use and access, familiarity with the platform or site, and providing targeted discussion questions, often involving self-reflection and application to students' own experience, for participants to share with their classmates while online (e.g., to facilitate and engage social interaction). These questions could create a purpose for interaction between students who do not know each other, by encouraging them to share similarities and differences in perceptions about a shared experience via social networking (e.g., in this case, the use of technology in their classrooms).

In this chapter, the social networking site, Facebook, was chosen as the virtual environment for the tele-collaboration as it was identified as a site that the majority of students could access easily (e.g., without having to navigate different universities' logon systems, or go through complex access processes). It was also identified as a site with which many students would have some familiarity due to the popularity of the use of Facebook for personal contacts (Hew, 2011). It was believed that previous familiarity could minimize the possible interference of the technology itself on interactions (e.g., the navigation of the system would be less problematic than having to learn a new system), and therefore minimize it as a disruptive factor in the study. In addition, based on the findings of Woodman and Kazoullis (2007), specific tasks were designed to encourage interaction between the two groups of participants, and to engage discussion on a specific topic (e.g., ICT in the language teaching classroom).

METHODOLOGY

Subjects

Participants in the study included nineteen pre- and in-service teachers studying in Masters of Education in Australia and Greece, and their two academic lecturers. Twelve of the students were studying in Greece, and seven were studying at the Australian university. While all of the participants from Greece were ethnically Greek, the 'Australian' group actually included participants from diverse cultural and linguistic backgrounds, including two students from China, one student from Malaysia, one student from the Philippines, one student from South Korea, one student from Saudi Arabia, and one Australian student. In total, there were five male participants and sixteen female participants.

Data Collection

A Facebook page was specially created for the project, and within the Page a specific discussion group called 'Scenario Discussions' was created. Weekly scenario questions were posted to stimulate discussion between the graduate students in Australia and Greece on issues in the use of technology for teaching languages via social networking to explore shared experiences: to discuss, share and interact with each other. Because participants shared a common profession (e.g., as language teachers), but did not know each other 'offline', discussion questions included issues which might be common to teachers in different countries such as access and use of technology in the classroom, and problem-solving via discussion of real-life issues facing teachers in different countries. To ensure participant privacy, access to both the Facebook page and the specific "Scenario Discussion" group within the Facebook page were controlled by the authors (who were also the course instructors). Only participants in the study could access and participate in activities. Approximately, once a week, a new "Discussion Question" was posted, and participants were invited to comment. All participants had 24/7 access to the site, so they were able to participate at their convenience. The study ran for approximately three months, which included the academic semesters of both institutions.

Analysis

Data in the larger study was analyzed in two ways. First, overall tendencies were observed in terms of number of participants, number and types of postings, number and types of postings/participant, etc. Second, 'target' postings – or those which triggered responses from participants – were identified and classified into four main categories: discussion questions, online questionnaires, resources, and other (Hew, 2011).

In this chapter, analysis focused on forum postings on Facebook in terms of (1) the types of activities; (2) the types of users; and (3) the content of responses. These responses were compared based on country of origin/teaching context, and are discussed in terms of similarities and differences of teaching contexts, countries of origin, and content of response. All quotes are provided as written by participants, without correction.

Results

The issue of access to ICT resources and/or the internet was a subject which generated the most discussion between participants. This result is perhaps not surprising, since all of the participants shared backgrounds as language teachers, and they were studying in courses on the use of technology for language teaching.

Access to ICT resources and/or the internet in educational contexts involve a number of different issues. For example, WHEN and/or WHERE the resources are available could potentially affect teaching. That is, teaching could be influenced by whether the teacher can use the internet at any time during their class, in the classroom – or do they need to pre-book a computer lab only once or twice a week? Similarly, are there restrictions on the amount of downloads or access to power/electricity? The amount/number of resources available relative to the size of the class can also be an issue (e.g., are there enough computers for the number of students, or do they need to share)? And of course, the condition of the resources (e.g., age of computers, number working, etc.) can also influence how easily or often they are used.

In fact, responses suggest that while most participants had some access in schools, access for students in school (e.g., during the school day) varied considerably, sometimes even within the same country. In other words, the differences may be seen by school (e.g., private vs. public, wealthy vs lower SES), rather than by country/region.

For example, teachers from China agreed both teachers and students had access to ICT in schools, in-class, and in extracurricular contexts. They also had social network access (albeit to local versions). Similarly, the teacher from South Korea indicated both teachers and students had access to ICT and social networks in schools and in extracurricular contexts, and 'most' in-class as well. The teachers from Greece also indicated that both teachers and students had access to social networks and in extracurricular contexts, and most had access to ICT in schools and in-class.

By contrast, the teacher from Australia, while agreeing that there was access to social networks and extracurricular access, characterized access in schools as 'some', access for students as 'limited', and in-class' as 'it depends'. Finally, the teacher from the Philippines indicated there was 'some' social network access and access in schools, but limited access for students in the school and in-class, although they were able to access it outside of the school.

In general, there were considerable similarities in terms of access across the different countries and teaching contexts. For example, in all of the countries represented in the sample, at least some access was available in schools, and all had access outside of the classroom (e.g., extracurricular access). However, there were also some interesting areas of variation by country. For example, the PRC and South Korea appeared to have the most general access to ICT and internet (noting, of course, the restrictions in the PRC on certain types of social networks). The PRC, South Korea and Greece appeared to have the best access for students. Interesting, as will be discussed below, in-class access was found to be the most contentious issue, with only the PRC appearing to have full access across different types of schools.

In the next section, some of these country-based differences will be discussed in more detail.

China

One key difference in terms of internet access was for those living in the People's Republic of China (PRC), where access to sites like Facebook, YouTube and Twitter is typically blocked. However, a number of sites with analogous functionality are available, as XZ comments

While in China we have no access to the popular websites, ie. Facebook, Youtube, Twitter, there are other similar substitutes available. For instance, the popular social networking websites include Renren, Kaixin, where people can keep with the latest news about their friends. Youku is the website where you can upload your own videos or watch others. [XZ]

XZ also noted the raising importance of mini-blogs:

Similar to Twitter, mini blogs are now gaining more and more popularity among people from all walks of life...All the above is accessible to our schools as well as our students by computers or mobiles.[XZ]

As noted above, in general terms, access in the PRC appears similar, if not better, to those in other countries for both students and teachers. Access was available for students and teachers in schools, in-class, and also in extracurricular contexts (often by smart phone), thus suggesting in this context the use of ICT for teaching purposes would be supported.

South Korea

Similarly, according to SK, in South Korea

..most schools have access to CMC. Also most of student [sic] can access to CMC at home easily or in the school computer labs. Sometimes, I asked my students to access special webpages to review and self-study what they'd learnt in the class. [SK]

Thus, access was available for students and teachers in schools, in-class, and also in extracurricular contexts (often by smart phone). South Korea is also well-known for fast access speeds, increasing the type of materials and activities that can be used. SK also indicated she used ICT to help her students both in and out of class, providing evidence for the potential for increased use of ICT and/or social networking for educational purposes.

Greece

In Greece, according to VK, "most schools have computers and internet access. And lots of schools have interactive whiteboards". However, AG suggests "when we have such equipment, they are not used properly in class or not used at all", a perspective supported by NM and JV.

NM says

I agree that almost all schools (at least those that I've worked at) have technological equipment that can be used for teaching but the point is that the percentage of teachers using them is disappointingly low...[NM]

The issue of access to ICT, but a lack of teacher use of ICT, and how this may be related to lack of teacher training, was of particular concern amongst the Greek students, although it was also echoed by other participants in the study, suggesting this is a significant underlying issue impacting ICT use for teaching.

It appears many school administrations believe providing technology(s) is enough to support the use of ICT in teaching. However, many of the teachers pointed out that even knowing how to use a particular technology or resource (e.g., Facebook) isn't the same as knowing how to use it to teach (or teach language). Therefore, often, there was also a perceived disconnection, or gap, between 'normal' in-class teaching techniques, and the online world.

The Philippines

In the context of the participants in the study, LQ from the Philippines was the most influenced by a general lack of access to resources. LQ notes that in the Philippines,

...due to limited CMC materials, students have to book for a schedule to access the computer in the computer laboratories provided for them and limit their usage for one hour usage for twice a day transaction. Internet cafes are also available outside the campus, but students need to pay fifteen pesos (equivalent to fifty cents AUD) per hour of usage. Lucky they are if the restaurants and coffee shops which have wifi don't have passwords [LQ]

Interestingly, LQ's observation seems to be the only example of a possible 'digital divide', where access may be limited by student income. Most other participants indicated their students had access either at home or outside of class in other ways.

LQ's comment also illustrates the complications in terms of access when students have to use computer labs. Clearly, such restrictions on access could influence the type and focus of possible pedagogical uses of ICT or internet.

Australia

KH, in her discussion of access to technology in the context of the Queensland (Australia) educational system, highlights more of the commonalities of across the various countries, citing issues related both to access, but also frustrating administrative issues, which may limit fully exploiting technology in the classroom. She states that "Queensland state schools have access to The Learning Place [an LMS] where teachers can set up Project Rooms...and Blackboard virtual classrooms". However, she also notes that although she has used YouTube at school, in general, "access to it is blocked for students". Similarly, she reports that "example sites for educators...(with) RSS feeds of 'breaking news'...no longer (are freely available)..(and can't) be accessed". In other works, it appears that some schools that purport to support the use of ICT and internet for educational purposes, often also create administrative roadblocks, or 'artificial' or 'context-specific' digital divides.

For example, while promoting computer use, many schools block students from using computers or mobile devices in class, even for pedagogical purposes. In many cases, the argument for restricting access appears to related to classroom management issues, rather than learning outcomes.

INTERNATIONAL PERCEPTIONS OF ISSUES IN THE USE OF ICT IN THE CLASSROOM

When participants were asked about key issues related to CALL or use of technology in teaching in their home countries, again more commonalities were seen than differences. In response to the question, "In your opinion, what are the key issues in your country's teaching context related to CALL or use of technology in teaching, some of the key issues identified included by the Greek teachers included: lack of training for teachers (n=3), use of new software (n=3), lack of hardware (n=3), student numbers (n=3), perception of use of technology (n=1), and administration/decision-making (n=1). Similar issues were identified by the Australian teacher (e.g., teacher confidence and skill with ICT) and the teacher from South Korea (e.g., teacher education and confidence with ICT).

Teacher Education

Thus, the key issues identified by the teachers from Greece, Australian and Korea related to the need for more teacher education with ICT to make teachers more confident with using ICT in the classroom. For example, KH notes that "in Queensland [Australia], teachers' levels of confidence and skill with technology and the availability of suitable resources seem to be the main issues. These findings are consistent with much of the literature on the use of ICT in language teaching (Godwin-Jones, 2010).

Within the Greek context, MM suggests "the teachers need immediate training on the use of ICT. Some of them have to start from '..and this is how the computer turns on'". NM adds that most teachers in Greece think "that technology is used only in Informatics (IT) and not in other fields [such as education]".NM also emphasized the fact that large class sizes also make teaching with ICT more challenging.

Finally, NP expresses the frustration of many educators, noting "every time when somebody new governs this place (it) all starts (again) from the beginning!".

And SK agrees, stating

(South) Korea has similar problem. Technology for teaching has been progressed a lot and so quickly but the teachers can't really follow it up. There are some teacher training programs but teachers don't really use them much as they normally like to use something that is already familiar (to) them...

Other issues identified by participants included issues related to lack of hardware and difficulties keeping up with new software.

DISCUSSION AND RECOMMENDATIONS

Findings support the use of Facebook for tele-collaboration in teacher education, and for research into ICT and language teaching. Results of the analysis provide support for use of Facebook discussion groups to encourage frank and open discussions of critical issues of interest to participants, including opportunities for constructive problem-solving by sharing and networking based on expertise. Results also illustrate similarities and differences in international issues related to the use of technology in the classrooms, and provide support for the use of Facebook for both tele- collaboration between teachers and/or graduate students, but also for data collection in research on teacher perceptions of issues related to the use of technology.

The Use of Facebook

The majority of participants were active on the Facebook site during the study, posting a number of times over the three month period. There were almost no questions about how to use the site itself, implying that participants had prior experience with social networking, and specifically Facebook, and its functionality. Even students from the PRC, who only had had access to Facebook while studying in Australia, appear to have had little difficulty adapting to Facebook, since they were familiar with the format and functions from their experience with the Chinese equivalent social networking sites. These findings support the use of Facebook for both the purposes of research, and for the pedagogical use in facilitating discussions about issues in language teaching amongst graduate students from different institutions and cultural backgrounds. Further, creating a specific place (e.g., Scenario discussions) for the discussions appears to have allowed participants to access and post on specific issues asynchronously (e.g., at different times) without the confusion of other issues in Facebook functionality (e.g., timeline, updates).

The Use of Scenario Discussion Questions

The use of specific or targeted Discussion Questions (or 'trigger questions') was also supported. Analysis of the types of questions which generated the post postings indicated that having specific issues which were personal and relevant motivated the most participants to contribute. In this context, Discussion Questions which focused on cross-cultural or international differences in education and technology were the most popular. These findings underline the importance of engaging in-service graduate students *as teachers* (e.g., as experts) on issues related to their personal experience in their own cultural contexts and own classrooms. Issues such as the impact of differential access to ICT and internet in different teaching contexts, and suggestions from participants about how to address challenges such as lack of training for teachers in ICT, imply a high level of engagement in the key issues of the courses, and a level of analysis and problem-solving appropriate to graduate level students. The questions which led to the highest response rates were those that allowed the participants to demonstrate their expertise in their identities as 'teacher/experts', not simply as 'graduate students/learners. These issues included ICT access in their teaching contexts; key issues related to ICT in their countries; how funding for ICT could be best spent in their teaching contexts. The types of questions, focusing discussion on common issues in diverse teaching contexts, did appear successful in creating an online community of teachers, discussing 'real world', or authentic, issues and problems.

INTERNATIONAL COMPARISON OF ISSUES IN THE USE OF ICT IN THE CLASSROOM

Findings reveal more similarities between the situations and perceptions of the participants from the different countries than differences. Although these results could reflect the origins and size of the sample, most participants indicated that while they and their students had access in general to computers and the internet, they did not necessarily have this access in the classroom. Even when technologies were available in schools, participants identified a critical need for professional development to increase teachers' use of ICT. These findings are relevant to educators and policy development as teacher training in the use of ICT is necessary for implementation of ICT or social networking in the language classroom.

Because of the impact of access issues on their day-to-day work, the discussion of the shared experience (and frustration) amongst many of the participants appears to have been a 'bonding experience' in terms of generating online discussions, reinforcing their professional identities as language teachers who faced shared difficulties and challenges, regardless of country or culture – and the ability to identify ways to circumvent some of these challenges, and creating a sense of community in the online context (e.g., Hew, 2011; Stafford et al., 1993).

FUTURE RESEARCH DIRECTIONS

This study strongly supports the use Facebook for tele-collaboration in teacher education, as well as a method to collect data on teacher perceptions using targeted discussion questions, and involving teachers (and/or graduate students) from around the world. Future research could further explore teacher perceptions of a number of different issues in the teaching of different topics and using different methodologies. Researchers could also explore the apparent gap between administrative policy and on-the-ground reality for classroom teachers.

CONCLUSION

This study supports the use of Facebook for tele-collaboration in teacher education, as well as an opportunity to collect data on teacher perceptions of ICT and language teaching. Postings reveal many similarities between the situations and perceptions of the participants from the different countries, suggesting that school systems around the world deal with the use of technology in the classroom in similar ways. Most participants indicated that while they and their students had general access to computers and the internet, they did not necessarily have this access in the classroom. Given the rising importance of e-literacy to the global economy, access to computers in the classroom needs to be addressed internationally.

Increasing access to computer-based functionality in the classroom could be accomplished by increased use to mLearning technologies (e.g., making use of smart phones, tablets and laptops), in pedagogically appropriate ways. For example, smart phones can provide individual access to the internet for task-based searches, dictionary and reference use, or access for specific learning sites. Smart phones can also replace the need to book video or audio recorders, literally putting a whole A/V department into students' and teachers' hands.

Similarly, participants identified a critical need for professional development to increase teachers' use of ICT. The implications for administrators and governments is the need to provide specific and targeted professional development such as curriculum and pedagogical task specifically developed to use mLearning devices if they want maximal use of technologies in the classroom. There may also be a need to change perceptions of devices such as smart phones, so that they are seen not just as for entertainment, but as, "personal learning devices".

In conclusion, the findings of this study are relevant to educators and policy development in terms of implementation of ICT or social networking in the language classroom.

REFERENCES

Attia, A., Aziz, N., Friedman, B., & Elhusseiny, M. (2011). Commentary: The impact of social networking tools on political change in Egypts 'Revolution 2.0. *Electronic Commerce Research and Applications, 10*(4), 369–374. doi:10.1016/j.elerap.2011.05.003

Belz, J. (2002). Social dimensions of telecollaborative foreign language study. *Language Learning & Technology, 6*(1), 60–81.

Carpenter, J., Green, M., & LaFlam, J. (2011). People or profiles: Individual differences in online social networking use. *Personality and Individual Differences, 50*(5), 538–541. doi:10.1016/j.paid.2010.11.006

Ellison, N., Steinfield, C., & Lampe, C. (2007). The benefits of Facebook friends: Social capital and college students use of online social network sites. *Journal of Computer-Mediated Communication, 12*(4), 1143–1168. doi:10.1111/j.1083-6101.2007.00367.x

Eysenbach, G. (2008). Medicine 2.0: Social networking, collaboration, participation, apomediation, and openness. *Journal of Medical Internet Research, 10*(3), e22. doi:10.2196/jmir.1030 PMID:18725354

Gangadharbatla, H. (2010). Facebook me: Collective self-esteem, need to belong, and internet self-efficacy as predictors of the attitudes toward social networking sites. *Journal of Interactive Advertising, 8*(2), 5–15. doi:10.1080/15252019.2008.10722138

Glynn, C., Huge, M., & Hoffman, L. (2012). All the news thats fit to post: A profile of news use on social networking sites. *Computers in Human Behavior, 28*(1), 113–119. doi:10.1016/j.chb.2011.08.017

Godwin-Jones, R. (2010). Emerging technologies: Literacies and technologies revisited. *Language Learning & Technology, 14*(3), 2–9.

Goodband, J., Solomon, Y., Samuels, P., Lawson, D., & Bhakta, R. (2011). Limits and potentials of social networking in academia: Case study of the evolution of a mathematics Facebook community. *Learning, Media and Technology*, 1–17.

Gosling, S., Augustine, A., Vazire, S., Holtzman, N., & Gaddis, S. (2011). Manifestations of personality in online social networks: Self-reported Facebook-related behaviours and observable profile information. *Cyberpsychology, Behavior, and Social Networking, 14*(9), 483–488. doi:10.1089/cyber.2010.0087 PMID:21254929

Harrison, R., & Thomas, M. (2009). Identity in online communities: Social networking sites and language learning. *International Journal of Emerging Technologies and Society, 7*(2), 109–124.

Hew, K. F. (2011). Students and teachers use of Facebook. *Computers in Human Behavior, 27*(2), 662–676. doi:10.1016/j.chb.2010.11.020

Hum, N., Chamberlin, P., Hambright, B., Portwood, A., Schat, A., & Bevan, J. (2011). A picture is worth a thousand words: A content analysis of Facebook. *Computers in Human Behavior, 27*(5), 1828–1833. doi:10.1016/j.chb.2011.04.003

Kabilan, M., Ahmad, N., & Abidan, M. (2010). Facebook: An online environment for learning English in institutions of higher education? *The Internet and Higher Education*, *13*(4), 170–187. doi:10.1016/j. iheduc.2010.07.003

Kaplan, A., & Haelein, M. (2010). Users of the world, unite! The challenges and opportunities of social media. *Business Horizons*, *53*(1), 59–68. doi:10.1016/j.bushor.2009.09.003

Madge, C., Meek, J., Wellens, J., & Hooley, T. (2009). Facebook, social integration and informal learning at university: It is more for socializing and talking to friends about work than for actually doing work. *Learning, Media and Technology*, *34*(2), 141–155. doi:10.1080/17439880902923606

Maranto, G., & Barton, M. (2010). Paradox and promise: MySpace, Facebook, and the sociopolitics of social networking in the writing classroom. *Computers and Composition*, *27*(1), 36–47. doi:10.1016/j. compcom.2009.11.003

Nosko, A., Wood, E., & Molema, S. (2010). All about me: Disclosure in online social networking profiles: The case of FACEBOOK. *Computers in Human Behavior*, *26*(3), 406–418. doi:10.1016/j.chb.2009.11.012

Orr, E., Sisic, M., Ross, C., Simmering, M., Arseneault, J., & Orr, R. (2009). The influence of shyness on the use of Facebook in an undergraduate sample. *Cyberpsychology & Behavior*, *12*(3), 337–340. doi:10.1089/cpb.2008.0214 PMID:19250019

Park, N., Kerk, K., & Valenzuela, S. (2009). Being immersed in social networking environment: Facebook groups, uses and gratifications, and social outcomes. *Cyberpsychology & Behavior*, *12*(6), 729–733. doi:10.1089/cpb.2009.0003 PMID:19619037

Pempek, T., Yemolayeva, Y., & Calvert, S. (2009). College students social networking experiences on Facebook. *Journal of Applied Developmental Psychology*, *30*(3), 227–238. doi:10.1016/j.appdev.2008.12.010

Qi, M., & Edgar-Nevill, D. (2011). Social networking searching and privacy issues. *Information Security Technical Report*, *17*, 74–78.

Roblyer, M., McDaniel, M., Webb, M., Herman, J., & Vince Witty, J. (2010). Findings on Facebook in higher education: A comparison of college faculty and student uses and perceptions of social networking sites. *The Internet and Higher Education*, *13*(3), 134–140. doi:10.1016/j.iheduc.2010.03.002

Ross, C., Orr, E., Sisic, M., Arseneault, J., Simmering, M., & Orr, R. (2009). Personality and motivations associated with Facebook use. *Computers in Human Behavior*, *25*(2), 578–586. doi:10.1016/j. chb.2008.12.024

Smith, W., & Kidder, D. (2010). Youve been tagged! (Then again, maybe not): Employers and Facebook. *Business Horizons*, *53*(5), 491–499. doi:10.1016/j.bushor.2010.04.004

Turkle, S. (2011). *Alone together: Why we expect more from technology and less from each other*. Basic Books.

Waters, R., Burnett, E., Lamm, A., & Lucas, J. (2009). Engaging stakeholders through social networking: How nonprofit organizations are using Facebook. *Public Relations Review*, *35*(2), 102–106. doi:10.1016/j. pubrev.2009.01.006

Weir, G., Toolan, F., & Smeed, D. (2011). The threats of social networking: Old wine in new bottles? *Information Security Technical Report*, *16*(2), 38–43. doi:10.1016/j.istr.2011.09.008

Woodman, K. (2004). Unlimited access: The real benefits of online learning. *International Journal of Learning*, *10*, 3025–3033.

Woodman, K. (2005). No borders: Virtual communities in online learning. *International Journal of the Humanities*, *1*, 1849–1861.

Woodman, K. (2009). Online learning and literacy development. *Proceedings of the 42nd Linguistics Colloquium*.

Woodman, K., & Kourtis-Kazoullis, V. (2007). Cyber-Self-Reflection: Developing learner autonomy in online programs. *Selected Papers from the 18th International Symposium on Theoretical and Applied Linguistics*.

Yan Yu, Y., Wen Tian, S., Vogel, D., & Chi-Wai Kwok, R. (2010). Can learning be virtually boosted? An investigation of online social networking impacts. *Computers & Education*, *55*(4), 1494–1503. doi:10.1016/j.compedu.2010.06.015

KEY TERMS AND DEFINITIONS

ICT: Information and communication technology; a term that includes any communication device of application.

Social Networking: The use of applications or websites to build social networks between people who share interests.

Tele-Collaboration: The use of technologies that facilitate interaction between remote groups.

TESOL: Teachers of English as a Second or Other Language.

Chapter 12
Contextual Issues in Groupware Applications for Educational Support Groups

Huizilopoztli Luna-García
Universidad Autónoma de Zacatecas – Campus Jalpa, Mexico

Guadalupe Lara-Cisneros
Universidad Autónoma de Zacatecas – Campus Jalpa, Mexico

Ricardo Mendoza-González
TecNM, Instituto Tecnológico de Aguascalientes, Mexico

Carlos R. Ordaz-García
Universidad Autónoma de Zacatecas – Campus Jalpa, Mexico

Laura C. Rodríguez-Martínez
TecNM, Instituto Tecnológico de Aguascalientes, Mexico

Sandra Mercado-Pérez
Universidad Autónoma de Zacatecas – Campus Jalpa, Mexico

Mario A. Rodríguez-Díaz
TecNM, Instituto Tecnológico de Aguascalientes, Mexico

Alejandro U. López-Orozco
Universidad Autónoma de Zacatecas – Campus Jalpa, Mexico

ABSTRACT

The objective of this chapter was to identify a set of contextual issues in groupware applications used by educational support groups. The analysis was performed through a Needfindings study where 20 active members of three Mexican federal educational-support groups called USAER were recruited. The analysis considered both users and functional vantage point. The participants (from one USAER) provided feedback and insights from their daily activities related to communication with others and resources access helping to define and understand users' scenarios. This information was classified and distilled as design ideas in low fidelity prototypes constructed by participants themselves under guidance from authors. Finally, prototypes were evaluated by the members of the other two USAER group providing their perception as expert users. The study derived in a set of particular contextual issues that directly influence interactions in group applications. These findings could be take into account by designers as a reliable starting point for well-designed User Interfaces for groupware.

DOI: 10.4018/978-1-5225-2616-2.ch012

INTRODUCTION

The working groups use different technologies as support tools for their activities (e.g., email, instant messaging, applications for data storage, social networking, text messaging, among others) to achieve specific objectives and meet goals group (Gräther et al., 2014). Available technologies allow members of working groups to communicate, interact and collaborate across a wide range of methods, minimizing common communication barriers as distance and time, and facilitating communication and exchange of information between group members, issues that are crucial to the effectiveness of a working group (Sagar, 2012).

Currently, the use of applications that allow communication, collaboration and interaction between multiple users play an important role in daily activities e.g. *groupware systems*; Ellis, Gibbs, & Rein (1991) suggest that society acquires much of its nature from the way that people interact and communicate through message exchange. Groupware systems or collaborative software refers to the use of techniques, methods and software tools that allow members of a working group to carry out their task and activities through data communication networks, either individual or collectively, and regardless of geographical location or time the activities are executed. Groupware systems or also knows as Computer-supported Cooperative Work (CSCW) are increasingly used due the facility to integrate knowledge among working groups and facilitate their communication. Groupware represent a great tool for people group-work since they have multiple possibilities oriented to improve interaction, collaboration, and communication between group members.

The term groupware was first defined by Johnson-Lenz in 1981 referring to *an intentional group processes plus software to support them,* later, in 1982 he defined groupware in his book «Groupware: computer Support for Business Teams» as a *computer-based system plus social work-groups processes* (Johnson-Lenz & Johnson-Lenz, 1998: 1982), other definitions of groupware are:

- (Berkenbrock, da Silva, & Hirata, 2009), it is software that allows the creation of cooperative work by using specific technologies to make the groups more productive.
- (Dix A., Finlay, Abowd, & Beale, 2004), groupware is a term for application written to support multi-user collaboration.
- (Ortega & Bravo, 2001), it is the hardware and software that support and enhance teamwork, therefore, groupware is a set of oriented products to group work, i.e., help groups of people work together.
- (Ellis, Gibbs, & Rein, 1991), computer-based systems that support groups of people engaged in a common task (or goal) and that provide an interface to a shared environment.

The goal of groupware is to assist groups to *facilitate communication, foster collaboration and improve coordination* of tasks and allow monitoring the process of building their common activities (Sosa, et al., 2006), (Ellis, Gibbs, & Rein, 1991). We define groupware as *a set of technologies integrated into a system that allows work groups to perform a common task using a shared environment,* i.e., this technology focuses on designing systems to support group work and the effect that technology on the working group. The purpose of all groupware systems is to provide the required functionality to allow *user to user* interactions, unlike the *user-system* interaction supported by the most conventional software systems (Noruega, 2009), (Ortega & Bravo, 2001), (Lococo & Yen, 1998).

According to Ellis, Gibbs, & Rein (1991) there is no a rigid dividing line between systems that are considered groupware and those who are not, due of its multiple and unique characteristics, therefore he proposed a taxonomy based on the functionality of the application level, which is represented by a groupware spectrum (see Figure 1) which identifies the level or approach degree (low or high) in which a specific system can be contemplated within the category of groupware systems.

The Figure 1 shows that the time-sharing systems and email systems are considered as low level within the groupware spectrum, due the lack of tools that allow shared activities in the work environment, conversely, the software review systems and electronic classroom allow performing tasks using the shared environment, such that, according to the spectrum of Figure 1, an application is in the range of Groupware, only if satisfy with the two determinated variables (common tasks and shared environment). Ellis et al., (1991) notes that some systems may become high-level groupware spectrum over time to advance the technology needed to implement new features. However, this representation only considers the functionality as a feature of groupware systems, advances in technology requires consideration of these and other variables for the design and development of groupware systems, for example, for mobile devices.

The groupware systems can be classified in several ways, however, the most used and known taxonomy is based on Johansen's (1991) notions of *time and space*, which is based on a 2x2 matrix where *time-space* considerations suggest four work categories as shown in Figure 2 (Dix et al., 2004).

As Figure 2 illustrates, if we consider time as the base, the applications are classified into *synchronous and asynchronous*; in synchronous applications, users access and modify shared data in real-time, while in asynchronous applications users collaborate in different time to access and modify shared data (Preguica, et al., 2005). If we take a space base, applications can be in the *same or a different place*. Similarly, the matrix includes four different types of interactions, i.e. *face-to-face, distributed synchronous, asynchronous and distributed asynchronous,* these are important concepts considered for

Figure 1. Dimensions of groupware, courtesy
Source: Ellis, Gibbs, & Rein, 1991

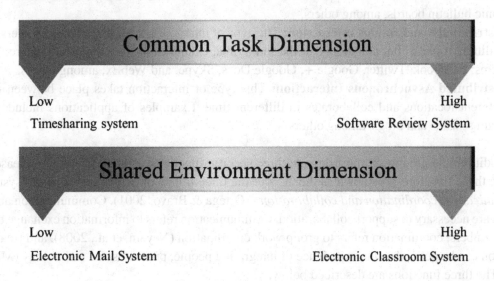

Figure 2. Space-Time groupware matrix
Source: Adapted from Johansen, 1991

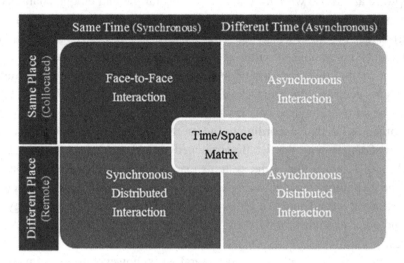

the development of a groupware application. It is important to note that a complete groupware system considers the needs of all quadrants of the matrix in Figure 2 (Ellis, Gibbs, & Rein, 1991). The four types of interaction are briefly described:

- **Face to Face Interaction**: In this type of interaction users are in the same place interacting through a specific medium, e.g., two users discussing how to use the functions of a smart board. Examples of other applications include electronic meeting and system support decision-making, among others.
- **Asynchronous Interaction:** This type of interaction is executed in the same place but at different times. As a continuation of the above example, users use the functions of the board individually and at different times. Other applications examples are: document management systems and electronic bulletin boards, among others.
- **Distributed Synchronous Interaction:** This type of interaction takes place between users located in different places but collaborate at the same time, examples of these applications are the platforms: Facebook, Twitter, Google +, Google Docs, Skype, and WebEx, among others.
- **Distributed Asynchronous Interaction:** This type of interaction takes place between users in different locations and collaborates in different time. Examples of applications include: email, forums, wikis and blogs, among others.

In addition, the groupware must provide three specific functions within a group to increase its efficiency, these functions are known as the 3C's or the three pillars on which a groupware-system rest *«communication, coordination and collaboration»* (Ortega & Bravo, 2001). Communication and coordination are necessary to support collaboration. Communication refers to information exchange between group members, coordination refers to group work coordination (Neyem, et al., 2008), and finally, collaboration can be defined as the experience of integrating people, processes and technology (Morabito, 2014). The three functions are described below:

- **Communication:** It is the most important groupware function, since it is the process in which messages are exchanged and information is shared. It is intended that it be effective, i.e., that sender and receives information perceived the same concept; and efficient in terms of resource spending. It is possible to identify a number of elements that can characterize this process, e.g. *participants, information and media,* also, is possible to recognize the different modes or types of communication-interaction, e.g., *face to face, synchronous, asynchronous or distributed.* (Noruega-García, 2009), (Sosa, Velázquez, Zarco, & Postiglioni, 2006), (Ortega & Bravo, 2001). In a groupware system the computer or mobile device acts as a means for transmitting information. According to Dix et al., (2004) good communication is not enough, participants must be able to cooperate and collaborate in activities and tasks of the working group.

- **Coordination:** Is the action to ensure that team is working together efficiently to achieve the workgroup´s goals. This includes distribution of tasks and review of its implementation. Coordination is seen as an activity in itself to be a necessary process when several people are involved in the same task. The effectiveness of communication and collaboration depends on coordination, i.e., *the organization, planning and synchronization of workgroup activities* (Noruega-García, 2009), (Geronimo-Castillo & Canseco, 2002).

- **Collaboration:** It is the intentional and coordinated participation of group-members. Collaboration refers to several people can work together on the same task to achieve a certain common purpose, i.e., *the collaboration consist in to work together to achieve the group's goals.* In a collaborative situation, the group-members seek to obtain results that derive in benefits for themselves and for other group members (Noruega-García, 2009), (Sosa, et al., 2006) (Ortega & Bravo, 2001).

BACKGROUND

Interactive technologies require several design considerations in order to provide an adequate user experience, most of them should be applied early during the design process. Groupware applications are not estrange to said assumption, in fact group-interaction context demands particular attention in design issues that should be tackled to ensure proper communication/interaction users-application-users.

According to above it is important to keeping in mind important concepts, paradigms, and strategies throughout the design process addressed to cover the main needs, tasks, and values from users by the design itself. Some of said insights and approaches were implemented for this research work and are following described.

Human-Computer Interaction

Broadly speaking, Human-Computer Interaction (HCI) is the part of Computer Sciences that provide specific techniques; methods; methodologies; and paradigms oriented to adequately perform the design, implementation, and evaluation of User Interfaces (UI) for both hardware and software technologies (SigChi, 1982; Carroll, 2002, Preece et al., 1994). HCI encompass an interdisciplinary approach integrating theories; paradigms; techniques; and concepts from knowledge areas such as Architecture; Art; Graphic Design; Industrial Design; Anthropology; Psychology; among others. This blend of knowledge makes HCI approaches applicable in a wide range of scenarios where well-designed technology for users is needed (Dix et al., 2003). Similarly, in (Preece et al., 1994) is emphasized that HCI pursuit the good design of systems (computer or not) which support and help people to complete their activities and tasks efficiently. In the same way, (Carroll, 2002) stated that HCI observes the study and practice of usability and relates with the understanding and development of technology that people would want to use, would may be capable to use, and would get effectiveness when use it.

The prestigious research group ACM-SigChi provides a definition for HCI specifically applied for computer development stating that HCI deal with every aspect related to the interaction between one or more humans and one or more computers using a program-interface. Said concept has been referred for more than 20 years and remains effective (SigChi, 1982).

These vantage-points reveal the importance of analyze and understand users as a crucial element during the design process of technology considering usage conditions required for users and capabilities constrains that could emerge during technology use. Concerns about incorporation of users through the design process represent the research focus of User Centered Design (UCD). UCD, is probably the more beneficial HCI paradigm for software development. UCD could be perceived as the basis for other important theory, the Usability Engineering (Lowdermilk, 2013; Nielsen & Budiu, 2012).

HCI and UCD relevance are even reflected in a part of ISO standards, specifically the norm ISO 13407 (Human-centered design processes for interactive systems). ISO 13407 guide interactive-systems development through a user-centered framework which can be adapted to several development life-cycles. This framework foster the application of proper techniques to design and evaluate technology for people. User-Centered development for interactive systems has the following basic stages:

1. **Needs Analysis:** This stage summarizes the purpose of the interactive system that is developing. Here is also defined the target audience for the system including those benefits achieved by the system use.
2. **Users and Tasks Analysis:** Here the particular audience characteristics are defined including age-range; education; experience with computers/systems; among other generals. When users are defined their specific tasks could be identified paying particular attention to their objectives and related activities to achieve them.
3. **Functional Analysis:** Here computer functionalities are realized bearing in mind the users' needs and keeping correspondence between computer functions and users tasks/activities.
4. **Requirements Analysis:** In this stage are described formal Software Engineering specifications for the interactive-system implementation. Said specifications include data dictionary; Entity-Relationship diagrams; Use-Cases; among others. It is crucial to maintain a strict observance of users' needs.
5. **Design:** Here could be provided some insights about the appearance of the user interface (UI) taking into account the results of previous stages. The sketches should reflect also an adequate organization of the content and information which must be showed with clarity and consistency. This stage allow to obtain the perception of users about the UI design.
6. **Prototyping:** Using feedback obtained by means of Design stage, it is possible to generate some global prototypes (Those useful to show the entire interactive system), and local prototypes (Those focused on specific modules of the interactive system). There are different kinds of prototypes including evolutive (Could be evolve to the final version of the interactive system); discardable (Provides guidance embodying an idea during a particular stage of the design process); high-fidelity

(Very close to the final version of the interactive system appearance); and low-fidelity (Similar to sketches from the design stage).

7. **Implementation:** UI designed and developed is implemented.
8. **Evaluation:** UI is analyzed by performing usability tests, e.g. Show the interface to a group of users and (by means of HCI techniques and tools) obtain its perception about their interactive experience.

Agreeing with (Lowdermilk, 2013), user-centered systems development do not be focused in data or widgets, but should be concerned in incorporate users throughout the design process. Said thought has been emphasized for over 20 years. Terry Winogard, HCI pioneer, states that developers should be focused in interaction among humans that occurs through computers, before starting any development (Winogard, 1994). This aspects suggests that HCI is accomplished into a social-organizational context. Different kinds of applications are required for different purposes, this scenario demands special attention in assignment tasks between humans and computers, being ensured that repetitive activities are assigned to computers; and creative activities correspond to users.

User eXperience (UX)

UX is a concept strongly related to UCD since involves all those interaction aspects between people and technology, its services, and its products. Don Norman and Jakob Nielsen, HCI and UX gurus, emphasize that an adequate UX consists understand the particular users' needs, which must be covered by the use of technology. Technology must avoid integrate excessive elements/features that could annoy users, designs must be simple and elegant, fostering enjoyment for users (Nielsen & Norman, 2014). In the same way, (Nielsen & Norman, 2014) considered that true UX goes beyond to provide users with they want, or provide them a features checklist; to achieve a high quality UX in products (technological or not) from a company, products and services must truly help people to adequately accomplish specific tasks.

Since technology must be adequate for people, an important concept has been mentioned in previous sections, usability. According to standard ISO 9241-11, usability represents the measure in that a product can be used by particular users to achieve specific objectives with effectiveness, efficiency, and satisfaction into a specific context.

Jakob Nielsen (considered the main contributor in usability worldwide) states that is very important differentiate UX from usability emphasizing that last one currently refers just to a quality attribute for user interfaces which, although is crucial, is just a piece from the entire puzzle for an adequate UX.

UX comprises all those elements related to the way on that people use an interactive product, a service, or an event, analyzing aspects such as: how they feel it in their hands; how they understand the utility of it; how they perceive it during use; how it helps them to their purposes; and how it fits in the whole use-context (Harston & Pyla, 2012).

UX leads to adequate functions and interaction flows emphasizing the good design idea, which consist in jointly understanding the whole set of senses involved in the users' perception about the interaction with some product and/or service (Harston & Pyla, 2012; Marsh, 2016).

Users' perception is usually influenced by previous and current experiences generating new experiences and modifying expectative. Therefore, the internal state of people impacts directly to their user experience (Norman, 2013).

Needfindings

Needfindings is a process that makes easier the design-context understanding for a particular technology. This process starts with "Audience Definition" phase which basically consist in analyzing tasks; activities; and needs of users. This feedback allows designer perceive the design problem from the vantage point of users expanding the solution-space and represents a reliable starting point for innovation since designers could generate insights that could be difficult to realize in other way (Dow et al., 2013).

Needfindings process lean upon specific techniques to properly define audience and contextualize the design idea all based on particular users´ needs, goals, activities, and values.

Needfindings is a flexible technique since it allows varying the process' tasks, e.g. the following tasks/stages are usually considered but not limited: Recruiting participants; Observation; Interview; Focus Group; Prototyping. Particularly, said stages were implemented in this research.

MAIN FOCUS OF THE CHAPTER

Issues, Controversies, Problems

It is crucial for working groups to encourage and maintain a good communication process among their members since the achievement of their particular group-goals depend on communication. This is not an easy enterprise, group-communications are complex and several variables interfere into the process having direct consequences in the working group ecology (Hall et al., 2015; Macias, 2003). This scenario is frequently seen into educational support groups, which are external working groups that help integration of children with special needs in primary schools.

Several technologies –*such as email; social networks; meeting applications; wikis; among others*– had been used for educational working groups trying to makes easier the distance-communication process and collaboration. Nevertheless, these alternatives working apart (Gräther, et al., 2014). One of the most known approaches in providing a compound of said tools is called groupware. This concept emerged in the 80's and emphasize the communication; collaboration; and cooperation among group members through an application that supports distance-interactions between group members (Sagar, 2012). Even if does not exist a standard definition for groupware applications several authors agree that a groupware system could be perceived as a set of specific technologies which allows groups to perform common task over a shared environment (Jeners & Prinz, 2014).

Groupware solved the separate-technologies issue; however, most of the times this is not enough since the original group communication complexity remains (Morabito, 2014). There are many pieces in the puzzle that should be harmonically integrated considering at least the following inspired by (Fechner, et al., 2015; Hall et al., 2015; Prates et al., 2015; Knowles et al., 2015):

1. Users should not perceive interactions on groupware just like simple user-system interactions. In other words, groupware interfaces should provide transparency allowing user-to-user interactions.
2. Environments of groupware should accord to activities, tasks, usage, and behavior from a particular working group.

Above second item could awake certain controversies; it is well known that each working group has their own features and manners, but also it is true that common group-communication issues had been identified (Wilson, 2007). In this vein, said discrepancy should be clarified.

SOLUTIONS AND RECOMMENDATIONS

As mentioned above, we implemented a Needfindings process considering the following stages: Recruiting participants; Observation; Interview; Focus Group; Prototyping. In this section we describe the implementation of every stage directly on a study case, which is used as an illustrative example and a proof of concept.

To investigate the contextual issues was conducted a case study and selected as study scenario the "Unit of Support Services for Regular Education "(USAER, for its Spanish acronym), which is focused in promoting integration of children with special educational needs to school in early education schools and regular basic education (SEP, 2006); Three support groups participated in different stages of the process, USAER Maria Montessori (#94), USAER Diego Tenamaxtli (#60), and USAER Gabriela Mistral (# 75), the first located in Tlachichila, and the last two in Nochistlán de Mejía, in the southeastern of Zacatecas state, Mexico. A total of 20 professional «real users» of the areas of *Communication, Psychology, Regular Education, Special Education, Social Work and Specialist* of the three USAER participated in the case study, also participated six experts in disciplines of *Design, Usability, Human-Computer Interaction (HCI) and User-Centered Design (UCD)*. In the first four stages of the process participated 11 members of USAER#94 and in the final stage *Conceptual Evaluation* attended the USAER#60 and USAER#75 with 9 members.

Stage 1. User Requirements: It refers to the *user needs* and it is the most important part of the design process, i.e., in this stage are established the foundation for the rest process and the working group needs are documented. Without an adequate requirements definition, it is impossible to continue on the right way in the definition and documentation of user requirements. The collection process requirements demand take the abstract requirements into useful needs.

The questions associated with the stage were: *How perform the work individually and collectively the group members?, What technologies are currently used to meet your needs? and What are the pros and cons of used technological services?*. To collect user requirements were performed unstructured interviews (individual needs) and focus groups (group needs) through the technique of brainstorming. Additionally, using the technic «experience sampling» the group of technical experts monitored the process of defining user requirements. Table 1 shows the User Requirements UR(1-21) and Members M(1-11) of USAER#94 who requested the requirements.

As shown in Table 1, in this stage 11 members of the USAER#94 participated, which determined 21 user requirements for the design of a groupware application that will help them to communicate, collaborate and develop activities-task individual and collective, and at the same time allowed to achieve the group's goals.

Stage 2. Functional Requirements: It means to the *applications needs*, i.e., technical specifications of the application. This stage is performed by the «technical experts» group. It is worth mention-

Table 1. User requirements «USAER#93»

UR	Requirement	M1	M2	M3	M4	M5	M6	M7	M8	M9	M10	M11
UR1	The application must include a space that keeps informed to the members group.	✓		✓	✓				✓			
UR2	Space to store different types of documents.	✓		✓	✓	✓			✓			✓
UR3	Notifications about the application activity.	✓										
UR4	Section that allows direct communication through chat.	✓		✓						✓		
UR5	Access to shared information.	✓	✓			✓				✓		✓
UR6	Videoconferencing.	✓		✓		✓			✓			
UR7	Notification of read message.	✓										
UR8	User profile.	✓				✓			✓			
UR9	Organization of shared information.				✓			✓	✓			
UR10	Register of access to page.							✓				
UR11	Notification of change in shared documents.				✓			✓				
UR12	Delivery Notification of documents according to established schedule.		✓								✓	
UR13	Forum.				✓			✓				
UR14	Search bottom.		✓		✓							
UR15	Collaborative document.				✓				✓		✓	
UR16	Multiple edition.				✓				✓		✓	
UR17	Notes section.					✓						
UR18	Schedule.					✓			✓			
UR19	Application access								✓	✓		
UR20	Color notifications								✓			
UR21	User registration									✓		

ing at this point that a user requirement can lead to several functional requirements. The question associated with this stage was: How could meet user needs to achieve the group's goals through a groupware application?

In this stage the functional requirements are classified according to the characteristics of the *Specific Functions of Groupware (GSF)*. Table 2 shows the list of functional requirements classified and the user requirement which satisfy.

Stage 3. Process Flows and Users Scenarios: It allows take into account the necessary steps for that a user or user-group complete a task. In this stage the design of the flows allowed to visualize the interactions between members of the working group and define the flow of communication, coordination and collaboration necessaries to perform an activity or task and meet the group objectives. In this stage were identified three principal actors and their information flows.

Table 2. Functional requirements classified according to Specific Functions of Groupware

Specific Function of Groupware	Functional Requirements	Accomplish with the User Requirement
Communication	The application displays information or relevant events to the working group.	UR1
	It allows group members receive notifications about important events, such as publications in the news section, among others.	UR3 UR11
	It allows 1:1 communication between two group members through text messages.	UR4
	It allows 1:N communication between group members through text messages.	UR4
	It displays users who are online, away, busy or disconnected in the chat.	UR4
	It allows display if a message sent through the chat was read by receiver through a symbol or color.	UR UR7
	It allows 1:1 communication between group members through video or audio conference.	UR6
	It allows 1:N communication between group members through video or audio conference.	UR6
	It allows send text messages, voice or video to members not connected in the application.	UR7
	Sign up in the application through the request of demographic data.	UR8 UR21
	It displays user registration information (user profile).	UR8
	It allows identify the user name that stored documents in the repository.	UR9
	It allows identify in a notification the user who perform an action on the platform (e.g., share a file) and it is sent automatically to other group members.	UR12
	It allows searching shared documents.	UR14
	It allows access to the platform through a username and password.	UR19
Coordination	It displays the date and time of access to application	UR4 UR10
	Sets different types of users, e.g. moderator, member group, guess, among others.	UR8
	It allows organizing the repository documents (e.g., areas, tasks, activities, among others).	UR9
	Keeps users informed about document delivery according to schedule established by the working group or the group moderator.	UR12
	It allows multiple editing in a collaborative document.	UR16
	Sets a specific identifier for each group member (e.g., color), in order to differentiate modifications/edits in a collaborative document.	UR16
	It allows taking text or audio notes during a conversation 1: 1, 1: N through voice or video conferencing.	UR17
	It allows scheduling meetings and important events for the workgroup.	UR18
	It allows classifying the importance level in sending notifications (e.g. normal, important, urgent)	UR20
Collaboration	It allows create and edit important events for group members.	UR1
	It allows access, store, view, and download documents from repository of shared objects.	UR2 UR5
	It allows establishing security filters on shared documents, limiting aspects such as access, viewing, editing, among others.	UR5
	It allows storing data (e.g., text, video and voice) in the 1:1, 1:N communications.	UR6
	It allows group members write questions, suggestions and/or recommendations.	UR13
	It allows create collaborative documents (collaboration between members in a shared space).	UR15

- **Actor 1. Classroom Teacher (Teacher of a Regular School).**
  - ◦ The information flow between the classroom teacher and the member's family.
    - ▪ The main activity of the classroom teacher is to identify the students with educational special needs, and then communicate this to his parents.
    - ▪ Provide information about the educational student progress and collaborate with the special activities and tasks planned for the special educational student.
  - ◦ The information flow between the classroom teacher and the support group.
    - ▪ Conduct the identified student to the support group.
    - ▪ Collaborate in the special activities and tasks planned to the special educational student
- **Actor 2. Family (Father/Mother (Student With Special Educational Needs)).**
  - ◦ The information flow between the member's family and the support group.
    - ▪ Authorize the attention of the support group to the student with educational special needs.
    - ▪ Collaborate in the special activities and tasks planned to the special educational student
- **Actor 3. Support Group (USAER).**
  - ◦ The information flow between the support group and the classroom teacher.
    - ▪ Organize, plan and coordinate the educational activities and tasks for the student with special educational needs.
  - ◦ The information flow between the support group and the family.
    - Provide information about initial evaluation considering the point of view of the specialist in Communication, Psychologist and Social Work.
    - Provide continuous information about the educational student progress.

Stage 4. Prototyping: Through design prototypes it is possible answer the question, How can users know what is trying to design if they cannot see?. With the participation of the members (USAER#94) were designed "paper prototypes" which allow transfer the functional requirements into something tangible, this allowed participants to initially display the graphical user interface of the application (see Figure 3a and 3c). Later, the group designed "low-fidelity" prototypes (Figure 3b and 3d). Figure 3 shows some user interface paper/low-fidelity prototypes

Stage 5. Conceptual Evaluation: In this stage were presented to the 9 members of the USAER#60 and USAER75 the low-fidelity prototypes made by participants of USAER#94 in the first four stages of the process, additionally, there were provided with a list of the next 24 design patterns to make the evaluation proposed by Luna et al., (2014.), see Table 3.

The process used to conduct the evaluation is described next:

1. **Description:** The low-fidelity prototypes were evaluated from the perspective of «user experience» in order to identify problems in the user interfaces and get feedback from expert users, also ensure the relevance of simulated interactions through the low-fidelity prototypes for the development of individual and collective activities of group members, furthermore the usability degree of the application.
2. **Participants:** In the evaluation participated six research professors with international recognition in usability, human-computer interaction and user-centered design, also the second group participated «9 professional expert users» of the USAER#60 and USAER#75 who did not participated in the first 4 stages.

Figure 3. Low-fidelity prototypes construction by participants

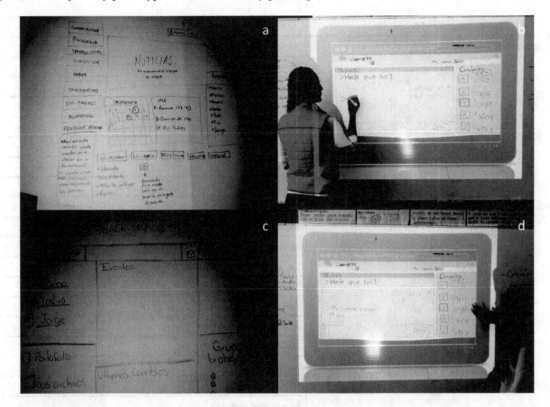

3. **Procedure:** The process to conduct the evaluation consists of the next three phases:

    a. **Phase 1. Training:** In this phase the evaluators explained to the expert users the purpose of the study and were provided with the formats «general information, list of design patterns, scenarios-tasks-subtasks, severity rating and problem description»; it is important to note that these formats are based on proposals of evaluations by Klemmer (2014) and usability by Nielsen (1993:2013).

    b. **Phase 2. Evaluation:** Expert users individually evaluated the low-fidelity prototypes using the design patterns of Table 3.

The feedback helped to determinate the usefulness and usability of the digital mockup in the development of working groups' activities, this feedback was complemented by a session of final comments between the group of evaluators and research team.

The 11 tasks and 35 subtasks that experts' users completed during the evaluation process are described below. The evaluators asked participants to simulate the tasks on the low-fidelity prototype, necessaries to perform the activities in a working group.

1. Register in the application:
    a. Register to use the application.
2. Application access:
    a. Access to the application.

Table 3. Conceptual evaluation based on groupware

Specific Function of Groupware	Design Pattern
Communication	Participation request
	Participation offer
	Participation absence
	Participation silent
	Environment conditioning
	Encouraging conditioning
	Encouraging feedback
	Communication status notification
Coordination	System access
	Member profile
	Member role
	List of members
	Task management
	Activity request
	Activity selection
	Direct assignment of activity
	Activity delegation
	Mediate the participation
	Information exchange
	Recording information
	Notification of activity status
	Notification of participation status
Collaboration	Complementary collaboration tools
	Notification of collaboration status

Source: Luna et al., 2014

3. User profile:
    a. Locate the option to edit the user profile.
4. Communicate through text messaging:
    a. Send a text message to all group members through chat application.
    b. Send a text message to only one group member.
    c. Send a text message to a group member with status "not connected".
    d. Click on forum menu.
    e. Create a comment in the forum.
    f. Read a comment in the forum.
5. Identify elements in the interface (interpreting chat interface):
    a. Identify elements in the chat window to provide some kind of feedback that lets users know who is writing (this allows you to switch the turn to write-reply to a text message during a conversation).

      b.   Identify the elements that create and save a personal text note or audio.

6.   Communicate using videoconferencing:
      a.   Activate camera (moderator role)
      b.   Access to a videoconferencing (member role).
      c.   Send request (moderator role) to other group members and add them to a videoconference.
      d.   Maximize the view of the group members connected in videoconferencing.
      e.   Click on the button «participation request».

7.   Identify elements in the interface (interpret videoconferencing interface):
      a.   Identify the user who requested to speech (raise the hand gesture).
      b.   Identify the interface item that displays the participation status of each group member.
      c.   Identify the item in the interface that allows moderator disable all the microphones group members (action silent).
      d.   Identify the interface item that displays the remaining time about the participation of a particular group member.
      e.   Identify the interface element that displays the group member whose turn in speaking.
      f.   Click on the button «record» videoconference.

8.   Share information:
      a.   Click on the «repository» menu.
      b.   Identify the button «add» document.
      c.   Identify and access to the personal storage area in repository.
      d.   Access to «restricted» folder in the personal area.

9.   Shared document (interpret shared interface):
      a.   Click on the «collaborating» menu.
      b.   Activate the option «shared document» in the drop-down menu.
      c.   Identify interface elements that let you show the collaboration between group members.
      d.   Maximize the shared «blackboard».

10.   Project Management:
      a.   Click on the «coordinate» menu.
      b.   Create a new project and assign members.
      c.   Create an activity and assign responsible.
      d.   Access to the project status.

11.   Application Exit:
      a.   Exit the application.

The evaluation identifies several simple interface usability problems. However, there are problems that require urgent attention, from the perception of the user experience the results were as follows:

- Member role, *clarify the function or role of each member in a meeting according to the USAER role.*
- Activity delegation, *provide additional mechanisms to delegate an activity according to the role of each member.*
- Information exchange, *improve the repository interface to avoid problems of interpretation in its items.*

- Notification of Collaboration status, *improve the interactive feedback provided and apply it in all the interfaces.*
- Activity request, *improve the «interaction cost» during the request process activity.*

After implementation tasks and subtasks, it should be noted that the 9 evaluators completed in its whole the tasks and subtasks scheduled.

FUTURE RESEARCH DIRECTIONS

Improve the prototype based on obtained feedback after the study; conduct a longitudinal usability study with other working groups in order to compare results; develop a software application based on the digital mockup and finally construct a strategy that allows the design of web and mobile applications to support the working group activities.

CONCLUSION

In this chapter were identified several contextual issues which should be considered in order to achieve a basic but well-designed user interfaces for groupware applications. Said aspects were addressed from two perspectives: the users' interactive requirements; and the functional requirements to support users' interactions.

The feedback and insights provided by participants (20 active members of a Mexican federal educational-support group called USAER) allow to match design-interaction to their daily activities related to communication with others and resources access.

Our findings suggested that even if the study was performed in an educational scenario, several activities and interactions could be considered as general since group communication principles matched with participants' perception. In this vein, results could help designers to achieve adequate interfaces for groupware in many scenarios providing a good starting-point for that reason.

REFERENCES

Baker, K., Greenberg, S., Gutwin, C., (2001). Heuristic Evaluation of Groupware Based on the Mechanics off Collaboration. *EHCI'01*, 123-139.

Berkenbrock, C., da Silva, A., & Hirata, C. (2009). Designing and Evaluating Interfaces for Mobile Groupware Systems. *Computer Supported Cooperative Work in Design, CSCWD*, 368-373.

Carroll, J. M. (2002). *Human-Computer Interaction in the new Millennium*. Addison-Wesley.

Dix, A., Finlay, J., Abowd, G. D., & Beale, R. (2004). *Human-Computer Interaction* (3rd ed.). Milan, Italy: Pearson Education/Prentice Hall.

Dow, S. P., Glassco, A., Kass, J., Schwarz, M., Schwartz, D. L., & Klemmer, R., S. (2010). Parallel prototyping leads to better design results, more divergence, and increased self-efficacy. *Transactions on Computer-Human Interaction (TOCHI), 17*(4).

Ellis, C. A., Gibbs, S. J., & Rein, G. (1991). Groupware: Some Issues and Experiences. *Communications of the ACM, 34*(1), 39–58. doi:10.1145/99977.99987

Fechner, T., Wilhelm, D. & Kray, C. (2015). Ethermap-Real-time Collaborative Map Editing. *CHI´15 Interactive & Multi-surface Maps*, 3583-3592. DOI: 10.1145/2702123.2702536

Gerónimo-Castillo, G., & Canseco, V. (2002). Breve Introducción a los Sistemas Colaborativos: Groupware & Workflow. *Temas - Universidad Tecnológica de la Mixteca*, 49-54.

Gräther, W., Laclavik, M., & Tomasek, M. (2014). Support for Collaboration between Large and Small & Medium Enterprises. In *Proceedings of ACM Conference on Supporting Groupwork, GROUP´14*, (pp. 288-290). Sanibel Island, FL: ACM Press. doi:10.1145/2660398.2663773

Hall, M. J., Jones, K., Bermell-Garcia, P., & David Hansen, D. (2015). Argumentation in virtual collaborative environments addressing complex issues through remote synchronous collaboration. In *Proceedings of 9th Annual IEEE International Systems Conference, SysCon*, (pp. 249-255). Vancouver, BC, Canada: IEEE Press.

Hartson, R., & Pyla, P. (2012). *The UX Book*. Morgan Kaufmann.

Jeners, N., & Prinz, W. (2014). Metrics for Cooperative Systems. *Proceedings of ACM Conference on Supporting Groupwork, GROUP´14*, (pp. 91-99). Sanibel Island, FL: ACM Press.

Johansen, R. (1991). Groupware: Furture Directions and Wild Cards. *Journal of Organizational Computing, 1*(2), 219–227. doi:10.1080/10919399109540160

Johnson-Lenz, P., & Johnson-Lenz, T. (1982). Groupware: The Process and Impacts of Design Choices. *Computer-Mediated Communication Systems: Status and Evaluation*.

Johnson-Lenz, P., & Johnson-Lenz, T. (1998). Groupware: Coining and Defining It. *SIGGROUP Bulletin, 19*(2), 34. doi:10.1145/290575.290585

Klemmer, S. (2014). *Human Computer Interaction*. The Design Lab, University of California, San Diego. Retrieved from http://goo.gl/OVNcFc

Knowles, B., Rouncefield, M., Harding, M., & Davies, N. (2015). Models and Patterns of Trust. *CSCW 2015, Trust & Anonynity*, 328-338.

Lococo, A., & Yen, D. C. (1998). Groupware: Computer Supported Collaboration. In Telematics and Informatics (pp. 85-101). Elsevier Science.

Lowdermilk, T. (2013). *User Centered Design A Developer's Guide to Building User-Friendly Applications*. Sebastopol, CA: O'Reilly Media.

Luna, H., Mendoza, R., Vargas, M., Muñoz, J., Álvarez, F. J., & Rodríguez, L. C. (2014). A Classification of Design Patterns to Support mobile Groupware Systems. *Proceeding of the 5th Mexican Conference on Human-Computer Interaction*. Doi:10.1145/2676690.2676691

Macías, G. J. (2003). *Teorías de la Comunicación Grupal en la Toma de Decisiones: Contexto y Caracterización*. Tesis Doctoral. Universitat Autónoma de Barcelona.

Marsh, J. (2016). *UX for Beginners: 100 Short Lessons to Get You Started*. Sebastopol, CA: O'Reilly.

Megasari, R., Kuspriyanto, K., Husni, E. M., & Widyantoro, D. H. (2015). Towards host to host meeting scheduling negotiation. *International Journal of Advances in Intelligent Informatics*, *1*(1), 23–29.

Mendoza, R. (2016). *User Centered Design Strategies for Massive Open Online Courses (MOOCs)*. Hershey, PA: IGI Global. doi:10.4018/978-1-4666-9743-0

Morabito, V. (2014). Digital Work and Collaboration. In *Trends and Challenges in Digital Business Innovation* (pp. 133–131). Milan: DOI; doi:10.1007/978-3-319-04307-4_7

Moreno-Rocha, M. A., & Peralta-Calvo, M. (2015). *La usabilidad y experiencia del usuario*. In *La Interacción Humano-Computadora en México* (p. 347). Pearson.

Neyem, A., Ochoa, S. F., & Pino, J. A. (2008). Coordination Patterns to Support Mobile Collaboration. Groupware: Design, Implementation, and Use. *14th International Workshop, CRIWG 2008*, 248-265. Doi:10.1007/978-3-540-92831-7_21

Nielsen, J. (1993). *Usability Engineering*. Mountain View, CA: Morgan Kaufmann.

Nielsen, J., & Budiu, R. (2013). *Mobile Usability*. New Riders.

Nielsen, J., & Norman, D. (2014). *User experience encompasses all aspects of the end-user's interaction with the company, its services, and its products*. Retrieved February 20, 2016, from: URL: https://www.nngroup.com/articles/definition-user-experience/

Norman, D. (2013). *The Design of Everyday Things: Revised and Expanded Edition*. New York: Basic Books.

Noruega-García, M. (2009). *Modelado y Análisis de Sistemas CSCW, Siguiendo un Enfoque de Ingeniería Dirigida por Odontologías*. Granada: Editorial de la Universidad de Granada.

Ortega, M., & Bravo, J. (2001). Trabajo Cooperativo con Ordenador. In *La Interacción Persona-Ordenador*. Castilla-La Mancha, España: Ediciones de la Universidad de Castilla - La Mancha.

Prates, R. O., Rosson, M. B., & de Souza, C. S. (2015). Interaction Anticipation: Communicating Impacts of Groupware Configuration Settings to Users. In *Proceedings of 5th International Symposium, End-User Development, IS-EUD*, (pp. 192-197). Madrid, Spain: Springer International Publishing. doi:10.1007/978-3-319-18425-8_15

Preece, J., Rogers, Y., Sharp, H., Benyon, D., Holland, S., & Carey, T. (1994). *Human Computer Interaction. United Sates*. Addison-Wesley Publishing Company.

Preguica, N., Martins, L., Domingos, E., & Duarte, S. (2005). Integrating Synchronous and Asynchronous Interactions in Groupware Applications. *LNCS*, *3706*, 89–104.

Sagar, A. B. (2012). Transparency Computation for Work Groups. *LNCS*, *7154*, 265–266.

SEP. (2006). *Orientaciones Generales para el Funcionamiento de los Servicios de Educación Especial - Integración Educativa.* Zacatecas: Secretaría de Educación Pública, Gobierno del Estado de Zacatecas.

SigCHI. (1982). *The ACM Special Interest Group on Computer-Human Interaction. Association for Computing Machinery.* Retrieved 20 February, 2016 from: http://www.sigchi.org

Sosa, M., Velázquez, I., Zarco, R., & Postiglioni, A. (2006). Modelo de Soporte para el Trabajo y Aprendizaje Colaborativo de Grupos de Investigación. *XII Congreso Argentino de Ciencias de la Computación*, 1034-1044.

Suarez, M.C. (2011). *SIRIUS: Sistema de Evaluación de la Usabilidad Web Orientado al Usuario y basado en la Determinación de Tareas Críticas* (Tesis Doctoral). Universidad de Oviedo, España.

UsabilityFirst. (2015). *Low-fidelity prototype.* Retrieved March 14, 2016, from http://goo.gl/2Ja8Ed

Usability.gov. (2015). *Improving the User Experience.* Retrieved March 14, 2016, from http://goo.gl/f3G6Ux

Wilson, G. L. (2007). *Grupos en Contexto, Liderazgo y Participación en Grupos Pequeños.* McGraw-Hill.

Winograd, T. (1994). Designing the Designer. *Human-Computer Interaction*, *9*(1), 128–132.

KEY TERMS AND DEFINITIONS

Good Design: Good design in products, services, or events allow people to achieve those things that are important for them, achieve their goals and values, and eventually get happiness.

Group Communication: It refers to the interaction between group members and it is the most important function of a group, since it is the process in which messages are exchanged and information is shared.

Groupware: A set of technologies integrated into a system that allows work groups to perform a common task using a shared environment.

Low-Fidelity Prototype: A prototype that is sketchy and incomplete, that has some characteristics of the target product but is otherwise simple, usually in order to quickly produce the prototype and test broad concepts.

Usability Testing: Usability testing refers to evaluating a product or service by testing it with representative users. Typically, during a test, participants will try to complete typical tasks while observers watch, listen and takes notes. The goal is to identify any usability problems, collect qualitative and quantitative data and determine the participant's satisfaction with the product (usability.gov).

USAER: Unit of Support Services for Regular Education, USAER» the purpose of this support group is to promote the integration of children with special educational needs to school in early education schools and regular basic education.

User Centered Design: Is an interactive methodology of software development, whose characteristic is ensure the usability of the software to be developed, placing the user at the center of the design process, and software development, from the initial concept to the final design.

Chapter 13

An Exploratory Study on the Interaction Beyond Virtual Environments to Improve Listening Ability When Learning English as a Second Language

Pablo A. Alcaraz-Valencia
Universidad de Guadalajara, Mexico

Laura S. Gaytán-Lugo
Universidad de Colima, Mexico

Sara C. Hernández Gallardo
Universidad de Guadalajara, Mexico

ABSTRACT

In this chapter, an exploratory research on people's interaction with a virtual environment as tool in a way in which listening comprehension occurs while improving English as a second language is addressed. Unlike technologies such as virtual environments, where users have to use hardware in order to get immersed inside of a fictional world, it is through holographic technologies that it is possible to extract virtuality and insert it into reality, and thus, have an approach to the real nature of the virtual world without using electronic devices. Why is it important to focus on the ability of listening to understand when people want to acquire English as a second language? What are the strategies that must be employed to improve this ability? What kind of advantages may users achieve through their interaction with holography? These are some of the questions that will to be answered in this chapter.

DOI: 10.4018/978-1-5225-2616-2.ch013

INTRODUCTION

Be proficient in English language provides access to a great library of ideas, scientific and technical resources in that language. Likewise, Richards (2008) mentions that English is the language of human communication that it is holding a growing demand in the incorporation of effective mechanisms to assist in its learning. According to experts, for non-native English speakers, mastering this language brings access to quality studies, especially abroad. English language proficiency offers more and better opportunities, not only in education but also in the workplace (Heredia & Chacón, 2015). English fluency empowers people, allowing them to make demands, to publicize achievements not only in their context but also in a globally, among others. In Latin American countries, overcome difficulties of learning English, it is a task with great personal, educational and social consequences. For example, in the case of Mexico, despite being the neighbor of the United States, Mexican people have low English level (Calderón, 2015). According to data produced by the results of the human capital in Mexico survey in 2008, the Center for Development Research (CIDAC, in Spanish) reported that 35% of respondents say they only have minimum English knowledge, while only 2% say master the language at a high level (Heredia, & Rubio, 2015).

In the struggle for trying to improve English skills as a second language, in recent decades, several researchers have tried to use different techniques and technological tools to support different educational practices. Examples ranging from "simple" technology as audiotapes, to more flamboyant technologies such as 3D virtual environments. However, the mere fact of integrating a technological tool to enhance different or several English skills, is nor efficient neither effective by itself. On the one hand, the selected technological tool needs to be accompanied by an instructional design, which in turn contains the necessary teaching strategies according to student needs in a certain context; and on the other hand, it should not represent a shock or a sudden change for the learner at the time to interact with it.

Therefore, as an exploratory study, in this book chapter we present the holographic technology as a mean of interaction to improve the listening ability named "listening to understand" on the acquisition of English as a second language. The chapter begins with a background, where results of different instruments applied in order to know English level reached by Mexicans are presented; as well as research projects that propose the use of several technological tools used as an educational support in order to improve English skills of different users or learners in particular contexts. After the above, there is a subsection that explains what does interaction mean, and then emphasize its importance as a means of communication between the learner and the technology used as educational tool support. Following the background, a section which defines listening, and listening to understand in a second language is presented. In this same section we argue about choosing the right strategies for effective improvement in the listening ability of the learner. After that, a set of references is shown in order to demonstrate that technologies by themselves do not represent an improvement, and that there are certain parameters that must be defined to choose the right technology for solving the problem that it is faced. Likewise, we introduce the context as one of the main variables to take into account in order to get good interactions; we explain the need of knowing the environment in which the learner is involve, as well as her experiences and knowledge of the world. On the next subsection, we argue about the opportunity to improve listening to understand ability by certain types of technologies and effective strategies, given way to the solution and recommendations section where holographic technology is proposed as a mean of interaction in order to improve the ability mention before. Finally, we present conclusions and future work.

BACKGROUND

English as a Second Language in Mexico

According to Heredia & Rubio (2015), for Mexicans, to count with English skills is imperative. Nowadays, Mexico is paying high costs for the lack of a national policy on teaching and learning English as a second language, because, in terms of public offering, for most of the students is very difficult to have access to an education where learning English through a quality program is included. In this sense, one of the main problems of the Mexican education system is that it does not have instruments or measures on the knowledge and use of English as a second language, and for that reason, it is impossible to have a reliable assessment.

Based on an official document of the Mexican Secretariat of Public Education (2008; 2015) concerning the teaching English language practices at basic level, both primary and secondary education, they can be identified: reading aloud, translation, vocabulary lists, and choral repetition, among other activities. Wrongly and with no success, Mexican education system expects that with these kind of exercises, Mexican students can achieve mastery of a foreign language.

Furthermore, in 2013 a survey applied by Consulta Mitofsky, a company that conducts periodic surveys of public opinion, reported that only 12% of Mexicans say speak English. The survey highlights that only 14.5% of the urban population declares speak English, while in rural communities this occurs in 2.4% of people. In northern Mexico, the survey shows that only one of each five says that speak and understand English very well, while to the south of the country the result was one out of twenty five.

Likewise, Mexicanos Primero (2014), a citizens' initiative, reports through the EF English Proficiency Index that Mexico is at "low level", standing at 39th position of the 63 countries evaluated for the 2014 edition.

Meanwhile, according to the results regarding performance after applying the TOEFL iBT in order to measure the ability to use and understand English as a second language at the university level, Mexico nationwide averaged 86 on a scale of 0 to 120 points between January and December 2014. This international assessment instrument evaluates how well people combines listening, reading, speaking, and writing skills in order to performance academic tasks, and each skill has a score range. The average per skill are: 23 points for listening skills, 22 points for oral skills, 21 points for reading skills, and 21 points for writing skills (ETS, 2015). However, while this average is acceptable to accomplish requirements for entry to secondary schools, language schools, programs four-year degree, and graduate programs; for immigration purposes or for employment schools where the language predominant is English, requirements are higher. According to the Central Intelligence Agency (CIA), it is estimated that only 0.8% of the total population fulfill all requirements to qualify with a score equal to or greater than 80 points in the TOEFL iBT.

In short, there are two types of operating problems in Mexico affect and hinder the acquisition of English as a second language. The first belongs to the public education system, which does not have a standardized instrument to assess which is the state in English as a second language of students attending any level of public and private education. Consequently, it is not possible to undertake efficiently and effectively, specific strategies in order to improve student skills regard to the acquisition of such language, without frustrating or hinder such process.

The Use of Technologies to Support English Learning

Nowadays, within educational practices that addresses the teaching and learning of English as a second language, it is common to incorporate different technology as a support tools. These technologies range from audio recordings, to the use of virtual environments.

Among the most popular examples it can be mentioned video games for educational purposes. At present, the use of video games for learning English language is common (Sørensen & Meyer, 2007; Anderson, Reynolds, Yeh, & Huang, 2008; Rankin, McNeal, Shute, & Gooch, 2008; Kuwada, 2010). For example Anderson et al. (2008) state that video games are one of the favorite support tools used by teachers. Meanwhile, Marsh (2011) explains that the use of these technologies is motivational and attractive to students.

On the other hand, there are also a lot of researches about the use of virtual environments to improve different skills when acquiring English as a second language (Lin, Shih, & Yang, 2005; Mayrath, Traphagan, Heikes, & Trivedi, 2007; Jiang, Liu, & Chen, 2010; Rashed, Lyons, & Bae, 2010; Popovici, 2011; Chung, 2012). De Freitas (2008) defines a virtual environment as an online, persistent, and interactive environment accessible by many users simultaneously. According to Ellis (1991), a virtual environment is defined as an interactive screen display in which images are enriched by special processing, which also involved non-visual elements such as audio and haptic, mixed to convince the user that she is immersed in a synthetic space. Some examples are the research project of Alcaraz-Valencia (2008) which used Second Life and Dive with students from high schools in order to improve their listening skills. Another example is the work of Pinto-Llorente, Sanchez-Gomez, & Garcia-Peñalvo (2015) who, through the creation of a virtual learning environment, improved English pronunciation of users.

Another popular tool is the multimedia software with educational purposes. In this sense, there is also a large repertoire of research and projects aiming to improve the acquisition of English as a second language through this kind of tool (Wickremaratne, Wimalaratne, & Goonetilleke, 2008; Tick, 2009; Alabbad, 2011; Reis, & Escudeiro, 2011; Chen, Chen, Chen, & Ku, 2015). One example of the use of multimedia software is the work of Khan (2014), who uses a software called Mongol Dip that helps people with visual impairments to operate windows operating system for computational tasks, and that provides an usable interface for impaired people in order to read out the contents of the document not only in the Bengali language but also in English, helping them to translate and learn vocabulary or sentences.

Digital stories are also a very popular tool used by teachers. For example, Verdugo, & Belmonte (2007) explain that, through and Internet/based technology, they created digital stories for Spaniards first graders, improving their English listening comprehension skills.

Interaction and Forms of Interaction

Although the word interaction is widely used, one of the major difficulties is that not all authors have an agreement about its definition; even though, there are important works that share similar definition of interaction. Simpson & Galbo (1986) explain that interactions are all kind of behavior in which people act upon each other. Wagner (1994) defines interaction as a reciprocal event that requires at least two objects and actions; this author adds that interaction occurs when these objects and events reciprocally influence each other. More recently, according to Dubberly, Haque, & Pangaro (2009) interaction is a way of framing the relationship between people and objects that were designed for them. All objects that were made for people and by people offer the possibility for interaction, and all design activities can be viewed as design for interaction. This remark, as it works for objects, it is also works for systems, message, among others. Meanwhile, Edmonds (2007) explains that interaction is not material, but experienced, perceived, understood, that nobody can touch, and for those reasons, to accomplish a "good" interaction it is really difficult.

In a LinkedIn forum, Rick Blunt affirms that to focus on the type of interactions that it needs to design, it needs to understand what it is trying to accomplish. In order to do that, he argues that Bloom's taxonomy should been taking into account. Bloom's taxonomy is hierarchical (from bottom to top), ordered in terms of increasing complexity of learning, and consists of the categories: creating, evaluating, analyzing, applying, understanding, and remembering (Blunt, 2014).

In the case of educational purposes there are instructional interactions and performance interactions. According to Wagner (1994) an instructional interaction is an event that occurs between a learner and a learner's environment. The purpose of an instructional interaction is that learners change their behavior toward an educational goal through some environment; this implies that instructional interaction is effective only when the learner modifies her behavior. Blunt (2014) adds that instructional are not just about to know, but to get ready in order to do something. Meanwhile this same author states that, unlike instructional interactions, performance interactions focus on doing, this means that, a performance interaction is effective only when the learner improve or modify some skill or ability.

TOWARDS IMPROVING LISTENING TO UNDERSTAND IN THE ADQUISITION OF ENGLISH AS A SECOND LANGUAGE

In order to improve listening comprehension as a part of English language acquisition by Mexican students there are a set of elements that must been taking into account: the state of the student, the context, the strategies, and the technology. In this section, we argue about the use of wrong and effective strategies in order to improve listening ability; we also explain the implications of not choosing the right technology as an educational support tool; and finally, we discuss about the need of knowing the context and experiences of the learner.

Listening Ability and the Use of Strategies

Although all the problems, that must be solved, regarding the acquisition of English as a second language in Mexico, Saricoban (1999) believes that listening is the ability that needs more attention and care, because it is from such skill that it makes possible the development of reading, speaking and writing. In this sense, Morley (1991) mentions that although the listening ability is seen as a critical element in the communication process and acquisition of a new language, its status still remains as one of the most difficult skill to acquire when people learn any language.

Rivers (1981) explains that listening is the skill that is most used. For example, it is used about twice or more than speaking, and from four to five times more that reading and writing. Therefore listening becomes an important element of learning a foreign language, as it helps the student to exhibit or not, the domain of the acquired language. Nevertheless, Burley-Allen (1989) mentions that the emphasis in the classroom about how the language is used, depends on the time of implementation. On average, students develop writing for twelve years, six to eight years for reading skills, one to two years for speaking, and for listening skills from zero to a midyear.

After a systematic review of definitions of listening in the process of English learning, that can be seen in detail in Table 1, (Pearson, 1983; Lund, 1990; Rubin, 1995; Goh, 1997; Rost, 2002; Goh, 2002; Vandergrift, 1999; Richards, & Schmidt, 2002), it concludes that listening is a process of interpretation, where the listener becomes an active entity that incorporates strategies to pay attention, facilitates, and evaluates not only what it receives through sound, but also relies on its ability to abstract in order to derive meaningful information from the preliminary messages available, and which in turns, it lies implicit in the environment and context in which the interlocutor interact.

Furthermore, listening involves implementing a set of sub mental processes that, according to O'Malley et al. (1989), and O'Malley & Chamot (1990), requires of a strategic recursive processing divided into three stages: (1) perception, (2) syntactic analysis, and (3) the implementation or use of the information received.

Rost (2005) mentions that the first stage of listening, consists in perceive, in a selective way, auditory information received to be stored in short-term memory. This memory has low capacity for holding information, therefore is filled constantly given the frequency which new information comes to be abide to analysis. At this stage, it is common that problems arise for those learning English as a second language, due to the segmentation of words and the recognizing of them, because of: speed, accents and increased other detractors as background noise, which dissipates the attention of the listener. A strategy to distinguish a good or bad performance at this stage is to check if they do not discriminate linguistic characteristics perceived in the audio input.

Table 1. Definitions of listening in learning English as a second language

Author	Definition	Gagne Taxonomy
(Pearson, 1983:5)	"Listening involves the simultaneous organization and combination of skills in Phonology, Syntax, Semantics, and knowledge of the text structure, all of which seem to be controlled by the cognitive process. Thus it can be said that though not fully realized, listening skill is essential in acquiring language proficiency"	(✓) Verbal information () Concept (✓) Rules () Problem solving () Cognitive strategy
Lund (1990)	Listening is to select a strategy to understand an audio text by: doing, choosing, transferring, responding, considering, extending, duplicating and chatting.	() Verbal information (✓) Concept () Rules () Problem solving () Cognitive strategy
(Rubin, 1995:7)	"Listening is conceived of as an active process in which listeners select and interpret information which comes from auditory and visual clues in order to define what is going on and what the speakers are trying to express"	() Verbal information (✓) Concept () Rules () Solución de problemas () Cognitive strategy
(Rost, 2002:24)	"Listening is the mental process of constructing meaning from spoken input"	() Verbal information () Concept () Rules (✓) Problem solving () Cognitive strategy
(Richards and Schmidt, 2002: 52)	"Listening comprehension (is) the process of understanding speech in a first or second language. The study of listening comprehension in second language learning focuses on the role of individual linguistic units (e.g., phonemes, words, grammatical structures) as well as the role of the listener's expectations, the situation and context, background knowledge and topic"	() Verbal information () Concept (✓) Rules () Problem solving () Cognitive strategy

Vandergrift (2007) mentions that the second stage to listening is to perform parsing, where information newcomer to the short-term memory is linked with information that was already processed and it is stored in long-term memory. The idea of this process is to create significant mental representations of gained information. At this stage, the listener does differentiate between an effective or non-effective syntactic processing, based on the amount of contextual information that can be analyzed such as words, messages, and phonology linguistic knowledge, syntax, and semantics.

Likewise, Rost (1990; 2005) mentions that the last step taken to listen, is to give usefulness to the newly processed information. An effective listener, structure the information holding in the long-term memory based on her prior knowledge, experiences, and knowledge about how the world works. The above through the mental representation of textual information perceived. In this last stage, the listener difference between a good or bad performance in accordance with the ability to outline the general knowledge of the subject matter, and then link it with the new acquired knowledge. The main idea of this final stage is to generate representations of the received information to transform it into meaningful knowledge, and not to knowledge susceptible to forget.

Likewise, both Serri, Boroujeni, & Hesabi (2012) and Rahimi (2012) identify three types of strategies used during the stages of listening to understand (perception, analysis and implementation): (1) socio affective strategies, which demand to clarify to the interlocutor when something was not understood and to read the emotions that appear in the conversation; (2) metacognitive strategies, which are the ones that organize and plan in order to assess the comprehension of the received text; and (3) cognitive strategies, which are based on an understanding of perspective approach, and refers to the way the information is understood, this can happen: as bottom-up way (joining words to find meaning), as top-down way (starting from a pre conceived idea to understand what is listening), or as interactive way (a mixture of the previous two approaches).

During the implementation of cognitive strategies (behaviors, techniques or actions), Lin (2000) mentions that the listener uses her personal knowledge and previous experiences about how the world works for: (1) to infer the speaker intention, (2) to generate assumptions about what will happen next, and (3) to verify these assumptions based on inference of relevant clues on the pronunciation of the speaker, and at the same time, non-verbal cues in the context of the conversation.

Table 2. Positive and negative strategies in order to process perceived audio input

Stages of Processing Auditory Input	Effective Strategy	Non-Effective Strategy
Perception	Keep focus on the information selection process	Process all the words, one by one, and to lose concentration because an unknown word or a less understandable word
Analysis	Analyze information from a bottom-up approach, top-down or a mixture of both	Analyze words or complete ideas continuously
Implementation	Using global knowledge about how the world works, experience and self-questioning	Not structure schematically information and generate ambiguity in the interpretation of the heard text, from an wrong internal contextualization

Source: Based on Hsueh-Jui Liu (2008)

Table 3. Listening to understand problems when undertake cognitive strategies

Hierarchy	Strategies	
	Bottom-Up	**Top-Down**
1	Recognize words limits	Use keywords to construct ideas from prior knowledge of the subject
2	Recognize vowels and consonants to identify words	Understand the roles of participants in a situation
3	Distinguish main words	Infer issues, resolutions, causes, effects and events sequences conversation
4	Recognize transitions between one idea and another	Distinguish between facts and opinions
5	Note patterns in word sequences	Insulate unimportant details for those that are important
6	Interpret stress and intonation of words	Understand the intention and tone of the conversation
7	Hold the audio input received	Construct ideas from knowledge
8	Acting at the time to receive orders, requests or instructions	Outlining and / or rank information

Source: Based on Serri, Boroujeni, & Hesabi (2012) and Rahimi (2012).

According to Abdelhamid (2007), cognitive strategies focus on four tasks: (a) understand the text untranslated, (b) focus on key words to understand new words, (c) support the main idea to understand all text and (d) rely on contextual or linguistic clues to predict or infer more information.

In other words, who tries to listen to understand when it is learning English as a second language, needs to master the execution of two types of processes that sometimes overlap, and which are unknown

Figure 1. Stages and listening strategies

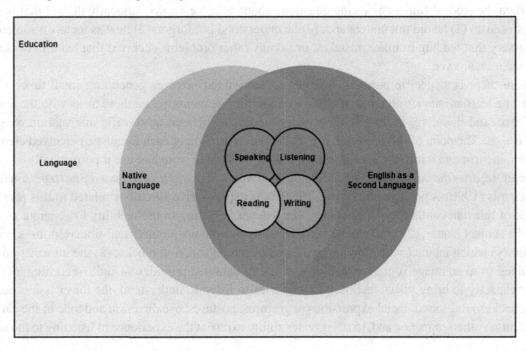

to those who translate what they listen to understand the information that is transmitted. The first process refers to the stages where the audio input information is processed, and the second concerns to the comprehension strategies undertaken during the process divided into stages.

Choosing the Right Technology for Listening Comprehension

The inability of listening comprehension texts in English as a second language, for those who translate the audio input is from the type of interaction established with the elements present in the environment where the conversation takes place; situation that result in the wrong implementation of strategies based on the complexity of the text heard, disable the processing stages of perceived audio input, disabling the processing stages of perceived audio input.

Ybarra and Green (2003) and Sharma (2009) mention that the acquisition of English as a second language needs support platforms both hardware and software that support in the development of experiences. The aim of this is streamline more significant learning outcomes compared to traditional mechanisms, such as: use computers, listen to radio, watch TV, watch videos online, use electronic audio players, implement sound recorders, to search for information online, implement voice or text mode dictionaries, real-time videoconference, writing emails, chat, among others.

Regarding to platforms employed as a listening comprehension support tool when acquiring English as a second language, the commonly such materials are mostly audio recordings. These elements do not always allow students a usable interaction in order to achieve specific goals of understanding based on the contextualization of the text they listen, with the baggage of past experiences; thus interfering with the immersion process, the quality of the generated inferences, and assumptions about the topic of conversation. At the end of the listening process, students have to answer comprehension questions. The first problem with this approach is that, in real life, almost always people know the reason why they listen something. In the same way, when a student is a beginner and interacts with a recording in order to understand, it probably do not know why is it doing. Then, immersed in a process of evaluation, when the student finish answering questions about what he knows, student will find that he was wrong because: (1) he did not understand, (2) he understood but forgot, (3) he was focus on something unnecessary that led him to make mistakes, or (4) any other problems occurred that led him to choose a less accurate answer.

Where there is a specific purpose, listening to understand involves generating small tasks which support the learner interaction through visual and auditory elements, relate these tasks with the learner experience, and therefore, at least achieve understanding of general or specific information received through texts. The point of this approach is to avoid the translation of each linguistic perceived element, and then, incorporate it into the speech, which it is impossible to store and use it permanently.

Therefore, *does the interaction with the media content is necessary to understand what a person listen to*? Richards (1990) is positive about that. The author explains five situations related to this premise: (1) lack of relevant content to put in context the listener, resulting in the inability to generate an idea about the subject matter; (2) Whoever wants to listen to understand, requires real-time responses (visual or auditory) which interact with, and not at the end of the information blocks; (3) the information that is obtained from an image is greater than the amount of data that provides an audio recording; (4) The greater capacity to bring visual feedback to who tries to listen to understand, the lower issues caused by: the background sound, facial expressions or gestures, postures, eye direction and tone of the caller's voice, among others, appears; and, (5) the greater ability to repeat the experience of listening to the audio input, with the same visual support, the greater the chances of not being distracted from background noise, pronunciation, murmurs and blanks given between the arrival of an idea and another.

In this sense, Ur (2005) proposes that in order to develop listening skills, it should have a preconceived idea about what is going to receive through the ear. This means, to know in advance the context in which a conversation allows the listener create excitement about the purpose of the conversation, leading to the possibility of expect from the speech of the speaker, certain phrases or words.

In a case study concerning problems in listening comprehension in high school students, Butt Sharif, Naseer-ud-Din, Hussain, Khan, & Ayesha (2010) propose to implement as software as hardware technology (visual and hearing support) so that students keep focus of study within the same auditory context, attention and immersed in the activity of both hardware technologies. The idea is to connect students with the topic of conversation through immersion with the surrounding environment, as it is in the physical context of student housing the elements during the analysis of the audio input, which will result in the level of understanding of the audio input received.

Similarly, both Oliver (2002) and Bannan-Ritland, Dabbagh,. & Murphy (2000) mention that the use of three-dimensional (3D) entities within virtual environments, supports contemporary theories of instructional design. Iuppa (2001) says that with the creation of 3D educational materials, it is possible to generate learning through the interaction between the student and the material; unlike the single implementation of sequences of images, sounds or readings, which only works as communication medium through information travels from one point to another. This is why, according to Winn (2002) technologies may "provide affordances that support instructional strategies that would not be possible without the technology".

The main point is that 3D educational material contains auditory and visual elements in order to interact with it, so that learning does not happen as a result of the single transmission of such information. In this order, learning is constructed by the user, as a result of the interaction with 3D educational material. In other words, the interaction with 3D objects, allows students to build their knowledge through three stages: (1) the reflection about what happens as a result of the interaction, (2) the link between the recent reflection with past interactions, and (3) predicting what will happen to future interactions. The latter based on a working model, where according to Reiser & Dempsey (2002), the instructor takes part only as an agent who is consulted and make it easier any task.

In addition to this, in practice, Alcaraz-Valencia (2008) mentions that learning in 3D virtual environments despite gather operational characteristics to provide context for those who need to enter situation, in order to obtain a visual and auditory support on which it is possible to understand the audio input received, 3D virtual environments are still far from being the solution to learning problems in the acquisition of English as a second language. The last mentioned, due to five issues that need to be resolved in order to validate and assess results which are generated on these interactive virtual environments, regarding learning to be obtained. In this sense, the first focus is that not all students of these platforms are frequent users of virtual technologies with entertainment or learning purposes, however, even having a close relationship with these technologies, a problem related to measuring usability that makes impossible to determine to what degree influences: (1) the efficiency and the effectiveness in the use of the virtual environment regarding to the potential of said interactive platform performance offered to the user. From the foregoing, are derived problems relating to select what kind of activities will take the user to construct their own knowledge. Activities such as: (2) monitoring the use of the virtual environment by the user; (3) monitoring the interaction between users participating in the activity; (4) monitoring each user interaction with the context itself (virtual environment) where the activity takes place, and

Figure 2. Virtual environments as a support tool when constructing learning based on learner interaction with other users. Visual and auditory elements, help in understanding what is listening when English as a second language is acquired

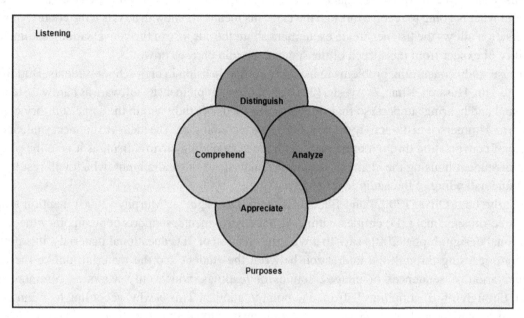

(5) monitoring the interaction established between who directs the activity (the assistant, the guide or teacher) and who are assisted (students).

In conclusion, a virtual collaborative environment does not offer support to identify what kind of interaction influence the performance of learners at the time to interact on the platform. This means that any improvement generated into the virtual environment could be due to an endless situations that not only is complex to qualify, but also is difficult to quantify, in order to determine what happened and in what degree influences the cognitive ability that the user modified .

The Importance of Context and Experience of the Learner: Avoiding Interaction Issues

Calderón (2015) mentions that education is not relevant when a learning model did not make sense to everyday life, or when both the context and the students point of view results impertinent for it. This implies that to not be aware of learner status, it will probably take him to get bad or insignificant results.

Context is essential to understanding and to make an interpretation of the text, as well as construct and communicate a message, since the personality of any person is linked to the environment in which it develops (Zilber, Tuval-Mashiach, & Lieblich, 2008). In fact Bruner (1990) emphasizes that learning about people, their lives and identities in the context in which they live is paramount in any investigation, because when human behavior is interpreted is necessary to consider physical, ethnic, historical, ideological, and gender. What is relevant to take into account the context is justified by the assumption that people do not construct their identity in a vacuum; rather they do so by social and cultural guides and norms (Tuval-Mashiach, 2014).

In this way, the context and the background of learners are also important at the time of choosing the technology as a support tool. Technologies do not cause learning by themselves, technologies give opportunities that may lead to learning if they are used in an effective way (Dickey, 2005; Dalgarno, & Lee, 2010; Dass, Dabbagh, & Clark, 2011).Difficulties on interaction between learners/users and technologies are very common, and they lead to bad results. For example, Dass et al. (2011) made a review of the use of virtual environments in order to improve different educational goals. They found that there are several studies (Mayrath, et al., 2007; Jarmon, Traphagan, Mayrath, & Trivedi, 2009; O'Connor, 2009; Wang, & Braman, 2009; Shen, & Eder, 2009; Wagner, & Ip, 2009) that evidence that demanding high levels of effort, to have technical navigation difficulties, to not explain to the students goals of the technological tool and activities, among others, represent a misstep in the chase of accomplish educational goals.

Other examples of problems that can occur by not taking into account the context of the person, can be found in Basto-Diaz Basto-Díaz, Madera-Ramírez, & Uicab-Ballote (2012) who explained, during their presentation, the problems they faced due to not considering the context when they were developing a serious game for math skills; for the original game they created a 3D environment, but they had to switch to a 2D environment when they had execution problems given the infrastructure of the schools they were working. In this sense, Hahorcade (2012; 2015) states that an important part of the design and development of technologies, is to ensure that the final product will leave the laboratory in order to achieve a social contribution through interaction with it.

As can be seen, context is useful in order to determine conditions and circumstances that may be relevant to generate useful interaction (Saracevic, 2010).

An Opportunity to Improve Listening Comprehension in a Significant Way

There are different factors that affects listening comprehension when learning a second language. Several authors have divided into categories (River, 1981; Dirven, & Oakeshott-Taylor, 1984; Samuels, 1984). For example, Boyle (1984) points out that the main elements that keep listening to understand a conversation in English as a second language are: (1) the lack of practice as the most important detractor in this process, (2) the linguistic knowledge of the language in question, (3) the general or personal experiences about how the world works (the background) to infer, to assume, to confirm or to refute hypotheses about the subject, (4) the motivation, (5) the memory and (6) the attention and the concentration on listening. Also, Teng (1993) simplified into four categories the factors that Boyle (1984) noted as part of the elements that affect listening comprehension: (1) factors in who listens (the reciver), (2) factors in the speaker (the transmitter), (3) factors on the stimuli and (4) factors in the context.

In this sense, Bacon (1992), Henner-Stanchina (1987), Murphy (1985), and Vandergrift (1996) suggest that on implementing consciously listening strategies, it will be possible to understand the texts that are heard, in order to avoid the fact of making a word by word translation of the perceived auditive text input. For this reason, Mendelsohn (1995) suggests that teachers not only need to provide students with auditory materials (based on varying degrees of difficulty) in which second language conversations happens, but also, it is necessary to give a greater weight on teaching strategies to control at will the analysis of the information received through the audio input.

Also, according to Vandergrift (2000), Teng (1998), O'Malley (1987) and Thompson, & Rubin (1996), about the listening comprehension of English as a second language, the usual focus is only situated on two aspects of the problem: (1) the cognitive comprehension strategies and (2) the instruction of them. Chang (2007) points out that listening strategies are seen only as a data input, while language acquisition corresponds to the process of digesting information, where all that matters is the ability of the listener to process the entry. From this perspective, the one who tries to understand what it is been heard in a second language, it is relegated to an isolated figure in the process of understanding where cognition is an individual phenomenon occurring separately to the environment or the context in which learning occurs.

Hansen, & Stansfield (1981), Willing (1993), Reid (1998), Branton (1999), Wintergerst, DeCapua, & Verna (2003), Ehrman, Leaver, & Oxford (2003) and Macaro Graham, & Vanderplank (2007) recommend to implement strategies to promote understanding of what is heard, via kinesthetic and context learning. This situation suggests the idea of implementing role activities where it is possible to work and interact with didactic elements present in the environment and put the user in context. This last in order to stimulate in a visual and auditory way during the immersion process with the activity that it is going to be performed.

From Genesee (1985) to Nieminen (2006), it is mentioned that one way to encourage the student during the acquisition of a new language, is to get in contact with real situations, where there is a need to speak in order to communicate. Roussou (2006), Bell (2008), Calongne (2008), Eschenbrenner, Nah, & Siau (2008), Girvan, & Savage (2010) and Kallonis & Sampson (2010) agree that adapting technological tools such as virtual reality combined with collaborative learning strategies, provide an alternative pathway in the generation of knowledge. In this sense, Zhang (2010) suggests that the implementation of collaborative activities, connect the participants and the environment that it is around (and vice versa). The idea of virtualizing environments is to enhance the intrinsic characteristics that exist in the real spaces (images and audio), and playing with them in order to carry out activities with a greater impact compared to that obtained in a traditional situation. For this reason, the graphics and sound features in a virtual environment are useful. They help to motivate and engage participants in the interaction process, through which immersion is generated and then, it is possible to obtain knowledge. According to Csiksgentmihalyi (1990), the idea is that the interaction inside of the virtual environment is directed in a way that boredom does not act against the activity that is going to be performed.

According Bizzocchi, & Paras (2005) virtual environments are effective when used for exploration. According to Norman (1993) the learning materials 3D presented in virtual environments are characterized by: (1) providing mechanisms to generate interaction and feedback, (2) presenting to the user an specific way to perform on tasks under defined procedures, (3) introducing elements that help the user to generate motivation, (4) providing activities that are not as difficult to perform and frustrate, or as simple to perform and get bored, (5) producing a sense of commitment to the activity being performed while experiencing the environment, (6) providing tools related to user capabilities, and activities to perform that help in order to not distract the attention on the user performance, and (7) generating an immersive experience without distractors agents. In this sense, Bizzocchi, & Paras (2005) mention that if accepted the requirements that Norman (1993) defined as necessary on a virtual learning environment, implicitly we are accepting that learning is linked to games. This last based on the idea that video games (virtual or not) are activities where it is possible to interact and to collaborate. Also, inside of them are hidden the necessary requirements to carry out any activity in a way that the results of the performance are less tedious versus doing the same activity in another way.

Figure 3. Listening comprehension and audio input processing

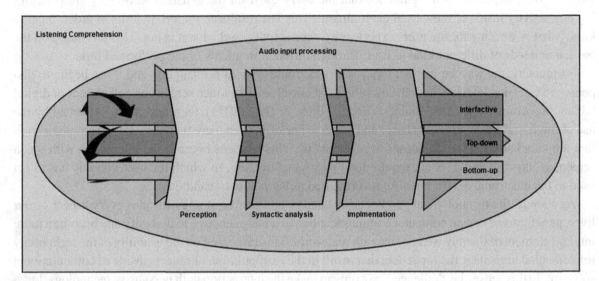

SOLUTIONS AND RECOMMENDATIONS

Holography is a way to retrieve the likeness of a subject from a record of its unfocused diffraction pattern (Collier, Burckhardt, & Lin, 1971). For Workman (2013) holography is a photographic technique that records the light scattered from an object, and then presents it in a way that appears three-dimensional. The word "hologram" comes from the Greek language, where "holos" means "all" and "grapho" corresponds to "recording". According to Jong (1999), a hologram is recording (or displaying) of two or three images that reflect different angles of an object. In this context, it is through the perspective that this phenomenon is conceived by the human brain as a single three-dimensional image, while it is observed. Based on the above, it is possible to create optical illusions to represent virtual environments that, while also synchronized with auditory information, it is possible for a user to dive inside a fictional environment where interaction is not limited to an electronic display device. Over this matter, holography requires mechanisms of communication so that the user can interact with holograms. On this last, the idea is to generate interaction by implementing computer vision algorithms that can connect the user actions over the hologram used, and later, link this to the communication system that controls the media content. All of this by not implementing an electronic device while the feedback occurs between the user's performance and the virtual reality enhanced by the holograms.

The problem is not that there are not efficient and effective mechanism to assist the user on the immersion with virtual environment, and then produce a contextualization by means of which certain level of depth is reached. The problem is that virtual reality, from where it is presented to the user, tends to require electronic devices that invade the physical space. Situation that has not even certainty about physiological or health impact, given the user's prolonged proximity to objects that emit thermal and electromagnetic radiation, such as virtual reality helmets and goggles. In addition, in situations where this kind of environments are meant to generate learning, virtual worlds do not provide support to determinate what kind of interaction and how this activity, influences the cognitive changes of the users. In this sense, a virtual environment does not result that much practical in order to get an overview about what is going on, between the guidance that the users get from the assistant while they are performing any activity inside of the virtual environment. This last results an important issue in order to get to know what is working for the users experience on the activity, and what it is not. This last based on the particular needs of different kind of users through different moments of the performed task.

Fortunately, the way we interact today with electronic devices is changing, and it has begun to dispense artifacts that interfere with the usability of themselves, like touch screens on cell phones or digital tablets. According to Richter, Blaha, Wiethoff, Baur, & Butz (2011), the interaction performed by the use of fingers on touch screens is faster and easier to perform, even more than the type of communication that requires hardware like a mouses or a keyboards. This happens because the interaction with touch screens is intuitive and does not require long periods of training, in which the user not only has to get used to the electronic device but also, it is required to learn how to handle it.

As soon as the technological gap becomes smaller and the technology invades every aspect of our lives, paradigms of human computer communication will change enough to diversify and become a more integral element of the way we interact with real world. This last based on the usability of the technology implemented to manage the input data that result in the manipulation of objects inside of computational software. In this sense, the challenge is not only to make the interaction with persuasive technology, but it is also easy to perform. Even more than the one that it is implemented without intervention of technology.

Moscovich (2007) mentions that the touch interaction allows users to communicate with computers quickly and fluidly, rather than do the same with "clicks". Still, for problems such as multi touch handling through two or three dimensional objects on touch screens, it is required from the user a figurative mental resolution to establish points of reference. In this sense, it is needed the same kind of proceeding in order to trigger and solve a sequential (or parallel) reasoning about how to interact with these digital material, and then, manipulate it to reach a specific level of interaction. In this sense, issues like those showed in the next question must not be an issue to solve: should I click on or over the object?, Should I drag it from right to left or from left to right?, Should I expand it from corners?, Why it is possible to expand the object from the left corner and it does not happen the same when I expand it from the right?, If it is a three dimensional object, am I able to put it upside down?, in this last case, why it does not respond to the laws of physics?

In this sense, holograms represent a possibility that, from our perspective, they gather the necessary requirements to establish interaction and immersion in an efficient and effective way. This last given the challenges that even the properties of touch interaction represent in order to fuse them, with educational materials when they get integrated to collaborative activities, and where the professor implements an audio and visual support when it is necessary. Thus, the properties of the 3D hologram are divided into three characteristics that benefits our vision of implementation to solve listening problems while it is intended to understand the auditive texts in a second language: (1) the holograms does not require electronic devices to interact with the media system. This minimizes the learning curve that the user experiments in order to interact with the technology. (2) The holograms can recreate virtual environments from which the user interacts and generates immersion with the context. And (3) holograms make possible to monitor the collaborative activity based on the attendance and the observation to determinate in real time, what works and what does not, according to how users respond over the work they are meant to accomplished about the activity performed. This leads to the possibility of merging a virtual environment with those activities meant to be performed within the traditional classroom, in order to give to the professor the responsibility to decide how to proceed when the virtualized educational material does not benefit the students needs.

FUTURE RESEARCH DIRECTIONS

Based on a systematic review of literature, it will be designed a construct that serves as the basis of a framework which will be transformed into a holographic tool of interaction, so that undergraduate students get to understand what they are listening in English as a second language. This process begins with the selection of a tool to determinate what is it the status of two thousand participants about the level of difficulty when there is a need of understanding the auditory input data when English learning happens. Later, it will be performed a statistical analysis to determinate how do the items of instrument get interrelated. The idea is to find out how the qualitative and quantitative dependencies work inside of the construct to validate it, and then, incorporate the resolution to a framework, which will be embedded into the technological and holographic tool of interaction. Finally, two groups of participants will be conformed. One of them will make use of the holographic tool, while the other group of participants will use the traditional educational support such as audio recordings on electronic devices. In this sense, it is intended to contrast the results of the type of interaction implemented when using holograms, and that one that it is implemented in the traditional classroom.

CONCLUSION

Start by giving importance to the context, the experiences and the background of the students mean that it has been made a diagnosis about the abilities status about what it is wanted to get better, and on what it is possible to achieve. This last based on the strategies implemented given the technological tools to establish interaction.

Interaction on virtual environments happens on different levels. This levels may change according to the elements interrelated in this process. In order interaction happens, a group of data must be transformed into perceptible stimulus for the user. The idea is to provide a way in which the user can transform information into knowledge based on the interaction with audio, visual, haptic and odoriferous interfaces. On this matter, interaction corresponds to the process in which a transaction of information happens between a virtual environment, a purpose on the performance and resolution of an activity and the users. In this sense, this last three elements constitutes the context, which implies the analysis of information that could be transformed into an experience. Based on the later, the immersion is a quality of the context in order to recreate experiences, from the fidelity of communication interfaces used in the interaction process.

What this chapter aims to improve is that students get to understand the audio input when learning English as a second language. This last based on the idea that students are capable of interact in order to solve problems from immersive experiences, and through holographic technology, bridged with collaborative activities.

The intention is to emphasize that learning occurs as part of the interaction between the user and the external environment (the holographic educational materials, the participants of the activity and the activity guide). In this sense, the goal is to generate a reflection that can be internalized in order to be used independently by implementing virtual environments through immersion with holography, versus the traditional educational materials used in this process. In this order, the essence of holographic interaction does not require prior knowledge about the use of this technology because the virtual environment is not contained within an electronic device such as a video screen on a touch pad. Also it does not require haptics to be manipulated through interfaces such as mouse or keyboard.

The idea is that who directs the undertaken activities has the control over the virtual platform of interaction through the type and amount of interactions that the participant can carry out given the context that surrounds the activity. The latter in order to determinate in real time what works for the participants to get knowledge, what does not serve in this purpose, and how this happen. The point is that the instructor could modulate in real time the direction of the activity by catching the student's level of skill or difficulty achieved during their activity performance, when it is required to understand the listened audio input on English as a second language.

REFERENCES

Abdalhamid, F. (2007). *Listening comprehension strategies of Arabic-speaking ESL learners*. Colorado State University.

Alabbad, A. M. (2011). Interactive computer/network-based program for teaching English as a foreign language in the elementary levels in Saudi Arabia. In *Multimedia Computing and Systems (ICMCS), 2011 International Conference on* (pp. 1-4). IEEE.

Alcaraz-Valencia, P. A. (2008). *Aplicaciones del despliegue auditivo en ambientes virtuales de colaboración como soporte en el aprendizaje de un segundo idioma* [Auditory applications deployment in virtual environments to support collaborative learning in a second language] (Unpublished Master's thesis). Universidad de Colima, México.

Anderson, T. A., Reynolds, B. L., Yeh, X. P., & Huang, G. Z. (2008). Video games in the English as a foreign language classroom. In *Digital Games and Intelligent Toys Based Education, 2008 Second IEEE International Conference on* (pp. 188-192). IEEE. doi:10.1109/DIGITEL.2008.39

Bacon, S. M. (1992). The relationship between gender, comprehension, processing strategies, and cognitive and affective response in foreign language listening. *Modern Language Journal*, 76(2), 160–178. doi:10.1111/j.1540-4781.1992.tb01096.x

Bannan-Ritland, B., Dabbagh, N., & Murphy, K. (2000). Learning object systems as constructivist learning environments: Related assumptions, theories, and applications. In D. A. Wiley (Ed.), *The Instructional Use of Learning Objects: Online Version*. Retrieved May 2, 2007, from http://reusability.org/read/chapters/bannan-ritland.doc

Basto-Díaz, L., Madera-Ramírez, F., & Uicab-Ballote, R. (2012). *Apoyo de la enseñanza y aprendizaje de las fracciones en un videojuego basado en Web*. Retrieved May 10, 2014, from: https://intranet.matematicas.uady.mx

Bell, M. W. (2008). Toward a definition of "virtual worlds". *Journal of Virtual Worlds Research*, 1(1).

Bizzocchi, J., & Paras, B. (2005). Game, motivation, and effective learning: An integrated model for educational game design. In *Changing Views*. Vancouver, BC: Worlds in Play, Conference of the Digital Games Research Association.

Blunt, R. (2014). *Interactivity vs Interaction in eLearning Design*. Retrieved January 4, 2016 from: https://www.linkedin.com

Boyle, J. P. (1984). Factors affecting listening comprehension. *ELT Journal, 38*(1), 34–38. doi:10.1093/elt/38.1.34

Branton, B. (1999). *Visual literacy literature review*. Retrieved December 26, 2001, from http://vicu.utoronto.ca/staff/branton/litreview.html

Bruner, J. S. (1990). *Acts of meaning* (Vol. 3). Harvard University Press.

Burley-Allen, M. (1989). *Listening, the forgotten skill*. Retrieved November 10, 2012, from: http://agris.fao.org/

Butt, M. M., Sharif, M. M., Naseer-ud-Din, M., Hussain, I., Khan, F., & Ayesha, U. (2010). Listening comprehension problems among the students: A case study of three govt. boy's higher secondary schools. *European Journal of Soil Science, 18*(2), 311–315.

Calderón, D. (2015). Introducción: el derecho a aprender inglés. *Sorry. El aprendizaje del inglés en México, Mexicanos Primero, 28*.

Calongne, C. M. (2008). Educational Frontiers: Learning in a virtual world. *EDUCAUSE Review, 43*(5), 36–48.

Chang, L. W. (2007). *A case study on four junior high school students' experiences in developing EFL listening strategies* (Unpublished Master's thesis). National Chengchi University, Taipei.

Chen, W. F., Chen, M. H., Chen, M. L., & Ku, L. W. (2015). A Computer-Assistance Learning System for Emotional Wording. *IEEE Transactions on Knowledge and Data Engineering, 99*, 1.

Chung, L. Y. (2012). Virtual Reality in College English Curriculum: Case Study of Integrating Second Life in Freshman English Course. In *Advanced Information Networking and Applications Workshops (WAINA), 2012 26th International Conference on* (pp. 250-253). IEEE.

CIDAC. (2008). *Encuesta CIDAC: Capital Humano en México*. Retrieved January 10, 2012, from: http://www.cidac.org/

Collier, R. J., Burckhardt, C. B., & Lin, L. H. (2006). Optical Holography. Academic.

Consulta Mitofsky. (2013). *Mexicanos y los idiomas extranjeros*. Retrieved July 8, 2014, from: http://consulta.mx/

Csikszentmihalyi, M. (1990). *Flow: The Psychology of Optimal Experience*. New York: Harper and Row.

Dalgarno, B., & Lee, M. J. (2010). What are the learning affordances of 3-D virtual environments? *British Journal of Educational Technology, 41*(1), 10–32. doi:10.1111/j.1467-8535.2009.01038.x

Dass, S., Dabbagh, N., & Clark, K. (2011). Using virtual worlds: What the research says. *Quarterly Review of Distance Education, 12*(2), 95.

Dickey, M. D. (2005). Three-dimensional virtual worlds and distance learning: Two case studies of Active Worlds as a medium for distance education. *British Journal of Educational Technology*, *36*(3), 439–451. doi:10.1111/j.1467-8535.2005.00477.x

Dirven, R., & Oakeshott-Taylor, J. (1984). Listening comprehension (Part I). *Language Teaching*, *17*(04), 326–343. doi:10.1017/S026144480001082X

Dubberly, H., Pangaro, P., & Haque, U. (2009). ON MODELING What is interaction? are there different types?. *Interactions, 16*(1), 69-75.

Edmonds, E. A. (2007). Reflections on the nature of interaction†. *CoDesign*, *3*(3), 139–143. doi:10.1080/15710880701251427

Education First. (2013). *Índice de Nivel en Inglés (EF EPI) Reporte 2013*. Retrieved January 4, 2015, from: http://www.ef.com.mx/

Education First. (2014). *Índice de Nivel en Inglés (EF EPI) Reporte 2014*. Retrieved January 4, 2015, from: http://www.ef.com.mx

Ehrman, M. E., Leaver, B. L., & Oxford, R. L. (2003). A brief overview of individual differences in second language learning. *System*, *31*(3), 313–330. doi:10.1016/S0346-251X(03)00045-9

Ellis, S. R. (1991). Nature and origins of virtual environments: A bibliographical essay. *Computing Systems in Engineering*, *2*(4), 321–347. doi:10.1016/0956-0521(91)90001-L

Eschenbrenner, B., Nah, F. F.-H., & Siau, K. (2008). 3-D Virtual Worlds in Education: Applications, Benefits, Issues, and Opportunities. *Journal of Database Management*, *19*(4), 91–110. doi:10.4018/jdm.2008100106

Genesee, F. (1985). Second Language Learning Through Immersion: A Review of U.S. Programs. *Review of Educational Research*, *55*(4), 541–561. doi:10.3102/00346543055004541

Girvan, C., & Savage, T. (2010). Identifying an appropriate pedagogy for virtual worlds: A Communal Constructivism case study. *Computers & Education*, *55*(1), 342–349. doi:10.1016/j.compedu.2010.01.020

Goh, C. C. (1997). Metacognitive awareness and second language listeners. *ELT Journal*, *51*(4), 361–369. doi:10.1093/elt/51.4.361

Goh, C. C. (2002). *Teaching listening in the language classroom*. Singapore: SEAMEO Regional Language Centre.

Hahorcade, J. P. (2012). Colima, Mexico: Interacciones Universales. In Congreso Internacional de Tecnologías de Información. Universidad de Colima.

Hahorcade, J. P. (2015). *Child-Computer Interaction*. Retrieved December, 2015, from: http://homepage.cs.uiowa.edu/~Hahorcade/

Hansen, J., & Stansfield, C. (1981). The relationship of field dependent-independent cognitive styles to foreign language achievement. *Language Learning*, *31*(2), 349–367. doi:10.1111/j.1467-1770.1981.tb01389.x

Henner-Stanchina, C. (1987). Autonomy as metacognitive awareness: suggestions for training self-monitoring on listening comprehension. *Mâ elanges Pâ edagogiques, 17*.

Heredia, B., & Rubio, D. (2015). Inglés y desigualdad social en México. *Sorry. El aprendizaje del inglés en México, Mexicanos Primero, 28*.

Hsueh-Jui, L. (2008). A study of the interrelationship between listening strategy use and listening proficiency levels, and learning style. *Articles, 5*, 84–104.

Iuppa, N. (2001). *Interactive design for new media and the web*. Boston: Focal Press.

Jarmon, L., Traphagan, T., Mayrath, M., & Trivedi, A. (2009). Virtual world teaching, experiential learning, and assessment: An interdisciplinary communication course in Second Life. *Computers & Education, 53*(1), 169–182. doi:10.1016/j.compedu.2009.01.010

Jeong, T. H. (1999). Basic principles and applications of holography. Lake Forest College.

Jiang, X., Liu, C., & Chen, L. (2010). Implementation of a project-based 3D virtual learning environment for English language learning. In *Education Technology and Computer (ICETC), 2010 2nd International Conference on* (Vol. 3, pp. V3-281). IEEE.

Kallonis, P., & Sampson, D. (2010). Implementing a 3D Virtual Classroom Simulation for Teachers' Continuing Professional Development. *Proceedings of the 18th International Conference on Computers in Education (ICCE 2010)*.

Khan, F. A., & Paul, B. (2014). Screen reading with Bangla & English audio assistance bi-lingual supported software 'Mongol Dip' for visually impaired people. In *Computer and Information Technology (ICCIT), 2014 17th International Conference on* (pp. 263-272). IEEE.

Kuwada, K. (2010). The effect of interactivity with a music video game on second language vocabulary recall. *About. Language Learning & Technology*, 74.

Lin, S. H. (2000). *A study of English listening comprehension strategies used by senior high school students in Taiwan* (Unpublished Master Thesis). National Kaohsiung Normal University, Kaohsiung, R.O.C.

Lin, Y. Y., Shih, Y. C., & Yang, M. T. (2005). VEC3D: A 3-D virtual English classroom for second language learning. In *Advanced Learning Technologies, 2005. ICALT 2005. Fifth IEEE International Conference on* (pp. 906-908). IEEE.

Lund, R. J. (1990). A taxonomy for teaching Second Language Listening. *Foreign Language Annals, 23*(2), 105–115. doi:10.1111/j.1944-9720.1990.tb00348.x

Macaro, E., Graham, S., & Vanderplank, R. (2007). A review of listening strategies: focus on sources of knowledge and on success. In A.D. Cohen & E. Macaro (Eds.), Language learner strategies: 30 years of research and practice, (pp. 165-186). Oxford University Press.

Mayrath, M., Sanchez, J., Traphagan, T., Heikes, J., & Trivedi, A. (2007). Using Second Life in an English course: Designing class activities to address learning objectives. In *Proceedings of world conference on educational multimedia, hypermedia and telecommunications* (Vol. 25).

Mendelsohn, D. (1995). Applying Learning Strategies in the second/foreign language listening comprehension lesson. In D. Mendelsohn & J. Rubin (Eds.), *A Guide for the Teaching of Second Language Listening*. San Diego, CA: Dominie Press.

Morley, J. (1991). *Listening Comprehension in Foreign Language Instruction*. Boston: Academic Press.

Moscovich, T. (2007). *Principles and applications of multi-touch interaction*. Brown University.

Murphy, J. M. (1985). *An Investigation into the Listening Strategies of ESL College Students*. Academic Press.

Nieminen, K. (2006). *Aspects of Learning Foreign Languages and Learning WITH Foreign Languages: Language Immersion and CLIL. Development Project Report*. Jyvaskyla, Finland: Jyvaskyla University of Applied Sciences.

O'Malley, J. M., & Chamot, A. U. (1990). *Learning strategies in second language acquisition*. London: Cambridge University Press. doi:10.1017/CBO9781139524490

OConnor, E. A. (2009). Instructional and design elements that support effective use of virtual worlds: What graduate student work reveals about Second Life. *Journal of Educational Technology Systems*, *38*(2), 213–234. doi:10.2190/ET.38.2.j

Oliver, R. (2002). *A teaching and learning perspective on learning objects*. Paper presented at Online Learning and Information Environments, Sydney, NSW.

OMalley, J. M., Chamot, A. U., & Kopper, L. (1989). Listening comprehension strategies in second language acquisition. *Applied Linguistics*, *10*(4), 418–437. doi:10.1093/applin/10.4.418

Pearson, P. D. (1983). *Instructional Implications of Listening Comprehension Research*. Urbana, IL: Center for the Study of Reading.

Pinto-Llorente, A. M., Sánchez-Gómez, M. C., & García-Peñalvo, F. J. (2015). Developing a VLE to enable the innovative learning of English pronunciation. In *Proceedings of the 3rd International Conference on Technological Ecosystems for Enhancing Multiculturality* (pp. 83-89). ACM. doi:10.1145/2808580.2808594

Popovici, S. (2011). The eGrammar clinic: A Moodle-based tutoring system for English as a second language. In *e-Education, Entertainment and e-Management (ICEEE), 2011 International Conference on* (pp. 50-54). IEEE. doi:10.1109/ICeEEM.2011.6137839

Rahimi, A. H. (2012). On the role of strategy use and strategy instruction in listening comprehension. *Journal of Language Teaching and Research*, *3*(3), 550–559. doi:10.4304/jltr.3.3.550-559

Rankin, Y. A., McNeal, M., Shute, M. W., & Gooch, B. (2008, August). User centered game design: evaluating massive multiplayer online role playing games for second language acquisition. In *Proceedings of the 2008 ACM SIGGRAPH symposium on Video games* (pp. 43-49). ACM. doi:10.1145/1401843.1401851

Rashed, D., Lyons, S., & Bae, H. K. (2010). Second Life in English as a Second Language Instruction. In *World Conference on E-Learning in Corporate, Government, Healthcare, and Higher Education* (No. 1).

Reid, J. (1998). Teachers as perceptual learning styles researchers. In J.M. Reid (Ed.), Understanding learning styles in the second language classroom, (pp. 15-26). Prentice-Hall Inc.

Reis, R., & Escudeiro, P. (2011). Educational software to enhance English language teaching in primary school. In *Information Technology Based Higher Education and Training (ITHET), 2011 International Conference on* (pp. 1-4). IEEE. doi:10.1109/ITHET.2011.6018684

Reiser, R. A., & Dempsey, J. V. (2002). *Trends and issues in instructional design and technology*. Merrill Prentice Hall.

Richards, J. C. (1990). *The Language Teaching Matrix*. Cambridge University Press. 10.1017/CBO9780511667152

Richards, J. C. (2008). *Teaching Listening and Speaking: From Theory to Practice*. New York: Cambridge University Press.

Richards, J. C., & Schmidt, R. (2002). *Longman Dictionary of Language Teaching and Applied Linguistics* (3rd ed.). Harlow, UK: Pearson Education Limited.

Richter, H., Blaha, B., Wiethoff, A., Baur, D., & Butz, A. (2011). Tactile feedback without a big fuss: simple actuators for high-resolution phantom sensations. In *Proceedings of the 13th international conference on Ubiquitous computing* (pp. 85-88). ACM. doi:10.1145/2030112.2030124

Rivers, W. M. (1981). *Listening Comprehension: Appraoch Design, Procedure*. TESOL Quartly.

Rost, M. (1990). *Listening in language learning*. Longman Group Limited.

Rost, M. (2002). *Teaching and researching listening*. Harlow, UK: Pearson Education. Longman.

Rost, M. (2005). L2 listening. In E. Hinkel (Ed.), *Handbook of research in second language teaching and learning*. Mahwah, NJ: Erlbaum Associates.

Roussou, M. (2006). Virtual reality and education: evaluating the learning experience. *Treballs d'Arqueologia*, (12), 69-85.

Rubin, J. (1995). An overview to a guide for the teaching of second language listening. In D. Mendelson & J. Rubin (Eds.), *A guide for the teaching of second language listening*. San Diego, CA: Dominie Press.

Samuels, S. J. (1984). Factors influencing listening: Inside and outside the head. *Theory into Practice*, 23(3), 183–189. doi:10.1080/00405848409543112

Saracevic, T. (2010). The notion of context in Information Interaction in Context. In *Proceedings of the third symposium on Information interaction in context* (pp. 1-2). ACM. doi:10.1145/1840784.1840786

Saricoban, A. (1999). The teaching of listening. *The Internet TESL Journal*, 5(12). Retrieved from http://iteslj.org/Articles/Saricoban-Listening.html

SEP (2008). *La enseñanza de idiomas en México. Diagnóstico, avances y desafíos. DGAR. Reunión nacional de control escolar*. Power point. Documento interno.

Serri, F., Boroujeni, A. J., & Hesabi, A. (2012). Cognitive, metacognitive, and social/affective strategies in listening comprehension and their relationships with individual differences. *Theory and Practice in Language Studies, 2*(4), 843. doi:10.4304/tpls.2.4.843-849

Sharma, P. (2009). *Controversies in using technology in language teaching*. Retrieved from http://www.teachingenglish.org.uk/articles/controversies-using-technology-language-teaching

Shen, J., & Eder, L. B. (2009). Intentions to use virtual worlds for education. *Journal of Information Systems Education, 20*(2), 225.

Simpson, R. J., & Galbo, J. J. (1986). Interaction and learning: Theorizing on the art of teaching. *Interchange, 17*(4), 37–51. doi:10.1007/BF01807015

Sørensen, B. H., & Meyer, B. (2007). Serious Games in language learning and teaching–a theoretical perspective. In *Proceedings of the 3rd international conference of the digital games research association* (pp. 559-566).

Teng, H. C. (1993). *Effects of culture-specific knowledge and visual cues on Chinese EFL students' listening comprehension*. Academic Press.

Tick, A. (2009). The MILES Military English learning system pilot project. In *Computational Cybernetics, 2009. ICCC 2009. IEEE International Conference on* (pp. 57-62). IEEE. doi:10.1109/ICCCYB.2009.5393930

Tuval-Mashiach, R. (2014). Life Stories in Context: Using the Three-Sphere Context Model To Analyze Amos's Narrative. *Narrative Works, 4*(1).

Ur, P. (2005). *Teaching Listening Comprehension*. Cambridge University Press.

Vandergrift, L. (1996). Listening Comprehension Strategies of Core French High School Students. *Canadian Modern Language Review, 52*(2), 200–223.

Vandergrift, L. (1999). Facilitating second language listening comprehension: Acquiring successful strategies. *ELT Journal, 53*(3), 168–176. doi:10.1093/elt/53.3.168

Vandergrift, L. (2007). Recent developments in second and foreign language listening comprehension research. *Language Teaching, 40*(03), 191–210. doi:10.1017/S0261444807004338

Verdugo, D. R., & Belmonte, I. A. (2007). Using digital stories to improve listening comprehension with Spanish young learners of English. *Language Learning & Technology, 11*(1), 87–101.

Wagner, C., & Ip, R. K. (2009). Action learning with Second Life-A pilot study. *Journal of Information Systems Education, 20*(2), 249.

Wagner, E. D. (1994). In support of a functional definition of interaction. *American Journal of Distance Education, 8*(2), 6–29. doi:10.1080/08923649409526852

Wang, Y., & Braman, J. (2009). Extending the classroom through Second Life. *Journal of Information Systems Education, 20*(2), 235.

Wickremaratne, J., Wimalaratne, G., & Goonetilleke, V. (2008). A Blend of Adaptive and Digital Learning Towards Language Proficiency. In *Information and Automation for Sustainability, 2008. ICIAFS 2008. 4th International Conference on* (pp. 173-178). IEEE. doi:10.1109/ICIAFS.2008.4783942

Willing, K. (1993). *Learning styles in adult migrant education*. Sydney: Macquarie University.

Winn, W. (2002). Research into practice: Current trends in educational technology research: The study of learning environments. *Educational Psychology Review, 14*(3), 331–351. doi:10.1023/A:1016068530070

Wintergerst, A. C., DeCapua, A., & Verna, M. A. (2003). Conceptualizing learning style modalities for ESL/EFL students. *System, 31*(1), 85–106. doi:10.1016/S0346-251X(02)00075-1

Workman, R. (2013). *What is a hologram?* Retrieve from: http://www.livescience.com/

Ybarra, R., & Green, T. (2003). Using technology to help ESL/EFL students develop language skills. *The Internet TESL Journal, 9*(3). Retrieved from http://iteslj.org/Articles/Ybarra-Technology.html

Zhang, Y. (2009). Cooperative Language Learning and Foreign Language Learning and Teaching. *Journal of Language Teaching and Research, 1*(1), 81-83.

Zilber, T. B., Tuval-Mashiach, R., & Lieblich, A. (2008). The embedded narrative navigating through multiple contexts. *Qualitative Inquiry, 14*(6), 1047–1069. doi:10.1177/1077800408321616

ADDITIONAL READING

Anderson, K. L. (1997). The Sound of Learning. *The American School Board Journal, 184*(10), 26–28.

Bachman, L. F. (2004). *Statistical analyses for language assessment*. Ernst Klett Sprachen. doi:10.1017/CBO9780511667350

Buck, G. (1991). The testing of listening comprehension: An introspective study1. *Language Testing, 8*(1), 67–91. doi:10.1177/026553229100800105

Buck, G. (1992). Listening Comprehension: Construct Validity and Trait Characteristics*. *Language Learning, 42*(3), 313–357. doi:10.1111/j.1467-1770.1992.tb01339.x

Buck, G. (2001). *Assessing listening*. Cambridge University Press. doi:10.1017/CBO9780511732959

Buck, G., & Tatsuoka, K. (1998). Application of the rule-space procedure to language testing: Examining attributes of a free response listening test. *Language Testing, 15*(2), 119–157.

Carrier, K. A. (2003). Improving high school English language learners second language listening through strategy instruction. *Bilingual Research Journal, 27*(3), 383–408. doi:10.1080/15235882.2003.10162600

Clark, H. H. (1996). *Using language*. Cambridge university press. doi:10.1017/CBO9780511620539

Clark, R. E., & Estes, F. (1999). The Development of Authentic Educational Technologies. *Educational Technology, 39*(2), 5–16.

Dix, A. (2009). *Human-computer interaction* (pp. 1327-1331). Springer US. Donato, L. Una experiencia en la adquisición de una segunda lengua. Retrieved from: http://servicios2.abc.gov.ar

Flagg, B. N. (2013). *Formative evaluation for educational technologies*. Routledge.

Gabbard, J. L., Hix, D., & Swan, J. E. (1999). User-centered design and evaluation of virtual environments. *Computer Graphics and Applications, IEEE, 19*(6), 51–59. doi:10.1109/38.799740

Goodman, J. W., & Lawrence, R. W. (1967). Digital image formation from electronically detected holograms. *Applied Physics Letters, 11*(3), 77–79. doi:10.1063/1.1755043

Holtzblatt, K., Wendell, J. B., & Wood, S. (2004). *Rapid contextual design: a how-to guide to key techniques for user-centered design*. Elsevier.

Johnson, E. (2001). Let's Hear It for Learning. *American School & University, 73*(11), 28–30.

Johnston, S. (2006). *Holographic Visions: A History of New Science: A History of New Science*. OUP Oxford. doi:10.1093/acprof:oso/9780198571223.001.0001

Krashen, S. (1982). *Principles and practice in second language acquisition* (Vol. 2). Oxford: Pergamon.

Lee, W. H. (1978). III Computer-Generated Holograms: Techniques and Applications. *Progress in optics, 16*, 119-232.

Lucente, M. E. (1993). Interactive computation of holograms using a look-up table. *Journal of Electronic Imaging, 2*(1), 28–34. doi:10.1117/12.133376

Lunner, T. (2003). Cognitive function in relation to hearing aid use. *International Journal of Audiology, 42*(sup1), S49–S58. doi:10.3109/14992020309074624 PMID:12918610

Maddux, C. D., Johnson, D. L., & Willis, C. W. (2001). Educational computing: Learning with tomorrow\'s technologies.

Nielsen, J. (1994). Usability inspection methods. In *Conference companion on Human factors in computing systems* (pp. 413–414). ACM. doi:10.1145/259963.260531

Norman, D. A. (2005). *Emotional design: Why we love (or hate) everyday things*. Basic books.

Norman, D. A. (2013). *The design of everyday things: Revised and expanded edition*. Basic books.

Norman, D. A., & Draper, S. W. (1986). *User centered system design*. Hillsdale, NJ.

Nunan, D. (1991). *Language teaching methodology: A textbook for teachers*. Prentice hall.

Obeidat, M. M. (2005). Attitudes and motivation in second language learning. *Journal of faculty of Education, 18*(22), 1-17.

Palviainen, J., & Väänänen-Vainio-Mattila, K. (2009). User experience in machinery automation: from concepts and context to design implications. In *Human Centered Design* (pp. 1042–1051). Springer Berlin Heidelberg. doi:10.1007/978-3-642-02806-9_119

Rubin, J. (1994). A review of second language listening comprehension research. *Modern Language Journal, 78*(2), 199–221. doi:10.1111/j.1540-4781.1994.tb02034.x

Seep, B., Glosemeyer, R., Hulce, E., Linn, M., & Aytar, P. (2000). Classroom Acoustics: A Resource for Creating Environments with Desirable Listening Conditions.

Seldowitz, M. A., Allebach, J. P., & Sweeney, D. W. (1987). Synthesis of digital holograms by direct binary search. *Applied Optics*, *26*(14), 2788–2798. doi:10.1364/AO.26.002788 PMID:20489962

Siebein, G. W., Gold, M. A., Siebein, G. W., & Ermann, M. G. (2000). Ten ways to provide a high-quality acoustical environment in schools. *Language, Speech, and Hearing Services in Schools*, *31*(4), 376–384. doi:10.1044/0161-1461.3104.376 PMID:27764477

Steuer, J. (1992). Defining virtual reality: Dimensions determining telepresence. *Journal of Communication*, *42*(4), 73–93. doi:10.1111/j.1460-2466.1992.tb00812.x

Vredenburg, K., Isensee, S., Righi, C., & Design, U. C. (2001). *An integrated approach*. Englewood Cliffs: Prentice Hall.

Weir, C. J. (2005). *Language Testing and Validation: an evidence-based approach*. Basingstoke: Palgrave Macmillan. doi:10.1057/9780230514577

Wickens, C. D., Hollands, J. G., Banbury, S., & Parasuraman, R. (2015). *Engineering psychology & human performance*. Psychology Press.

Williams, E. (2006). Teaching reading: Individual and social perspectives. *Current trends in the development and teaching of the four language skills*, 355-383.

KEY TERMS AND DEFINITIONS

Context: Underlying information to an object, person, or situation scenario, which allows serve as a starting point to generate inferences or assumptions about a subject, all of this based on our past experiences.

Hologram: An image that cheats the brain's visual perception in order to recreate three dimensional objects in our own dimension.

Holography: A photographic technique that produces the recording of an object from three different planes in order to be interpreted by the human brain as one.

Instructional Interactions: Transaction process of information between a person, the context and purpose, in order to generate an experience that is susceptible to become knowledge.

Interaction: Transaction process of information between a person, the context and a purpose.

Listening Comprehension: To pay attention when listening to undertake strategies that lead a person to understand the perceived audio input.

Listening: The necessary activity of hearing sounds when it is intended or desired to understand audio verbal messages.

Strategies: Orderly interactions that lead to the fulfillment of goals or objectives.

Virtual Environment: Recreation of reality (or an alternative reality) encapsulated into a software program.

Chapter 14
Use of Large Multi-Touch Interfaces:
A Research on Usability and Design Aspects

Mehmet Donmez
Middle East Technical University, Turkey

Serkan Alkan
Middle East Technical University, Turkey

Kursat Cagiltay
Middle East Technical University, Turkey

Fuat Bolukbas
Middle East Technical University, Turkey

Goknur Kaplan Akilli
Middle East Technical University, Turkey

ABSTRACT

This study explores the design considerations and usability factors of using large multi touch interfaces. In this study, an experimental approach incorporating a large multi touch interface environment was used. End user usability test sessions supported with glasses type eye tracker and interview sessions were conducted. The data were collected from one expert and three non-expert users by implementing a task on a military training application. Two analysis methods were used, analysis for eye movement data of users and analysis for interviews. This study revealed that users were generally focusing at the center of the screen while using the large multi touch display. The most common gestures were Tap and Drag which are single touch input gestures. It was easy to adapt to the system by recalling the previous experiences from mobile devices, to manage the area on the screen, and to interact with two hands thanks to display size.

INTRODUCTION

The increasing use of touch devices has bought significant changes on Human Computer Interaction (HCI). Users have started to use touch technology in their daily lives as an inevitable consequence of increasing usage of smart devices. Because of this trend, the needs of users have been changed in terms

DOI: 10.4018/978-1-5225-2616-2.ch014

of the display size of devices. Users started to request for using larger display size with multi touch capability. According to Martin-Dorta, Saorin and Contero (2011), using touch screen interfaces increases the motivation and satisfaction of the students during the interactive courses.

The use of devices with touch ability like smart phones and smart boards is increasing day by day, because using devices by touching is easier and more collaborative than traditional usage of devices by using keys, keyboard and mouse. According to Wahab and Zaman (2013), multi touch interactive tables are started to be essential technology for collaborative works. As a consequence of this increase, the demand for larger multi touch devices emerged. It necessitates the studies on this issue.

There is a need to investigate the usability factors of large multi touch displays, because the gestures used on large multi touch displays should be different from the usual touch gestures which are used on smaller displays like smart phones or tablet PCs. Besides, user preferences on using large multi touch displays can be different from the user preferences on smaller multi touch displays. Most of the multi touch devices are designed for single person use. Although the small displays have primary role in disseminating multi touch gestures, Very Large Displays (VLDs) need new definitions and suggestions to integrate these gestures in those sizes. Creating a usable interfaces for VLDs, a series of experiments should be conducted. In this study, basic usability methods are integrated with the eye tracking technology to record and analyze bases of user responses. The findings highlight the users' attitudes and behaviors toward a newly produced VLDs. Besides, the findings are important to design of next generation large multi touch displays. In addition, there are not many studies about the design of VLDs in the HCI literature. One of the aims of the current study is to suggest answers about the design guidelines for VLDs.

LITERATURE REVIEW

This part includes five main sections, namely the history of touch displays, larger touch displays and usage, technology of touch displays, gesture standards for touch devices and Very Large Displays (VLDs), and the current VLDs.

History of Touch Displays

At the beginning of the post PC era, the idea of tablet PCs was created well-known patent disputes between two main players, namely Apple and Samsung in the market (Hey & Pápay, 2014). During these lawsuits, Samsung showed Stanley Kubricks' 50 years old "A Space Odyssey" movie as a proof against Apple claims in which a tabletop screen is shown explicitly. Although the tablet PC seen in this scene is no more than an LCD display, it creates the sense of using screen as an input device. Afterwards any developments in interactive large displays were announced "dreams come true" by referencing the movies in which interactive tools depicted.

This shows that there is a breakdown between technological and conceptual development in the subject of multi touch screens. The developmental tracks of tablet computers and touch screen technologies followed different routes before incorporated into a device. For example, the first patent which can be linked to the use of screens as an input devices can be dated back 1915, a century ago (Goldberg, 1915). Pen is the first input tool used instead of keyboard among computers in earlier models at 50s (Dimond, 1957). Although many different models or mediums produced as prototypes for modern touch screens, they won't become a part of daily life until first introduction of iPhone by Apple in 2007 (Grissom, 2008).

After the introduction and the success of the finger controlled touch screens, many models followed iPhone. Today, there are many different types and sizes of touch screens available at the market. It took more than 40 years to develop devices which respond to user touch at table or board size.

According to developing technology and demands of people, touch displays are changing in terms of size, type, purpose of usage in addition to technology behind the screen. At the very beginning of the touch displays, there were capacitive displays (Jain, Bhargava, & Rajput, 2013). It was developed by E.A. Johnson at the Royal Radar Establishment, Malvern, U.K. After that, touch screen technology was improved day by day. In 1982, the first multi touch system was developed in University of Toronto (Buxton, 2009). Afterwards, the first multi touch display which is based on a transparent capacitive array of touch sensors placed on a Cathode Ray Tube (CRT) was developed by Bob Boie in 1984 (Buxton, 2009). After the release of the Nintendo DS in 2004, the popularity of the touch screens started to increase (Jain et al., 2013). With the increase of the popularity of the touch screens, commercial usage of the multi touch screens started to become widespread. One of the leading company was Microsoft Corporation. Microsoft Corporation developed a commercial multi touch system, namely Microsoft Surface (Dietz & Eidelson, 2009). This system is a tabletop computing system and uses infrared (IR) light and series of cameras to detect the interaction of user with the multi touch system. After that, Microsoft PixelSense which has similar technology with Microsoft Surface was released. Microsoft PixelSense uses IR sensors and computer vision to detect the touches. Besides, it has a much thinner tabletop system (Bordin, Zancanaro, & Angeli, 2013).

Larger Touch Displays and Usage

The early models of the smartphones with touch screens have about 3-4 inch displays. But shortly after, the size of the screens is getting larger as a result of user demand. Today many smartphones come to market with a display about 5 inch or more. Same trend can be tracked in tablet computers also. But, sizes in inches in the market are not satisfactory when multi person interactivity is required.

This trend is consistent with developing technology, people' needs are changing day by day and being more sophisticated, so large wall displays started to enter people' lives and they are taking the place of standard desktop monitors (Malik, Ranjan, & Balakrishnan, 2005). The cause of this change is that there is a need for using sophisticated single-user and multi-user applications on larger place than the standard desktop monitors. In addition, Thompson, Nordin, and Cairns (2012) stated that the more the screen size is larger, the more the involving experience is provided. Besides, large displays with high-resolution help users to reach more information simultaneously and easily (Andrews, Endert, & North, 2010). According to Czerwinski, Tan, and Robertson (2002), larger displays can be used to handle a greater field of view. Czerwinski et al. (2003) stated that working on complex, multiple window tasks with larger displays increases the productivity and satisfaction of users significantly. Also, they reported that users work significantly faster on larger displays while completing multiple step cognitively loaded tasks. Using a large display provides benefits for managing multiple windows by showing on display simultaneously (Bi, Bae, & Balakrishnan, 2014). Besides, working on large display enhances the concentration of the users on the task.

According to Bi et al. (2014), VLDs might be beneficial about ergonomic issues. For example, users are limited to move their heads or to change their sitting position in front of the single monitor usage. On the other hand, users are more relaxed about their body position in front of the large screens.

The factors given above show that, demand for VLDs will continue to increase in following years. Although there are some commercial products with interactive VLDs available as tabletop or walltop in the market already, the empirical research about these products is not common in the literature to provide input to the designers or companies. This study aims to provide explicit cues for the usability and designing issues of very large displays at the end.

The devices with touch sense capability which are used in daily life are smart phones, tablet PCs, laptops and desktop PCs with touch sense displays. The screen sizes of these devices vary from 3 inches to 27 inches when the market comparison is done via the Internet. One of the most important questions for engineers and researchers who are capable of manufacturing these VLDs is who needs a display about 2 meters at diagonal or larger. The answer to this question does not come from the consumers directly. Consumers who want to have a VLD systems know that they need something like VLD, but the details and technical specifications of these systems are not clear to them. Smaller displays are easier to use, but it is hard to handle simultaneous tasks on these displays rather than one task at a time. When the displays are getting larger, many problems occur such as placement of the tasks, unused spaces, low effectiveness and productivity etc. However, these problems do not retain people having large screens.

Today, the use of VLDs is not very common. But probability of meeting with a VLD is getting higher everyday even in a rock bar or a fair. Although they are not frequent today, they will be a part of our daily life soon when the barriers in design, technology and cost are overcomed. The cost of a VLD system is fairly high today, but there are signs that they will be available with different prices and sizes in the market soon.

VLDs have a wide range of areas to be used, namely business, education and public places. Although idea of VLDs is seem to be attractable, the productivity and the effectiveness of these VLDs are not clear yet.

VLDs have many possible applications. Ni et al. (2006) listed eight class for the possible use of VLDs. This is neither final nor exclusive list, but it gives an idea about how wide the areas of VLD use. Despite, they made this classification for only for displays, interactivity in current study can be considered as an asset. The command and control tasks are the first situation that require very high resolution according to Ni et al. (2006). These control centers can be either military or research oriented. Second use of VLDs are design studios such as automobile design in which the product and environment should be seen in its actual size. Geospatial Imagery and Videos; Scientific Visualization; Collaboration and Tele-immersion; Education and Training; Immersive Applications; and Public Information Displays are the other possible applications of VLDs.

Technology of Touch Displays

Technology of touch displays has been changed up to nowadays. Jain et al. (2013) state that there are various technologies which are used in touch displays:

Capacitive Touch-Screen Technology: Capacitive touch-screen technology provides clear display (Kolokowsky & Davis, 2009). It has two types, namely surface capacitance technology and projected capacitance technology. Surface capacitance technology consists of four sensors at the corners of the screen. These sensors identify the touch by checking the changes on the capacitance. In order to use this technology, there is a need to touch the screen via conductive object like a finger. The other type of the capacitive touch-screen technology, projected capacitance technology, has more advantages than the surface capacitance technology. It provides much more positional accuracy. Besides, it is capable to identify multiple touches simultaneously.

Resistive Touch-Screen Technology: Resistive touch-screens are the most common and the cheapest touch technology (Kolokowsky & Davis, 2009). This technology is based on pressure on the screen and it can react to touch by a finger or any other object which is a conductive or a non-conductive object.

Surface Acoustic Wave Technology: Surface acoustic wave technology is based on sound waves traveling along the screen (Hao & Kui, 2014). The corruption on the sound waves is used to determine the coordinates of touch point. This technology has shorter reaction time and long service life, but it has high cost and it is difficult to integrate this technology with small sized and medium sized terminals.

Infrared Touch-Screen Technology: Infrared (IR) touch technology is based on an IR frame which is an IR emitter at the four sides of the screen (Wei, Liu, He, & Wei, 2011). IR emitter provides horizontal and vertical IR matrix. In order to determine the coordinates (X, Y) of touch point, the controller can calculate the coordinates where the IR matrix is blocked by a finger or any other objects.

METHODOLOGY

Participants and Study Setting

The number of users who know how to use application was limited that there were four participants. The test engineer of the application was selected as expert user. Three of the developers of the application were selected as non-expert users.

For this study, a software related to military tactical operations was selected and installed on a VLD. The reason for selecting this software is that it includes different custom touch gestures to use during the study. Before the tests, three non-expert users were matched with the expert user in order like Test Group 1 (EU and NEU 1), Test Group 2 (EU and NEU 2) and Test Group 3 (EU and NEU 3). Therefore, the test was conducted 3 times. During the tests, participants were asked to sit as it is seen in the Figure 1. Both of the participants were asked to wear glasses type eye tracking devices for recording the eye movement data of them. Also, the test environment was recorded with two video cameras (one from the side of the device and one from the backside of the participants) to identify the usage behaviors of participants. Subsequent to tests, a short interview around 20 minutes was conducted and recorded with each user about their experiences during the tests.

In this study, two Tobii Glasses 1 Eye Tracker device and a large multi touch display were used. Eye tracker device which uses reflector and infrared detector camera tracks right eye of the participant and collect data about where the participant is looking, how long and how many times s/he looks at which location.

Data Collection and Data Analysis

The task for this study consists of three steps. The first step is that two different smugglers, who are controlled by the user on the control computer, enter from the border line by cutting the wires. Each smuggler starts to move inside the border line through different directions. As the second step of the task, each of the two users, expert user and non-expert user, selects one of the guardhouses and starts to follow one of the smugglers. As the third and final step of the task, each user arrests and handcuffs one

Figure 1. The test setting

of the smugglers. While users were doing the task, their eye movements were recorded for the analysis of the data in order to interpret their attitudes, behaviors, task completion times, and their successes.

For data collection, two different methods were applied. The first method was end user usability testing. The participants were asked to complete the given task by using the software which was located on the large multi touch display. During the end user usability testing, one expert user (EU) and one non-expert user (NEU) used the software simultaneously. The same test was repeated for three times. After end user usability testing, the interviews were done with expert user and non-expert users as a second method by taking their voice recordings. At the beginning of the interview session, the retrospective review with each user of Test 1 was done in order to strengthen the data. They were asked to watch his/her own video recording which includes their eye movements, and to explain what and why they were doing. Subsequent to retrospective review, users were interviewed in order to collect information about their experiences with the VLD.

As the first step of data analysis, the eye movement data were analyzed for Test 1 and Test 2. During the analysis of these data, the video recordings from eye tracking device were reviewed on the software of such device and coded manually to identify the users' line of vision. Manual coding provided counts and durations of users' line of vision and gestures performed by users. After the manual coding, the data for each user were divided into 10 equal time intervals in order to examine the data more efficiently. In addition, these video recordings were divided into 4 equal Area of Interests (AOIs) in order to analyze the fixation counts and fixation durations of users for each AOI. As the second step of the data analysis, the interview data were analyzed for Test 1, Test 2 and Test 3. Firstly, interview records were transcribed into text. Then, retrospective review data were separated from the interview data and grouped according to time intervals. Retrospective review data were used to support the results coming from the first step of the data analysis. After separating retrospective review data, the coding was done by the researcher.

RESULTS

The results of Test 1 and Test 2 are examined under 10 time intervals. The AOI results of Test 1 and Test 2 indicate that expert user was mostly working on upper side of the screen which includes objects and right side of the screen which includes right menu, while non-expert users were mostly working on left side of the screen which includes left menu and objects. There are three menu areas which are placed on the right side of the screen, left side of the screen and middle bottom side of the screen. The differences between menu inside durations and menu outside durations have similar pattern after the 60% of the task according to Time Intervals (TI) for both EU and NEU 1 for Test 1. Likewise, the differences between menu inside durations and menu outside durations have similar pattern after the 40% of the task according to Time Intervals (TI) for both EU and NEU 2 for Test 2. In addition, the results of Test 1 and Test 2 show that EU, NEU 1 and NEU 2 were looking at the out of menu area more than menu area in durations among the total task for Test 1 and Test 2. Besides, EU was moving around the area more than NEU 1 and making selections a little bit more than NEU 1 in counts in Test 1. Counts data for Tap gesture on EU is a little bit higher than on NEU 1. Counts data for Zoom Out gesture and Rotate gesture for EU 1 are smaller than for NEU 1. However, counts data for Zoom In gesture, Select gesture and Drag gesture for EU are higher than for NEU 1. Likewise, EU was moving around the area more than NEU 2 and making selections more than NEU 2 in counts in Test 2. Counts data for Tap gesture on EU is a little bit higher than on NEU 2. Counts data for Zoom Out gesture and Drag gesture on EU is higher than on NEU 2. Counts data for Zoom In gesture for EU are higher than for NEU 2. Counts data for Select gesture on EU 1 is equal to the data on NEU 2. Counts data for Rotate gesture on EU 1 do not exist, while such data on NEU 2 exist.

According to interview results, users tried to transfer previous habits from smart devices. Therefore, it was easy to adapt gestures for users. Also, it was easy to select objects, to see the area, to see the objects, and to move camera to see the area. In addition, some users were used to use touch devices with one hand, but it was easier for them to use large multi touch display with two hands. Besides, the device uses infrared (IR) frame to sense touch gestures. Because of the size of the screen, sometimes the other fingers can be sensed as touch gestures by the device. There can be made enhancement about gesture sensitivity of the device.

CONCLUSION

Discussion and Conclusion

The results of this study showed that users who used the large multi touch display system transferred their previous habits. These habits were based on their usage of mobile devices. Bellucci, Malizia, and

Aeto (2014) figured out that touch gestures for large touch surfaces can be generated from the gestures for small devices like mobile devices, because it provides user acceptance about such gestures.

According to the results of this study, it was easy to select objects, manage the area, see the objects on the screen, and interact with two hands. These results comply with the results of a study in literature which pointed out that the most cited reasons of users for liking the public large multi touch system, which was provided for the study, were its simplicity/ease of use (12.9%), interactivity (12.4%) and multi touch (10.1%) (Jacucci, Morrison, & Richard, 2010). In addition, Liu and Chapuis (2014) pointed out that wall size display system is significantly effective for managing the difficult tasks.

According to the results of this study, users were satisfied about using the large multi touch display system. This result complies with the result of a study which found out that user satisfaction was improved notably and they felt more comfortable about using drag and drop operations on large multi touch system rather than using traditional drag and drop operations on a desktop PC via mouse operations (Doeweling, 2010). Besides, another study stated that all of the participants of the study were satisfied with their work on large multi touch display system, because they felt they worked effectively (Jakobsen & HornbÆk, 2014).

According to the data from tracked area and the data from the AOIs of users, eye movements of both users were around the center of the screen. It means that the focus of the users was in line with the eye level of users. This result complies with the result of a study in the literature which stated that 81% of the mouse events of the users were around the center of the screen, when they worked on large display (Bi & Balakrishnan, 2009). These results show that notifications or pop-up windows should be around the center of the screen.

The gesture counts for Test 1 and Test 2 show that the most common used gesture is tap gesture for all users. In addition, the usage counts of tap gesture and drag gesture which are single input gestures are higher than the other gestures. The study of Epps, Lichman, and Wu (2006) stated that the frequency of usage of tap gesture was 70.1% for all tasks. According to Chaboissier, Isenberg, and Vernier (2011), the usage of single touch input on a large multi touch screen occurred more than multi touch input. These results show that designers should take into account that the most common gestures for large multi touch display based systems are one handed single touch gestures.

During the analysis of the eye tracking data of users, it was observed that users preferred to use both of their hands for multi touch gestures like Zoom In gesture, Zoom Out gesture and Rotate gesture. It means that users used both of their hands to perform multi touch gestures instead of single hand. This is because the size of the display was larger and it took time to perform gestures like Zoom In, Zoom Out and Rotate by using single hand. These results show that developers should consider two handed usage of gestures, while defining multi touch gestures for applications developed for large multi touch display based systems.

Contribution of the Study

This study contributes to the Human Computer Interaction literature by stating the usability factors of large multi touch displays and the suggestions for the design of these displays. The findings of the study showed that it is easy to adapt to use large multi touch displays for users. Also, the management of the data in these displays is easy because it enables users to see more data simultaneously than smaller displays. In addition, expert users make more interaction than non-expert users in terms of usage of touch gestures. Moreover, the design of the display can be changed in accordance of users' needs because there are unused spaces on the display in this study. These results can be a guide for manufacturers and developers of the systems and for applications which are appropriate for these kind of devices.

REFERENCES

Andrews, C., Endert, A., & North, C. (2010). *Space to think: large high-resolution displays for sense-making*. Retrieved from http://dl.acm.org/citation.cfm?id=1753336

Bellucci, A., Malizia, A., & Aeto, I. (2014). Light on horizontal interactive surfaces: Input space for tabletop computing. *ACM Computing Surveys*, *46*(3), 1–42. Retrieved from http://dl.acm.org/citation.cfm?id=2500467 doi:10.1145/2500467

Bi, X., Bae, S., & Balakrishnan, R. (2014). WallTop: Managing Overflowing Windows on a Large Display. *Human-Computer Interaction*, 1–59. Retrieved from http://www.tandfonline.com/doi/abs/10.1080/07370024.2013.812411

Bi, X., & Balakrishnan, R. (2009). Comparing usage of a large high-resolution display to single or dual desktop displays for daily work. *The SIGCHI Conference*, 1005. doi:10.1145/1518701.1518855

Bordin, S., Zancanaro, M., & De Angeli, A. (2013). *Touching dante: a proximity-based paradigm for tabletop browsing*. Retrieved from http://dl.acm.org/citation.cfm?id=2499172

Buxton, B. (2009). Retrieved from http://www.billbuxton.com/multitouchOverview.html

Chaboissier, J., Isenberg, T., & Vernier, F. (2011). RealTimeChess: Lessons from a participatory design process for a collaborative multi-touch, multi-user game. *Conference ITS*, *11*(November), 97–106. doi:10.1145/2076354.2076374

Czerwinski, M., Smith, G., Regan, T., Meyers, B., Robertson, G., & Starkweather, G. (2003). *Toward characterizing the productivity benefits of very large displays* (Vol. 3). Proc. Interact.

Czerwinski, M., Tan, D. S., & Robertson, G. G. (2002). Women Take a Wider View. In Proceedings of {ACM} {CHI} 2002 (Vol. 4, pp. 195–202). doi:10.1145/503376.503412

Dietz, P., & Eidelson, B. (2009). *SurfaceWare: dynamic tagging for Microsoft Surface*. Retrieved from http://dl.acm.org/citation.cfm?id=1517717

Dimond, T. L. (1957). Devices for reading handwritten characters. *IRE-ACM-AIEE '57 (Eastern): Proceedings of the Eastern Joint Computer Conference: Computers with Deadlines to Meet*, 232–237. doi:10.1145/1457720.1457765

Doeweling, S. (2010). Drop-and-drag: easier drag & drop on large touchscreen displays. *Proceedings of the 6th Nordic Conference*, 158–167. http://doi.org/ doi:10.1145/1868914.1868936

Epps, J., Lichman, S., & Wu, M. (2006). A study of hand shape use in tabletop gesture interaction. *CHI '06 Extended Abstracts on Human Factors in Computing Systems - CHI EA '06*, 748. 10.1145/1125451.1125601

Goldberg, H. E. (1915). *Controller*. Retrieved May 28, 2015, from http://www.freepatentsonline.com/1117184.pdf

Grissom, S. (2008). iPhone application development across the curriculum. *Journal of Computing Sciences in Colleges*, *24*(1), 40–46.

Hao, X., & Kui, H. (2014). A Low-Power Ultra-Light Small and Medium Size Acoustic Wave Touch Screen. *Applied Mechanics and Materials*, *513-517*, 4072–4075. doi:10.4028/www.scientific.net/AMM.513-517.4072

Hey, T., & Pápay, G. (2014). The Computing Universe: A Journey through a Revolution. Cambridge University Press. Retrieved from https://books.google.com/books?id=NrMkBQAAQBAJ&pgis=1 doi:10.1017/CBO9781139032643

Jacucci, G., Morrison, A., & Richard, G. (2010). *Worlds of information: designing for engagement at a public multi-touch display*. Retrieved from http://dl.acm.org/citation.cfm?id=1753669

Jain, A., Bhargava, D., & Rajput, A. (2013). Touch-screen technology. *International Journal of Advanced Research in Computer Science and Electronics Engineering*, *2*(January), 74–78. Retrieved from http://www.ijarcsee.org/index.php/IJARCSEE/article/view/309

Jakobsen, M. R., & HornbÆk, K. (2014). Up close and personal: Collaborative work on a high-resolution multitouch wall display. *ACM Transactions on Computer-Human Interaction*, *21*(2), 1–34. doi:10.1145/2576099

Kolokowsky, S., & Davis, T. (2009). *Touchscreens 101: Understanding Touchscreen Technology and Design*. Retrieved from http://www.cypress.com/?docID=17212

Liu, C., & Chapuis, O. (2014). *Effects of display size and navigation type on a classification task*. doi:10.1145/2556288.2557020

Malik, S., Ranjan, A., & Balakrishnan, R. (2005). Interacting with large displays from a distance with vision-tracked multi-finger gestural input. *Proceedings of the 18th Annual ACM Symposium on User Interface Software and Technology - UIST '05*, 43. doi:10.1145/1095034.1095042

Martin-Dorta, N., Saorin, J., & Contero, M. (2011). Web-based Spatial Training Using Handheld Touch Screen Devices. *Journal of Educational Technology & Society*, *14*, 163–177. Retrieved from http://www.ifets.info/others/download_pdf.php?j_id=52&a_id=1160

Ni, T., Schmidt, G. S., Staadt, O. G., Livingston, M. A., Ball, R., & May, R. (2006). *A survey of large high-resolution display technologies, techniques, and applications*. Proceedings - IEEE Virtual Reality. doi:10.1109/VR.2006.20

Thompson, M., Nordin, A., & Cairns, P. (2012). *Effect of touch-screen size on game immersion*. Retrieved from http://dl.acm.org/citation.cfm?id=2377952

Wahab, N., & Zaman, H. B. (2013). The Significance of Multi-Touch Table in Collaborative Setting: How Relevant this Technology in Military Decision Making. *Applied Mechanics and Materials*, *278-280*, 1830–1833. doi:10.4028/www.scientific.net/AMM.278-280.1830

Wei, Z., Liu, W., He, Q., & Wei, N. (2011). *The design of infrared touch screen based on MCU*. Retrieved from http://ieeexplore.ieee.org/xpls/abs_all.jsp?arnumber=5949041

KEY TERMS AND DEFINITIONS

Human-Computer Interaction (HCI): HCI is the study of how people interact with computers, i.e., mobile phone, tablet Pcs, etc., and to what extent computers are or are not developed for successful interaction with human beings.

Interaction Design: Interaction design focuses on creating engaging interfaces with well thought out behaviors, for children, adults, animals, robots, etc.

Interface: Traditionally, the word interface is a shared boundary or connection between two dissimilar objects, devices or systems through which information is passed.

Touch Display: It is a computer display screen that is also an input device. The screens are sensitive to pressure, a user interacts with the computer by touching pictures or words on the screen, for instance, a iPhone.

Usability: Usability or Engineering of the Usability means making products and systems easier to use, and matching them more closely to user needs and requirement.

Chapter 15
A Multi–Agent Model for Personalizing Learning Material for Collaborative Groups

Pablo Santana-Mansilla
National Scientific and Technical Research Council, Argentina & National University of Santiago del Estero, Argentina

Rosanna Costaguta
National University of Santiago del Estero, Argentina

Silvia Schiaffino
National Scientific and Technical Research Council, Argentina & National University of the Center of Buenos Aires Province, Argentina

ABSTRACT

The use of computer-supported collaborative learning (CSCL) environments in teaching and learning processes has increased during the last decade. These environments have various collaboration, communication and coordination tools that students and teachers can use without depending on the time and place where they are. However, having software tools that support group learning does not guarantee successful collaboration because factors such as insufficient knowledge of study contents can impair learning. The analysis of group interactions should allow teachers to recognize obstacles in the learning process, but when there are a lot of interactions the manual analysis is unfeasible owing to time and effort required. This chapter presents a multi-agent model that personalizes the delivery of learning material when groups of collaborative students manifest lack of knowledge. In addition, this chapter describes results of experiments conducted to evaluate the feasibility of using Lucene for retrieving learning material written in English and Spanish.

DOI: 10.4018/978-1-5225-2616-2.ch015

INTRODUCTION

With the rapid development of knowledge-based society the importance that is given to collaborative knowledge creation has increased. In this context, CSCL has become a new form of education where students learn through interaction with people who may be located in different temporal and spatial contexts (Suh & Lee, 2006). However, availability of software tools that support group learning does not guarantee that students collaborate, since factors such as insufficient knowledge in the content area, lack of access to appropriate resources, lack of knowledge on how to use resources, skills deficit, and problems with course materials, may obstruct the learning process of students (Costaguta, García, & Amandi, 2011; Olivares, 2007; Onrubia & Engel, 2012; O'Rourke, 2003; Orvis & Lassiter, 2006; Varvel, 2007). According to Varvel (2007) e-tutors (teachers) are responsible for identifying these obstacles in group learning so as to assist students at the right time and with the appropriate methods.

In CSCL environments a complete record of the activities and interactions of students is available. Further analysis of this set of activities and interactions should enable e-tutors recognize the presence of obstacles in the learning process mentioned above. But when there is a considerable amount of interactions manual analysis is virtually impossible due to the time and effort required (Chen, 2006; Rosé et al., 2008). Furthermore, coordination of discussions imposes to CSCL e-tutors a huge effort, both temporal and cognitive, especially when there are several groups working simultaneously (Schwarz & Asterhan, 2011). If we also take into account that the e-tutors may not log in the course site for a long time due to health problems, travel, connection problems, among others, it is clear that the group learning process would be slowed down if students were not able to solve the obstacles that arise during an activity or course (Souali, Afia, Faizi, & Chiheb, 2011).

Based on what we mentioned in the last paragraph, a multi-agent model to deal specifically with the problem of insufficient knowledge in the content area is proposed. In the proposed model, an agent will analyze group interactions to identify themes or content areas where students have doubts or difficulties. Once detected the failure of knowledge, another agent will suggest students study materials (power point presentations, books, monographs, web pages, videos, and so on) that can be consulted to resolve the problem or difficulty. In these cases the system will alert the teacher to assist students to achieve completeness of the task or activity.

With this multi-agent model it is intended to alleviate the workload of teachers, as well as to help students to be less dependent on the teacher. For students, having a system that recommends them to review the contents would help them better manage their own time, since often they are limited in this aspect and they do not have the possibility of reviewing all the study material. This situation is exacerbated when one considers that many college students combine their studies with part-time jobs.

Once gaps in knowledge have been recognized, the subsequent recommendation of learning materials is not easy especially when working with materials written in more than one language. The search and retrieval of information from materials written in multiple languages is precisely the main focus of this work. This chapter assesses the feasibility of using Lucene as multilingual search engine within the multi-agent model for recommending study material.

The rest of the chapter begins with a theoretical background section as it introduces the notion of software agent, describes the types of communication interfaces used in CSCL tools, refers to the techniques for analyzing interactions through communication interfaces based on natural language, explains the concept as well as a taxonomy of recommender systems, presents the methods commonly used to search multilingual documents, and describes some previous research related to our proposal. Once introduced the preliminary notions, the multi-agent model to recommend study material is described in detail. Then we describe the experimentation process with different analyzers and filters of Lucene[1]. After that, the user interface suggested to implement the proposed multi-agent model is presented. Finally, we present our conclusions and further work.

BACKGROUND

The Notion of Software Agent

In spite of the fact that there is no universally accepted definition of the term agent, it is usually accepted that an agent is any entity that perceives its environment through sensors and acts upon that environment through actuators (Russell & Norvig, 2010). Agents can be biologic (people or animals, for example), robotic, or computational. A human agent has eyes, ears, and other organs for sensors and hands, legs, vocal tract, and so on for actuators. A robotic agent could have cameras and infrared range finders for sensors and motors for actuators.

Various attributes are associated with agents in different domain applications yet, according to Nwana (1996) there are three ideal and primary attributes that agents should exhibit: autonomy, cooperation, and learning. Autonomy refers to the principle that agents can operate on their own without the need for human guidance. A key element of their autonomy is their proactivity, i.e. their ability to 'take the initiative' instead of reacting in response to their environment (Nwana, 1996). Cooperation is social ability that agents possess, which means the ability to interact with other agents and possibly humans via some communication language. Agent learning refers to agents' capability of improving their performance over time as they react and/or interact with their external environment. In (Nwana, 1996) the author argues that a key attribute of any intelligent agent is its ability to learn.

This chapter is concerned with a particular type of agents, software agents. A software agent is a computer program designed to carry out some task on behalf of a user (Coppin, 2004). As the aim of our multi-agent model is personalizing the delivery of learning material for collaborative learning groups, we are working with a special kind of software agents known as pedagogical agents. Pedagogical agents could be defined as autonomous and/or interface agents that support human learning in the context of an interactive learning environment (Chen & Wasson, 2005). Essentially, interface agents act as an autonomous personal assistant that cooperates with the user in accomplishing some task in a software application such as a spreadsheet or an operating system (Nwana, 1996). In order to support and provide assistance to the user, interface agents observe and monitor the actions taken by the user in the interface, learn new 'shortcuts', and suggest better ways of doing the task (Nwana, 1996).

A common way of exploiting the potential power of agents is by combining many agents in one multi-agent system. A multi-agent system can be defined as a set of agents that work and communicate together to achieve individual and common goals (Soh, Khandaker, & Jiang, 2010). Each agent in a multi-agent system has incomplete information and is incapable of solving the entire problem on its own, but combined together, the agents form a system that has sufficient information and ability to solve the problem (Coppin, 2004). Communication and collaboration are desirable properties of multi-agent systems, since multi-agent systems do not have a centralized control mechanism for solving the problem.

User Interfaces Employed in CSCL Environments

In CSCL environments, student-student and student-teacher interactions occur through semi-structured interfaces (such as dialogue acts, sentence opener, menu-based and diagrams) or free text interfaces.

Semi-structured interfaces are quite popular in distributed collaborative learning environments due to its ease of use and the fact that they reduce the amount of natural language processing necessary to understand the collaboration (Chen, 2006; Soller, Monés, Jermann, & Muehlenbrock, 2005; Tchounikine, Rummel, & McLaren, 2010). However, there is research showing that the semi structured interfaces undermine the collaborative process because they restrict the types of communicative acts, make the communication slow (Chen & Wasson, 2005; Constantino-González, Suthers, & Escamilla-De-Los-Santos, 2003), and create relational stress (Olivares, 2007). Additionally restricting users to communicate using semi-structured interfaces can lead to misunderstanding the dialogue when students use interface options incorrectly (Chen & Wasson, 2005; Constantino-González et al., 2003; Tchounikine et al., 2010).

As shown in Figure 1, when sentence openers are used it is necessary for students to start their contributions selecting a suggestive phrase (for example: "Do you think," "I believe", "Let's try" and "Please show me ") and then enter the rest of the sentence in their own words (Goodman et al., 2005). This strategy identifies the intention of a contribution in a conversation without fully understanding the meaning of the underlying dialogue acts (Goodman et al., 2005; Soller, 2001). However, opening statements suffer from additional problems that occur in other semi structured interfaces, namely recognition of only the primary intention of each contribution, change in the nature of the interaction and steep learning curve.

- Recognition of only the primary intention of each contribution: because each sentence opener typically is associated with only one intention (e.g. suggest or justify), an interface based on sentence openers can only represent the primary intention (Soller et al., 2005). This means that if for example a student begins a sentence with the sentence opener corresponding to the dialogue act "motivate" and then in the same sentence the student introduces a second dialogue act "reject", the sentence opener approach would only recognize the dialogue act "motivate" since it cannot capture complex intentions (Goodman et al., 2005).
- Change in the nature of the interaction: requiring users to select sentence openers before writing the rest of their contribution can tempt them to change the meaning of their contribution to match the meaning of the opening sentence (Soller, 2001). It is therefore essential that the opening statements allow a broader communication range in relation to the learning task.
- Steep learning curve: if students have no prior experience with the use of opening statements, they may invest considerable time during the first sessions by reading the list of sentences available to find the most appropriate for their contribution (Soller, 2004). To avoid that students have difficulty in locating the phrases they need in the interface we should train them in the use of sentence openers in real situations (Israel & Aiken, 2007).

Free text-based interfaces have the advantage of not restricting the interaction nor requiring users to have to explicitly indicate the type of contribution they want to make. However, in a free text interface it is not possible to use the interface itself to make inferences about the interaction process, and therefore it is necessary to use natural language processing and text mining techniques.

Figure 1. Sentences openers in the ICSS system
Source: (Israel & Aiken, 2007)

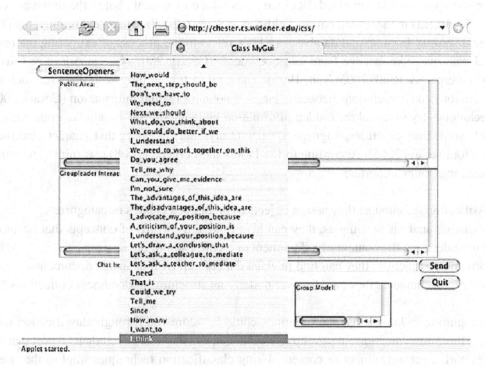

Analysis of Natural Language Interactions

Natural languages are the languages used by humans to, among other things, communicate. Unlike the formal languages (such as C ++, Java or Prolog) natural languages are characterized as ambiguous, i.e., a sentence in natural language can have more than one meaning and in some cases determining the correct meaning can be difficult (Coppin, 2004).

Natural language processing is an area of research and application that explores how computers can be used to understand and manipulate text or voice in natural language (Chowdhury, 2005). The foundations of natural language processing consist of various disciplines, namely: information science and computer science, linguistics, mathematics, electrical and electronic engineering, artificial intelligence, robotics, and psychology (Chowdhury, 2005). Researchers in the field of natural language processing are interested in knowing how humans understand and use language because in this way they can develop appropriate techniques and ensure that computer systems understand and handle natural languages while performing their tasks (Chowdhury, 2005).

The area of natural language processing includes tasks such as token decomposition, Part-of-Speech Tagging (POST), suppression of stop words, stemming, identifying lemmas, entity recognition, classification of entities, determining the limits of the sentence, phrase recognition, correcting spelling mistakes, and text summary.

Alternatively to the use of natural language processing, the analysis of communications in CSCL environments based on free text interfaces could be addressed through text mining. As with data mining, text mining seeks to extract useful information from data sources through the exploration and identification of interesting patterns. However, text mining data sources are collections of documents and therefore it does not seek patterns in formalized data records as with data mining, but in the unstructured textual data in the documents in these collections (Feldman & Sanger, 2007). Then, text mining, also known as knowledge discovery from textual databases (KDT), refers to the process of extracting interesting and non-trivial patterns or knowledge from text documents (Césari, 2007; García-Adeva & Calvo, 2006; Hotho, Nürnberger, & Paaß, 2005; Tan, 1999). The goal of text mining is to discover such things as trends, deviations and associations between "large" amount of textual information (Césari, 2007). Text mining techniques try to reveal the hidden information by methods that are able to cope with the large number of words and structures, vagueness, uncertainty, and fuzziness that characterize the natural language (Hotho et al., 2005). According to Do-Prado and Ferneda (2008) text mining techniques can be organized into four categories:

- Classification techniques: they assign objects to predefined classes or categories.
- Association analysis techniques: they can help to identify words of concepts that occur together, and to understand the content of a document or a collection of documents.
- Information extraction: they can find relevant data or expressions inside documents.
- Clustering techniques: they can discover underlying structures in document collections.

The recognition of knowledge shortcomings could be addressed through classification techniques that process the communications in a group to establish in which messages students report that they have difficulties with a certain subject or content. Using classification techniques implies that we need to gather a collection of documents to train classifiers. In this collection of documents each message sent by the students will have to be manually associated to a category or type of knowledge shortcoming.

Given the issues raised by Aranha and Passos (2008) a text mining process consists of 4 macro steps shown in Figure 2: gathering, pre-processing, indexing, and mining.

Figure 2. Steps of a text mining process
Source: (Aranha & Passos, 2008)

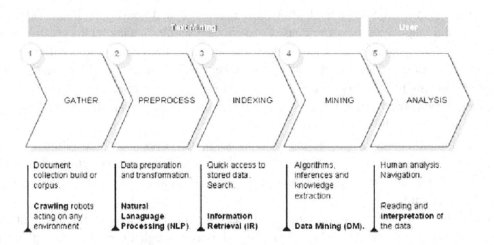

- **Gathering:** The aim is to identify and select the domain in which the text mining technique is applied, so that they can collect data that will compose the text database.
- **Pre-Processing:** It is responsible for obtaining a structured or semi-structured document representation, usually in the form of an attribute-value table that can be sent to knowledge discovery algorithms. Although it can be quite costly, the pre-processing step is absolutely necessary for the success of the process of text mining.
- **Indexing:** It is characterized by using information retrieval methods that increase the performance of the process.
- **Mining:** It aims to find useful or previously unknown patterns or information in the documents. For the extraction of patterns similar techniques to the traditional data mining process, like clustering and classification, are used.

Text mining and natural language processing are closely linked in the sense that many of the techniques of natural language processing (POST, suppression of stop words, stemming, lemmatization, etc.) are used for the pre-processing step of text mining.

One issue that should be considered is that while text mining methods and natural language processing allow to analyze free text-based interactions in a non-intrusive way for students and for teachers, these approaches are limited by their ability to understand natural human conversation (Soller et al., 2005). Besides the text mining techniques cannot be used generically as they have to adapt to each domain of learning and they often require considerable time and effort by humans (Barros & Verdejo, 2000; Soller et al., 2005).

The Notion of Recommender Systems

Recommender systems development initiated from a rather simple observation: to make daily and routine decisions people often rely on recommendations provided by others (Felfernig, Friedrich, & Schmidt-Thieme, 2007). For example, it is common to rely on what one's friends recommend when selecting a book to read; employers count on recommendation letters when making recruiting decisions; and when selecting a film to watch, individuals tend to read and rely on the movie reviews that appear on printed or digital newspapers (Rocco, Rokach, & Shapira, 2011). Recommender systems assist and augment this natural social process because they support users by identifying interesting products, information and services in situations where the number and complexity of offers surpass the user's capability to survey them and reach a decision (Felfernig et al., 2007).

The term "Recommender Systems" includes all software tools and techniques that provide suggestions for items most likely to be interesting to users or relevant to their needs (Rocco et al., 2011; Konstan, 2004). "Item" is the general term used to denote what the system recommends to users. A recommender system normally focuses on a specific type of item (e.g., CDs, books, movies, or news) and accordingly its design, its graphical user interface, and the core recommendation technique used to generate the recommendations are all customized to provide useful and effective suggestions for that specific type of item (Rocco et al., 2011). Interest in recommender systems has dramatically increased owing to the demand for personalization technologies from large and successful e-commerce applications such as amazon.com, netflix.com and tripadvisor.com (Felfernig et al., 2007). Nowadays recommender applications suggest everything from news, web sites, CDs, books, and movies to more complex items such as financial services, digital cameras, or e-government services.

Despite having their roots in information retrieval, from the mid-1990s recommender systems have become an independent research area of their own (Gedikli, 2013). According to Konstan (2004) recommender systems were developed to address two challenges that could not be addressed by existing keyword-based information filtering systems. First, they deal with the problem of overwhelming numbers of on-topic documents (all of which would be selected by a keyword filter) by filtering based on human judgement about the quality of those documents. Second, they addressed the problem of filtering non-text documents, such as music and images, based on human taste.

Having introduced the notion of recommender systems, it is convenient to define the recommendation problem more precisely. Supposing $U = \{u_1, ..., u_n\}$ is the set of users and $I = \{i_1, ..., i_m\}$ is the set of items that can be recommended to the users. Furthermore let $\hat{r} : U \times I \to S$ be a utility function which measures the usefulness $\hat{r}_{u,i}$ of item i to user u and returns a ranking in a totally ordered set S consisting of real numbers or nonnegative integers. In the recommender system literature the utility of an item is usually represented by a rating value that represents the degree a particular user likes a given item. According to Gedikli (2013) the recommendation problem consists of selecting for each user $u \in U$ a not-yet-rated item $i'_u \in I$ that maximizes the utility function $\hat{r}$:

$$\forall u \in U, \ i'_u = \underset{i \in I}{\arg\max} \ \hat{r}_{u,i} \tag{1}$$

Since the utility function of equation (1) is used to predict the interest of a user in a particular item, $\hat{r}$ could be considered as a prediction function. Therefore $\hat{r}_{u,i}$ stands for the predicted rating value of user u for item i. In this context, the user u is called target user and the item i is called target item. The target user is also known as the active user.

Recommender systems process various kinds of data in order to build their recommendations. As a general classification these data refer to three kinds of objects: items, users, and transactions (relations between users and items) (Rocco et al., 2011).

- **Items:** They are the objects that are recommended. They may be characterized by their complexity and their value or utility. For instance, in the case of a news item the complexity is determined by its structure, the textual representation, and its time-dependent importance. The value of an item may be positive if the item is useful for the user or negative if the item is not appropriate and the user made a wrong decision when selecting it.

- **Users:** Users of a recommender system usually have different goals and characteristics. Recommender systems exploit a range of information about the users in order to personalize the recommendations and the human-computer interaction. User data constitutes the user model or user profile that encodes her/his preferences and needs. The user model always plays a central role because no personalization is possible without a convenient user model (Rocco et al., 2011). Since a user model may include relations between users (such as the trust level of these relations), recommender systems might recommend items based not only on preferences and needs but also based on relations.

- **Transactions:** They are data that store important information generated during the interaction between a user and the recommender system. These data are useful for the recommendation generation algorithm that the system is using. For instance, a transaction log may contain a reference to the item selected by the user and a description of the context for that particular recommendation. A transaction may also include an explicit or implicit feedback the user has provided. Ratings are the most popular form of feedback that a recommender system collects. In the explicit collection of ratings, the user is asked to provide her/his opinion about an item on a rating scale. In contrast, when dealing with implicit ratings the system aims to infer the opinion of the users based on the user's actions.

Previously it was mentioned that in a recommendation system the core recommendation technique used to generate the recommendations is customized to provide useful and effective suggestions for a specific type of item. Depending on the way the core function is implemented, it is possible to distinguish between six classes of recommender systems (Rocco et al., 2011):

- **Content-Based:** The system recommends items that are similar to the ones that the user liked in the past (Rocco et al., 2011). The similarity of items is calculated based on the features associated with the compared items. A content-based recommender system suggests all items on the basis of purchasing or activities information available from the current user, yet it cannot provide serendipitous recommendations (Felfernig et al., 2007). Content-based recommendation has two advantages: it does not require large user groups to achieve reasonable recommendation accuracy, and new items can be recommended once item attributes are available (Jannach, Zanker, Felfernig, & Friedrich, 2011).

- **Collaborative Filtering:** This approach recommends to the active user the items that other users with similar tastes liked in the past (Rocco et al., 2011). These systems suppose that if users shared the same interests in the past (if they viewed or bought the same books, for example) they will also have similar tastes in the future (Jannach et al., 2011). Therefore, if user A and B have a purchase history that overlaps strongly and user A has recently bought a book that B has not yet seen, the basic rationale is to propose this book also to B. Collaborative filtering is considered to be the most popular and widely implemented technique in recommender systems (Rocco et al., 2011).

- **Demographic:** This type of system recommends items based on the demographic profile of the user (age, language, country and so on) since they assume that different recommendations should be generated for different demographic niches (Rocco et al., 2011).

- **Knowledge-Based:** Some application domains, such as consumer electronics and financial services, involve large numbers of one-time buyers. This means that it is impossible to rely on the existence of a purchase history, a prerequisite for collaborative and content-based filtering approaches (Jannach et al., 2011). Nevertheless, more detailed and structured content (including technical and quality features) may be available to support the selection of appropriate items. Knowledge-based systems exploit that additional knowledge because they generate recommendations based on specific domain knowledge about how certain item features satisfy needs and preferences of users and, ultimately, how the item is useful for the user (Rocco et al., 2011). In knowledge-based approaches the explicit representation of knowledge lets recommender systems calculate solutions that fulfill certain requirements of customers, as well as it lets explain solutions to customers and support customers when the system can't find a solution (Felfernig et al., 2007).

- **Community-Based:** Since evidence suggests that people tend to rely more on recommendations from their friends than on recommendations from similar but anonymous individuals, this type of system recommends items based on the preferences of the user's friends (Rocco et al., 2011). Community-based recommender systems need to acquire and model information about the social relations of the users and the preferences of the user's friends (Rocco et al., 2011).
- **Hybrid Recommender Systems:** These recommender systems combine two or more of the above mentioned techniques so as to use the advantages of one technique and fix the disadvantages of other ones (Rocco et al., 2011). For example, collaborative filtering methods suffer from new-item problems, i.e., they cannot recommend items that have no ratings (Rocco et al., 2011). However, this does not limit content-based approaches since the prediction for new items is based on their description that is typically easily available.

It is also worth noting that sometimes the user utility for an item depends on contextual variables (Rocco et al., 2011). For instance, the utility of an item for a user can be influenced by the domain knowledge of the user (e.g., expert vs. beginning users of a notebook), or can depend on the time when the recommendation is requested. Also, the user could be more interested in items (e.g., a restaurant, a supermarket or a museum) closer to his current location. When recommendations must be adapted to these specific additional details of contextual variables, it becomes harder and harder to correctly estimate what the right recommendations are (Rocco et al., 2011).

At first glance it might seem that the multi-agent model described in this chapter should be implemented as a content-based recommender system because the aim is to suggest learning materials that help students to solve their lack of knowledge about certain topics. Nonetheless, there are factors such as nationality and learning style that influence the kind of study material that is most appropriate for a student or student group. On the one hand, in collaborative learning courses o activities with international students it is very common that all members of a group do not share a native language or that students do not have the same level of proficiency of the language in which the course is taught. On the other hand, it is known that the type of learning material most suitable for each person is strongly influenced by their learning style (Felder & Silverman, 1988). This means that a combination of knowledge-based, content-based and demographic recommendation techniques would be the most suitable approach to suggest learning materials that are relevant to interests and needs of students. Additionally it might be useful to include in the student model contextual issues such as device type (notebook, PC, smartphone, etc.), speed connection, knowledge level, and so on. Suppose for example a scenario where a student with visual learning style accesses to the CSCL environment through a mobile device with 2G connection. In spite of being a video a suitable kind of learning material for the visual learning style, the long download time of the video with a 2G connection could lead to replace the video with a web page full of text and drawings because this type of content would load faster.

Methods for Searching Multilingual Documents

Multilingual Information Retrieval (MIR) is a sub-domain of Information Retrieval that addresses the problem of making queries in a certain language and retrieving documents in several languages (Korra, Sujatha, Chetana, & Kumar, 2011). The most commonly used strategy for solving this problem is translation. Since the language of the query differs from the documents and it is necessary to compare the performance of the query representation with the documents representation to establish how similar they are, we should decide between translating the query to the language of the documents or translating the documents to the query language (Korra et al., 2011). The translation of documents or the query can be done by using translation resources such as bilingual dictionaries, machine translation systems, and parallel corpora.

- **Dictionary-Based Translation:** Machine-readable bilingual dictionaries have become increasingly available and are often used in the translation modules of MIR engines. A dictionary-based approach to translation is relatively simple (when compared to other alternatives) but suffers from two major weaknesses: ambiguity and lack of coverage (Zhou, Truran, Brailsford, Wade, & Ashman, 2012). Bilingual dictionaries usually contain multiple translations for any given term and selecting the "correct" translation from a list of competing candidate terms is a crucial but nontrivial task (Zhou et al., 2012). Solutions to this selection task have specialized toward two mutually exclusive techniques: single selection translators and multiple selection translators. While single selection translators try to find the single best translation for each term, multiple selection translators are open to the possibility of more than one translation of each term and address the issue of ambiguity via the reweighting of terms (Zhou et al., 2012). Regarding vocabulary coverage, certain types of words (e.g., newly coined terms, technical terms, compound words, proper names, acronyms, and abbreviations) are under-represented in bilingual dictionaries. These out-of-vocabulary (OOV) terms can severely degrade the retrieval effectiveness of a MIR engine (Zhou et al., 2012).

- **Machine Translation (MT):** It is the automatic translation of free-text from one natural language to another. MT systems have become extremely popular in MIR over the last years due to the wide availability of MT systems and the linguistic resources required to train them (Zhou et al., 2012). In spite of this recent popularity and excellent results obtained in experiments, MT systems are still some distance from solving the MIR problem. First of all, the effectiveness of statistical MT systems is heavily dependent on the languages involved. For resource-poor languages (e.g., Thai) or language pairs with little in common (e.g., English and Chinese), MIR effectiveness can be as low as 50 percent of the monolingual baseline (Zhou et al., 2012). Secondly, the output of a MT system is usually one word per term. This sort of literal mapping ignores the availability of multiple expressions in the target language, leaving some translations incomplete (Zhou et al., 2012). Finally, MT systems generally pay too much attention to syntactic structure, which is unimportant when translating queries (Zhou et al., 2012). Furthermore, OOV terms often have a significant impact on retrieval effectiveness, but are usually ignored by MT systems (Zhou et al., 2012).

- **Corpus-Based Translation:** A parallel text is a document written in one language and presented next to its translation in another. Large collections of parallel texts are referred to as parallel corpora. When using parallel corpora for translation, the basic technique involves a side-by-side analysis of the corpus and the production of a set of translation probabilities for each term (Zhou et al., 2012). One of the main disadvantages of the corpus-based approach to translation is the difficulty in obtaining suitable document collections. Parallel corpora can be extremely time-consuming to produce, even when restricted to specific information domains (Zhou et al., 2012).

Considering the shortcomings of translation methods that have been used in MIR and that it is intended to recommend study materials written in more than one language, a strategy or mechanism to search for learning resources, without translating neither the query nor the study materials, is needed. It is considered that a possible solution to this dilemma could be the inclusion of Lucene as a component of the "Study Materials Searching" agent in the multi-agent model shown in Figure 3. Lucene has word processing resources that are independent of language as well as language-specific resources. Therefore, it is necessary to establish which resource or combination of resources allows Lucene to search on an inverted index built from documents written in more than one language.

The fact of working with study materials written in more than one language is one of the most challenging aspects of the development process of the "Study Materials Searching" agent because it raises questions such as: Should we use analyzers for each language?, should we use a generic parser that is independent of the language?, should we build a single index for all languages or a separate index for each language?, should we allow to search by language?, among others.

Related Work

Considering that in the e-learning domain there are a number of context variables (such as user attributes, domain characteristics, and what kind of learning is desired) that should be considered before a recommender system is deployed, simply transferring a recommender system from an existing (e.g. commercial) content to e-learning may not accurately meet the needs of the targeted users (Nikos Manouselis, Drachsler, Vuorikari, Hummel, & Koper, 2011). For this reason, in this subsection we focus our discussion on recommender systems that have been introduced in order to propose learning resources to students or teachers. Table 1 summarizes some work that are related to the multi-agent model presented in this chapter.

In spite of all research projects shown in Table 1 argue that they seek to recommend learning resources (clues, explanations, bibliographic material, activities, etc.), the proposal of Reuter and Durán (2014) cannot really be considered a recommender system but rather a framework in which the use of information search and retrieval techniques prevails. Reuter and Durán (2014) assume that the active student will be able to erase all his/her doubts if he/she is shown similar questions made previously by other students, yet Reuter and Durán (2014) do not know if the answers to those questions allowed students erase their doubts in the past. This means that Reuter and Durán (2014) did not incorporate explicit or implicit feedback mechanisms in order to evaluate the usefulness of answers that peers of the active student or even the teacher gave. Other limitation of this research is that the user profile was not considered, therefore no recommendation system is possible. In the rest of the projects summarized in Table 1 it can be seen that it is quite common the use of a hybrid approach to generate the recommendations, i.e., the combination of recommendation techniques. Regarding the use of the software agent technology, Souali et al. (2011) included two software agents: one for extracting terms and keywords from the learner's request and the other for recommending the suitable resources (direct responses, lessons, explanations, or even clues) that would meet his/her needs. While Dascalu et al. (2015) incorporated a software agent that offers suggestions of educational bibliographic materials and tools in order to help the learner to better navigate through educational resources.

A general observation that can be noted from Table 1 is that Reuter and Durán (2014) and Abel et al. (2010) are the only ones that consider the communication between students in order to suggest learning resources. In the rest of the research works suggestions are made based on the analysis of students' search string (Rodríguez et al., 2015; Souali et al., 2011), evaluation of users about the utility of learning resources (Ghauth & Abdullah, 2009; Manouselis et al., 2010), navigation history (Khribi et al., 2008), the activities of users in the e-learning platform (Dascalu et al., 2015; Klašnja-Milićević et al., 2011).

Table 1. Comparison of recommender systems for e-learning

Research Projects	Description	Techniques	Communication	Type of Support
Reuter & Duran (Reuter & Durán, 2014)	A recommendation framework that aims to assist students in solving their doubts about topics of a university course, through a process that leverages questions and answers raised previously by other students taking the same course.	Text mining. Information search and retrieval.	Forum	Student
Souali et al. (Souali et al., 2011)	A recommender system capable of analyzing the learners' requests and providing them with the most appropriate learning resources (direct answers, courses, clues or explanations) that meets their needs.	Software agents. Content-based recommendation Information search and retrieval.	---	Student
Ghauth & Abdullah (Ghauth & Abdullah, 2009)	A framework that works on the idea of recommending learning materials based on the similarity of content items and good learners' average rating strategy.	Content-based recommendation Recommendation based on good learners' average ratings.	---	Student
CELEBRATE (Manouselis, Vuorikari, & Van-Assche, 2010)	A learning resources' collaborative filtering service for an online community of teachers in Europe.	Collaborative filtering based on multi-attribute.	---	Teacher
Khribi et al. (Khribi, Jemni, & Nasraoui, 2008)	It computes on-line automatic recommendations to an active learner based on his/her recent navigation history, as well as exploiting similarities and dissimilarities among user preferences and among the contents of the learning resources.	Web usage mining techniques (clustering and association rule mining) Information search and retrieval. Content-based and collaborative filtering.	---	Student
Comtella-D (Abel et al., 2010)	A generic personalization framework for the e-learning focused discussion forum.	Collaborative filtering. Ontologies. Rubed-based recommendation.	Forum	Student
Protus (Klašnja-Milićević, Vesin, Ivanović, & Budimac, 2011)	A recommender system that suggests online learning activities to learners based on their learning style, knowledge and preferences.	Clustering. Sequential pattern mining. Collaborative filtering.	---	Student
Rodríguez et al. (Rodríguez, Duque, & Ovalle, 2015)	A knowledge-based recommender systems that uses a clustering technique in order to suggest learning objects according to learning style, evaluation by other users and students prior knowledge.	Knowledge-based recommendation. Clustering.	---	Student
U-learn (Dascalu et al., 2015)	A recommender agent that suggests learning materials and learning tools according to students' profile and learning styles.	Software agents. Collaborative-filtering.	---	Student

Considering only the use of tools for communication between students, the multi-agent model described in this chapter approaches the work of Reuter and Durán (2014) due to the interaction between students occurs through an interface based on free text and an analysis of the interaction process is performed with text mining. Nevertheless, unlike Reuter and Durán (2014) in the multi-agent model described in the following section the user is not required to explicitly indicate his or her information need because the Lack of Knowledge Detector agent (see Figure 3) should be able to identify shortcomings in knowledge based on analysis of group chats.

Paying attention to the column titled "Type of support" in the Table 1 one can notice that the nine recommender systems were designed so as to help students or assist teachers. Therefore, the proposed multi-agent model differs from the systems of Table 1 when considering support to collaboration. Learning resources suggested by the Study Materials Recommender agent (see Figure 3) aim that students can overcome any doubts or difficulties with topics that are required to complete a task or learning activity, and that way they contribute to improve the process of group learning.

MODEL FOR RECOMMENDATION OF STUDY MATERIAL

As it was previously mentioned manual analysis of group's interactions should allow teachers to identify difficulties during the learning process. Nevertheless, processing by hand information recorded by CSCL systems is extremely time intensive for two reasons. First, developing the coding schemes with categories (type of learning problems, skills, behavior, and so on) that can be assigned to actions, messages, interactions, etc., of students is a lengthy process requiring several iterations of development, revision, and improvement until human analysts can apply them reliably (Dönmez et al., 2005). Second, the tedious part of manual analysis worsens as the number of students and exchanged messages grows and it is very difficult to follow the thread of discussion, the flow of ideas, and contributions of each student (Chen, 2006; Dönmez et al., 2005; Rosé et al., 2008).

Considering what was stated in the previous paragraph, Figure 3 shows a schema of the multi-agent model proposed to automatically detect weaknesses in students' knowledge and recommend study material, which can help fill in those gaps in the knowledge of students.

Figure 3. Graphical representation of multi-agent model for study material recommendation

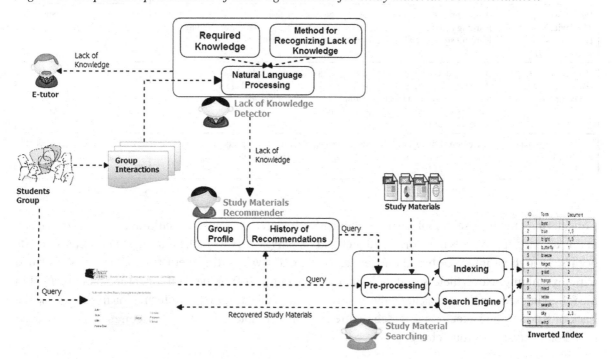

In the model there is a *Lack of Knowledge Detector* agent that monitors group interactions in order to identify issues or contents that create difficulties or doubts in students and that are required to complete an activity. To examine the interactions in search of knowledge gaps text mining techniques can be used, also a simpler approach based on keywords might be applied. With the second alternative phrases such as "I have doubts", "It is not clear", "I do not understand", "This technique is very complicated", etc., would be saying that students have difficulties with the topics covered by the underlying course or activity. When analyzing the group communications the *Lack of Knowledge Detector* agent also needs to consider the *Required Knowledge* and some *Method for recognizing lack of knowledge* in order to distinguish situations where the keywords (in case you use this technique) indicate and do not indicate missing knowledge. It could be the situation where a student does not know a topic but one of his colleagues has previous knowledge on it.

Once the lack in the knowledge of students is detected, the *Lack of Knowledge Detector* agent informs the e-tutor and *Study Materials Recommender* agent the theme or content that students should learn. After being notified of a lack of student knowledge, the *Study Materials Recommender* agent will consult the *Study Material Searching* agent about study materials that contain information on the topic that students need to learn. Once the searching agent indicates the learning material that could be useful to students, the *Study Materials Recommender* agent will select material considering the profile of the group (learning styles, native language, disabilities, etc.) and the history of recommendations. After making the selection, the *Study Materials Recommender* agent will contact the student group to suggest materials that could be consulted. In addition to intervening at the request of the *Lack of Knowledge detector* agent the *Study Material Searching* agent is activated when students wish to seek learning materials on a particular topic.

The *Study Material Searching* agent will be responsible for pre-processing queries of both students and the *Study Materials recommender* agent (identifying tokens, removing stop words, making conversion to lowercase, etc.). To index the study materials and search the inverted index, the *Study Materials Searching* agent will use Lucene for the analysis and retrieval of information on study materials written in more than one language.

A remarkable feature of the proposed multi-agent model is that the recognition of knowledge gaps will be done non-intrusively, i.e. the group dynamics is not affected. Assessing the level of knowledge of students is usually done with techniques such as questionnaires (Shishehchi, Banihashem, & Zin, 2011), but this method implies that students deviate from the activities being undertaken to focus on answering the questionnaire.

SEARCH IN MULTILINGUAL DOCUMENTS USING LUCENE

As mentioned in the introduction, this study is intended to assess the capabilities of Lucene to analyze and retrieve information about learning materials written in more than one language. While the idea is that the study materials can be written in several languages and be of multiple types (power point presentations, monographs, web pages, etc.), as an initial assessment of Lucene we chose to work only with information on books written in English and Spanish. Specifically, we considered about 200 books belonging to the library of the Department of Informatics, Faculty of Sciences and Technologies (FCEyT) at National University of Santiago del Estero, Argentina (UNSE). Of those 200 books, 76% are written in Spanish and the remaining 24% in English. In the subsections below we define the fields that are part of the inverted index, the fields that can be searched are detailed, the notion of relevance is introduced together with the metrics used to evaluate the results of the searches, and the results of experimentation with various Lucene analyzers and filters are described.

Definition of Index Fields

In the library of the Department of Informatics, for each book a plain text file containing the following information is kept:

- **Authors:** Name of the authors separated by comma.
- **Title:** Title under which the book was published.
- **Editorial:** Name of the publisher.
- **Year:** The year in which the book was published.
- **Originals Quantity:** Number of copies of the book the library has.
- **Original Code:** Alphanumeric code that locates the book on the shelves of the library.
- **ISBN:** The ISBN number could be registered with digits separated by dashes or digits without dashes.
- **Date Added to Library:** Date when the book was acquired.
- **Index:** Table of contents of the book.

Based on the plain text files that contain information about the books we had to determine which fields were to be indexed and which were to be stored without indexing. In the process of defining the fields the first objective was to reduce the size of the index, so that the information sent by the *Study Materials Searching* agent is kept to a minimum, both in response to queries sent by the *Study Materials Recommender* agent and those made by students. Once the information from plain text files was analyzed, we found that the inverted index had to contain the path and language fields. The path field specifies the location of the text file with information about the book. This field allows access to the ISBN number and the table of contents when the user wants to see more details of a particular book. The language field indicates the language in which the text file is written. Table 2 shows the characteristics of the fields with information about the books that are part of the inverted index.

Fields Employed to Search the Inverted Index

Only four out of eight inverted index fields described in Table 2 were employed to seek information about books. Detail of searches that can be performed by author name, book title, contents, and ISBN number are given below.

In queries by author name, we considered that the inverted index should contain occurrences not only equal to the text of the query but also similar to it. The search for similar names is possible thanks to a fuzzy search operator (~) that calculates the similarity of terms based on the algorithm of Levenshtein distance (Hatcher & Gospodnetic, 2005). With the addition of fuzzy search operator the syntax to search by author name is: "Authors: AuthorName OR Authors: AuthorName ~".

Table 2. Description of the fields in the inverted index

Field	Features
Authors	Type of field: TextField Field.Store.YES: as search result, the authors of the books are shown to users. Field.Index.YES: searches based on the authors of the books are made.
Title	Type of field: TextField Field.Store.YES: as search result, the title of the books is shown to users. Field.Index.YES: searches based on the title of the books are made.
ISBN	Type of field: StringField Field.Store.NO: the ISBN of the books is not shown to users as search result Field.Index.YES: searches based on the ISBN of the books are made.
Year	Type of field: StringField Field.Store.YES: as search result, the year of publication of the books is shown to users. Field.Index.NO: no searches are made with this field.
Index	Type of field: TextField Field.Store.NO: the index of the books is not shown to users as search result. Field.Index.YES: searches based on the content index are made.
Editorial	Type of field: StringField Field.Store.YES: as search results, the editorial is shown to users. Field.Index.NO: it is only necessary to recover the name of the publisher of each book and no searches are done with this field.
Path	Type of field: StringField Field.Store.YES: the inverted index stores the path to access the text file that contains information of each book, but this is not shown to users. Field.Index.NO: no searches are made with this field.
Language	Type of field: StringField Field.Store.NO: the language in which the book is written is not shown to users. Field.Index.YES: searches can be made using this field.

When searching for the title field the fuzzy operator search was also used, therefore, the expression for the title search would be: "Title: BookTitle OR Title: BookTitle ~".

Through an expression of the type "ISBN: BookISBN OR ISBN: BookISBN~" exact and approximates matches are searched for the ISBN number field.

The most complex type of query performed is done by keywords, because it involves considering the fields Author, Title, ISBN and Index, and determining the presence of terms that are part of the query. This means that keyword actually does not refer to a field but rather includes a number of fields. With the addition of the fuzzy search operator, search by keywords has the following structure: "(Authors: keyword OR Authors: keyword ~) ^ 1.6 OR (Title: keyword OR Title: keyword ~) ^ 2 OR (Index: keyword OR Index: keyword ~) ^ 1 OR (ISBN: keyword OR ISBN: keyword ~) ^ 1.3".

The ^ operator (boosting operator) was included in the above expression to ensure a variation of the importance given to documents retrieved by the search depending on the field in which query terms appear. The use of boosting may require a study in a real use scenario to determine which field or aspect of the book information users give greater importance, or use more frequently to perform searches. Nevertheless, in this chapter, we consider that in the search results books that contain the query terms in the Title field should appear first, followed by books where the query terms appear in the Authors and ISBN number fields, and finally the books that have the query terms in the Index field.

Evaluation of Search Results Considering Relevance

Determining the relevance of query results is a subjective task that depends on factors such as: being of the correct topic, being appropriate in time, coming from a reliable source, and satisfying user goals. This indicates that a good assessment of the relevance of the results obtained by the *Study Material Searching* agent should be performed with real users, i.e. students working in a CSCL environment. Since we did not have the possibility of an evaluation with real users, to compare the different resources provided by Lucene for information retrieval, we considered the following two notions of relevance that are less subjective than considering whether the results are useful for the intended use of the user:

- A document is relevant if the words in the query appear frequently in the document, in any order.
- If the words in the query do not appear frequently in the document, we consider that the document is relevant when there is not a difference higher than 30% among the characters in the query and the characters in the document words.

Table 3 illustrates the notion of relevance with a query using author name and its results. Bold characters in the second column of Table 3 represent characters in the author name of retrieved documents that match the query string. In this example title field is not relevant to assess relevance due to search is made by author name.

Analyzer Selection Process

This subsection introduces, first, the metrics used to evaluate the results obtained from Lucene to different test queries. Next, the values of these metrics for different analyzers, filters, and combinations of filters and analyzers are presented. Analyzers are resources of Lucene whose work is to parse each field of data into indexable tokens or keywords. While filtering is a mechanism of narrowing the search space, allowing only a subset of the documents to be considered as possible query matches (Hatcher & Gospodnetic, 2005). They can be used to implement search-within-search features to successively search within a previous set of query match or to constrain the document search space for security or external data reasons (Hatcher & Gospodnetic, 2005). For instance, a security filter allows users to only see search results of documents they own even if their query technically matches other documents that are off limits.

Table 3. Examples of the notion of relevance

Query	Search results	% Matching	Relevant?
James Baeza	Author: **Baeza James** Title: Administracion. 6ta Edicion	100%	Yes
	Author: Arnold Ken, **Baeza Jane** Title: Object-Oriented Simulation: Reusability, Adaptability, Maintainability	80%	Yes
	Author: Senn **James** A. Title: Análisis y Diseño de Sistemas de información	50%	No
	Author: Hammer Michael, **Baez** Marian Title: Reingeniería	40%	No

Evaluation Metrics

To compare search results obtained by applying different analyzers and filters available in Lucene the precision and recall metrics (Konchady, 2008) were used. Precision refers to the fraction of retrieved documents that are relevant to the query, i.e. the portion of retrieved documents that comply with the notion of relevance introduced in section *Evaluation of Search Results Considering Relevance*. Meanwhile, the recall indicates the fraction of relevant documents retrieved among all relevant documents stored in the inverted index.

The values of precision and recall metrics were calculated from 86 test queries designed to assess the capabilities of Lucene. These test queries are distributed as follows: 15 to evaluate searches by Authors field, 15 to evaluate searches by Title field, 8 to evaluate searches by ISBN field and 48 to evaluate keyword based searches.

Experimenting With Lucene Analyzers and Filters

This subsection describes a few experiments that were conducted with different analyzers and filters of Lucene in order to establish which combination allows reaching the best values for the precision and recall metrics.

Experiments With the StandardAnalyzer

The StandardAnalyzer breaks the text into tokens (through StandardTokenizer), converts it to lowercase (using LowerCaseFilter) and removes stop words (with StopFilter). During removal of stop words we replaced the Lucene stop words list with the stop words included in text mining software tm^2. Table 4 contains the value of precision and recall metrics obtained for different search fields when using StandardAnalyzer, as well as the average values for all the search fields.

Experiments With the SimpleAnalyzer

SimpleAnalyzer combines LowerCaseFilter with LetterTokenizer to convert text to lowercase and separate it into tokens. Table 5 shows the precision and recall for test queries when documents and queries are processed with SimpleAnalyzer.

Table 4. Precision and recall values for queries using Standard Analyzer

Search field	Precision	Recall
Authors	0,700925926	0,916667
Title	0,159775154	0,966667
ISBN	1	0,875
Keyword	0,445478933	0,764238
Average	0,576545003	0,880643

Table 5. Precision and recall values when using SimpleAnalyzer

Search field	Precision	Recall
Authors	0,700925926	0,916667
Title	0,070947866	0,966667
ISBN	1	0,875
Keyword	0,516419024	0,755558
Average	0,572073204	0,878473

SimpleAnalyzer differs from StandardAnalyzer in that it does not include the operation of removing stop words. In order to determine whether the removal of stop words led to the same precision and recall values shown in Table 5, we combined StopFilter and SimpleAnalyzer. To achieve this combination we had to create an extension of the Analyzer class that includes the functionality of LowerCaseFilter, StopFilter, and LetterTokenizer in one analyzer. Table 6 shows the precision and recall values for SimpleAnalyzer, when considering stop words removal in English, while Table 7 shows the results when Spanish and English stop words are deleted.

Experiments With the SnowballAnalyzer

Using SnowballAnalyzer the text of a document is converted to lowercase (LowerCaseFilter) and stop words are removed (StopFilter). SnowballAnalyzer not only recognizes the different types of tokens present in the documents (StandardTokenizer) but also replaces the tokens by its root or stem form. For example, the words "consist", "consisted", "consistency", "consistent", "consistently" and "consisting" are reduced to stem "consist". Since SnowballAnalyzer provides stemming algorithms specific to each language, Spanish documents were processed with the stemming algorithm for Spanish, while English documents were processed with the stemmer for English. Table 8 shows the values of precision and recall for searches using SnowballAnalyzer.

Table 6. Precision and recall values when combining SimpleAnalyzer with English stop words removal

Search field	Precision	Recall
Authors	0,788888889	0,916667
Title	0,159672472	0,933333
ISBN	1	0,875
Keyword	0,524958534	0,743405
Average	0,618379974	0,867101

Table 7. Precision and recall values when combining SimpleAnalyzer with English and Spanish stop words removal

Search field	Precision	Recall
Authors	0,722222222	0,916667
Title	0,191201343	0,9
ISBN	1	0,875
Keyword	0,623178033	0,715014
Average	0,6341504	0,85167

Table 8. Precision and recall values when using SnowballAnalyzer

Search field	Precision	Recall
Author	0,744444444	0,916667
Title	0,121646835	1
ISBN	1	0,875
Keyword	0,445848036	0,823365
Average	0,577984829	0,903758

Experiments With the SpanishAnalyzer

The fact that SpanishAnalyzer has algorithms for tokenizing and stemming that are specific to the Spanish language offers advantages when processing texts in Spanish. However, applying these algorithms to documents in English can lead to unpredictable results. For this reason, we decided to process documents in Spanish with SpanishAnalyzer and apply StandardAnalyzer to documents in English. During the stop words removal SpanishAnalyzer considered the list of stop words in Spanish included in the tm software while StandardAnalyzer was based on English stop words of tm. The values of the two relevant evaluation metrics applied to the results of the searches performed by combining SpanishAnalyzer with StandardAnalyzer are included in Table 9.

Experiments With the EnglishAnalyzer and SpanishAnalyzer

The last combination of analyzers we evaluated was EnglishAnalyzer and SpanishAnalyzer. Each of these analyzers has tokens decomposition and stemming algorithms specific for each language. For this reason, Spanish documents were analyzed with SpanishAnalyzer and English documents were processed with EnglishAnalyzer. The results for precision and recall are shown in Table 10.

Comparison of Results

Figures 4 and 5 show the average precision and recall values for experiments conducted with StandardAnalyzer, SimpleAnalyzer, SnowballAnalyzer, SpanishAnalyzer, EnglishAnalyzer and SpanishAnalyzer of Lucene. Analyzing these two figures, we can say that there are no substantial differences in the relevance of search results when you use one or another analyzer. The recall is always higher than 0.85, therefore we can say that with any of the analyzers or combination of analyzers it is possible to recover almost all of the documents that are relevant to the query. The precision in most cases is lower than 0.6, and while this value is acceptable, it indicates that about 40% of the results displayed to users are not relevant to their query.

Considering only the precision values in Figure 4, SimpleAnalyzer outperforms other analyzers because about 0.63 of results are relevant. The values in Tables 5, 6, and 7 clearly indicate that the removal of stop words improves the precision of searches because, with the addition of stop words removal in Spanish and English, it increased from 0.57 (SimpleAnalyzer without stop words removal) to 0.63. In turn, this increase in precision does not decrease recall values (see Figure 5).

Table 9. Precision and recall values when using SpanishAnalyzer and StandardAnalyzer

Search field	Precision	Recall
Author	0,744444444	0,916667
Title	0,115749151	0,933333
ISBN	1	0,875
Keyword	0,486102754	0,79584
Average	0,586574087	0,88021

Table 10. Precision and recall values when using SpanishAnalyzer and EnglishAnalyzer

Search field	Precision	Recall
Author	0,744444444	0,916667
Title	0,128336196	1
ISBN	1	0,875
Keyword	0,461371392	0,802119
Average	0,583538008	0,898446

Figure 4. Precision for searches with different analyzers

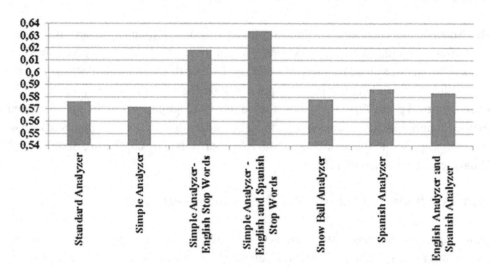

Figure 5. Recall for searches with different analyzers

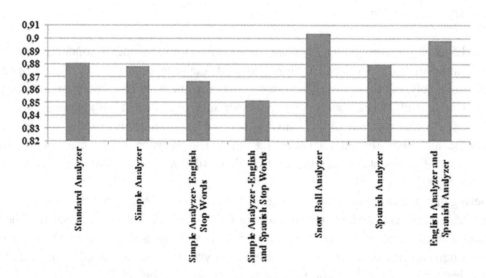

A review of the values in Tables 4 to 10 shows that while the precision for queries using the Title field does not exceed 0.19, in searches with the rest of the fields precision is always greater than 0.44. This means that queries for the Title field are a kind of Achilles heel for any of the analyzers. In order to improve the precision of searches using Title we decided to apply the Porter stemming algorithm (Hatcher & Gospodnetic, 2005) instead of the stemming algorithms used by SnowballAnalyzer, EnglishAnalyzer and SpanishAnalyzer. The results of these new experiments are discussed in the next subsection.

Improving Precision With PorterStemFilter

For improving the precision of searches based on the Title field when both documents and queries are subjected to the Porter stemming algorithm (PorterStemFilter), an extension of Lucene Analyzer class was created. Through this extension PorterStemFilter with LowerCaseTokenizer, StandardTokenizer, StopFilter, and LowerCaseFilter were combined. The metrics of precision and recall for results of searches that were made by coupling the four above-mentioned resources to PorterStemFilter are shown in Table 11.

The two cells with bold numbers in Table 11 show the highest precision and recall values that could be reached when using Title for searching. As it can be seen the most suitable strategy for improving the effectiveness of searches by title involves applying PorterStemFilter with StandardTokenizer and StopFilter (considering Spanish and English stop words). The precision value of 0.28 on the highlighted cell represents an increase of 47% taking into account that with the rest of the analyzers we obtained a maximum value of 0.19. Meanwhile, the recall is maintained within the values achieved with other analyzers.

Analyzing the fourth column of Table 11, we thought that PorterStemFilter with StandardTokenizer improved the relevance of search results, at least for the Title field, because this combination had been generated an inverted index that had higher amount of terms that the indices created by combining PorterStemFilter with other filters. However, in Figure 6 it is clearly shown that there is no direct relationship between the number of index terms and the relevance of search results. Precision can either improve or worsen with increasing the number of terms in the index.

Having it determined that the combination of PorterStemFilter with StandardTokenizer and StopFilter (with stop words removal in English and Spanish) improves the relevance of search results by title, we applied this combination of filters to search by author, ISBN and keyword in order to check whether the effect this combination had had in searches by title still remained. Table 12 reflects the values of precision and recall in searches by author, ISBN and keyword.

Table 11. Precision and recall values for searches by Title using PorterStemFilter

Combination of Filters	Precision	Recall	Number of Terms in the Index
PorterStemFilter – LowerCaseTokenizer	0,060297548	0,9	11763
PorterStemFilter-LowerCaseTokenizer- StopFilter with English stop words removal	0,118608388	1	11573
PorterStemFilter-LowerCaseTokenizer- StopFilter with Spanish and English stop words removal	0,154940214	1	11385
PorterStemFilter- StandardTokenizer	0,145454926	0,966667	20345
PorterStemFilter-StandardTokenizer–LowerCaseFilter	0,068436596	1	15863
PorterStemFilter-StandardTokenizer- LowerCaseFilter-StopFilter with English stop words removal	0,120936808	0,933333	15641
PorterStemFilter- StandardTokenizer - LowerCaseFilter - StopFilter with Spanish and English stop words removal	0,155218863	1	15489
PorterStemFilter – StandardTokenizer- StopFilter with English stop words removal	0,2369131	0,966667	19953
PorterStemFilter - StandardTokenizer - StopFilter with Spanish and English stop words removal	**0,279647474**	**0,966667**	19653

Figure 6. Relationship between precision and number of index terms for searches using title

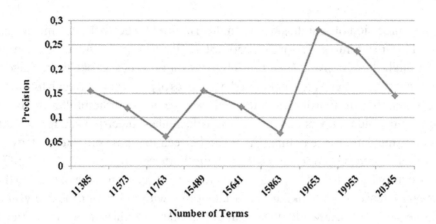

Comparing Table 12 with the values in Table 7, we can observe that: the relevance of search results for Author also improved; there are no changes in search by ISBN; and there is a decrease in the accuracy of the results when using keywords that somewhat compensates with a small increase in the recall. The average precision and recall values of Table 12 are 3% higher than those achieved by SimpleAnalyzer (Table 7). Thus, it could be concluded that for information processing of books written in English and Spanish we should use: StandardTokenizer, StopFilter with English and Spanish stop words, and PorterStemFilter. However, the problem with this combination of resources provided by Lucene is that searches are case sensitive.

When StandardTokenizer, StopFilter and PorterStemFilter are used the text is not converted to lowercase. This means that if a user searches for the word "Sommerville" and then performs another query by replacing the letter "S" for lowercase equivalent, i.e. "somerville", he can get completely different results. In fact, they will be results for the query "Sommerville" if the word "Sommerville" was present in the document collection and hence in the inverted index. Similarly, for the query "sommerville" are displayed books that have the word "sommerville" but not books in which the word "Sommerville" appears. SimpleAnalyzer does not suffer from the drawback of case sensitive searches because it converts the text to lowercase using LowerCaseFilter.

Table 12. Precision and recall values when PorterStemFilter is combined with StandardTokenizer and StopFilter

Search Field	Precision	Recall
Author	0,788888889	0,916667
Title	0,279647474	0,966667
ISBN	1	0,875
Keyword	0,541919152	0,731982
Average	0,652613879	0,872579

Based on the discussion in the preceding paragraphs, it is possible to conclude that the most appropriate strategy is to process both documents (information from books) and queries using SimpleAnalyzer complemented with the removal of stop words in English and Spanish (StopFilter).

DESCRIPTION OF USER INTERFACE FOR THE PROPOSED MULTI-AGENT MODEL

The user interface proposed for the multi-agent model to recommend study material could be similar to that shown in Figure 7. On the left, a chat tool that would show users a list of group posts during a conversation and would give them the possibility of sending new messages. The *Lack of Knowledge Detector* agent is responsible for monitoring these messages and looking for evidence of a lack in the knowledge required to complete a task or activity. Once notified about the topic that causes difficulties or doubts to students, the *Study Materials Recommender* agent would show on the right side of the interface materials that students should revise. The *Study Materials Searching* agent would also be accessible directly from the interface to give students the opportunity to search materials on their own.

Thus far, we have not implemented neither the three agents of the proposed model nor the chat user interface in Figure 7. Nevertheless, we have implemented an application that uses SimpleAnalyzer to search for books in Spanish and English. The user interface of this application is the same that will be used by the *Study Material Searching* agent and it is described below with an example.

To search for a book, the user has to enter the search string (left search button) and select the field by which he wants to search: author, title, ISBN or all fields (see Figure 8). This last option implies that searches are simultaneously made by Authors, Title, ISBN and index fields. Assuming that the text to search in books of the Department of Informatics was "java", and we are looking for all fields, the recovered books would be those shown in Figure 9.

Figure 7. User interface of the proposed multi-agent model

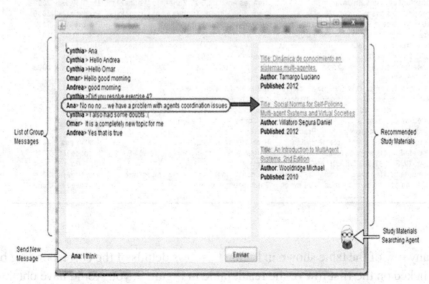

Figure 8. Study Material Searching agent user interface

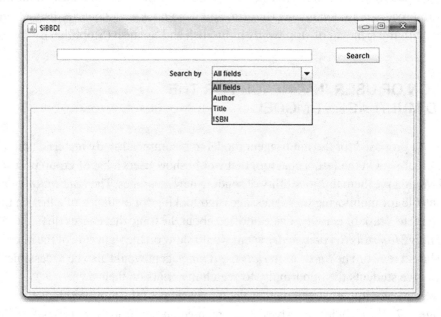

Figure 9. Results of a search with the Study Material Searching agent

Title	Author	Editorial	Published
Estructura de datos y algoritmos en JAVA	Goodrich Michael T., Tamassia Roberto	Compañia ...	2002
Estructura de Datos En Java	Joyanes Aguilar Luis , Zahonero Martínez Ig...	Mc Graw Hill	2008
Creación de sitios Web con XML y Java	Maruyama Hiroshi, Tamura Kent, Uramoto N...	Prentice Hall	2000
El Lenguaje de la Programacion Java. 3er E...	Arnold Ken, Gosling James	Pearson	2002
Ingenieria de Software Orientada a Objetos c...	Weitzenfeld Alfredo	Thomson I...	2003
Programación en java 2 : Algoritmos, estruct...	Joyanes Aguilar Luis, Zahonero Martínez Ign...	Mc Graw Hill	2002
J2ME. Manual de usuario y tutorial	Froufe Quintas Agustin	Alfaomega ...	2004
Fundamentos de Programación. Algoritmos,...	Joyanes Aguilar Luis	Mc Graw Hill	2003
UML y Patrones	Larman Craig	Pearson - ...	2003
Sistemas de tiempo real y lenguajes de pro...	Burns Alan, Wellings Andy	ADDISON-...	2003
Desarrollo de software dirigido por modelos...	Pons Claudia, Giandini Roxana Silvia, Pérez ...	Universida...	2010
El gran libro de Android avanzado	Tomás Jesús , Carbonell Vicente ,Vogt Carst...	Marcombo	2013
Sistemas distribuidos. Conceptos y diseño. ...	Coulouris George, Dollimore Jean , Kindber...	Pearson	2007
Mobile Design and Development. Practical C...	Mikkonen Tommi	O'Reilly	2009
Compiladores: Teoría e Implementación	Ruiz Catalán Jacinto	AlfaOmega	2010
Discrete-Event System Simulation. 5 ta edici...	Banks Jerry , Carson John S. , Nelson Barry ...	Prentice Hall	2010
REAL-TIME SYSTEMS DESIGN AND ANALYS...	Laplante Phillip	IEEE Pres	2004
E-commerce: Negocios, Tecnologia, Socied...	Laudon Kenneth C., Guercio Traver Carol	Prentice Hall	2009
Sistemas operativos modernos. 3er Edición	Tanenbaum Andrew S.	Prentice Hall	2009

A click on any row of the table shown in Figure 9, shows details of the corresponding book. Assuming you have clicked on the first row of the result table in Figure 9, you would have obtained additional information on the book "Data Structure and Algorithms in Java" as shown in Figure 10.

Figure 10. Details of the selected book

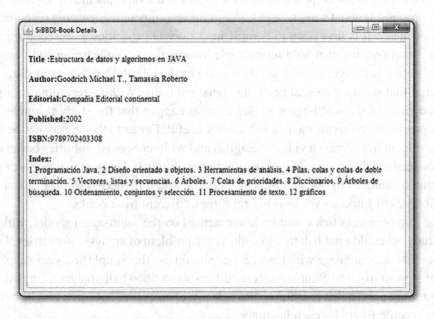

CONCLUSION

This work not only allowed us to propose a multi-agent model that customizes the retrieval of study material for collaborative groups of students, taking into account the needs of them, but also allowed us to experiment with tools available in Lucene to analyze and retrieve documents written in English and Spanish.

One of the first issues we should keep working on is to improve the accuracy of search results using the Title. The precision is always kept low because of the way in which the query to search for the Title field was built. Searches by Title recover not only books whose title field exactly matches the search string, but also books that have in the Title field some of the words that are part of the query. This causes that for each of this type of query, users are provided with more results than those that are really necessary to satisfy their information needs. For example, a search for the title field with the string "Operating System Administration" would result in the book whose title is "Operating System Administration" but also books with the words "Operating", "Systems" and "Administration" as part of their title.

On the other hand, two possible modifications to the search process that may enhance the precision and recall are: automatic language detection and synonym expansion for queries. Currently if a user performs a title search for the string "Introduction to Programming", the user will get as a result the book whose title contained the string "Introduction to Programming". However, the collection of books we considered contains a book titled "Programming Fundamentals. Algorithms and Data Structures", with almost the same issues that the book "Introduction to Programming". Consequently, it might be useful to include in the list of results not only the book "Introduction to Programming" but also "Programming Fundamentals. Algorithms and Data Structures". In this situation the words "Introduction" and "Fundamentals" can be taken as synonymous since books that have these words in their title often refer to basic or essential issues of the area or discipline they belong to.

Although in this chapter we emphasized on information retrieval capacities of Lucene, we should not forget that our proposal is about a multi-agent system for recommending learning resources in a personalized way. This means it is necessary to complement Lucene capacities with recommendation based on students or group profiles (that hold for example information about learning style, native language, domain of non-native language, knowledge level, and physical disabilities) so as to suggest to students learning material that satisfy their real needs and personal traits. Without techniques for personalizing the recommendations of the multi-agent model it could happen that the study resources suggested to students meet precision and recall metrics but are not useful. For instance, it may not be a good option to suggest to a student from Spain a video in English and without Spanish subtitles because that student could hardly understand the video if he/she does not know English. During the process of incorporating recommendation techniques to our multi-agent model it would be necessary to evaluate analysis and recovery capabilities of Lucene over learning resources different from books.

Beyond the improvements that could be implemented on the multi-agent model, with the development of this study we could establish that to address the problem of analysis and retrieval of documents written in more than one language with Lucene, one should use the SimpleAnalyzer supplemented with suppression of stop words. The SimpleAnalyzer differs from SnowballAnalyzer, EnglishAnalyzer and SpanishAnalyzer not only in that it achieves better levels of relevance in search results but also because it does not use specific filters for each language.

Another aspect that distinguishes SimpleAnalyzer, and that somehow justifies its best performance, is that it does not apply stemming. Stemming harms the relevance of search results because it increases the similarity of terms that are not similar actually. Consider for example the Spanish word "programación" and the English word "programming" that can be reduced to stem "program". If stemming is applied, a search with the word "programación" would result in all documents that have the word "programación" but also documents with the word "programming". But the word "programming" only shares 60% of the characters with "programación", and therefore does not comply with the notion of relevance introduced in section *Evaluation of Search Results Considering Relevance*.

Contrary to what happens with the operation of stemming, stop words removal does not increase the similarity between terms that are not really similar but it prevents these situations. Suppose that we have two books authored by "De la Mora" and "De la Mont". A query with the string "De la Mora" over an inverted index built without applying suppression of stop words, would retrieve books written by "De la Mora" and "De la Mont". The query string shares with "De la Mora" 100% of the characters while with "De la Mont" shares 75% of the characters, so both books meet the criteria of relevance. With the removal of stop words in Spanish, "De la Mora" becomes "Mora". Due to this transformation only the term "Mora" would be relevant because the term "Mont" shares 50% of the characters with the query string. Finally, it should be noted that the multi-agent model proposed in this chapter will soon be implemented as part of a thesis at National University of Santiago del Estero.

REFERENCES

Abel, F., Bittencourt, I. I., Costa, E., Henze, N., Krause, D., & Vassileva, J. (2010). Recommendations in online discussion forums for e-learning systems. *IEEE Transactions on Learning Technologies*, *3*(2), 165–176. doi:10.1109/TLT.2009.40

Aranha, C., & Passos, E. (2008). Automatic NLP for Competitive Intelligence. In H. A. Do-Prado & E. Ferneda (Eds.), *Emerging Technologies of Text Mining: Techniques and Applications* (pp. 54–76). IGI Global. doi:10.4018/978-1-59904-373-9.ch003

Barros, B., & Verdejo, M. (2000). Analysing student interaction processes in order to improve collaboration. The DEGREE approach. *International Journal of Artificial Intelligence in Education, 11*(3), 221–241.

Bin Ghauth, K. I., & Abdullah, N. A. (2009). Building an e-learning recommender system using Vector Space Model and good learners average rating. In *Proceedings - 2009 9th IEEE International Conference on Advanced Learning Technologies, ICALT 2009* (pp. 194–196). Riga: IEEE.

Césari, M. I. (2007). *Cartografiado de Textos. Protocolo de Exploración y Visualización de datos textuales aplicados a la Minería de Textos* (Unpublished master's thesis). Universidad Politecnica de Madrid, España.

Chen, W. (2006). Supporting teachers intervention in collaborative knowledge building. *Journal of Network and Computer Applications, 29*(2-3), 200–215. doi:10.1016/j.jnca.2005.01.001

Chen, W., & Wasson, B. (2005). Intelligent Agents Supporting Distributed Collaborative Learning. In F. Lin (Ed.), *Designing Distributed Learning Environments with Intelligent Software Agents* (pp. 33–66). IGI Global. doi:10.4018/978-1-59140-500-9.ch002

Chowdhury, G. G. (2005). Natural language processing. *Annual Review of Information Science & Technology, 37*(1), 51–89. doi:10.1002/aris.1440370103

Constantino-González, M., Suthers, D. D., & Escamilla-De-Los-Santos, J. D. (2003). Coaching Web-based Collaborative Learning based on Problem Solution Differences and Participation. *International Journal of Artificial Intelligence in Education, 13*(2-4), 263–299.

Coppin, B. (2004). *Artificial Intelligence Illuminated*. Jones and Bartlett Publishers.

Costaguta, R., García, P., & Amandi, A. (2011). Using Agent for Training Students Collaborative Skills. *IEEE Latin America Transactions, 9*(7), 1118–1124. doi:10.1109/TLA.2011.6129712

Dascalu, M.-I., Bodea, C.-N., Moldoveanu, A., Mohora, A., Lytras, M., & de Pablos, P. O. (2015). A recommender agent based on learning styles for better virtual collaborative learning experiences. *Computers in Human Behavior, 45*, 243–253. doi:10.1016/j.chb.2014.12.027

Do-Prado, A. H., & Ferneda, E. (2008). *Emerging Technologies of Text Mining : Techniques and Applications*. IGI Global. doi:10.4018/978-1-59904-373-9

Dönmez, P., Rosé, C., Stegmann, K., Weinberger, A., & Fischer, F. (2005). Supporting CSCL with automatic corpus analysis technology. In *Proceedings of th2005 Conference on Computer Support for Collaborative Learning: Learning 2005: The next 10 Years!* (pp. 125–134). International Society of the Learning Sciences. doi:10.3115/1149293.1149310

Felder, R., & Silverman, L. (1988). Learning and teaching styles in engineering education. *English Education, 78*(7), 674–681.

Feldman, R., & Sanger, J. (2007). *The text mining handbook: advanced approaches in analyzing unstructured data*. Cambridge University Press.

Felfernig, A., Friedrich, G., & Schmidt-Thieme, L. (2007). Recommender Systems. *IEEE Intelligent Systems*, *22*(May/June), 18–21. doi:10.1109/MIS.2007.52

García-Adeva, J. J., & Calvo, R. (2006). Mining text with pimiento. *IEEE Internet Computing*, *10*(4), 27–35. doi:10.1109/MIC.2006.85

Gedikli, F. (2013). *Recommender Systems and the Social Web. Leveraging Tagging Data for Recommender Systems*. Springer.

Goodman, B. A., Linton, F. N., Gaimari, R. D., Hitzeman, J. M., Ross, H. J., & Zarrella, G. (2005). Using Dialogue Features to Predict Trouble During Collaborative Learning. *User Modeling and User-Adapted Interaction*, *15*(1-2), 85–134. doi:10.1007/s11257-004-5269-x

Hatcher, E., & Gospodnetic, O. (2005). *Lucene in Action*. Manning Publications.

Hotho, A., Nürnberger, A., & Paaß, G. (2005). A Brief Survey of Text Mining. *LDV Forum - GLDV Journal for Computational Linguistics and Language Technology*, *20*, 19–62.

Israel, J., & Aiken, R. (2007). Supporting Collaborative Learning With An Intelligent Web-Based System. *International Journal of Artificial Intelligence in Education*, *17*, 3–40.

Jannach, D., Zanker, M., Felfernig, A., & Friedrich, G. (2011). *Recommender Systems: An Introduction*. New York: Cambridge University Press.

Khribi, M. K., Jemni, M., & Nasraoui, O. (2008). Automatic Recommendations for E-Learning Personalization Based on Web Usage Mining Techniques and Information Retrieval. In P. Díaz-Kinshuk, I. Aedo, & E. Mor (Eds.), *IEEE International Conference on Advanced Learning Techniques* (Vol. 8, pp. 241 – 245). Santander, Cantabria: IEEE. doi:10.1109/ICALT.2008.198

Klašnja-Milićević, A., Vesin, B., Ivanović, M., & Budimac, Z. (2011). E-Learning personalization based on hybrid recommendation strategy and learning style identification. *Computers & Education*, *56*(3), 885–899. doi:10.1016/j.compedu.2010.11.001

Konchady, M. (2008). *Building Search Applications: Lucene, Lingpipe, and Gate*. Mustru Publishing.

Konstan, J. A. (2004). Introduction To Recommender Systems : Algorithms and Evaluation. *ACM Transactions on Information Systems*, *22*(1), 1–4. doi:10.1145/963770.963771

Korra, R., Sujatha, P., Chetana, S., & Kumar, M. N. (2011). Performance Evaluation of Multilingual Information Retrieval (MLIR) System over Information Retrieval (IR) System. In *IEEE-International Conference on Recent Trends in Information Technology (ICRTIT 2011)* (pp. 722–727). Chennai, Tamil Nadu: IEEE Press.

Manouselis, N., Drachsler, H., Vuorikari, R., Hummel, H., & Koper, R. (2011). Recommender Systems in Technology Enhanced Learning. In F. Rocco, L. Rokach, B. Shapira, & P. Kantor (Eds.), *Recommender Systems Handbook* (pp. 387–415). Springer. doi:10.1007/978-0-387-85820-3_12

Manouselis, N., Vuorikari, R., & Van-Assche, F. (2010). Collaborative recommendation of e-learning resources: An experimental investigation. *Journal of Computer Assisted Learning*, 26(4), 227–242. doi:10.1111/j.1365-2729.2010.00362.x

Nwana, H. S. (1996). Software agents: An overview. *The Knowledge Engineering Review*, 11(03), 205–244. doi:10.1017/S026988890000789X

O'Rourke, J. (2003). *Tutoring in open and distance learning: a handbook for tutors*. Vancouver: The Commonwealth of Learning.

Olivares, O. J. (2007). Collaborative vs. Cooperative Learning: The Instructor's Role in Computer Supported Collaborative Learning. In K. L. Orvis & A. L. R. Lassiter (Eds.), *Computer-Supported Collaborative Learning: Best Practices and Principles for Instructors* (pp. 20–39). Information Science Publishing.

Onrubia, J., & Engel, A. (2012). The role of teacher assistance on the effects of a macro-script in collaborative writing tasks. *International Journal of Computer-Supported Collaborative Learning*, 7(1), 161–186. doi:10.1007/s11412-011-9125-9

Orvis, K. L., & Lassiter, A. L. R. (2006). Computer-Supported Collaborative Learning: The Role of the Instructor. In S. P. Ferris & S. H. Godar (Eds.), *Teaching and learning with virtual teams* (pp. 158–179). Information Science Publishing. doi:10.4018/978-1-59140-708-9.ch007

Reuter, B. F., & Durán, E. (2014). Framework de recomendación automática de contenidos en foros de discusión para entornos de e-learning. In C. Cubillos, C. Rusu, & D. Gorgan (Eds.), *Proceedings of the 7th Euro American Conference on Telematics and Information Systems - EATIS '14* (pp. 1–2). Valparaíso: ACM Digital Library. doi:10.1145/2590651.2590689

Rocco, F., Rokach, L., & Shapira, B. (2011). Introduction to Recommender Systems Handbook. In F. Rocco, L. Rokach, B. Shapira, & P. Kantor (Eds.), *Recommender Systems Handbook* (pp. 1–35). Springer.

Rodríguez, P., Duque, N., & Ovalle, D. A. (2015). Multi-agent System for Knowledge-Based Recommendation of Learning Objects Using Metadata Clustering. In J. Bajo, K. Hallenborg, P. Pawlewski, V. Botti, N. Sánchez-Pi, N. D. D. Méndez, & V. Julian et al. (Eds.), *Highlights of Practical Applications of Agents, Multi-Agent Systems, and Sustainability-The PAAMS Collection* (Vol. 524, pp. 356–364). Springer. doi:10.1007/978-3-319-19033-4_31

Rosé, C., Wang, Y.-C., Cui, Y., Arguello, J., Stegmann, K., Weinberger, A., & Fischer, F. (2008). Analyzing collaborative learning processes automatically: Exploiting the advances of computational linguistics in computer-supported collaborative learning. *International Journal of Computer-Supported Collaborative Learning*, 3(3), 237–271. doi:10.1007/s11412-007-9034-0

Russell, S., & Norvig, P. (2010). *Artificial Intelligence: A Modern Approach* (3rd ed.). Prentice Hall.

Schwarz, B. B., & Asterhan, C. S. (2011). E-Moderation of Synchronous Discussions in Educational Settings: A Nascent Practice. *Journal of the Learning Sciences*, 20(3), 395–442. doi:10.1080/1050840 6.2011.553257

Shishehchi, S., Banihashem, S. Y., & Zin, N. A. M. (2011). A Proposed Semantic Recommendation System for E-Learning. A Rule and Ontology Based E-learning Recommendation System. In A. K. Mahmood, H. B. Zaman, P. Robinson, S. Elliot, P. Haddawy, S. Olariu, & Z. Awang (Eds.), *2010 International Symposium in Information Technology (ITSim)* (pp. 1–5). Kuala Lumpur: IEEE Press.

Soh, L.-K., Khandaker, N., & Jiang, H. (2008). I-MINDS: A multiagent system for intelligent computer- supported collaborative learning and classroom management. *International Journal of Artificial Intelligence in Education*, *18*(2), 119–151.

Soller, A. (2001). Supporting Social Interaction in an Intelligent Collaborative Learning System. *International Journal of Artificial Intelligence in Education*, *12*(1), 40–62.

Soller, A. (2004). Computational Modeling and Analysis of Knowledge Sharing in Collaborative Distance Learning. *User Modeling and User-Adapted Interaction*, *14*(4), 351–381. doi:10.1023/B:USER.0000043436.49168.3b

Soller, A., Monés, A. M., Jermann, P., & Muehlenbrock, M. (2005). From Mirroring to Guiding: A Review of State of the Art Technology for Supporting Collaborative Learning. *International Journal of Artificial Intelligence in Education*, *15*(4), 261–290.

Souali, K., El Afia, A., Faizi, R., & Chiheb, R. (2011). A new recommender system for e-learning environments. In *International Conference on Multimedia Computing and Systems -Proceedings* (pp. 1–4). Ouarzazate: IEEE Press. doi:10.1109/ICMCS.2011.5945630

Suh, H.-J., & Lee, S. W. (2006). Collaborative Learning Agent for Promoting Group Interaction. *ETRI Journal*, *28*(4), 461–474. doi:10.4218/etrij.06.0105.0235

Tan, A.-H. (1999). Text Mining: The state of the art and the challenges. In *Proceedings of the PAKDD 1999 Workshop on Knowledge Disocovery from Advanced Databases* (pp. 65-70).

Tchounikine, P., Rummel, N., & McLaren, B. M. (2010). Computer Supported Collaborative Learning and Intelligent Tutoring Systems. In R. Nkambou, J. Bourdeau, & R. Mizoguchi (Eds.), *Advances in Intelligent Tutoring Systems* (Vol. 308, pp. 447–463). Springer-Verlag Berlin Heidelberg. doi:10.1007/978-3-642-14363-2_22

Varvel, V. E. (2007). Master Online Teacher Competencies. *Online Journal of Distance Learning Administration*, *10*, 1–47.

Zhou, D., Truran, M., Brailsford, T., Wade, V., & Ashman, H. (2012). Translation techniques in cross-language information retrieval. *ACM Computing Surveys*, *45*(1), 1–44. doi:10.1145/2379776.2379777

KEY TERMS AND DEFINITIONS

Collaborative Learning: Unstructured group process that promotes the independence of students, an atmosphere of dissent, and the free exchange of ideas so as to create new knowledge or generate solutions for a problem or task. During this group process the teachers do not emphasize in providing the correct answer or saying which members of the group are right, yet in making a minimal pedagogical intervention in order to redirect the group work towards a productive direction or monitoring which members are not interacting.

Computer-Supported Collaborative Learning: Research field product of the union between class-based collaborative learning and computer-mediated communication that explores the problems and factors that influence learning in computer-mediated collaborative configurations. It also studies the ways of designing technology to support collaborative learning processes between students.

Group Learning: Group of people that interact with the purpose of sharing knowledge and getting its members to learn from each other.

Information Retrieval: It is the discipline whose aim is developing systems that store huge numbers of documents so as to enable efficient retrieval of those documents that are relevant to the information needs of their users.

Interaction: Reciprocal action between two or more individuals or objects. In a collaborative situation the interaction requires people to actively respond to each other, explaining ideas and generating returns.

Natural Language Processing: Field of study that seeks to understand the way in which humans understand and use the language with the aim of developing techniques and tools to make computer systems understand and manipulate natural languages while performing tasks.

Personalization: It is the action of tailoring information or services provided by a system to the needs (or interests) of a particular user or a set or users.

Recommender System: Software application that provides suggestions for products (CDs, books, movies, etc.) or services (e-government, financial, healthcare and son on) most likely to be relevant to the needs or personal traits of the users.

Software Agent: A computer program designed to carry out some task on behalf of a user or other program. The basic attributes of a software agent are: autonomy (agents can operate without the need for human guidance), cooperation (ability to interact with other software agents and humans), and learning (capability of improving their performance over time).

Text Mining: A process that allow the extraction of useful and previously unknown patters from a collection of text documents.

ENDNOTES

1 https://lucene.apache.org/core/
2 http://tm.r-forge.r-project.org/

Chapter 16
Scientific Information Superhighway vs. Scientific Information Backroads in Computer Science

Francisco V. Cipolla-Ficarra
Latin Association of Human-Computer Interaction, Spain & International Association of Interactive Communication, Italy

Donald Nilson
University of Oslo, Norway

Jacqueline Alma
Electronic Arts, Canada

ABSTRACT

In the current appendix present a first heuristic study about the scientific publications related to computer science and the human factors that make that some contents travel through highways and others in back roads of scientific information. We also present the first elements which generate that parallel information of the scientific work for financial and/or commercial reasons. Finally, a set of rhetoric questions link two decades of experiences in the university educational context, research and development (R&D) and Transfer of Technology (TOT) in the Mediterranean South and make up a first evaluation guide.

INTRODUCTION

If we analyze some data bases where are indexed the scientific works in the computer science context, and all its derivations (multimedia, Web 2.0, computer graphics, scientific visualization, etc.), of the authors, we can see quickly that whether the authors have travelled through a highway of the scientific publications or not. We understand as highways of the scientific publications those that through associations such ACM (Association for Computing Machinery –www.acm.org) or IEEE (Institute of Electrical

DOI: 10.4018/978-1-5225-2616-2.ch016

and Electronics Engineers –www.ieee.org), to mention a couple of examples are automatically indexed in their data bases. In the current work we do not go into the details of how those works are indexed, in relation to the names and/or surnames of their authors, which in the Spanish case of the double surnames in many cases two different pages can be seen in the digital library. In one of them the surnames are separate and in others together, through the use of a hyphen. They even change the historic affiliation of the author or co-author of those works, as can be seen in the Figures 1 and 2.

Another of the problems is the reliability of the indexed information as they appear in the Figures 1 and 2 in the total of works. In short, the indexation method does not offer a reliable information to the potential users who access that digital library.

Aside from these technical remarks, the works that accumulate in that page may have been published by that association, which makes them easy to distinguish, since they have the logo up front and those stemming from magazines, books chapters, etc. Which have been accepted in the current database. The acceptation of those works derives from the intensity of the influence that the scientific committee of the magazine, book, conference or workshop has towards that association in order to get its sponsoring. Through it those works will be automatically included in the database. In other cases, the included works stem from associations of peers, such as ACM, IEEE, etc. or from projects deriving from data bases such as the initials DBLP (Digital Bibliogrpahy & Library Project).

In the DBLP it is easy to observe the amount of works that an author has, classified in decreasing order from the temporal point of view and where that register originated, that is, if it belongs to a conference (letter c), a journal (letter j), etc. At the end, there is the alphabetic index of the authors with which he has collaborated. Here it can also be seen how sometimes that index doesn't follow an alphabetic order. In the Figure 3, we see how the co-author "de-Castro-Lozano" occupies the last place in the table, when in fact he should be among the authors a and b. Once again, a reliability mistake can be seen at the moment of accessing the information stored in the hyperbase.

Figure 1. The author, whose surnames are linked by a hyphen, appears affiliate to the Barcelona University

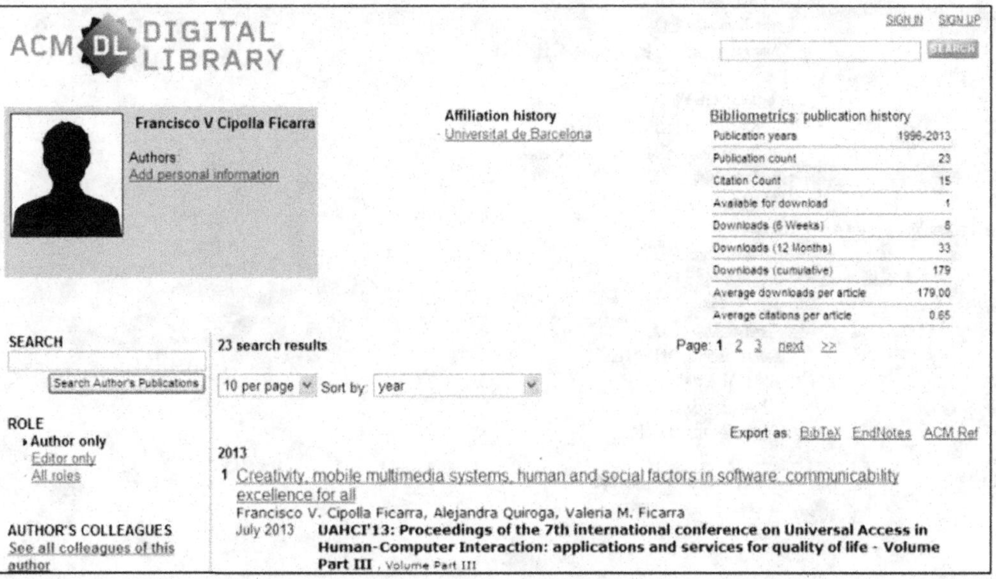

Figure 2. The same author appears affiliated historically to another two universities: Stanford (USA) y Pompeu Fabra (Spain)

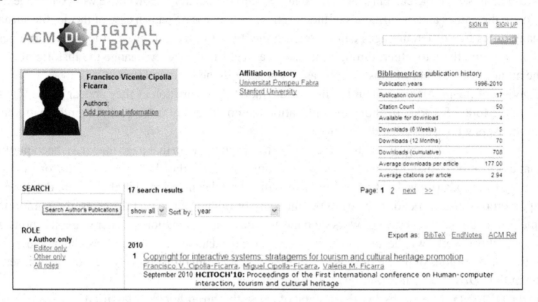

Figure 3. Failing in the alphabetic order of the authors listing

1	Jacqueline Alma [c43] [c38] [c35] [c32]
2	Silvia Bernatené [c16]
3	Huang Chih-Fang [e4]
4	Miguel Cipolla-Ficarra [e6] [e5] [e4] [c43] [c42] [c38] [c35] [c32] [e3] [e2] [c25] [c22] [c21] [c20] [c18] [c17] [e14] [c11] [p2] [p1] [c9]
5	Rodolfo Fernández-Ziegler [c16]
6	Valeria M. Ficarra [c44] [c42] [c41] [c36] [c29] [c26] [c20]
7	Daniel Alberto Giulianelli [c14]
8	Mario Greco [c16]
9	Tyler Harder [c11]
10	Mauricio Pérez Jiménez [e3]
11	Florian Kammüller [e6]
12	Andreas Kratky [e5] [e4] [c40] [c36] [e3] [e2]
13	Gary Marchionini [c2]
14	Punyashloke Mishra [c2]
15	Kim Nguyen [c2]
16	Emma Nicol [e3] [e2] [c29] [c22] [c21]
17	Jorge Fernández Niello [c16]
18	Blair Nonnecke [c2]
19	Jennifer Preece (Jennifer J. Preece, Jenny Preece) [c2]
20	Alejandra Quiroga [c44]
21	Lucy Richardson [c27] [c22]
22	Rocio A. Rodriguez [c13]
23	Joaquim Romo [c15]
24	Kim H. Veltman [e6] [e5] [e4]
25	Pablo M. Vera [c18]
26	Domen Verber [e6]
27	Maria Villarreal [c23] [c16]
28	Ernesto Vivas [c15]
29	Carlos de-Castro-Lozano [e3] [e2]

Now in our study we have sent a questionnaire with five questions to a group made up by 30 computer science and electronics university professors of the south of Europe, asking them basically what are the databases which they consider as having a greater current scientific prestige, and 83.5% of those polled have answered the associations a and b. Only 16.5% have answered dblp. Although the three may be regarded in the current academic context as highways for scientific information, the third was regarded by some as a back road. Besides, in the open questions asked, it has been made apparent that many scientific works of tge mid past century haven't been indexed. Consequently, many researches that have been carried out by inventors and discoverers of new fields for electronic and/or computer science investigation do not appear online. This is a data, it constitutes an important factor since it influences in those members of the current scientific committees, who only look up online the information of the works they are evaluating, without knowing that there are in paper support journals or books with information previous to that which they are looking up, in certain fields of scientific knowledge. In other cases, many works with a high level of originality, innovation, relevance, transcendence are failed because they include a bibliography that doesn't have online access. Evidently, this is a very important human factor in the conformation of the evaluators committee of the scientific works. These mistakes may lead a young scientist to spend a large part of his life in back roads in the scientific context.

Other databases of great interest in the scientific sector are: EI COMPENDEX and Inspec. The former, EI COMPENDEX its initials mean Engineering Index and COMPuterized ENgineering inDEX.. Their origins go back to 1884, and it indexes scientific literature pertaining to engineering materials, compiled by hand under the original title of Engineering Index. As Compendex, it is now published by the publishing house Elsevier (www.elsevier.com). It is a database which surpasses 16 million registers and yearly incorporates a million of registers stemming from the main engineering branches, mainly, as well as other areas of knowledge belonging to the formal and factual sciences. The Inspec has its origin in 1967 as a major indexing database of scientific and technical literature, published by the Institution of Engineering and Technology (IET) and formerly by the Institution of Electrical Engineers (IEE). Inside that database is stored the information related to computer science, physics, engineering, etc. That is, works of research stemming from astronomy, electronics, communications, ergonomics, computers & computing, computer science, control engineering, electrical engineering, information technology, and physics. Currently, there are other databases stemming from the search engines. For instance: Google Scholar (scholar.google.com) It is a subproduct of Google specialized in searching and identifying published bibliographical material of a scientific –academic character. Finally, there are those deriving from the editorial context or from the information in paper support such as Thomson Reuters, etc.

THE SCIENTIFIC PUBLICATIONS IN THE COMPUTER SCIENCE CONTEXT OF THE NEW MILLENNIUM: THE TRIAD OF THE HUMAN, SOCIAL AND FINANCIAL FACTORS

Before the end of the first decade of the new millennium, with the drop of financial resources in the public university area, especially that aimed at research, has prompted an increase of the scientific publications in journals or books. This phenomenon can be easily proved by looking up the dblp of those authors who have published their research works since the 90s, for instance. The reason is the costs. Besides, the presentations must be carried out in situ, since the virtual presentations, for instance, through videoconferences, in some scientific contexts are not possible.

All of this has bolstered the phenomenon of the group publications, which do not necessarily relate to interdisciplinary works, but rather to human or social factors. This kind of publications which are indexed in the databases of the highways of scientific information lack any legal value at the moment of granting the enablement of university professors for the teaching of computer science, in some countries of the EU, as is the case of Spain from 2002 onwards and through the National Agency of Assessment Quality and Certification (ANECA –www.aneca.es). The place that the petitioner of the accreditation in that listing is essential. That is, the former are the valid ones and the rest practically lack any value. In the figure, abc, the first two people are regarded as main authors. The rest of the co-authors do not have a great legal value when it comes to issuing enablements for university teaching in Spain, since 2002.

Another of the factors of the triad that derives from the analysis of the dblp database is that many authors not only do not have a continuity line in their research in keeping with the lines of interest that is detected across time, but besides it makes a constant reusability of the same works to increase the number of registers inside the database. This is a typical phenomemnon of those research works related to the study of queries for the databases, for instance. The goal pursued by some of its co-authors is to increase quickly the number of registers in the database. Some examples in Figures 4, 5, 6 and 7. That

Figure 4. It is a classic example from where the second author onwards the rest of co-authors have no university legal value in Spain

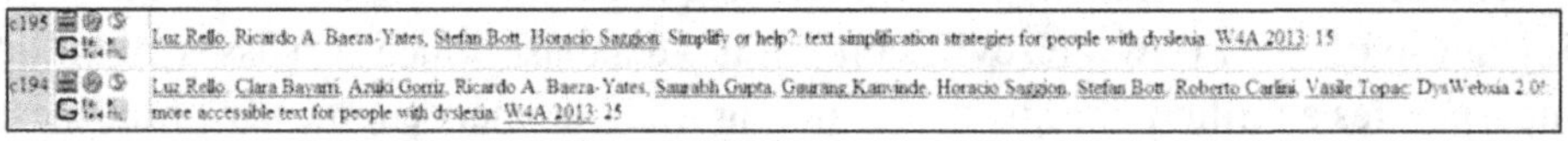
c195 Luz Rello, Ricardo A. Baeza-Yates, Stefan Bott, Horacio Saggion: Simplify or help? text simplification strategies for people with dyslexia. W4A 2013: 15

c194 Luz Rello, Clara Bayarri, Azuki Gorriz, Ricardo A. Baeza-Yates, Saurabh Gupta, Gaurang Kanvinde, Horacio Saggion, Stefan Bott, Roberto Carlini, Vasile Topac: DysWebxia 2.0!: more accessible text for people with dyslexia. W4A 2013: 25

Figure 5. The author and/or co-authors resort to the reusability of scientific information

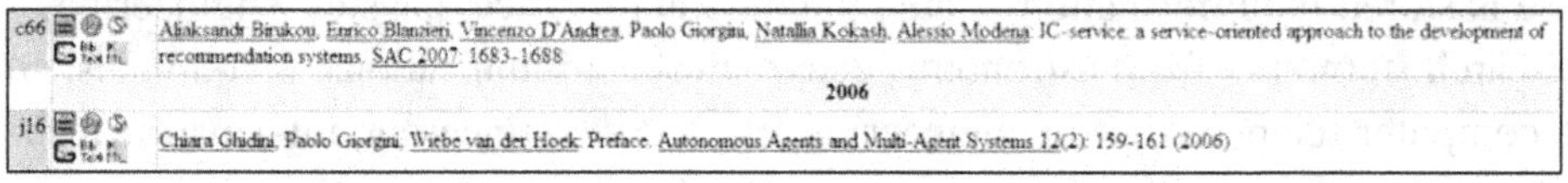
c66 Aliaksandr Birukou, Enrico Blanzieri, Vincenzo D'Andrea, Paolo Giorgini, Natallia Kokash, Alessio Modena: IC-service: a service-oriented approach to the development of recommendation systems. SAC 2007: 1683-1688

2006

j16 Chiara Ghidini, Paolo Giorgini, Wiebe van der Hoek: Preface. Autonomous Agents and Multi-Agent Systems 12(2): 159-161 (2006)

Figure 6. The logical programming and the queries for database allows a myriad options which enrich the possibilities of variants in the publication of computer science articles

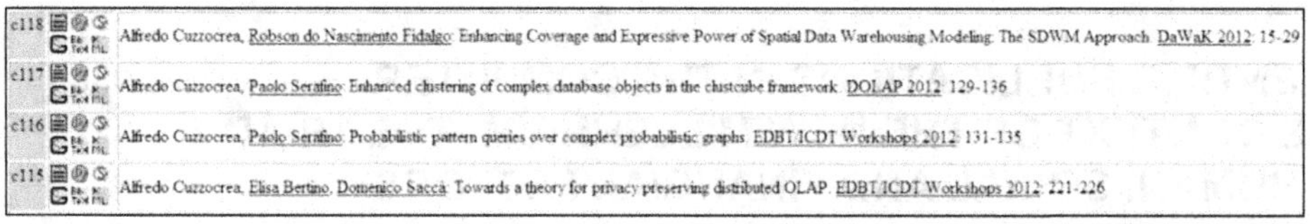
c118 Alfredo Cuzzocrea, Robson do Nascimento Fidalgo: Enhancing Coverage and Expressive Power of Spatial Data Warehousing Modeling: The SDWM Approach. DaWaK 2012: 15-29

c117 Alfredo Cuzzocrea, Paolo Serafino: Enhanced clustering of complex database objects in the clustcube framework. DOLAP 2012: 129-136

c116 Alfredo Cuzzocrea, Paolo Serafino: Probabilistic pattern queries over complex probabilistic graphs. EDBT/ICDT Workshops 2012: 131-135

c115 Alfredo Cuzzocrea, Elisa Bertino, Domenico Saccà: Towards a theory for privacy preserving distributed OLAP. EDBT/ICDT Workshops 2012: 221-226

Figure 7. One poster with 15 co-authors

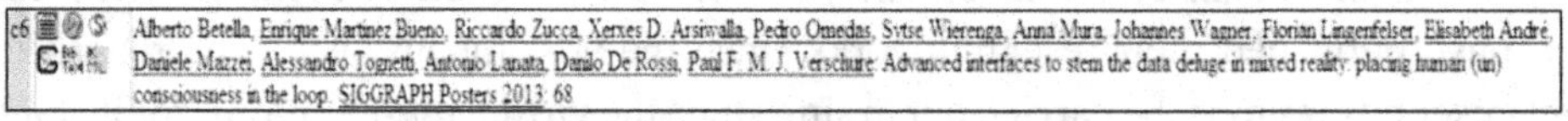
c6 Alberto Betella, Enrique Martinez Bueno, Riccardo Zucca, Xerxes D. Arsiwalla, Pedro Omedas, Sytse Wierenga, Anna Mura, Johannes Wagner, Florian Lingenfelser, Elisabeth André, Daniele Mazzei, Alessandro Tognetti, Antonio Lanata, Danilo De Rossi, Paul F. M. J. Verschure: Advanced interfaces to stem the data deluge in mixed reality: placing human (un) consciousness in the loop. SIGGRAPH Posters 2013: 68

is why their works are not extensive in those cases, only posters or works in progress, whose extension in pages ranges between 1 and 5. Obviously, they are not papers of book chapters. Only yet another item inside a database, which may belong to the group of the highways of scientific information. Besides, many of those items do not constitute neither future lines of research or learned lessons from experiments that have been carried out, for instance.

As a rule, the more authors appear in the item, the less extended is the work. A classical example are the posters that are presented from the south of Europe in the Siggraph or other works of graphic computing in magazines of the same publisher, that is, ACM. Many of those authors or co-authors are PhD students and theoretically with those publications they have started to circulate through the highways of scientific information, but in those groups also exists academic endogamy, parochialism, the dynamic persuader, etc. Next we mention some examples stemming from DBLP.

In Figure 8, can be seen how a graduate in physics turns into an expert in human-computer interaction, exercising for decades all the negative techniques in human and social behaviour of the dynamic persuader inside the scientific context (stalking, bullying, etc.). As origin of that transformation he uses the disabled users, forcing them inside the Spanish and Latin American borders to follow his new lines of research. That is, a radial and vertical structure is generated in the contests of the research related to the human-computer interaction, within and without the borders where those leaders and pressure groups are to be found. The goal they pursue is the destruction of the democratization of the sciences, although apparently in the database are indexed many registers yearly as co-authors of the works. The items where he appears as a single author are very scarce, because his function is not technical but political. That is, an authoritarian and destructive policy. The horizontality and democratization of knowledge does not exist in those groups. All the members of those radial and vertical structures have mostly their works indexed in the databases belonging to the highways of scientific information. Another example in Figure 11 from civil structure to podcasting and disbled, children, teenagers, etc. users. The readers interested in these structures and systems can find widely detailed examples in the following references (Cipolla-Ficarra, et al., 2013a; Cipolla-Ficarra, 2013b).

In the previous example we have observed the case of isolated authors who group with the passing of time. Simultaneously, we have other cases which respond to university endogamy such as can be the couples, fathers and sons, brothers, etc., and all the rest of family links which can exist in the academic context. This reality is usually very common as the genesis of the pressure groups known generically as parochialism (Cipolla-Ficarra, Ficarra, & Cipolla-Ficarra, 2012; Cipolla-Ficarra, & Ficarra, 2014). Although their members declare diverging interests among themselves, they all will converge on the same item or register of the database. Obviously, they do not relate to the notions of interdisciplinarity,

Figure 8. Metamorphosis of a graduate in physics into an expert in human computer interaction through the Spanish and Latin American disabled people

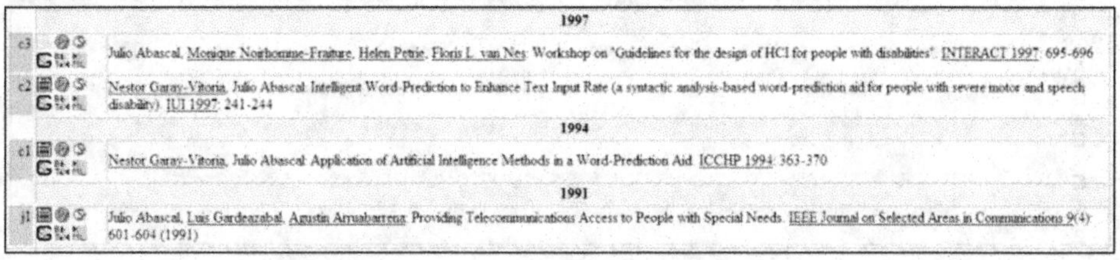
1997

c3 Julio Abascal, Monique Noirhomme-Fraiture, Helen Petrie, Floris L. van Nes: Workshop on "Guidelines for the design of HCI for people with disabilities". INTERACT 1997: 695-696

c2 Nestor Garay-Vitoria, Julio Abascal: Intelligent Word-Prediction to Enhance Text Input Rate (a syntactic analysis-based word-prediction aid for people with severe motor and speech disability). IUI 1997: 241-244

1994

c1 Nestor Garay-Vitoria, Julio Abascal: Application of Artificial Intelligence Methods in a Word-Prediction Aid. ICCHP 1994: 363-370

1991

j1 Julio Abascal, Luis Gardeazabal, Agustin Arruabarrena: Providing Telecommunications Access to People with Special Needs. IEEE Journal on Selected Areas in Communications 9(4): 601-604 (1991) transdisciplinarity, etc., of the sciences, but rather to family relationships (Cipolla-Ficarra, & Ficarra, 2012; & Cipolla-Ficarra, & Kratky, 2012). In the examples of Figures 9 and 10, the endogamy is presented with different degrees of intensity.

All these examples of a negative sign for the sciences make apparent the economic interests derived from the pressure groups which exert their influence on the rest of the scientific community. The financial resources are essential so that their works are indexed in databases pertaining to the highways of scientific information. Consequently, generating unidirectional and/or authoritarian structures is positive for those who make up the summit of power, since they can submit projects requesting regional, state European or other financial subsidies, knowing that they are the only ones who have the absolute control in a state or regional territory. If one observes their section of acknowledgements, all their works are subsidized by ministries, private businesses, European bodies, etc. All those who do not belong to those radial, vertical and authoritarian structures are automatically excluded and their research works, even if they are original, will have a lower category, because they travel in the back roads of the scientific publications and they will be prey to constant plagiarism.

An evolution online of a project of the 80s is DBLP (DataBase systems and Logical Programming). It is a computer science bibliography website hosted at Universität Trier (Germany). With the passing of time these initials have turned into a project called "Digital Bibliography & Library Project", with

Figure 9. Example of works indexed where exists a high endogamy or inmarriage. Besides, one international event with 4 works accepted –AVI 2012

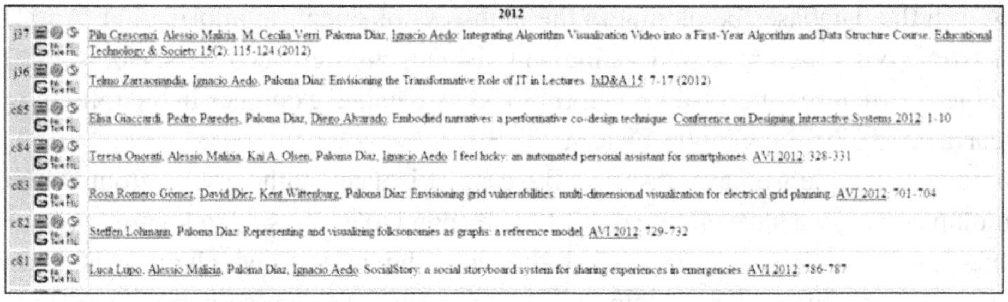

	2012
j37	Pilu Crescenzi, Alessio Malizia, M. Cecilia Verri, Paloma Diaz, Ignacio Aedo: Integrating Algorithm Visualization Video into a First-Year Algorithm and Data Structure Course. Educational Technology & Society 15(2): 115-124 (2012)
j36	Telmo Zarraonandia, Ignacio Aedo, Paloma Diaz: Envisioning the Transformative Role of IT in Lectures. IxD&A 15: 7-17 (2012)
c85	Elisa Giaccardi, Pedro Paredes, Paloma Diaz, Diego Alvarado: Embodied narratives: a performative co-design technique. Conference on Designing Interactive Systems 2012: 1-10
c84	Teresa Onorati, Alessio Malizia, Kai A. Olsen, Paloma Diaz, Ignacio Aedo: I feel lucky: an automated personal assistant for smartphones. AVI 2012: 328-331
c83	Rosa Romero Gómez, David Diez, Kent Wittenburg, Paloma Diaz: Envisioning grid vulnerabilities: multi-dimensional visualization for electrical grid planning. AVI 2012: 701-704
c82	Steffen Lohmann, Paloma Diaz: Representing and visualizing folksonomies as graphs: a reference model. AVI 2012: 729-732
c81	Luca Lupo, Alessio Malizia, Paloma Diaz, Ignacio Aedo: SocialStory: a social storyboard system for sharing experiences in emergencies. AVI 2012: 786-787

Figure 10. Example of indexed works where a moderate endogamy or inmarriage exists. Besides, local event CHI Italy 2013 with 4 works accepted with the same author/s

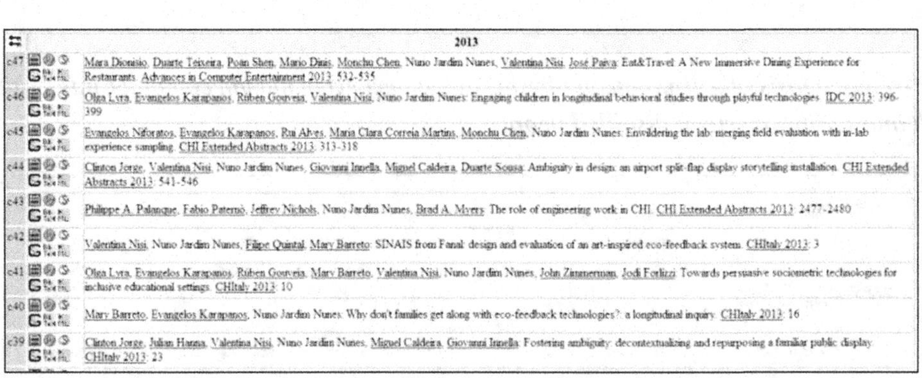

	2013
c47	Mara Dionisio, Duarte Teixeira, Poan Shen, Mario Dinis, Monchu Chen, Nuno Jardim Nunes, Valentina Nisi, José Paiva: Eat&Travel: A New Immersive Dining Experience for Restaurants. Advances in Computer Entertainment 2013: 532-535
c46	Olga Lyra, Evangelos Karapanos, Rúben Gouveia, Valentina Nisi, Nuno Jardim Nunes: Engaging children in longitudinal behavioral studies through playful technologies. IDC 2013: 396-399
c45	Evangelos Niforatos, Evangelos Karapanos, Rui Alves, Maria Clara Correia Martins, Monchu Chen, Nuno Jardim Nunes: Enwildering the lab: merging field evaluation with in-lab experience sampling. CHI Extended Abstracts 2013: 313-318
c44	Clinton Jorge, Valentina Nisi, Nuno Jardim Nunes, Giovanni Innella, Miguel Caldeira, Duarte Sousa: Ambiguity in design: an airport split-flap display storytelling installation. CHI Extended Abstracts 2013: 541-546
c43	Philippe A. Palanque, Fabio Paternò, Jeffrey Nichols, Nuno Jardim Nunes, Brad A. Myers: The role of engineering work in CHI. CHI Extended Abstracts 2013: 2477-2480
c42	Valentina Nisi, Nuno Jardim Nunes, Filipe Quintal, Mary Barreto: SINAIS from Fanal: design and evaluation of an art-inspired eco-feedback system. CHItaly 2013: 3
c41	Olga Lyra, Evangelos Karapanos, Rúben Gouveia, Mary Barreto, Valentina Nisi, Nuno Jardim Nunes, John Zimmerman, Jodi Forlizzi: Towards persuasive sociometric technologies for inclusive educational settings. CHItaly 2013: 10
c40	Mary Barreto, Evangelos Karapanos, Nuno Jardim Nunes: Why don't families get along with eco-feedback technologies?: a longitudinal inquiry. CHItaly 2013: 16
c39	Clinton Jorge, Julian Hanna, Valentina Nisi, Nuno Jardim Nunes, Miguel Caldeira, Giovanni Innella: Fostering ambiguity: decontextualizing and repurposing a familiar public display. CHItaly 2013: 23

Figure 11. Example of a big metamorphosis from civil engineering to archaeology, podscanting, etc. to disabled people and education for children, teenagers, adults, etc. for instance

European subsidies, and currently the title "the DBLP Computer Science Bibliography" does not only denote the evolution of the project, but it also connotes how German publishers make use of it for their publications to be automatically indexed in the databases of the ACM and/or IEEE. Many authors submit their works in congresses backed by that German publisher because they have guaranteed that their works will also be indexed in the USA.

AN HEURISTIC GUIDE DERIVED FROM THE RHETORIC QUESTIONS

Although rhetoric has its origin in the social sciences, it can orient us to reach a greater transparency in the information stored in the current databases of the scientific works. In the figures of the presented examples it is possible to realize how the human and social factors, with a negative sense, are present in the field of the publications belonging to the highways of scientific information. Although part of the figures have darkened areas because of privacy reasons, they denote the veracity of the data that have allowed to carry out the research. Next are listed a first set of rhetorical questions, which der8ive from the education, research and development and technology transfer between university and/or industry and vice versa in the last two decades:

- How is it possible that a same author in the university educational context can carry out simultaneously so many scientific works along the year and that they do not keep among themselves any correlation, whether from the theoretical or the practical point of view?
- How is it possible that in certain themes of scientific knowledge, for instance, interactive design aimed at children, the same authors are always to be found and always the same work format, that

is, a long paper (no papers, short papers, demos, etc.) in publications belonging to the highways of scientific information?

- How is it possible that doctorates are granted without the PhD candidate having a minimum of autonomous publications or own works indexed in the databases of high scientific level?

- How is it possible that in the new millennium, algorithms, methods and computer science techniques are not generated to wipe out the problem that around a 20–40 of the authors with Spanish names and/or surnames have badly indexed their works in the scientific databases?

- How can it be that the high level databases, sometimes index automatically and other times they do not, the proceedings, books, journals .etc. derived from certain international conferences not affiliated to the abc or cd association?

- How can it be that the retired and advanced in age university professors keep on appearing as co-authors of scientific works where their theoretical or practical contribution is equal to zero?

- How can it be that the institutions of the local, provincial, regional, national continental or international government finance projects to research centres where endogamy, plagiarism, etc are rife?

- How can it be that the European Union finances R&D projects in educational environments or of technology transfer, public and private, where there are conflicts with labour, civil and penal justice?

- How can it be that the members of a research group accept the indiscriminate incorporation of co-authors, who haven't cooperated at all with the indexed work?

- How can it be that many research works of the last decades of the 20th century are not indexed in the commercial scientific databases?

- How can it be that scientific groups of evaluators are made up in the conferences with the sponsoring of associations that index automatically, where they fail works because they have references prior to the current decade or which are not digitalized?

- How can it be that the evaluation committees are made up in high level impact conferences where their members lack the knowledge and/or experiences in the main and secondary topics of the conference?

These questions, following some techniques of descriptive statistics, will be broken down across time, until making up a first table of heuristic evaluation, of the indexation of the scientific works belonging to the high level or scientific excellence databases. These two latter notions have changed negatively from the point of view of the social factors in the computer science context of the European South during the transition from the 20th to the 21st century.

LESSONS LEARNED

Currently there is a tendency in the scientific sector of quantifying but not qualifying the research works, since the online databases appeared, where are indexed automatically the research works in book support, journals, proceedings, etc. Not everything that circulates in the highways of scientific information, inside the context of computer science and all its derivations belongs to scientific excellence, since even the authorship of those works may lack validity. The motley production by different sectors of the formal and factual sciences, the high number of indexed works, the presence of endogamy (family, friends, etc.), the duplication of information of authors with Spanish surnames and/or names but with different contents of their publications, the appearance of publications made by college professors of a very high age or deceased, and so on denotes that there is no 100% control of the quality in the indexed information. There is also an exaggerated tendency of the stardom factor of the dynamic persuader, through the inscription to a myriad new online websites, which offer for free the services of including the published works. The goal is to see increase not only the total number of publications, but also the number of the quotes of their own works. This is a line of research in the future, where the high level databases will be analyzed, those online like Google Scholar or other organizations devoted to indexing the scientific works in the American continent, for instance. At the same time a universe of study will be generated to investigate the Garduña factor, parochialism and the dynamic persuader.

CONCLUSION

The second decade of the new millennium makes apparent how the divide among scientific publications is increasing the division among the research groups, due to the financing of works. This divide does not only concern the current scientists, but also the new generations of scientists, who will only consider the quantitative aspect of their works online. The epistemological principles such as whether the scientific knowledge is clear and precise, or the veracity of the information among others are usually not present if the indexes that make up those databases are analyzed. The data stored indexed in a database are unreal where there is a reference to a person in Europe who works in a private enterprise, holding high responsibility managerial jobs and he also devotes himself to the management of R&D European projects, transfer of technology between the university and the entrepreneurial sector, university public teaching, direction of doctor theses, organization of international congresses, etc. And then he is besides co-author or author of over 20 yearly publications, as it appears in DBLP. In short, many of the epistemological principles of the formal and factual sciences are to be found in the scientific works that travel in the back roads, since their authors and/or co-authors lack the necessary funds to travel through the alleged highways of scientific information, where the authors are not the real authors of the works indexed in the databases.

REFERENCES

Cipolla-Ficarra, F. (2013a). *Emerging Software for Interactive Interfaces, Database, Computer Graphics and Animation*. Bergamo: Blue Herons Editions.

Cipolla-Ficarra, F. (2013b). *Computer Engineering and Innovations in Education for Virtual Learning Environments, Intelligent Systems and Communicability*. Bergamo: Blue Herons Editions.

Cipolla-Ficarra, F., & Ficarra, V. (2012). Motivation for Next Generation of Users Versus Parochialism in Software Engineering. In *Proc. Second International Conference on Advances in New Technologies, Interactive Interfaces and Communicability*. Heidelberg, Germany: Springer.

Cipolla-Ficarra, F., & Ficarra, V. (2014). Anti-Models for Universitary Education: Analysis of the Catalans Cases in Information and Communication Technologies. In *Advanced Research and Trends in New Technologies, Software, Human-Computer Interaction and Communicability*. Hershey, PA: IGI Global. doi:10.4018/978-1-4666-4490-8.ch005

Cipolla-Ficarra, F., Ficarra, V., & Cipolla-Ficarra, M. (2012). New Technologies of the Information and Communication: Analysis of the Constructors and Destructors of the European Educational System. In *Proc. Second International Conference on Advances in New Technologies, Interactive Interfaces and Communicability*. Heidelberg, Germany: Springer.

Cipolla-Ficarra, F., & Kratky, A. (2012). Computer Graphics for Students of the Factual Sciences. In *Proc. First International Symposium Communicability, Computer Graphics and Innovative Design for Interactive Systems*. Heidelberg, Germany: Springer. doi:10.1007/978-3-642-33760-4_7

Chapter 17
Rendering and Video Games

Francisco V. Cipolla-Ficarra
Latin Association of Human-Computer Interaction, Spain & International Association of Interactive Communication, Italy

Jacqueline Alma
Electronic Arts, Canada

Miguel Cipolla-Ficarra
International Association of Interactive Communication, Italy

ABSTRACT

We present a study of the triad rendering computer made static and/or dynamic images, video games and adult users who interact with a personal computer. Besides, there is a diachronic study of the basic components to design the virtual 3D characters which are included in the video games. The link of the evolution of the interactive games is also analyzed and especially the interactive design characteristics related to the content, navigation, structure and layout. Finally, a table is presented with those components stemming from the rendering of the scenes for the video games, which motivate their fruition by the adult users.

INTRODUCTION

The video game industry keeps on manufacturing versions of its larest novelties in DVD support, because there are adults users who prefer to interact with them through the computer (Edvardsen & Kulle, 2010). Some of them, from the keyboard, that is, without using the joystick. Some of the psychological motivations from the point of view of the user are due to the fact that the videogames make them live again the fiction of past times, that is, childhood, adolescence or youth, where they interacted directly from the personal computer at school or in the home. Users who have interacted with videogames such as Myst, Tomb Raider, SimCity, The Sims, Resident Evil, Tetris, Pac Man, etc. (Edvardsen, & Kulle, 2010). At the moment of the pauses while they learned the use of the applications aimed at office automation such as the words processors, spreadsheets, databases, etc., that is to say, WordStar, WordPerfect, Lotus 1-2-3, Dbase II or rather the programming in BASIC, Cobol, Fortran, Assembler, etc. In other

DOI: 10.4018/978-1-5225-2616-2.ch017

words, they were born in the era of audiovisual communication, like television and cinema, they were immersed in the process of metamorphosis from the analogical information to the digital one, where the pastime with the traditional games (chess, checkers, cards, minesweeper, etc.), and some of them were already included in the options of the operative systems such as the versions of Windows of the 90s (Cipolla-Ficarra, 2010).

The current chapter starts with a state of the art and the evolution of rendering from the graphic software and the hardware in the PCs, to know the essential components for the emulation and simulation of reality, through graphic computing. Later on we research the basic principles of the three-dimensional characters and their behaviour, investigating in the first studies carried out by the Thalmann couple and some of the basic principles for 3D modelling of the virtual characters. Then is examined the evolution of the PC interactive videogames considering them from the point of view of communicability and user experience design (UX). The categories of interactive design are also considered such as the content with the narrative; the structure and the transformations with the passing of time, among hypertext, multimedia, hypermedia, navigation and the immersion of the user in the different contexts or scenes, etc. All these elements have allowed to draw up a table with those elements of the rendering which the adults users regard as positive to motivate them in the fruition of the contents, irrespective of the way in which they have been structured. Finaly, there are the sections of learned lessons and conclusions.

RENDERING: STATIC AND DYNAMIC FRAME

Traditionally, rendering is regarded as the process of generating a static image (frame) or dynamic (a set of frames) in a video format through the calculation of the lightening of the components in a 3D and/or 2D (Cipolla-Ficarra, 1996). In other words, generating an image from the mathematical description of the scene in the scene 3D and/or 2D, through algorithms which define the color in each pixel of the digital image. The description refers to a set of data related to the geometry 2D and/or 3D from the point of view of the observer, the optical characteristics of the surfaces, visible to the observer, illumination, etc. (Newman & Sproull, 1979: Soh & Tan, 2008; Furtado, Santos, & Ramalho, 2011). The term calculation implies mathematic equations for the simulation and emulation of reality, in natural weather phenomena such as fog, snow, rain, and so on which are included in the static or dynamic image. The mathematics used for the rendering includes: the Montecarlo method, lineal algebra, calculation and numerical analysis, the digital analysis of signals, etc. The set of algorithms make up what is colloquially known in computer graphics as "the engine" of the rendering. Generally, in relation to the engine a commercial software is capable of making the calculation of the illumination, for instance, in more or less time. Aside from the hardware used, the final quality of the static and/or dynamic images depends on them, with a high final quality, which makes currently the users of interactive systems unable to tell apart quickly a digital photograph of reality or an image made through geometric objects in 2D or 3D in the computer. Now at the end of the 20th century, when in the stage previous to the definitive creation of the scenes were completed (representation, wireframe), the stage called rendering (Newman & Sproull, 1979), that is, were included the texture bitmap, lights, bump mapping, and so on giving as a result a final image or frame. In the case of the computer animations, with cinematographic purposes or not, there was a high number of frames.

These images obtained from the rendering can be classified alphabetically and in relation to a set of visible phenomena in:

Figure 1. Commercial software to carry out computer animations such as 3D studio, where the different options included within the rendering can be seen (3D model of wired trees)

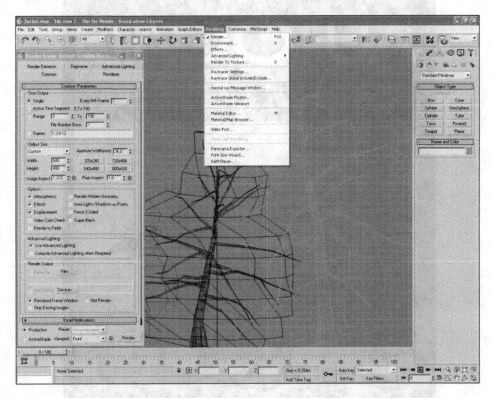

Figure 2. Result of the rendering of a scene stored in a database

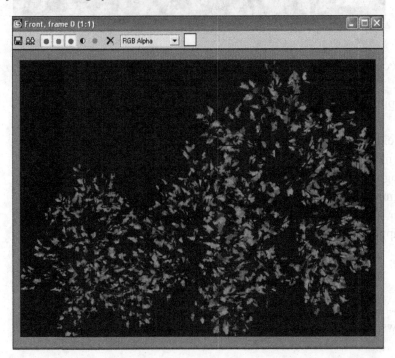

Figure 3. Rendering result for Spanish magazine cover in 1997(author: Francisco V. C. Ficarra)

- Ambient Occlusion,
- Anisotropy,
- Bump Mapping,
- Caustic,
- Depth of Field,
- Displacement Mapping,
- Distance Fog,
- Global Illumination,
- Motion Blur,
- Normal Mapping,
- Reflection,
- Refraction,
- Shading,
- Shadows,
- Soft Shadows,

Figure 4. Rendering result for Spanish magazine cover in 1998 (author: Francisco V. C. Ficarra)

- Subsurface Scattering,
- Texture Mapping. and
- Transparency.

Now if the algorithms are grouped in relation to the problem to be solved in graphic computing (Newman & Sproull, 1979), there are two large groups: the radiosity that is related to the mathematics of the finite elements and the ray tracing, which is related to pirobalistic maths. Both groups make up a reliable structure for the management of the equations related to the rendering in graphic computing. In the real time applications, carried out with personal computers, a complete elaboration of the scenes is not necessary. That is to say, getting very high quality images in the making process of the 3D animation project, for instance. In these cases it is possible to resort to the texture mapping (zero illumination), since the intrinsic color of an object has a greater influence on its aspect; and the direct illumination, that is, that only the light which goes from the source of the illumination to the surface is considered, without taking into account the reflections generated on the objects which may be present in the scene. Some of the algorithms used in these cases are: Painter's Algorithm, Z- Buffering, Global Illumination, Volume Rendering, etc. In the case of carrying out a rendering of a high number of images for a 3D animation film one resorts to the render farm, that is, a network of computers connected among each other. The software RenderMan, created by Pixar Animation Studios (www.pixar.com) is one of the most widespread for these tasks. Other commercial engines for the rendering are Mental Ray, Vray, Brazil, Final Render, POV-Ray and Maxwell Render.

STRATEGIES OF SOFTWARE, HARDWARE AND INTERACTIVE DESIGN FOR THE PRODUCTION OF THREE-DIMENSIONAL VIDEO GAMES

At the end of the 20th century, the results of the animation project could not be visualized in real time, especially when working in a graphic commercial hardware and software belonging to the middle range from the point of view of cost, but high in relation to the quality of the results, for instance, the 3D Studio (i.e., Figures 1, 2, 3 and 4). Nevertheless, in the new millennium the advance of the commercial software of the middle range has started to modify that reality leaning on the current video plates equipped with processors which allow to visualize in real time the final rendering of a 3D scene. However, in that range of hardware, it can only be applied to simple scenes, not being applicable yet for scenes of greater complexity, since this requires a too high calculation power. This is the main reason why the three-dimensional designers choose to create the 3D environment with a simpler form of visualization and then generate the slow rendering process and thus achieve the intended final results. The rendering time depends to a great extent on the parameters established in the materials and lights, as well as on the configuration of the rendering engine and the hardware where the software works. In short, the rendering process in a personal computer requires the CPU in a high number of operations. Consequently, it is slow. However, this time can be reduced and assisted in real time, through the use of the 3D accelerators of the graphic cards for the three-dimensional games, for instance.

Usually each 3D application counts with its own rendering engine, but it is necessary to explain that there are plug-ins which devote themselves to make the calculation inside the program, using special formulas (a plug-in is a software components that adds a specific feature to an existing software application). This is the case of the known engines Mental Ray, Vray, Brazil, Final Render, etc. Now in the case of the videogames, normally "pre-rendered" images are used to generate the textures and thus help the hardware, whether it is a console or a PC working in the virtual environment, with a much higher speed (even so the current games have a great demand in their processors, video plate and RAM memory.

The pre-rendering is based on the use of the image or texture in a game that was rendered through a graphic engine much more powerful than that used in the videogame, that is, a professional one. Consequently, the graphic engine of the game only takes care of calculating the position of that texture and not of all its content. In other words, it is much easier for a computer to calculate pixels than a large set of polygons with textures and where lights, glints, shadows, transparencies, reflects and so on converge.

This resource was very much used mainly in games of the 20th century, which were a mixture of 3D and 2D. At that time, the only thing that the graphic engine calculated in three dimensions were the dynamic objects (characters, objects which could be kept or used, etc.) while the backgrounds were an immobile texture. Collision boxes were used so that a character could simulate being hitting the objects of that immobile texture and thus not go through them. The main drawback of this method was tgat a free camera could not be used, but the field of vision of the player was based on a lot of predetermined positions of the camera bearing in mind the position of the character. This method was used a lot if the first games of series like Resident Evil, for instance.

Currently the pre-rendering is only used to insert textures to 3D objects. For instance, making the pre-rendering to a wall on which there is a shadow, it is achieved that the graphic engine doesn't have to calculate in each photogram the position and all the characteristics of the shadow, if not only the image previously allocated to the object. Also for other minimal details, although possibly in the future it will not be needed because it strips the graphics of dynamism. In the example of the shadow of the pre-rendering previously mentioned, that shadow couldn't be modified, in other aspects like the light or the position of the object that is generating it, since the graphic engine is not calculating it any longer.

The procedure to make a 3D scene through the computer, in which a transformation takes place, such as can be the special effect of an explosion, is made up of three key elements: the object, in which the position must be considered, the orientation, the size, the shape, the color and the transparency. The camera, in which the position of the viewer must be considered, the point of interest and the point of view. For instance, in Resident Evil, it is a videogame in third person and the user of the computer watches the protagonist, which bestows a greater appeal to what happens in her environment. Lastly, there is the source of light, in which its intensity must be regarded as well as the position.

Now the studies carried out by Daniel Thalmann and Nadia Magnenat Thalmann in the 90s have allowed to generate graphic computing systems capable of generating computer animations (Magnenat-Thalman & Thalmann, 1993) where there are human beings, whose behaviour take into account variables of the context where they are immersed. They are studies based on the excellence of interdisciplinarity, where aspects and methods of mechanics, robotics, physiology, psychology and artificial intelligence converge. The common denominator of their works consisted in drawing up systems where the virtual characters made with the computer had a natural behaviour, increasing the complexity and improving the realism of the context and very especially paid attention to the facial expressions, the deformation of the body and the hands, during the movement.

VIRTUAL CHARACTERS: OLD AND NEW EXCELLENT EXAMPLES

Following the experiments carried out by the Thalmann couple, such as can be the animation "Rendez-vous a Montreal" (Magnenat-Thalman & Thalmann, 1993), where a virtual encounter takes place between Marylyn Monroe and Humphrey Bogart we can analyze the traditional composition of the 3D characters who have been incorporated into the videogames, for instance. Since the 20th century, one of the great goals of computer animation consists in generating human characters through the computer that have a high level of realism, to such a degree that the human eye can not tell whether it is real or not. In that sense, some examples of the second decade of the new millennium are to be found in the publicity sector, like the female character Antonella to promote the sale of the Ford Verbe car.

In the 90s the geometric and mathematic models used in graphic computing did not adapt very well to the shapes of the human body, nor did the movements of the joints, due to the role of the muscles. In this sense a commercial products which tried to solve the muscles issues in the computer animation of the low cost range were the 3D plug-ins of "Reyes infografica" in Madrid (Cipolla-Ficarra, 1999). A more costly method at the time was rotoscoping, also known as brute force method. It is a method that consists in the natural representation of the human movement, from which derives the motion capture technique, for instance. Without any doubt, these were techniques and methods very used in the cinema

Figure 5. A photogram of the animation "Rendez-vous a Montreal", when Monroe and Bogart meet in Canada

Figure 6. Photograms/frames of the publicity of the car Ford Verbe, where a 3D character by the name of Antonella presents the main characteristics of the car in the city of Rome, Italy Source: www.nytimes. com/slideshow/2009/07/19/automobiles/0719-fiesta_index.html

Figure 7. Photograms/frames of the publicity of the car Ford Verbe, where a 3D character by the name of Antonella presents the main characteristics of the car in the city of Rome, Italy Source: www.nytimes. com/slideshow/2009/07/19/automobiles/0719-fiesta_index.html

Figure 8. Photograms/frames of the publicity of the car Ford Verbe, where a 3D character by the name of Antonella presents the main characteristics of the car in the city of Rome, Italy.\ Source: www.nytimes. com/slideshow/2009/07/19/automobiles/0719-fiesta_index.html

and the videogames of the late 20th century. Now a human body in 3D with movement which emulates reality can be carried out with three "classical" models: stick figures, surface models and volume models. A brief description of each one of them to contrast the basic principles, which have influenced the design of characters in 3D, is the following:

- **Stick Figure:** It is a human skeleton built up with segments and joints. The final image that results is not realistic and there are human movements that can't be represented since it lacks depth, such as torsion and contact. A model built with that technique was Hipi. Hipi is the protagonist of an animation film titled "Dream Flight", made by Nadie and Daniel Thalmann in collaboration with Philippe Bergeron in 1982 (Magnenat-Thalmann & Thalmann, 1993).
- **Surface Figures:** The skeletons can be covered with an upper layer, with a flat or curve shape. In this way the movements that modify the surface are visible and the hidden lines of the segments and the joints can be eliminated. A classical example is Cyberman (1978) of the Chrysler Corporation firm. This example has been built by the motor industry to study the positions and movements of the drivers.
- **Volume Figures:** The body is depicted with simple rotation. In general cylinders can be used with the models designed by Evans (1976), Poter and Willmert (1975) ellipsoids with the models designed by Herbison-Evans (1978-1982) and spheres with the model designed by Badler (1979-

Figure 9. Hipi sitting in the woods

Figure 10. Hippi flying

1980). With those models, and bearing in mind the cost factor for the modification in the case of failings, in the elaboration of the 3D characters were already used some design strategies, such as:

- ◦ Knowing the parts which will make up the limbs, hands and feet, that is, to build them as a single object or consider the fingers and toes in a separate way. If there are more components and they are smaller and malleable, a greater realism can be obtained in the details, for instance:

- ◦ Using the symmetry, as in the case of the face, although in reality it is not perfectly symmetric, etc.

- ◦ Bearing in mind the following recommendations: the spine must be as straight as possible, the same as the legs and the arms. The arms must be as perpendicular as possible to the body. The fingers must be separated between themselves and the thumbs must form a 45 degrees angle with the side of the hand.

Each one of these software and hardware components turned the 2D, 3D computer-made characters into a kind of borderline in the context of graphic computing, where interdisciplinarity was the key for the advances of the behaviour computer animation, for instance. Those studies would be the key for the momentum of the videogames sector in the new millennium.

INTERACTIVE COMMUNICATION AND VIDEO GAMES

Although the interaction between user and computer is natural since its inception, with the advance of the hypertext the multimedia and hypermedia gained a greater relevance in the cultural environment with the appearance of the graphic interfaces and the implicit possibility, open in the 80s, of carrying out tasks of the graphic arts in paper support, which included the creative aspect, for instance (Van Lent, 2008; Levis, 1997). Then, in the countries of the Mediterranean in Europe, multimedia became a topic of conversation, and later on the interactive systems to include virtual reality, which with the democratization of the internet of the 90s started to draw the attention of the potential users of commercial products, especially for the generation of 3D characters who could move in computer-generated environments. The purpose of those characters was to show the functionality or eventual options in architectonical environments, the use of mechanic devices, etc. That's to say, environments in where from the arts they switched to architecture or industrial engineering. That kind of knowledge entailed, as in the behaviour computer animation, the interchange of knowledge and/or experiences between technicians and artists. However, in the south of Europe, the real specialists were sidelined so that the products and/or services deriving from those computer-made creations, animated or not, as are the experts in social communication.

When in 1993 the electronic game of the greatest cultural impact, appeared, Myst, the interactive systems aimed at the online and offline hypermedia entertainment started to develop in a frenzy until at the beginning of the new millennium the virtual enterprises that arose with the democratization of the internet, and the so-called new economy springing up around the new technologies fell apart with the same speed with which it had developed, thus ending with almost all the cultural interactive initiatives, excepting the videogames (Levis, 1997). Which was the only sector of the multimedia that still grew in Europe. Aside from the social and/or social factors from the software and the hardware it could be seen how the offline multimedia interactive systems (DVD, Playstation, etc.) they kept on democratizing the circulation of the videogames among the potential users in the whole planet (Levis, 1997). Besides, the telecommunications allowed a faster online transmission, through the use of the ADSL and also the commercial applications to program multimedia systems, they democratized the dynamism in the presentations, for instance, for instance, with Flash or MMDirector. But this ease in the context of the user experience desgn or programming had not tu2rned into a larger production of original contents, nor in a deepening of the interactive language. For instance, in the late 80s the investigations of the hypertext focused on the usability of the system and not from the clearly literary perspective. This is perhaps because the interactive means rather than literary is audiovisual. To such an extent that the references for a possible interactive fiction must be found above all in the electronic games.

However, the professionals and the industry of these games have been very far from artistic/fun creation (Van Lent, 2008). This is the divide between technicians and artists, and also the lack of incorporation of communication experts, what has scattered the research of the narrative possibilities of the interactive means for decades. Little by little, the academic environment of the audiovisual of the Mediterranean European countries started to regard the games as culture. A statement which is true to some extent, since the interactive game, where communicability is present, may interrelate in a bidirectional way leisure and culture.

Historically, after the momentum of the 90s, its progress has been very limited, especially in the south of Europe because of factors which are exogenous to technique. Wild mercantilism made the term multimedia be synonymous with getting profits in the short term, generating low quality multimedia interactive systems, and turning the general public away from their consumption, due to the costs-quality equation. Aside from this negative European reality, Brenda Laurel (Laurel, 2004; Laurel, 2013), and Janet Murray (Murray, 2011) among others claim that in the cultural environment the most significant thing about the computer science revolution but that the realization of its potentialities is still to arrive.

One of the models of the interactive narrative with an excellent level of communicability, for instance, and coming from the world of games is SimCity (Cipolla-Ficarra, 2014). In this game there is no previous story, but it is built as interacts in such a way that every player experiences a different narrative or experience. This formula, originally applied to the evolution of a city, has also been applied with great success to other scenarios, such as are The Sims. It is the simulation of family life. It is an interactive experience which is closer to fiction in the traditional sense. Besides, it means the application to narrative of a digital quality: the generation of original contents, since there would be no two equal cities or families among different users. Another playing model to be taken into account are the MUDs (Multi User Dungeons) where the experiences evolve in keeping with the interactions such as SimCity, but besides, they are developed inside a community of players, in such a way that one doesn't only play against the computer, but against other players, turning entertainment into a socialization space.

In these interactive systems the compatibility between narrative and playability entails a constant evaluation of the components where the stage of inception and design of the system. There are important differences at a theoretical level. For instance, the differences in the treatment of time: in narrative one relates, usually in a past tense, whereas the game develops in the present tense. Narrative jumps in time, and besides, it usually compresses it. In contrast, in a game the experience follows a strictly real time. There are also differences in the way of treating the space that surrounds the action: the special environment is an essential part of a game; in contrast, in a narration it may become irrelevant.

Now a videogame consists in a formal structure which may be totally devoid of narrative content and yet keep on working (Pac Man, Tetris, etc.). In contrast, a fiction handles plenty of elements which do not look easy at all to formalize, for instance, the coding of the behaviour of a character. Simultaneously, one of the foundations of narrative is the separation between the world told by the authors and the existential world of the reader; the success of the narrative depends on the more or less effective achievement of this separation and the suspension of the disbelief in face of what is told, to which tends, naturally, any reader. Now in an interactive the reader makes progress the story through interactions, which entails a connection between both worlds, and it is the degree of sensation of immersion of the users what makes the interaction time with the game increase or decrease as time passes in front of the PC, for instance. The deeper is the immersion of the player, the greater is the feeling he/she has of being inside the game, and the greater is, therefore, its credibility. The immersive sensation has a very important implication to draw the attention in the interaction and motivate the fruition. the identification of the player. However, the greater the identification is, the less interesting become the other players, the less empathy they must generate, and the lesser is, in short, the power of the story and its narrativity. In such a way that the immersion, one of the elements of interactive communications in the PC videogames, is not akin to narrative, but rather goes against it. Therefore, one of the ways to limit the identification of the use with the content of the videogame and thus bolster the attractive of the rest of the charactes in a fiction consists in changing the point of view. In the games in the first person (Myst) the user is the main character of the story, and therefore, the identification is maximal. In contrast, in the games in third person, the user controls the main character (Tomb Raider) or watches the protagonist (Resident Evil), which bestows more attractive to what happens in her environment. In few words, perhaps, the interactive fiction, which is not synomymous of literary fiction (although it has many of its components) tends to replace the pleasure of telling by the pleasure of interaction.

The table represents the results obtained through a heuristic evaluation, with adult users, when they interacted with a PC through the keyboard in a communicability lab in the city of Barcelona, Spain. The total of videogames analyzed for PC was 80. The listing of the commercial products evaluated are into the Appendix. The heuristic techniques of the evaluation are formularies for direct observation, questionnaires and interviews (Nielsen & Mack, 1994). The results obtained, in our universe of study, make apparent the importance that has in the first place the central element (virtual character or object), shape or color, with which the user identifies and the degree of emulation/simulation of the movements. In the anthropomorphism or personification of the characters, the behaviour computer animation of those

Table 1. Results of the Heuristic Evaluation

Components:	%
1) Central Element (character or object)	85
- Sharp	60
- Color	55
- Behaviour computer animation	70
2) Realism (emulation or simulation)	75
- Illumination	65
- Effects	55
- Textures	40
3) Special effect (fx)	70
- Chemistry and/or physics	65
- Nature phenomena	55

characters can surpass the empathy achieved through the shapes. The second position is the realism of the graphic context where the action develops, regarding the illumination and all its associated effects, such as the texture of the materials that make up the surfaces of the objects. Third, the special effects, taking the first place those derived from chemistry and/or physics such as explosions, fires, collisions, and so on which precede nature phenomena such as mist, rain, snow, etc.

LESSONS LEARNED

In the triad rendering, videogames and adult users we can seen how the principles enunciated about behaviour animation, the basic design for the 3D characters and the interactive contents aimed at leisure, literature has taken a second place with relation to the audiovisual and interactive communication.

This is due to the fact that the human being prefers the audiovisual contents among the "new technologies" of the ICT (information and communication technology) sector. Through the television and the cinema, for instance, in the 20th century, a generation of users has been generated with a wide culture for the constant consumption of static and/or dynamic information in an analogical or digital support. Although they are adult users and who in keeping with the current classifications of those born or not in the digital era, z generation, and other nominations to exclude them because they prefer the PC to an iPod or a Tablet PC, they still belong to a generation of explorers and enjoyers of multimedia and augmented reality contents, for example, with a high percentage of quality. This qualitative factor is due to the fact that many of them are not only users of the commercial software, but have also been programmers of their personal computers. That is, they fell when in an interactive system there is presence or absence of quality. This intuition is verified after interacting during a few minutes with it. They are those who keep on looking in the software, for instance, those attributes of the interactive system such as the prediction of the behaviour of the dynamic means at the moment of the navigation, the inference of the contents and the drawing of isotopies among the different sections that make up the structure of the interactive system. Therefore, in the new millennium, they still remain faithful consumers of all those videogames which contain the four mainstays of computer animation, that is, originality, universality, simplicity and humor.

CONCLUSION

The algorithms and the programming languages which make up the engines of rendering have made up the advance of graphic computing in the daily life of millions of users of the interactive services, in the era of the expansion of communicability. One of the most dynamic sectors in the communicability has been the videogames sector, where software and hardware have been constantly in evolution, almost free of those exogenous and/or endogenous factors stemming from the financial and/or economic, local and global and which have slowed down the democratization of virtual reality, for example. An evolution of the hardware that always precedes the software, but which in our case of study it has been seen how users of computers of the 80s, 90s and early 2000s are still used at the moment of interacting with the video games. In this sense, they have also been the first in interacting with videogames such as: Myst, SimCity, Tetris, Tomb Raider, etc. Those are videogames that have set a tendency across time in each one of the categories of interactive design. However, it is in the category of the layout where the rendering is present. The rendering engines have increased the level of demand of the users towards the producers, in the final quality that the video games must have. A quality which increases communicability, regardless of the hardware platform that is used, that is, personal computers, tablet PCs, video consoles, iPhone, etc. The results of the emulation or simulation processes of reality in graphic computing applied to the videogames context, denotes the existence of users who even today prefer the PCs rather than the video consoles or multimedia mobile phones, for instance.

ACKNOWLEDGMENT

The authors would like to express their deepest gratitude to Maria Ficarra. Thanks a lots to Alejandra Quiroga, Jim Carré, Donald Nilson, and Carlos for their valuable comments and suggestions to improve the quality of the research work.

REFERENCES

Chatham, R. (2007). Games for Training. *Communications of the ACM*, *50*(7), 36–43. doi:10.1145/1272516.1272537

Cipolla-Ficarra, F. (1996). A User Evaluation of Hypermedia Iconography. In Proceedings Computer-graphics. Paris: GRASP.

Cipolla-Ficarra, F. (1999). Investigación y desarrollo en la infografia empresarial. [In Spanish]. *AutoCAD Magazine*, *60*, 62–66.

Cipolla-Ficarra, F. (2010). *Quality and Communicability for Interactive Hypermedia Systems: Concepts and Practices for Design*. Hershey, PA: IGI Global. doi:10.4018/978-1-61520-763-3

Cipolla-Ficarra, F. (2014). *Advanced Research and Trends in New Technologies, Software, Human-Computer Interaction and Communicability*. Hershey, PA: IGI Global. doi:10.4018/978-1-4666-4490-8

Edvardsen, F., & Kulle, H. (2010). *Educational Games: Design, Learning and Applications*. New York: Nova.

Furtado, A., Santos, A., Ramalho, G., & de Almeida, E. S. (2011). Improving Digital Game Develpoment with Software Product Lines. *IEEE Software*, *28*(5), 30–37. doi:10.1109/MS.2011.101

Laurel, B. (2004). *Design Research: Methods and Perspectives*. Cambridge, MA: MIT Press.

Laurel, B. (2013). *Computers as Theatre*. Addison-Wesley Professional.

Levis, D. (1997). *Los videojuegos, un fenómeno de masas*. Barcelona: Paidós. (in Spanish)

Magnenat-Thalmann, M., & Thalmann, D. (1993). *Virtual Worlds and Multimedia*. New York: Wiley.

Murray, J. (2011). *Inventing the Medium: Principles of Interaction Design as a Cultural Practice*. Cambridge, MA: MIT Press.

Newman, W., & Sproull, R. (1979). *Principles of Interactive Computer Graphics*. New York: McGraw Hill.

Nielsen, J., & Mack, R. (1994). *Usability Inspections Methods*. New York: Wiley. doi:10.1145/259963.260531

Soh, J., & Tan, B. (2008). Mobile Gaming. *Communications of the ACM, 51*(3), 35–39. doi:10.1145/1325555.1325563

Van Lent, M. (2008). The Business of Fun. *IEEE Computer, 41*(2), 97–103. doi:10.1109/MC.2008.64

ADDITIONAL READING

Billinghurst, M., Grasset, R., & Looser, J. (2005). Designing Augmented Reality Interfaces. *Computer Graphics, 39*(1), 17–21. doi:10.1145/1057792.1057803

Birn, J. (2000). *Digital Lighting & Rendering*. Indianapolis: New Riders.

Brenda, L. (1990). *The Art of Human-Computer Interface Design*. Boston: Addison-Wesley.

Brenda, L. (1991). *Computers as Theatre*. Boston: Addison-Wesley.

Cipolla-Ficarra, F., & Cipolla-Ficarra, M. (2008). Interactive Systems, Design and Heuristic Evaluation: The Importance of the Diachronic Vision. In *Proceedings New Directions in Intelligent Interactive Multimedia* (pp. 625–634). Heidelberg: Springer-Verlag. doi:10.1007/978-3-540-68127-4_64

Cipolla-Ficarra, F., Cipolla-Ficarra, M., & Harder, T. (2008). Realism and Cultural Layout in Tourism and Video Games Multimedia Systems. In *Proceedings of the 1st ACM Workshop on Communicability Design and Evaluation in Cultural and Ecological Multimedia System*, New York: ACM Press, 461-470 doi:10.1145/1462039.1462043

Colman, D., & Vertegaal, R. (2008). Organic User Interfaces: Designing Computers in Any Way, Shape, or Form. *Communications of the ACM, 51*(6), 48–53. doi:10.1145/1349026.1349037

Demel, J., & Miller, M. (1984). *Introduction to Computers Graphics*. Boston: PWS Engineering.

Fernandez, I. (2001). *Macromedia Flash Animation & Cartooning: A Creative Guide*. New York: McGraw Hill.

Frohlich, D. The Design Space of Interface (1991). In *Proceedings Eurographics Workshop Multimedia: Systems, Interaction and Application*. Stockhom: Springer-Verlag, 53-69

Goes, J. et al.. (1999). *Warping & Morphing of Graphical Objects*. San Francisco: Morgan Kaufmann Publishers.

Gulz, A., & Haake, M. (2006). Design of Animated Pedagogical Agents –A look at their look. *International Journal of Human-Computer Studies, 64*(4), 322–339. doi:10.1016/j.ijhcs.2005.08.006

Höysniemi, J., Hämäläinen, P., Turkki, L., & Rouvi, T. (2005). Childrens Intuitive Gestures in Vision-Based Action Games. *Communications of the ACM, 48*(1), 44–50. doi:10.1145/1039539.1039568

Lord, P., & Sibley, B. (1998). *Cracking Animation*. London: Thames and Hudson.

Maestri, G. (2000). *Character Animation*. Indianapolis: New Riders.

Obrenovicc, Z., Gasevic, D., & Eliens, A. (2008). Stimulating Creativity through Opportunistic Software Development. *IEEE Computer Software*, *25*(6), 64–70. doi:10.1109/MS.2008.162

Sebeok, T. (2001). *Global Semiotics*. Bloomington: Indiana University Press.

Van Welbergen, H., Nijholt, A., Reidsma, D., & Zwiers, J. (2006). Presenting in Virtual Worlds: An Architecture for a 3D Anthropomorphic Presenter. *IEEE Intelligent Systems*, *21*(5), 47–53. doi:10.1109/MIS.2006.101

KEY TERMS AND DEFINITIONS

Communicability: A qualitative communication between the user and the interactive system, such as mobile phones, augmented reality, immersion multimedia, hypermedia, among others. The extent to which an interactive system successfully conveys its functionality to the user.

Computer Graphics: Or graphic computing are graphics created using software and hardware. The use of a computer to produce and manipulate pictorial imagen on a video screen, for example.

Computer Animation: It is the creation of moving images or dynamics images (animation) using a computer.

Interactive System: It is a computer device made up by a CPU and peripherals, whose functioning requires a constant interaction with the user. Currently these systems tend to their miniaturization and/or invisibility, the mobility and wireless connectability among them.

Motivation: Is the set of the dynamics means and of the structure resources that strengthen navigation in the interactive system. Motivation seeks to concentrate the attention of the user on the need to pursue her/his enjoyment of the system. Attention on the fram must be maintained, that is, the user must retain lasting expectations regarding the inferface.

Rendering: The process of adding realism to a computer graphics (static and/or dynamics images) by adding three-dimensional qualities such as texture, shadows, illumination, etc., and variations in color and shade, for example.

Video Game: Is an electronic game that involves human interaction with one or more user/s interface/s to generate audio-visual feedback, for example, on a video device.

APPENDIX

Videogames Analyzed for PC

Title	Release Date	Publisher
1. Age of Empires II: The Age of Kings	1999	Microsoft
2. Age of Empires III	2005	Microsoft
3. Age of Empires	1997	Microsoft
4. Age of Mythology	2002	Microsoft
5. American McGee's Alice	2000	Electronic Arts
6. Anno 1503	2003	Sunflowers
7. Anno 1602	1998	Sunflowers
8. Battlefield 1942	2002	Electronic Arts
9. Black & White	2001	EA Games
10. Blade Runner	1997	Virgin Interactive
11. Civilization III	2001	Infogrames
12. Civilization IV	2005	2K Games & Aspyr
13. Civilization V	2010	2K Games & Aspyr
14. Command & Conquer 3: Tiberium Wars	2007	Electronic Arts
15. Command & Conquer: Red Alert	1996	Virgin Interactive
16. Command & Conquer: Tiberian Sun	1999	Electronic Arts
17. Cossacks II: Napoleonic Wars	2005	CDV Software
18. Counter-Strike	1999	Valve Corporation
19. Counter-Strike: Source	2004	Electronic Arts
20. Crysis Warhead	2008	Electronic Arts
21. Crysis	2007	Electronic Arts
22. DayZ	2013	Bohemia Interactive
23. Deer Hunter	1997	WizardWorks Software
24. Doom 3	2004	Activision
25. Doom II: Hell on Earth	1994	GT Interactive
26. Doom	1993	id Software
27. Dungeon Siege	2002	Microsoft Game Studios
28. Empire Earth	2001	Sierra Entertainment
29. Euro Truck Simulator 2	2012	SCS Software
30. Europa Universalis IV	2013	Paradox Interactive
31. EverQuest	1999	Sony Online Entertainment
32. Far Cry	2004	Ubisoft
33. Frogger	1997	Hasbro Interactive
34. Full Throttle	1995	LucasArts
35. Guild Wars 2	2012	NCsoft
36. Guild Wars	2005	NCsoft
37. Half-Life	1998	Sierra Entertainment
38. Harry Potter and the Philosopher's Stone	2001	Electronic Arts
39. Hotel Giant	2002	JoWood Productions
40. Imperivm: Great Battles of Rome	2005	FX Interactive
41. Killing Floor	2009	Tripwire Interactive
42. Machinarium	2009	Amanita Design
43. Mafia: The City of Lost Heaven	2002	Gathering of Developers
44. Magicka	2011	Paradox Interactive
45. Microsoft Flight Simulator X	2006	Microsoft Game Studios
46. Monopoly	1995	Leisure Genius
47. Myst	1993	Brøderbund
48. Patrician III: Rise of the Hanse	2003	Encore

Conclusion

The temporal dimension is a very interesting component to evaluate all those discoveries and inventions which have allowed great breakthroughs or setbacks in the history of humankind. In our days the dilemma can focus on the distribution of those benefits among the population pyramid of a local community or in the global village. For instance, if we examine it from the human-computer interaction (which is not synonymous with the experience of the user or usability engineering), the use of multimedia mobile phones in the cities with millions of inhabitants, we can set common denominators among the different kinds of users in relation to age, educational level, financial resources, etc. We will also see how international marketing fosters constantly the purchase of the latest models, even though millions of users only know approximately 1 or 5% of the potential functions of those devices.

However, if later on we examine segments of the adult or elderly population, hit or not by the big international financial crisis since the end of the last decade, the mobile phones with reduced multimedia components turn out to be safer at the moment of the cyber attacks international or domestic. That is, there is a comeback to the primitive function of those devices such as talking on the phone and/or send short text messages. Now how is this regression possible in the second decade of the new millennium? The motivations are to be found in the good or bad use of the technological breakthroughs and those who manage or control such uses, or rather abuse. The switch from freedom to debauchery in the cyberspace, perhaps, will endanger the freedom of navigating in the internet for millions of cybernauts in the midterm.

Something identical happens with creativity inside the human-computer interaction (HCI). In many occasions it is easy to detect the empire of mediocrity until plagiarism, since the sport of some of its members comes down to two verbs: "copy and paste". How is it possible that the originality and creativity is not the common denominator in the current HCI seen the boundless inclusion of professionals, variegated and exotic, belonging to the formal sciences? The reason is very simple, they are not interested in that scientific sector and much less in what happens to their population basis. HCI is yet another aggregate to their listings of academic interest to give a humanistic shade to the curriculum vitae. Their sights are aimed at the peak of the population, or rather, the elite groups, with great power in decision making, in particular to get financial resources.

Resources that only serve to foster the phenomenon of the digital divide, and a new generation frustrated with several academic degrees of the native digitals. These are some of the consequences of the lax boundaries that mathematics, physics and certain engineering degrees have in the 21st century. It is this laxness that is seriously affecting not only this domain of scientific knowledge such as human-computer interaction, but also the whole coherent and lucid future of the NICT (New Information and Communications Technology). So nobody should be surprised if in a myriad geographical spaces (academic-scientific) on the rim of the European Mediterranean the training of professionals and the correct use of all the technological breakthroughs in the framework of the ICT (Information and Communications Technology) have lost their bearings, specifically in the last two decades and in fields such as: the HCI, the design and development of the interfaces, computer graphics, the generation of original multimedia contents, multimedia engineering, computer and/or systems engineering, mathematics, physics, the fine arts, industrial design, telecommunications, videogames, primary, secondary and college education, healthcare and a long etc. In that geographical space the Garduña factor has generated a ghetto of caliphs, perverting the epistemological principles of the sciences. They have imposed their antiscientific laws and they will last for decades.

Their main premise is "no one can do us anything". That is, total immunity in the face of their wild, inhuman and destructive behaviour, since all that shines autonomously by its originality, creativity, modesty and honesty must be eliminated. In other words, it is the supremacy of mediocrity in the main disciplines that make up the human-computer interaction and the ICTs, which range from education to research and development (R&D), including the transfer of knowledge between university and industry/ business and vice versa. This is another of the elements to be taken into account when one investigates the potentiality or the success percentage of the new start-ups &spin-offs among those located in the west coast of the USA and those that are born in the Old World. The greatest success will concentrate on the Pacific coast compared with the coasts of the European continent, as it happened before with the virtual firms. It isn't only a matter of bigger financial resources but rather the lack of the Garduña factor.

Aside from this conjuncture, mostly invariable with the passing of the years, decades and centuries, now such expressions as "educational excellence", "highly qualified personnel", "fast workplace outlet, sure and stable", among so many other slogans, lose their grip or credibility in the face of a reality not liquid as it was well defined by Zygmunt Bauman (2000), but rather in a gaseous and sometimes nauseating state. These deeds tending to establish subsets or endless divisions, fortunately, even in our days, find a boomerang effect in each of the continents of the planet. That is, researchers, professors, students, etc., who are aware of these opaque realities as it has been possible to see in each one of the works selected to make up the current handbook. Each one of the key words of those works constitutes a point of reference for the current and future generations of professionals interested in the constant growth of the sciences to the service of the common good, whether it is local or global. Therefore, their learned lessons, conclusions and future lines of research are cardinal points in the ocean of the formal and factual sciences.

The professionals of the formal and factual sciences, linked to the technological breakthroughs, will have to be essential in the reduction of the digital divide, the social exclusion of the professionals who have a short, middle or long trajectory of training and working experience, and the reduction of local and global property. Students, professors, researchers, mathematicians, physicists, chemists, mechanics, engineers, graduates, etc., have to be original and avant-garde protagonists in the genesis of the innovation and development skills of the new technologies. They must in a constant and positive way lead the way in trying to elaborate new processes, products and services to fill up those real and non-virtual spaces that the local and global population is daily requesting from them. Although it is true that several agents participate in the innovating and creative activities, sometimes with competing interests, it is essential to include the businessman (i.e., industrialist, commercial, etc.) in a bidirectional relationship among peers with the educational-scientific field. Where each one of these agents takes an egalitarian position so that this communication process between production of goods and/or services, technology and sciences, has a constructive and lasting feedback. It is also necessary that this triad guarantees and carries out the greatest possible access to the population pyramids in the matter of the latest scientific and technological breakthroughs aimed at healthcare (prevention and cure of diseases) and education (knowing how to find in time where the real sources of creative, theoretical and practical knowledge are).

New and interesting horizons are opening up from the point of view of the sciences where the dignity, freedom, equality and mutual respect among the human beings must remain at the summit of the motivations. Although in a myriad occasions, the human cost to be paid is very high for believing and working for certain social and technological utopias, we think and maintain that said stimuli mustn't decay in the view of certain gaseous realities. In the synergy and positive energy among thousands of people will be facilitated the passage through the information highways so that they keep on researching, discovering and inventing solutions in a disinterested way, with the purpose of improving the quality of life of the population. In that framework, communicability, human-computer interaction, the NICTs, electronics, mechanics, computer science, robotics, and the rest of disciplines that make up the formal and factual sciences will keep on playing a transcendental role. Lastly, a selection of sentences of famous personalities of the history of mankind that allow us to reflect in front of all those who entertain themselves provoking or putting a spike in the wheels of the scientific, technological and educational cart: "You can have anything you want – if you want it badly enough. You can be anything you want to be, do anything you set out to accomplish if you hold to that desire with singleness of purpose" (Abraham Lincoln); "The difference between what we do and what we are capable of doing would suffice to solve most of the world's problems" (Mahatma Gandhi); "Human subtlety will never devise an invention more beautiful, more simple or more direct than does nature because in her inventions nothing is lacking, and nothing is superfluous" (Leonardo da Vinci); "The most exciting phrase to hear in science, the one that heralds new discoveries, is not 'Eureka!' but 'That's funny'..." (Isaac Asimov); "When I was a child, my mother said to me, 'If you become a soldier, you'll be a general. If you become a monk, you'll end up as the Pope.' Instead, I became a painter and wound up as Picasso" (Pablo Picasso).

REFERENCES

Bauman, Z. (2000). *Liquid Modernity*. Oxford, UK: Blackwell Publishers.

Compilation of References

Abdalhamid, F. (2007). *Listening comprehension strategies of Arabic-speaking ESL learners*. Colorado State University.

Abel, F., Bittencourt, I. I., Costa, E., Henze, N., Krause, D., & Vassileva, J. (2010). Recommendations in online discussion forums for e-learning systems. *IEEE Transactions on Learning Technologies*, *3*(2), 165–176. doi:10.1109/TLT.2009.40

Abernethy, A. P., & Hesse, B. W. (2011). Guest editor's introduction to the special section on information technology and evidence implementation. *Translational Behavioral Medicine*, *1*(1), 11–14. doi:10.1007/s13142-011-0014-6 PMID:24073027

Adelskold, G., Alklett, K., Axelsson, R., & Blomgren, G. (1999). Problem- based distance learning of energy issues via computer network. *Distance Education*, *20*(1), 129–143. doi:10.1080/0158791990200110

Afanas'eva, N. A. (2008). Self-organization is a factor in the success of learning activity. *Fundamental'nye issledovanija*, *2*. Retrieved from http://cyberleninka.ru/article/n/samoorganizatsiya-faktor-uspeshnosti-uchebnoy-deyatelnosti

Agha, L. (2014). The effects of health information technology on the costs and quality of medical care. *Journal of Health Economics*, *34*, 19–30. doi:10.1016/j.jhealeco.2013.12.005 PMID:24463141

Aharony, N. (2010). Twitter use in libraries: An exploratory analysis. *Journal of Web Librarianship*, *4*(4), 333–350. doi:10.1080/19322909.2010.487766

Ajzen, I. (1991). The theory of planned behavior. *Organizational Behavior and Human Decision Processes*, *50*(2), 179–211. doi:10.1016/0749-5978(91)90020-T

Aksit, K., Kade, D., Özcan, O., & Ürey, H. (2014). Head-worn Mixed Reality Projection Display Application. In *Proceedings of the 11th Conference on Advances in Computer Entertainment Technology*. ACM.

Alabbad, A. M. (2011). Interactive computer/network-based program for teaching English as a foreign language in the elementary levels in Saudi Arabia. In *Multimedia Computing and Systems (ICMCS), 2011 International Conference on* (pp. 1-4). IEEE.

Alcaraz-Valencia, P. A. (2008). *Aplicaciones del despliegue auditivo en ambientes virtuales de colaboración como soporte en el aprendizaje de un segundo idioma* [Auditory applications deployment in virtual environments to support collaborative learning in a second language] (Unpublished Master's thesis). Universidad de Colima, México.

Al-ghamdi, H. A. K., & Al-ghamdi, A. A. K. (2015). The role of virtual communities of practice in knowledge management using Web 2.0. *Procedia Computer Science*, *65*, 406–411. doi:10.1016/j.procs.2015.09.102

Alley, L. R., & Jansak, K. E. (2001). The ten keys to quality assurance and assessment in Online Learning. *Journal of Interactive Instruction Development*, 3-18.

Allinson, J., & Hayes, C. (1996). The cognitive style index, a measure of intuition-analysis for organizationresearch. *Journal of Management Studies, 33*(1), 119–135. doi:10.1111/j.1467-6486.1996.tb00801.x

Alquraini, H., Alhashem, A. M., Shah, M. A., & Chowdhury, R. I. (2007). Factors influencing nurses' attitudes towards the use of computerized health information systems in Kuwaiti hospitals. *Journal of Advanced Nursing, 57*(4), 375–381. doi:10.1111/j.1365-2648.2007.04113.x PMID:17291201

Al-Zoube, M. (2009). E-Learning on the Cloud. *Int. Arab J. e-Technol, 1*(2), 58-64.

Ammenwerth, E., Stefan, G., Gabriele, H., Burkle, T., & Konig, J. (2003). Evaluation of health information systems: Problems and challenges. *International Journal of Medical Informatics, 71*(2), 125–135. doi:10.1016/S1386-5056(03)00131-X PMID:14519405

Ander-egg, E. (1986). *Techniques of Social Investigation*. Buenos Aires: Hvmanitas.

Anderson, T. A., Reynolds, B. L., Yeh, X. P., & Huang, G. Z. (2008). Video games in the English as a foreign language classroom. In *Digital Games and Intelligent Toys Based Education, 2008 Second IEEE International Conference on* (pp. 188-192). IEEE. doi:10.1109/DIGITEL.2008.39

Andreadis, A., Hemery, A., Antonakakis, A., Gourdoglou, G., Mauridis, P., Christopoulos, D., & Karigiannis, J. N. (2010). Real-time motion capture technology on a live theatrical performance with computer generated scenery. *Informatics (pci), 14th panhellenic conference on. IEEE*, 148–152. doi:10.1109/PCI.2010.14

Andreoni, G. (2010). Sustainable Children's Product Experience. In F. Ceschin, C. Vezzoli, & J. Zhang (Eds.), *Proceedings of Sustainability in Design: Now!* (pp. 1184–1195). Bangalore, India: LENS.

Andrews, C., Endert, A., & North, C. (2010). *Space to think: large high-resolution displays for sensemaking*. Retrieved from http://dl.acm.org/citation.cfm?id=1753336

Andrews, C., Endert, A., & North, C. (2010). Space to think: Large high-resolution displays for sensemaking. In *CHI '10: Proceedings of the SIGCHI conference on human factors in computing systems* (pp. 55-64). ACM. doi:10.1145/1753326.1753336

Andriole, S. J. (2010). Business impact of Web 2.0 technologies. *Communications of the ACM, 53*(12), 67–79. doi:10.1145/1859204.1859225

Ang, R. P. (2016). Cyberbullying: Its prevention and intervention strategies. In D. Sibnath (Ed.), *Child safety, welfare and well-being: Issues and challenges* (pp. 25–38). Springer. doi:10.1007/978-81-322-2425-9_3

Anisova, T. L., Markov, V. K., & Ustinova, L. V. (2014). The use of presentation method in mathematics at University. *Sovremennye problemy nauki i obrazovanija, 2*. Retrieved from http://www.science-education.ru/pdf/2014/2/342.pdf

Anohina, A., & Grundspenkis, J. (2009). *Scoring concept maps: an overview*. Paper presented at the International Conference on Computer Systems and Technologies. CompSysTech'09. Retrieved from http://stpk.cs.rtu.lv/sites/all/files/stpk/alla/IV.8.pdf

Aoyama, I., Utsumi, S., & Hasegawa, M. (2011). Cyberbullying in Japan: Cases, government reports, adolescent relational aggression and parental monitoring roles. In Q. Li, D. Cross, & P. K. Smith (Eds.), *Bullying in the global playground: Research from an international perspective*. Oxford, UK: Wiley-Blackwell.

Aranha, C., & Passos, E. (2008). Automatic NLP for Competitive Intelligence. In H. A. Do-Prado & E. Ferneda (Eds.), *Emerging Technologies of Text Mining: Techniques and Applications* (pp. 54–76). IGI Global. doi:10.4018/978-1-59904-373-9.ch003

Arcà, M. (2009). *Insegnare biologia*. Pisa, Italy: Naturalmente Scienza.

Ardito, C., Buono, P., Costabile, M. F., & Desolda, G. (2015). Interaction with large displays: A survey. *ACM Comput. Surv., 47*(3), 46:1-46:38. doi:10.1145/2682623

Ardizzone, P., & Rivoltella, P. C. (2008). *Media e tecnologie per la didattica*. Milano, Italy: Vita e Pensiero.

Aricak, T., Siyahhan, S., Uzunhasanoglu, A., Saribeyoglu, S., Ciplak, S., Yilmaz, N., & Memmedov, C. (2008). Cyberbullying among Turkish adolescents. *Cyberpsychology & Behavior, 11*(3), 253–261. doi:10.1089/cpb.2007.0016 PMID:18537493

Arkhipova, L. M. (2012). Comics as an innovative method for the activation of cognitive sphere of students with mental retardation in the process of teaching history. *Jaroslavskij pedagogicheskij vestnik, 4*(2), 106-110.

Armitage, C. J., & Conner, M. (2001). Efficacy of the theory of planned behaviour: A meta-analytic review. *The British Journal of Social Psychology, 40*(4), 471–499. doi:10.1348/014466601164939 PMID:11795063

Aronson, I. D., Marsch, L. A., & Acosta, M. C. (2013). Using findings in multimedia learning to inform technology-based behavioral health interventions. *Translational Behavioral Medicine, 3*(3), 234–243. doi:10.1007/s13142-012-0137-4 PMID:24073174

Arslan, S., Savaser, S., Hallett, V., & Balci, S. (2012). Cyberbullying among primary school students in Turkey: Self-reported prevalence and associations with home and school life. *Cyberpsychology, Behavior, and Social Networking, 15*(10), 527–533. doi:10.1089/cyber.2012.0207 PMID:23002988

Arthur, C. (2013). *Google Launches tool to help users plan for digital afterlife*. Online article: http://www.theguardian.com/ technology/2013/apr/12/google-inactive-account-manager-digital-death

Attia, A., Aziz, N., Friedman, B., & Elhusseiny, M. (2011). Commentary: The impact of social networking tools on political change in Egypts 'Revolution 2.0. *Electronic Commerce Research and Applications, 10*(4), 369–374. doi:10.1016/j.elerap.2011.05.003

Augmented Reality Livens Up Museums I Innovation I Smithsonian. (n.d.). Retrieved from http://www.smithsonianmag.com/innovation/augmented-reality-livens-up-museums-22323417/?no-ist

Ayas, T., & Horzum, M. B. (2010). *Cyberbullg / victim scale development study*. Retrieved from: http://www.akademik-bakis.org

Bacon, S. M. (1992). The relationship between gender, comprehension, processing strategies, and cognitive and affective response in foreign language listening. *Modern Language Journal, 76*(2), 160–178. doi:10.1111/j.1540-4781.1992.tb01096.x

Badmaeva, N. C. (2000). *Motivational factors of formation of cognitive and memory abilities*. Ulan-Udje: Izd-vo VSGTU.

Baker, K., Greenberg, S., Gutwin, C., (2001). Heuristic Evaluation of Groupware Based on the Mechanics off Collaboration. *EHCI '01*, 123-139.

Balashova, J. V. (2011). *Cognitive and personality features of students of internal and distance education* (Unpublished candidate dissertation). Moscow.

Baldacci, M. (2001). *Metodologia della ricerca pedagogica*. Milano, Italy: Paravia Bruno Mondadori.

Bannan-Ritland, B., Dabbagh, N., & Murphy, K. (2000). Learning object systems as constructivist learning environments: Related assumptions, theories, and applications. In D. A. Wiley (Ed.), *The Instructional Use of Learning Objects: Online Version*. Retrieved May 2, 2007, from http://reusability.org/read/chapters/bannan-ritland.doc

Barbiero, G. (2012). Ecologia Affettiva per la Sostenibilità. *Culture della Sostenibilità, 10*, 126–139.

Barlett, C. P., & Gentile, D. A. (2012). Long-term psychological predictors of cyber-bullying in late adolescence. *Psychology of Popular Media Culture, 2*, 123–135. doi:10.1037/a0028113

Barlett, C. P., Gentile, D. A., Anderson, C. A., Suzuki, K., Sakamoto, A., Yamaoka, A., & Katsura, R. (2013). Cross-cultural differences in cyberbullying behavior: A short-term longitudinal study. *Journal of Cross-Cultural Psychology, 45*(2), 300–313. doi:10.1177/0022022113504622

Barros, B., & Verdejo, M. (2000). Analysing student interaction processes in order to improve collaboration. The DEGREE approach. *International Journal of Artificial Intelligence in Education, 11*(3), 221–241.

Barry, A., Thomas, G., Debenham, P., & Trout, J. (2012). Augmented reality in a public space: The natural history museum, london. *Computer, 45*(7), 42–47. doi:10.1109/MC.2012.106

Basto-Díaz, L., Madera-Ramírez, F., & Uicab-Ballote, R. (2012). *Apoyo de la enseñanza y aprendizaje de las fracciones en un videojuego basado en Web.* Retrieved May 10, 2014, from: https://intranet.matematicas.uady.mx

Bates, D. W., & Gawande, A. A. (2003). Improving safety with information technology. *The New England Journal of Medicine, 348*(25), 2526–2534. doi:10.1056/NEJMsa020847 PMID:12815139

Bauer, A. M., Thielke, S. M., Katon, W., Unützer, J., & Areán, P. (2014). Aligning health information technologies with effective service delivery models to improve chronic disease care. *Preventive Medicine, 66*, 167–172. doi:10.1016/j.ypmed.2014.06.017 PMID:24963895

Bauman, S., Toomey, R. B., & Walker, J. L. (2013). Associations among bullying, cyberbullying, and suicide in high school students. *Journal of Adolescence, 36*(2), 341–350. doi:10.1016/j.adolescence.2012.12.001 PMID:23332116

Bauman, S., Underwood, M. K., & Card, N. A. (2013). Definitions: Another perspective and a proposal for beginning with cyberaggression. In S. Bauman, D. Cross, & J. Walker (Eds.), *Principles of cyberbullying research: Definitions, measures, methodology* (pp. 26–40). New York, NY: Routledge.

Bauman, Z. (2000). *Liquid Modernity.* Oxford, UK: Blackwell Publishers.

Bayar, Y., & Ucanok, Z. (2012). School social climate and generalized peer perception in traditional and cyberbullying status. *Educational Sciences: Theory and Practice, 12*, 2352–2358.

Beckman, L., Hagquist, C., & Hellstrom, L. (2012). Does the association with psychosomatic health problems differ between cyberbullying and traditional bullying? *Emotional & Behavioural Difficulties, 17*(3-4), 421–434. doi:10.1080/13632752.2012.704228

Belanger, E., Bartlett, G., Dawes, M., Rodriguez, C., & Hasson-Gidoni, I. (2012). Examining the evidence of the impact of health information technology in primary care: An argument for participatory research with health professionals and patients. *International Journal of Medical Informatics, 81*(10), 654–661. doi:10.1016/j.ijmedinf.2012.07.008 PMID:22910233

Belavin, V. A., Golicyna, I. N., & Kucenko, S. N. (2000). The effectiveness of using simulative training systems in Technical University. *Obrazovatel'nye tehnologii i obshhestvo, 3*(2), 161-174.

Bell, M. W. (2008). Toward a definition of "virtual worlds". *Journal of Virtual Worlds Research, 1*(1).

Bellucci, A., Malizia, A., & Aeto, I. (2014). Light on horizontal interactive surfaces: Input space for tabletop computing. *ACM Computing Surveys, 46*(3), 1–42. Retrieved from http://dl.acm.org/citation.cfm?id=2500467 doi:10.1145/2500467

Belz, J. (2002). Social dimensions of telecollaborative foreign language study. *Language Learning & Technology, 6*(1), 60–81.

Benedek, J., & Miner, T. (2002). Measuring Desirability: New methods for evaluating desirability in a usability lab setting. *Proceedings of Usability Professionals Association, 2003,* 8–12.

Benedek, W., Veronika, B., & Matthias, K. (2008). *Internet Governance and the Information Society.* Eleven International Publishing.

Bennett, S., Bishop, A., Dalgarno, B., Waycott, J., & Kennedy, G. (2012). Implementing Web 2.0 technologies in higher education: A collective case study. *Computers & Education, 59*(2), 524–534. doi:10.1016/j.compedu.2011.12.022

Berdnikova, I. A. (2007). Conditions for increase of efficiency of educational material acquisition. *Materialy konferencii «Stanovlenija sovremennoj nauki».* Retrieved from http://www.rusnauka.com/17_SSN_2007/Pedagogica.htm

Bergehel, H. (1997). Cyberspace 2000: Dealing with Information Overload. *Communications of the ACM, 40*(2), 19–24. doi:10.1145/253671.253680

Berkenbrock, C., da Silva, A., & Hirata, C. (2009). Designing and Evaluating Interfaces for Mobile Groupware Systems. *Computer Supported Cooperative Work in Design, CSCWD,* 368-373.

Berner, E. S. (2008). Ethical and legal issues in the use of health information technology to improve patient safety. *HEC Forum, 20*(3), 243–258. doi:10.1007/s10730-008-9074-5 PMID:18803020

Berners-Lee, T. (2014). *World wide Web needs bill of rights.* Retrieved from http://www.bbc.co.uk/news/uk-26540635

Berners-Lee, T. (1999). *Weaving the Web.* New York: Harper.

Berthon, P. R., Pitt, L. F., Plangger, K., & Shapiro, D. (2012). Marketing meets Web 2.0, social media, and creative consumers: Implications for international marketing strategy. *Business Horizons, 55*(3), 261–271. doi:10.1016/j.bushor.2012.01.007

Bespalko, V. P. (1989). *Augends of educational technology.* Moscow.

Bhattacherjee, A., & Hikmet, N. (2007). Physicians' resistance toward healthcare information technology: A theoretical model and empirical test. *European Journal of Information Systems, 16*(6), 725–737. doi:10.1057/palgrave.ejis.3000717

Bigus, J. (2014, December 28). *Interactivity and Web-Based Courseware.* Retrieved from http://www.bigusbooks.com/mastersportfolio/products/InteractivityAndWebBasedCourseware.pdf

Bin Ghauth, K. I., & Abdullah, N. A. (2009). Building an e-learning recommender system using Vector Space Model and good learners average rating. In *Proceedings - 2009 9th IEEE International Conference on Advanced Learning Technologies, ICALT 2009* (pp. 194–196). Riga: IEEE.

Bi, X., Bae, S., & Balakrishnan, R. (2014). WallTop: Managing Overflowing Windows on a Large Display. *Human-Computer Interaction,* 1–59. Retrieved from http://www.tandfonline.com/doi/abs/10.1080/07370024.2013.812411

Bi, X., & Balakrishnan, R. (2009). Comparing usage of a large high-resolution display to single or dual desktop displays for daily work. *The SIGCHI Conference,* 1005. doi:10.1145/1518701.1518855

Bizzocchi, J., & Paras, B. (2005). Game, motivation, and effective learning: An integrated model for educational game design. In *Changing Views.* Vancouver, BC: Worlds in Play, Conference of the Digital Games Research Association.

Black, A. (2005). The use of asynchronous discussion: Creating a text of talk. *Contemporary Issues in Technology & Teacher Education.*

Bloom, B. S., & Krathwohl, D. R. (1956). *Taxonomy of educational objectives; the classification of educational goals. Handbook I: Cognitive Domain.* Addison-Wesley.

Blunt, R. (2014). *Interactivity vs Interaction in eLearning Design.* Retrieved January 4, 2016 from: https://www.linkedin.com

Bodenheimer, T. (2008). Coordinating care: A perilous journey through the health care system. *The New England Journal of Medicine, 358*(10), 1064–1071. doi:10.1056/NEJMhpr0706165 PMID:18322289

Bodenheimer, T., Wagner, E., & Grumbach, K. (2002). Improving primary care for patients with chronic illness: The chronic care model. *Journal of the American Medical Association, 288*(14), 1775–1779. doi:10.1001/jama.288.14.1775 PMID:12365965

Boettcher, J. (1999). *Nuggets about: the shift to web-based teaching and learning.* Florida State University.

Bonanno, R. A., & Hymel, S. (2013). Cyber bullying and internalizing difficulties: Above and beyond the impact of traditional forms of bullying. *Journal of Youth and Adolescence, 42*(5), 685–697. doi:10.1007/s10964-013-9937-1 PMID:23512485

Bonk, C., & Zhang, K. (2006). Introducing the R2D2 model: Online learning for the diverse learners of this world. *Distance Education, 27*(2), 249–264. doi:10.1080/01587910600789670

Bordin, S., Zancanaro, M., & De Angeli, A. (2013). *Touching dante: a proximity-based paradigm for tabletop browsing.* Retrieved from http://dl.acm.org/citation.cfm?id=2499172

Borgna, E. (2009). *Le emozioni ferite.* Milano, Italy: Feltrinelli.

Borisova, L. G. (2001). *Pedagogical conditions of formation of educational activity style of schoolchild* (Unpublished candidate dissertation). Kaliningrad.

Borkowski, J., Carr, M., & Pressely, M. (1987). Spontaneous strategy use: Perspectives from metacognitive theory. *Intelligence, 11*(1), 61–75. doi:10.1016/0160-2896(87)90027-4

Bosova, L. L., & Zubchenok, N. E. (2013). Electronic textbook: yesterday, today, tomorrow. *Obrazovatel'nye tehnologii i obshhestvo, 16*(3), 697-712.

Boulos, M. N. K., & Wheeler, S. (2007). The emerging Web 2.0 social software: An enabling suite of sociable technologies in health and health care education. *Health Information and Libraries Journal, 24*(1), 2–23. doi:10.1111/j.1471-1842.2007.00701.x PMID:17331140

Boulton, M., Lloyd, J., Down, J., & Marx, H. (2012). Predicting undergraduates self-reported engagement in traditional and cyberbullying from attitudes. *Cyberpsychology, Behavior, and Social Networking, 15*(3), 141–147. doi:10.1089/cyber.2011.0369 PMID:22304402

Boyle, J. P. (1984). Factors affecting listening comprehension. *ELT Journal, 38*(1), 34–38. doi:10.1093/elt/38.1.34

Bradbury, R. (1953). *Fahrenheit 451.* Milan: Mondadori.

Branton, B. (1999). *Visual literacy literature review.* Retrieved December 26, 2001, from http://vicu.utoronto.ca/staff/branton/litreview.html

Bridges, J. F. P. (2006). Lean systems approaches to health technology assessment. *PharmacoEconomics, 24*(2), 101–109. PMID:23389493

Brighi, A., Guarini, A., Melotti, G., Galli, S., & Genta, M. L. (2012). Predictors of victimisation across direct bullying, indirect bullying and cyberbullying. *Emotional & Behavioural Difficulties, 17*(3-4), 375–388. doi:10.1080/13632752. 2012.704684

British Museum - Augmented Reality. Beyond the Hype. (n.d.). Retrieved from http://www.museum-id.com/idea-detail. asp?id=336

Brown, S. A. (2012). Seeing Web 2.0 in context: A study of academic perceptions. *The Internet and Higher Education, 15*(1), 50–57. doi:10.1016/j.iheduc.2011.04.003

Bruck, S., & Watters, P. A. (2009). Estimating cybersickness of simulated motion using the simulator sickness questionnaire (ssq): A controlled study. In *Computer Graphics, Imaging and Visualization, CGIV'09. Sixth International Conference on*, (pp. 486–488). IEEE.

Bruner, J. (1966). *Toward a Theory of instruction*. Roma, Italy: Armando Editore.

Bruner, J. S. (1990). *Acts of meaning* (Vol. 3). Harvard University Press.

Brushlinskii, A. V., & Volovikova, M. I. (1983). About the interactions of procedural (dynamic) and personal (motivational) aspects of thinking. In D. Kovach et al. (Eds.), *Psychological researches of cognitive processes and personality* (pp. 84–96). Moscow: Nauka.

Buckingham, D. (2003). Media Education: Literacy, Learning and Contemporary Culture. Cambridge, UK: Polity Press.

Buckingham, D., & Willet, R. (Eds.). (2009). *Video Cultures. Media Technology and Everyday Creativity*. London: Palgrave Macmillian.

Bunge, M. (1981). *The science: Your Method and Your Philosophy*. Buenos Aires: Siglo XXI.

Burley-Allen, M. (1989). *Listening, the forgotten skill*. Retrieved November 10, 2012, from: http://agris.fao.org/

Burton, K. A., Florell, D., & Wygant, D. B. (2013). The role of peer attachment and normative beliefs about aggression on traditional bullying and cyberbullying. *Psychology in the Schools, 50*(2), 103–114. doi:10.1002/pits.21663

Buslova, N. S., Vychuzhanina, A. J., Klimenko, E.V., & Sheshukova, L.A. (2014). Semiotic features of presentation of information messages. *Sovremennye problemy nauki i obrazovanija, 3*. Retrieved from http://www.science-education. ru/117-13476

Butt, M. M., Sharif, M. M., Naseer-ud-Din, M., Hussain, I., Khan, F., & Ayesha, U. (2010). Listening comprehension problems among the students: A case study of three govt. boy's higher secondary schools. *European Journal of Soil Science, 18*(2), 311–315.

Buxton, B. (2009). Retrieved from http://www.billbuxton.com/multitouchOverview.html

Cakmakci, O., Ha, Y., & Rolland, J. P. (2004). A compact optical see-through head-worn display with occlusion support. *Proceedings of the 3rd IEEE/ACM International Symposium on Mixed and Augmented Reality*, 16–25. doi:10.1109/ ISMAR.2004.2

Calderón, D. (2015). Introducción: el derecho a aprender inglés. *Sorry. El aprendizaje del inglés en México, Mexicanos Primero, 28*.

Calongne, C. M. (2008). Educational Frontiers: Learning in a virtual world. *EDUCAUSE Review, 43*(5), 36–48.

Calvani, A. (Ed.). (2007). *Fondamenti di didattica. Teoria e prassi dei dispositivi formativi*. Roma, Italy: Carocci Editore.

Canfield, A. A., & Lafferty, L. C. (1974). *Learning styles inventory*. Birmingham, MI: Humanics Media.

Canova, G. (Ed.). (2002). *Storia del cinema Italyno 1965-1969* (Vol. 11). Venezia-Roma, Italy: Marsilio Editore.

Cappadocia, M. C., Craig, W. M., & Pepler, D. (2013). Cyberbullying: Prevalence, stability and risk factors during adolescence. *Canadian Journal of School Psychology, 28*(2), 171–192. doi:10.1177/0829573513491212

Carpenter, J., Green, M., & LaFlam, J. (2011). People or profiles: Individual differences in online social networking use. *Personality and Individual Differences, 50*(5), 538–541. doi:10.1016/j.paid.2010.11.006

Carr, N. (2010). *The Shallows. What the Internet is Doing to Our Brains.* New York: W.W. Norton.

Carroll, J. M. (2002). *Human-Computer Interaction in the new Millennium.* Addison-Wesley.

Casey, D. M. (2008). A journey to legitim acy: The historical developm ent of distance education through technology. *TechTrends*, 45–51.

Cassidy, W., Brown, K., & Jackson, M. (2012a). Making kind cool: Parents suggestions for preventing cyber bullying and fostering cyber kindness. *Journal of Educational Computing Research, 46*(4), 415–436. doi:10.2190/EC.46.4.f

Cassidy, W., Brown, K., & Jackson, M. (2012b). Under the radar: Educators and cyberbullying in schools. *School Psychology International, 33*(5), 520–532. doi:10.1177/0143034312445245

Cassirer, E. (2009). *Saggio sull'uomo.* Roma, Italy: Armando Editore.

CD-Rom QUITSA-TO. (2003). *Catequilla: The Real Middle of the world.* Quito.

Cerioli, L. (2002). *Funzione educativa e competenze relazionali. Genitori, figli, insegnanti.* Milano, Italy: Franco Angeli.

Césari, M. I. (2007). *Cartografiado de Textos. Protocolo de Exploración y Visualización de datos textuales aplicados a la Minería de Textos* (Unpublished master's thesis). Universidad Politecnica de Madrid, España.

Chaboissier, J., Isenberg, T., & Vernier, F. (2011). RealTimeChess: Lessons from a participatory design process for a collaborative multi-touch, multi-user game. *Conference ITS, 11*(November), 97–106. doi:10.1145/2076354.2076374

Chalufour, I., & Worth, K. (2004). *Building structure with young children.* St. Paul, MN: Redleaf Press.

Chamberlin, L., & Parish, T. (2011). MOOCs: Massive Open Online Coursesor Massive and Often Obtuse Courses? *E- learn Magazine.*

Chang, L. W. (2007). *A case study on four junior high school students' experiences in developing EFL listening strategies* (Unpublished Master's thesis). National Chengchi University, Taipei.

Chang, B. L., Bakken, S., Brown, S. S., Houston, T. K., Kreps, G. L., Kukafka, R., & Stavri, P. Z. et al. (2004). Bridging the digital divide: Reaching vulnerable populations. *Journal of the American Medical Informatics Association, 11*(6), 448–457. doi:10.1197/jamia.M1535 PMID:15299002

Charmet, P. G. (2009). *Fragile e spavaldo. Ritratto dell'adolescente di oggi.* Roma-Bari, Italy: Laterza.

Chatham, R. (2007). Games for Training. *Communications of the ACM, 50*(7), 36–43. doi:10.1145/1272516.1272537

Chatti, M. A., Jarke, M., & Frosch-Wike, D. (2007). The future of e-learning: A shift to knowledge networking and social software. *International Journal of Knowledge and Learning, 3*(4/5), 404–420. doi:10.1504/IJKL.2007.016702

Chau, P. Y. K., & Hu, P. J. (2001). Information technology acceptance by individual professionals: A model comparison approach. *Decision Sciences, 32*(4), 699–719. doi:10.1111/j.1540-5915.2001.tb00978.x

Chaves, M. S., Gomes, R., & Pedron, C. (2012). Analysing reviews in the Web 2.0: Small & medium hotels in Portugal. *Tourism Management, 33*(5), 1286–1287. doi:10.1016/j.tourman.2011.11.007

Chellappan, E., Erden, E., & Urey, H. (2010). Laser-based displays: A review. *Applied Optics, 49*(25), 79–98. doi:10.1364/AO.49.000F79 PMID:20820205

Chen, I. J., Yang, K. F., Tang, F. I., Huang, C. H., & Yu, S. (2007). Applying the technology acceptance model to explore public health nurses' intentions towards web-based learning: A cross-sectional questionnaire survey. *International Journal of Nursing Studies, 465*(6), 869–878. PMID:17482191

Chen, S. C., Yen, D. C., & Hwang, M. I. (2012). Factors influencing the continuance intention to the usage of Web 2.0: An empirical study. *Computers in Human Behavior, 28*(3), 933–941. doi:10.1016/j.chb.2011.12.014

Chen, W. (2006). Supporting teachers intervention in collaborative knowledge building. *Journal of Network and Computer Applications, 29*(2-3), 200–215. doi:10.1016/j.jnca.2005.01.001

Chen, W. F., Chen, M. H., Chen, M. L., & Ku, L. W. (2015). A Computer-Assistance Learning System for Emotional Wording. *IEEE Transactions on Knowledge and Data Engineering, 99*, 1.

Chen, W., & Wasson, B. (2005). Intelligent Agents Supporting Distributed Collaborative Learning. In F. Lin (Ed.), *Designing Distributed Learning Environments with Intelligent Software Agents* (pp. 33–66). IGI Global. doi:10.4018/978-1-59140-500-9.ch002

Chernokova, T. E. (2011). Metacognitive psychology: the problem of a research subject. *Vestnik Severnogo (Arkticheskogo) federal'nogo universiteta. Serija Gumanitarnye i social'nye nauki, 3*, 153-158.

Chickering, A. W., & Gamson, Z. F. (1987). Seven principles for good practice in undergraduate education. *AAHE Bulletin*, 3–6.

Choi, S., Lim, C., & Leem, J. (2002). *Effects of Different Types of Interaction on Learning Achievement, Satisfaction and Participation in Web-Based Instruction, Innovations in Education and Teaching International*. Academic Press.

Chowdhury, G. G. (2005). Natural language processing. *Annual Review of Information Science & Technology, 37*(1), 51–89. doi:10.1002/aris.1440370103

Christopher, B. (2013). *Learning about social learning in MOOCs: From statistical analysis to generative model*. Academic Press.

Chung, L. Y. (2012). Virtual Reality in College English Curriculum: Case Study of Integrating Second Life in Freshman English Course. In *Advanced Information Networking and Applications Workshops (WAINA), 2012 26th International Conference on* (pp. 250-253). IEEE.

Churchill, D. (2011). Web 2.0 in education: A study of the explorative use of blogs with a postgraduate class. *Innovations in Education and Teaching International, 48*(2), 149–158. doi:10.1080/14703297.2011.564009

Chu, S. K. W., Woo, M., King, R. B., Choi, S., Cheng, M., & Koo, P. (2012). Examining the application of Web 2.0 in medical-related organisations. *Health Information and Libraries Journal, 29*(1), 47–60. doi:10.1111/j.1471-1842.2011.00970.x PMID:22335289

CIDAC. (2008). *Encuesta CIDAC: Capital Humano en México*. Retrieved January 10, 2012, from: http://www.cidac.org/

Cipolla-Ficarra, F. (1996). A User Evaluation of Hypermedia Iconography. In Proceedings Computergraphics. Paris: GRASP.

Cipolla-Ficarra, F. (1993). Cartografía e Infografía: Una Convergencia Magistral. [In Spanish]. *Imaging*, *10*(December), 24–31.

Cipolla-Ficarra, F. (1999). Investigación y desarrollo en la infografia empresarial. [In Spanish]. *AutoCAD Magazine*, *60*, 62–66.

Cipolla-Ficarra, F. (2010). *Quality and Communicability for Interactive Hypermedia Systems: Concepts and Practices for Design*. Hershey, PA: IGI Global. doi:10.4018/978-1-61520-763-3

Cipolla-Ficarra, F. (2011). The Expansion Era of the Communicability: First Nations for the Local and Global Promotion of Cultural and Natural Heritage. In *Proc. Human-Computer Interaction, Tourism and Cultural Heritage* (pp. 25–37). Heidelberg, Germany: Springer. doi:10.1007/978-3-642-18348-5

Cipolla-Ficarra, F. (2013a). *Emerging Software for Interactive Interfaces, Database, Computer Graphics and Animation*. Bergamo: Blue Herons Editions.

Cipolla-Ficarra, F. (2013b). *Computer Engineering and Innovations in Education for Virtual Learning Environments, Intelligent Systems and Communicability*. Bergamo: Blue Herons Editions.

Cipolla-Ficarra, F. (2014). *Advanced Research and Trends in New Technologies, Software, Human-Computer Interaction and Communicability*. Hershey, PA: IGI Global. doi:10.4018/978-1-4666-4490-8

Cipolla-Ficarra, F. (2015). *Handbook of Research on Interactive Information Quality in Expanding Social Network Communications*. Hershey, PA: IGI Global. doi:10.4018/978-1-4666-7377-9

Cipolla-Ficarra, F., & Ficarra, V. (2012). Motivation for Next Generation of Users Versus Parochialism in Software Engineering. In *Proc. Second International Conference on Advances in New Technologies, Interactive Interfaces and Communicability*. Heidelberg, Germany: Springer.

Cipolla-Ficarra, F., & Ficarra, V. (2014). Anti-Models for Universitary Education: Analysis of the Catalans Cases in Information and Communication Technologies. In *Advanced Research and Trends in New Technologies, Software, Human-Computer Interaction and Communicability*. Hershey, PA: IGI Global. doi:10.4018/978-1-4666-4490-8.ch005

Cipolla-Ficarra, F., Ficarra, V., & Cipolla-Ficarra, M. (2012). New Technologies of the Information and Communication: Analysis of the Constructors and Destructors of the European Educational System. In *Proc. Second International Conference on Advances in New Technologies, Interactive Interfaces and Communicability*. Heidelberg, Germany: Springer.

Cipolla-Ficarra, F., & Kratky, A. (2012). Computer Graphics for Students of the Factual Sciences. In *Proc. First International Symposium Communicability, Computer Graphics and Innovative Design for Interactive Systems*. Heidelberg, Germany: Springer. doi:10.1007/978-3-642-33760-4_7

Clark, D. (1989). An Analysis of TCP Processing Overhead. Biography. *IEEE Communications Magazine*, 29.

Claxton, K. P., & Sculpher, M. J. (2006). Using value of information analysis to prioritise health research. *Pharmaco-Economics*, *24*(11), 1055–1068. doi:10.2165/00019053-200624110-00003 PMID:17067191

Cobb, S. V. G., Nichols, S., Ramsey, A., & Wilson, J. R. (1999). Virtual reality-induced symptoms and effects (vrise). *Presence (Cambridge, Mass.)*, *8*(2), 169–186. doi:10.1162/105474699566152

Coeckelbergh, M. (2013). E-care as craftsmanship: Virtuous work, skilled engagement, and information technology in health care. *Medicine, Health Care, and Philosophy*, *16*(4), 807–816. doi:10.1007/s11019-013-9463-7 PMID:23338289

Collier, R. J., Burckhardt, C. B., & Lin, L. H. (2006). Optical Holography. Academic.

Colvin-Sterling, S. (2016). The correlation between temperament, technology preference, and proficiency in middle school students. *Journal of Information Technology Education: Research, 15*, 1–18.

Computing curricula. The overview report. (2005). Retrieved from http://www.acm.org/education/curric_vols/CC2005-March06Final.pdf

Constantino-González, M., Suthers, D. D., & Escamilla-De-Los-Santos, J. D. (2003). Coaching Web-based Collaborative Learning based on Problem Solution Differences and Participation. *International Journal of Artificial Intelligence in Education, 13*(2-4), 263–299.

Consulta Mitofsky. (2013). *Mexicanos y los idiomas extranjeros*. Retrieved July 8, 2014, from: http://consulta.mx/

Coppin, B. (2004). *Artificial Intelligence Illuminated*. Jones and Bartlett Publishers.

Corcoran, L., Connolly, I., & OMoore, M. (2012). Cyberbullying in Irish schools: An investigation of personality and self-concept. *The Irish Journal of Psychology, 33*(4), 153–165. doi:10.1080/03033910.2012.677995

Costaguta, R., García, P., & Amandi, A. (2011). Using Agent for Training Students Collaborative Skills. *IEEE Latin America Transactions, 9*(7), 1118–1124. doi:10.1109/TLA.2011.6129712

Cronin, J. J. (2009). Upgrading to Web 2.0: An experimental project to build a marketing wiki. *Journal of Marketing Education, 31*(1), 66–75. doi:10.1177/0273475308329250

Csikszentmihalyi, M. (1990). *Flow: The Psychology of Optimal Experience*. New York: Harper and Row.

Curelaru, M., Iacob, I., & Abalasei, B. (2009). *School bullying: Definition, characteristics, and intervention strategies*. Lumean Publishing House.

Curry, D. B. (2014, December 28). *Collaborative, Connected and Experiential Learning: Reflections of an Online Learner*. Retrieved from http://www.mtsu.edu/~itconf/proceed01/2.html

Czerwinski, M., Tan, D. S., & Robertson, G. G. (2002). Women Take a Wider View. In Proceedings of {ACM} {CHI} 2002 (Vol. 4, pp. 195–202). doi:10.1145/503376.503412

Czerwinski, M., Smith, G., Regan, T., Meyers, B., Robertson, G., & Starkweather, G. (2003). *Toward characterizing the productivity benefits of very large displays* (Vol. 3). Proc. Interact.

Czerwinsky Domenis, L. (2000). *La discussione intelligente*. Trento, Italy: Erickson.

Dabbagh, N., & Kitsantas, A. (2012). Personal learning environments, social media, and self-regulated learning: A natural formula for connecting formal and informal learning. *The Internet and Higher Education, 15*(1), 3–8. doi:10.1016/j.iheduc.2011.06.002

Dalgarno, B., & Lee, M. J. (2010). What are the learning affordances of 3-D virtual environments? *British Journal of Educational Technology, 41*(1), 10–32. doi:10.1111/j.1467-8535.2009.01038.x

Dallari, M. (2008). *In una notte di luna vuota. Educare pensieri metaforici, laterali, impertinenti*. Trento, Italy: Erickson.

Daniel, J. (2012). Making sense of MOOCs: Musings in a m aze of m yth, paradox and possibility. *Journal of Interactive Media in Education, 2012*(3), 18. doi:10.5334/2012-18

Dasarathy, B., Sullivan, K., Schmidt, D. C., Fisher, D. H., & Porter, A. (May de 2014). The past, present, and future of MOOCs and their relevance to software. *Proceedings of the on Future of Software Engineering*, 212-224. doi:10.1145/2593882.2593897

Dascalu, M.-I., Bodea, C.-N., Moldoveanu, A., Mohora, A., Lytras, M., & de Pablos, P. O. (2015). A recommender agent based on learning styles for better virtual collaborative learning experiences. *Computers in Human Behavior, 45,* 243–253. doi:10.1016/j.chb.2014.12.027

Dass, S., Dabbagh, N., & Clark, K. (2011). Using virtual worlds: What the research says. *Quarterly Review of Distance Education, 12*(2), 95.

Davis, F. D., & Venkatesh, V. (1995). *Measuring user acceptance of emerging information technologies: An assessment of possible method biases.* Paper presented at the 28th Annual Hawaii International Conference on System Sciences, Maui, HI. doi:10.1109/HICSS.1995.375675

Davis, F. D. (1989). Perceived usefulness, perceived ease of use, and user acceptance of information technology. *Management Information Systems Quarterly, 13*(3), 319–340. doi:10.2307/249008

Davis, K., Doty, M. M., Shea, K., & Stremikis, K. (2009). Health information technology and physician perceptions of quality of care and satisfaction. *Health Policy (Amsterdam), 90*(2/3), 239–246. doi:10.1016/j.healthpol.2008.10.002 PMID:19038472

Davison, R. M., Ou, C. X. J., Martinsons, M. G., Zhao, A. Y., & Du, R. (2014). The communicative ecology of Web 2.0 at work: Social networking in the workspace. *Journal of the Association for Information Science and Technology, 65*(10), 2035–2047. doi:10.1002/asi.23112

Davis, S. (2009). *Interactive drama using cyberspaces.* Drama Education with Digital Technology.

Davydov, V. V. (1986). *Problems of developmental teaching: The experience of theoretical and experimental psychological research.* Moscow: Pedagogika.

De Kerckhove, D. (1999). *The Skin of Culture: Investigating the New Electronic Reality.* London: Kogan Page.

Dehling, T., & Sunyaev, A. (2014). Secure provision of patient-centered health information technology services in public networks–leveraging security and privacy features provided by the German nationwide health information technology infrastructure. *Electronic Markets, 24*(2), 89–99. doi:10.1007/s12525-013-0150-6

Dehue, F., Bolman, C., & Vollink, T. (2008). Cyberbullying: Youngsters experiences and parental perception. *CyberPscyhology & Behavior, 11*(2), 217–223. doi:10.1089/cpb.2007.0008 PMID:18422417

Dehue, F., Bolman, C., Vollink, T., & Pouwelse, M. (2012). Cyberbullying and traditional bullying in relation to adolescents' perceptions of parenting. *Journal of Cyber Therapy and Rehabilitation, 5,* 25–34.

deLara, E. W. (2012). Why adolescents dont disclose incidents of bullying and harassment. *Journal of School Violence, 11*(4), 288–305. doi:10.1080/15388220.2012.705931

Dent, B., Torguson, J., & Hodler, T. (2008). *Cartography Thematic Map Design.* New York: McGraw Hill.

Descartes, R. (1637). *Discourse on the Method of Rightly Conducting the Reason, and Seeking Truth in the Sciences.* Cambridge, UK: Cambridge University Press.

Descartes, R. (1641). *Mediations on First Philosophy.* Cambridge, UK: Cambridge University Press.

Diamanduros, T., & Downs, E. (2011). Creating a safe school environment: How to prevent cyberbullying at your school. *Library Media Connection, 30*(2), 36–38.

Diaz, L. A. (2009). Are the functions of teachers in e-learning and face-to-face learning environments really different? *Journal of Educational Technology & Society.*

Dickey, M. D. (2005). Three-dimensional virtual worlds and distance learning: Two case studies of Active Worlds as a medium for distance education. *British Journal of Educational Technology, 36*(3), 439–451. doi:10.1111/j.1467-8535.2005.00477.x

Dietz, P., & Eidelson, B. (2009). *SurfaceWare: dynamic tagging for Microsoft Surface.* Retrieved from http://dl.acm.org/citation.cfm?id=1517717

Dim, E., & Kuflik, T. (2014). Automatic detection of social behavior of museum visitor pairs. *ACM Trans. Interact. Intell. Syst., 4*(4), 17:1-17:30. doi:10.1145/2662869

Dimond, T. L. (1957). Devices for reading handwritten characters. *IRE-ACM-AIEE '57 (Eastern): Proceedings of the Eastern Joint Computer Conference: Computers with Deadlines to Meet,* 232–237. doi:10.1145/1457720.1457765

D'Incerti, D., Santoro, M., & Varchetta, G. (2007). *Nuovi schermi di formazione.* Milano, Italy: Guerini & Associati.

Dirven, R., & Oakeshott-Taylor, J. (1984). Listening comprehension (Part I). *Language Teaching, 17*(04), 326–343. doi:10.1017/S026144480001082X

Dix, A., Finlay, J., Abowd, G. D., & Beale, R. (2004). *Human-Computer Interaction* (3rd ed.). Milan, Italy: Pearson Education/Prentice Hall.

Dixon, S. (2007). *Digital performance: a history of new media in theater, dance, performance art, and installation.* MIT Press.

Doebbeling, B. N., Chou, A. F., & Tierney, W. M. (2006). Priorities and strategies for the implementation of integrated informatics and communications technology to improve evidence-based practice. *Journal of General Internal Medicine, 21*(2), S50–S57. doi:10.1007/s11606-006-0275-9 PMID:16637961

Does Technology Cut Us Off From Other People? (n.d.). Retrieved from http://greatergood.berkeley.edu/article/item/does_technology_cut_us_off_from_other_people#

Doeweling, S. (2010). Drop-and-drag: easier drag & drop on large touchscreen displays. *Proceedings of the 6th Nordic Conference,* 158–167. http://doi.org/ doi:10.1145/1868914.1868936

Dominici, P. (2014). *Dentro la Società Interconnessa. Prospettive etiche per un nuovo ecosistema della comunicazione.* Milano, Italy: Franco Angeli.

Dönmez, P., Rosé, C., Stegmann, K., Weinberger, A., & Fischer, F. (2005). Supporting CSCL with automatic corpus analysis technology. In *Proceedings of th2005 Conference on Computer Support for Collaborative Learning: Learning 2005: The next 10 Years!* (pp. 125–134). International Society of the Learning Sciences. doi:10.3115/1149293.1149310

Doolin, B. (2004). Power and resistance in the implementation of a medical management information system. *Information Systems Journal, 14*(4), 343–362. doi:10.1111/j.1365-2575.2004.00176.x

Do-Prado, A. H., & Ferneda, E. (2008). *Emerging Technologies of Text Mining : Techniques and Applications.* IGI Global. doi:10.4018/978-1-59904-373-9

Dorsey, M. (2011). *Pearson Assignments: Quizzes, Tests, and Homework Explained.* Retrieved from http://www.myaccountinglabcommunity.com/custom/scripts/google-search-init.js

Dougherty, M., & Meyer, E. T. (2014). Community, tools, and practices in web archiving: The state-of-the-art in relation to social science and humanities research needs. *Journal of the Association for Information Science and Technology, 65*(11), 2195–2209. doi:10.1002/asi.23099

Dow, S. P., Glassco, A., Kass, J., Schwarz, M., Schwartz, D. L., & Klemmer, R., S. (2010). Parallel prototyping leads to better design results, more divergence, and increased self-efficacy. *Transactions on Computer-Human Interaction (TOCHI), 17*(4).

Dowling, R. A. (2013). Health information technology in urologic care: Current status and implications for quality of care. *Current Urology Reports, 14*(6), 535–540. doi:10.1007/s11934-013-0356-3 PMID:23881730

Drexler, W. (2010). The networked student model for construction of personal learning environments: Balancing teacher control and student autonomy. *Australasian Journal of Educational Technology, 26*(3), 369–385. doi:10.14742/ajet.1081

Drusian, M., & Riva, C. (Eds.). (2010). *Bricoleur High tech. I giovani e le nuove forme di comunicazione.* Milano, Italy: Guerini & Associati.

Druz, I. N. (2013). The formation of future engineers' readiness to profession using new technologies of modeling. *Vestnik Har'kovskogo nacional'nogo avtomobil'no-dorozhnogo universiteta, 60,* 12-16.

Dubberly, H., Pangaro, P., & Haque, U. (2009). ON MODELING What is interaction? are there different types?. *Interactions, 16*(1), 69-75.

Duff, W. (1997). *The Indian History of British Columbia: The Impact of the White Man.* Victoria: Royal British Columbia Museum.

Dvoryadkina, S. N. (2011). Conceptual ideas of model of learning the probability theory and statistics focused on complex training of students of technical and humanitarian sciences. *Teorija i praktika obshhestvennogo razvitija, 7,* 168-172.

Eccleston, D., & Griseri, L. (2008). How does Web 2.0 stretch traditional influencing patterns? *International Journal of Market Research, 50*(5), 591–616. doi:10.2501/S1470785308200055

Eco, U. (1977). *A Theory of Semiotics.* Bloomington, IN: Indiana University Press.

Eden, S., Heiman, T., & Olenik-Shemesh, D. (2013). Teachers perceptions, beliefs and concerns about cyberbullying. *British Journal of Educational Technology, 44*(6), 1036–1052. doi:10.1111/j.1467-8535.2012.01363.x

Edmonds, E. A. (2007). Reflections on the nature of interaction†. *CoDesign, 3*(3), 139–143. doi:10.1080/15710880701251427

Edoh, T. O., & Teege, G. (2011). Using information technology for an improved pharmaceutical care delivery in developing countries. Study case: Benin. *Journal of Medical Systems, 35*(5), 1123–1134. doi:10.1007/s10916-011-9717-y PMID:21519942

Education First. (2013). *Índice de Nivel en Inglés (EF EPI) Reporte 2013.* Retrieved January 4, 2015, from: http://www.ef.com.mx/

Education First. (2014). *Índice de Nivel en Inglés (EF EPI) Reporte 2014.* Retrieved January 4, 2015, from: http://www.ef.com.mx

Edvardsen, F., & Kulle, H. (2010). *Educational Games: Design, Learning and Applications.* New York: Nova.

Ehrman, M. E., Leaver, B. L., & Oxford, R. L. (2003). A brief overview of individual differences in second language learning. *System, 31*(3), 313–330. doi:10.1016/S0346-251X(03)00045-9

e-Learners.com. (2014, December 28). *Synchronous vs. asynchronous classes.* Retrieved from http://www.elearners.com/online-education-resources/online-learning/synchronous-vs-asynchronous-classes/

Elledge, L. C., Williford, A., Boulton, A. J., DePaolis, K. J., Little, T. D., & Salmivalli, C. (2013). Individual and contextual predictors of cyberbullying: The influence of childrens provictim attitudes and teachers ability to intervene. *Journal of Youth and Adolescence*, *42*(5), 698–710. doi:10.1007/s10964-013-9920-x PMID:23371005

Ellis, C. A., Gibbs, S. J., & Rein, G. (1991). Groupware: Some Issues and Experiences. *Communications of the ACM*, *34*(1), 39–58. doi:10.1145/99977.99987

Ellison, N., Steinfield, C., & Lampe, C. (2007). The benefits of Facebook friends: Social capital and college students use of online social network sites. *Journal of Computer-Mediated Communication*, *12*(4), 1143–1168. doi:10.1111/j.1083-6101.2007.00367.x

Ellis, S. R. (1991). Nature and origins of virtual environments: A bibliographical essay. *Computing Systems in Engineering*, *2*(4), 321–347. doi:10.1016/0956-0521(91)90001-L

Epps, J., Lichman, S., & Wu, M. (2006). A study of hand shape use in tabletop gesture interaction. *CHI '06 Extended Abstracts on Human Factors in Computing Systems - CHI EA '06*, 748. 10.1145/1125451.1125601

Erdur-Baker, O. (2010). Cyberbullying and its correlation to traditional bullying, gender and frequent and risky usage of internet-mediated communication tools. *New Media & Society*, *12*(1), 109–125. doi:10.1177/1461444809341260

Eschenbrenner, B., Nah, F. F.-H., & Siau, K. (2008). 3-D Virtual Worlds in Education: Applications, Benefits, Issues, and Opportunities. *Journal of Database Management*, *19*(4), 91–110. doi:10.4018/jdm.2008100106

Esposito, L. (2012). Le TIC e la promozione della competenza digitale. La nuova sfida della scuola 2.0. *OPPInformazioni*, *113*, 1–10.

European Commission, DG Education and Culture. (2004). *Study on Innovative Learning Environments in School Education*. Final Report.

Eysenbach, G. (2008). Medicine 2.0: Social networking, collaboration, participation, apomediation, and openness. *Journal of Medical Internet Research*, *10*(3), e22. doi:10.2196/jmir.1030 PMID:18725354

Fanti, K. A., Demetriou, A. G., & Hawa, V. V. (2012). A longitudinal study of cyberbullying: Examining risk and protective factors. *European Journal of Developmental Psychology*, *8*(2), 168–181. doi:10.1080/17405629.2011.643169

Faust, D. F., & Courtenay, B. C. (2002). Interaction in the intergenerational freshman class: What matters. *Educational Gerontology*, *28*(5), 401–422. doi:10.1080/03601270290081362-2038

Fechner, T., Wilhelm, D. & Kray, C. (2015). Ethermap-Real-time Collaborative Map Editing. *CHI'15 Interactive & Multi-surface Maps*, 3583-3592. DOI: 10.1145/2702123.2702536

Felder, R., & Silverman, L. (1988). Learning and teaching styles in engineering education. *English Education*, *78*(7), 674–681.

Feldman, R., & Sanger, J. (2007). *The text mining handbook: advanced approaches in analyzing unstructured data*. Cambridge University Press.

Felfernig, A., Friedrich, G., & Schmidt-Thieme, L. (2007). Recommender Systems. *IEEE Intelligent Systems*, *22*(May/June), 18–21. doi:10.1109/MIS.2007.52

Ferreira-Soaje, V. (2011). *Cerro Colorado: Una Luz de Otros Tiempos*. Córdoba: Ediciones del Boulevard. In Spanish

Ferri, P. (2011). *Nativi Digitali*. Milano, Italy: Bruno Mondadori Editore.

Festl, R., Schwarkow, M., & Quandt, T. (2013). Peer influence, internet use and cyberbullying: A comparison of different context effects among German adolescents. *Journal of Children and Media*, 7(4), 446–462. doi:10.1080/17482 798.2013.781514

Fieschi, M. (2002). Information technology is changing the way society sees health care delivery. *International Journal of Medical Informatics*, 66(3), 85–93. doi:10.1016/S1386-5056(02)00040-0 PMID:12453562

Fishbein, M., & Ajzen, I. (1975). *Belief, attitude, intention, and behavior: An introduction to theory and research*. Reading, MA: Addison–Wesley.

Foucault, M. (1975). *Discipline and Punishment*. Milan: Einaudi.

Fox, G., & Pierce, M. (2009). Grids challenged by a Web 2.0 and multicore sandwich. *Concurrency and Computation*, 21(3), 265–280. doi:10.1002/cpe.1358

Franza, A. M. (1988). *Retorica e metaforica in pedagogia. Milano, Italy: Unicopli- (1993). Giovani satiri e vecchi sileni*. Milano, Italy: Unicopli.

Frederickson, B. B. L. (2013, March 23). Your phone vs. your heart. *The New York Times*.

Frolov, I. N. (2011). E-didactics as a theoretical basis of e-learning. *V mire nauchnyh otkrytij. Serija: «Problemy nauki i obrazovanija»*, 2(14), 135-142.

Fuchs, C. (2011). New media, Web 2.0 and surveillance. *Social Compass*, 5(2), 134–147. doi:10.1111/j.1751-9020.2010.00354.x

Fuji, K. T., & Galt, K. A. (2008). Pharmacists and health information technology: Emerging issues in patient safety. *HEC Forum*, 20(3), 259–275. doi:10.1007/s10730-008-9075-4 PMID:18803019

Furtado, A., Santos, A., Ramalho, G., & de Almeida, E. S. (2011). Improving Digital Game Develpoment with Software Product Lines. *IEEE Software*, 28(5), 30–37. doi:10.1109/MS.2011.101

Future Learn. (2013). *Future learn launches*. Retrieved January 04, 2015, from http://futurelearn.com/feature/futurelearn-launches

Gagliardi, R., Gabbari, M., & Gaetano, A. (2010). *La scuola con la LIM: guida didattica per la lavagna interattiva multimediale*. Brescia, Italy: La Scuola.

Gambini, A., Pezzotti, A., & Broglia, A. (2008). Sussidiari ed esperienze didattiche di tipo pratico: due modi contrapposti con cui affrontare a scuola la complessità dei temi ambientali. In G. Giordani, V. Rossi, & P. Viaroli (Eds.), *Ecologia Emergenza Pianificazione. Proceedings of XVIII Congresso Nazionale della Società Italiana di Ecologia, Parma, 1-3 settembre 2008* (pp. 280-288). Retrieved from http://www.dsa.unipr.it/sitecongresso/node/9

Gambini, A., Pezzotti, A., & Samek Lodovici, P. (2005). An online Biology course: A teaching-learning experiment. *Je-LKS*, 1(2), 223–231.

Gangadharbatla, H. (2010). Facebook me: Collective self-esteem, need to belong, and internet self- efficacy as predictors of the attitudes toward social networking sites. *Journal of Interactive Advertising*, 8(2), 5–15. doi:10.1080/152520 19.2008.10722138

García-Adeva, J. J., & Calvo, R. (2006). Mining text with pimiento. *IEEE Internet Computing*, 10(4), 27–35. doi:10.1109/MIC.2006.85

Gardois, P., Colombi, N., Grillo, G., & Villanacci, M. C. (2012). Implementation of Web 2.0 services in academic, medical and research libraries: A scoping review. *Health Information and Libraries Journal*, *29*(2), 90–109. doi:10.1111/j.1471-1842.2012.00984.x PMID:22630358

Garrison, D., & Kanuka, H. (2004). Blended learning: Uncovering its transformative potential in higher education. *The Internet and Higher Education*, *7*(2), 95–105. doi:10.1016/j.iheduc.2004.02.001

Gauthier, K. (2014). Starting the conversation: A health information technology tool to address pediatric obesity. *The Journal for Nurse Practitioners*, *10*(10), 813–819. doi:10.1016/j.nurpra.2014.06.007

Gedikli, F. (2013). *Recommender Systems and the Social Web. Leveraging Tagging Data for Recommender Systems*. Springer.

Geigel, J., & Schweppe, M. (2004). Theatrical story telling in a virtual space. *Proceedings of the 1st ACM workshop on Story representation, mechanism and context*, 39–46. doi:10.1145/1026633.1026642

Genesee, F. (1985). Second Language Learning Through Immersion: A Review of U.S. Programs. *Review of Educational Research*, *55*(4), 541–561. doi:10.3102/00346543055004541

Gerónimo-Castillo, G., & Canseco, V. (2002). Breve Introducción a los Sistemas Colaborativos: Groupware & Workflow. *Temas - Universidad Tecnológica de la Mixteca*, 49-54.

Ghislandi, P. (Ed.). (2012). eLearning: Theories, Design, Software, Applications. Rijeka, Croatia: InTech Europe.

Gibson, W. (1984). *Neuromancer*. New York: Ace Books.

Girvan, C., & Savage, T. (2010). Identifying an appropriate pedagogy for virtual worlds: A Communal Constructivism case study. *Computers & Education*, *55*(1), 342–349. doi:10.1016/j.compedu.2010.01.020

Glasgow, R. E., Bull, S. S., Piette, J. D., & Steiner, J. F. (2004). Interactive behavior change technology: A partial solution to the competing demands of primary care. *American Journal of Preventive Medicine*, *27*(2), 80–87. doi:10.1016/j.amepre.2004.04.026 PMID:15275676

Glukhareva, T. V. (2008). Individualization in teaching mathematics students. *Vestnik KemGU*, *4*, 43–45.

Glynn, C., Huge, M., & Hoffman, L. (2012). All the news thats fit to post: A profile of news use on social networking sites. *Computers in Human Behavior*, *28*(1), 113–119. doi:10.1016/j.chb.2011.08.017

Godwin-Jones, R. (2010). Emerging technologies: Literacies and technologies revisited. *Language Learning & Technology*, *14*(3), 2–9.

Goebert, D., Else, I., Matsu, C., Chung-Do, J., & Chang, J. Y. (2011). The impact of cyberbullying on substance use and mental health in a multiethnic sample. *Maternal and Child Health Journal*, *15*(8), 1282–1286. doi:10.1007/s10995-010-0672-x PMID:20824318

Goh, C. C. (1997). Metacognitive awareness and second language listeners. *ELT Journal*, *51*(4), 361–369. doi:10.1093/elt/51.4.361

Goh, C. C. (2002). *Teaching listening in the language classroom*. Singapore: SEAMEO Regional Language Centre.

Goldberg, H. E. (1915). *Controller*. Retrieved May 28, 2015, from http://www.freepatentsonline.com/1117184.pdf

Goldstein, M. K. (2008). Using health information technology to improve hypertension management. *Current Hypertension Reports*, *10*(3), 201–207. doi:10.1007/s11906-008-0038-6 PMID:18765090

Goldwater, J., & Harris, Y. (2011). Using technology to enhance the aging experience: A market analysis of existing technologies. *Ageing International, 36*(1), 5–28. doi:10.1007/s12126-010-9071-2

Golub, O. V., & Fokina, E. A. (2013). Optimization of mental and cognitive activity in solving analytical and diagnostic tasks. *Fundamental'nye issledovanija, 11*, 525-528.

Goodband, J., Solomon, Y., Samuels, P., Lawson, D., & Bhakta, R. (2011). Limits and potentials of social networking in academia: Case study of the evolution of a mathematics Facebook community. *Learning, Media and Technology*, 1–17.

Goodman, B. A., Linton, F. N., Gaimari, R. D., Hitzeman, J. M., Ross, H. J., & Zarrella, G. (2005). Using Dialogue Features to Predict Trouble During Collaborative Learning. *User Modeling and User-Adapted Interaction, 15*(1-2), 85–134. doi:10.1007/s11257-004-5269-x

Gosling, S., Augustine, A., Vazire, S., Holtzman, N., & Gaddis, S. (2011). Manifestations of personality in online social networks: Self-reported Facebook-related behaviours and observable profile information. *Cyberpsychology, Behavior, and Social Networking, 14*(9), 483–488. doi:10.1089/cyber.2010.0087 PMID:21254929

Gould, L. S. (2009). What Web 2.0 means to you. *Automotive Design & Production, 121*(6), 36–37.

Gradinger, P., Strohmeier, D., & Spiel, C. (2009). Traditional bullying and cyberbullying. *The Journal of Psychology, 217*, 205–213.

Grant, R. W., Campbell, E. G., Gruen, R. L., Ferris, T. G., & Blumenthal, D. (2006). Prevalence of basic information technology use by U.S. physicians. *Journal of General Internal Medicine, 21*(11), 1150–1155. doi:10.1111/j.1525-1497.2006.00571.x PMID:16879417

Gräther, W., Laclavik, M., & Tomasek, M. (2014). Support for Collaboration between Large and Small & Medium Enterprises. In *Proceedings of ACM Conference on Supporting Groupwork, GROUP'14*, (pp. 288-290). Sanibel Island, FL: ACM Press. doi:10.1145/2660398.2663773

Gregorc, A. R. (1982). *Style delineator*. Maynard, MA: Gabriel Systems.

Grigg, D. W. (2012). Definitional constructs of cyberbullying and cyber aggression from a triagnulatory overview: A preliminary study into elements. *Journal of Aggression, Conflict and Peace Research, 4*(4), 202–215. doi:10.1108/17596591211270699

Grissom, S. (2008). iPhone application development across the curriculum. *Journal of Computing Sciences in Colleges, 24*(1), 40–46.

Gruzelier, J., Inoue, A., Smart, R., Steed, A., & Steffert, T. (2010). Acting performance and flow state enhanced with sensory-motor rhythm neurofeedback comparing ecologically valid immersive VR and training screen scenarios. *Neuroscience Letters, 480*(2), 112–116. doi:10.1016/j.neulet.2010.06.019 PMID:20542087

Gu, J., Churchill, D., & Lu, J. (2014). Mobile Web 2.0 in the workplace: A case study of employees' informal learning. *British Journal of Educational Technology, 45*(6), 1049–1059. doi:10.1111/bjet.12179

Guri-Rosenblit, S. (2005). Distance education and e-learning: Not the same thing. *Higher Education, 49*(4), 467–493. doi:10.1007/s10734-004-0040-0

Gusakova, E. M. (2013). Electronic interactive whiteboard: software and technical characteristics impacting efficiency of education. *Integracija obrazovanija, 1*(70), 89-93.

Hahorcade, J. P. (2015). *Child-Computer Interaction*. Retrieved December, 2015, from: http://homepage.cs.uiowa.edu/~Hahorcade/

Hahorcade, J. P. (2012). Colima, Mexico: Interacciones Universales. In Congreso Internacional de Tecnologías de Información. Universidad de Colima.

Hall, M. J., Jones, K., Bermell-Garcia, P., & David Hansen, D. (2015). Argumentation in virtual collaborative environments addressing complex issues through remote synchronous collaboration. In *Proceedings of 9th Annual IEEE International Systems Conference, SysCon*, (pp. 249-255). Vancouver, BC, Canada: IEEE Press.

Handsfield, L. J., Dean, T. R., & Cielocha, K. M. (2009). Becoming critical consumers and producers of text: Teaching literacy with Web 1.0 and Web 2.0. *The Reading Teacher, 63*(1), 40–50. doi:10.1598/RT.63.1.4

Hanna, L., Risden, K., Czerwinski, M., & Alexander, K. J. (1999). The role of usability research in designing children's computer products. In A. Druin (Ed.), *The design of children's technology* (pp. 4–26). San Francisco, CA: Kaufmann.

Hannum, W., & Briggs, L. (1982). How does instructional system design differ from traditional instruction? *Educational Technology*, 9–14.

Hansen, J., & Stansfield, C. (1981). The relationship of field dependent-independent cognitive styles to foreign language achievement. *Language Learning, 31*(2), 349–367. doi:10.1111/j.1467-1770.1981.tb01389.x

Hao, X., & Kui, H. (2014). A Low-Power Ultra-Light Small and Medium Size Acoustic Wave Touch Screen. *Applied Mechanics and Materials, 513-517*, 4072–4075. doi:10.4028/www.scientific.net/AMM.513-517.4072

Hao, Y., & Lee, K. S. (2015). Teachers' concern about integrating Web 2.0 technologies and its relationship with teacher characteristics. *Computers in Human Behavior, 48*, 1–8. doi:10.1016/j.chb.2015.01.028

Harris, J. M., Mishra, P., & Koehler, M. (2009). Teachers technological pedagogical content knowledge and learning activity types: Curriculum-based technology integration reframed. *Journal of Research on Technology in Education, 41*(4), 393–416. doi:10.1080/15391523.2009.10782536

Harrison, A. F., & Brainson, R. M. (1984). *The art of thinking*. Berkley Books.

Harrison, C., Benko, H., & Wilson, A. D. (2011). OmniTouch: wearable multitouch interaction everywhere. *Proceedings of the 24th annual ACM symposium on User interface software and technology*, 441–450.

Harrison, R., & Thomas, M. (2009). Identity in online communities: Social networking sites and language learning. *International Journal of Emerging Technologies and Society, 7*(2), 109–124.

Hartson, R., & Pyla, P. (2012). *The UX Book*. Morgan Kaufmann.

Hatcher, E., & Gospodnetic, O. (2005). *Lucene in Action*. Manning Publications.

Hayhoe, M., & Ballard, D. (2005). Eye movements in natural behavior. *Trends in Cognitive Sciences, 9*(4), 188–194. doi:10.1016/j.tics.2005.02.009 PMID:15808501

Held, R. M., & Durlach, N. I. (1992). Telepresence, presence: Teleoperators and virtual environments. MIT Press.

Hendrix, D., Chiarella, D., Hasman, L., Murphy, S., & Zafron, M. L. (2009). Use of Facebook in academic health sciences libraries. *Journal of the Medical Library Association: JMLA, 97*(1), 44–47. doi:10.3163/1536-5050.97.1.008 PMID:19159005

Henner-Stanchina, C. (1987). Autonomy as metacognitive awareness: suggestions for training self-monitoring on listening comprehension. *Mâ elanges Pâ edagogiques, 17.*

Herbart, J. F. (1809). *La Pedagogia generale derivata dal fine dell'educazione*. Firenze, Italy: La Nuova Italia.

Heredia, B., & Rubio, D. (2015). Inglés y desigualdad social en México. *Sorry. El aprendizaje del inglés en México, Mexicanos Primero, 28.*

Herrington, J., Reeves, T. C., & Oliver, R. (2014). Authentic Learning Environments. In J. M. Spector, M. D. Merril, J. Elen, & M. J. Bishop (Eds.), *Handbook of Research on Educational Communications and Technology* (pp. 401–412). New York, NY: Springer. doi:10.1007/978-1-4614-3185-5_32

Hew, K. F. (2011). Students and teachers use of Facebook. *Computers in Human Behavior, 27*(2), 662–676. doi:10.1016/j.chb.2010.11.020

Hey, T., & Pápay, G. (2014). The Computing Universe: A Journey through a Revolution. Cambridge University Press. Retrieved from https://books.google.com/books?id=NrMkBQAAQBAJ&pgis=1 doi:10.1017/CBO9781139032643

Hikmet, N., Bhattacherjee, A., Menachemi, N., Kayhan, V. O., & Brooks, R. G. (2008). The role of organizational factors in the adoption of healthcare information technology in Florida hospitals. *Health Care Management Science, 11*(1), 1–9. doi:10.1007/s10729-007-9036-5 PMID:18390163

Hikmet, N., & Chen, S. K. (2003). An investigation into low mail survey response rates of information technology users in health care organizations. *International Journal of Medical Informatics, 72*(1), 29–34. doi:10.1016/j.ijmedinf.2003.09.002 PMID:14644304

Hillman, D. C., Willis, D. J., & Gunawardena, C. N. (1994). Learner-interface interaction in distance education: An extension of contemporary models and strategies for parishioners. *American Journal of Distance Education, 8*(2), 30–42. doi:10.1080/08923649409526853

Hinchliffe, L. J., & Leon, R. (2011). Innovation as a framework for adopting Web 2.0 marketing approaches. In D. Gupta & R. Savard (Eds.), *Marketing libraries in a Web 2.0 world* (pp. 58–65). Berlin, Germany: De Gruyter Saur. doi:10.1515/9783110263534.57

Hinduja, S., & Patchin, J. W. (2007). Offline consequences of online victimization. *Journal of School Violence, 6*(3), 89–112. doi:10.1300/J202v06n03_06

Hinduja, S., & Patchin, J. W. (2008). Cyberbullying: An exploratory analysis of factors related to offending and victimization. *Deviant Behavior, 29*(2), 129–156. doi:10.1080/01639620701457816

Hinduja, S., & Patchin, J. W. (2010). Bullying, cyberbullying, and suicide. *Archives of Suicide Research, 14*(3), 206–221. doi:10.1080/13811118.2010.494133 PMID:20658375

Hinduja, S., & Patchin, J. W. (2012). Cyberbullying: Neither and epidemic nor a rarity. *European Journal of Developmental Psychology, 9*(5), 539–543. doi:10.1080/17405629.2012.706448

Hinduja, S., & Patchin, J. W. (2013). Social influences on cyberbullying behaviors among middle and high school students. *Journal of Youth and Adolescence, 42*(5), 711–722. doi:10.1007/s10964-012-9902-4 PMID:23296318

Hinrichs, U., Schmidt, H., & Carpendale, S. (2008). EMDialog: Bringing information visualization into the museum. *Visualization and Computer Graphics. IEEE Transactions on, 14*(6), 1181–1188. doi:10.1109/TVCG.2008.127

Hokoda, A., Lu, H. A., & Angeles, M. (2006). School bullying in Taiwanese adolescents. *Journal of Emotional Abuse, 6*(4), 69–90. doi:10.1300/J135v06n04_04

Holodnaya, M. A. (2004). *Cognitive styles. The nature of individual mind.* St. Petersburg: Peter.

Hornecker, E. (2010). Interactions around a contextually embedded system. In *TEI '10: Proceedings of the fourth international conference on tangible, embedded, and embodied interaction* (pp. 169-176). ACM. doi:10.1145/1709886.1709916

Hotho, A., Nürnberger, A., & Paaß, G. (2005). A Brief Survey of Text Mining. *LDV Forum - GLDV Journal for Computational Linguistics and Language Technology, 20*, 19–62.

Hrastinski, S. (2008). Asynchronous & synchronous e-learning. *EDUCAUSE Quarterly*, 51–55.

Hsueh-Jui, L. (2008). A study of the interrelationship between listening strategy use and listening proficiency levels, and learning style. *Articles, 5*, 84–104.

Hsu, I. C. (2013). Multilayer context cloud framework for mobile Web 2.0: A proposed infrastructure. *International Journal of Communication Systems, 26*(5), 610–625. doi:10.1002/dac.1365

Hua, H., Gao, C., & Rolland, J. P. (2002). *Imaging properties of retro-reflective materials used in head-mounted projective* displays (HMPDs). In *AeroSense 2002* (pp. 194–201). International Society for Optics and Photonics. doi:10.1117/12.478871

Huang, C., Fu, T., & Chen, H. (2010). Text-based video content classification for online video-sharing sites. *Journal of the American Society for Information Science and Technology, 61*(5), 891–906. doi:10.1002/asi.21291

Huang, Y., & Chou, C. (2010). An analysis of multiple factors of cyberbullying among junior high school students in Taiwan. *Computers in Human Behavior, 26*(6), 1581–1590. doi:10.1016/j.chb.2010.06.005

Hui, G., & Hayllar, M. R. (2010). Creating public value in e-government: A public-private-citizen collaboration framework in Web 2.0. *Australian Journal of Public Administration, 69*(s1), S120–S131. doi:10.1111/j.1467-8500.2009.00662.x

Hum, N., Chamberlin, P., Hambright, B., Portwood, A., Schat, A., & Bevan, J. (2011). A picture is worth a thousand words: A content analysis of Facebook. *Computers in Human Behavior, 27*(5), 1828–1833. doi:10.1016/j.chb.2011.04.003

Hunger Statistics. (2013). *United Nations World Food*. Programme.

Hung, M., Conrad, J., Hon, S. D., Cheng, C., Franklin, J. D., & Tang, P. (2013). Uncovering patterns of technology use in consumer health informatics. *Wiley Interdisciplinary Reviews: Computational Statistics, 5*(6), 432–447. doi:10.1002/wics.1276 PMID:24904713

Hung, S. Y., Tsai, J. C. A., & Chuang, C. C. (2014). Investigating primary health care nurses' intention to use information technology: An empirical study in Taiwan. *Decision Support Systems, 57*, 331–342. doi:10.1016/j.dss.2013.09.016

Isenberg, P., Fisher, D., Paul, S., Morris, M. R., Inkpen, K., & Czerwinski, M. (2012). Co-Located collaborative visual analytics around a tabletop display. *Visualization and Computer Graphics, IEEE Transactions on, 18*(5), 689-702. doi:10.1109/TVCG.2011.287

Ishkov, A. D. (2004). *Learning activity of a student: psychological factors of success*. Moscow: Izdatel'stvo ASV.

Israel, J., & Aiken, R. (2007). Supporting Collaborative Learning With An Intelligent Web-Based System. *International Journal of Artificial Intelligence in Education, 17*, 3–40.

Iuppa, N. (2001). *Interactive design for new media and the web*. Boston: Focal Press.

Jacucci, G., Morrison, A., & Richard, G. (2010). *Worlds of information: designing for engagement at a public multi-touch display*. Retrieved from http://dl.acm.org/citation.cfm?id=1753669

Jacucci, G., Morrison, A., Richard, G. T., Kleimola, J., Peltonen, P., Parisi, L., & Laitinen, T. (2010). Worlds of information: Designing for engagement at a public multi-touch display. In *CHI '10: Proceedings of the SIGCHI conference on human factors in computing systems* (pp. 2267-2276). ACM. doi:10.1145/1753326.1753669

Jain, A., Bhargava, D., & Rajput, A. (2013). Touch-screen technology. *International Journal of Advanced Research in Computer Science and Electronics Engineering*, 2(January), 74–78. Retrieved from http://www.ijarcsee.org/index.php/IJARCSEE/article/view/309

Jakobsen, M. R., & HornbÆk, K. (2014). Up close and personal: Collaborative work on a high-resolution multitouch wall display. *ACM Transactions on Computer-Human Interaction*, 21(2), 1–34. doi:10.1145/2576099

James, J., Ingalls, T., Qian, G., Olsen, L., Whiteley, D., Wong, S., & Rikakis, T. (2006). Movement-based interactive dance performance. *Proceedings of the 14th annual ACM international conference on Multimedia*, 470–480. doi:10.1145/1180639.1180733

James, R. (2014). ICT's participatory potential in higher education collaborations: Reality or just talk. *British Journal of Educational Technology*, 45(4), 557–570. doi:10.1111/bjet.12060

Jang, H., Song, J., & Kim, R. (2014). Does the offline bully-victimization influence cyberbullying behavior among youths? Application of general strain theory. *Computers in Human Behavior*, 31, 85–93. doi:10.1016/j.chb.2013.10.007

Jannach, D., Zanker, M., Felfernig, A., & Friedrich, G. (2011). *Recommender Systems: An Introduction*. New York: Cambridge University Press.

Jarmon, L., Traphagan, T., Mayrath, M., & Trivedi, A. (2009). Virtual world teaching, experiential learning, and assessment: An interdisciplinary communication course in Second Life. *Computers & Education*, 53(1), 169–182. doi:10.1016/j.compedu.2009.01.010

Jean-Jacques, M., Persell, S. D., Thompson, J. A., Hasnain-Wynia, R., & Baker, D. W. (2012). Changes in disparities following the implementation of a health information technology-supported quality improvement initiative. *Journal of General Internal Medicine*, 27(1), 71–77. doi:10.1007/s11606-011-1842-2 PMID:21892661

Jeners, N., & Prinz, W. (2014). Metrics for Cooperative Systems. *Proceedings of ACM Conference on Supporting Groupwork, GROUP '14*, (pp. 91-99). Sanibel Island, FL: ACM Press.

Jenkins, H. (2010). *Culture partecipative e competenze digitali*. Milano, Italy: Edizioni Angelo Guerini e Associati.

Jensen, C. B. (2008). Power, technology and social studies of health care: An infrastructural inversion. *Health Care Analysis*, 16(4), 355–374. doi:10.1007/s10728-007-0076-2 PMID:18085441

Jeong, T. H. (1999). Basic principles and applications of holography. Lake Forest College.

Jiang, X., Liu, C., & Chen, L. (2010). Implementation of a project-based 3D virtual learning environment for English language learning. In *Education Technology and Computer (ICETC), 2010 2nd International Conference on* (Vol. 3, pp. V3-281). IEEE.

Johansen, R. (1991). Groupware: Furture Directions and Wild Cards. *Journal of Organizational Computing*, 1(2), 219–227. doi:10.1080/10919399109540160

Johnson-Lenz, P., & Johnson-Lenz, T. (1982). Groupware: The Process and Impacts of Design Choices. *Computer-Mediated Communication Systems: Status and Evaluation*.

Johnson-Lenz, P., & Johnson-Lenz, T. (1998). Groupware: Coining and Defining It. *SIGGROUP Bulletin*, 19(2), 34. doi:10.1145/290575.290585

Joinson, A. (1998). Causes and implications of behavior on the Internet. In J. Gackenbach (Ed.), *Psychology and the Internet: Intrapersonal, interpersonal, and transpersonal implications* (pp. 43–60). San Diego, CA: Academic Press.

Joshi, A., & Trout, K. (2014). The role of health information kiosks in diverse settings: A systematic review. *Health Information and Libraries Journal*, *31*(4), 254–273. doi:10.1111/hir.12081 PMID:25209260

Kabilan, M., Ahmad, N., & Abidan, M. (2010). Facebook: An online environment for learning English in institutions of higher education? *The Internet and Higher Education*, *13*(4), 170–187. doi:10.1016/j.iheduc.2010.07.003

Kade, D., Özcan, O., & Lindell, R. (2013a). Towards Stanislavski-based Principles for Motion Capture Acting in Animation and Computer Games. *Proceedings of CONFIA 2013, International Conference in Illustration and Animation*, 277–292.

Kade, D., Özcan, O., & Lindell, R. (2013b). An Immersive Motion Capture Environment. *Proceedings of the ICCGMAT 2013 International Conference on Computer Games, Multimedia and Allied Technology*, 73, 500-506.

Kalashnikova, A. V. (2013). Understanding of scientific text by students in terms of individual psychological characteristics of personality. *Gumanitarnye nauchnye issledovanija, 7*. Retrieved from http://human.snauka.ru/2013/07/3522

Kallonis, P., & Sampson, D. (2010). Implementing a 3D Virtual Classroom Simulation for Teachers' Continuing Professional Development. *Proceedings of the 18th International Conference on Computers in Education (ICCE 2010)*.

Kam, H. J., & Katerattanakul, P. (2014). Structural model of team-based learning using Web 2.0 collaborative software. *Computers & Education*, *76*, 1–12. doi:10.1016/j.compedu.2014.03.003

Kangas, K., Seitamaa-Hakkarainen, P., & Hakkarainen, K. (2007). The artifact project: History, science, and design inquiry in technology enhanced learning at elementary level. *Research and Practice in Technology Enhanced Learning*, *2*(03), 213–237. doi:10.1142/S1793206807000397

Kannampallil, T. G., Franklin, A., Mishra, R., Almoosa, K. F., Cohen, T., & Patel, V. L. (2013). Understanding the nature of information seeking behavior in critical care: Implications for the design of health information technology. *Artificial Intelligence in Medicine*, *57*(1), 21–29. doi:10.1016/j.artmed.2012.10.002 PMID:23194923

Kanuka, H., & Anderson, T. (1998). Online social interchange, discord, andknowledge construction. *Journal of Distance Education*, *13*(1), 57–74.

Kaplan, A., & Haelein, M. (2010). Users of the world, unite! The challenges and opportunities of social media. *Business Horizons*, *53*(1), 59–68. doi:10.1016/j.bushor.2009.09.003

Kaptelinin, K. K., & Bannon L. (1997). Activity theory: Basic concepts and applications. *Human-Computer Interaction*, 189–201.

Karginova, F. D. (1999). *Taking into account the individual characteristics of students as a factor of increase of efficiency of foreign language acquisition* (Unpublished candidate dissertation). Vladikavkaz.

Kasemsap, K. (2014). The role of social media in the knowledge-based organizations. In I. Lee (Ed.), *Integrating social media into business practice, applications, management, and models* (pp. 254–275). Hershey, PA: IGI Global. doi:10.4018/978-1-4666-6182-0.ch013

Kasemsap, K. (2015). The role of cloud computing adoption in global business. In V. Chang, R. Walters, & G. Wills (Eds.), *Delivery and adoption of cloud computing services in contemporary organizations* (pp. 26–55). Hershey, PA: IGI Global. doi:10.4018/978-1-4666-8210-8.ch002

Kasemsap, K. (2016a). The roles of e-learning, organizational learning, and knowledge management in the learning organizations. In E. Railean, G. Walker, A. Elçi, & L. Jackson (Eds.), *Handbook of research on applied learning theory and design in modern education* (pp. 786–816). Hershey, PA: IGI Global. doi:10.4018/978-1-4666-9634-1.ch039

Kasemsap, K. (2016b). Creating product innovation strategies through knowledge management in global business. In A. Goel & P. Singhal (Eds.), *Product innovation through knowledge management and social media strategies* (pp. 330–357). Hershey, PA: IGI Global. doi:10.4018/978-1-4666-9607-5.ch015

Kearsley, G. (1995). The nature and value of interaction in distance learning. *Distance Education Research Symposium 3: Instruction.*

Kelders, S. M., Kok, R. N., Ossebaard, H. C., & van Gemert-Pijnen, J. E. W. C. (2012). Persuasive system design does matter: A systematic review of adherence to web-based interventions. *Journal of Medical Internet Research, 14*(6), 2–25. doi:10.2196/jmir.2104 PMID:23151820

Khalil, H., & Ebner, M. (2013). Interaction Possibilities in MOOCs – How Do They Actually Happen? *International Conference on Higher Education Development,* 1-24.

Khan, F. A., & Paul, B. (2014). Screen reading with Bangla & English audio assistance bi-lingual supported software 'Mongol Dip' for visually impaired people. In *Computer and Information Technology (ICCIT), 2014 17th International Conference on* (pp. 263-272). IEEE.

Kho, N. D. (2011). Social media in libraries: Keys to deeper engagement. *Information Today, 28*(6), 31–32.

Khribi, M. K., Jemni, M., & Nasraoui, O. (2008). Automatic Recommendations for E-Learning Personalization Based on Web Usage Mining Techniques and Information Retrieval. In P. Díaz-Kinshuk, I. Aedo, & E. Mor (Eds.), *IEEE International Conference on Advanced Learning Techniques* (Vol. 8, pp. 241 – 245). Santander, Cantabria: IEEE. doi:10.1109/ICALT.2008.198

Kidd, L., Cayless, S., Johnston, B., & Wengstrom, Y. (2010). Telehealth in palliative care in the UK: A review of the evidence. *Journal of Telemedicine and Telecare, 16*(7), 394–402. doi:10.1258/jtt.2010.091108 PMID:20813893

Kilic, Z., Kaya, O. N., & Dogan, A. (2004). *Effects of students' pre- and post-laboratory concept maps on students' attitudes toward chemistry laboratory in university general chemistry.* Paper presented at the International Conference on Chemical Education, Istanbul, Turkey.

Kilo, C. M. (2005). Transforming care: Medical practice design and information technology. *Health Affairs, 24*(5), 1296–1301. doi:10.1377/hlthaff.24.5.1296 PMID:16162576

Kim, H., Takahashi, I., Yamamoto, H., Kai, T., Maekawa, S., & Naemura, T. (2013). MARIO: Mid-Air augmented re-ality interaction with objects. In Advances in computer entertainment (pp. 560-563). Springer International Publishing. doi:10.1007/978-3-319-03161-3_53

Kimaro, H. C., & Sahay, S. (2007). An institutional perspective on the process of decentralization of health information systems: A case study from Tanzania. *Information Technology for Development, 13*(s4), 363–390. doi:10.1002/itdj.20066

Kim, D. J., Yue, K., Hall, S. P., & Gates, T. (2009). Global diffusion of the Internet XV: Web 2.0 technologies, principles, and applications: A conceptual framework from technology push and demand pull perspective. *Communications of AIS, 24*(1), 657–672.

Kincaid, H. (2012). *The Oxford Handbook of Philosophy of Social Science.* Oxford, UK: Oxford University Press. doi:10.1093/oxfordhb/9780195392753.001.0001

Kiseleva, T. V. (2011). Poetic educational texts is a modern and effective tool which facilitate acquisition of educational material (for example mathematics). *Mezhdunarodnyj zhurnal prikladnyh i fundamental'nyh issledovanij, 8,* 82-84.

Kitsantas, A., & Dabbagh, N. (2011). The role of Web 2.0 technologies in self-regulated learning. *New Directions for Teaching and Learning, 2011*(126), 99–106. doi:10.1002/tl.448

Klašnja-Milićević, A., Vesin, B., Ivanović, M., & Budimac, Z. (2011). E-Learning personalization based on hybrid recommendation strategy and learning style identification. *Computers & Education, 56*(3), 885–899. doi:10.1016/j.compedu.2010.11.001

Klemmer, S. (2014). *Human Computer Interaction.* The Design Lab, University of California, San Diego. Retrieved from http://goo.gl/OVNcFc

Knowles, B., Rouncefield, M., Harding, M., & Davies, N. (2015). Models and Patterns of Trust. *CSCW 2015, Trust & Anonynity*, 328-338.

Kochenderfer-Ladd, B., & Pelletier, M. (2008). Teachers views and beliefs about bullying: Influences on classroom management strategies and students coping with peer victimization. *Journal of School Psychology, 46*(4), 431–453. doi:10.1016/j.jsp.2007.07.005 PMID:19083367

Kodzhaspirova, G. M., & Petrov, K. V. (2001). *Technical means of learning and methods of their use: manual for students of higher pedagogical educational institution.* Moscow: Izdatel'skij centr «Akademija».

Kolb, D. A. (1984). *Experimental learning: Experience as a source of learning and development.* Englewood Cliffs, NJ: Prentice-Hall.

Kolokowsky, S., & Davis, T. (2009). *Touchscreens 101: Understanding Touchscreen Technology and Design.* Retrieved from http://www.cypress.com/?docID=17212

Konchady, M. (2008). *Building Search Applications: Lucene, Lingpipe, and Gate.* Mustru Publishing.

Konstan, J. A. (2004). Introduction To Recommender Systems : Algorithms and Evaluation. *ACM Transactions on Information Systems, 22*(1), 1–4. doi:10.1145/963770.963771

Korra, R., Sujatha, P., Chetana, S., & Kumar, M. N. (2011). Performance Evaluation of Multilingual Information Retrieval (MLIR) System over Information Retrieval (IR) System. In *IEEE-International Conference on Recent Trends in Information Technology (ICRTIT 2011)* (pp. 722–727). Chennai, Tamil Nadu: IEEE Press.

Kostromina, S., & Gnedykh, D. (2012). The innovative approach in using the visual aids in modern education. *Scientific enquiry in the contemporary world: Theoretical basics and innovative approach, 3*, 291-293.

Kostromina, S. (2013). Academic skills as a basis for self-organization of human activity. *Procedia: Social and Behavioral Sciences, 86*(6), 543–550. doi:10.1016/j.sbspro.2013.08.611

Kostromina, S., & Gnedykh, D. (2016). Students psychological characteristics as factor of effective acquisition of visualization in e-learning. *Procedia: Social and Behavioral Sciences, 217*, 34–41. doi:10.1016/j.sbspro.2016.02.016

Kotova, S. S., & Shakhmatova, O. N. (2007). Students' psychological features of self-organization of learning activity. *Nauchnye issledovanija v obrazovanii, 4.* Retrieved from http://cyberleninka.ru/article/n/psihologicheskie-osobennosti-samoorganizatsii-uchebnoy-deyatelnosti-studentov

Kowalski, R. M., & Limber, S. P. (2007). Electronic bullying among middle school students. *The Journal of Adolescent Health, 41*(6), 22–30. doi:10.1016/j.jadohealth.2007.08.017 PMID:18047942

Kowler, E. (Ed.). (1990). *Eye Movements and Their Role in Visual and Cognitive Processes.* Amsterdam: Elsevier Science Publisher B.V.

Kratky, A. (n.d.). Transparent touch – interacting with a multi-layered touch-sensitive display system. Springer Berlin Heidelberg.

Kuchma, V. R., Teksheva, L. M., Vjatleva, O. A., & Kurganskij, A. M. (2012). Features of information perception via electronic device for reading (reader). *Voprosy shkol'noj i universitetskoj mediciny i zdorov'ja, 1,* 39-46.

Kudryashova, V. G. (2009). Improvement of self-organization skills of learning activities in teaching biology as the basis for development of students' general educational competence. *Srednee professional'noe obrazovanie, 3,* 37-39.

Kurilovas, E., & Dagiene, V. (2010). *Evaluation of quality of the learning software: Basics, concepts, methods.* Saarbrücken, Germany: LAP LAMBERT Academic Publishing.

Kurilovas, E., & Juskeviciene, A. (2015). Creation of Web 2.0 tools ontology to improve learning. *Computers in Human Behavior, 51,* 1380–1386. doi:10.1016/j.chb.2014.10.026

Kurzwel, R. (2005). *The Singularity is Near.* London: Penguin Books.

Kuwada, K. (2010). The effect of interactivity with a music video game on second language vocabulary recall. *About. Language Learning & Technology,* 74.

Kwan, G. C. E., & Skoric, M. M. (2013). Facebook bullying: An extension of battles in school. *Computers in Human Behavior, 29*(1), 16–25. doi:10.1016/j.chb.2012.07.014

La Torre, G., de Waure, C., de Waure, A., & Ricciardi, W. (2013). The promising application of health technology assessment in public health: A review of background information and considerations for future development. *Journal of Public Health, 21*(4), 373–378. doi:10.1007/s10389-013-0557-8

Lacey, C., Chun, S., Terrones, L., & Huang, J. S. (2014). Adolescents with chronic disease and use of technology for receipt of information regarding health and disease management. *Health Technology, 4*(3), 253–259. doi:10.1007/s12553-014-0076-9

Laftman, S. B., Modin, B., & Ostberg, V. (2013). Cyberbullying and subjective health: A large-scale study of students in Stockholm, Sweden. *Children and Youth Services Review, 35*(1), 112–119. doi:10.1016/j.childyouth.2012.10.020

Lakkala, M., Ilomaki, L., & Palonen, T. (2007). Implementing virtual, collaborative inquiry practices in a middle school context. *Behaviour & Information Technology, 26*(1), 37–53. doi:10.1080/01449290600811529

Landis, C. (2007). Friending our users: Social networking and reference services. In S. Steiner & L. Madden (Eds.), *The desk and beyond: Next generation reference services.* Chicago, IL: Association of College and Research Libraries.

Lanier, J. (2013). *Who Owns the Future.* London: Penguin Books.

Laurel, B. (1991). *Computers as Theatre.* Boston: Addison-Wesley Publishing.

Laurel, B. (2004). *Design Research: Methods and Perspectives.* Cambridge, MA: MIT Press.

Lazareva, O. V. (2012). To the question about the influence of metacognitive processes in comprehension of scientific text. *Vestnik JuUrGU, 31,* 13–17.

Lazuras, L., Barkoukis, V., Ourda, D., & Tsorbatzoudis, H. (2013). A process model of cyberbullying in adolescence. *Computers in Human Behavior, 29*(3), 881–887. doi:10.1016/j.chb.2012.12.015

Lee, J., McCullough, J. S., & Town, R. J. (2013). The impact of health information technology on hospital productivity. *The Rand Journal of Economics, 44*(3), 545–568. doi:10.1111/1756-2171.12030

Lefkowitz, L. S., & Lesser, V. R. (1988). Knowledge acquisition as knowledge assimilation. *International Journal of Man-Machine Studies, 29*(2), 215–226. doi:10.1016/S0020-7373(88)80047-6

Leggett, J., & Schnase, J. (1994). Viewing Dexter with Open Eyes. *Communications of the ACM, 37*(2), 76–86. doi:10.1145/175235.175241

Lenhart, A. (2015). *Teens, social media & technology overview 2015.* Retrieved from: http://www.pewinternet.org/2015/04/09/teens-social-media-technology-2015/

Leontiev, A. N. (1978). *Activity, consciousness, and personality.* Retrieved from https://www.marxists.org/archive/leontev/works/1978/index.htm

Levis, D. (1997). *Los videojuegos, un fenómeno de masas.* Barcelona: Paidós. (in Spanish)

Levy, M. (2009). Web 2.0 implications on knowledge management. *Journal of Knowledge Management, 13*(1), 120–134. doi:10.1108/13673270910931215

Liarokapis, F., & White, M. (2005). Augmented reality techniques for museum environments. *The Mediterranean Journal of Computers and Networks, 1*(2), 90–96.

Liestol, G., & Morrison, A. (2013). Views, alignment and incongruity in indirect augmented reality. *IEEE Xplore,* 23-28. doi:10.1109/ISMAR-AMH.2013.6671263

Li, L., Adelstein, B. D., & Ellis, S. R. (2009). *Perception of image motion during head movement.* New York: ACM Press.

Li, L., Xu, L., Jeng, H. A., Naik, D., Allen, T., & Frontini, M. (2008). Creation of environmental health information system for public health service: A pilot study. *Information Systems Frontiers, 10*(5), 531–542. doi:10.1007/s10796-008-9108-1

Lilleker, D. G., & Jackson, N. A. (2010). Towards a more participatory style of election campaigning: The impact of Web 2.0 on the UK 2010 general election. *Policy & Internet, 2*(3), 69–98. doi:10.2202/1944-2866.1064

Lin, S. H. (2000). *A study of English listening comprehension strategies used by senior high school students in Taiwan* (Unpublished Master Thesis). National Kaohsiung Normal University, Kaohsiung, R.O.C.

Lin, Y. Y., Shih, Y. C., & Yang, M. T. (2005). VEC3D: A 3-D virtual English classroom for second language learning. In *Advanced Learning Technologies, 2005. ICALT 2005. Fifth IEEE International Conference on* (pp. 906-908). IEEE.

Li, Q. (2007). Bullying in the new playground: Research into cyberbullying and cybervictimization. *Australasian Journal of Educational Technology, 23*(4), 435–454. doi:10.14742/ajet.1245

Li, Q. (2008). A cross-cultural comparison of adolescents experience related to cyberbullying. *Educational Research, 50*(3), 223–234. doi:10.1080/00131880802309333

Liu, C., & Chapuis, O. (2014). *Effects of display size and navigation type on a classification task.* doi:10.1145/2556288.2557020

Livingstone, S., Haddon, L., Gorzig, A., & Olafsson, K. (2011). *EU Kids On Line. Final report.* London: London School of Economics.

Locke, J. (1693). *Some Troughts Concerning Education.* Torino, Italy: Utet.

Lococo, A., & Yen, D. C. (1998). Groupware: Computer Supported Collaboration. In Telematics and Informatics (pp. 85-101). Elsevier Science.

Lorence, D. (2007). Why there can be no sustainable national healthcare IT program without a translational health information science. *Journal of Medical Systems, 31*(6), 557–562. doi:10.1007/s10916-007-9099-3 PMID:18041292

Lorence, D. P., & Greenberg, L. (2006). The zeitgeist of online health search. *Journal of General Internal Medicine, 21*(2), 134–139. PMID:16336621

Lorenzo, G. (2005). *An overview of e-portfolios*. EDUCASE Learning Initiative.

Lovell, N. H., & Celler, B. G. (1999). Information technology in primary health care. *International Journal of Medical Informatics*, *55*(1), 9–22. doi:10.1016/S1386-5056(99)00016-7 PMID:10471237

Lowdermilk, T. (2013). *User Centered Design A Developer's Guide to Building User-Friendly Applications*. Sebastopol, CA: O'Reilly Media.

Lowe, B., D'Alessandro, S., Winzar, H., Laffey, D., & Collier, W. (2013). The use of Web 2.0 technologies in marketing classes: Key drivers of student acceptance. *Journal of Consumer Behaviour*, *12*(5), 412–422. doi:10.1002/cb.1444

Luna, H., Mendoza, R., Vargas, M., Muñoz, J., Álvarez, F. J., & Rodríguez, L. C. (2014). A Classification of Design Patterns to Support mobile Groupware Systems. Proceeding of the 5th Mexican Conference on Human-Computer Interaction. Doi:10.1145/2676690.2676691

Lund, R. J. (1990). A taxonomy for teaching Second Language Listening. *Foreign Language Annals*, *23*(2), 105–115. doi:10.1111/j.1944-9720.1990.tb00348.x

Luppicini, R. (2013). *The Emerging Field of Technoself Studies. In Handbook of Research on Technoself: Identity in a Technological Society* (pp. 1–25). Hershey, PA: IGI Global. doi:10.4018/978-1-4666-2211-1.ch001

Macaro, E., Graham, S., & Vanderplank, R. (2007). A review of listening strategies: focus on sources of knowledge and on success. In A.D. Cohen & E. Macaro (Eds.), Language learner strategies: 30 years of research and practice, (pp. 165-186). Oxford University Press.

Macedo, D., & Steinberg, S. (Eds.). (2007). *Media Literacy: a reader*. New York: Peter Lang.

Machackova, H., Dedkova, L., & Mezulanikova, K. (2015). Brief report: The bystander effect in cyberbullying incidents. *Journal of Adolescence*, *43*, 96–99. doi:10.1016/j.adolescence.2015.05.010 PMID:26070168

Machackova, H., Dedkova, L., Sevcikova, A., & Cerna, A. (2013). Bystanders support of cyberbullied schoolmates. *Journal of Community & Applied Social Psychology*, *23*(1), 25–36. doi:10.1002/casp.2135

Macías, G. J. (2003). *Teorías de la Comunicación Grupal en la Toma de Decisiones: Contexto y Caracterización*. Tesis Doctoral. Universitat Autónoma de Barcelona.

MacKay, B., & Watters, C. (2012). An examination of multisession web tasks. *Journal of the American Society for Information Science and Technology*, *63*(6), 1183–1197. doi:10.1002/asi.22610

MacKenzie, I. S. (2012). *Human-computer interaction: An empirical research perspective*. Newnes.

Maddux, J. E. (1999). Expectancies and the social cognitive perspective: Basic principles, processes, and variables. In I. Kirsch (Ed.), *How expectancies shape experience* (pp. 17–40). Washington, DC: American Psychological Association. doi:10.1037/10332-001

Madge, C., Meek, J., Wellens, J., & Hooley, T. (2009). Facebook, social integration and informal learning at university: It is more for socializing and talking to friends about work than for actually doing work. *Learning, Media and Technology*, *34*(2), 141–155. doi:10.1080/17439880902923606

Magnenat-Thalmann, M., & Thalmann, D. (1993). *Virtual Worlds and Multimedia*. New York: Wiley.

Mak, S., Williams, R., & Mackness, J. (2010). Blogs and Forums as Communication and LearningTools in a MOOC. *Proceedings of the 7th International Conference on Networked Learning*, 275-284.

Malik, S., Ranjan, A., & Balakrishnan, R. (2005). Interacting with large displays from a distance with vision-tracked multi-finger gestural input. *Proceedings of the 18th Annual ACM Symposium on User Interface Software and Technology - UIST '05*, 43. doi:10.1145/1095034.1095042

Manouselis, N., Drachsler, H., Vuorikari, R., Hummel, H., & Koper, R. (2011). Recommender Systems in Technology Enhanced Learning. In F. Rocco, L. Rokach, B. Shapira, & P. Kantor (Eds.), *Recommender Systems Handbook* (pp. 387–415). Springer. doi:10.1007/978-0-387-85820-3_12

Manouselis, N., Vuorikari, R., & Van-Assche, F. (2010). Collaborative recommendation of e-learning resources: An experimental investigation. *Journal of Computer Assisted Learning*, 26(4), 227–242. doi:10.1111/j.1365-2729.2010.00362.x

Mantorova, I. V. (2002). *Presentation of educational information by means of multimedia tools as a factor of improving the quality of learning* (Unpublished candidate dissertation). Karachaevsk.

Mantovani, S. (Ed.). (2000). *La ricerca sul campo in educazione. I metodi qualitativi*. Milano, Italy: Paravia Bruno Mondadori.

Mantovani, S., & Ferri, P. (Eds.). (2008). *Digital Kids. Come i bambini usano il computer e come potrebbero usarlo genitori e insegnanti*. Bologna, Italy: ETAS.

Maragliano, R. (Ed.). (2000). *Tre ipertesti su multimedialità e formazione*. Roma-Bari, Italy: Laterza.

Maragliano, R. (Ed.). (2004). *Pedagogie dell'e-learning*. Roma-Bari, Italy: Laterza.

Maranto, G., & Barton, M. (2010). Paradox and promise: MySpace, Facebook, and the sociopolitics of social networking in the writing classroom. *Computers and Composition*, 27(1), 36–47. doi:10.1016/j.compcom.2009.11.003

Markova, A. K. (1999). *Psychological characteristics of learning motivation at schoolchildren*. Pedagogicheskaja psihologija. Hrestomatija. Cheljabinsk: Izd-vo JuUrGU.

Marks, R. B., Sibley, S. D., & Arbaugh, J. B. (2005). A structural equation model of predictors for effective online learning. *Journal of Management Education*, 29(4), 531–563. doi:10.1177/1052562904271199

Marsh, J. (2016). *UX for Beginners: 100 Short Lessons to Get You Started*. Sebastopol, CA: O'Reilly.

Martin-Dorta, N., Saorin, J., & Contero, M. (2011). Web-based Spatial Training Using Handheld Touch Screen Devices. *Journal of Educational Technology & Society*, 14, 163–177. Retrieved from http://www.ifets.info/others/download_pdf.php?j_id=52&a_id=1160

Martin, E., Vinyals, O., Friedland, G., & Bajcsy, R. (2010). Precise indoor localization using smart phones. *Proceedings of the international conference on Multimedia*, 787–790.

Maskinskov, A. B. (2003). *The influence of theoretical and empirical thinking styles on the process of acquisition of foreign language by students* (Unpublished candidate dissertation). Kursk.

Mason, K. (2008). Cyberbullying: A preliminary assessment for school personnel. *Psychology in the Schools*, 45(4), 323–348. doi:10.1002/pits.20301

Mason, R. P., Pegler, C., & Weller, M. (2004). E-portfolios: An assessment tool for online courses. *British Journal of Educational Technology*, 35(6), 717–727. doi:10.1111/j.1467-8535.2004.00429.x

Massa, R. (1990). La Clinica della formazione. In R. Massa (Ed.), *Istituzioni di pedagogia e scienze della formazione* (pp. 481–583). Roma-Bari, Italy: Laterza.

Massa, R. (1992). *La Clinica della formazione*. Milano, Italy: FrancoAngeli.

Massa, R. (1997). *Cambiare la scuola. Educare o istruire?* Roma, BA, Italy: Laterza.

Massa, R. (2004). *Le tecniche e I corpi verso una scienza dell'educazione.* Milano, Italy: Unicopoli.

Massa, R., & Cerioli, L. (Eds.). (1999). *Sottobanco. Le dimensioni nascoste della vita scolastica.* Milano, Italy: Franco Angeli.

Matyukhina, V. M. (1984). *Motivation of learning in midchildhood.* Moscow: Pedagogika.

May, C., Mort, M., Williams, T., Mair, F., & Gask, L. (2003). Health technology assessment in its local contexts: Studies of telehealthcare. *Social Science & Medicine, 57*(4), 697–710. doi:10.1016/S0277-9536(02)00419-7 PMID:12821017

Mayrath, M., Sanchez, J., Traphagan, T., Heikes, J., & Trivedi, A. (2007). Using Second Life in an English course: Designing class activities to address learning objectives. In *Proceedings of world conference on educational multimedia, hypermedia and telecommunications* (Vol. 25).

McAuley, A., Stewart, B., Siemens, G., & Cormier, D. (2010). Massive Open Online Courses Digital ways of knowing and learning. *The MOOC model For Digital Practice.*

McCabe, C., Edlin, R., & Hall, P. (2013). Navigating time and uncertainty in health technology appraisal: Would a map help? *PharmacoEconomics, 31*(9), 731–737. doi:10.1007/s40273-013-0077-y PMID:23877738

McCloud, S. (1994). Understanding comics. The invisible art. New York: Academic Press.

McCracken, H. (2002). The importance of learning communities in motivating and retaining online learners. *Motivating and retaining adult learners online*, 65-74.

McGraw, D. (2009). Privacy and health information technology. *The Journal of Law, Medicine & Ethics, 37*(s2), 121–149. doi:10.1111/j.1748-720X.2009.00424.x PMID:19754656

McKenna, K. Y. A., & Bargh, J. A. (2000). Plan 9 from cyberspace: The implications of the internet for personality and social psychology. *Personality and Social Psychology Review, 4*(1), 57–75. doi:10.1207/S15327957PSPR0401_6

McLoughlin, C., & Lee, M. J. W. (2008). The Three P's of Pedagogy for the Networked Society: Personalization, Partecipation and Productivity. International Journal of Teaching and learning in Higher Education, 20(1), 10-27.

McLuhan, M. (1964). *Understanding Media: The Extensions of Man.* Berkeley, CA: Gingko Press.

McLuhan, M. (1967). *The Mechanical Bride: Folklore of Industrial Man.* London: Duckworth Overlook.

McLuhan, M., & Powers, B. (1989). *The Global Village: Transformations in World Life and Media in the 21st Century.* Oxford, UK: Oxford University Press.

McNamara, D. S., & O'Reilly, T. (n.d.). *Learning - knowledge acquisition, representation, and organization.* Retrieved from http://education.stateuniversity.com/pages/2165/Learning-KNOWLEDGE-ACQUISITION-REPRESENTATION-ORGANIZATION.html

McQuade, C. S., Colt, P. J., & Meyer, B. N. (2009). *Cyber bullying: Protecting kids and adults from online bullies.* Westport, CT: Praeger.

Meador, W. S., Rogers, T. J., ONeal, K., Kurt, E., & Cunningham, C. (2004). Mixing dance realities: Collaborative development of live-motion capture in a performing arts environment. *Computers in Entertainment, 2*(2), 12–12. doi:10.1145/1008213.1008233

Megasari, R., Kuspriyanto, K., Husni, E. M., & Widyantoro, D. H. (2015). Towards host to host meeting scheduling negotiation. *International Journal of Advances in Intelligent Informatics, 1*(1), 23–29.

Mei, Y. Y., Marquard, J., Jacelon, C., & DeFeo, A. L. (2013). Designing and evaluating an electronic patient falls reporting system: Perspectives for the implementation of health information technology in long-term residential care facilities. *International Journal of Medical Informatics, 82*(11), e294–e306. doi:10.1016/j.ijmedinf.2011.03.008 PMID:21482183

Meloni, J. (2010). Tools for synchronous and asynchronous classroom discussion. *The Chronicle of Higher Education.*

Mendelsohn, D. (1995). Applying Learning Strategies in the second/foreign language listening comprehension lesson. In D. Mendelsohn & J. Rubin (Eds.), *A Guide for the Teaching of Second Language Listening.* San Diego, CA: Dominie Press.

Mendoza, R. (2016). *User Centered Design Strategies for Massive Open Online Courses (MOOCs).* Hershey, PA: IGI Global. doi:10.4018/978-1-4666-9743-0

Miller, A. A. (2010). The use of e-book (electronic textbook) in training of students of technical disciplines. *Mir nauki, kul'tury, obrazovanija, 3,* 161-162.

Mitchell, K. J., Ybarra, M., & Finkelhor, D. (2007). The relative importance of online victimization in understanding depression, delinquency, and substance use. *Child Maltreatment, 12*(4), 314–324. doi:10.1177/1077559507305996 PMID:17954938

Mohr, D. C., Cuijpers, P., & Lehman, K. (2011). Supportive accountability: A model for providing human support to enhance adherence to eHealth interventions. *Journal of Medical Internet Research, 13*(1), e30. doi:10.2196/jmir.1602 PMID:21393123

Moledo, L., & Olszevicki, N. (2015). *History of Scientific Ideas: From Tales of Miletus to God Machine.* Buenos Aires: Planeta.

Monk, A., Wright, P., Haber, J., & Davenport, L. (1993). *Improving Your Human-Computer Interface: A Practical Technique.* Upper Saddle River, NJ: Prentice Hall.

Montague, K., Hanson, V. L., & Cobley, A. (2012). Designing for individuals: Usable touch-screen interaction through shared user models. In *ASSETS '12: Proceedings of the 14th international ACM SIGACCESS conference on computers and accessibility* (pp. 151-158). ACM. doi:10.1145/2384916.2384943

Montano, B. S. J., Carretero, R. G., Entrecanales, M. V., & Pozuelo, P. M. (2010). Integrating the hospital library with patient care, teaching and research: Model and Web 2.0 tools to create a social and collaborative community of clinical research in a hospital setting. *Health Information and Libraries Journal, 27*(3), 217–226. doi:10.1111/j.1471-1842.2010.00893.x PMID:20712716

Monty, R. A., & Senders, J. W. (Eds.). (1976). *Eye Movements and Psychological Processes.* Lawrence Erlbaum.

Moore, M. G. (1989). Editorial: Three types of interaction. *American Journal of Distance Education, 3*(2), 1–6. doi:10.1080/08923648909526659

Morabito, V. (2014). Digital Work and Collaboration. In *Trends and Challenges in Digital Business Innovation* (pp. 133–131). Milan: DOI; doi:10.1007/978-3-319-04307-4_7

Moreno-Rocha, M. A., & Peralta-Calvo, M. (2015). *La usabilidad y experiencia del usuario. In La Interacción Humano-Computadora en México* (p. 347). Pearson.

Morley, J. (1991). *Listening Comprehension in Foreign Language Instruction.* Boston: Academic Press.

Morrison, G. D. (2007). A CMOS camera-based man-machine input device for large-format interactive displays. In SIGGRAPH '07: ACM SIGGRAPH 2007 courses (pp. 65-74). ACM. doi:10.1145/1281500.1281686

Moscovich, T. (2007). *Principles and applications of multi-touch interaction.* Brown University.

Mottana, P. (1997). *Dissolvenze, le immagini della formazione.* Bologna, Italy: Clueb. - (2003). Clinica della formazione (Voce). In M. Laeng (Ed.), *Enciclopedia pedagogica.* Brescia, Italy: La Scuola.

Mottana, P. (2002). *L'opera dello sguardo. Braci di pedagogia immaginale.* Bergamo, Italy: Moretti & Vitali Editore.

Mouttapa, M., Valente, T., Gallagher, P., Rohrbach, L. A., & Unger, J. B. (2004). Social network predictor of bullying and victimization. *Adolescence, 39,* 315–335. PMID:15563041

Mouttham, A., Kuziemsky, C., Langayan, D., Peyton, L., & Pereira, J. (2012). Interoperable support for collaborative, mobile, and accessible health care. *Information Systems Frontiers, 14*(1), 73–85. doi:10.1007/s10796-011-9296-y

Müller, J., Bailly, G., Bossuyt, T., & Hillgren, N. (2014). MirrorTouch: Combining touch and mid-air gestures for public displays. In *MobileHCI '14: Proceedings of the 16th international conference on human-computer interaction with mobile devices & services* (pp. 319-328). ACM. doi:10.1145/2628363.2628379

Multimodal learning through media: What the research says. (2008). Retrieved from http://www.cisco.com/c/dam/en_us/solutions/industries/docs/education/Multimodal-Learning-Through-Media.pdf

Murphy, J. M. (1985). *An Investigation into the Listening Strategies of ESL College Students.* Academic Press.

Murray, J. (2011). *Inventing the Medium: Principles of Interaction Design as a Cultural Practice.* Cambridge, MA: MIT Press.

Murray, J. H. (1997). *Hamlet on the holodeck: The future of narrative in cyberspace.* Simon and Schuster.

Murray, M. P. (2012). tudent Interactionwith Online Course Content: Build It and They Might Come. *Journal of Information Technology Education,* 125–142.

Murray, M., Pérez, J., Geist, D., & Hedrick, A. (2012). Student Interactionwith Online Course Content: Build It and They Might Come. *Journal of Information Technology Education, 11*(1), 125–142.

Najaftorkaman, M., Ghapanchi, A. H., Talaei-Khoei, A., & Ray, P. (2015). A taxonomy of antecedents to user adoption of health information systems: A synthesis of thirty years of research. *Journal of the Association for Information Science and Technology, 66*(3), 576–598. doi:10.1002/asi.23181

Naseikina, L. F. (2010). Interactive electronic textbooks at modern open education. *Vestnik orenburgskogo gosudarstvennogo universiteta, 5*(111), 30-35.

Nassar, M. A., & Meawad, F. (2010). An augmented reality exhibition guide for the iphone. *IEEE Xplore,* 157-162. doi:10.1109/IUSER.2010.5716742

Navarro, P., & Shoemaker, J. (2000). Performance and perceptions of distance learners in cyberspace. *American Journal of Distance Education, 14*(2), 15–35. doi:10.1080/08923640009527052

Nedlund, A. C., & Garpenby, P. (2014). Puzzling about problems: The ambiguous search for an evidence based strategy for handling influx of health technology. *Policy Sciences, 47*(4), 367–386. doi:10.1007/s11077-014-9198-1

Nelson, T. (1974). *Computer Lib / Dream Machines.* Redmond, WA: Tempus Books of Microsoft Press.

Nesset, V., & Large, A. (2004). Children in the information technology design process: A review of theories and their applications. *Library & Information Science Research, 26*(2), 140–161. doi:10.1016/j.lisr.2003.12.002

Nesta, F., & Mi, J. (2011). Library 2.0 or library III: Returning to leadership. *Library Management, 32*(1/2), 85–97. doi:10.1108/01435121111102601

Netesov, S. I. (2012). Graphic visualization on the lessons of jurisprudence with the use of information and communication technologies. *Informacijni tehnologiï i zasobi navchannja, 1*(27). Retrieved from http://www.journal.iitta.gov.ua

Newman, W., & Sproull, R. (1979). *Principles of Interactive Computer Graphics*. New York: McGraw Hill.

Neyem, A., Ochoa, S. F., & Pino, J. A. (2008). Coordination Patterns to Support Mobile Collaboration. Groupware: Design, Implementation, and Use. *14th International Workshop, CRIWG 2008*, 248-265. Doi:10.1007/978-3-540-92831-7_21

Nielsen, J., & Norman, D. (2014). *User experience encompasses all aspects of the end-user's interaction with the company, its services, and its products*. Retrieved February 20, 2016, from: URL: https://www.nngroup.com/articles/definition-user-experience/

Nielsen, J. (1990). Big Playbacks from 'Discount' Usability Engineering. *IEEE Software, 7*(3), 107–108.

Nielsen, J. (1992). The Usability Engineering Life Cycle. *IEEE Computer, 25*(3), 12–22. doi:10.1109/2.121503

Nielsen, J. (1993). *Usability Engineering*. Cambridge, MA: Academic Press.

Nielsen, J., & Budiu, R. (2013). *Mobile Usability*. New Riders.

Nielsen, J., & Landauer, T. K. (1993). A mathematical model of the finding of usability problems. In *Proceedings ACM INTERCHI'93 Conference*, (pp. 206-213). doi:10.1145/169059.169166

Nielsen, J., & Mack, R. (1994). *Usability Inspections Methods*. New York: Wiley. doi:10.1145/259963.260531

Nieminen, K. (2006). *Aspects of Learning Foreign Languages and Learning WITH Foreign Languages: Language Immersion and CLIL. Development Project Report*. Jyvaskyla, Finland: Jyvaskyla University of Applied Sciences.

Nikiforou, M., Georgiou, S. N., & Stavrinides, P. (2013). Attachment to parents and peers as predictors of bullying and victimization. *Journal of Criminology, 2013*, 1–9. doi:10.1155/2013/484871

Ni, T., Schmidt, G. S., Staadt, O. G., Livingston, M. A., Ball, R., & May, R. (2006). *A survey of large high-resolution display technologies, techniques, and applications*. Proceedings - IEEE Virtual Reality. doi:10.1109/VR.2006.20

Normand, J.-M., Servières, M., & Moreau, G. (2012). A new typology of augmented reality applications. In *AH '12: Proceedings of the 3rd augmented human international conference* (pp. 18:1-18:8). ACM. doi:10.1145/2160125.2160143

Norman, D. (2013). *The Design of Everyday Things: Revised and Expanded Edition*. New York: Basic Books.

Norman, D. A. (1999). *The Invisible Computer*. MIT Press.

Normand, J.-M., Spanlang, B., Tecchia, F., Carrozzino, M., Swapp, D., & Slater, M. (2012). Full body acting rehearsal in a networked virtual environment - A case study. *Presence (Cambridge, Mass.), 21*(2), 229–243. doi:10.1162/PRES_a_00089

Northrup, P. T. (2002). Online learners' preferences for interaction. *TheQuarterly Review of Distance Education, 3*(2), 219–226.

Noruega-García, M. (2009). *Modelado y Análsis de Sistemas CSCW, Siguiendo un Enfoque de Ingeniería Dirigida por Odontologías*. Granada: Editorial de la Universidad de Granada.

Nosko, A., Wood, E., & Molema, S. (2010). All about me: Disclosure in online social networking profiles: The case of FACEBOOK. *Computers in Human Behavior, 26*(3), 406–418. doi:10.1016/j.chb.2009.11.012

Nouri, H., & Shahid, A. (2005). The effect of PowerPoint presentations on student learning and attitudes. *Global Perspectives on Accounting Education, 2*, 53–73.

Novak, J. D., & Gowin, D. B. (1984). *Learning how to learn*. New York, NY: Cambridge University Press. doi:10.1017/CBO9781139173469

Nugumanova, A. M., & Khamitova, G. H. (2013). The study of impact of teaching using multimedia technologies on visual analyzer among students of Medical University. *Prakticheskaja medicina, oftal'mologija, 1-3*(13). Retrieved from http://pmarchive.ru/izuchenie-vliyaniya-multimedijnyx-texnologij-prepodavaniya-na-sostoyanie-zritelnogo-analizatora-u-studentov-medicinskogo-universiteta/

Nurminsky, I. I., & Gladysheva, N. K. (1991). *Statistical regularities of forming of knowledge and abilities at pupils*. Moscow: Pedagogika.

Nussbaum, M. (2010). *Non per profitto. Perché le democrazie hanno bisogno della cultura umanistica*. Bologna, Italy: Il Mulino.

Nwana, H. S. (1996). Software agents: An overview. *The Knowledge Engineering Review, 11*(03), 205–244. doi:10.1017/S026988890000789X

O'Leary, D. E. (n.d.). *Technologies for knowledge assimilation*. Retrieved from https://msbfile03.usc.edu/digitalmeasures/doleary/intellcont/technologies-assimilation-1.pdf

O'Malley, J. M., & Chamot, A. U. (1990). *Learning strategies in second language acquisition*. London: Cambridge University Press. doi:10.1017/CBO9781139524490

O'Rourke, J. (2003). *Tutoring in open and distance learning: a handbook for tutors*. Vancouver: The Commonwealth of Learning.

Oberhelman, D. (2007). Coming to terms with Web 2.0. *Reference Reviews, 21*(7), 5–6. doi:10.1108/09504120710836473

OConnor, E. A. (2009). Instructional and design elements that support effective use of virtual worlds: What graduate student work reveals about Second Life. *Journal of Educational Technology Systems, 38*(2), 213–234. doi:10.2190/ET.38.2.j

Oculus, V. R. (2014). *Next-gen virtual reality*. Retrieved April 24, 2014, from http://www.oculusvr.com/rift

Okoniewski, A. E., Lee, Y. J., Rodriguez, M., Schnall, R., & Low, A. F. H. (2014). Health information seeking behaviors of ethnically diverse adolescents. *Journal of Immigrant and Minority Health, 16*(4), 652–660. doi:10.1007/s10903-013-9803-y PMID:23512322

Olivares, O. J. (2007). Collaborative vs. Cooperative Learning: The Instructor's Role in Computer Supported Collaborative Learning. In K. L. Orvis & A. L. R. Lassiter (Eds.), *Computer-Supported Collaborative Learning: Best Practices and Principles for Instructors* (pp. 20–39). Information Science Publishing.

Oliver, R. (2002). *A teaching and learning perspective on learning objects*. Paper presented at Online Learning and Information Environments, Sydney, NSW.

Olweus, D. (1993). *Bullying at school. What we know and what we can do*. Malden, MA: Blackwell Publishing.

OMalley, J. M., Chamot, A. U., & Kopper, L. (1989). Listening comprehension strategies in second language acquisition. *Applied Linguistics, 10*(4), 418–437. doi:10.1093/applin/10.4.418

Onrubia, J., & Engel, A. (2012). The role of teacher assistance on the effects of a macro-script in collaborative writing tasks. *International Journal of Computer-Supported Collaborative Learning, 7*(1), 161–186. doi:10.1007/s11412-011-9125-9

Orlov, J. M. (1984). *Need and motivational factors of efficiency of students' educational activity at University* (Unpublished candidate dissertation). Moscow.

Orr, E., Sisic, M., Ross, C., Simmering, M., Arseneault, J., & Orr, R. (2009). The influence of shyness on the use of Facebook in an undergraduate sample. *Cyberpsychology & Behavior*, *12*(3), 337–340. doi:10.1089/cpb.2008.0214 PMID:19250019

Ortega, M., & Bravo, J. (2001). Trabajo Cooperativo con Ordenador. In La Interacción Persona-Ordenador. Castilla-La Mancha, España: Ediciones de la Universidad de Castilla - La Mancha.

Orvis, K. L., & Lassiter, A. L. R. (2006). Computer-Supported Collaborative Learning: The Role of the Instructor. In S. P. Ferris & S. H. Godar (Eds.), *Teaching and learning with virtual teams* (pp. 158–179). Information Science Publishing. doi:10.4018/978-1-59140-708-9.ch007

Orwell, G. (1949). *Nineteen Eight-Four*. London: Penguin Books.

Osmundson, E., Chung, G. K. W. K., Herl, H. E., & Klein, D. C. D. (1999). *Knowledge mapping in the classroom: A tool for examining the development of students' conceptual understandings*. Los Angeles, CA: University of California.

Ovchinnikova, O. M. (2013). Structural and logical charts in learning of foreign economic terminology. Filologicheskie nauki. *Voprosy teorii i praktiki, 11*(29), 122-127.

Padavano, D. G. (2005). Student Satisfaction with Faculty-Student Interaction. *Sloan-C International Conferences on Asynchronous Learning 2005*.

Pallin, D. J., Sullivan, A. F., Kaushal, R., & Camargo, C. A. (2010). Health information technology in US emergency departments. *International Journal of Emergency Medicine, 3*(3), 181–185. doi:10.1007/s12245-010-0170-3 PMID:21031043

Palloff, R. M., & Pratt, K. (2003). *The virtual student: a profile and guide to working with online learners*. San Francisco: Jossey-Bass.

Paquay, L., Altet, M., Charlier, E., & Perrenoud, P. (2001). *Former des ensegnants professionnels*. Bruxelles, Belgique: De Boeck Université.

Pare, G., Sicotte, C., & Jacques, H. (2006). The effects of creating psychological ownership on physicians' acceptance of clinical information systems. *Journal of the American Medical Informatics Association, 13*(2), 197–205. doi:10.1197/jamia.M1930 PMID:16357351

Parkhomenko, M. V. (2003). *Fundamentals of organization of content acquisition in midchildhood* (Unpublished candidate dissertation). Rjazan'.

Park, N., Kerk, K., & Valenzuela, S. (2009). Being immersed in social networking environment: Facebook groups, uses and gratifications, and social outcomes. *Cyberpsychology & Behavior*, *12*(6), 729–733. doi:10.1089/cpb.2009.0003 PMID:19619037

Parmigiani, D. (2009). *Tecnologie di gruppo. Collaborare in classe con I media*. Trento, Italy: Erickson.

Paschal, A. M., Oler-Manske, J., Kroupa, K., & Snethen, E. (2008). Using a community-based participatory research approach to improve the performance capacity of local health departments: The Kansas immunization technology project. *Journal of Community Health, 33*(6), 407–416. doi:10.1007/s10900-008-9116-6 PMID:18587634

Patchin, J. W., & Hinduja, S. (2006). Bullies move beyond the schoolyard: A preliminary look at cyberbullying. *Youth Violence and Juvenile Justice, 4*(2), 148–169. doi:10.1177/1541204006286288

Patel, V. L., & Cohen, T. (2008). New perspectives on error in critical care. *Current Opinion in Critical Care, 14*(4), 456–459. doi:10.1097/MCC.0b013e32830634ae PMID:18614912

Patel, V. L., Kushniruk, A. W., Yang, S., & Yale, J. F. (2000). Impact of a computerized patient record system on medical data collection, organization and reasoning. *Journal of the American Medical Informatics Association*, 7(6), 569–585. doi:10.1136/jamia.2000.0070569 PMID:11062231

Păuleþ-Crãiniceanu, L. (2014). Integrating the Web 2.0 technologies in Romanian public universities. Towards a blended learning model that addresses troubled student-faculty interaction. *Procedia: Social and Behavioral Sciences*, 142, 793–799. doi:10.1016/j.sbspro.2014.07.618

Pearson, P. D. (1983). *Instructional Implications of Listening Comprehension Research*. Urbana, IL: Center for the Study of Reading.

Pejsahov, N. M., & Shevcov, M. N. (1991). *Practical psychology (the scientific basis): textbook*. Kazan': Izd-vo Kazansk. un-ta.

Pempek, T., Yemolayeva, Y., & Calvert, S. (2009). College students social networking experiences on Facebook. *Journal of Applied Developmental Psychology*, 30(3), 227–238. doi:10.1016/j.appdev.2008.12.010

Perren, S., Dooley, J., Shaw, T., & Cross, D. (2010). Bullying in school and cyberspace: Associations with depressive symptoms in Swiss and Australian adolescents. *Child and Adolescent Psychiatry and Mental Health*, 4(1), 1–10. doi:10.1186/1753-2000-4-28 PMID:21092266

Petrova, S. I., & Stepanova, Z. B. (2005). Japanese comics as the text type (category of informativeness). *Vestnik JaGU*, 2(4), 47–51.

Pezzotti, A., & Gambini, A. (2012). Indicatori di qualità per l'analisi della comunicazione di un corso online. *TD – Tecnologie Didattiche*, 20(2), 90-98.

Pezzotti, A., Broglia, A., & Gambini, A. (2014). Realizzazione di un learning object per favorire la cooperazione online. In T. Minerva & A. Simone (Eds.), *Politiche, Formazione, Tecnologie. Proceedings of IX Convegno della Sie-L, Roma, 12-13 ottobre 2013* (pp. 168-171). Roma, Italy: SIe-L Editore.

Phillips, L. M., Norris, S. P., & Macnab, J. S. (2010). *Visualization in mathematics, reading and science education*. Springer.

Piaget, J. (1983). Chapter. In P. Mussen (Ed.), Handbook of Child Psychology: Vol. 1. Piaget's theory (4th ed.). New York: Wiley.

Picciano, A. G. (2002). Beyond student perceptions: issues of interaction, presence, and performance in an online course. *JALN*, 21-40.

Pieri, M., & Diamantini, D. (2014). An e-learning Web 2.0 experience. *Procedia: Social and Behavioral Sciences*, 116, 1217–1221. doi:10.1016/j.sbspro.2014.01.371

Ping, Y., Li, H., & Gagnon, M. P. (2009). Health IT acceptance factors in long-term care facilities: A cross-sectional survey. *International Journal of Medical Informatics*, 78(4), 219–229. doi:10.1016/j.ijmedinf.2008.07.006 PMID:18768345

Pinto-Llorente, A. M., Sánchez-Gómez, M. C., & García-Peñalvo, F. J. (2015). Developing a VLE to enable the innovative learning of English pronunciation. In *Proceedings of the 3rd International Conference on Technological Ecosystems for Enhancing Multiculturality* (pp. 83-89). ACM. doi:10.1145/2808580.2808594

Pontecorvo, C., Ajello, A. M., & Zucchermaglio, C. (Eds.). (2004). *Discutendo si impara. Interazione e conoscenza a scuola*. Roma, Italy: Carocci Editore.

Popova, Z.I. (2008). Computer learning system. *Izvestija Volgogradskogo gosudarstvennogo tehnicheskogo universiteta*, 10(7), 154-156.

Popovici, S. (2011). The eGrammar clinic: A Moodle-based tutoring system for English as a second language. In *e-Education, Entertainment and e-Management (ICEEE), 2011 International Conference on* (pp. 50-54). IEEE. doi:10.1109/ICeEEM.2011.6137839

Pornari, C. D., & Wood, J. (2010). Peer and cyber aggression in secondary school students: The role of moral disengagement, hostile attribution bias, and outcome expectancies. *Aggressive Behavior, 36*(2), 81–94. doi:10.1002/ab.20336 PMID:20035548

Porter, L. R. (1997). *Creating the virtual classroom: Distance learning with the internet.* New York: John Wiley & Sons, Inc.

Prates, R. O., Rosson, M. B., & de Souza, C. S. (2015). Interaction Anticipation: Communicating Impacts of Groupware Configuration Settings to Users. In *Proceedings of 5th International Symposium, End-User Development, IS-EUD*, (pp. 192-197). Madrid, Spain: Springer International Publishing. doi:10.1007/978-3-319-18425-8_15

Preece, J., Rogers, Y., Sharp, H., Benyon, D., Holland, S., & Carey, T. (1994). *Human Computer Interaction. United Sates.* Addison-Wesley Publishing Company.

Preguica, N., Martins, L., Domingos, E., & Duarte, S. (2005). Integrating Synchronous and Asynchronous Interactions in Groupware Applications. *LNCS, 3706*, 89–104.

Premazzi, V. (2010). *L'integrazione online. Nativi e migranti fuori e dentro la rete. Rapporto Fieri.* Torino, Italy: Forum internazionale ed Europeo di Ricerche sull'immigrazione.

Prensky, M. (2009). H. Sapiens Digital: From Digital Immigrants and Digital Natives to Digital Wisdom. Innovate, 5(3).

Prensky, M. (2001). Digital natives, digital immigrants. *On the Horizon, 9*(5), 1–6. doi:10.1108/10748120110424816

Protti, D., Johansen, I., & Perez-Torres, F. (2009). Comparing the application of health information technology in primary care in Denmark and Andalucia, Spain. *International Journal of Medical Informatics, 78*(4), 270–283. doi:10.1016/j.ijmedinf.2008.08.002 PMID:18819836

Puskar, K. R., Aubrecht, J., Beamer, K., & Carozza, L. J. (2004). Implementing information technology in a behavioral health setting. *Issues in Mental Health Nursing, 25*(5), 439–450. doi:10.1080/01612840490443428 PMID:15204889

Qi, M., & Edgar-Nevill, D. (2011). Social networking searching and privacy issues. *Information Security Technical Report, 17*, 74–78.

Radley, A. (2013). Computers as Self. In *CD Proceedings Fourth International Workshop in Human-Computer Interaction, Tourism and Cultural Heritage in Rome, Italy.* Bergamo: Blue Herons Editions.

Radley, A. (2015). *Self as Computer.* Chalerston: BluePrints.

Rahimi, A. H. (2012). On the role of strategy use and strategy instruction in listening comprehension. *Journal of Language Teaching and Research, 3*(3), 550–559. doi:10.4304/jltr.3.3.550-559

Rahimi, E., van den Berg, J., & Veen, W. (2015a). A learning model for enhancing the student's control in educational process using Web 2.0 personal learning environments. *British Journal of Educational Technology, 46*(4), 780–792. doi:10.1111/bjet.12170

Rahimi, E., van den Berg, J., & Veen, W. (2015b). Facilitating student-driven constructing of learning environments using Web 2.0 personal learning environments. *Computers & Education, 81*, 235–246. doi:10.1016/j.compedu.2014.10.012

Randeree, E., & Mon, L. (2007). Web 2.0: A new dynamic in information services for libraries. *Proceedings of the American Society for Information Science and Technology, 44*(1), 1–6. doi:10.1002/meet.145044039

Rankin, Y. A., McNeal, M., Shute, M. W., & Gooch, B. (2008, August). User centered game design: evaluating massive multiplayer online role playing games for second language acquisition. In *Proceedings of the 2008 ACM SIGGRAPH symposium on Video games* (pp. 43-49). ACM. doi:10.1145/1401843.1401851

Rao, S., Brammer, C., McKethan, A., & Buntin, M. (2012). Health information technology: Transforming chronic disease management and care transitions. *Primary Care: Clinics in Office Practice*, *39*(2), 327–344. doi:10.1016/j.pop.2012.03.006 PMID:22608869

Rashed, D., Lyons, S., & Bae, H. K. (2010). Second Life in English as a Second Language Instruction. In *World Conference on E-Learning in Corporate, Government, Healthcare, and Higher Education* (No. 1).

Razmerita, L., Kirchner, K., & Sudzina, F. (2009). Personal knowledge management. *Online Information Review*, *33*(6), 1021–1039. doi:10.1108/14684520911010981

Reeve, C. (2000). Presence in virtual theater. *Presence (Cambridge, Mass.)*, *9*(2), 209–213. doi:10.1162/105474600566727

Regan, E. C., & Price, K. R. (1994). The frequency of occurrence and severity of side-effects of immersion virtual reality. *Aviation, Space, and Environmental Medicine*. PMID:8074626

Reid, J. (1998). Teachers as perceptual learning styles researchers. In J.M. Reid (Ed.), Understanding learning styles in the second language classroom, (pp. 15-26). Prentice-Hall Inc.

Reinecke, D., & Finn, L. L. (2015). Video lectures in online graduate education: Relationship between use of lectures and outcome measures. *Journal of Information Technology Education: Research*, *14*, 113–121.

Reinert, H. (1976). One picture is worth a thousand words? Not necessarily! *Modern Language Journal*, *60*, 160–168.

Reis, R., & Escudeiro, P. (2011). Educational software to enhance English language teaching in primary school. In *Information Technology Based Higher Education and Training (ITHET), 2011 International Conference on* (pp. 1-4). IEEE. doi:10.1109/ITHET.2011.6018684

Reis, A., Pedrosa, A., Dourado, M., & Reis, C. (2013). Information and communication technologies in long-term and palliative care. *Procedia Technology*, *9*, 1303–1312. doi:10.1016/j.protcy.2013.12.146

Reiser, R. A., & Dempsey, J. V. (2002). *Trends and issues in instructional design and technology*. Merrill Prentice Hall.

Reski, N., Nordmark, S., & Milrad, M. (2014). Exploring new interaction mechanisms to support information sharing and collaboration using large multi-touch displays in the context of digital storytelling. *IEEE Xplore*, *176-180*. doi:10.1109/ICALT.2014.59

Reuter, B. F., & Durán, E. (2014). Framework de recomendación automática de contenidos en foros de discusión para entornos de e-learning. In C. Cubillos, C. Rusu, & D. Gorgan (Eds.), *Proceedings of the 7th Euro American Conference on Telematics and Information Systems - EATIS '14* (pp. 1–2). Valparaiso: ACM Digital Library. doi:10.1145/2590651.2590689

Reynolds, R., Ali, M., & Jayyousi, T. (2008). Mining the Social Fabric of Archaic Urban Centers with Cultural Algorithms. *IEEE Computer*, *47*(1), 64–72. doi:10.1109/MC.2008.25

Rheingold, H. (1985). *Tools for Thought*. MITPress.

Richards, J. C. (1990). *The Language Teaching Matrix*. Cambridge University Press. 10.1017/CBO9780511667152

Richards, B. (2009). A social software/Web 2.0 approach to collaborative knowledge engineering. *Information Sciences*, *179*(15), 2515–2523. doi:10.1016/j.ins.2009.01.031

Richards, J. C. (2008). *Teaching Listening and Speaking: From Theory to Practice*. New York: Cambridge University Press.

Richards, J. C., & Schmidt, R. (2002). *Longman Dictionary of Language Teaching and Applied Linguistics* (3rd ed.). Harlow, UK: Pearson Education Limited.

Richmond, A. S., Krank, H. M., & Cummings, R. (2006). A brief research report: Thinking styles of online distance education students. *International Journal of Technology in Teaching and Learning, 2*(1), 58–64.

Richter, H., Blaha, B., Wiethoff, A., Baur, D., & Butz, A. (2011). Tactile feedback without a big fuss: simple actuators for high-resolution phantom sensations. In *Proceedings of the 13th international conference on Ubiquitous computing* (pp. 85-88). ACM. doi:10.1145/2030112.2030124

Rideout, V. J., Roberts, D. F., & Foehr, U. G. (2005). *Generation M: Media in the lives of 8-18-year-olds: Executive summary.* Menlo Park, CA: Henry J. Kaiser Family Foundation.

Riffenburgh, B. (2014). *Mapping the World: The Story of Cartography.* London: Carlton Publishing Group.

Riva, M. G. (2008). *L'insegnante professionista dell'educazione e della formazione.* Pisa, Italy: ETS Edizioni.

Rivers, W. M. (1981). *Listening Comprehension: Appraoch Design, Procedure.* TESOL Quartly.

Rivoltella, P. C. (Ed.). (2014b). Tecnologie digitali e management scolastico. Autonomia e dirigenza, 23.

Rivoltella, P. C. (2012a). Bambini, anziani e linguaggi elettronici. InRivoltella, P. C. (Ed.), *Progetto Generazioni. Bambini e anziani: due stagioni della vita a confronto.* Pisa, Italy: ETS Edizioni.

Rivoltella, P. C. (Ed.). (2003). *Costruttivismo e pragmatica della comunicazione on-line: socialità e didattica in internet.* Trento, Italy: Erickson.

Rivoltella, P. C. (Ed.). (2006a). *Media Education. Modelli, esperienze, profilo disciplinare.* Roma, Italy: Carocci.

Rivoltella, P. C. (Ed.). (2006b). *Screen Generation. Gli adolescenti e le prospettive dell'educazione nell'età dei media digitali.* Milano, Italy: Vita e Pensiero.

Rivoltella, P. C. (Ed.). (2014a). *Smart Future. Didattica, media digitali e inclusione.* Milano, Italy: Franco Angeli.

Robert, I. (1994). *Modern information technologies in education: didactic problems; prospects for use.* Moscow: Shkola-Press.

Robinson, A. H. (1995). *Elements of Cartography.* New York: John Whiley & Sons.

Roblyer, M., McDaniel, M., Webb, M., Herman, J., & Vince Witty, J. (2010). Findings on Facebook in higher education: A comparison of college faculty and student uses and perceptions of social networking sites. *The Internet and Higher Education, 13*(3), 134–140. doi:10.1016/j.iheduc.2010.03.002

Rocco, F., Rokach, L., & Shapira, B. (2011). Introduction to Recommender Systems Handbook. In F. Rocco, L. Rokach, B. Shapira, & P. Kantor (Eds.), *Recommender Systems Handbook* (pp. 1–35). Springer.

Rodríguez, P., Duque, N., & Ovalle, D. A. (2015). Multi-agent System for Knowledge-Based Recommendation of Learning Objects Using Metadata Clustering. In J. Bajo, K. Hallenborg, P. Pawlewski, V. Botti, N. Sánchez-Pi, N. D. D. Méndez, & V. Julian et al. (Eds.), *Highlights of Practical Applications of Agents, Multi-Agent Systems, and Sustainability-The PAAMS Collection* (Vol. 524, pp. 356–364). Springer. doi:10.1007/978-3-319-19033-4_31

Rogozynska, N. S., & Kozak, L. M. (2013). Information support of a technology for automated monitoring of the state of population health. *Cybernetics and Systems Analysis, 49*(6), 941–950. doi:10.1007/s10559-013-9585-1

Rollett, H., Lux, M., Strohmaier, M., Dosinger, G., & Tochtermann, K. (2007). The Web 2.0 way of learning with technologies. *International Journal of Learning Technology, 3*(1), 87–107. doi:10.1504/IJLT.2007.012368

Romashkina, N. V., Mishina, E. A., & Dolgaja, T. I. (2010). The organization of learning activity at lessons of physics in the logic of scientific knowledge using the interactive whiteboard. *Uchenye zapiski Zabajkal'skogo gosudarstvennogo universiteta. Serija: Fizika, matematika, tehnika, tehnologija, 2,* 82-85.

Rosé, C., Wang, Y.-C., Cui, Y., Arguello, J., Stegmann, K., Weinberger, A., & Fischer, F. (2008). Analyzing collaborative learning processes automatically: Exploiting the advances of computational linguistics in computer-supported collaborative learning. *International Journal of Computer-Supported Collaborative Learning, 3*(3), 237–271. doi:10.1007/s11412-007-9034-0

Rosenberg, D., & Grafton, A. (2012). *Cartographies of Time: A History of the Timeline.* New York: Princeton Architectural Press.

Rosen, L. D. (2007). *Me, Myspace, and I: Parenting the Net Generation.* New York: Palgrave Macmillan.

Ross, A. (2016). *The Industries of the Future.* New York: Simon & Schuster.

Ross, C., Orr, E., Sisic, M., Arseneault, J., Simmering, M., & Orr, R. (2009). Personality and motivations associated with Facebook use. *Computers in Human Behavior, 25*(2), 578–586. doi:10.1016/j.chb.2008.12.024

Rost, M. (1990). *Listening in language learning.* Longman Group Limited.

Rost, M. (2002). *Teaching and researching listening.* Harlow, UK: Pearson Education. Longman.

Rost, M. (2005). L2 listening. In E. Hinkel (Ed.), *Handbook of research in second language teaching and learning.* Mahwah, NJ: Erlbaum Associates.

Rousseau, J. J. (1762). Emile ou De L'éducation. In *Opere.* Firenze, Italy: Sansoni.

Roussou, M. (2006). Virtual reality and education: evaluating the learning experience. *Treballs d'Arqueologia,* (12), 69-85.

Rubin, J. (1995). An overview to a guide for the teaching of second language listening. In D. Mendelson & J. Rubin (Eds.), *A guide for the teaching of second language listening.* San Diego, CA: Dominie Press.

Rubinstein, S. L. (2005). *Fundamentals of general psychology.* St. Petersburg: Peter.

Rubio, R., Martín, S., & Morán, S. (2010). Collaborative web learning tools: Wikis and blogs. *Computer Applications in Engineering Education, 18*(3), 502–511. doi:10.1002/cae.20218

Russell, B. (1963). *Skeptical Essays.* Chicago: University of Chicago Press.

Russell, S., & Norvig, P. (2010). *Artificial Intelligence: A Modern Approach* (3rd ed.). Prentice Hall.

Saadé, R. G., & AlSharhan, J. (2015). Discovering the motivations of students when using an online learning tool. *Journal of Information Technology Education: Research, 14,* 283–296.

Sabinina, A. A. (2009). Educational text: Structure and pragmatics. *Izvestija Rossijskogo gosudarstvennogo pedagicheskogo universiteta im. A.I. Gercena, 97,* 222–224.

Sadaf, A., Newby, T. J., & Ertmer, P. A. (2012). Exploring pre-service teachers' beliefs about using Web 2.0 technologies in K-12 classroom. *Computers & Education, 59*(3), 937–945. doi:10.1016/j.compedu.2012.04.001

Sagar, A. B. (2012). Transparency Computation for Work Groups. *LNCS, 7154,* 265–266.

Sahin, M. (2010). Teachers perceptions of bullying in high schools: A Turkish study. *Social Behavior and Personality, 38*(1), 127–142. doi:10.2224/sbp.2010.38.1.127

Saleem, J. J., Patterson, E. S., Militello, L., Render, M. L., Orshansky, G., & Asch, S. M. (2005). Exploring barriers and facilitators to the use of computerized clinical reminders. *Journal of the American Medical Informatics Association*, *12*(4), 438–447. doi:10.1197/jamia.M1777 PMID:15802482

Salvendy, G. (2012). *Handbook of Human Factors and Ergonomics*. New York: John Wiley. doi:10.1002/9781118131350

Samuels, S. J. (1984). Factors influencing listening: Inside and outside the head. *Theory into Practice*, *23*(3), 183–189. doi:10.1080/00405848409543112

Santrock, J. W. (2004). *Life-Span development*. Boston, MA: McGraw-Hill College.

Saracevic, T. (2010). The notion of context in Information Interaction in Context. In *Proceedings of the third symposium on Information interaction in context* (pp. 1-2). ACM. doi:10.1145/1840784.1840786

Saricoban, A. (1999). The teaching of listening. *The Internet TESL Journal, 5*(12). Retrieved from http://iteslj.org/Articles/Saricoban-Listening.html

Sawoski, P. (2010). The Stanislavski system growth and methodology. Santa Monica College.

Scalvini, S., Baratti, D., Assoni, G., Zanardini, M., Comini, L., & Bernocchi, P. (2014). Information and communication technology in chronic diseases: A patient's opportunity. *Journal of Medicine and the Person*, *12*(3), 91–95. doi:10.1007/s12682-013-0154-1

Schmid, R., & Zambarbieri, D. (Eds.). (1991). *Oculomotor Control and Cognitive Processes – Normal and Pathological Aspects*. Amsterdam: Elsevier Science Publisher B.V.

Schneckenberg, D., Ehlers, U., & Adelsberger, H. (2011). Web 2.0 and competence-oriented design of learning: Potentials and implications for higher education. *British Journal of Educational Technology*, *42*(5), 747–762. doi:10.1111/j.1467-8535.2010.01092.x

Schreurs, B., & de Laat, M. (2014). The network awareness tool: A Web 2.0 tool to visualize informal networked learning in organizations. *Computers in Human Behavior*, *37*, 385–394. doi:10.1016/j.chb.2014.04.034

Schwarz, B. B., & Asterhan, C. S. (2011). E-Moderation of Synchronous Discussions in Educational Settings: A Nascent Practice. *Journal of the Learning Sciences*, *20*(3), 395–442. doi:10.1080/10508406.2011.553257

Sebeok, T. (2001). *Global Semiotics*. Bloomington, IN: Indiana University Press.

Segal, K. (2012). *Insanely Simple*. London: Penguin.

Seo, D., & Lee, J. (2016). Web_2.0 and five years since: How the combination of technological and organizational initiatives influences an organizations long-term Web_2.0 performance. *Telematics and Informatics*, *33*(1), 232–246. doi:10.1016/j.tele.2015.07.010

SEP (2008). *La enseñanza de idiomas en México. Diagnóstico, avances y desafíos. DGAR. Reunión nacional de control escolar*. Power point. Documento interno.

SEP. (2006). *Orientaciones Generales para el Funcionamiento de los Servicios de Educación Especial - Integración Educativa*. Zacatecas: Secretaría de Educación Pública, Gobierno del Estado de Zacatecas.

Sequist, T. D. (2011). Health information technology and disparities in quality of care. *Journal of General Internal Medicine*, *26*(10), 1084–1085. doi:10.1007/s11606-011-1812-8 PMID:21809173

Sequist, T. D., Cook, D. A., Haas, J. S., Horner, R., & Tierney, W. M. (2008). Moving health information technology forward. *Journal of General Internal Medicine*, *23*(4), 355–357. doi:10.1007/s11606-008-0551-y PMID:18373129

Serri, F., Boroujeni, A. J., & Hesabi, A. (2012). Cognitive, metacognitive, and social/affective strategies in listening comprehension and their relationships with individual differences. *Theory and Practice in Language Studies, 2*(4), 843. doi:10.4304/tpls.2.4.843-849

Sevcikova, A., Machackova, H., Wright, M. F., Dedkova, L., & Cerna, A. (2015). Social support seeking in relation to parental attachment and peer relationships among victims of cyberbullying. *Australian Journal of Guidance & Counselling, 15*, 1–13. doi:10.1017/jgc.2015.1

Shapka, J. D., & Law, D. M. (2013). Does one size fit all? Ethnic differences in parenting behaviors and motivations for adolescent engagement in cyberbullying. *Journal of Youth and Adolescence, 42*(5), 723–738. doi:10.1007/s10964-013-9928-2 PMID:23479327

Shariff, S., & Hoff, D. L. (2007). Cyber bullying: Clarifying legal boundaries for school supervision in cyberspace. *International Journal of Cyber Criminology, 1*, 76–118.

Sharma, P. (2009). *Controversies in using technology in language teaching.* Retrieved from http://www.teachingenglish. org.uk/articles/controversies-using-technology-language-teaching

Shen, J., & Eder, L. B. (2009). Intentions to use virtual worlds for education. *Journal of Information Systems Education, 20*(2), 225.

Shih, Y. C. T., Pan, I. W., & Tsai, Y. W. (2009). Information technology facilitates cost-effectiveness analysis in developing countries. *PharmacoEconomics, 27*(11), 947–961. doi:10.2165/11314110-000000000-00000 PMID:19888794

Shishehchi, S., Banihashem, S. Y., & Zin, N. A. M. (2011). A Proposed Semantic Recommendation System for E-Learning. A Rule and Ontology Based E-learning Recommendation System. In A. K. Mahmood, H. B. Zaman, P. Robinson, S. Elliot, P. Haddawy, S. Olariu, & Z. Awang (Eds.), *2010 International Symposium in Information Technology (ITSim)* (pp. 1–5). Kuala Lumpur: IEEE Press.

Shneiderman, B. (2002). Creativity Support Tools. *Communications of the ACM, 45*(10), 116–120. doi:10.1145/570907.570945

Shoemaker, G., Tsukitani, T., Kitamura, Y., & Booth, K. S. (2010). Body-centric interaction techniques for very large wall displays. In *NordiCHI '10: Proceedings of the 6th nordic conference on human-computer interaction: Extending boundaries* (pp. 463-472). ACM. doi:10.1145/1868914.1868967

Shoemaker, G., Tsukitani, T., Kitamura, Y., & Booth, K. S. (2012). Two-Part models capture the impact of gain on pointing performance. *ACM Trans. Comput.-Hum. Interact., 19*(4), 28:1-28:34. doi:10.1145/2395131.2395135

Siegel, D. J. (1999). *La mente relazionale. Neurobiologia dell'esperienza interpersonale.* Milano, Italy: Raffaello Cortina Editore.

SigCHI. (1982). *The ACM Special Interest Group on Computer-Human Interaction. Association for Computing Machinery.* Retrieved 20 February, 2016 from: http://www.sigchi.org

Sijtsema, J. J., Ashwin, R. J., Simona, C. S., & Gina, G. (2014). Friendship selection and influence in bullying and defending. *Effects of moral disengagement. Developmental Psychology, 50*(8), 2093–2104. doi:10.1037/a0037145 PMID:24911569

Simoens, S., & Laekeman, G. (2005). Applying health technology assessment to pharmaceutical care: Pitfalls and future directions. *Pharmacy World & Science, 27*(2), 73–75. doi:10.1007/s11096-004-4098-7 PMID:15999914

Simonson, M. S. (2012). *Teaching and learning at a distance: Foundations of distance education.* Boston: Pearson.

Simpson, R. J., & Galbo, J. J. (1986). Interaction and learning: Theorizing on the art of teaching. *Interchange*, *17*(4), 37–51. doi:10.1007/BF01807015

Sini, C. (2000). Idoli della conoscenza. Torino, Italy: Raffaello Cortina Ed.

Sinsky, C. A., Willard-Grace, R., Schutzbank, A. M., Sinsky, T. A., Margolius, D., & Bodenheimer, T. (2013). In search of joy in practice: A report of 23 high-functioning primary care practices. *Annals of Family Medicine*, *11*(3), 272–278. doi:10.1370/afm.1531 PMID:23690328

Sittig, D. F. (2006). Potential impact of advanced clinical information technology on cancer care in 2015. *Cancer Causes & Control*, *17*(6), 813–820. doi:10.1007/s10552-006-0020-z PMID:16783609

Sjurso, I. R., Fandream, H., & Roland, E. (2016). Emotional problems in traditional and cyber victimization. *Journal of School Violence*, *15*(1), 114–131. doi:10.1080/15388220.2014.996718

Skylar, A. (2009). A Comparison of asynchronous online text-based lectures and synchronous interactive web conferencing lectures. *Issues in Teacher Education*, 69–84.

Slater, M., Howell, J., Steed, A., Pertaub, D.-P., & Garau, M. (2000). Acting in virtual reality. *Proceedings of the third international conference on Collaborative virtual environments*, 103–110. doi:10.1145/351006.351020

Slater, M., & Wilbur, S. (1997). A framework for immersive virtual environments (five): Speculations on the role of presence in virtual environments. *Presence (Cambridge, Mass.)*, *6*(6), 603–616. doi:10.1162/pres.1997.6.6.603

Smith, A., & Rogers, S. (2008). Web 2.0 and official statistics: The case for a multi-disciplinary approach. *Statistical Journal of the IAOS*, *25*(3/4), 117–123.

Smith, P. K., Del Barrio, C., & Tokunaga, R. S. (2013). Definitions of bullying and cyberbullying: How useful are the terms? In S. Bauman, D. Cross, & J. Walker (Eds.), *Principles of cyberbullying research: Definitions, measures, methodology* (pp. 26–40). New York, NY: Routledge.

Smith, P. K., Mahdavi, J., Carvalho, M., Fisher, S., Russell, S., & Tippett, N. (2008). Cyberbullying: Its nature and impact in secondary school pupils. *Journal of Child Psychology and Psychiatry, and Allied Disciplines*, *49*(4), 376–385. doi:10.1111/j.1469-7610.2007.01846.x PMID:18363945

Smith, W., & Kidder, D. (2010). Youve been tagged! (Then again, maybe not): Employers and Facebook. *Business Horizons*, *53*(5), 491–499. doi:10.1016/j.bushor.2010.04.004

Snigireva, T. A., & Grishanova, I. A. (2014). An integrated approach in evaluation the quality of knowledge structure of a student. *Fundamental'nye issledovanija, 11-6*, 1382-1385.

Soh, J., & Tan, B. (2008). Mobile Gaming. *Communications of the ACM*, *51*(3), 35–39. doi:10.1145/1325555.1325563

Soh, L.-K., Khandaker, N., & Jiang, H. (2008). I-MINDS: A multiagent system for intelligent computer- supported collaborative learning and classroom management. *International Journal of Artificial Intelligence in Education*, *18*(2), 119–151.

Sokolova, I. J., & Ivanova, T. V. (2014). The development of personal potential of students in preparation for professional activity. *Professional'noe obrazovanie v Rossii i za rubezhom, 1*(13), 86-91.

Soller, A. (2001). Supporting Social Interaction in an Intelligent Collaborative Learning System. *International Journal of Artificial Intelligence in Education*, *12*(1), 40–62.

Soller, A. (2004). Computational Modeling and Analysis of Knowledge Sharing in Collaborative Distance Learning. *User Modeling and User-Adapted Interaction*, *14*(4), 351–381. doi:10.1023/B:USER.0000043436.49168.3b

Soller, A., Monés, A. M., Jermann, P., & Muehlenbrock, M. (2005). From Mirroring to Guiding: A Review of State of the Art Technology for Supporting Collaborative Learning. *International Journal of Artificial Intelligence in Education*, *15*(4), 261–290.

Solomon, M. R. (2007). Regional health information organizations: A vehicle for transforming health care delivery? *Journal of Medical Systems*, *31*(1), 35–47. doi:10.1007/s10916-006-9041-0 PMID:17283921

Solomon, M. R. (2008). Information technology to support self-management in chronic care. *Disease Management & Health Outcomes*, *16*(6), 391–401. doi:10.2165/0115677-200816060-00004

Song, D., & Lee, J. (2014). Has Web 2.0 revitalized informal learning? The relationship between Web 2.0 and informal learning. *Journal of Computer Assisted Learning*, *30*(6), 511–533. doi:10.1111/jcal.12056

Sørensen, B. H., & Meyer, B. (2007). Serious Games in language learning and teaching–a theoretical perspective. In *Proceedings of the 3rd international conference of the digital games research association* (pp. 559-566).

Sosa, M., Velázquez, I., Zarco, R., & Postiglioni, A. (2006). Modelo de Soporte para el Trabajo y Aprendizaje Colaborativo de Grupos de Investigación. *XII Congreso Argentino de Ciencias de la Computación*, 1034-1044.

Souali, K., El Afia, A., Faizi, R., & Chiheb, R. (2011). A new recommender system for e-learning environments. In *International Conference on Multimedia Computing and Systems -Proceedings* (pp. 1–4). Ouarzazate: IEEE Press. doi:10.1109/ICMCS.2011.5945630

Sourander, A., Brunstein, A., Ikonen, M., Lindroos, J., Luntamo, T., Koskelainen, M., & Helenius, H. et al. (2010). Psychosocial risk factors associated with cyberbullying among adolescents: A population-based study. *Archives of General Psychiatry*, *67*(7), 720–728. doi:10.1001/archgenpsychiatry.2010.79 PMID:20603453

Spinelli, A. (2009). *Un'officina di uomini. La scuola del costruttivismo*. Napoli, Italy: Liguori.

Stabile, M., & Cooper, L. (2013). Review article: The evolving role of information technology in perioperative patient safety. Canadian Journal of Anesthesia/Journal canadien d'anesthésie, 60(2), 119–126. doi:10.1007/s12630-012-9851-0

Stafinski, T., Menon, D., Philippon, D. J., & McCabe, C. (2011). Health technology funding decision-making processes around the world. *PharmacoEconomics*, *29*(6), 475–495. doi:10.2165/11586420-000000000-00000 PMID:21568357

Stahl, J. E. (2008). Modelling methods for pharmacoeconomics and health technology assessment. *PharmacoEconomics*, *26*(2), 131–148. doi:10.2165/00019053-200826020-00004 PMID:18198933

Stanislavski, C. (2013). *Building a character*. A&C Black.

Starfield, B., Shi, L., & Macinko, J. (2005). Contribution of primary care to health systems and health. *The Milbank Quarterly*, *83*(3), 457–502. doi:10.1111/j.1468-0009.2005.00409.x PMID:16202000

Steen, H. L. (2008). Effective eLearning design. *Journal of Online Learning and Teaching*, *4*(4), 526–532.

Steptoe, W., Normand, J.-M., Oyekoya, O., Pece, F., Giannopoulos, E., Tecchia, F., & Slater, M. et al. (2012). Acting rehearsal in collaborative multimodal mixed reality environments. *Presence (Cambridge, Mass.)*, *21*(4), 406–422. doi:10.1162/PRES_a_00109

Sterling, S. L. (2001). *Sustainable Education: Re-visioning Learning and Change*. Bristol, UK: Green Books, Ltd. for the Schumacher Society.

Stewart, I. (2012). *Seventeen Equations that Changed the World*. London: Profile Books.

Stoll, L. C., & Block, R. Jr. (2015). Intersectionality and cyberbullying: A study of cybervictimization in a Midwestern high school. *Computers in Human Behavior*, *52*, 387–391. doi:10.1016/j.chb.2015.06.010

Strohmeier, D., Aoyama, I., Gradinger, P., & Toda, Y. (2013). Cybervictimization and cyberaggression in Eastern and Western countries: Challenges of constructing a cross-cultural appropriate scale. In S. Bauman, D. Cross, & J. L. Walker (Eds.), *Principles of cyberbullying research: Definitions, measures, and methodology* (pp. 202–221). New York: Routledge.

Styliaras, G., Koukopoulos, D., & Lazarinis, F. (2011). *Handbook of Research on Technologies and Cultural Heritage: Applications and Environments*. Hershey, PA: IGI Global. doi:10.4018/978-1-60960-044-0

Su, A., Yang, S., Hwang, W., & Zhang, J. (2010). A Web 2.0-based collaborative annotation system for enhancing knowledge sharing in collaborative learning environments. *Computers & Education*, *55*(2), 752–766. doi:10.1016/j.compedu.2010.03.008

Suarez, M.C. (2011). *SIRIUS: Sistema de Evaluación de la Usabilidad Web Orientado al Usuario y basado en la Determinación de Tareas Críticas* (Tesis Doctoral). Universidad de Oviedo, España.

Suh, H.-J., & Lee, S. W. (2006). Collaborative Learning Agent for Promoting Group Interaction. *ETRI Journal*, *28*(4), 461–474. doi:10.4218/etrij.06.0105.0235

Suhih, A. E., & Korytchenkova, N. I. (2008). Theoretical analysis of cognitive characteristics in psychology. *Vestnik KemGU. Psihologija*, *4*, 97–100.

Suler, J. (2004). The online disinhibition effect. *Cyberpsychology & Behavior*, *7*(3), 321–326. doi:10.1089/1094931041291295 PMID:15257832

Sultan, N. (2013). Knowledge management in the age of cloud computing and Web 2.0: Experiencing the power of disruptive innovations. *International Journal of Information Management*, *33*(1), 160–165. doi:10.1016/j.ijinfomgt.2012.08.006

Svensson, M., & Lagerros, Y. (2010). Motivational technologies to promote weight loss from Internet to gadgets. *Patient Education and Counseling*, *79*(3), 356–360. doi:10.1016/j.pec.2010.03.004 PMID:20378298

Takahashi, T. B., Takahashi, S., Kusunoki, F., Terano, T., & Inagaki, S. (2013). Making a hands-on display with augmented reality work at a science museum. *IEEE Xplore*, 385-390. doi:10.1109/SITIS.2013.69

Tamburini, D. (2010). Linguaggio cinematografico e comunicazione formativa. In *Adolescenti e media: cinema, televisione e ruolo della scuola*. Milano, Italy: Centro Filippo Buonarroti.

Tan, A.-H. (1999). Text Mining: The state of the art and the challenges. In *Proceedings of the PAKDD 1999 Workshop on Knowledge Disocovery from Advanced Databases* (pp. 65-70).

Tangen, D., & Campbell, M. (2010). Cyberbullying prevention: One primary schools approach. *Australian Journal of Guidance & Counselling*, *20*(02), 225–234. doi:10.1375/ajgc.20.2.225

Tattersall, A. (2011). How the web was won … by some. *Health Information and Libraries Journal*, *28*(3), 226–229. doi:10.1111/j.1471-1842.2011.00945.x PMID:21831222

Tauscher, J., Davis, W. O., Brown, D., Ellis, M., Ma, Y., Sherwood, M. E., & Coy, J. W. et al. (2010). Evolution of mems scanning mirrors for laser projection in compact consumer electronics. In *MOEMS-MEMS* (pp. 75940A–75940A). International Society for Optics and Photonic. doi:10.1117/12.843095

Tchounikine, P., Rummel, N., & McLaren, B. M. (2010). Computer Supported Collaborative Learning and Intelligent Tutoring Systems. In R. Nkambou, J. Bourdeau, & R. Mizoguchi (Eds.), *Advances in Intelligent Tutoring Systems* (Vol. 308, pp. 447–463). Springer-Verlag Berlin Heidelberg. doi:10.1007/978-3-642-14363-2_22

Technical Illusions. (2015). *CastAR*. Retrieved March 18, 2015, from http://castar.com

Teng, H. C. (1993). *Effects of culture-specific knowledge and visual cues on Chinese EFL students' listening comprehension*. Academic Press.

The Hidden Dimension. (1990). New York: Anchor Books.

Thompson, M., Nordin, A., & Cairns, P. (2012). *Effect of touch-screen size on game immersion*. Retrieved from http://dl.acm.org/citation.cfm?id=2377952

Tick, A. (2009). The MILES Military English learning system pilot project. In *Computational Cybernetics, 2009. ICCC 2009. IEEE International Conference on* (pp. 57-62). IEEE. doi:10.1109/ICCCYB.2009.5393930

Ting, Z. L. K., Lim, Y. P., & Sharji, E. A. (2013). Young visitors' preferences for touch screen design in museums. *IEEE Xplore, 288-291*. doi:10.1109/ICICM.2013.55

Todorov, T. (1989). *Nous et les autres. La réflextion francaise sur la diversité humaine*. Torino, Italy: Edizioni Paperbacks Sienze sociali, Einaudi.

Toledano, S., Werch, B. L., & Wiens, B. A. (2015). Domain-specific self-concept in relation to traditional and cyber peer aggression. *Journal of School Violence, 14*(4), 405–423. doi:10.1080/15388220.2014.935386

Totura, C. M. W., MacKinnon-Lewis, C., Gesten, E. L., Gadd, R., Divine, K. P., Dunham, S., & Kamboukos, D. (2009). Bullying and victimization among boys and girls in middle school: The influence of perceived family and school contexts. *The Journal of Early Adolescence, 29*(4), 571–609. doi:10.1177/0272431608324190

Travis, D. (2008). *Measuring satisfaction: Beyond the usability questionnaire*. Retrieved April 12, 2015, from http://www.userfocus.co.uk/articles/satisfaction.html

Trepka, M. J., Newman, F. L., Huffman, F. G., & Dixon, Z. (2010). Food safety education using an interactive multimedia kiosk in a WIC setting: Correlates of clients satisfaction and practical issues. *Journal of Nutrition Education and Behavior, 42*(3), 202–207. doi:10.1016/j.jneb.2008.10.001 PMID:20149752

Troeshestova, D. A., & Ivanova, M. V. (2013). The selection of interactive methods of training for students of the specialty "Mathematics" on the basis of psychological and pedagogical monitoring. *Vestnik Chuvashskogo universiteta, 2*, 141-145.

Tung, F. C., Chang, S. C., & Chou, C. M. (2008). An extension of trust and TAM model with IDT in the adoption of the electronic logistics information system in HIS in the medical industry. *International Journal of Medical Informatics, 77*(5), 324–335. doi:10.1016/j.ijmedinf.2007.06.006 PMID:17644029

Turkle, S. (2011). *Alone together: Why we expect more from technology and less from each other*. Basic Books.

Tuval-Mashiach, R. (2014). Life Stories in Context: Using the Three-Sphere Context Model To Analyze Amos's Narrative. *Narrative Works, 4*(1).

Tzeng, H., Ming, H., & Yin, C. Y. (2008). Nurses' solutions to prevent inpatient falls in hospital patient rooms. *Nursing Economics, 26*(3), 179–187. PMID:18616056

UDHR. (1948). *Universal Declaration of Human Rights*. UN General Assembly.

Ugazio, V. (2012). *Storie permesse, storie proibite. Polarità semantiche familiari e psicopatologie. Nuova edizione ampliata, aggiornata e rivista*. Torino, Italy: Bollati Boringhieri.

Ulanovskaja, K. A., Kaljuzhnov, E. J., & Antropov, I. V. (2013). Individualization of evaluation of knowledge quality. *Izvestija Volgogradskogo gosudarstvennogo tehnicheskogo universiteta, 12-2*(105), 130-133.

University of Southern California. (2007). *Flatworld project*. Retrieved April 24, 2014, from http://ict.usc.edu/projects/flatworld

Urey, H., Chellappan, K. V., Erden, E., & Surman, P. (2011). State of the art in stereoscopic and autostereoscopic displays. *Proceedings of the IEEE, 99*(4), 540–555. doi:10.1109/JPROC.2010.2098351

Ur, P. (2005). *Teaching Listening Comprehension*. Cambridge University Press.

Usability.gov. (2015). *Improving the User Experience*. Retrieved March 14, 2016, from http://goo.gl/f3G6Ux

UsabilityFirst. (2015). *Low-fidelity prototype*. Retrieved March 14, 2016, from http://goo.gl/2Ja8Ed

Van Lent, M. (2008). The Business of Fun. *IEEE Computer, 41*(2), 97–103. doi:10.1109/MC.2008.64

van Schaik, P., Bettany-Saltikov, J. A., & Warren, J. G. (2002). Clinical acceptance of a low-cost portable system for postural assessment. *Behaviour & Information Technology, 21*(1), 47–57. doi:10.1080/01449290110107236

Vandergrift, L. (1996). Listening Comprehension Strategies of Core French High School Students. *Canadian Modern Language Review, 52*(2), 200–223.

Vandergrift, L. (1999). Facilitating second language listening comprehension: Acquiring successful strategies. *ELT Journal, 53*(3), 168–176. doi:10.1093/elt/53.3.168

Vandergrift, L. (2007). Recent developments in second and foreign language listening comprehension research. *Language Teaching, 40*(03), 191–210. doi:10.1017/S0261444807004338

Varvel, V. E. (2007). Master Online Teacher Competencies. *Online Journal of Distance Learning Administration, 10*, 1–47.

Veltman, K. (2006). *Understanding New Media*. Calgary: University of Calgary Press.

Veltman, K. (2006). *Understanding New Media: Augmented Knowledge and Culture*. Calgary: University of Calgary Press.

Veltman, K. (2014). *Alphabets of Life*. Maastricht: Virtual Maastrict McLuhan Institute.

Veltman, K. (2014). *The Alphabets of Life*. Maastricht: Virtual Maastricht McLuhan Institute.

Venkatesh, V., Zhang, X., & Sykes, T. A. (2011). "Doctors do too little technology": A longitudinal field study of an electronic healthcare system implementation. *Information Systems Research, 22*(3), 523–546. doi:10.1287/isre.1110.0383

Verdugo, D. R., & Belmonte, I. A. (2007). Using digital stories to improve listening comprehension with Spanish young learners of English. *Language Learning & Technology, 11*(1), 87–101.

Virga, P. H., Jin, B., Thomas, J., & Virodov, S. (2012). Electronic health information technology as a tool for improving quality of care and health outcomes for HIV/AIDS patients. *International Journal of Medical Informatics, 81*(10), e39–e45. doi:10.1016/j.ijmedinf.2012.06.006 PMID:22890224

Virkus, S. (2008). Use of Web 2.0 technologies in LIS education: Experiences at Tallinn University, Estonia. Program: Electronic Library and Information Systems, 42(3), 262–274.

Vucovich, L. A., Gordon, V. S., Mitchell, N., & Ennis, L. A. (2013). Is the time and effort worth it? One library's evaluation of using social networking tools for outreach. *Medical Reference Services Quarterly, 32*(1), 12–25. doi:10.1080/02763869.2013.749107 PMID:23394417

Vumyatnin, V. M., Demkin, V. P., Mozhaeva, G. V., & Rudenko, T. V. (2002). Multimedia courses: methodology and technology of development. *Otkrytoe i distancionnoe obrazovanie, 3*(7), 34-61.

Vuzix. (2014). *Vuzix*. Retrieved April 24, 2014, from http://www.vuzix.com

Wade, A., & Beran, T. (2011). Cyberbullying: The new era of bullying. *Canadian Journal of School Psychology*, *26*(1), 44–61. doi:10.1177/0829573510396318

Wagner, C., & Ip, R. K. (2009). Action learning with Second Life-A pilot study. *Journal of Information Systems Education*, *20*(2), 249.

Wagner, E. D. (1994). In support of a functional definition of interaction. *American Journal of Distance Education*, *8*(2), 6–29. doi:10.1080/08923649409526852

Wagner, J., Nancel, M., Gustafson, S. G., Huot, S., & Mackay, W. E. (2013). Body-centric design space for multi-surface interaction. In *CHI '13: Proceedings of the SIGCHI conference on human factors in computing systems* (pp. 1299-1308). ACM. doi:10.1145/2470654.2466170

Wahab, N., & Zaman, H. B. (2013). The Significance of Multi-Touch Table in Collaborative Setting: How Relevant this Technology in Military Decision Making. *Applied Mechanics and Materials*, *278-280*, 1830–1833. doi:10.4028/www.scientific.net/AMM.278-280.1830

Walsh, K., & Callan, A. (2011). Perceptions, preferences, and acceptance of information and communication technologies in older-adult community care settings in Ireland: A case-study and ranked-care program analysis. *Ageing International*, *36*(1), 102–122. doi:10.1007/s12126-010-9075-y

Walter, Z., & Lopez, M. S. (2008). Physician acceptance of information technologies: Role of perceived threat to professional autonomy. *Decision Support Systems*, *46*(1), 206–215. doi:10.1016/j.dss.2008.06.004

Wang, Y., & Braman, J. (2009). Extending the classroom through Second Life. *Journal of Information Systems Education*, *20*(2), 235.

Waterson, P. (2014). Health information technology and sociotechnical systems: A progress report on recent developments within the UK National Health Service (NHS). *Applied Ergonomics*, *45*(2), 150–161. doi:10.1016/j.apergo.2013.07.004 PMID:23895916

Waterson, P. E., Glenn, Y., & Eason, K. D. (2012). Preparing the ground for the "Paperless Hospital": A case study of medical records management in a UK Outpatient Services department. *International Journal of Medical Informatics*, *81*(2), 114–129. doi:10.1016/j.ijmedinf.2011.10.011 PMID:22088601

Waters, R., Burnett, E., Lamm, A., & Lucas, J. (2009). Engaging stakeholders through social networking: How nonprofit organizations are using Facebook. *Public Relations Review*, *35*(2), 102–106. doi:10.1016/j.pubrev.2009.01.006

Wei, Z., Liu, W., He, Q., & Wei, N. (2011). *The design of infrared touch screen based on MCU*. Retrieved from http://ieeexplore.ieee.org/xpls/abs_all.jsp?arnumber=5949041

Weiner, M., & Biondich, P. (2006). The influence of information technology on patient-physician relationships. *Journal of General Internal Medicine*, *21*(1), 35–39. doi:10.1111/j.1525-1497.2006.00307.x PMID:16405708

Weir, G., Toolan, F., & Smeed, D. (2011). The threats of social networking: Old wine in new bottles? *Information Security Technical Report*, *16*(2), 38–43. doi:10.1016/j.istr.2011.09.008

Wenger, E. (1998). *Communities of practice: Learning, meaning, and identity*. Cambridge, UK: Cambridge University Press. doi:10.1017/CBO9780511803932

Wickremaratne, J., Wimalaratne, G., & Goonetilleke, V. (2008). A Blend of Adaptive and Digital Learning Towards Language Proficiency. In *Information and Automation for Sustainability, 2008. ICIAFS 2008. 4th International Conference on* (pp. 173-178). IEEE. doi:10.1109/ICIAFS.2008.4783942

Wiener, N. (1950). *The Human Use of Human Beings*. Boston: Hougthon Mifflin.

Willing, K. (1993). *Learning styles in adult migrant education*. Sydney: Macquarie University.

Wilson, E. O. (1993). *The Biophilia Hypothesis*. Washington, DC: Island Press.

Wilson, E. V., & Lankton, N. K. (2004). Modeling patients' acceptance of provider-delivered e-health. *Journal of the American Medical Informatics Association*, *11*(4), 241–248. doi:10.1197/jamia.M1475 PMID:15064290

Wilson, G. L. (2007). *Grupos en Contexto, Liderazgo y Participación en Grupos Pequeños*. McGraw-Hill.

Winn, W. (2002). Research into practice: Current trends in educational technology research: The study of learning environments. *Educational Psychology Review*, *14*(3), 331–351. doi:10.1023/A:1016068530070

Winograd, T. (1994). Designing the Designer. *Human-Computer Interaction*, *9*(1), 128–132.

Wintergerst, A. C., DeCapua, A., & Verna, M. A. (2003). Conceptualizing learning style modalities for ESL/EFL students. *System*, *31*(1), 85–106. doi:10.1016/S0346-251X(02)00075-1

Winter, S., & Kramer, N. C. (2012). Selecting science information in Web 2.0: How source cues, message sidedness, and need for cognition influence users' exposure to blog posts. *Journal of Computer-Mediated Communication*, *18*(1), 80–96. doi:10.1111/j.1083-6101.2012.01596.x

Wirtz, B. W., Schilke, O., & Ullrich, S. (2010). Strategic development of business models: Implications of the Web 2.0 for creating value on the Internet. *Long Range Planning*, *43*(2/3), 272–290. doi:10.1016/j.lrp.2010.01.005

Witmer, B. G., & Singer, M. J. (1998). Measuring presence in virtual environments: A presence questionnaire. *Presence (Cambridge, Mass.)*, *7*(3), 225–240. doi:10.1162/105474698565686

Wittgenstein, L. (1967). Ricerche filosofiche. Torino, Italy: Einaudi.

Wong, D. S., Chan, H. C. O., & Cheng, C. H. (2014). Cyberbullying perpetration and victimization among adolescents in Hong Kong. *Children and Youth Services Review*, *36*, 133–140. doi:10.1016/j.childyouth.2013.11.006

Woodman, K., & Kourtis-Kazoullis, V. (2007). Cyber-Self-Reflection: Developing learner autonomy in online programs. *Selected Papers from the 18th International Symposium on Theoretical and Applied Linguistics*.

Woodman, K. (2004). Unlimited access: The real benefits of online learning. *International Journal of Learning*, *10*, 3025–3033.

Woodman, K. (2005). No borders: Virtual communities in online learning. *International Journal of the Humanities*, *1*, 1849–1861.

Woodman, K. (2009). Online learning and literacy development. *Proceedings of the 42nd Linguistics Colloquium*.

Workman, R. (2013). *What is a hologram?* Retrieve from: http://www.livescience.com/

Wotzko, R., & Carroll, J. (2009). *Digital theatre and online narrative*. Drama Education with Digital Technology.

Wright, M. F. (2015). Cyber victimization and adjustment difficulties: The mediation of Chinese and American adolescents' digital technology usage. *CyberPsychology: Journal of Psychosocial Research in Cyberspace, 1*(1), article 1. Retrieved from: http://cyberpsychology.eu/view.php?cisloclanku=2015051102&article=1

Wright, M. F. (2013). The relationship between young adults beliefs about anonymity and subsequent cyber aggression. *Cyberpsychology, Behavior, and Social Networking, 16*(12), 858–862. doi:10.1089/cyber.2013.0009 PMID:23849002

Wright, M. F. (2014a). Cyber victimization and perceived stress: Linkages to late adolescents' cyber aggression and psychological functioning. *Youth & Society.*

Wright, M. F. (2014b). Predictors of anonymous cyber aggression: The role of adolescents beliefs about anonymity, aggression, and the permanency of digital content. *Cyberpsychology, Behavior, and Social Networking, 17*(7), 431–438. doi:10.1089/cyber.2013.0457 PMID:24724731

Wright, M. F. (2014c). Longitudinal investigation of the associations between adolescents popularity and cyber social behaviors. *Journal of School Violence, 13*(3), 291–314. doi:10.1080/15388220.2013.849201

Wright, M. F. (in press). Adolescents' cyber aggression perpetration and cyber victimization: The longitudinal associations with school functioning. *Social Psychology of Education.*

Wright, M. F., Kamble, S., Lei, K., Li, Z., Aoyama, I., & Shruti, S. (2015). Peer attachment and cyberbullying involvement among Chinese, Indian, and Japanese adolescents. *Societies, 5*(2), 339–353. doi:10.3390/soc5020339

Wright, M. F., & Li, Y. (2012). Kicking the digital dog: A longitudinal investigation of young adults victimization and cyber-displaced aggression. *Cyberpsychology, Behavior, and Social Networking, 15*(9), 448–454. doi:10.1089/cyber.2012.0061 PMID:22974350

Wright, M. F., & Li, Y. (2013a). Normative beliefs about aggression and cyber aggression among young adults: A longitudinal investigation. *Aggressive Behavior, 39*(3), 161–170. doi:10.1002/ab.21470 PMID:23440595

Wright, M. F., & Li, Y. (2013b). The association between cyber victimization and subsequent cyber aggression: The moderating effect of peer rejection. *Journal of Youth and Adolescence, 42*(5), 662–674. doi:10.1007/s10964-012-9903-3 PMID:23299177

Wu, I. L., & Chen, J. L. (2005). An extension of trust and TAM model with TPB in the initial adoption of on-line tax: An empirical study. *International Journal of Human-Computer Studies, 62*(6), 784–808. doi:10.1016/j.ijhcs.2005.03.003

Wu, J. H., Wang, S. C., & Lin, L. M. (2007). Mobile computing acceptance factors in the healthcare industry: A structural equation model. *International Journal of Medical Informatics, 76*(1), 66–77. doi:10.1016/j.ijmedinf.2006.06.006 PMID:16901749

Xia, Z. D. (2009). Marketing library services through Facebook groups. *Library Management, 30*(6/7), 469–478. doi:10.1108/01435120910982159

Yalcinkaya, A. D., Ürey, H., Brown, D., Montague, T., & Sprague, R. (2006). Two-axis electromagnetic microscanner for high resolution displays. *Microelectromechanical Systems Journalism, 15*(4), 786–794.

Yan Yu, Y., Wen Tian, S., Vogel, D., & Chi-Wai Kwok, R. (2010). Can learning be virtually boosted? An investigation of online social networking impacts. *Computers & Education, 55*(4), 1494–1503. doi:10.1016/j.compedu.2010.06.015

Yanchar, S., & Slife, B. D. (2004). Teaching critical thinking by examining assumptions: An instructional framework. *Teaching of Psychology, 31*(2), 85–90. doi:10.1207/s15328023top3102_2

Yang, Y., Kankanhalli, A., & Chandran, S. (2015). A stage model of information technology in healthcare. *Health Technology, 5*(1), 1–11. doi:10.1007/s12553-015-0097-z

Ybarra, R., & Green, T. (2003). Using technology to help ESL/EFL students develop language skills. *The Internet TESL Journal, 9*(3). Retrieved from http://iteslj.org/Articles/Ybarra-Technology.html

Ybarra, M. L., Diener-West, M., & Leaf, P. (2007). Examining the overlap in internet harassment and school bullying: Implications for school intervention. *The Journal of Adolescent Health, 1*(6), 42–50. doi:10.1016/j.jadohealth.2007.09.004 PMID:18047944

Ybarra, M. L., & Mitchell, K. J. (2004). Online aggressor/targets, aggressors, and targets: A comparison of associated youth characteristics. *Journal of Child Psychology and Psychiatry, and Allied Disciplines, 45*(7), 1308–1316. doi:10.1111/j.1469-7610.2004.00328.x PMID:15335350

Ye, J., Stevenson, G., & Dobson, S. (2014). USMART: An unsupervised semantic mining activity recognition technique. *ACM Trans. Interact. Intell. Syst., 4*(4), 16:1-16:27. doi:10.1145/2662870

Yi, M. Y., Jackson, J. D., Park, J. S., & Probst, J. C. (2006). Understanding information technology acceptance by individual professionals: Toward an integrative view. *Information & Management, 43*(3), 350–363. doi:10.1016/j.im.2005.08.006

Yi, Z. (2014). Australian academic librarians' perceptions of effective Web 2.0 tools used to market services and resources. *Journal of Academic Librarianship, 40*(3/4), 220–227. doi:10.1016/j.acalib.2014.02.009

Yousef, W. S. M., & Bellamy, A. (2015). The impact of cyberbullying on the self-esteem and academic functioning of Arab American middle and high school students. *Electronic Journal of Research in Educational Psychology, 23*(3), 463–482.

Yu, S., & Yang, K. F. (2006). Attitudes toward web-based distance learning among public health nurses in Taiwan: A questionnaire survey. *International Journal of Nursing Studies, 43*(6), 767–774. doi:10.1016/j.ijnurstu.2005.09.005 PMID:16253261

Yusop, F. D. (2015). A dataset of factors that influence preservice teachers' intentions to use Web 2.0 technologies in future teaching practices. *British Journal of Educational Technology, 46*(5), 1075–1080. doi:10.1111/bjet.12330

Zakharova, I. G. (2003). *Information technologies in education: textbook for students of higher educational institutions.* Moscow: Izdatel'skij centr «Akademija».

Zaman, M., Anandarajan, M., & Dai, Q. (2010). Experiencing flow with instant messaging and its facilitating role on creative behaviors. *Computers in Human Behavior, 26*(5), 1009–1018. doi:10.1016/j.chb.2010.03.001

Zambarbieri, D. (2003). E-TRACKING; Eye tracking analysis in the evaluation of e-learning systems. In *Proceedings of HCI International Conference*, (pp. 617-621).

Zambarbieri, D., & Carniglia, E. (2012). Eye movement analysis of reading from computer displays, eReaders and printed books. *Ophthalmic & Physiological Optics, 32*(5), 390–396. doi:10.1111/j.1475-1313.2012.00930.x PMID:22882151

Zapalska, A., Bugaj, M., Flanegin, F., & Rudd, D. (2004). *Student Feedback on Distance Learning with the Use of WebCT.* Computers in Higher Education Economics Review.

Zaporozhets, A. A. (1986). *Selectas.* Moscow: Pedagogika.

Zhang, Y. (2009). Cooperative Language Learning and Foreign Language Learning and Teaching. *Journal of Language Teaching and Research, 1*(1), 81-83.

Zhang, A., & Aasheim, Ch. (2011). Academic success factors: An IT student perspective. *Journal of Information Technology Education: Research, 10*, 309–331.

Zhang, Y. (2013). Toward a layered model of context for health information searching: An analysis of consumer-generated questions. *Journal of the American Society for Information Science and Technology*, *64*(6), 1158–1172. doi:10.1002/asi.22821

Zhou, D., Truran, M., Brailsford, T., Wade, V., & Ashman, H. (2012). Translation techniques in cross-language information retrieval. *ACM Computing Surveys*, *45*(1), 1–44. doi:10.1145/2379776.2379777

Zhou, Z., Tang, H., Tian, Y., Wei, H., Zhang, F., & Morrison, C. M. (2013). Cyberbullying and its risk factors among Chinese high school students. *School Psychology International*, *34*(6), 630–647. doi:10.1177/0143034313479692

Zilber, T. B., Tuval-Mashiach, R., & Lieblich, A. (2008). The embedded narrative navigating through multiple contexts. *Qualitative Inquiry*, *14*(6), 1047–1069. doi:10.1177/1077800408321616

About the Contributors

Francisco V. Cipolla-Ficarra is a professor, reaserh and writer. PhD-Ing. Area: Multimedia (1999). B.A. in Social Communication (1988). B.A. in Computer Programming and Systems Analysis (1983). Manager and coordinator of the first Human-Computer Interaction Lab. in Barcelona, Spain (1997 – 1999). Professor in American and European universities, technical and professional colleges (1981 – present), subjects: computer science, computer graphics and animation, human-computer interaction, design and multimedia. Scientific journalist and writer (1989 – present). CEO: Blue Herons Editions. Coordinator of AInCI (*International Association of Interactive Communication* –www.ainci.com) and ALAIPO (*Latin Association International of Human-Computer Interaction* –www.alaipo.com). Main research interests: HCI, communicability, quality, auditory and evaluation of interactive systems, computer graphics and animation, social communication, semiotics, e-learning, video games, ecological and cultural heritage. ACM and IEEE member.

* * *

Goknur Kaplan Akilli is an Assistant Professor in the Department of Computer Education and Instructional Technology at the Middle East Technical University (METU), Ankara,Turkey. She holds a Ph.D. in Instructional Technology from Penn State University, Pennsylvania USA. She is one of the co-founders of the SIMGE research group. Her research and interest focus on Instructional Design (analysis, design, development, implementation and evaluation), games and simulations, communities of practice. Qualitative Research, Design-Based Research, Mixed Methods, Social Network Analysis. Usability and Usability testing, Participatory Design. Mathematics Teaching (Abstract concepts, problem building and solving, mathematics teaching via games).

Pablo A. Alcaraz-Valencia is an imaginative, creative, constructive and conscientious programmer, systems engineer, teacher and doctoral student. He was born and raised in Colima, Mexico. As a Teacher, he has worked at the University of Colima on various disciplines of engineering. As a programmer, he has worked at the software development department of the National Center for Digital Publishing and Development of Information Technologies (CENEDIC), in Colima, Mexico. Currently, his major field of study is centered on the implementation and usage of graphics and sound features, based on 3D holograms to enhance the "listening" ability on English learning as a second language.

Serkan Alkan is psychologist in the Middle East Technical University. He received a B.S. degree in Psychology and M.S. & PhD degrees in Computer Education and Instructional Technology from

METU, Ankara, Turkey. He worked as instructor in Kocaeli University, and managed Measurement and Evaluation Unit in a Private Education Institution before joining METU in 2000. Currently he is a risk manager at "Capacity Development of Employees and Employers via Information and Communication Technologies (ICT)" project and deputy manager at METU - Design Factory. His main research interests are multimedia learning, human-computer interaction, technology sharing, design thinking and MOOCs.

Jacqueline Alma lives and works in Vancouver (BC), Canada. She was a professor at the HEC Montréal École de Gestion, British Columbia Institute of Technology, and Vancouver Film School. She received her B.A., master's and doctorate degree in Computing & IT from the Simon Fraser University and University of British Columbia. The main areas of the interest are computer science, database, interactive design, video games, computer animation, cinema digital and business technology management.

Fuat Bölükbaş received his B.Sc. degree from Department of Computer Engineering of Karadeniz Technical University (KTU) in 2009. He has been working in Simsoft since 2013. He has taken important roles in different projects such as tactical game simulations and graphical user interface software for complicated systems. His research interests include human computer interaction and artificial intelligence.

Kursat Cagiltay is Professor of the Department of Computer Education and Instructional Technology at the Middle East Technical University (METU), Ankara, Turkey. He holds a double Ph.D. in Cognitive Science and Instructional Systems Technology from Indiana University, Bloomington USA. He is the founder of three research groups at METU: Simulations and Games in Education (SIMGE), HCI research group and Educational Neuroscience/Neurotechnology. His research focuses on, Human Computer Interaction, Instructional Technology, Social and Cognitive issues of electronic games, socio-cultural aspects of technology, technology enhanced learning, Human Performance Technologies, Educational Neuroscience/Neurotechnology. He is the director of METU's Audio/Visual Research Center.

Miguel Cipolla-Ficarra is a professor and research. PhD. Area: Power Electronic Engineering (1996). B.A. Electronic Engineering – Telecommunications (1990). B.A. Electric Engineering (1999). Professor in European universities, technical and professional colleges (1987 – present). Software project manager: design, development and implementation of algorithms. Product manager, application engineer and technical sales engineer in international projects. Director of laboratory in F&F Multimedia Communic@tions Corp. Technical manager in AInCI (*International Association of Interactive Communication* –www.ainci.com) and ALAIPO (*Latin Association International of Human-Computer Interaction* –www.alaipo.com). Main research interests: interfaces, usability engineering, interactive systems, telecommunication, computer sciences, networks, industrial design, programmation, automation, motors on microprocessor, ecological energy, e-commerce and computer aided education.

Fiammetta Costa graduated in Architecture at Politecnico di Milano, Italy in 1993 where she also obtained a PhD degree in Industrial Design in 1999, she is currently researcher at the Design Department of Politecnico di Milano, Italy. Principal areas of her research interests are environmental design and user research methods. She participated in several international research programs and coordinated research projects in collaboration with Industrial Companies.

Rosanna Costaguta is member of the IIISI Research Institute and a Professor in the Department of Informatics at the Universidad Nacional de Santiago del Estero, in Santiago del Estero, Argentina. She received her Specialist in Higher Education Teaching Degree in 2001 from Universidad Católica de Cuyo, her Master in Software Engineering Degree in 2002 from Universidad Politécnica de Madrid and her PhD in Computer Science in 2008 from Universidad Nacional del Centro de la Provincia de Buenos Aires. Her main research interests include: intelligent agents, particularly interface agents; data mining and machine learning techniques for user profiling and personalization; computer-supported collaborative learning, particularly personalized with software agents.

Mehmet Donmez is a Research Assistant of the Department of Computer Education and Instructional Technology at the Middle East Technical University (METU), Ankara, Turkey. He received a B.S. degree in Computer Education and Instructional Technology, M.S. degree in Information Systems from METU, Ankara, Turkey. Currently, he is a Ph.D. student in Computer Education and Instructional Technology at METU, Ankara, Turkey. His research focuses on eye-tracking research, human computer interaction, instructional technology, and educational neuroscience/neurotechnology.

Annastella Gambini graduated in Biology and in Biological Researches. She worked at the University of Milan Italy (Department of Biology), in 1999 she has gone as a researcher at Department of Human Sciences for Education "Riccardo Massa", University of Milano-Bicocca, Italy. She is Associate Professor at the same Department where she's teaching Biology and Teaching Biology. She is a member of scientific societies as SiTe, SBI, Siel, EECERA. To develop the activities of an Environment Educational Centre, realized to follow some innovative learning practices, she produced CD-ROM, DVD and informatics objects, guides and books for different student levels (from primary school to University). She has also a research branch on the assessment on the online courses for university students.

Laura S. Gaytán-Lugo is a professor at the University of Colima in Mexico, appointed at the School of Mechanical and Electrical Engineering. She focuses on Human-Computer Interaction. Her research interests include serious games, user experience design, crowd-computer interaction and evaluation methods. She holds a Ph.D. in Information Technologies from the University of Guadalajara and is a member of Mexico's National System of Researchers. She is also a member of the Mexican Association on Human Computer Interaction (AMexIHC). Recently, she was named ambassador of the ACM SIGCHI.

Daria Gnedykh is a researcher at the Department of Personality Psychology of St Petersburg State University in Russia. She received a Ph.D in Educational Psychology from St Petersburg State University. Her research interests focus on e-learning, human–computer interaction, educational technology. The area of her interest includes psychology of learning activity, cognitive learning processes, neurodidactics/brain-based education.

Sara C. Hernández is a Mexican research professor at the University of Guadalajara. Her initial training was as a teacher of primary education. She completed a specialty in interpretative methodology. She studied a psychology degree and two masters: one in psychology and the other in educational research. Her PhD was centered on higher education problems. She has held several leadership positions in the field of education: she was the coordinator for Master's in Higher Education at the University of Guadalajara, the director for the Centre for Educational and Social Research under the administration of the national ministry of education. She got UDUAL´s Honorable Mention Award for the academic quality of his research. Today, she is recognized as teacher with the PROMEP´s profile, awarded by the Mexican Ministry of Education.

Sandra Jiménez earned her Career of Strategic Information Systems in 2014, She holds a Master Degree in Networks and System from the Universidad Politécnica de Aguascalientes. Sandra´s research interest focus (but not limited) on Human-Computer interaction oriented in Massive Online Open Courses (MOOCs); usability; intelligent software; data bases; and software engineering.

Daniel Kade holds a PhD in computer science with specialization in interaction design from Mälardalen University (2016). Furthermore, he holds a Licentiate degree (Mälardalen University, 2014), a M.Sc. (University of Applied Sciences Darmstadt, 2011) and a B.Sc. (University of Applied Sciences Hamburg, Université Paul Verlaine, Metz, 2009) in computer science. His research interests are within ubiquitous computing, multimedia, mixed reality, interaction design and bridging the gap between design and engineering practices. Daniel´s research is focused on mixed reality applications, applicable to areas such as motion capture, gaming and simulators. Moreover, Daniel looks at user experiences and interactions associated with the prototypes built.

Kijpokin Kasemsap received his BEng degree in Mechanical Engineering from King Mongkut's University of Technology, Thonburi, his MBA degree from Ramkhamhaeng University, and his DBA degree in Human Resource Management from Suan Sunandha Rajabhat University. Dr. Kasemsap is a Special Lecturer in the Faculty of Management Sciences, Suan Sunandha Rajabhat University, based in Bangkok, Thailand. Dr. Kasemsap is a Member of the International Economics Development and Research Center (IEDRC), the International Foundation for Research and Development (IFRD), and the International Innovative Scientific and Research Organization (IISRO). Dr. Kasemsap also serves on the International Advisory Committee (IAC) for the International Association of Academicians and Researchers (INAAR). Dr. Kasemsap is the sole author of over 250 peer-reviewed international publications and book chapters on business, education, and information technology. Dr. Kasemsap is included in the TOP 100 Professionals–2016 and in the 10th edition of 2000 Outstanding Intellectuals of the 21st Century by the International Biographical Centre, Cambridge, England.

Vasilia Kourtis-Kazoullis is an Associate Professor in the Department of Primary Education at the University of the Aegean in Greece, where she teaches undergraduate and undergraduate courses. Her research field is "Bilingualism and Learning in Electronic Environments". She has designed several electronic language learning environments for European projects.

Svetlana Kostromina is a Professor in St Petersburg State University, Russia. She completed her Ph.D. at the age of 29 at Moscow State Pedagogical University and Dr. of Sciences at the age of 39 at St Petersburg State University. She is a professor at the Department of Personality Psychology. She is a President of St Petersburg Psychological Society. Her research interests are: human-computer interaction, psychology of training (issues of acquisition, cognition and formation of students` metacognitive skills) and neurodidactics/brain-based education.

Andreas Kratky is assistant professor in the Interactive Media and Games Division and the Media Arts and Practice Division of the School for Cinematic Arts of the University of Southern California. Kratky's work is broadly interdisciplinary and comprises research in human computer interaction and in digital humanities as well as numerous award winning media art projects. His work has been shown internationally in Europe, the USA, Japan, and Korea in institutions like the ICA in London, ICC in Tokyo, HDKW in Berlin, Centre George Pompidou in Paris, or RedCAT in Los Angeles. Andreas Kratky's research is widely published and several of his art works are published as interactive media on DVD and in art catalogues.

Guadalupe Lara-Cisneros is a Researcher/Professor of full time in the Department of Electrical Engineering, Campus Jalpa in the Autonomous University of Zacatecas, México. He has had coordinator's positions of Campus of the UAZ, as well as in charge of the computer centers, and manager of the programs in the Department of Electrical Engineering, he has taught basic courses of programming, computer networks and security, introduction to the internet, computer organization. Member of the Computer Academy.

Rikard Lindell is an associate professor in computer science with specialisation in interaction design. His research interest is in digital material and materiality of programming language code as a design material. Rikard's primary domain is embodied interaction and new interfaces for musical expressions, exploring the materiality of code through digital art and new interface technologies for multimedia content and creative work in cooperation. Rikard is also working on research commercialisation with experience of the tedious process of transforming an interactive research prototype to a reliable software with a sustained focus on the user experience and attending the experiential qualities of the design process.

Alejandro U. López-Orozco has a Master's Degree in Science and Computational Technologies (Autonomous University of Aguascalientes), he is a Researcher/Professor in the Department of Electrical Engineering Campus Jalpa at the Autonomous University of Zacatecas, México. He has given several courses at bachelor level, mainly related to databases, web programming and desktop applications. His research interests are web programming, mobile technology and educational technology.

Huizilopoztli Luna-García is a Researcher and Professor in the Department of Electrical Engineering, Campus Jalpa at the Autonomous University of Zacatecas, México. He has a Ph.D. in Computer Science with a specialization in Human-Computer Interaction from the Technological Institute of Aguascalientes. Prof. Luna-Garcia holds a Master degree in Sciences and Information Systems from the Autonomous University of Aguascalientes and a Bachelor degree in Computer Systems Engineering from the Technological Institute of Zacatecas. His research interests are in human-computer interaction, usability, user experience, user centered design, design patterns, mobile technology and educational technology.

Alessandra Mazzola graduated in Pedagogical Sciences at University of Milano-Bicocca in 2005. In 2008 post-graduated in Forensic Criminology at the LIUC – Libera Università Carlo Cattaneo of Castellanza, Italy. Since 2014, Research Fellow in Design at Politecnico di Milano, Italy. Current research interests: design and technologies for education and health; eye tracking in human behavior analysis; interaction design.

Ricardo Mendoza-Gonzalez is a Researcher/Professor at the Instituto Tecnológico de Aguascalientes (Mexico). He holds a Ph.D. in Computer Science (Universidad Autónoma de Aguascalientes, México, 2009), a Master degree in Computer Science (Universidad Autónoma de Aguascalientes, México, 2008), and a Bachelor of Computer Science (Instituto Tecnológico de Aguascalientes, México, 2004). He collaborates with researchers of the University of Ontario Institute of Technology (UOIT, Canada), and Universidad Autónoma de Aguascalientes (Mexico). His current research interests include several topics on: human-computer interaction, information security, usability, artificial intelligence, and software engineering.

Sandra Mercado-Pérez has a Master's Degree in Science (Cinvestav) and a Bachelor in Computer Systems Engineering (Technological Institute of Zacatecas), she is a Researcher/professor in the Department of Electrical Engineering, Campus Jalpa at the Autonomous University of Zacatecas, Mexico. Since 2005 she has given diverse courses at Bachelor's level, all related to programming basics. She has published his research in journals and national congress contributions. Her research interests are applied computing, mobile technology and educational technology.

Galina Molodtsova is a researcher and associate professor at the Department of Psychology of Education and Pedagogy of St Petersburg State University in Russia. She holds a Ph.D in Theory and Methods of Professional Education from Russian State Pedagogical University. Her research interest lies on multimedia learning, human–computer interaction and educational technology. Other areas of interest include optimization of learning techniques and processes for teachers` professional development.

Sabrina Muschiato graduated in Architecture at Politecnico di Milano, Italy, where she also obtained a PhD degree in Industrial Design in 2005. Since 1999, she's been collaborating with the Ergonomics & Design Research team, developing studies in Ergonomics for Healthcare products and services and in Design for All. She also works as architect and designer with Companies of the Healthcare and Social Welfare sector, suggesting experimental and innovative solutions based on her research since 1995.

Donald Nilson holds a B.A. in computer science from University of Oslo, Norway, and a master in games for learning from New York University, and he is a PhD student in Norway. He has an industrial and commercial experience in the fields of new media, graphic design, video game programming, chilhood education, software and systems engineering. His main research interests are video games for learning, special education, artificial intelligence, cyber behaviour, big data, computer graphics, augmented reality, and human-computer interaction.

Ordaz-García is a Researcher/Professor in the Department of Electrical Engineering, Campus Jalpa at the Autonomous University of Zacatecas, México. He has a Master in Information Technologies with a specialization in Networking at the Inter-American University for Development and a Bachelor in Computer Systems Engineering (Technological Institute of Zacatecas). His research interests are e-government, mobile technology and educational technology.

Oğuzhan Özcan is the current director of KUAR, and currently full professor of design at Koç University's Department of Media and Visual Arts, and the director of the Koç University – Arçelik Research Center for Creative Industries (KUAR). Özcan has degrees in architecture (BA, Mimar Sinan

University, 1985), computer-aided architecture and design (MA, Straclyde University), and multimedia design (Mimar Sinan University, 1993). He is the first Turkish faculty awarded by UNESCO as an Aschberg Fellow. In the last 30 years, in Turkey, he has founded and directed the first communication design undergraduate program, the first Interactive Media Design Graduate Program, and the first PhD program in Art and Design. He continues to lead a team of interaction design researchers at the Koç University Design Lab and coordinates an interdisciplinary PhD Program called Design Technology & Society since 2011.

Antonella Pezzotti graduated in Natural Sciences at University of Milan, Italy in 2001 and a PhD in Educational and Communication Sciences in 2011. She has been working for years (also as a research fellow) at the Department of Educational Human Sciences "Riccardo Massa", University of Milano-Bicocca, Italy on the realization of learning environments and teaching devices (online courses, learning objects, multimedia objects) making use of new technologies. She has developed a model for analyzing asynchronous discussions in virtual learning environments.

Annamaria Poli graduated in Architecture at Politecnico di Milano, Italy in 1991 and she also obtained a PhD degree in Bioengineering in 2007. She is currently researcher at Department of Educational Human Sciences "Riccardo Massa", University of Milano-Bicocca, Italy. Member of Scientific Committee: SETECEC, HCITOCH, CCGIDIS, ADNTIIC, ESIHSE, RDINIDR, MSIVISM, and HI-ASCIT. Current research interests: human visual perception and image language, Emerging Interactive Technologies, Computer Arts and Creativity, Computer Graphics, Cinema and Digital Technologies in Educational contests. She is author of several papers and experimental work among wich mention: A.Poli, *Food Perception Without Colors, 2016*; *Una doppia origine nell'esercizio dello sguardo*, 2012; *Cinema e disabilità visive*, 2009; *Analysis, design and development of aid for overcoming colour vision/perception barriers*, 2007; *Il computer pensato per i bambini*, 2006.

Alan Radley is a writer, lecturer and inventor who is based in the UK. Alan holds a Ph.D. in Physics from University College London (UCL). He was the optical designer for the High Resolution Optical Spectrograph, which is part of the International Gemini Telescope project. Whilst at Logic PLC, Alan was the data scientist for the NASA/ESA XMM satellite observatory. Alan has taught undergraduate and postgraduate courses in physics, astronomy, and computing, and also in innovation and technology. He has developed the concept of the Lookable User Interface, and he was granted a patent for his Hologram Mirror. At present Alan is working on two forthcoming books, which analyze the myriad of influences / relationship(s) between, self and computer.

Mario A. Rodríguez-Díaz earned his M.Sc. in 2009 and his Ph.D. in 2015 both in Exact Sciences, Systems and Information from the Universidad Autónoma de Aguascalientes. Currently, he works at Instituto Tecnológico de Aguascalientes, where he teaches courses in computer programming and image processing, he also works at Traffic System developing software for the broadcasting industry. His main interests are image processing, computer vision, pattern recognition, information theory, automata theory, video games and artificial intelligence.

Laura C. Rodríguez-Martínez earned her Ms. in Computing Sciences in 2006 and her Ph.D. in Computing Sciences in 2009 from the Autonomous University of Aguascalientes, Mexico. She is a full-time Professor and Researcher in Institute of Technology of Aguascalientes (ITA) since 2010. Before joining ITA she worked as Software Engineer in Mexican Private Enterprises since 1992 to 2006. Her current teaching and research interest include Service-Oriented Software Engineering, Software-System Development Life Cycle and Graphical User Interface Processes Design.

Pablo Santana-Mansilla is member of the IIISI Research Institute at the Universidad Nacional de Santiago del Estero and he has a doctoral scolarship from National Council for Scientific and Techno-logical Research of Argentina (CONICET). He received his Bachelor in Information Systems Degree in 2013 from Universidad Nacional de Santiago del Estero and hi is currently working toward his PhD in Computer Science studies at Universidad Nacional del Centro de la Provincia de Buenos Aires. His main research interests include: computer-supported collaborative learning, software agents, text mining, and performance support systems. His PhD thesis is concerned with the automatic training of teachers that work in computer-supported collaborative learning platforms.

Silvia Schiaffino is a Researcher at the National Council for Scientific and Technological Research of Argentina (CONICET). She is also member of ISISTAN Research Institute and a Professor in the Department of Computer Science at the Universidad Nacional del Centro de la Provincia de Buenos Aires, Tandil, Argentina. She received her Master in Systems Engineering Degree in 2001 and her PhD in Computer Science in 2004 from this institution. Her main research interests include: intelligent agents, recommender systems, social networks, personalized assistance, and machine learning techniques for user profiling and personalization.

Carlo Emilio Standoli graduated in Industrial Design at Politecnico di Milano, Italy in 2011, where he received his Master Degree in Industrial Design and his Ph.D. in Design. Currently he is a Research Fellow at the Design Department. He works with the TeDH (Technology and Design in Healthcare) Research Group, and he is involved in basic and applied research in the Healthcare field, in the Wearable Monitoring Systems field and in the Human Factor and Human-Product Interaction field. He is involved in Research Projects funded by the European Commission and other National and Local boards.

Daniela Tamburini graduated in Pedagogy at the Università Cattolica del Sacro Cuore of Milan and obtained a Master in Development of Clinical Skills in Educational and Training Professions at the Università Degli Studi of Milano-Bicocca. She has taught in several public and private institutions in-cluding the Scuola Magistrale Salesiana and at the Università degli Studi of Milano-Bicocca, Faculty of Sociology (Laboratories of Cinematic Language and Communications Systems). She works on research projects developing particular applications of the Clinica di Formazione in educational, training and school fields. Since 2012 she has been the director of Sperimenta, the Centro Studi di Cinema e Formazione in Milan. She also collaborates with the Università Degli Studi of Milano-Bicocca as a consultant within the research project "A school with cinema for the enhancement of learning and teaching".

Hakan Ürey is a Professor of Electrical Engineering at Koç University, Istanbul. He received the BS degree from Middle East Technical University and MS and Ph.D. degrees from Georgia Institute of Technology all in Electrical Engineering. He worked for Microvision Inc in Seattle for 5 years before joining Koç University. He is the inventor of more than 50 issued and pending patents in the areas of displays, imaging systems, sensors, and microtechnologies. He received the prestigious European Research Council Advanced Grant in 2013 to develop next generation wearable and 3D display technologies.

Karen Woodman is a Senior Lecturer in TESOL in the School of Cultural and Professional Learning at QUT. At QUT, she was the Coordinator of the Master of Education (TESOL) and Master of Education (TEFL) from 2008-2012. She is a member of many professional associations, and she is involved with the promotion and development of the fields of ESOL teacher education. Karen's research interests also include a number of related issues in second language acquisition, including learning disabilities in ESL, online teaching and learning, neurolinguistic issues in SLA, gender and culture in the ESL classroom, and the experience of international students in graduate and HDR studies.

Michelle Wright joined the CSC (Child Study Center - PennState University) in 2015, after spending the previous two and a half years as a Postdoctoral Research Fellow at the Institute for Children, Youth, and Family at Masaryk University in the Czech Republic. She received her Ph.D. in Experimental Psychology with a focus on Development Psychology from DePaul University, and her Masters in General Psychology from Auburn Montgomery. She possesses extensive research knowledge and experience involving children's, adolescents' and young adults' offline and online emotional risks, particularly bullying and cyberbullying. At the CSC, Michelle works with faculty on innovative ways of collecting data and delivering interventions.

Daniela Zambarbieri, degree in Electronic Engineering from the Politecnico di Milano in 1978. Researcher at the University of Pavia 1978-1992. Since 1992 Associate Professor of Biomedical Instrumentation at the University of Pavia. Member of the editorial board of Journal of Eye Movements Research. Coordinator of the European project E-TRACKING (Eye Movement Analysis in the Evaluation of e-Learning systems IST 2001-32323). Current research interests: oculomotor control system, eye-head coordination; eye tracking inhuman behavior analysis, eye movement analysis in reading.

Index

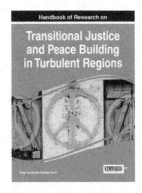
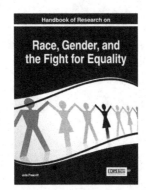

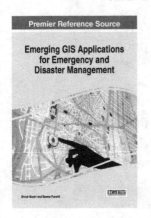

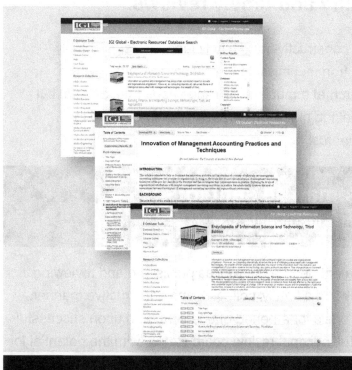

Printed in the United States
By Bookmasters